The process of learning

The process of learning

Second edition

John B. Biggs

Professor of Education
University of Newcastle

Ross Telfer

Associate Professor of Education
University of Newcastle

PRENTICE–HALL OF AUSTRALIA

Prentice-Hall, Inc., *Englewood Cliffs, New Jersey*
Prentice-Hall of Australia Pty Ltd, *Sydney*
Prentice-Hall Canada, Inc., *Toronto*
Prentice-Hall Hispanoamericana, S.A., *Mexico*
Prentice-Hall of India Private Ltd, *New Delhi*
Prentice-Hall International, Inc. *London*
Prentice-Hall of Japan, Inc., *Tokyo*
Prentice-Hall of Southeast Asia Pte Ltd, *Singapore*
Editora Prentice-Hall do Brasil Ltda, *Rio de Janeiro*

Typeset by Creative Typographics Pty Ltd,
Hobart, Tasmania.

Printed and bound in Australia by
Brown Prior Anderson Pty Ltd,
Burwood, Victoria.

Cover design by Mass Marketing Pty Ltd.

2 3 4 5 91 90 89 88

ISBN 0 7248 1002 1

National Library of Australia
Cataloguing-in-Publication Data

Biggs, J. B. (John Burville), 1934–
    The process of learning.

    2nd ed.
    Bibliography.
    Includes index.

    1. Learning, Psychology of. 2. Educational psychology.
    I. Telfer, Ross, 1937–   . I. Title.

370.15'23

CONTENTS

model in action. Summary. **Section B.** Who is responsible for self-direction? Situations that enhance metalearning. Assessing learning outcomes qualitatively. Summary. Further reading. Questions.

PREFACE

As a foundation discipline of education, educational psychology is an essential part of teacher education. However, the link between educational psychology and what happens in classrooms is not always clear to teacher–education students. Because psychology does not *prescribe* what classroom teachers do, many students and teachers believe it to be irrelevant and so dismiss it. In this book, we intend to demonstrate that this belief is false.

In both first and second editions, we maintained a distinction between the basic principles being discussed and the applications to educational practice. Section A of each chapter deals with the general principles; Section B deals with how these principles may be applied to Australian school systems and to topics of current concern in the Australian context such as maintaining classroom discipline, multicultural education, lifespan education, reading and writing skills, the education of the gifted, values and moral education, evaluating the quality of school learning, school-based assessment and so on.

So that readers may relate directly to the context they know, we have deliberately used Australian sources and references when we could. We believe it is important that teachers should realise that there is in fact a wealth of Australian research that can be drawn upon to improve the quality of education.

Since the first edition appeared, a great deal of educationally relevant research has been carried out. We found increasingly, however, that the task of updating the first edition was not simply a matter of cutting out the old and pasting in the new. Not only had new topics been researched, but new approaches to research had emerged. Our rewrite became a massive rethink.

One important new dimension of research comes from what cognitive psychologists call 'metacognition'. In experiencing the cognitive processes of attending to something, learning, remembering and making decisions, the human learner may also become *aware* that one is engaging in these processes; that metacognitive knowledge may be used to control and improve the learning process. The implications for education are impressive and may be seen in certain approaches to teaching reading, writing and problem solving, as well as in improving learning and study skills in general.

The second strand comes from the general area of ethnography. This is research that is carried out from within the learner's own framework rather than from that of an observing scientist. Research into the frameworks children use to understand the physical world has important implications for teaching science and mathematics, and that into the frameworks children use for their social interactions with each other and with adults has interesting implications for classroom management.

It is important to note too that the relation between school and society has shifted. The management structures of schools generally are moving more into line with those used in society as a whole. Rather than creating its own isolated little world, with its own rules, bureaucracies and ways, and its sharp distinctions between children and adults, the school is becoming more like the rest of society. Indeed the philosophy of adult and continuing education is beginning to permeate schools, and, of course, in both school and society, high technology is creating possibilities that are only just beginning to be understood for teaching, learning and assessment. Such developments make the model of the self-aware learner all the more readily applicable to school learning.

How to use this book

In order to help readers themselves become more self-aware of where they are going, and of how to judge whether or not they think they have got there, we have organised the book into five parts. Parts 1 and 5 comprise single chapters about schools, teachers and teaching: Parts 2, 3 and 4 are about learners and learning. Part 1 might be seen as *Presage*, Parts 2, 3 and 4 as *Process*, and Part 5 as *Product*. These 'three Ps' make up what we call the 3P model of learning which we describe in due course. The book itself makes up a 3P model of teaching: what schools are about (presage), how learners learn (process) and how the reader may integrate that material to become an effective teacher (product).

We hope that the new structure and content of the book makes it easier to reconcile knowing about learning, knowing about teaching and knowing therefore how to teach more effectively.

Other features include the following:

- A general overview of each part indicates how the chapters in that part integrate and form a particular theme.
- Each chapter is provided with an overview at the beginning, to give an idea of what is to be covered.
- Each chapter has a set of questions at the end to allow the reader (a) to self-test on factual coverage of content, and (b) to provide for discussion topics to help understand and apply the ideas expressed.
- The order of coverage is quite flexible.

On the last point, the order of coverage depends on the teaching method used. The sequence in the chapter headings as they appear is logical for a basically expository approach and for obtaining a broad overview of educational psychology. However, when our faculty switched to a problem-based approach, we found that a different sequence worked better. When students went out to schools early in the course they came back demanding to know not about theories of learning or development, but about how to manage a class. The chapter of first immediate interest then became Chapter 8. Then, as curriculum topics need designing and evaluating, attention is focussed on those chapters that have most impact on the decisions of current and changing concern: Chapter 5 for science and maths emphasis, Chapter 6 for language (reading, essay writing, second language learning), Chapter 7 for social science, Chapter 9 for dealing with the gifted and talented, Chapter 10 for issues to do with evaluation, Chapters 4 and 8 for general course design and classroom management, while Chapters 2 and 3, on learning and motivation, underpin most decisions.

We are grateful to many people for their assistance in producing this book. Formal acknowledgement to those firms and individuals for permission to reproduce previously published text and artwork is given elsewhere. Here we would like to express our thanks to several people, colleagues and ex-students, whose comments and suggestions have been useful:

Patricia Aslen
Eddie Braggett
Mary Coates
John Kirby
Pam Mahoney
Candida Peterson

Finally we express our appreciation to the editorial staff at Prentice-Hall of Australia, whose professionalism saw the book through an extremely tight schedule precisely on time.

John Biggs
Ross Telfer

Newcastle

ACKNOWLEDGEMENTS

The authors and publisher have made an effort to trace the source of copyright for material used in this book; however, they would be glad to hear of any errors or omissions in the following list.

Pages 3, 77, 84, 94 (top), 112, 119, 141 (top and bottom), 276, 296, 302, 340 (top and bottom), 359 (top and bottom), 373, 407, 433, 457 (bottom), 502, 511 (top and bottom), 515 and 517: Photos by permission of the Community Relations Unit of the New South Wales Department of Education.

Pages 17 and 18:   From *Taim Belong Masta* (Episode: Masta Me Laik Work), first broadcast May 1981, Australian Broadcasting Corporation.

Page 24:   J. A. Peddiwell, *The Saber-Tooth Curriculum*, McGraw-Hill, New York, 1939.

Pages 26, 27 and 28:   S. F. Bourke and R. Lewis, *Australian Studies in School Performance, Vol. II — Literacy and Numeracy in Australian Schools*, AGPS, 1976.

Pages 43 and 237 (top and bottom): Photos by permission of Bruce Turnbull, Faculty of Medicine, University of Newcastle.

Pages 55 and 56:   G. Nuthall and A. A. Lee, *Measuring and Understanding the Way Children Learn in Class*, Technical Report: Teaching Research Project, University of Canterbury, Christchurch, New Zealand, 1982.

Page 90:   M. Pines, E. Aronson and D. Kafry, *Burn-out — From Tedium to Personal Growth*, Free Press, New York, 1981.

Page 94 (bottom), 170, 291 and 452: Photos by permission of Murdoch University.

Page 122:   S. H. Lovibond, T. Mithiran and W. G. Adams, 'The Effects of Three Experimental Prison Environments on the Behaviour of Non-convict Volunteer Subjects', *Australian Psychologist*, **14**, 1979.

Page 131:   R. Telfer, *Program Equity and Participation — A Report of an Evaluation Study of Garokan High School*, Research Report, Department of Education, University of Newcastle, 1985.

Page 134:   From the *Alumni Papers*, **2**, No. 4, p. 26, February 1986, University of New South Wales.

Pages 145 and 146:   From *How to Solve it: A New Aspect of Mathematical Method*, © 1945, © 1973 renewed by Princeton University Press, second edition © 1957 by G. Polya; excerpt, pp. xvi–xvii, reprinted with permission of Princeton University Press.

Page 156:   D. Watkins and J. Hattie, 'An Arts Undergraduate', *Human Learning*, 1985.

Page 158:   P. Ramsden, *The Experience of Learning*, Scottish Universities Press, Edinburgh, 1984.

Pages 165 and 166:   Freely adapted draft of the story of a talk by Garth Boomer.

Page 190:   Photo by permission of Ken Scott, Faculty of Education, University of Newcastle.

Page 203:   From *The Weekend Magazine*, 10 July 1971.

Page 220:   Table adapted from Table 9.3 in *Towards a Science of Science Teaching* by Michael Shayer and Philip Adey, reprinted by permission of Heinemann Educational Books Ltd, London.

Pages 221 and 482:   From *The Development of a Set of SOLO Items for High School Science*, by K. Collis and H. Davey, © 1985.

Page 223:   *The Magic Triangle for Ohm's Law* from a thesis by R. Killen, 1983.

Page 234: Photo by permission of Freedman Studios, Newcastle.

Page 235: 'Reflections of a MAS', from the *Gazette* of the University of Newcastle, 1985.

Page 258: From *Teacher* by Sylvia Ashton-Warner, published by Virago Press, London, 1980.anguage in Education, No. 1, Tasmanian

Department of Education, 1975; C. R. Cooper and L. Odell, *Research on Composing: Points of Departure*, National Council of Teachers of English, Urbana, Ill., 1978.

Page 279: Ali Eyian, *An Autobiography*, Form 6, University High School, Melbourne.

Page 305: M. B. Katz, *The Irony of Early School Reform*, Harvard University Press, Cambridge, Mass., 1968.

Page 306: From 'Curbs on Political Discussion in Schools', *The Australian*, 18 November 1975.

Page 310: I. Wallace, D. Wallechinsky and A. Wallace, *The Book of Lists — 3*, Corgi Books, London, 1984.

Page 312: Photo by permission of Tim DeNeefe.

Page 315: From *The Newcastle Herald*, 14 March 1986.

Page 319: From 'Children's Understanding or Friendship Issues: Developmental by Stage or Sequence?' by M. Schofield and N. Kafer, *Journal of Social and Personal Relationship*, **2**, 1985, pp. 151–65, Sage Publication.

Pages 321, 322, 323 and 325: From *Life in the Classroom and Playground* by B. Davies, © 1982, Routledge and Kegan Paul.

Page 329: From *The Social Animal* by E. Aronson, p. 206, © 1984, fourth edition, W. H. Freeman and Co.

Page 331: From *Freedom to Learn in the 80s* by C. Rogers, © 1983, Charles E. Merrill Publishing Co.

Pages 338 and 339: From *Towards Non-sexist Education — Policies and Guidelines for Schools*, New South Wales Department of Education, Sydney, 1980.

Page 345: From 'The Irrelevance of Literacy' by E. Fesl, *Education News*, p. 15, 18 May 1983.

Pages 363, 377 and 578: From *Teachers' Work* by R. W. Connell, © 1985, p. 14, George Allen and Unwin.

Pages 364: H. W. Dettman, *Discipline in Secondary Schools in Western Australia: Report of the Committee*, Education Department, Perth, 1972.

Page 366: By permission of *The Newcastle Herald*, 25 January 1986.

Pages 394 and 395: From 'For and Against Corporal Punishment', *Education News*, 11 February 1985.

Page 426: A. R. Jensen, 'How Much Can We Boost IQ and Scholastic Achievement?', *Harvard Educational Review*, 1969.

Page 439: From *Educational and Psychological Characteristics of Students Gifted in English*, prepared by Marnie O'Neill and Joanne Reid for the Commonwealth Schools Commission under the aegis of 'Projects of National Significance — Gifted Children', 1985.

Page 442: E. P. Torrance and R. E. Myers, *Creative Learning and Teaching*, Harper & Row, New York, 1970.

Page 446: E. J. Braggett, *Education of Gifted and Talented Children: Australian Provision*, 1985.

Page 448: Freely adapted from G. H. Reavis, *The Animal School*, Contemporary Thought on Public School Curriculum, Brown, Iowa, 1968.

Pages 450 and 451: From 'Towards Improving Learning Strategies and Personal Adjustment with Computers', by A. Ryba and J. Chapman, *The Computing Teacher*, pp. 48–53, August 1983.

Page 460:   K. Green and S. Stager, paper presented to Higher Education Research and Development Society of Australasia, New Zealand, 1985.

Page 473:   J. P. Keeves, J. K. Matthews and S. F. Bourke, *Educating for Literacy and Numeracy in Australian Schools*, Australian Education Reports, No. 11, ACER, Hawthorn, Victoria, 1978.

Page 503:   By permission of *The Australian*, 21–22 December 1985.

Page 520:   From 'Trivial Relevance Imposing Mediocrity on Students', *The Weekend Australian*, p. 3, 22–23 March 1986.

Pages 529 and 530:   From *The Sun Herald*, 26 January 1986.

Page 531:   From 'The Shape of Schools to Come' by Frank Canu, *The Sydney Morning Herald*, 8 May 1979.

Part 1

Presage: Schools and learning

Teaching, like any professional practice, requires the integration of two different kinds of knowing: *knowing-that* and *knowing-how*. Knowing the principles of thermodynamics to the point where the workings of a car engine are clearly understood does not mean knowing how to get it going when it refuses to start. The first kind of knowing — knowing-that — is *declarative* knowledge; we can declare what we know about car engines to someone else. Such knowledge may certainly help us to work out sensible strategies for diagnosing the problem, but the know-how of an experienced mechanic is more reassuring. Knowing-how, or *procedural* knowledge, comes with experience. But that does *not* mean that declarative knowledge is irrelevant. The more we know about cars, the richer will be the experience and the faster will be the pay-offs from experience.

This book is mostly concerned with knowing *about* learners: about how they think, about their information processing capacities, about their ability to work out strategies to handle perceived problems, about their motives, about the way they develop, about the ways they interrelate with each other and about what they want from life. Knowing about learning (even knowing about teaching) does not mean that one then knows how to teach (or even about how to learn), but it certainly helps. Knowing about learners and their learning will make the pay-offs, from practice teaching and real-life teaching, roll in that much thicker and faster.

1

Unfortunately, it is sometimes difficult to convince student teachers of this at the beginning of their pre-service training. They want to know *how*. Right now. All that declarative knowledge (psychology, for example) simply means that academics are at their favourite game of requiring students to jump through hoops. Eventually, most students come to a different view, but it does take time and, unless one is careful, a barrier can be erected between the learning endorsed by institutions and that used in the business of life. Nevertheless, the barrier between knowing-that and knowing-how can be lowered by contextual and problem-based learning, and by encouraging students to reflect: these are matters dealt with in later chapters, especially Chapter 4.

For the moment we are concerned with teachers, not learners. The first thing teachers need to know is where they are going. What are schools for? And how can psychology help teachers in furthering the aims of schooling? These are 'presage' questions, addressed in Chapter 1 (Part 1). After that, we move into Parts 2, 3 and 4, which contain nine chapters about learners: these involve 'process' questions. Then, in Chapter 11 (Part 5), we return to teachers again: the product. Parts 1 and 5 link the declarative knowledge about learners with informed and professionally driven practice. The complete link, though, takes a long time and always continues to develop.

The link between theory and practice is conceptualised here by the distinction between *espoused theory* and *theory-in-use* (Argyris, 1976). Any decision is driven by some sort of theory or reason, whether it be commonsense or the astrology column in the daily paper. This is what we refer to as the theory-in-use. Espoused theory is what we *say* are the reasons (i.e. the relevant declarative knowledge). Professions have their espoused theories based on research and their foundation disciplines. Professionalisation means transforming espoused theory into the theory-in-use.

1

Psychology and schooling

OVERVIEW

Schools serve two broad functions: those concerned with *educational* outcomes (with children learning, and with the preservation and enrichment of culture) and those concerned with non-educational issues (with keeping people in jobs and children off street corners). Important though the latter may be, they are not our present concern.

This book deals with the first function. In this chapter, we describe the types of learning that are the special concern of schools. These are learnings that are difficult, that are important to society and that students need special help to acquire. Professional teachers need to think in terms of how people learn, which is where psychology comes in.

This chapter answers the following questions:

- Why does the family teach the child to speak but not to read?
- Why are most children not naturally interested in school subjects?
- What domains of learning are the concerns of schools?
- To what extent are Australian students considered to reach 'acceptable standards of literacy and numeracy'?
- What role does psychology play in contributing towards an espoused theory of education?
- What ways of thinking about human nature underlie current school practices?

When you have finished this chapter, you should be able to:

1. Watch a teacher in action and say if that teacher holds to Theory X or Theory Y.
2. Explain why you think teaching is a profession rather than a craft.
3. List six types of learning undertaken by schools and group them in four categories.
4. Distinguish between prepared and unprepared learning.
5. Distinguish between content and process learning.
6. Differentiate espoused theory from theory-in-use.

SECTION A

WHY HAVE SCHOOLS?

This book is about the role psychology may play in improving the quality of education. *Psychology* is the science (and perhaps art) of understanding human learning and other behaviour; *education* is concerned with facilitating human learning through the agency of a teacher. It seems reasonable, then, that some understanding of psychology may help the work of the teacher.

However, before we explain psychology's role, we first need to ask a more general question. Why do we have schools at all — what are they *for*? This is a question about which almost every member of the community has some ideas. Of the many answers that have been given, the following is a representative list (not in any order of significance):

1. *The enrichment of culture.* Civilisation is based on bodies of knowledge, the discoveries of scientists and thinkers, and the creations of artists — in short, culture. This richness would be lost if it were not passed on to the perceptive youth of each generation. Universities, libraries, museums, books and audiovisual media are the repositories of this heritage; schools are the medium for inducing the young to appreciate, use and subsequently enlarge this cumulative achievement.

2. *Socialisation.* Schools also exist to train people in the skills, knowledge, attitudes and values of society. Responsible citizens should not only know about important social institutions — the police force, banking, parliament and so on — but also entertain certain positive feelings (e.g. respect) towards them. In our pluralist society, school is the one institution where all future citizens may learn both the knowledge and the values of citizenship. Many argue that this is a legitimate and important role of the school.

3. *Vocational.* Schools teach students the skills necessary for entering the workforce. This function includes not only literacy (the ability to read and write) and numeracy (the ability to calculate simple arithmetical problems), but more specialised skills such as typing, book-keeping, woodwork, metalwork and so on. Technical schools particularly emphasise the latter aspects of schooling.

4. *Individual development.* Schools are not, however, just for the benefit of society as a whole: they help individuals to enrich their lives. Schools nurture and develop particular artistic, scientific or other talents that individual students may possess. While this may eventually lead to better employment prospects, it is not the immediate aim. The emphasis is rather on discovering the talents students possess and providing the opportunity for enlarging them. It is argued (see Karmel Report, 1973) that such development is intrinsically valuable, both for the individuals concerned and for the society in which they will eventually play an active part. The school can also provide these opportunities for students who might not otherwise encounter them (i.e. those from underprivileged or socially disadvantaged homes which would be unlikely to provide the conditions leading to the development of potential).

5. *Childminding.* In modern society, one and frequently both parents have a role outside the home. Thus the school is the major (if not only) institution which gives parents a breather from strictly parental responsibilities. It is also increasingly recognised that the school can provide experiences in areas that can no longer be assumed to be provided in the home, such as sex education, peer interaction, personal hygiene and so on.

6. *Easing the labour market.* If it were not for compulsory schooling, the labour market would be swamped by individuals seeking employment. As the compulsory schooling age is raised, so the demand by youth of that age for employment is decreased. This is particularly relevant when unemployment is high.

7. *The provision of employment.* Schools provide jobs for an extremely large number of people. Education, with its associated bureaucracies and feeder industries, is

one of the greatest employers in the Western world. If it were not for schools, unemployment would be higher still.

We can see that the above seven functions fall into two distinct groups: the first four are concerned with the effects of *learning* on the young and on society; the rest are concerned with non-educational, or *non-learning*, outcomes. In this book, we shall concentrate on the effects of learning and, even then, with only a narrow range of learnings: specifically, those with which the school is concerned. But what kinds and contents of learning are the concern of schools?

PREPAREDNESS FOR LEARNING

Seligman (1970) told of a seemingly commonplace, if unpleasant, incident in a restaurant. He ate some sauce bearnaise and shortly afterwards was violently ill. He could not eat sauce bearnaise for some considerable time afterwards, despite the fact that he knew that there was no objective reason not to eat sauce bearnaise again (he knew the immediate cause of illness to be gastro-enteritis).

Let us now turn to the 'Grandad' treatment for juvenile drinking. In rural United States, Grandad and his adolescent grandson sit eyeball to eyeball across the kitchen table with a bottle of sour-mash whisky between them — Sonny is to match Grandad, tumbler for tumbler. It is said that by the time the bottle is empty, the lad will not drink again for many years (presumably Grandad is used to the stuff).

What do these examples show? They show that such learning:

- is very rapid;
- lasts for a very long time;
- is therefore *efficient*;
- is related to *survival*.

There is survival in instantly learning to avoid foods that make us ill. To generalise: we learn things that have survival value more easily than things that do not.

Possibly we are biologically prepared for certain kinds of learnings. Table 1.1 lists some of the things that seem particularly easy (A) and particularly difficult (B) for us to learn. What distinguishes the prepared learnings from the unprepared? The prepared learnings are 'close to the bone': they are concerned with learning skills, usually in a family or small-group context. Learning to walk, to talk, to carry out simple skills, to recognise the emotional states of others, whether the teacher is a parent or other close associate, have been easily done from ancient times. Verbal communication and mechanical tools were widely used by *Homo habilis* three million years ago. Such a learning context is still characteristic of people today — up to about four or five years of age. This is *learning-how* or *procedural* knowledge: learning perceptual–motor skills that engage the world directly.

The unprepared learnings are derivative: they are concerned not with immediate action upon objects but with action upon *symbols* which stand for real objects. This is *learning-that* or declarative knowledge: learning about the world. These unprepared

Table 1.1   Learnings for which we are prepared and unprepared

A   *Prepared learnings*
Learning to avoid certain foods
Learning to walk
Learning to talk
Learning to read emotions from facial and bodily gestures: recognising friendliness, hostility,
    fear, love
Learning to imitate people who are significant to us
Learning how to do simple acts and skills

B   *Unprepared learnings*
Learning by verbal instruction of how-to-do skills
Learning from strangers or from people we dislike, when they explain verbally rather than
    demonstrate by example
Learning to read and write
Learning how to use other symbol systems
Learning how to understand symbolic manipulations
Learning by rote things we do not understand
Learning to decide between several options when we cannot see the immediate
    consequences of each
Learning to change habitual behaviour by logical argument (e.g. giving up smoking when you
    know it is bad for you)
Learning complex problems in the abstract

learnings are organised into bodies of knowledge called subjects or disciplines (e.g. mathematics, biology, history, fine arts, language, psychology and so on). They constitute our cultural heritage (what other people have discovered) and are preserved in symbolic form so that they need not be learned afresh by each new generation. Further, they tend not to be learned in the immediacy and warmth of the family.

In short, prepared learnings are *direct*: one learns in the first person. Unprepared learnings are *indirect*: they involve learning in the third person.

Look at it another way. Concrete (learning-how) skills are related to survival: people who did not easily learn how to talk, how to read emotion and distinguish friendly from hostile gestures, and how to learn basic hunting, cooking and other skills, would not survive for as long as those who learned such things easily. This relationship has extended for over 150,000 generations: time enough for natural selection to take a hand. Perhaps we are now prepared by our biology to learn these things.

Unprepared learnings — learning-that — are not so readily related to survival. No one actually dies or has fewer children, by virtue of being unable to do mathematics or to read. Learning-that is also very much younger in our evolutionary history. One of the earliest known symbolic writing systems is that of the Ebla, who flourished in the Middle East about 6,000 years ago — a mere 300 generations — and even then, writing was restricted to special castes. Universal education is, in Western countries, only five generations old.

So biology can have had little hand in preparing the average individual for learning-that. In fact, people show enormous variation in their aptitude for learning to read and write — possibly because the genetic factors involved are unevenly distributed and have yet to be ironed out by natural selection. In order to compensate for this uneven distribution, it is necessary to assist nature with formal instruction, the latter being taught in institutions called schools. Schools are there to help people to master unprepared learnings — those things they would not otherwise learn and which it is believed to be important that they should learn.

There is little point in setting up schools to teach students things they would learn at home or in their immediate community. Let us just look at learning to use words. Most people achieve a high and consistent degree of mastery within the first four years of life of learning to *talk*. There is a much wider variation in mastery of learning to *read*. If left to themselves or to tuition by parents, some children will learn to read easily and fluently; others learn with extreme difficulty, even though they may cope very successfully in other ways. Children thus do not go to school in order to learn how to speak, but they do go in order to learn how to read —because, in the latter case, nature is not working so hard for them. Why blame schools and modern methods (or traditional methods, or for that matter, any sort of methods) for not teaching children to read as fluently and as easily as they can talk? Ginsburg and Opper (1969, pp. 224–5) are a little unfair when they say:

> In the first two years of life, for example, the infant acquires a primitive concept of causality, of the nature of objects, of relations, of language and of many things, largely without the benefit of formal instruction or adult 'teaching' ... an infant ... is curious, interested in the world around him and eager to learn. It is quite evident that these are characteristics of older children as well ... Consequently, it is quite safe to permit the child to structure his own learning. The danger arises precisely when the school attempts to perform the task for him. To understand this point, consider the absurd situation that would result if traditional schools were entrusted with teaching the infant what he spontaneously learns during the first years ... One can speculate as to the outcome of such a program of training!

The last speculation of these authors is easily resolved: if schools *did* provide such a program of early training, the children would learn just the same. The program would simply be unnecessary.

Learning to read is a different matter. If left to learn 'spontaneously', some children do learn to read, most do not. This kind of learning — based on human intervention between the learner and the world in the form of a system of symbols — is one for which most people are not biologically prepared. Hence, such learning needs to be aided or accelerated by another process: *teaching*. And in view of the fact that the sum total of human invention is now enormous, the teacher has to be a specialist.

A MANAGER OF MANY KINDS OF LEARNING

Years ago, in the village school or in the one-teacher school in the outback, teachers were quite likely to be a well-known member of a small community. They interacted with the child for six years or longer and had some chance of creating a warm, personal context for learning, acting *in loco parentis* (as a parent substitute). People tend to learn easily in such a context.

Today, high schools are large and are organised (significantly) by subject department — not by class, year or other basis that encourages or prolongs teacher–student interaction. The contacts students have with a teacher (who usually commutes to work from another community) are made and broken several times a day. The pattern is repeated with a new set of teachers the following year. Subject matter is usually all-important, not the formation of bonds between teacher and student.

This appears inevitable, in view of the role of schools. Given our complex society and such new media of instruction as microcomputers, it is necessary that students cope with a learning context that is less personal than that in which they accomplished their 'learnings-how' as little children. Schools thus provide — and depend upon — a more impersonal structure to promote learning, a structure that involves making indirect learning easier for the learner. Thus, it is necessary for someone of superior knowledge to take professional responsibility for decisions about what will be learned in what order, at what point the learning is deemed adequate, and what procedures and learning materials (such as books, maps, tapes, diagrams, etc.) might be helpful. Above all, unprepared learning requires motivational support. Whereas prepared learning is simply doing what comes naturally, learners of academic content most often need 'persuading' to learn indirectly. Such learning may therefore require an elaborate structure if it is to take place efficiently.

Sometimes, however, that structure becomes slightly too prominent; a little more warmth and intimacy might make learning in the third person that much easier. But then we have a conflict if (as frequently happens) intimacy and warmth get in the way of the role of manager. Whether we like it or not, the orchestration of all that structure makes the teacher a *manager of learning*. The legal obligation is now less that of an absent parent and more that of a *professional*, who is held accountable to exercise 'reasonable care' and judgment.

What, then, are all these learnings that the teacher is to manage? What are the important roles of schools? Schools are places where, first of all, learning is to take place that would not otherwise occur. Mostly, such learning is unprepared, and relates to abstract and established knowledge. School learning might, however, also include quite different learnings, such as those that once occurred in the extended family but are now excluded in anonymous urbanised living conditions. Finally, schools address learnings that may occur elsewhere, such as the workplace, but which may more conveniently be learned in school. Our list of learnings looks something like this:

- learning abstract knowledge at second hand;
- learning to interact with other people — learning about feelings, values and morality;
- learning about oneself — one's strengths, weaknesses and goals in life;
- learning vocational and saleable skills;
- learning how to make use of leisure time;
- learning things throughout the lifespan that either did not exist when one was a child or were not learned for some other reason.

Four kinds of learning

All these learnings, as varied as they are, may be categorised under four headings:

- *cognitive learning*, such as acquiring knowlege;
- *affective learning*, or learning about feelings, values and emotions;
- *content learning*, as set out in syllabuses, such as the topics treated in a particular history course;
- *process learning*, which is concerned with how results are achieved. (What is happening to the way we *think* as we study history, physics or literature?)

Effective process learning can take place only on the basis of a firm foundation of content learning (Biggs, 1973a). Students have to know mathematics really well before they can derive new and elegant solutions. Nevertheless, there is an important distinction to be made, once the basic content foundations are laid, between content and process targets of learning. Too great a reliance on content learning results in a 'rear-vision mirror' approach to education (McLuhan, 1970). Trying to cope with the future on the basis of content learning is like driving by looking through the rear-vision mirror. If the road is straight (i.e. nothing is changing), it works very well. As soon as there is a change, the rear vision can no longer serve as a guide to future action.

Alvin Toffler (1971) was, like McLuhan, a persuasive futurologist. If, as he puts it, 'Today's fact may be tomorrow's misinformation', then teaching the wisdom of the ages — content learning — would be wasteful of time and resources. That 'wisdom' is already decaying into superstition. Toffler believed that, on the affective side, students should be taught how to involve themselves more directly with the lives of other people, and, on the cognitive side, to develop strategies that will enable them to cope at first hand with novelty and the absence of precedent.

Four functions of schooling

Writers such as McLuhan and Toffler emphasise various aspects of schooling that need to be noted. We may put all these views together to obtain a two-way table: aim (process or content) by domain (cognitive or affective), as outlined in Table 1.2.

Table 1.2   Domains and targets of schooling

	Content aim	Process aim
Cognitive domain	1 Traditional subject matter and disciplines	2 Problem-solving approaches, discovery learning
Affective domain	3 Explicit teaching of traditional values	4 Values clarification; concern with feelings

Four functions of schooling may thus be distinguished:

1. *Content learning in the cognitive domain.* This is the most widely accepted and traditional role of schooling. It involves the passing down of our cultural and scientific heritage, usually by expository teaching methods in the conventional subject areas.

2. *Process learning in the cognitive domain.* This aspect always has been present in schooling, but usually with skills and strategies being limited to particular subjects. It has usually been assumed that in situations providing little guidance or formal structure — such as discovery learning — students will evolve their own coping strategies (Bruner, 1966).

3. *Content learning in the affective domain.* This used to be an explicit function of public schooling. Nowadays, State education systems often claim 'neutrality' in this area, whereas most private schools are quite definite about their emphasis on the teaching of traditional values. In fact, as we shall see many times throughout this book, it is impossible to be neutral. Official statements claiming neutrality are themselves value-ridden.

4. *Process learning in the affective domain.* This area is of increasing concern — in both positive and negative ways. The aim is to provide experiences, such as group discussion, games and role-playing, that help students clarify their own ideas of right and wrong. For example, a problem might be presented that involves a moral dilemma where the guidelines from the community are in conflict both with each other and with self-interest.

Not everybody agrees that all four aspects should be the legitimate functions of public schooling, particularly as far as the affective domain is concerned. Our point is that responsible educators have at some time or another identified these functions of the school: they indicate the kinds of learning that *may* take place. Teachers should be aware of them and of the conditions under which they may be promoted.

IS TEACHING A PROFESSION?

What is the difference between a witchdoctor and a medical practitioner? Both might note the appropriate symptoms in their patients; both might alleviate those symptoms by administering compounds containing quinine. In one case, the quinine is contained in chewed-up bark and, in the other, in a capsule, but that is not the issue.

The essential difference lies in the reasons *why* the treatment is given. While each practitioner would have an explanation, only one fits the comprehensive network of knowledge and procedures that we call *science*. It would not do even if the witchdoctor gives the perfectly logical and non-magical reason that chewing the bark of the cinchona tree has usually worked in the past. Such an answer is based on the inductive principle: if such-and-such works for this disorder, it is likely to do so again. That is not, however, a theory.

The cure rate of folk medicine or witchdoctoring might even be little different from that of your friendly neighbourhood general practitioner. Yet in our culture the latter is regarded as a professional and the witchdoctor is not.

We are then faced with the question: what is the difference between a profession and a craft or trade? Ultimately, it comes down to two interrelated issues (Telfer and Rees, 1975):

- a protected 'licence to practise';
- an intensive education in the underlying theoretical knowledge that gives validity to the skills and expertise required to practise.

How does teaching fare as a profession? All State education departments certainly require evidence of credentials before teachers can be employed and these credentials depend upon the satisfactory completion of a course of studies at a college or university. These studies, further, include psychology as the scientific study of learning. Thus, to the extent that education is based on psychological (and other) theory, it would seem that teaching may be regarded as a profession.

However, things are not as simple as this. As long ago as 1899, William James said:

> I say moreover that you make a great, a very great mistake, if you think that psychology, being the science of the mind's laws, is something from which you can deduce definite programs and schemes and methods of instruction for immediate schoolroom use. Psychology is a science and teaching is an art; and sciences never generate arts directly out of themselves. (James, 1962, p. 3)

Nevertheless, psychology is not, in James' view, irrelevant to education. It is important in the particular sense that:

> Teaching must *agree* with the psychology, but need not necessarily be the only kind of teaching that would so agree; for many diverse methods of teaching may equally well agree with psychological laws. (ibid.)

Here, then, is the beginning of the answer to the question. Although teaching may well be an art, it does appear that there is a theory behind the practice of that art. Teachers, of course, have to know their subject matter; they also have to know certain theoretical knowledge about the nature of learning. To that extent, then, teaching is a profession.

Espoused theory and theory-in-use

An important distinction needs to be made between the explicit theory underlying teaching and the practice that takes place anyway on the basis of tradition, wisdom, habit and the intuition of the individual teacher. In simple terms, this could be seen as the distinction between *teacher education* and *teacher training*. Argyris (1976) captured this distinction with his terms *espoused theory* — which is the 'official' and explicit theory behind a particular practice — and *theory-in-use* — which is the actual reason for the practice. All activities, even witchcraft, have a theory-in-use; only professions have an espoused theory. A professional decision is one where the theory-in-use is the espoused theory.

This espoused theory may or may not coincide with the theory-in-use. For example, a State education department may impose external examinations because the Minister for Education wants to please the business lobby, who find external examinations very convenient for the purposes of job selection. Espoused theory, on the other hand, using research evidence, may suggest that external examinations positively motivate only a small minority of students, causing many others to drop out early or adopt test-taking strategies of short-term value, producing results that are predictably inconsistent with official departmental aims. In this case, the decision cannot claim to be a *professional* one.

To take a different example, a particular teacher may use the technique of praising students for doing good work and ignoring their mistakes, because it was the way he or she was taught and thus formed the personal theory that students do better when they feel good about things. In this case, there is good coincidence between the theory-in-use and espoused theory, or more precisely, the two espoused theories, those of self-concept and operant conditioning (see Chapter 3).

Clearly, it is better when the individual's (or the State department's) theory-in-use coincides with espoused theory, so that practice is theoretically explicit and coherent. We believe that this is gradually taking place and, as it does, education becomes more a profession and less a craft or a political exercise. Suppes (1974, p.4) made the point strikingly: '... education needs to develop its own deeply structured theories ... that drastically reduce, if not eliminate, the need for wisdom'.

FROM THEORY TO PRACTICE

Two main sets of forces affect the nature and quality of an individual's teaching. The first is individual, involving what that teacher knows and can do; the second is social, involving the teacher as a member both of a general community and of a professional body.

These forces are depicted in Figure 1.1. Theory-in-use is represented as a map of Australia in order to emphasise that practice is unique to a particular country. While the body of knowledge that validates the teaching profession is international, countries have educational systems of a certain stamp. Applications that work in one teaching system may not work in another. In Chapter 9, for example, we see that for cultural reasons behaviour modification works rather differently in the United States than it does in Australia. Let us examine these individual and social forces.

Individual forces

General life experiences. These consist of those things — such as upbringing, values, schooling, etc. — that determine the sort of person the teacher is. We teach the way we do because we were taught that way ourselves. The factors and the resulting values are learned informally — before and during the teaching experience itself, and independently of formal training as a teacher.

General education. Education is regarded here from a liberal-arts point of view. It is not so much what the teacher is to know (see below for further discussion) but that the study of one subject in depth, or other culturally valued subjects in breadth, will make one 'a better sort of person'. There are two main outcomes to such an education:

1. *The value system of an educated person.* In other words, one would want the emerging teacher to operate ethically, compassionately and with lack of prejudice, to be concerned to act professionally rather than industrially, to recognise the contribution that may be made by other subjects and disciplines, to be open to, but cautiously critical of, innovation, and so on.

2. *A model of human nature.* A teacher, as a person whose profession is founded upon human interaction, will have some sort of theory-in-use about humanity: what people are like, how they learn, what their motives are. Liberal-arts studies, both implicitly and explicitly, help a person construct such a model. While the relevance of psychology and sociology is obvious, such diverse subjects as history, geography, economics, politics, biology and even mathematics, all make their contribution to the student's understanding of what humans are like.

These first two components are not particularly related to education as such. They are chiefly concerned with building up what will become a personal philosophy (**5**, see Figure 1.1), which will contribute to one's theory-in-use. The teacher has not studied anything (so far) for its particular relevance to education. It is the next two components that are specifically concerned with educational applications. They lead directly to the teacher's espoused theory.

Content disciplines. These are the subjects that teachers are to teach. They need to know them well in order to teach effectively. There is, however, some controversy about how well 'well' is, particularly at high school level. Traditionalists (with one model of human nature) place this level considerably higher than humanists (with a different model): one claims to teach 'mathematics', the other to teach 'children'. Despite the word games, however, all teachers teach both — the most adamant teacher of 'children' teaches them *something*. Part of professional teacher education is thus devoted to building up competence in the subjects the teacher plans to teach.

Educational foundations. Several disciplines are regarded as 'foundations' of educational practice. These disciplines are directed at three main contexts:

- *the individual context,* consisting of psychology, particularly what psychology has to say about development, learning, motivation and individual differences (this book addresses this context);
- *the social context,* consisting of sociology, history and economics;
- *the value context,* consisting of philosophy and ethics.

Components **3** and **4** in Figure 1.1 together form **6** — the espoused theory of education. This might be called 'educology' or the 'logos' of education (Biggs, 1976). Content knowledge and some knowledge of foundations interact to form curriculum theory, instructional design, evaluation, and a host of skills and techniques related to the teaching of particular subjects, using appropriate media.

Espoused theory (**6**) and personal philosophy (**5**) combine to shape theory-in-use. Eventually, experience (practice teaching and in-service) tend to merge all three, so that the way one operates 'naturally' would, in an ideal world, be the same as that dictated by professional considerations.

Figure 1.1   Forces influencing the nature and quality of teaching

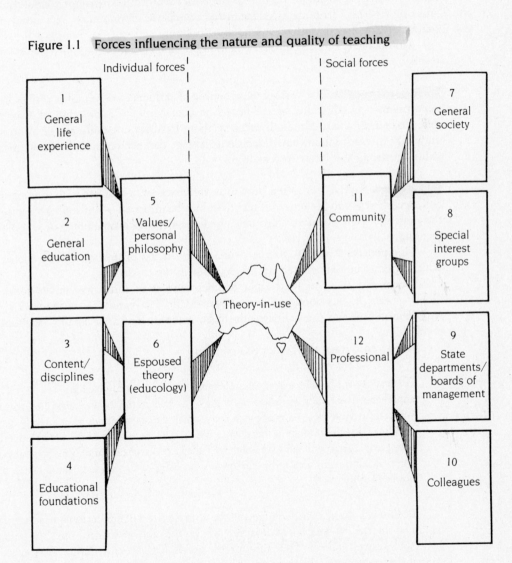

Social forces

General society. Schools fulfil society's expectations and needs with varying degrees of success. What happens in schools is obviously a function of this network of values, expectations and needs.

Special-interest groups. As well as exerting a general effect (**5**), special groups within society focus community expectations, producing specific pressures on the school and teacher. Such special-interest groups include parent and citizen groups, school councils and other formal structures by means of which the community in general or in particular can directly influence school procedures.

Components **7** and **8** combine, then, to provide **11**, the community's view of the teacher's theory-in-use.

State departments. One very obvious source of influence on school practices is 'the department' (or education office/board of management in the case of Catholic/independent schools). Although recently there has been a significant devolution of authority towards school-based decision-making, the influence of the department is still very strong and likely to remain so.

Colleagues. A final, and often powerful, influence on a teacher is that exerted by colleagues' beliefs and practices. This effect may be informal — through interaction in the staffroom — or formal — through a professional association, union or school staff meeting.

Components **9** and **10** interact, then, to form the professional components **12**, which directly influence a teacher's behaviour in the classroom.

There are, then, at least eight distinct sources of influence on the teacher's theory-in-use. In this book, we concentrate on the left-hand side of Figure 1.1, the individual forces and the contribution to be made in that area by the discipline of psychology.

It may encourage the reader to note that:

> Fortunately for you teachers, the elements of the mental machine can be clearly apprehended and their workings easily grasped. And, as the most general elements and workings are just those parts of psychology which the teacher finds most directly useful, it follows that the amount of this science which is necessary for all teachers need not be very great ... A general view is enough, provided it be a true one; and such a general view, one may say, might almost be written on the palm of one's hand (James, 1962, p. 5; original edition, 1899).

Both psychological knowledge and the complexities of educational practice have increased in the 80 years since James wrote the above words, but his point is nevertheless well taken. The amount of psychological knowledge that directly contributes to espoused theory is not indeed very great. This book, at any rate, will fit in 'the palm of a teacher's hand'.

But more to the point is not the amount of psychology content, but *how it is used*. As a glance at Figure 1.1 will show, psychology may affect the theory-in-use by a person's philosophy and values (**5**) as well as by espoused theory (**6**). Given that a teacher knows the subject matter and can teach it, that person will still be a better teacher for having studied psychology and formed a model of human nature around that study. To know, for example, that children think *differently* about the world than adults do (see Chapter 5) results in the construction of a different model of what people are like.

MODELS OF HUMAN NATURE

Why do people do things as they do? Because that is the way the human being is made. If we ask what way is *that*, different people will come up with quick, off-the-cuff generalisations based on their own particular model.

McGregor (1960), working in the context of business, distinguished two directly opposed models of human nature. According to Theory X, people are basically lazy and greedy. In order for them to work at all, they need to be motivated by rewards and pay-offs, with severe punishments administered to prevent them stepping outside acceptable codes of conduct. People are not to be trusted; they are basically evil and self-seeking. They must therefore be supervised constantly and be continually reminded of the unpleasant consequences of deviant or unco-operative behaviour.

According to Theory Y, on the other hand, people are basically good. If left to themselves, they will do those things that will develop their talents and will co-operate with other people to develop theirs. People do bad things because of a self-fulfilling prophecy: the assumption that they cannot be trusted makes people act untrustworthily.

The crucial difference between the two models hinges on this question of trust. Theory X says: 'You will get best results if you do *not* trust people!', while Theory Y says: 'You will get best results if you *do* trust people!' It is clear that a teacher acting on the assumptions of Theory X will come up with a greatly different work-space and pattern of interaction than one operating on Theory Y (see Box 1.1).

BOX 1.1   SOME EXAMPLES OF THEORY X AND THEORY Y

Theory X
'If you hit somebody or showed physical power you had their respect. It was well known we caught them a swift clout over the ear if they did something wrong. We also applied a boot to the area where it did most good. Actually of course my father used to chastise me much more severely than we were allowed to punish them. Other punishments inflicted were doing extra tasks ... or stopping their tobacco for the week.'

'It was a matter of control; teaching the lads what you wanted done. They all knew the score and you had to thump them ... mostly with the open hand, make a lot of noise and wouldn't cut their skin like a closed fist.'

Theory Y

'I really preferred to have married people working. Once a married man and his wife came along they would like to stay and build gardens; I used to give them land for gardens. I encouraged village crafts and cultural efforts such as dancing. Every night you could hear the throb of drums; it was very pleasant ... I never had any trouble the whole time I was there.'

'I got keen on land development. Why not divide some of it between me and a man who's been working for me for 10 or 15 years? ... I made certain conditions ... I stipulated that they should clear their land, plant it with coconuts and cover crop, and build a home within two years. Eventually I transferred the land to them ... now they're running a plantation in as modern a way as any European plantation I've ever seen ... It was my way of saying "thanks" to the lads who'd worked well for me ...'

Source: Interviews with ex-plantation owners, from *Taim Bilong Masta* (Episode, 'Masta me Laik Work'), Australian Broadcasting Corporation, April 1981.

The theory that one adopts depends not so much on psychological theory as on the commonsense philosophy developed through one's life experiences and value system (see **5** in Figure 1.1). McGregor arrived at his two types on the basis of business experience. Psychologists also have their set of models or theories based on other kinds of evidence.

Three broad schools of psychological thought are currently relevant to education:

- *behaviourist* psychology;
- *cognitive* psychology;
- *humanist* psychology.

A few years ago, we might have included Freudian psychology in the list, but the Freudian school of psychoanalysis (and its many derivatives) is not now of much concern to educators. Each of the three schools is 'true' — at least for one purpose or another. Psychologists cannot say with a unified voice: 'This is what we are. This is how we work!' What we can say is that each one of these models is convenient for tackling one aspect or another of the educational task.

Behaviourism: the reacting person

Behaviourism is a very influential school of thought which dominated psychology until very recently. It explains human behaviour in terms of how people *react* to their environment. If the environment is rewarding (i.e. if a certain course of action has a satisfying result) people will tend to persist with that behaviour. If the environment is unrewarding, people will pursue a different course of action. Thus the emphasis is on what people *do*, not on what they think or feel: behaviourists study observable behaviour and its relationship to observable stimuli in the environment, rather than unobservable contents of the mind. This objective focus was derived from experiments, with both animals and humans performing simple tasks in highly structured and controlled situations. What goes on inside an individual is seen in terms of a telephone switchboard: an incoming call originating from one instrument (the stimulus) is linked via the switchboard (conditioning) to another receiving instrument (response). Many different stimuli will be linked to many responses over a period.

Two major processes were put forward to account for learning: *classical* and *operant* (or instrumental) conditioning (for fuller descriptions, see Chapter 3). The word 'conditioning' is used because it is a *condition* that if something happens in the environment (e.g. a reward, a pairing of two stimuli), then people behave in a predictable way.

Many educators — whether or not they know much about behaviourist psychology — have a philosophy that is very compatible with this model of 'reaction' and firmly believe in high-structure educational environments. They will accordingly find much in the behaviourists' procedures and recommendations that gives form and coherence to their own thinking and practice. We shall examine some of these in Section B.

Cognitivism

The cognitivist model assumes that people try to *make sense* out of their environment rather than react unthinkingly to it. They attend to certain aspects of the environment that are in some way important to them and neglect others. They think about those aspects and extract their meaning. They solve problems and make decisions. Whereas behaviourists talk about the environment in terms of stimuli, cognitivists talk about the environment as *conveying information*, which is then 'processed'. The 1960s boom in computer technology provided cognitivists with a much better metaphor and terminology than the telephone switchboard underlying much behaviourist thinking (Biggs, 1968).

Cognitivists thus emphasise internal processes rather than external responses and are correspondingly more willing to admit the importance of innate factors. A critically important aspect is the study of the development of intellectual functioning. Cognitivists argue that with growth and critical experiences, the mental structures of children (through which they process information) themselves grow increasingly complex, and help them to extract deeper and richer meanings from the world as they grow older (see Chapter 5).

Many educators find this model (based on the notion that we primarily try to make sense out of experience) very compatible with their own views about the role of schools. If (to put it bluntly) the human organism is a computer that programs itself to handle increasingly complex problems, then school should provide carefully selected experiences that allow the child sufficient freedom to learn how to cope with them, and thus grow in information processing range and power. There is much Theory Y thinking here. Educators using this model would be more interested in how a problem is handled (process learning) rather than whether the correct answer is obtained (content learning).

Humanism

Humanist psychology (sometimes called 'third force' psychology) finds its roots in Jean Jacques Rousseau's 'noble savage'. If behaviourism's metaphor is the telephone switchboard and cognitivism's the computer, that of humanism is a native bush garden. The best potentials in people will be realised if, like the seeds of a native plant, they are allowed freedom to grow in their own way, with minimal clipping, pruning and artificial fertiliser. Humanism is even closer to Theory Y than is cognitivism.

This model was given a sharp boost in the 1960s. As the counter culture rejected the straight, logical and materialist ways of thinking of the establishment, which seemed scientifically and politically to be pushing the human race into self-created disaster, they emphasised feelings and interpersonal interaction based upon mutual respect and co-operation. Educationally, humanists would provide low-structure environments, and encourage children to develop their own potential in their own way and to respect that of others. In this model, cognitive learnings, both content and process, are given a low priority.

These three models of what people are like are clearly very different, but each has something to offer the educator: school has a function to perform in each of the areas of reacting, thinking and feeling.

In other words, in order to fulfil the common aims of schooling, it is necessary to adjust teaching strategies according to aims: to provide high structure to teach particular contents; to lower that structure to provide challenging situations that will stretch and develop students' problem-solving strategies; and also to foster individual potential and interpersonal good feeling. It is a matter of using the model that best fits the particular purpose — the latter will vary according to the particular task in hand and the particular student. Some students tend to be more 'reactive' than others: they like high structure, and work best when the task is clear and the options few. Other students work best when they try to work out for themselves how best to solve problems. In any case, all students could do with more good feelings, towards both themselves and others.

In this book, we draw unashamedly on various aspects of psychology which appear to us to offer most to the enlightened practice of education. People are reacting, thinking *and* feeling beings: accordingly, all three psychological schools of thought have something to say. If at times we appear to emphasise the thinking aspect, it is because that is an emphasis reflected in the statements of aims in most (if not all) school systems. It might also reflect the model of human nature most espoused by the authors.

SUMMARY

In this section, we have looked at the role of the school and the part which psychology might have to play in education.

Why have schools? Seven commonly agreed functions or aims of schooling were outlined. These fell into two groups. The first involved change of some kind with respect to the learner: vocational, individual development, transmitting culture and socialisation. The second group was industrial in intent: childminding, easing pressure on the labour market and providing employment. Our concern is with those aims that involve the student as a *learner*.

Preparedness for learning. We suggested that some kinds of things (prepared learnings) are easier to learn than others (unprepared learnings). Prepared learnings are basic to survival, and are related to our direct interaction with the world and other people, particularly those to whom we are naturally close. Unprepared learnings are to do with cultural inventions which are organised into subject matters. Such unprepared learnings require abstract thought and the ability to learn in this way varies widely between people. If unprepared learnings are to be learned — and the notion of civilisation itself demands that they should be — then special institutions need to be set up to assist in the process. This is one major reason for schools, although not the only one.

A manager of many kinds of learning. Schools exist because they do a job that no other institution does. A large part of that job is to teach abstract disciplines. But there are other parts of that job, such as learning to interact with other people, and learning the rules of society and life skills that enable work and enrich leisure. These learnings are of content and of process. They are cognitive and affective. They require a skilful manager, that is, a professional manager of learning.

Is teaching a profession? It has to be! We start, then, with the assumption that teaching *is* a profession, not just a craft. While all practitioners, professional or otherwise, have an implicit theory-in-use to guide their behaviour, professionals have as well an espoused theory that is based on scientific research.

From theory to practice. The way a teacher teaches is a result of many things. Two main groups of factors are distinguished: individual and social. The individual factors include personality, informal and non-professional training, which lead to one's personal philosophy, and professional training, which leads to the espoused theory. Social factors define the total cultural context in which the teacher works, and this is made up of components from department policies, roles, traditions, community attitudes and expectations, and membership of professional associations.

Models of human nature. All teachers have some kind of model of human nature, either implicit or explicit, incorporating a belief about how human beings 'work'. One way of typifying such models is in terms of how close they come to Theory X ('Do not trust') or Theory Y ('Trust'). People develop these models on all sorts of grounds and they constitute one important aspect of a total philosophy of life. Psychology can contribute to these models' relevance to teaching.

Psychologists have grouped themselves, in the main, around three models of human nature. The behaviourists concentrate on people as reacting to a highly structured environment. In this model, people tend to be passive and their options are few. Cognitivists concentrate on people as thinkers and problem-solvers in an environment that signals information to them. Humanists concentrate on how people feel about themselves and their relationships with others.

While educators may well have their preferences for one or other of these models, all three in fact have something to say about educational practice. As we shall see in Section B, each model is highly compatible with existing and recognisable models of schooling.

SECTION B

THE AIMS OF AUSTRALIAN STATE SCHOOL SYSTEMS

Education systems have their own answers to the question 'Why do we have schools?' According to the New South Wales Department of Education:

> The central aim of education which, with home and community groups, the school pursues is to give individual development in the context of society through recognisable stages of development towards
>
> perceptive understanding,
> mature judgment,
> responsible self-direction and
> moral autonomy.
>
> (Vaughan, 1973, p. 14)

The impact of this splendid-sounding set of aims is, however, dulled somewhat by the foreword to this document by the then Director-General:

> It must be emphasised that in accepting the statement and endorsing it for wider issue, the boards are in no way committed to any derivable courses of action.

The Victorian Minister for Education, for his part, prefaced a 1980 statement of aims with the reminder:

> A clear statement of aims and objectives in Victoria has never to this date been published. (*Victorian Education Gazette*, 13 February 1980)

He went on to outline the following aim:

> The central aim of education in Victoria is to provide educational experiences of the best possible quality, for children, youth and adults. Through these experiences they will have the fullest opportunity to —
> (a) reach an understanding of themselves and society (educational opportunity);
> (b) develop to their highest level of intellectual, emotional and social competence (educational achievement);
> (c) achieve socially responsible self-direction (education and values); and
> (d) build an abiding sense of community throughout our society (education and community).

Coincidence with the New South Wales statement can be seen in the references to individual development in the societal context and responsible self-direction. In fact, the aims of the education systems in New South Wales, Tasmania, Victoria and Western Australia are essentially similar.

The intentions of these education departments can be summarised in the form of nine objectives:

1. *academic achievement* (maximising the pupil's grasp of fundamental, school-based skills);
2. *further education* (encouraging children to enjoy learning and to pursue it);
3. *critical thought* (the ability to make objective and rational decisions on a range of issues);
4. *independence* (providing varying degrees of autonomy);
5. *creativity* (self-expression and participation in school-based cultural activities);
6. *leisure and health* (using the environment or physically and mentally healthy activities);
7. *social interaction* (the ability to communicate clearly and appropriately in society);
8. *group membership* (encouraging participation in formal and informal groups, with recognition of accompanying restraints and responsibilities);
9. *acculturation* (an introduction to the traditional philosophical bases of Australian society, such as Christianity and democracy).

There tends to be a good deal of controversy over these kinds of objectives. On the one hand, it is disputed whether or not the aims are appropriate; on the other, whether they are being realised. Almost half a century ago, a satiric essay drew attention to the way in which conservative influences can lead to out-of-date curricula in schools (Peddiwell, 1939). In the essay, a tribal leader introduced formal education which aimed to teach survival skills such as catching fish, clubbing horses and scaring off sabre-tooth tigers. An approaching ice age led to the disappearance of the stream, displacement of the horses by antelopes and extinction of the tiger. But the tribal elders insisted on the retention of the traditional curriculum because of its 'eternal verities' (see Box 1.2).

To what extent do Australian curricula rest upon 'eternal verities'? A survey of 1,567 members of societal groups (teachers, students, parents, business people and unionists) in six Australian States sought their views on what they expected of schools, teachers and teaching (Campbell and Robinson, 1979). There was a great deal of consensus and seven conclusions were drawn from the study (Campbell, 1980):

1. There is no general dissatisfaction with the educational values being espoused by schools. Only a small group of vocal and highly visible 'fundamentalists' draw attention to views and doctrines they find offensive.
2. The main function of schools is not to prepare children for work. Rather they should prepare people for society in terms of both coping with, and contributing to, its experiences. Living, not earning a living, is the focus for schools.
3. While teachers cannot simply do their own thing, they are not there to carry out the educational directives of governments.
4. Although the basic curriculum should be primarily concerned with the established basics of reading, writing, spelling and arithmetic, there should also be emphasis on discovering new knowledge and developing enquiry skills.
5. Teachers have a responsibility to ensure that children develop values of respect for authority, hard work, restraint and preparation for the future (the 'work ethic').
6. Children may be motivated by teacher directions, firm discipline and structure, but more effective motivators are:

   • teacher warmth, supportiveness and respect;
   • challenging learning tasks;
   • opportunities for co-operative participation;
   • feelings that they are needed and valued in activities.

7. The teacher should continue the traditional role of instructing and demonstrating, but should also work with the children.

In short, schools were seen as human learning communities, as well as institutions maintaining academic standards and traditional values. This seems rather a tall order. To what extent are schools succeeding?

Attainments in literacy and numeracy

A study by the Australian Council for Educational Reserach (ACER) measured pupils' attainments in literacy and numeracy (Bourke and Keeves, 1977). The skills tested were those considered essential for participation in Australian society. As well as estimating the number of Australians who could not attain these basic skills, the study sought to identify relationships between such variables as age, grade, ethnic origin, sex, language

BOX 1.2 THE SABRE-TOOTH CURRICULUM

The radicals persisted a little in their questioning. 'Fishnet-making and using, antelope-snare construction and operation, and bear-catching and -killing', they pointed out, 'require intelligence and skills — things we claim to develop in schools. They are also activities we need to know. Why can't the schools teach them?'

But most of the tribe, and particularly the wise old men who controlled the school, smiled indulgently at this suggestion. 'That wouldn't be *education*,' they said gently.

'But why wouldn't it be?' asked the radicals.

'Because it would be mere training,' explained the old men patiently. 'With all the intricate details of fish-grabbing, horse-clubbing and tiger-scaring — the standard cultural subjects — the school curriculum is too crowded now. We can't add these fads and frills of net-making, antelope-snaring, and — of all things — bear-killing.'

'But, damn it,' exploded one of the radicals, 'how can any person with good sense be interested in such useless activities? What is the point of trying to catch fish with the bare hands when it just can't be done any more? How can a boy learn to club horses when there are no horses left to club? And why in hell should children try to scare tigers with fire when the tigers are dead and gone?'

'Don't be foolish,' said the wise old men, smiling most kindly smiles. 'We don't teach fish-grabbing to grab fish; we teach it to develop a generalised agility which can never be developed by mere training. We don't teach horse-clubbing to club horses; we teach it to develop a generalised strength in the learner which he can never get from so prosaic and specialised a thing as antelope-snare-setting. We don't teach tiger-scaring to scare tigers; we teach it for the purpose of giving that noble courage which carries over into all the affairs of life and which can never come from so base an activity as bear-killing.'

All the radicals were silenced by this statement, all except the one who was most radical of all. He felt abashed, it is true, but he was so radical that he made one last protest.

'But — but anyway,' he suggested, 'you will have to admit that times have changed. Couldn't you please *try* these other more up-to-date activities? Maybe they have *some* educational value after all?'

Even the man's fellow radicals felt that this was going a little too far.

The wise old men were indignant. Their kindly smiles faded. 'If you had any education yourself,' they said severely, 'you would know that the essence of true education is timelessness. It is something that endures through changing conditions like a solid rock standing squarely and firmly in the middle of a raging torrent. You must know that there are some eternal verities and the sabre-tooth curriculum is one of them!'

Source: J.A. Peddiwell, 1939.

in the home and test performance. The sample consisted of 6,628 10-year-old pupils in 272 schools and 6,247 14-year-olds in 257 schools — representative of State, Catholic and independent schools across the country.

The reading tests indicated that at the 10-year-old level, 3 per cent (7,500 students) could not read a simple sentence; at the 14-year-old level, the figure was 0.8 per cent (2,000 students). Some 34 per cent of the 10-year-olds and 25 per cent of the 14-year-olds lacked the skills necessary to read a school textbook, reference book or magazine. Yet few Australian upper-primary or secondary schools provide courses in reading.

Boxes 1.3 and 1.4 show how the 14-year-olds tackled two of the test items. Differences in performance of students at government and non-government schools favoured the latter, but these differences were attributed to socio-economic or

---

BOX 1.3   TEST ITEM: BASIC NUMERACY

Task: Using the four basic arithmetical operations with whole numbers.
Sub-task: Using addition and subtraction to solve problems met in everyday
             life.

22 Here are some winning ticket numbers in a lottery.

100 PRIZES AT $1,000 EACH:

748	14922	25743	35975	40852	50048	61959	69653	79710	90234
1808	18357	26847	35978	41690	50913	61988	73021	79926	90320
3434	18901	26981	36173	42004	53092	62375	74324	84357	91157
5457	22508	28088	36492	42152	53644	64190	75074	84868	91894
6459	23678	29179	37415	42183	55311	67982	76490	85723	92206
8038	24088	29625	37757	46730	56410	68068	76598	86422	92369
9209	24147	30832	38675	47232	57401	68736	76753	87011	94520
8297	24966	33420	39627	47345	57482	68891	77674	87408	95040
10170	25312	35123	39724	47424	57645	69302	78429	88766	98032
14284	25647	35369	40391	49179	61854	69569	79000	89178	98361

Which number closest to 85000 won a prize?   Answer _____

	% Correct (C)	% Incorrect (I)	% No Attempt (NA)
Australia	77	21	2

	C	I	NA
Male	78	20	1
Female	76	22	2

	C	I	NA
Metro	78	20	2
Non-metro	76	23	2

	C	I	NA
Govt.	76	23	2
Cath.	81	18	1
Indep.	87	12	1

	C	I	NA
English (E) only	79	20	1
E + North European	76	24	0
E + South European	68	27	5
E + 'Other language	67	26	8
No English	58	29	13

Comments

1. Although the level of student performance on this item was not high, it is higher than the levels for Items 25 and 33 which also involved use of the four operations with whole numbers.
2. Students at government schools had a lower level of performance than students at Catholic schools who, in turn, had a lower level of performance than students at independent schools.
3. Students from non-English-speaking homes had a particularly low level of performance.

BOX 1.4   TEST ITEM: BASIC LITERACY

Task: Comprehending what is read.
Sub-task: Deriving the inferential meaning of a clause or phrase from the context in which it appears.

27 The headline on the front page, **Pay grab sparks off security clamp,** means
- ☐ sparks came off a clamp when it was grabbed and dropped.
- ☐ bandits grabbed the pay off some electric sparks.
- ☐ the payroll robbery will make the company take more care.
- ☐ the pay grabbers put the security men in a clamp.

	% Correct (C)	% Incorrect (I)	% No Attempt (NA)
Australia	74	22	5

	C	I	NA
Male	76	20	5
Female	72	24	4

	C	I	NA
Metro	74	22	5
Non-metro	74	22	5

	C	I	NA
Govt.	72	23	5
Cath.	76	20	4
Indep.	84	12	4

	C	I	NA
English (E) only	75	21	5
E + North European	70	26	4
E + South European	63	33	4
E + Other language	52	43	5
No English	60	27	13

Comments

1. This item is one of the few for which males performed higher than females (see also Items 17 and 26). The item content may favour the male students. This sex difference is not recorded by the 10-year-old students who were also asked to do this item.
2. Performance varied moderately with both languages in the home and type of school attended. Students attending independent schools performed better than other students.

Source: S.F. Bourke and R. Lewis, 1976.

socio-cultural advantage of their home background. Students from inner-suburban and some rural regions performed at a very low level.

Aboriginal students in Aboriginal schools in the Northern Territory recorded low levels of performance in the reading and number tests. This result introduced the dilemma of whether teachers should maintain and consolidate use of the Aboriginal language or English (see Chapter 6). The researchers regarded the lack of mastery of the skills tested as a severe disadvantage in participation as adults in Australian life (Bourke and Keeves, 1977, p. 269). The performance of Aboriginal students in conventional schools marked them, too, as a handicapped group. Their results were below those of the average Australian student of the same age.

Migrant students (who had at least one parent born outside Australia, and whose home language was either not English or a language in addition to English) constituted 14 per cent of the 10-year-old sample and 11 per cent of the 14-year-old sample. Of these, substantial numbers (59 per cent of the 10-year-old migrants and 43 per cent of the 14-year-olds) failed to master the reading tests but achieved greater mastery of the number test. The researchers pointed out:

> There is little point in emphasising identification of learning problems if the schools are not prepared or not able to help the student overcome the disability (p. 272).

When the results of the ACER studies were released, there was a great deal of consternation in the press, particularly by the Australian Council for Educational Standards (ACES). For example, Williams (1977, p. 9) wrote:

> The time is ripe for, and the situation demands, a clear statement, by a national body, of the minimum literacy and numeracy standards schools must be attempting to impart. *Given such a statement progress could be quite rapid* — particularly if funding were to be contingent upon the realisation of these objectives.

This suggestion was not taken up. In 1985, journalist Greg Sheridan felt it appropriate to write in the *Weekend Australian* (9–10 February 1985):

> Australian education is a disaster. An Australian Council of Education Research survey done a few years ago reported that one-sixth of the 14-year-olds sampled were unable to read a simple sentence, while a further quarter had only partly mastered reading skills.
>
> Having failed at education, the Australian school system seems to be turning towards a mixture of entertainment and propaganda. Bread and circuses, plus a little radical hot-gospelling, are no substitute for a decent education.

We take up the point about 'radical hot-gospelling' in Chapter 7 when we discuss values in education. But are attainment levels really any worse than years ago? In 1981 there was a flurry of correspondence in the *Sydney Morning Herald* (3, 4, 5, 10 September 1981) referring to 'declining standards', including some more ACER data showing 'no change' between 1975 and 1980. Doneau (n.d.) has published norming data and Higher School Certificate (HSC) examiners' comments over the years, which indicate that, if anything, general literacy and numeracy standards have *improved* over the last 30 to 40 years.

Adult illiteracy. One kind of evidence bearing on the 'declining standards' question relates to adult illiteracy. During World War II, conscripts (aged from 18 to 40) were given educational tests. The results were detailed in the Duncan Report (1944, in White, 1978): 4 per cent of these conscripts were totally illiterate (corresponding to 0.8 per cent of the 1975 14-year-olds), and 20 per cent 'partially' literate. Thirty years later, Goyen (1974) surveyed 2,000 Sydney adults on a door-to-door basis and asked them to read material on the pretext of carrying out market research. She found (among those who agreed to participate) that 3.6 per cent of all Australian-born respondents were illiterate (being unable to read, for example, STD dialling instructions), and of those born in non-English-speaking countries, 43.5 per cent were illiterate. In all, she estimates that about 10 per cent of Sydney dwellers are functionally illiterate. Interestingly, older illiterates greatly outnumbered young ones. Thus, while too many students still go through school and remain illiterate today, there were many more still who were slipping through in the so-called 'good old days'.

MODELS OF SCHOOLING

In Section A, we distinguished three models of human nature and suggested a parallel with various models of schooling. Now, we are considering the following questions: what models of schooling exist in Australia, and how do they relate to the models that see human nature as based on reaction, thought and feeling?

Reaction

There are two seemingly different models of schooling that fall under this first heading. However, both assume that learning is achieved through reacting to a highly structured environment. The actual structure of the learning situation is closed: the contents to be learned are contained within the system. Such an assumption is entirely compatible with the aim of content learning — learning is highly structured, and its contents can be defined, assimilated and applied. To this quite reasonable and widespread aim, we next add part of Theory X: the student will not learn this material unless coerced into doing so. We then have our historically first model of schooling.

Traditional schools. Throughout the civilised world, schools sprang from what we call here the 'traditional' model. The aims of schooling in this model are content learning in the cognitive and affective domains. Only recently in this country has the traditional model been seriously questioned as the basis of compulsory secular schooling. There have been 'progressive' schools since the turn of the century; in the 1930s, the New Education Fellowship enjoyed something of a vogue; and a few independent non-traditional schools have flourished for years. But the *majority* of Australian children went through the traditional system. What are the characteristics of this model?

    Aims.   Content learning, concentrating on the skills of basic literacy and numeracy; the basics of some science, geography and history; and the values (e.g. conformity to authority) that make up 'good citizenship'. The good content learners went on to more content learning; the not-so-good joined the workforce after three to four years in high school or central school.

    Methods.   In keeping with the aim of content learning, methods were expository — presenting information to as large a number of students as possible (which mostly meant as high a student–teacher ratio as teacher unions and some parents would tolerate). Discipline therefore tended to be coercive, not only because of Theory X, but to maintain the viability of a high student–teacher ratio. It was assumed that many, if not most, students would learn only if there were no alternatives. Also in keeping with Theory X, punishment for deviance outweighed reward for compliance. Reward was usually reserved for the successful minority, in the form of prizes, scholarships, approval and wider job opportunities.

    Structure.   Likewise in keeping with Theory X, students were presented with two options: obey the rules or else. Most students took the desired alternative. Elective subjects were few. Regulations governed dress, mode of entry and departure from the school premises as well as mode of addressing staff. Attendance at and duration of lessons were strictly controlled. It is interesting that teachers were not exempt from departmental assumptions deriving from Theory X: they were transferred and promoted from school to school by departmental edict, were also subject to dress regulations, and public criticism of either policy or practice was forbidden.

In recent years, aspects of this model have been modified — in some States (and in some schools in all States) quite markedly. Nevertheless it began as, and remains in some forms, the nearest to a universal model for Australian school systems.

The founders of compulsory schooling, in their wisdom, thought that people would have to be forced to learn; their basic assumption that people — or at least students — were fundamentally reactors, not agents. The second model that shares this assumption suggests a significantly different model of schooling.

Behavioural engineering. We have called this second model 'behavioural engineering' and it incorporates features suggested by behaviourist psychology. The emphasis has shifted from moulding the *student* to structuring the *situation* and the *task*. It is Theory X without the venom.

Aims.   Content learning, expressed in terms of behaviour change (see below).

Methods.   Various — any which enhance the learning of content. Motivation maintained non-coercively by positive reinforcement (e.g. reward, see Chapter 3) and (if possible) immediate feedback of results. Tasks usually detailed and arranged into small steps.

Structure.   Very high, but entirely focused on the task and learning context, not on implicit or affective aspects.

Instead of elaborating on these particular points, let us take some examples of the behavioural engineering approach.

Instructional design. Instruction is closed. The objectives of each learning episode (a lesson, lab class, demonstration, field trip, discussion, etc.) are assumed to be specifiable in advance if they are worth anything at all. In other words, the students' behaviour (here is the main link with behaviourism) should be *different* in some clearly specifiable way after instruction than it was before. Hence, the term *behavioural objective* (Mager, 1961) was used.

Each learning episode is stated in terms of a clear behavioural objective: 'The student will be able to perform correctly eight out of 10 sums involving the addition of three two-digit numbers.' If, after the lesson in question, the student can reach the criterion (which is clearly stated in the objective), the teacher then moves on to the next episode. If not, the student goes through the episode until the objective is reached.

Instruction thus has a clear-cut design, as illustrated in Figure 1.2. The teacher states the objectives (**1**) taking into account the student's 'entering behaviours' (**2**) — behaviours that are needed in order to achieve the specified objectives and that the student can already perform. Appropriate entering behaviours for the objective in question would include: 'can recognise and write all numbers from 0 to 99'; 'can recite accurately the sums and differences of pairs of numbers from 0 to 9'; 'can perform the operation of carrying from units to tens'; and so on. The teacher then provides instruction (**3**) in the new sum, concentrating on the additional 'behaviour' not included

Figure 1.2   A flowchart for the closed instructional model

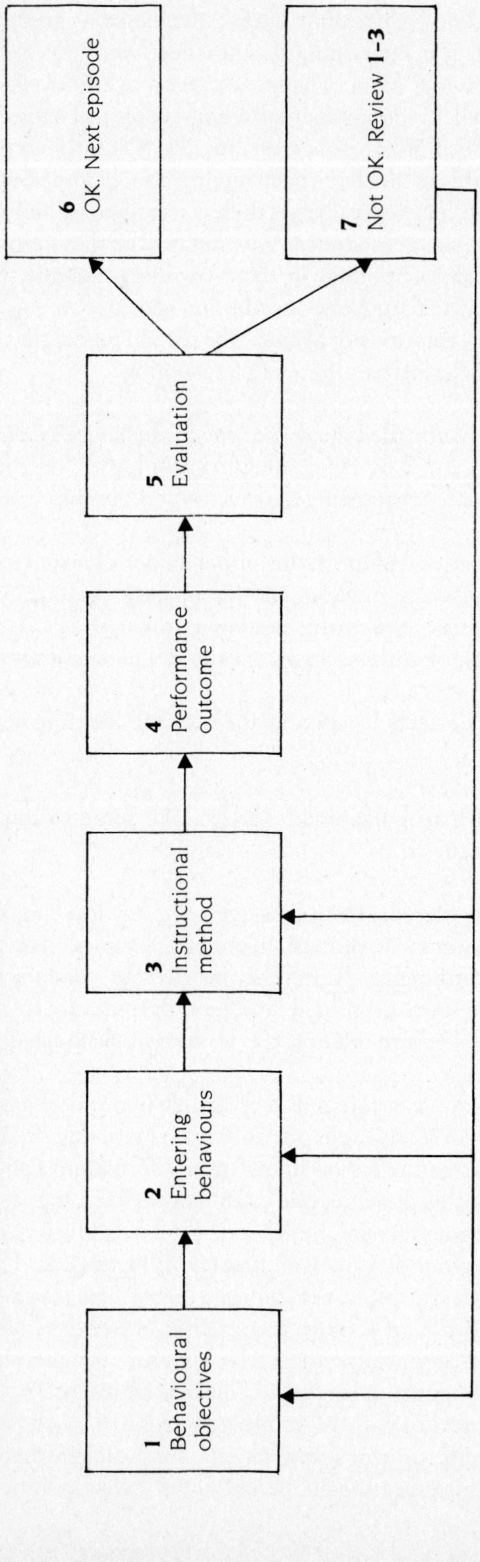

| 1 Behavioural objectives | 2 Entering behaviours | 3 Instructional method | 4 Performance outcome | 5 Evaluation |

6 OK. Next episode

7 Not OK. Review 1–3

in the entering behaviours (i.e. cumulating the addend, as the entering behaviours referred only to pairs of numbers in the sum). The student performs the 10 sums (**4**) and performance is evaluated (**5**). If performance reaches criterion, the teacher moves on to the next learning episode (**6**); if it does not, the teacher then reviews what might have gone wrong at steps **1** to **3** (**7**). Thus the model provides a strategy for retracing the steps to diagnose the difficulty.

It will be noted how the terminology of the objectives avoids unobservable processes: the verbs 'understand', 'appreciate', 'think', 'work out', etc., do not appear. It is not that these are unimportant, but rather that for effective instruction the student must show 'understanding' (in this example, by carrying out the sums correctly). Such terms are unnecessary if the teacher has designed the objectives appropriately.

Critics (e.g. McDonald–Ross, 1973) often charge that this approach over-simplifies complex concepts, but the learning objectives need not be as simple as in this example. A teacher may define appreciation of Shakespeare's literary style in behavioural terms as: 'The student will be able to identify correctly eight out of 10 sonnets, five of which are written by Shakespeare, and five by a contemporary.' Some may regard the appreciation of literary style as involving much more than successfully accomplishing what that task implies, but the correct identification (to specified standards) cannot be seen as a trivial accomplishment. In the case of motor skills, the use of behavioural objectives is eminently sensible and has been used successfully by one of the authors in such a complex task as learning to fly an aeroplane (Telfer, 1979b).

Different examples of this general approach are the variants known as personalised system of instruction or PSI (Keller, 1968), precision teaching (Kunzelmann, 1970) and mastery learning (Block, 1971). All these methods require:

- the specification in advance of what constitutes good learning, although not necessarily in behavioural terms;
- a period of instruction;
- evaluation in terms of the original specification of objectives.

Evaluation using these methods is called *criterion-referenced*. The student is evaluated in terms of an objective criterion, not in relation to others in the class (see Chapter 10). Instruction is thus what is called individualised and is quite different from the traditional model, which relies on class-based (*norm-referenced*) instruction and evaluation. Clearly some students will need more time, and more re-runs, to reach the required standard than will others.

Programmed instruction (PI). This technique involves structuring the task so that it is broken into small steps, each of which is tested. The tests are constructed so that most students have a 90 per cent chance of passing the next step if they have successfully completed the previous one (Skinner, 1968). The theory is that the task is so tightly structured that the student makes few mistakes and is continually rewarded — by the in-built success rate — throughout the task.

Programmed instruction may be presented on the page, or the steps can be incorporated in a mechanical or electronic device to which the student responds by pressing a key. Such teaching machines have reached a very high level of sophistication in computer-assisted instruction (CAI), where students can have elaborate 'conversations' with the machine about the task and their performance.

Behaviour modification. Behaviour modification is not so much a method of instruction as a means of motivating students. The basic principle is to reward every desirable response the student makes and, in most applications, to ignore deviant responses. This technique is discussed at length in Chapter 8.

Accountability. The accountability movement is not a method of teaching so much as a means of evaluating and controlling the schooling process itself: it has more political than educational implications. Nevertheless, it arises directly out of the behaviourist 'reacting' philosophy.

It is in fact quite an old policy, known last century in this country as 'payment by results' — which in effect meant that the teacher's salary depended on the examination results of the students. As the teacher's job is to teach, that job is not being done if the students do not learn; therefore the salary is not being earned. The notion did not last very long in that form. However, modern versions of accountability are gaining currency in the United States, as for example in the idea that the school is legally responsible if an intelligent adolescent completes school and is functionally illiterate. We have not gone that far yet in Australia, but recent studies show that Australian teachers are becoming increasingly concerned about their professional responsibilities and accounting to others for them (Telfer, 1980, 1981).

Thought

The emphasis in the preceding section was on content learning; here it is on process learning. The appropriate target for learning is how the student solves problems and makes decisions, rather than whether or not the right answer is obtained. To this extent, then, the situation is open: it is not always possible (or desirable) to specify in advance what is to be learned. Several State education departments give this aspect prominence in their statements of aims, although all would still acknowledge that content learning also has its rightful place in the school experience.

Open schools
Aims.   Process learning: in the cognitive domain, this would take the form of problem-solving strategies, self-directed learning and extraction of personal meaning from an experience, and in the affective domain, developing a self-concept of competence (see Chapter 3).

Methods.   Discovery and enquiry methods rather than exposition: the student is given sufficient information to solve the problem, but is not told the processes to use. The emphasis is on activity, self-selected tasks, 'centre of interest' and group discussion.

Structure.   Moderately high in terms of task presentation. If discovery methods are to work, the teacher has to be very careful to design the situation so that the student does not become lost or discouraged through insufficient information. Structure may be high or low on non-instructional issues (e.g. dress, school regulations), although teachers in these schools usually prefer low structure in such areas.

Open education recalls the analogy of learning to swim. Extremely low structure teaching would throw the learner in the deep end; very high structure would keep the supporting hand permanently under the learner's stomach. Open education should provide just that amount of support that leads to solo swimming at the earliest possible time.

The 'supporting hand' can be withdrawn at any of several points in the instructional program: setting of goals, selecting suitable tasks, acquiring information, solving problems and evaluating outcomes. Many younger students, however, definitely feel insecure in such a model: they want to be told what to do, how to do it and when it is good enough to stop doing it (see Chapter 2). There is a fine line between 'spoon-feeding' and being left alone to the point of feeling unable to cope.

The cognitivist model can be accommodated either in particular lessons, or in a total school environment of an appropriate kind. An open school is designed to provide the flexibility that is usually required by discovery-type programs: one group may work co-operatively here, two combined classes might be taught there (thus releasing a teacher for small-group supervision) with an individual doing private study in the quiet withdrawal room over there.

Feeling

The environment created for the 'feeling' model is often confused with that for 'thinking'. Open-space design is desirable for both, but in fact aims, methods and structures are quite different.

Free schools. The total educational environment which caters for the feeling aspect is identified in Australia as a 'free school'. Examples are Currumbena in Sydney and the Education Reform Association school (ERA) in Melbourne.

Aims. Almost total concentration on the affective domain. It is believed that cognitive learning will take care of itself once individuals feel good about themselves and have a personal need to solve a problem. They will then organise themselves to do so.

Methods. Based on 'centre of interest' and on personal relationships. A student expresses interest in a particular topic or issue, and pursues it either alone or in co-operation with other students who have expressed like interests. The teacher acts as resource: encouraging (above all) and providing information when required. Evaluation is not intended to point out failure but simply to provide supportive comment. On the question of the role of the teacher, Carl Rogers, one of the most influential humanist educators, says that significant learning 'rests not upon his lectures and presentations ... [but] upon certain attitudinal qualities which exist in the personal relationship between the facilitator and the learner' (Rogers, 1969, p. 106).

Structure. Low, in all areas. Formal teaching is provided if students desire it, but there is no compulsion to attend lessons. Structures relating to interpersonal conduct are variable. A. S. Neill's Summerhill school imposed no rules for behaviour beyond

'You can do anything you like as long as you don't interfere with anyone else' (Neill, 1960). In order to interpret how this worked in practice, the students set up a council to determine particular cases of 'interference'. While the result was sometimes as punitive as in a more traditional school, the point is that such structure as did exist was erected by the students themselves.

Some of the aims of humanism can be realised by particular lessons in otherwise traditional schools. Man: a Course of Study (MACOS), to some extent, and Social Education Materials Project (SEMP), to a greater extent, are kits for high-school use that may be used in social-science courses in otherwise traditional classrooms. (This was not, however, the case in one otherwise traditional State system: both MACOS and SEMP were banned from Queensland schools in 1978. For discussion of this issue, see Smith and Knight, 1978 and Duhs, 1979). Likewise, recent English and, especially, drama courses emphasise affective outcomes, often employing encounter-group techniques in which students are encouraged to express their feelings for each other without inhibition. These and some other techniques are discussed in Chapter 7.

SUMMARY

The aims of Australian State school systems. Australian school systems share the content and process aims enumerated in Section A. As a result of a large nationwide survey, it was noted Australians are generally satisfied with the values espoused by schools. There was consensus that:

- Schools should prepare students for society rather than concentrate solely on the narrower vocational aims.
- Schools should be concerned both with basic literacy and numeracy and with broader process-oriented aspects.
- Teachers should provide direction but also warmth and challenge.

Small wonder there was consensus: the schools are perceived to be doing what most people want them to do. But *are* they doing what they say they are? Aims are one thing, achieving them is another. One director-general of education made it clear that endorsing a set of aims 'in no way' implied courses of action for achieving them. It is particularly interesting, then, to see how far the endorsed aims are in fact reached by present schooling systems.

There is much reason for concern about literacy and numeracy if 25 per cent of 14-year-old students in Australian schools cannot read a school textbook, reference book or magazine; and nearly 1 per cent cannot read a simple sentence. However, this is not, as some fundamentalists would like to think, a recent phenomenon and specifically the result of modern methods: there is evidence that adult illiteracy is much higher than 1 per cent, and progressively higher in *older* age groups.

Society today is so much more complex than it was even 20 years ago: schools have a correspondingly more difficult job to do and teachers need to be more knowledgeable and capable; that is, more professional.

Models of schooling. Three main schools of psychological thought were suggested as being relevant to education and, specifically, as providing the theoretical underpinning for various models of schooling, of which the traditional model of yesteryear is only one.

The view based on reaction has philosophical affinities with two models of schooling: traditional and behavioural engineering. Both models rely heavily on external structure. The traditional model applies the structure to the study so that behaviour is constrained, while the engineering model applies the structure to the situation and task.

The model of schooling that is based on thought as paramount is quite different. It provides for a higher degree of self-direction, but in a situation that is carefully designed to challenge the learner's developing intellectual potential. Open schooling is compatible with the aims and structure of this model. The model that emphasises the importance of feelings draws its theoretical inspiration from humanist psychology and is exemplified in free and alternative schools.

FURTHER READING

On school in the context of society
R. Bates and E. Kynaston, *Thinking Aloud: Interviews with Australian Educators*, Deakin University Press, Geelong, Victoria, 1983.
R. W. Connell, *Teachers' Work*, George Allen & Unwin, Sydney, 1985.
P. H. Karmel, *Schools in Australia: Report of the Interim Committee for the Australian Schools Commission*, AGPS, Canberra, 1973.

Bates and Kynaston conducted interviews with 36 leading Australian teachers, academics, writers and administrators, giving their views on education. While some of the interviews are dated — many interviewees smarting from the big cut-backs of 1981–82 — most are still active and hold even more exalted positions. It is an interesting view of Australian education from the top down.

Connell's book is a fascinating account of the lives and thoughts of several Australian teachers. Here is the actuality of teaching, and how teachers learned both to adapt and to maintain their ideals in some very unpromising environments, including the Sydney western suburbs. A 'must' reading for all intending teachers.

The Karmel Report incorporates the first major official rethink for Australian education for decades and likewise should be read by all intending teachers. You will then be able to see it as it *is* (Connell) and as it *should be* (Karmel).

On standards in Australian schools
S. Doenau, *Have School Standards Declined?* Edvance Publications, Pennant Hills, NSW (undated).
J. P. Keeves, J. K. Matthews and S. F. Bourke, *Educating for Literacy and Numeracy in Australian Schools*, Australian Council for Educational Research, Hawthorn, Victoria, 1978.

Keeves et al. is a report of an Australia-wide, representative sample of 10- and 14-year-olds tested in reading, writing and number by the Australian Council for Educational Research. The results are surprising and often sobering.

Doenau is a hastily compiled and privately published compilation of evidence (test norms, examiners' reports, etc.) strongly suggesting that standards have *not* declined in the last 10 or 50 years — rather the contrary is the case.

On models of schooling
Reacting

R. Mager, *Preparing Instructional Objectives*, Fearon, San Francisco, Calif., 1961.
M. D. Merrill (ed.), *Instructional Design: Readings*, Prentice-Hall, Englewood Cliffs, N.J., 1971.
R. M. Gagné and L. J. Briggs, *Principles of Instructional Design*, Holt, Rinehart & Winston, New York, 1974.

Mager's book is small, easy to read and one of the first significant statements on behavioural objectives. Merrill has collected many significant readings on different aspects of instructional design, from objectives to evaluation, and is highly recommended. Gagné and Briggs offer an integrated analysis of all stages of closed instructional design.

Thinking

J. S. Bruner, *Towards a Psychology of Instruction*, University Press, Cambridge, Mass., 1966.
D. W. McNally, *Piaget, Education and Teaching*, Hodder & Stoughton, Sydney, 1975.

Bruner is concerned with the relationship between cognitive psychology and educational practice in broad terms, with some particular applications to maths and social studies, McNally with the influence of Piagetian thought on Australian schools.

Feeling

R. M. Jones, *Fantasy and Feeling in Education*, New York University Press, New York, 1968.
A. S. Neill, *Summerhill*, Hart, New York, 1960.
D. A. Read and S. B. Simon (eds), *Humanistic Education Sourcebook*, Prentice-Hall, Englewood Cliffs, N.J., 1975.
C. R. Rogers, *Freedom to Learn*, Merrill, Columbus, Ohio, 1969.

Jones is an account of using MACOS in a more affective way than usual (Jones thinks Bruner's MACOS is too intellectual). Read and Simon is a general manual. Neill and Rogers are both grand pioneers in this area: Neill's story is about one of the most famous free schools ever; Rogers emphasises humanistic psychology in educational practice.

QUESTIONS

Questions for self-testing

1. What are the major functions of schools in society? List at least seven answers which have been suggested.
2. Provide three examples of learnings for which we are biologically prepared and three examples of unprepared learnings.
3. What four categories of learning do schools provide? Give at least one example of learning for each category.

4. For the cognitive and affective domains, distinguish between a content aim and a process aim.
5. Give an example of conflict between espoused theory and theory-in-use in a school or education system.
6. What are some of the influences on a teacher's choice of theory-in-use? Identify seven sources.
7. Distinguish between McGregor's Theory X and Theory Y models.
8. How is the term 'conditioning' related to the word 'condition'?
9. Distinguish between behaviourism, cognitivism and humanism.
10. Describe programmed instruction.
11. How does an open school differ in aims, method and structure from a free school?

Questions for discussion

1. You have been given a free hand to design what you regard as the ideal school. Provide brief details of its aims, method and structure, and justify your choice.
2. Is the description 'manager of learning' an understatement of the role of a classroom teacher?
3. At a social gathering you are discussing career choices with a medical student and a law student. It is rather forcefully pointed out to you that teachers receive a salary (not charging a fee for service) and are employed in a bureaucracy which regularly supplies clients. How, then, you are asked, can teachers call themselves 'professionals'? What can you say?
4. 'I'll tell you one thing,' says The Most Venerable Staff Member as you begin practice teaching, 'it didn't take me long to find out that the educational psychology we studied had nothing to do with real teaching. And I'll bet nothing much has changed 20 years later, or has it?' How will you respond? Note that this question is repeated after Chapter 11. Compare your present answer to what you will say then.
5. To what extent are the functions of the school and its accountability affected by changing roles of the family, peer group, media and church as agencies of socialisation?
6. A study of Victorian secondary schools (Carpenter and Western, 1984) identified the following proportions of students who had high results:

Government schools	19%
Catholic schools	18%
Independent schools	28%

A Queensland study (Beswick, Hayden and Schofield, 1983) provided a different distribution:

Government schools	21%
Catholic schools	20%
Independent schools	21%

What conclusions would you draw from these two sets of results? What do you think the correlates of success at school would be? (You might like to make use of your library and the original studies to help you answer these questions.)

For more information see:

P. Carpenter, 'Does the school make a difference?', *Education News* **19**, 12 March 1985, 12–15.

P. G. Carpenter, and J. S. Western, '*Origins, Aspirations and Early Career Attainments*', Report to the Department of Education and Youth Affairs, Canberra, 1984.

D. Beswick, M. Hayden, and H. Schofield, *Evaluation of the Tertiary Education Assistance Scheme*, Australian Government Printer, Canberra, 1983.

Part 2

The individual learner

In the Russian language, teaching and learning are seen as so inter-related that the one word *obuchenie* may refer to either teaching, or learning, or both. In English, we use two separate words, which allows us the opportunity of thinking about one process independently of the other. That in turn allows teachers to go through the motions of teaching without thinking about whether or not the students are going through the motions of learning. In Part 2, we try and redress the balance by looking at what those 'motions of learning' might be in the context of teaching. What motivates students? Why do they attend to some things and not others? How do they read in and store information? How do they use it in the future? What limitations on memory capacity might there be?

Psychologists have built up a considerable amount of knowledge about three basic processes of cognition. A general term to describe them is derived from computers: *information processing*. A fixed-capacity information-processing system is a helpful way of describing how information is coded, stored and subsequently recalled. That description is useful for teachers to know in broad outline.

Humans differ from computers, however, in three main ways:

- They 'program' themselves.
- Their processes are activated internally, not from a power supply.
- They can be made aware of the fact that these processes are occurring internally and can use that knowledge to direct and control their own learning.

Chapter 2 discusses the basic cognitive processes of selectively attending to an information-rich environment, and organising it in various ways to suit prior experience and knowledge. The 'energy' that activates all these processes may, however, get out of control when threatening things happen, such as taking exams, or practice teaching. We discuss ways of handling that situation when it occurs for students, student teachers and teachers themselves.

Why do learners learn things? Why does anyone do anything? Chapter 3 discusses the question of *motivation* of processes: what kinds of motives there are, how different motives lead to different kinds of learning and what conditions lead to the more appropriate kinds of motivation. In particular, the question of the effect of extrinsic motivation on intrinsic is discussed.

Put the principles of learning and motivation together, add an institutional context, then the learner's perspective on it all, and Chapter 4 is the result. Students in varying degrees become aware of their motives for learning (or for not learning) and devise strategies for dealing with the situation in which they find themselves. Whereas Chapter 2 dealt with learning as a *cognitive* process, Chapter 4 deals with the *metacognitive* dimension.

This metacognitive dimension is used to construct a model of learning, from the point of view of the learner. This presage-process-product (or '3P') model of student learning is used to look analytically at how common teaching decisions affect the learner's approach to the task, which are conceived as deep, surface and achieving approaches. Deep approaches lead to structurally rich outcomes and positive feelings of satisfaction and involvement, surface approaches lead to fragmented outcomes and to feelings of alienation, and achieving approaches lead to maximised grades.

Institutions of learning, and those who teach in them, are caught in a bind: their major task is to teach declarative knowledge. Learners thus have little to bring from their own experienced world of procedural knowledge, and unless they happen to be intrinsically interested in particular content, tend to engage 'school' knowledge at a surface level. Further, the running of institutions requires procedures that greatly encourage the natural inclination of students to surface learn what they are ignorant about. Course structures, fixed time slots, accreditation procedures, busywork, and compulsory routines readily produce cynicism. Every teaching decision has at least two perspectives: the teacher's and the student's (not to mention the administration's and the public's). Teachers need to take both perspectives into account.

Chapters 2, 3 and 4 thus lay the foundation for understanding the individual learner from two perspectives: from that of the psychologist looking in, and that of the student looking out. We look at process from three angles: information processing, motivational processes and metacognitive processes. But learners change as they grow and develop; they interact with other learners and form values and feelings about their world. We therefore continue with the process theme—developmental and social processes — in Chapters 5 and beyond.

2

Learning, memory and activation

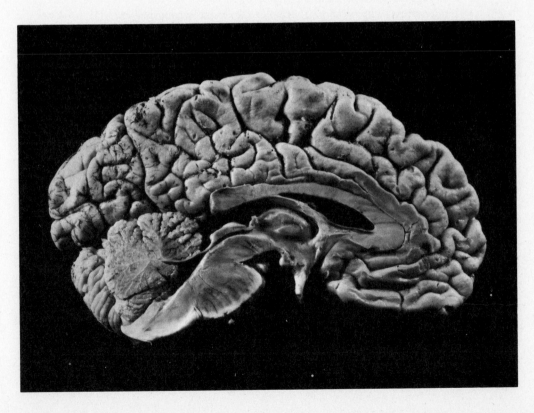

OVERVIEW

Sometimes we find it easy to remember names, numbers, addresses and dates. On other occasions, just as we need the information, our memory lets us down. Why does this occur? How are memory and learning related?

It is usually far easier to get teenage boys to read motorcycle magazines than *Meanjin Quarterly*. Why do students pay attention to some things and not to others? What attention-grabbers can teachers use when teaching boring or unpopular subjects? Questions addressed by this chapter include the following:

- How much information can we store in our memories?
- Do we learn by our mistakes?
- Does our memory's capacity determine our intelligence?
- Do pupils react differently to examinations, to open classrooms, or to highly structured classrooms?
- In what way do teachers accommodate these differences?
- Do teachers experience common patterns of anxiety?
- What can be done to alleviate student and teacher anxieties?
- How can students learn to beat examination nerves?
- Can jogging increase mental performance?
- Under stress, why would a footballer tackle the wrong player?
- How can the school counsellor help the classroom teacher and the individual pupil?

When you have finished this chapter, you should be able to do the following:

1. Describe three broad stages of learning.
2. Describe three memory systems.
3. Explain the three factors which determine whether or not we pay attention.
4. Explain how a communication gap can occur between teacher and student.
5. Provide three properties of working memory.
6. Distinguish between rote and meaningful learning.
7. Link the processes of dismembering and remembering.
8. By means of a simple diagram, show how the arousal system links with the sensory register and working memory.
9. Distinguish between the energising and interfering effects of arousal.
10. Explain the Yerkes-Dodson Law concerning arousal, task complexity and the quality of performance.
11. Describe the effect of over-learning on learner stress.
12. Distinguish between trait anxiety and state anxiety.
13. Distinguish between teacher burn-out and teacher rust-out, and describe how to avoid both.
14. List four important roles of the school counsellor.
15. Describe three basic methods of employing variability as a teaching technique.

SECTION A

We deal in this chapter with two sorts of processes: the *cognitive processes* of paying attention, learning by rote and learning by understanding, being conscious of what we are learning, memorising and recalling things that we have learned; and *activating* all these cognitive processes.

Activation refers to the energy that drives the system. Sometimes we are low, listless and uninterested in learning, while at other times we are on a high, willing, and 'rarin' to go' — not go anywhere in particular, just 'go'. *Motivation*, on the other hand is concerned with going somewhere quite definite, with learning something in particular. Motivation specifies the object of the verb 'to learn'; activation does not. Motivation is dealt with in the following chapter, activation in the present one, along with the cognitive processes.

This chapter concerns cognitive and activating processes located at three main stages.

- *input processes*, concerned with paying attention, learning and storing information;
- *output processes*, concerned with memorising and recalling previously learned material;
- *activation processes*, concerned with energising all these different stages.

THREE STAGES IN LEARNING: INPUT PROCESSES

The learning process has three broad stages: attending to particular stimuli in an environment busy with activity; processing the information presented by the selected stimuli; and storing it so that it may be used later.

Attending. In any situation, we experience a huge variety of sensations: the amount that we *could* learn is impossibly large. A massive amount of information is received through our five senses, but it is registered only briefly. We have to select from this 'register' of sensory impressions, as we are distinctly limited in the number of things we can attend to at once. For example, it is not possible to read the paper and listen to the news at the same time, nor to attend to someone's conversation while we are daydreaming. We attend selectively, to only one train of thought at a time.

Processing. When we make up our minds to attend, something must then be done with that information. We think about it. To be more specific: we rehearse it by repeating it over and over again, or code it by linking it to something we already know. On being introduced to Fred Austin, for example, we can remember his name by repeating 'Fred Austin, Fred Austin, Fred Austin...' over and over, or by thinking 'Fred, ah yes, he reminds me of my Uncle Fred. Austin: that's right, Uncle Fred, used to have an Austin A40...' This second way of remembering is usually better, although problems can arise. If Uncle Fred had sold the A40 and bought a Mini Minor our new acquaintance would probably not be very amused at being addressed as 'Fred Morris'. Whether we code or rehearse, however, it is done consciously in working memory.

Storing. After processing, we need to store the information in the long-term memory in such a way that it can be recalled to consciousness when required in future.

Opinions differ as to how best we may construe these three stages of learning, and how they interact with each other. First, there is the *structural* model of memory espoused by Atkinson and Shiffrin (1968), according to which each of the three levels of memory has its own storage system. Second, there is the *levels of processing* model of Craik and Lockhart (1972), which suggests that how well something is remembered depends on the quality of the process used to memorise in the first place. Both views have been very influential, but both grossly oversimplify (Baddeley, 1976). The current view, as indeed in psychology in general, is *functional*: one selects the kind of model that best suits our particular purposes.

We are concerned here with presenting a model of memory that best suits classroom learning. That is, we need to understand the conditions that affect:

- paying attention to the task at hand;
- consciously thinking about doing the task;
- remembering on cue important features of the task, or conclusions that might be drawn from the experience.

A useful way of conceptualising these functions is in terms of a modified Atkinson–Shiffrin model, referring to three different memory *systems*, rather than stores, with each system working on a different time scale.

The first system is the *sensory register*, which is concerned with how we pay attention by selecting, or 'precoding', information that is important to us. The time scale here is very short, no more than a second.

The second system is *working memory*, which corresponds to our attention span or memory of the very recent past. It is the surface of the everflowing 'stream of consciousness', as William James (1890) describes it, and is of limited capacity. An item floating on the surface of the stream is visible for only a minute or so, and in that time it needs to be processed in various ways if it is to be retained.

The final system is *long-term memory*, where processed information is stored and may be available for recall for periods as long as a lifetime.

These three systems carry out different functions and it is convenient to treat them separately. Nevertheless, they are inextricably linked, in particular by a central *plan*, or executive, which plays a role both in governing *what* we attend to (in the sensory register) and in *how* we attend to it (in the working memory), while the plan itself comprises what we have learned in the past (long-term memory). We might portray the systems and their interconnections as shown in Figure 2.1.

Figure 2.1   Three memory systems in processing input

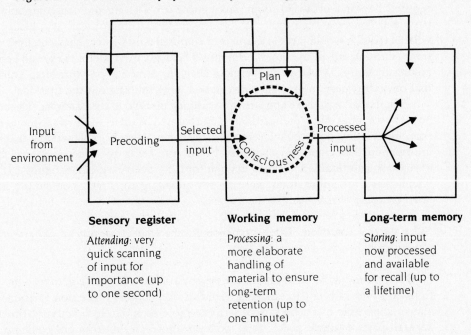

Sensory register	**Working memory**	**Long-term memory**
Attending: very quick scanning of input for importance (up to one second)	*Processing*: a more elaborate handling of material to ensure long-term retention (up to one minute)	*Storing*: input now processed and available for recall (up to a lifetime)

The sensory register

Ultra-short-term storage is carried out in what is usually called the sensory register (Atkinson and Shiffrin, 1968). All sensory impressions are retained for a period lasting up to one second, depending on several factors, such as the strength of the stimulus. Sperling (1960) showed that people can retain large numbers of digits for about one-third of a second, after which the retention rate drops dramatically to about seven or eight digits as they move from the sensory register to working memory.

The properties of the sensory register may lead teachers to believe they have the attention of their students when they do not. Johnny is gazing out of the window, apparently miles away; his teacher knows that he is not attending.

Teacher: ...and so Captain Cook was killed on the landing at Hawaii ...
Johnny! What were the last words I said?
Johnny: And-so-Captain-Cook-was-killed-on-the-landing-at-Hawaii.
Teacher: Hmmmm. At least look as if you're paying attention then.

The teacher was sure that Johnny was daydreaming. Johnny in fact wasn't paying attention, but the teacher had given him a sensory-register test, not a probe of his attention-paying working memory. Johnny, on hearing his own name, simply hauled in the jumble of words that was still echoing around in his sensory register and read them off. He could play it back, but that doesn't mean he was paying attention.

The cocktail-party phenomenon illustrates more properties of the sensory register. I am in a crowded room, talking to a small group and conscious only of its particular conversational topic. If a multi-directional microphone was placed right where I stand, it would pick up a jumble of confused noises — yet I have focused on one track, shutting out all the others. But now I hear my own name: the group behind is talking about me. 'Me!' I think. Without changing direction or expression, I tune into that obviously more interesting conversation, now shutting out the first one.

On the surface, there appears to be nothing unusual in the example. The curious point, however, is that I 'preheard' my name before I heard it — if I was so intent on the first conversation, how could I have heard my name? A likely explanation is that all the information that could be physically heard was being received at a level below awareness, and retained just long enough for it to receive a quick scanning to decide which pieces of information were worth attending to. I was consciously aware, however, only of the result of the process.

Why we pay attention. Three factors determine whether or not we pay attention to something.

1.   *Mental set.* Mental set is established by a deliberate plan (e.g. to read this page, to listen to the radio or to talk to a friend). It is a conscious decision to attend. It is almost impossible to attend satisfactorily to more than one such activity. But as the cocktail-party example makes clear, concentration can slip from one conversational train to another or, with the best will in the world, we simply go off daydreaming when we really should be listening to what a speaker is telling us.

2.   *The physical properties of the stimulus.* 'Low-key' stimuli, such as a flat monotonous voice, a dimly lit picture, or a blurred or opaque image, are hard to attend to. Bright lights and loud sounds are easy to attend to. Perhaps even more important than sheer signal strength, *variation* in the stimulus and changing stimuli hold our attention very successfully. Effective public speakers, for instance, constantly change the pitch, volume and pace of their words.

3.   *Physiological or internal states.* We pay attention to the smell of cooking when we are hungry. When we are anxious, we attend both to our feelings of stress and discomfort and to outside stimuli that may conceivably spell threat. Such stimulation is very distracting and may make us perform badly.

What do these three conditions add up to? Each one spells out some way in which external stimuli may be important to us — because we decide they are, because they are physically insistent or because they have biological survival value. The process that occurs at the gateway of consciousness — sorting out the important from the unimportant stimuli — is called *precoding*.

Precoding is a kind of importance filter (Deutsch and Deutsch, 1963) or allocator of priorities. It is as though all the inputs to the sensory register are stacked upright so that the most important one is always the tallest at any given moment, and it is that one that enters working memory; the rest drop unlamented through the floor. In order to maintain attention on a particular line of inputs —that is, to concentrate on the task at hand — the trick is to ensure that task input is always the tallest.

A communication gap. What *I* decide to be important may be quite different from what someone else decides to be important. While physically we might be in the same situation, our different perspective or different backgrounds make it likely that we will have different priorities and hence literally see a different world. When we discuss it afterwards, and find we disagree about even the simplest things, each may conclude that the other is just plain stupid. That may or may not be true; the real point is that each has been working on different information, and we are bound to disagree.

Teaching involves communication; for communication between teacher and pupil to take place, each must have similar plans, so that their mental sets are similar and each will precode similar information as important. In that way, each will attend to the same things. However, Holt (1970) argued that such identity of purpose between student and teacher is unlikely.

> For children, the central business of school is not learning, whatever this vague word means; it is getting the daily tasks done, or at least out of the way, with a minimum of effort and unpleasantness. The children don't care how they dispose of it. If they can get it out of the way by doing it, they will do it; if experience has taught them that this does not work very well, they will turn to other means, illegitimate means, that wholly defeat whatever purpose the task-giver may have had in his mind (p. 47).

Holt illustrates this in the following example. Teacher and student are each employing quite incompatible plans, even under the most favourable circumstances of one-to-one interaction and goodwill:

> I remember the day not long ago when Ruth opened my eyes. We had been doing math, and I was pleased with myself because, instead of telling her answers and showing her how to do problems, I was 'making her think' by asking her questions. It was slow work. Question after question met only silence. She said nothing, did nothing, just sat and looked at me through those glasses, and waited. Each time, I had to think of a question easier and more pointed than the last, until I finally found one so easy that she would feel safe in answering it. So we inched our way along until suddenly, looking at her as I waited for an answer to a question, I saw with a start that she was not even thinking about it. She was coolly appraising me, weighing my patience, waiting for that next, sure-to-be-easier question. I thought, 'I've been had!'.

How do teachers get their students to adopt the same plan and thus the same precoding priorities, to see the same inputs as the tallest? This is probably the most important question in teaching. It is a large part of 'motivating' students: getting them to do what the teacher sees as important. One way of doing this is for teachers to accept students' priorities, whatever they may be, as is done in some of the more radical free schools. This practice assumes that learning *something* is better than actively resisting learning anything. Another method is to try to convince students that a rewarding career hinges upon close attention to the lesson of the moment. A third is to make them terrified of the consequences of not paying attention. These issues are dealt with in Chapters 3 and 8.

Another answer is more cognitive than motivational. The teacher may induce the appropriate mental set by introducing the material to be learned with statements of objectives, pre-tests, advance organisers and other devices such as overviews. All of these are intended in various ways to 'prime' the learner to take special note of what is to come. We shall examine some of these in Section B.

Working memory

The most important feature of working memory is that it is of limited capacity. This limitation may be construed in two ways. Consider, for example, the following mental arithmetic problem: 333 multiplied by itself. Logically, it involves only knowing that $3 \times 3 = 9$ and knowing how to add up — a 9-year-old should be able to do it easily. However, most adults find it difficult. Clearly, this is not because it demands special knowledge, but rather because we need to hold the various steps in mind.

The familiar digit span test will give a good idea of some of the main features of working memory. Glance at the first row of digits below, and read from left to right at the rate of about one digit per second, saying the digit to yourself. Then close your eyes and write the series on a scrap of paper.

$$4 \quad 5 \quad 7 \quad 0 \quad 9$$

Now repeat the performance for the following series, dealing with each series at a time.

(a) 6 4 0 3 9 5 1
(b) 4 2 1 7 3 9 6 0
(c) 5 8 3 0 1 7 9 2 6
(d) 1 3 5 7 2 4 6 8 1 3 5 7 2 4 6 8

Which series was the hardest? Which the easiest? Most people find c the hardest and d the easiest. But d needs much more space than c: d has 16 digits and c only nine. Of course, this need not be the issue. Usually there are not 16 'things to remember' in d, there are *four* (odd numbers, even numbers, 8 the largest number, repeat). The series was coded into a more economical form, using previous knowledge as the basis for the code.

How do people remember other series (if the digits don't correspond to a known telephone number or some other relevant number)? One possibility is just to let the mind go blank and 'hold', without doing anything. This method is suitable if it is only necessary to hold the material for 30 seconds but, if any distraction occurs, the material will be dislodged from working memory and impossible to retrieve from long-term memory. (A familiar example of this is when we look up a phone number in the directory, pause momentarily and think of something else — and then find we have to look up the number again.) Alternatively, one can keep the number by repeating (recycling) it until it is no longer required. Such repetition — called rehearsal — will also help fix the number in long-term memory. If the number can also be coded in whole or in part, then so much the better.

Digit span and age. The number of random digits one can hold is referred to as one's digit span, which is remarkably constant for a given individual. Digit span is typically over four digits at age five, rising to six at age 10, settling at around seven in adults. This constancy led to a 'slots' theory of short-term memory: that the average person has the 'magical number seven (plus or minus two)' (Miller, 1956).

Unfortunately for this theory, the number of 'slots' seemed to vary according to the items in the test. Whereas adults can hold seven unrelated digits, they typically hold only six letters and five unrelated words (Dempster, 1981). Further, Case (1985) in a series of studies showed that by teaching adults a new number language, their span reduced to that of six-year-olds doing the same task. Chi (1978) showed that 10-year-old chess experts remembered fewer digits than a group of adults (who were not expert at chess), but the children far surpassed the adults in remembering chess positions that were exposed in a typical span task. In other words, variation in digit span is attributable to familiarity with the content. The main reason children have smaller spans than adults, then, is that adults usually have a much larger knowledge base, and more experience to automatise their knowledge and coding processes (Case, 1985).

Rote and meaningful learning. Two kinds of processing, then, ensure that material is learned for later recall: rehearsal and coding. Coding may be used where the material has some kind of structure, and the individual has the relevant background knowledge to make use of that structure. Obviously, someone who didn't know the difference between odd and even numbers would be unable to make use of that code in remembering the above series.

Rehearsal has the same compressing, or chunking, function as coding. It is used in physical skills, and in verbal tasks where there is no intrinsic structure to the material or where the individual is unable to use what structure there is. Rehearsal is also used when the learner wants to make sure that learning is verbatim, or 100 per cent accurate: it is applied to the actual words used, without reference to their meaning, and is thus called *rote* learning. Actors, for instance, will rote-learn their lines — not because they do not understand them but simply to ensure accuracy.

Meaningful learning — by coding — is much more economical, more stable and usually more enjoyable than rote learning. It is applied to the meanings of the words, rather than the words themselves. Material learned by coding may be reproduced in a new version: the meaning remains the same, but the words may be different. This in fact, is a crucial test that distinguishes rote from meaningful learning: rote-learned material cannot be replayed in a greatly changed way (obviously one can use synonyms for individual words), whereas material that has been learned with understanding can be rephrased and transformed.

This point about transformation highlights a distinct weakness in evaluation procedures in school. Teachers in general *value* accurate, verbatim responses. This is partly because of a confusion between accuracy of wording and accuracy in meaning, but also because it is much easier to mark for accuracy of wording — when teachers attempt to assess a student's transformations, they themselves have to be very sure of their subject matter. Consequently, we do tend to give credit for correctly recalled material, rather than for how well or ingeniously the student can apply that material in new situations.

Recoding. Coding takes place on the basis of previous knowledge, and may be very rapid and unconscious (as when an experienced reader interprets a sentence without consciously analysing the meaning of each word), or slow and quite deliberate (as when we try and decipher the meaning of a new word from its context).

That last example, deciphering a new word, raises an important issue. How can we code a new experience when nothing quite like it has occurred previously? It all depends on how much the new experience has in common with earlier ones. If there is a very great deal in common, we might code the new experience as 'Uh-huh. Thingamajig again' (William James again). Or we might note some differences, and in trying to make sense out of them, recombine our past experience in new ways, as when trying to work out the meaning of a new word from its context. That recombination is called *recoding*.

Each new experience, then, is *matched* to what is already known. It is unlikely that the match will be exact, but there are varying degrees of *mismatch*. When the mismatch is optimal, growth will occur: there is a change in code structure (called *recoding*) to reconcile novel elements of the new experience with the elements of the old. Piaget called this process 'accommodation'. Not only is the new content learned, but the learner's codes have changed in a more complex, more sophisticated direction.

One important aspect of recoding is its direct link with intrinsic motivation (i.e. our personal interest and involvement in a task). A task that demands no recoding is boring: we have seen it all before, nothing new is happening. If there is some mismatch, so that recoding is required, the individual is challenged: the situation becomes interesting, even exciting. If the mismatch is too great, it becomes overwhelming and threatening; and if there is total mismatch, the situation becomes incomprehensible and is unlikely to evoke interest. The degree of intrinsic motivation experienced by a student thus depends upon the match between current experience and the knowledge gained from previous ones. It is sometimes possible for teachers to design experiences that create the appropriate degree of mismatch for students. There are, however, great difficulties in this, particularly in whole-class teaching that does not allow for differences between individual learning rates. The whole question of intrinsic motivation is dealt with at length in Chapter 3, and we shall return to it there.

Finally, all these processes of coding, rehearsal and recoding are integrated with each other, and with attentional and memory-retrieval processes, by means of the executive plan. It is the plan that gives continuity to our cognition beyond the life of working memory itself. We may or may not be conscious of the plan itself, that is, be aware of our way of thinking as well as of what we are thinking about. Awareness of the plan is called *metacognition*, which is dealt with further in Chapter 4.

OUTPUT PROCESSES: MEMORISING AND RECALL

The so-called input processes discussed above explain how information is selected for learning, how it is treated in working memory by various mixtures of coding, recoding and rehearsal, and stored in long-term memory. As we have seen, there is a very close relationship between input and output — what comes out depends on how it went in —but more to the point, what goes in depends on what is already there. Nevertheless, what happens in long-term memory and how we remember things raise a different set of questions, which we deal with in the present section.

Theories of forgetting

Long-term memory — or rather its opposite, forgetting — has been studied for many years. In fact, many present-day theories of forgetting were originally described by Ebbinghaus (1913). Trace decay theory makes intuitive sense to the layperson; it states that memory traces stored in the brain spontaneously deteriorate over time 'rather like a mark in a pat of butter will gradually disappear in a warm room' (Baddeley, 1976, p. 59). Of course, that is not the whole story, as some memories are retained with extraordinary clarity over many decades, while others have gone within days, but it seems fairly clear that under certain conditions, something similar to a fading does occur.

Another theory, for years believed to be the sole cause of forgetting (see for example, McGeoch and Irion, 1951), is that of associative interference, and its two forms, retroactive and proactive inhibition. For example, if you take a driving test in the State of Victoria, you must look in the rear vision mirror, not over your shoulder, at traffic behind when changing lanes — otherwise you fail the test. In the Province of Alberta, you must always look over your shoulder when changing lanes — otherwise you fail the test. It is easy to imagine how easy it would be to 'forget' whether to look or not to look — simply by getting the rules confused. Assuming you learned to drive in Victoria first, then 'forgetting' to look when in Alberta would be an example of proactive inhibition. What had already been learned is interfering with present learning. If you were back in Victoria again, looking would be an example of retroactive inhibition: the interposed Albertan experience 'acted backwards' and interfered with what you once knew. Clearly, the greater the similarity between two sets of learning, the more likely it is that interference would occur.

To take an example nearer the classroom, if a student learns the French for 'cat' (*chat*) and then the Spanish word (*gato*), the interference (or inhibition) is said to be retroactive if the student recalls the French word: it might appear as *ghat* instead of *chat*, or as *château*. In the first case, the Spanish meaning has acted backwards (or retroactively) to change the 'c' and 'g'; and in the second, to create a double confusion between the sound of the word *gato* and a quite different French word, *château*. If, on the other hand, the student is required to recall the last (Spanish) word, then proactive interference may occur, for instance, if it is recalled as *cato*.

Such 'forgettings' occur very easily, and no doubt play a large part in everyday forgetfulness, particularly where isolated or arbitrary units are used, such as foreign words. Associative interference is less likely to occur with material that has been carefully learned and related to other knowledge. In fact, when we know a subject well, the more we read, the more clearly do we sort out and place details. It is in the early stages, before we have built up this knowledge network, that associative interference is most likely to cause confusions and difficulties.

Teachers should therefore be very careful when presenting new material in the early stages of a subject. They should keep it plain and simple, avoiding details that may be easily confused with each other. If there is any likelihood of confusing similar-sounding names or events, attempts should be made to separate them as far as possible, filling in the interval with quite different materials. For example, it is desirable to avoid presenting in the same lesson homophones such as 'there', 'their' and 'they're'; or 'to', 'two' and 'too'.

Memorising through what we already know. Trace decay and associative interference theories focus on the negative aspect of *forgetting*. The third kind of theory, then, reflects more the positive aspect of remembering: *the main determinant of what we remember is what we already know*. We have seen examples of this already in Chi's experiment with the 10-year-old chess experts: whether in the short term or in the long term, the children who knew a lot about chess remembered the presented positions far more effectively than the ignorant adults.

Another side to this view of remembering is given by Bartlett's (1932) classic studies. He gave his students (Cambridge undergraduates) several meaningful prose passages to read. He then studied the changes in the passages as the students reproduced them later, usually on several occasions. One common form of change, Bartlett called 'conventionalisation': people remember an event as they think it ought to have happened, rather than as it is actually said to have occurred. One of Bartlett's stories, for example, was a North American Indian folk-tale in which a supernatural event occurred at noon. His subjects distorted this event to fit their own codes, most English students reporting the events as having occurred at midnight.

Exactly the same thing happens in courts of law when leading questions are asked; such questions as 'Was the accused still striking the victim when you arrived?' set up certain expectations that the event to be remembered must have occurred in a certain way. Thus witnesses may swear in all sincerity that they 'remember' the accused doing something that is in line with that expectation, rather than what actually occurred.

The knowledge-based view of memory leads to two kinds of process (DiSibio, 1982): constructivist and reconstructivist. According to the constructivist process, limitations of working memory cause information to be selected and abstracted at input, and the information is then stored in long-term memory with little change thereafter. According to the reconstructivist process, such as the Bartlett experiments or the 'led' witness, changes occur at *recall* as well as at input. Again it is clear that both processes occur.

Dismembering and reconstruction

There are many examples of reconstruction. Consider recovery of memory following amnesia after a head injury. It seems that in time surrounding parts of the brain learn to 'cover' for the injured part, and a version of the event (which may not correspond exactly to what happened) may be recalled.

A striking example of this kind of reconstruction is given by Piaget and Inhelder (1973). They gave some children a seriation task (putting sticks of different lengths in order to form a kind of staircase). The children were then asked to draw the staircase from memory — immediately, and again some months later (see Figure 2.2). On immediate recall, four-year-olds tended to draw the sticks of varying but roughly equal length; five-year-olds produced groups of small, medium and large sticks; six-year-olds reproduced the staircase correctly. The six-year-olds had reached a new stage of development (called 'concrete–symbolic', see Chapter 5) and were able to encode the series correctly.

Six to eight months later, however, we see a different story. Those who had in the meantime reached the concrete–symbolic stage and therefore had recoded on a massive scale, now drew a proper staircase (see B in Figure 2.2.). Those who had not recoded, however, drew the same representation as before. In other words, the children's memories of what they had seen changed according to how their codes had changed.

If remembering involves *re*assembling component parts, it implies that the original learning was *dis*assembled. In fact, that is what some psychologists (Neisser, 1967; Pribram, 1969) suggest: experience is dismembered, stored along several dimensions, then reassembled or reconstructed.

Dimensions of dismembering. Dismembering experiences to store them away for later reconstruction takes place in two main ways. First, we seem to remember in terms of the *content* of the episode — what it was about — and in terms of the *context* in which it took place. We can remember, for instance, not only what someone said, but where it was and who was there at the time. Or, more infuriatingly, we cannot remember what was said, but we are certain of the episodic features (Tulving, 1972). Frequently, such partial recall can be used to prompt more accurate reconstruction of the episode.

Second, there are many dimensions along which an episode can be dismembered, ranging from quite specific visual details, to abstract word meanings. Some psychologists suggest that the details are lost first, and we retain increasingly more generalised and abstract representations of an event (Ausubel, 1968), although this is certainly not true of children's recall of lesson content. Nuthall and Lee (1982), for example, found that children recalled a smattering of detail when they had long forgotten the point the detail was meant to illustrate (see Box 2.1). In general, it is likely that the more dimensions used to encode material the better for subsequent recall.

The following dimensions may be distinguished, from the most concrete to the most abstract:

1.   *Enactive* memory concerns the retention of motor responses and it seems to be remarkably stable. Once learned, is it possible (short of brain damage) to forget how to ride a bicycle? A frequent phenomenon is going to the telephone and dialling a particular number, but being unable to recall the number verbally prior to dialling it.

2.   *Sensory* memory is of the specific sensations, other than muscular, that make up the original bits of raw experience. Neisser refers to these as serving the function of the 'bone chips' that paleontologists use to reconstruct the whole skeleton of a dinosaur: they use a few fossilised pieces of bone and their knowledge of anatomy and of dinosaurian lifestyles. They might be wrong in detail but right in general outline. Koestler's (1969) term for sensory memory is 'picture strip', the storage of high fidelity detail such as the 'wart on grandma's nose'. Children are much better than adults at storing such detail, in the form of eidetic imagery (or 'photographic memory'). These picture strips are mostly visual, but not entirely. We remember tunes, and the timbre of people's voices, but not as well as we remember words or pictures. In fact, humans do not remember pure sensory input such as smells and tastes as well as other animals. The

Figure 2.2   Recalling a seriation task

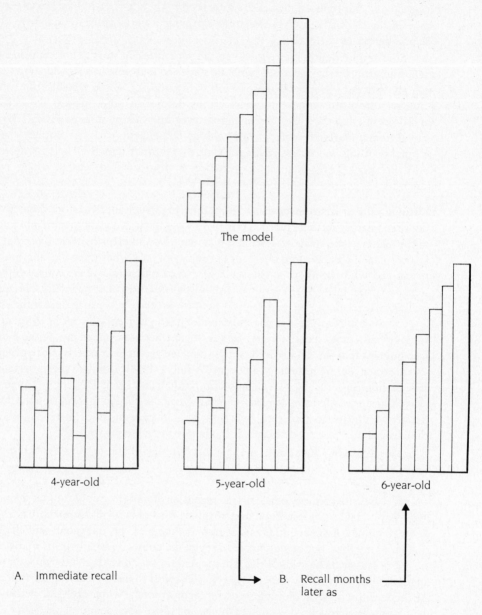

The model

4-year-old   5-year-old   6-year-old

A.   Immediate recall   B.   Recall months
                                    later as

terminology of wine buffs ('minty', 'lifted fruit', 'sweaty saddles') is not entirely pretension, but an attempt to code with words sensations that are elusive. True 'palate memory' is, alas, rare.

3.   Affective. We remember feelings and emotions associated with an event. Indeed, these may be overwhelming — why else do we watch nostalgia movies? —and certainly they are often clearly and accurately coded with an event. It is often much easier to recall the 'feel' of an event than its details ('Yes, I was happy then, I know. But why... I can't quite remember...'). Perhaps stranger is the nostalgia for desperately unhappy times: the survivors, few now, of the Great War, who trek annually to the old battlefields of Flanders where once, their mental and physical suffering was intense.

BOX 2.1   WHAT DO CHILDREN REMEMBER FROM LESSONS? MEMORY OF CLASS ACTIVITY WITHOUT ITS POINT

On some occasions there is evidence that the memory for the relevant content is there, but not in the form needed by the pupil to answer the question. This might be because the content has become too generalised (lacking in detail) and necessary distinctions have been forgotten, or because the detail is still there but the purpose or conclusion of the activity has been forgotten. The following transcript is an example of the former kind. The test item was concerned with the meaning of the word 'fauna'.

Pupil: I put native plants. I think, um... oh, I can remember Mr H saying flora and fauna. I remember him teaching about that but I still get muddled up which one. And I don't know why I put native plants, but I just did.

An example of the latter kind can be seen in the following exchange, The interviewer uses a prompt to elicit recall of an activity in which the teacher demonstrated the effects of air pollution.

Interviewer: Do you remember the incense?
Pupil: Yeah.
Interviewer: Now, why did he do that?...
Pupil: Well, we went into the 'flea-pit' and everyone was all smelling and everyone was going 'Oh God!' and all that, and we were looking on top of the door, and it was all put around the top of the door and everything. It was all up there.
Interviewer: Why was it there? What did it make you think of?
Pupil: Um... Some people thought it didn't smell very nice, some people thought it smelled like flowers and that, and, um, some people just didn't like it and went outside and that sort of thing.
Interviewer: Did it have anything to do with conservation?
Pupil: I think it did. I'm not sure, and I can't remember.

Source: Nuthall and Lee, 1982, pp. 11–12.

4.   *Temporal.* Time is a dimension that has both contextual and abstract aspects. For example it is easy to remember things in the order in which they happened. If I want to recall what I did last Friday at 5 p.m., I can usually do so by starting at some useful reference point that I can remember (such as a class or lunch) and then tracing through the events thereafter. Interestingly, the same strategy works for events that do not even form part of one's own personal experience. History students, for example, find it easier to encode and recall the prime ministers since federation in terms of succession rather than in a more logical scheme, such as grouping according to political party or platform.

5.   *Spatial.* Spatial encoding is an abstraction from visual sensation. Whereas straight sensory encoding would retain the actual images, spatial encoding retains relationships between objects and events. Some material is easily codable in this form. For example, directions to get from A to B in a strange city are much more economically coded in terms of a map or sketch than in terms of a list of verbal instructions (such as 'Turn left at the first corner, then straight on for three blocks ...' etc.). Other material, not inherently visual, can still be better understood if coded spatially; for example, Figure 2.1 represents the memory systems in terms of a flowchart.

6.   *Semantic.* Semantic encoding refers to word meaning, and is probably the most important and the most complex aspect of human memory. Semantic memory is organised in quite complex hierarchies from simple, concrete meanings of single words, through meanings of sentences and of paragraphs, to the quite abstract moral of a complex story or the theme of a scientific treatise. One of the most important issues in school learning is targeting the appropriate level of semantic meaning. Frequently, students interpret an historical event too literally, remembering the details but not the sense of historical inevitability, or remembering in detail that they burned magnesium and it gained weight ... 'because, um, hot things get bigger and so they weigh more, or something like that' (see also Box 2.1).

7.   *Logical.* The most abstract frameworks are purely logical. Memory is helped considerably if material is encoded in terms of its inherent logical structure: it is much easier to remember logical arguments than illogical ones. The Piaget experiment referred to above of course uses a logical structure (seriation) to store the memory of the original pattern: and if the child is too immature to be able to use this structure, the pattern is misremembered.

Figure 2.3 represents how a learning episode may be dismembered into these seven dimensions. Obviously, not all dimensions will be used. Depending on the nature of the episode and on the capabilities and prior knowledge of the learner, one or more of the dimensions will be used, and in varying levels of abstraction. At the most concrete level, the specific sensations, emotions and motor responses will be recorded, giving a fusion of both content and context. Temporal and spatial relations offer the next level of abstraction, whereby the learner begins to separate out contextual from content aspects of the episode; while content becomes more firmly abstracted with focus on meaning and logical structure.

Good learning thus implicates (a) a *variety of dimensions* being used for encoding; and (b) the *highest levels of abstraction* that the learner can handle. In turn, good teaching should involve all possible means of encoding: striking images and diagrams to give a

Figure 2.3   How learning is dismembered and remembered

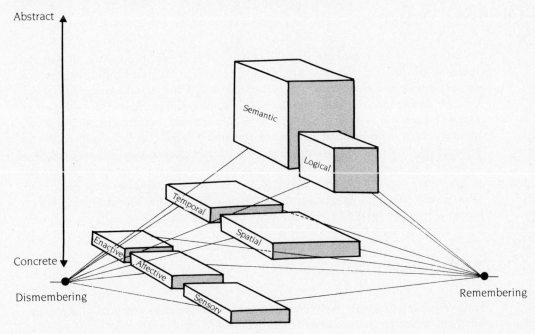

spatial encoding; use of mnemonic devices; presenting material in a logical step-by-step structure. Finally, simple repetition should not be forgotten, especially for those raw picture strips of detail. The American TV series *Sesame Street* illustrates how visual and auditory surprise can avoid dullness yet hammer home the message with much repetition.

Generativity in learning and recall. Overall, this form of reconstruction calls for activity or, as Wittrock (1977) called it, *generativity.* Generativity implies the active construction of meaning for stimuli using verbal, visual imagery and any other form of multiple processing. The more aspects of previous experience that can be linked to an item, and the more ways in which that item can be coded, the better it will be remembered. Wittrock showed, for example, that when children were asked to generate headings for each paragraph of a story they were set to read, their recall of the story material was greatly increased. According to this approach, then, merely reading the text would not be as effective for later recall as underlining important sentences; underlining, in turn, would be less effective than writing out those sentences; copying sentences would be less effective than rewriting them in your own words and using your own examples; while most effective, as we shall see in Chapter 4, is to teach the material to someone else. *Activity* is important in learning because it helps link the content being learned with existing knowledge; it provides cross-links between different methods of encoding the material; and, as will be explained further in Chapter 4, it helps students become *metacognitive,* or aware of their own learning processes.

ACTIVATING PROCESSES: THE CONCEPT OF AROUSAL

So far, we have been looking at 'cold' cognition: selecting, processing, storing and recalling information. We now turn to 'hot' cognition: the source of the energy that drives the system, and the effects it has on the system. The key is the concept of *arousal*.

Let us introduce a fourth system into that portrayed in Figure 2.1 — the *arousal system* (Figure 2.4) — which is linked with both sensory register and with working memory. It will be recalled that when something is precoded as 'important' the message goes straight to working memory for further processing. This is marked as pathway 1 in Figure 2.4. In addition, however, another signal goes to the arousal system (pathway 2). It is this boost to arousal that distinguishes important from unimportant messages in relation to motivation. Finally, the arousal system affects working memory (pathway 3) in the ways described below.

The orienting response

Some messages are more likely than others to be precoded as potentially important. First, any *variation* from the current input will be precoded as important (e.g. a sudden noise against a quiet background, or sudden quiet amidst prolonged noise, such as the

Figure 2.4   The relation between arousal and information processing systems

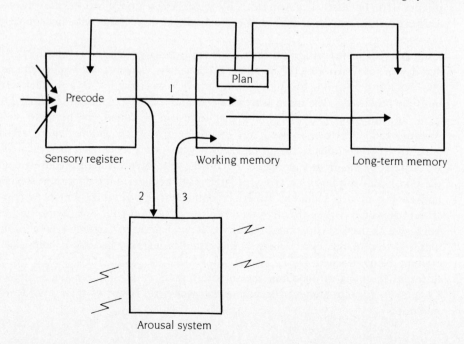

clock that we 'hear' ticking only when it stops). Such variations signal that something *different* is happening. We are biologically wired up to be sensitive to things that are different, because such variations in the environment may well be vital for survival. Other important signals may include stimuli that are relevant to a prevailing physiological or psychological set: for example, the sound of our own name, or the smell of food when we are hungry. Precoding gives an initial boost to the arousal system most obviously when, for example, we hear such phrases as: 'Pay attention!', 'Fire!', 'You there!', 'Help', and so on.

The special kind of response to unusual precoding of this nature is called the orienting response; the individual becomes oriented to a new and important event. At the same time, arousal is increased to help handle the new situation. Input comes from any or all of our sense organs, and it takes two routes to the brain. The first is to the cortex, where it is interpreted and stored (as discussed earlier in this chapter) for decision-making, problem-solving or other cognitive processes. The second is to the reticular arousal system (RAS), which is located in the brain stem. This system consists of dense neuronal fibres that operate not in a specific cognitive manner, as do the cortical cells, but simply to increase readiness for general activity.

Energising and interfering effects of arousal

When the arousal system is stimulated, as happens in the orienting response, two general things also happen: cortical processes are directly energised to cope more efficiently with the message which has been received, and the autonomic nervous system is activated to release adrenalin to the bloodstream. There follow increases in sweating, heart-rate, rate of breathing and blood flow to the larger muscle systems; pupils dilate and digestive processes are withheld. These changes are useful for emergency action requiring immediate energy, such as fighting or running away. The system returns to normal when the energy has been expended.

Today, however, most of the stress we endure is psychological rather than physical, and emergency action does not usually demand an immediate, high-energy output. Hence we are forced to deal with emotional or stressful situations with bodily functions that have to be ignored or suppressed in our civilised settings. Moreover, if adrenalin stimulates high heart-rate and shuts down the digestive processes, constant stress may lead to one or both of two general kinds of physical breakdown: heart attack and stomach ulcers. People who by nature have particularly unstable or active autonomic nervous systems, and who are also subject to a stressful, competitive work environment, are most likely to be at risk. Even before that breakdown stage, the immediate effects of such autonomic arousal are likely to be distracting and to interfere with effective performance.

Arousal, then, tends to have two effects: an energising effect which enhances performance, and an interfering effect, from an overactive autonomic system, which detracts from performance. The interfering effect greatly increases at higher levels of arousal. The arousal system is comparable to the brightness control of a television set, and performance to the picture quality of the tube. If the brightness control is turned down (i.e. arousal is low) there is no clear picture. As the brightness is increased the picture becomes clearer, is clearest at some optimal midpoint, but then becomes progressively washed out.

Arousal and performance

The general relationship between arousal and performance is described by an inverted U-curve (Figure 2.5). If we plot arousal against performance quality, we see that at very low levels of arousal, performance is poor (at extreme levels, of course, we are asleep). As arousal increases, performance improves up to an optimal point after which it deteriorates with increasing arousal. On the upward slope, the energising effects of arousal predominate; on the descending slope, the interfering effects take over (Humphreys and Revelle, 1984).

It is obviously important for teachers to try and strike the best balance, so that pupils are energised to the highest level possible before interference occurs. For example, a teacher is questioning a student in class: it is possible that gentle probing will lead to a good response. However, if the questioner becomes heavy or sarcastic, the student is likely to become flustered; if answers are forthcoming at all, they will probably be confused or incorrect.

This familiar example can also help illustrate some other relevant factors, such as the nature of the task and the personality of the student. Very simple questions, to which the student knows the answers, are less likely to be affected adversely than complex questions, the answers to which require the integration of a lot of information. Similarly, anxious students are more likely to be adversely affected by heavy public questioning than less anxious students.

Anxiety and performance. This aspect of arousal — *anxiety* — has received a great deal of attention in the educational setting (e.g. Biggs, 1962; Gaudry and Spielberger, 1971; Sarason et al., 1960). As with arousal in general, anxiety has an inverted-U relationship to performance. Low anxiety is a state in which you 'couldn't care less' and consequently do not bother to try. High anxiety disrupts performance; you try too hard, become confused, the mind 'goes blank'. With a middling degree of anxiety, however, performance is best for that person for that task. As we shall see below, some tasks are best performed at lower levels of anxiety while others can withstand quite a high level. Furthermore, different people are characteristically anxious or non-anxious as part of their personality, and consequently react to and cope with stress in quite different ways.

Exertion and mental performance. Another, quite different, form of arousal has been receiving more attention recently — exertion arousal (i.e. the arousal engendered by heavy physical exertion such as jogging). Several writers (e.g. Fixx, 1977) have described the 'high' sometimes experienced by trained long-distance runners. This would seem, on the basis of individual reports, to lead to good mental performance — up to a point. That point is the peak in Figure 2.5 after which mental (and ultimately physical) performance declines.

Figure 2.5   General relation between arousal and quality of performance (the inverted U)

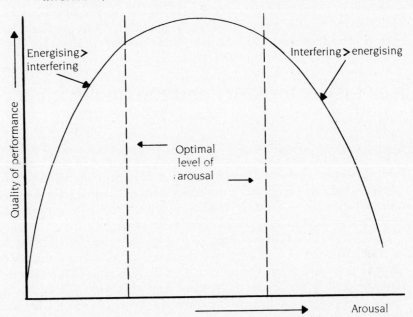

In a series of studies initially carried out on some aspirants to the Australian Olympic Team, Davey (1973) noted that under extreme stress highly experienced athletes sometimes made 'stupid' decisions, such as changing into the wrong lane, sprinting too soon or tackling the wrong player. Davey then set up an experiment using physical education students, giving them two tasks to perform during continual exertion on an exercycle. The tasks were:

- spotting odd-even-odd sequences in strings of digits, which demands high concentration;
- a working-memory task, requiring the immediate repetition of digits.

He found that performance on the first task increased dramatically for the first four minutes of hard pedalling (about equivalent to running a fast 800 metres): working memory was unaffected. After this time, however, most subjects declined rapidly on both tasks.

Wall (in progress) showed that these findings generalise to school subjects. She gave memory, spatial and arithmetic tasks to 60 primary (Year 5) students after various intervals of pedalling on a bicycle ergometer, up to a maximum of four minutes. The children were divided, on the basis of a sports day performance, into 'fit', 'medium fit' and 'unfit'. The familiar U-curve began to emerge in the case of the unfit and the medium fit — but even then, after four minutes of hard exercise, the children were still *better* at spatial reasoning and arithmetic tasks than when they were at rest. The scores of the fit children were still on the increase.

These studies have most interesting implications — ones that are contrary to conventional wisdom about the timetabling of PE lessons. For example, children might concentrate better if the more academic subjects were timetabled *after* PE (as long as it is not too strenuous, and that now seems unlikely). A fast jog might be a good idea before an examination. This is an interesting area for further research.

Arousal, task complexity and the quality of performance

The Yerkes–Dodson Law, formulated in the early part of this century, states that simple tasks are performed better under high degrees of motivation or arousal, while complex tasks are performed better under relatively low degrees of motivation; as in our earlier example, a simple question is more likely to be answered satisfactorily under stressful questioning than a complex question.

The inverted-U curve of Figure 2.5 now looks rather different for the two kinds of task. It narrows for a complex task: the peak in performance is reached quickly with increasing arousal, it lasts a short time, then declines rapidly. It broadens for a simple task: the peak in performance is reached somewhat later with increasing arousal, is maintained longer, and then declines relatively slowly. In short, when doing a simple task, a person can operate efficiently at much higher levels of arousal than when doing a complex task.

What do we mean by 'simple' and 'complex'? These terms reflect the *amount of working memory* required in order to perform a task satisfactorily. Simple tasks require little working memory, complex tasks rather more. It would therefore follow that any means of reducing the working memory load during a task would help the interfering effects of anxiety, particularly in the case of complex tasks. Consequently, Sieber (1969) suggested that mnemonic devices — diagrams, notes, outlines and general ways of organising complex ideas into smaller, manageable chunks — are useful for counteracting the anxiety experienced in performing a task. After-dinner speakers, particularly those who are at all nervous, find notes very useful for countering anxiety, even if they never use them in the event.

While arousal helps activate performance, too much arousal 'hurts' working memory (Humphreys and Revelle, 1984). The reason for the pain is clear: we can only attend to so many things at a time. With increasing anxiety, we become aware of the physiological and psychological side-effects of arousal — we notice that our heart is pounding, that we have butterflies in the stomach, and that we feel helpless. These general I-feel-awful cues simply take over working memory to the exclusion of information relevant to the task. However, because complex tasks require more relevant cues for adequate processing than do simple tasks, such cures are displaced earlier when performing a complex task than is the case with simple tasks. The performer in a complex task is in effect operating with less working memory than is needed — hence performance suffers. In simple tasks, on the other hand, reduced working memory will not matter so much and thus energising (improvement) will continue for longer.

Trait and state anxiety

People differ markedly in their tendency to react to stress: some people over-react, and hence tend to seek quietness and solitude in order to work comfortably; others take stress in their stride, and indeed seem to go out of their way to seek excitement and stimulation. Some pupils, for example, seem quite distressed by being questioned in public, while others actively seek the limelight.

Psychologists usually make a distinction between *trait* anxiety and *state* anxiety. Trait anxiety refers to a *general readiness* to react with anxiety to most situations. State anxiety refers to the anxiety *actually experienced* in a particular situation.

Trait anxiety, or general anxiety as it is sometimes called, is a characteristic predisposition of some people to react with anxiety. It is very likely part of their physiology, particularly of the reticular arousal system and of the autonomic nervous system, and is probably inherited. This is not to say, of course, that people cannot develop ways of keeping their general anxiety under reasonable control. Sometimes these ways are useful and help them to adapt; for example, finding out more information about a potential threat. On the other hand, anxiety may not be easily contained or controlled, and then it is experienced as state anxiety.

State anxiety is associated with a *particular situation*. Testing is a particularly common example, which strikes some students whenever their competence is laid on the line — by questionning in class or by formal testing. Teaching itself is another; experienced teachers feel anxious when 'outsiders' come into the classroom, and as we see in Section B, many student teachers suffer crippling anxiety when they stand in front of a class for the first few times.

This last example illustrates that state anxiety can be managed. If the first few sessions do not culminate in the feared catastrophe, the anxiety dissipates, confidence is restored, and the student will begin to look forward to teaching, all the more so for having beaten the initial anxiety. Conquered fear results in a better adaptation to the task than not having experienced it at all. The control of state anxiety, and test and teacher anxiety in particular, are taken up in Section B.

SUMMARY

In this chapter, we have looked at input processes, with the three corresponding systems of memory; at output processes; and at how the whole system is activated.

Input processes. In the sensory register, material is sorted out very quickly according to its current importance to the individual. This is called precoding. Importance is 'decided' according to various priorities:

1. the plan of the individual, which is more or less a conscious choice of what to do;
2. the physical attributes of the stimulus: their intensity or variability;

3. the internal physiological states (hunger, anxiety, etc.) which signal biological importance.

Individuals vary greatly in what they consider to be important. Consequently their plans differ and frequently a communication gap results. One of the major problems in teaching is bridging the communication gap between teacher and student.

Working memory may be regarded as an area in which information is held — either singly or as 'chunks' — while we think about it. If the information is not processed fairly quickly it fades beyond recall. The number of chunks that can be held in working memory at any given time increases with age, and is about seven or eight in adults, depending on the familiarity of the content.

Rehearsal is the process used in rote learning, *coding* that in meaningful learning. When material is rote-learned, it is difficult to recall it in a different order, structure or wording to that of the original. In meaningful learning, learners are able to explain the content in their own words and in their own way.

Meaningfulness of learning can vary considerably, depending on how the learner relates content to previously learned codes. Often there is some degree of mismatch between current content and previous learning, and recoding might take place. This process involves the alteration of existing codes to fit the demands of a new experience, and is related to the degree of intrinsic motivation experienced during learning.

Output processes. An experience or event that is to be committed to memory is either coded or rehearsed, usually both. Aspects of that experience are dismembered into various components of differing levels of concreteness.

At the most concrete level are the enactive, emotional and sensory experiences, usually coded in the context of when and where. Semantic encoding, which refers to the meaning and content of the learning, may vary considerably in abstractness, from literal to quite metaphoric or remote meanings.

This model allows for regular and consistent faults in memorising, such as 'conventionalisation', when we remember things as we think they 'ought' to have happened. Other sources of error in memory are *interference*, due to confusion between similar details, and *fading* of detail. Students are thus likely to remember quite different and seemingly unrelated aspects of a lesson.

Learning is thus *generative*; errors can be avoided by active involvement on all aspects of learning so that concrete and abstract components are linked.

Activation processes. Stimuli in general, and particularly varying stimuli, act upon both the cortex and the arousal system. Increasing arousal has two effects: it energises cortical functions and it causes (increasingly at high levels) autonomic or emotional responses that may interfere with cognitive functioning. Interference effects vary according to differences between both tasks and individuals. Task differences are determined by the amount of memory load the task makes on the individual, which in turn is a function of familiarity and skill with the task. Simple tasks are performed effectively at much higher levels of arousal than complex tasks. Facilitating the achievement of complex tasks is to a large extent a matter of making the individual's response as automatic as possible, thus decreasing memory load.

Individuals differ widely in the way in which their arousal systems react to stimulation and in how they themselves handle changes in arousal. Trait anxiety refers to readiness to react with anxiety, and state anxiety refers to experienced anxiety in particular kinds of situations.

SECTION B

All the material dealt with in Section A has implications for classroom practice. We are talking about how students maintain their attention to what is going on around them, select and learn some aspects with varying degrees of accuracy and understanding, and remember them, also with varying degrees of accuracy and understanding. There is so much to unpack and talk about here that we have to be very selective ourselves.

Much of this material on cognitive processing is relevant to how students perceive their learning environment, what the task is and how they derive their own approaches to learning. This whole question of students' awareness of themselves as learners places an important new perspective on the management of learning. These are referred to as the metacognitive aspects of learning, and are dealt with in Chapter 4.

Here, then, we restrict ourselves to some of the more important cognitive processes and to their activation. The cognitive processes which teachers have most to do with are: directing attention, optimising the use of working memory, encouraging meaningful rather than rote processes through generic or surface coding (see below) and memorising. We then deal with the management of anxiety, as experienced by both student and teacher.

DIRECTING ATTENTION

What can teachers do to encourage the students to 'pay attention'? Two general classes of strategy are discussed here. The first relies on the orienting response which is extrinsic to the nature of the task itself, and refers to the way the task is presented. The second uses the task content itself to keep the students' attention on line.

Orienting the students

The orienting response is based on surprise. Arousal leaps at the unexpected. One of the writers was present at a conference at which a research paper was to be presented. It was after dinner and everyone was tired. The researcher preceded the paper by presenting some test slides of his results. The trial data were not, however, presented as a three-way analysis of covariance of the critical flicker-fusion data: they were of

Playboy centrefolds. His audience oriented rapidly. The arousal was extrinsic, but there was an attentive audience that night.

This incident clearly illustrates the element of surprise, or *variation*. Like surprise, a variation can be defined as a departure from the expected. The technique used by teachers who deliberately introduce variation into lessons is known as *variability*.

Although what is 'expected' can vary according to the particular circumstances, variability can be considered in terms of three components: the teacher's manner or style; the media and materials of instruction; and the interaction between teacher and pupils (Turney et al., 1983).

Variability in style of teaching. The variations in a teacher's personal style are essentially either verbal or non-verbal.

1.   Verbal variations. To be 'interesting', a speaker should vary speed of delivery (e.g. slowing down for emphasis) and volume (increasing it for importance or — a double surprise — speaking the climax very softly so that the audience strains to hear). Tone and pitch provide further contrasts with volume and speed: for example, the teacher's voice can range from sharp emphasis to quiet encouragement. Variation of grammatical style and use of questions at unpredictable moments during the lesson are further examples of ways of creating the unexpected.

2.   Non-verbal variations. Non-verbal variability can reinforce verbal techniques. Having reminded the class that the climax of the radio play will occur unexpectedly, the English teacher raises a hand just as the lines commence. As a pupil struggles to identify the error in solving the mathematics problem, the teacher silently goes to the board and underlines the key step in coloured chalk.

Non-verbal communication can take the form of facial expressions of approval or disapproval, head or body movements conveying the same message, and gestures. The movement of a teacher around the classroom is itself a form of variation and non-verbal communication. Unobtrusive shifting from the front of the room when a pupil viewpoint is being presented, delivering part of the lesson while standing next to an inattentive pupil, and quickly giving attention to the pupil who is having difficulties, are all examples. Eye contact with pupils is another form of variability: the pupil may be slumped in the back row, confident of anonymity, when the brush of eye contact says otherwise.

Variability in media and materials of instruction. There are three types of teaching material: visual, aural and tactile.

1.   Visual variations. Visual resources include film, actual objects, pictures, maps, charts, videotape, television, overhead projector transparencies and duplicated materials. There is also the school's environment: field trips and excursions take advantage of it to add purpose, variety and interest to lessons — if they are conducted properly (see below).

2.   Aural variations. When is noise a form of pollution? How loud is a noise of five decibels? How does Chaucerian English differ from modern English? How does Greig convey the dawning of day in *Peer Gynt*? Don't just say: illustrate. All of these questions can be answered in a classroom by means of recordings of sound or interviews.

In varying proportions, teacher talk and pupil talk are the main aural components in a lesson. Teacher talk, according to research findings, comprises one-half to two-thirds of all classroom interaction time (Dunkin and Biddle, 1974). Given that, perhaps teacher talk is the first component to consider for variation: especially if pupil interest and surprise is the criterion.

3. *Tactile variations.* It is common practice in some secondary-school subjects (e.g. science, industrial arts, technical drawing, home science and textiles) for actual objects to be handled. It is in the less obvious subjects that this variation can provide the greatest impetus to pupil interest.

Variability in interaction of pupils and teacher. The final source of variation is the interaction of the teacher and the pupils. This can be considered as a continuum: at one extreme is teacher talk, at the other is independent work by pupils. In between are such variations as group work, pupil presentations to the rest of the class, teacher assistance and so on. Interaction offers the teacher a means of maintaining surprise. The lesson may begin with the teacher introducing the subject, then the groups are formed to discuss it and reach a conclusion which individuals convey to the whole class. Such a lesson has a smooth and purposeful change of interaction every 10 or 15 minutes. However, room design, departmental furniture, noise and rigid timetabling may restrict the effective use of this technique.

Maintaining attention

Once the students are oriented and helped to remain so with variation in the presentation of the material, attention can be held by the intrinsic content. That battle is part over if teacher and student agree on what is important. When the *learner* chooses the content there is no problem. When the *teacher* does the choosing, however, the learner may have to be convinced.

The 'centres of interest' approach to the curriculum uses the first technique. The teacher uses material in which the students are already interested (e.g. playing games, calculating football results, building a play area, when in fact the aim is to increase speed and accuracy in number manipulation). Freire (1970) used such a technique to teach illiterate Brazilian peasants to read. Assembling a group in the village square, he used words of intense common interest, especially those concerned with political disputes involving the local patron. Most of the group became functionally proficient readers after 30 hours of such instruction (Freire's persecution as a subversive was another consequence).

The technique has also been used by Ashton-Warner (1980), the Mt Gravatt Developmental Reading Program (Hart, 1976), and the widely used *Breakthrough to Literacy* materials (Mackay, 1971). For example, in Ashton-Warner's 'organic reading' program, five-year-old Maori children were asked for their 'own' words (i.e. those which had private importance). Each youngster built up a 'key vocabulary' on a set of cards, each word being written on the child's 'own' card. The cards were then rearranged to form stories based on the individual's own chosen words.

A vital aspect of teaching is selling the task to the learner, and the learner's scale of importance is the key. Good conversationalists recognise the importance of tapping the listener's interests whenever they can.

Embedded questions and overviews. The teacher can highlight what is likely to be important before and during instruction by asking questions and giving overviews at various stages, as we have done throughout this book (see questions for discussion at the end of this chapter and Chapter 4). In Chapter 4 we look at self-questioning in much more detail, particularly where the student has control. Here we look at what the teacher can do simply to channel the learner's attention, rather than inducing comprehension (although the two processes closely intertwine). The following is derived largely from reviews by Hartley and Davies (1976), Faw and Waller (1976), and Hamilton (1985).

1. *Pre-testing.* Before a lesson, or a passage of reading, sets of questions on the content of the lesson or passage are given to alert the students to the significant points (and the ones likely to be tested). Pre-testing works for relatively short teaching episodes, and particularly for bright or mature students who have some prior knowledge of the content (otherwise the questions are meaningless). This technique works by focusing attention onto specifics. If the lesson or passage is meant to be exploratory, pre-testing tends to inhibit students from looking at different aspects and is not advised.

2. *Behavioural objectives.* As outlined in Chapter 2, behavioural objectives are statements of behaviours that are to be expected at the end of a learning episode. They specify both the conditions under which the behaviour is to be shown, and the standard of performance that represents attainment of the objective. Objectives are designed for the benefit of the teacher, but if they are communicated to the student, they do appear to help learning, particularly when the content is rambling or abstract: objectives aid students in structuring the material.

3. *Overviews.* Overviews have been used for a very long time by teachers. These are simple statements of the main points to be dealt with, rather like synopses at the beginning of a paper. They put, in abbreviated form, points and issues which will be elaborated in the material to follow. Again, the evidence is that overviews do enhance learning, probably not so much through priming the attention of learners, as through the mechanisms of repetition and familiarisation. Because the overview is written at much the same level as the material itself, the student encounters the important concepts twice.

4. *Advance organisers.* These are overviews of a special kind, suggested by Ausubel (1968). An overview is written at the same level as the main material, whereas an advanced organiser is a short passage that gives an abstract theoretical framework to the material that follows. An advance organiser provides the *concepts* that will be used by the learner to understand the material to be learned.

Advance organisers help the learner when the material to be learned is both novel and complex, and for this reason they are probably not very useful for students much below senior high school. Ausubel (1978) himself claimed, however, that advance organisers have been used successfully with children as young as six years of age.

5.   *Inserted questions.* Questioning need not be restricted to the beginning or end of a lesson. It may occur at various points, so that the learner is periodically stopped and questioned *during* the course of learning. This, too, seems to be an effective procedure.

Depending on the lesson, overviews and embedded questions seem useful aids to learning. Gagné (1978) summarised their use, pointing out that 'Reminding learners of relevant knowledge prior to reading may have dramatic effects' (p. 645), partly by priming their attention to topics of particular importance, and by reminding them of what they already know which may be of help in handling the material. This second issue borders closely on metacognitive aspects of learning, which are dealt with more fully in Chapter 4.

OPTIMISING THE USE OF WORKING MEMORY

An issue that continually reappears is the limited capacity of working memory. A good general strategy is to make sure that, wherever possible, working memory is concerned with the more important rather than the less important aspects of a problem. For example, in driving a manual car, the beginner has many things to think about at once: remembering the road rules, using signals, and so on. Under these conditions, the learner might easily forget — as anyone who has accompanied an L-driver will testify — to do something crucial, such as applying the brake in an emergency. Experienced drivers have practised these things for so long that they are automatic: they can easily reserve some working-memory space for such things as the road rules, or even for such irrelevant activities as conversation.

The principle is the same for simple sums. A young student, say an eight-year-old, can solve the two sums, 7 + 9 and 16 + 5, but not 7 + 9 + 5. To do so correctly, an extra slot in working memory is needed to *hold* the result of the first addition (7 + 9), and then add in the remaining 5. An older child — who has had practice, much practice — chunks the 7 + 9 into one unit, so that the problem becomes, in effect, (7 + 9) + 5; in other words, 16 + 5.

Students should therefore be encouraged rather than discouraged from using space-saving devices, such as crutches in mechanical arithmetic (which some teachers will still frown upon). By writing a tiny 1 in the tens column, the student will remember to include the 10 that is to be carried from the units column. Experienced students are likely to carry the figure without thinking about it, but beginners certainly will not. It is senseless to insist that working memory be cluttered with material that can more efficiently be 'remembered' on a piece of paper.

Working memory is particularly likely to be crowded when the individual is in a stressful situation, such as an exam. A good strategy for relieving the strain (and for allaying anxiety) is to jot down points as soon as they come to mind: they can then be written into the essay at the appropriate time. If one tries to keep them in the head, they are almost certain to be lost. This particular use of space-saving to cope with anxiety is dealt with in more detail in a later section.

One of the most effective ways of improving learning and problem-solving is to cut down wherever possible on working-memory load. This is not 'spoon-feeding'; it is making sure that our limited minds are given the opportunity of handling more complex problems than they otherwise would.

ENCOURAGING MEANINGFUL LEARNING

Teaching is the process of organising and relating new information to the learner's previous experience, stimulating him to construct his own representation for what he is encountering... (Wittrock, 1977, p. 177).

...methods of teaching should be designed to stimulate students actively to construct meaning from their own experience rather than stimulating them to reproduce the knowledge of others (p. 180).

Here Wittrock has captured the essence of the teaching process in relation to the model of memory we considered in Section A. We shall illustrate this general theme, and the applications of the model itself, in this section.

Generic and surface codes

It follows from the generative model of memory that the more meaningful material is, the better it will be retained; and the more meaningful it is, the greater the number of connections with previous knowledge. In other words, meaningfulness varies, particularly according to the elaborateness of coding (see also Craik and Tulving, 1975). It is helpful to distinguish between two kinds of coding: surface and generic.

Surface codes are not strongly linked with previous knowledge and operate at a low level of abstraction (see Figure 2.3). Material coded in this way is narrow in its range of application or in its transferability to different fields. In order for such material to be remembered, rehearsal will often be required as well: surface coding includes a high proportion of rote learning.

Generic codes, on the other hand, connect with the individual's existing knowledge at many points, and operate at a high level of abstraction — that is, semantic encoding at a thematic level, or logical encoding.

Generic coding can have two meanings. First, generic codes can refer to the *structure of the subject matter* to be learned (e.g. the concept of directed numbers in mathematics, of place value in arithmetic, of tragic hero in drama and so on). Such lists of codes read like a curriculum statement.

The second meaning is more personal. A generic code also describes whether the appropriate links are made *within the cognitive structure of the individual*. Ideally, the aim of education would be to bring the individual's understanding of the code as close as possible to an expert's elucidation of the curriculum code. The distinctions between surface and generic coding, and between objective (curriculum) and personal coding, are brought out in the following classroom examples.

Example 1

In a Year 6 arithmetic lesson, the teacher says: 'Now take five from three.' The student's first response is 'You can't' — existing number codes cannot stretch that far. Teacher then says, 'Oh, yes you can!' Now what?

One way of handling the problem is for the student to do a bit of recoding and conclude 'OK, then, teacher is a liar.' This solves the immediate problem, but it is not a good solution because it undermines everything else that has been learned from that teacher. The teacher might respond by introducing concrete instances where the student *does* take five from three: as in an overdrawn bank account, or when two degrees of frost occur. To comprehend these examples, a crucial piece of recoding is required, especially concerning the concept of zero. Instead of being the empty set — the absence of something — zero can mean a position on a scale in the directed number system. By stepping up and down that scale, the student learns that all those things that could be done with the old system (of natural numbers) can still be done, plus many new things with directed numbers. The mismatch produced by those experiences has led to recoding to form a new generic code.

Example 2

The formula 'A base plus acid gives a salt plus water' has been taught. The following exam question is set: 'What happens when dilute hydrochloric acid is added to potassium hydroxide?' The example originally given in class involved sulphuric acid and sodium hydroxide, giving sodium sulphate and water.

To surface coders, 'acid' means sulphuric acid; 'base' means caustic soda, which cannot cover the different ingredients. Generic coders would relate the formula to other items in their knowledge network: 'A base: ah yes, that's a metallic ion and a hydroxyl ion; an acid, that's a hydrogen ion plus a radical; a salt is a metallic ion plus a radical ... now it doesn't matter what metal is in question, I think, so if we recombine ...' These students are using the acid-plus-base-gives-salt-plus-water formula as a means of reviving a whole lot of other relevant information. Most important, the problem is related to a much broader and abstract set of principles, from which the solution to many specific problems can be derived.

Example 3

Year 7 history students may learn that 'Australia was first settled by the British because they needed prison space.' It is unlikely, however, that this proposition would mean much to them; it is certainly irrelevant to their experience of Australia. The statement becomes coded into a narrow set of equally unreal propositions about convicts, rum and Bligh. Year 12 students, on the other hand, might well see many implications: these could include the choice of sites for some of the capital cities; the kind of industries developed; the kind of society that might evolve from one based upon prisons, the military and an aristocracy; the likely effects of such a social structure on the psychology of the typical Australian (if there were such a person); contrasts with modern Australian society, with a different history of settlement; and so on. Thus, the statement might to knowledgeable and mature students become a generic code of some importance, and with a wide degree of extension.

The place of detail. Each subject has its own generic codes, and these should become the focus of teaching where possible. To avoid surface-code learning, students should be asked to think up their own examples and to apply them to new situations; to write *in their own words* what they think is the gist of the material being learned. In this way, they are forced to extend the meaning of a paragraph or sentence in the light of both their own interpretation and knowledge.

It is important to note that although background knowledge, facts and detail are important, they are — in generic-code learning — simply a means to an end. In surface-code learning, however, the facts become an end in themselves, and one is likely to end up being unable to see the wood for the trees. The relationship between factual detail and general principle is well illustrated by Lashley (1960):

> ...every memory becomes part of a more or less extensive organisation. When I read a scientific paper, the new facts presented become associated with the field of knowledge of which it is a part. Later availability of the specific items of the paper depend on a partial activation of the whole body of associations. If one has not thought of a topic for some time, it is difficult to recall details. With a review or discussion of the subject, however, names, dates and references which seemed to have been forgotten rapidly become available to memory (p. 497).

Encoding across different modalities: Multiple embodiment

Both generic and surface coding are concerned with the interconnections of codes with existing knowledge, irrespective of the *modality* of the coding. Most of the above examples were concerned with the semantic mode.

We saw in Section A, however, that cross-modal coding is useful: for example, tagging the bouquet and flavour of wine with verbal labels. Most subjects have become associated with modalities that suit their subject matter: arithmetic and mathematics with numerical and letter symbols; English expression with verbal symbols. Some subjects straddle two modalities: history uses verbal symbols and temporal structuring; creative writing frequently uses verbal means to elicit strong visual and other sensory images. Such multi-modal coding should help the understanding and retention of subject matter.

The idea of coding an event or concept in different domains is similar to the *multiple-embodiment* principle suggested by Dienes (1963). He believed that concepts are formed through a process of abstraction from concrete experience, and the more varied that experience, the more powerful the concept formed. Consequently, he devised material and games that illustrated certain basic mathematical concepts — or generic mathematical codes — which had a considerable vogue in several Adelaide primary schools.

The following example is one of many such illustrations, and is taken from work carried out with Bruner at Harvard University (Bruner, 1964; Dienes, 1963). The materials were cut out of thick plastic, and consisted of small 'unit' squares of constant size; 'strips' of plastic that could be any length, but were unit width; and 'squares' with sides that were as long as the strip (see Figure 2.6A). The dimensions of the strip may vary from set to set; the only constraint is that once a particular strip length has been selected, it must also apply to the sides of the square. If we let x be the length of the strip, then, the dimensions of the pieces are: the square is $x \times x$ (or x^2, as it is written); the strip is $x \times 1$, or just plain x; and the unit is 1×1, or 1.

It is now possible to make a spatial model of quadratic functions by making a rectangle. Let us say we are given the expression $2x^2 + 8x + 6$ (the parts of the expression are shown in Figure 2.6B). They have to be arranged, however, to form a rectangle (Figure 2.6C), and when this is done, it may be seen that such a rectangle has one side of length $2x + 2$, and the other $x + 3$. It can also be seen that such a rectangle is the same as $2x^2 + 8x + 6$ (because it is composed of precisely those parts).

It might be argued that it would be much quicker to do the problem in the old symbolic way: lay out the brackets, which will have to have $2x$ beginning one, and x the other $(2x + \quad)(x + \quad)$. The factors of 6 are 1 and 6 or 2 and 3. We then fiddle around with these combinations, until the addition of xs $(2x + 2)(x + 3)$ makes $8x$. While this method may be quicker, it has fewer connections with other items of knowledge. The spatial method, on the other hand, links immediately to several known geometrical concepts. For example, the area of 'size' of a rectangle is the length multiplied by the breadth; when the two sides of a rectangle are the same, the result is a square (hence x^2 is x '*squared*'); all these things are true whatever the size of the square or rectangle. Many students find it quite exciting to discover that algebra 'sums' can be done by geometry or by other physical representations. (Dienes also explains other ways of solving quadratics, for example, by using cups and beans, and hooks on a balance.)

How successful is the multiple-embodiment approach? Biggs (1966) found that children taught for two years by this method were superior to closely matched, traditionally taught children in terms of (a) positive attitudes to maths; (b) conceptual understanding; and (c) computing skill. The last finding was unexpected, as the children were not taught the rules, facts and tables of calculation as such: it seems that they were able to work out the answers to sums on the basis of their understanding of the concepts involved. The longer the children had been exposed to the method the greater were the benefits; and children with the lowest IQs benefited the most from long exposure to the method.

The generative model of learning explains these findings. The more cross-links into other modes of representation, the more likely students will be able to comprehend and extend their knowledge. The principle of illustrating in as varied a manner as possible is not restricted to mathematics. Any attempt to use activity, illustration, concrete example, the field trip, the experiment, audiovisual aids, and so on, simply helps them to use more, and wider areas, of their brains. Learning is bound to be more efficient, more secure, and more usable as a result.

Do students learn from excursions? The typical field trip or excursion appears ideal in helping students to integrate their academic knowledge with their experience of the real world. After a series of lessons on a natural feature, the teacher takes the students into the field with a list of demonstrations or features the students are to note, the teacher acting as 'tour guide'. The results are usually disappointing (Mackenzie and White, 1982).

Figure 2.6   Factorising quadratic functions with concrete materials

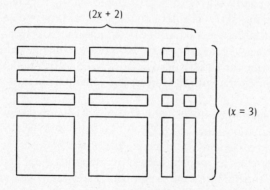

Squares
$(x \times x)$

Strips
$(x \times 1)$

Units
(1×1)

A   Squares, strips and units

$2x^2$'s   and $8x$'s   and   6 ones

B   The parts of the expression $2x^2 + 8x + 6$

$(2x + 2)$

$(x = 3)$

C   Making a rectangle of sides $(2x + 2)(x + 3)$

Mackenzie and White argued that observation and demonstration are insufficient. On the basis of Wittrock's generative model, and a memory model not unlike that presented here (Gagné and White, 1978) in that it emphasises multiple encoding, Mackenzie and White devised a 'processing' excursion which required the students to be actively involved, including unusual actions such as wading through a mangrove swamp, tasting leaves for salinity, scrambling over cliff platforms. All activities were

*Carefully designed excursions
require active involvement linked
to previously learned material.*

designed to link with a lesson on coastal geography and were designed to *generate* information to be observed and recorded. Three classes of mixed Year 8 and Year 9 students were given the detailed lesson, addressing 35 objectives. Two classes were then taken on an excursion, one class being given the usual 'guided tour' of demonstration and observations, the other, the processing excursion.

The results, according to the authors, were 'remarkable'. There were no differences between the three classes immediately after the lesson, but three months after, with the excursion intervening, the processing class recalled 90 per cent of the original lesson, the traditional excursion class recalled 58 per cent and the third class who simply had the lesson with no excursion, 51 per cent. There was also a special test designed to see if students linked experiences or observations with the facts taught in the lesson: the processing excursion group was far better at this than the others.

In other words, the passive, 'demo' kind of excursion was little, if any, better than having no excursion at all. A carefully designed excursion, requiring active involvement in episodes that demonstrated previously taught material, was very successful in helping students not only to retain that material, but to make the connection between their formal knowledge and their experience of the world.

The general point is much the same as that underlying the use of the Dienes material: requiring students to *act*, in as many different modes as possible, to illustrate a set of concepts, operations or principles. In the absence of that activity, the students will learn formal knowledge insecurely and as alien to the very world to which it is meant to apply. Gunstone and White (1981), for example, found that students who had passed HSC physics were frequently unable to apply their knowledge to make sense out of simple demonstrations: this, however, raises a whole new set of issues and we return to them in Chapter 6.

IMPROVING MEMORISING

Ways in which students may themselves improve their memorising are dealt with in Chapter 4. Here we deal with two aspects that are more directly under the teacher's control. The first relates to the basic point that what is remembered is a function of what was originally learned; the second, to the use of mnemonics.

Being careful of what goes in

In the tradition of Bartlett's work on reconstruction, Howe (1970a) read his students an excerpt from a modern novel and they then wrote down what they remembered of it. Immediately after they had done so, the original version was re-read. The following week, the students again wrote their version of the passage, and again the original was re-read. This pattern — writing down and re-reading — was repeated for four weeks. One might have expected that under such conditions the students would check their errors against each re-reading. In fact, however, the students reproduced each time *a version of their first reproduction,* despite the fact that they had had four opportunities to correct their initial errors. Howe reported that the students were aware of doing this, but found the tendency very hard to resist.

The implications of this study are quite important. Teachers need to be very careful about what they say the first time round. If they find they were mistaken and try to correct the mistake, it will be difficult to get the second version across. (This could be explained in terms of associative interference, in view of the likely similarity between the correct and incorrect versions.) Similarly, teachers who have given the class a test and then read out the correct answers may be disappointed. While logically one might expect that the students who had incorrect answers would write the corrections in and remember them, what seems to happen is that the students confuse their mistakes with the corrections.

One solution is to make sure students do not make mistakes in the first place: this is precisely the teaching strategy recommended by Skinner, and employed in mastery learning. Another solution, as Howe (1972) pointed out, is to analyse the *reasons* for those mistakes: recode the codes that produced the errors, rather than simply concentrating on the errors. In other words, much 'forgetting' takes place when the material is *learned*: it is inadequate learning rather than forgetting. For example, a very common mistake is the confusion between two codes governing the formation of plural verbs: 'When the subject of the sentence is plural, the verb is plural' (generic code); 'When the word just before the verb is plural the verb is plural too' (surface code). Most young students use the second code: it is clear, concrete and it works most of the time. In the case of collective nouns, however, it does not work — as when students write 'The case of oranges are dear.' Simply to correct them will only result in confusion; it is obviously preferable for them to learn and apply the real code — that it is the *case* that is dear, not the oranges.

Mnemonics

So far we have been talking about coding that makes use of structure that is *intrinsic* to the content. We know that rehearsal or rote learning is applied to material that has no evident or usable structure — such as numbers, dates, formulae, etc. — but can *coding* be used to help memorise such material? It certainly can, and its use in such situations is achieved by *mnemonics*. A mnemonic system imposes a structure where none exists, and thus encourages ease of learning, firm lodging in long-term memory, and ease of retrieval, which are normally the prerogatives of meaningful learning.

A simple example of a mnemonic is when a word is formed from the first letters of the target words: the Great Lakes become HOMES (Huron, Ontario, Michigan, Erie, Superior); or the colours of the spectrum become that spunky Minister for Ethnic Affairs, Roy G. Biv (red, orange, yellow, green, blue, indigo, violet). The reverse can also be applied by turning target letters into sentences: the notes in the treble staff are thus recalled as '*E*very *G*ood *B*oy *D*eserves *F*ruit' (the five lines) and *D*irty *F*ilthy *A*nimals *C*an't *E*at *G*rass (the adjacent notes).

There are more elaborate mnemonic systems. Typically, easily visualised objects are attached, by rote learning, to a number or letter, and the function of memory is to retain the mixture of visual images rather than the original numbers.

Thus, Bower (1970) suggested an easy way to remember the day's shopping list, by associating each item with a particular location — behind the door, on the floor, on the kitchen table, and so on.

Using techniques such as these, it certainly is possible to 'amaze yourself and your friends' as the advertisements promise; the only (non-financial) catch is that they do require a lot of time and trouble to acquire. Whether such elaborate mnemonics are really *educationally* useful, however, may be debatable.

ANXIETY ON BOTH SIDES OF THE TEACHER'S DESK

From trait to state

People who are high in trait anxiety may or may not actually *experience* anxiety in a particular state or situation. Wrightsman (1962) divided a group of students into high and low trait-anxious and gave them an intelligence test, telling one group (stressed) that the results were so important they could affect their college careers, and the other group (unstressed) that the results were only needed for norming the test and would not be looked at individually. The low-anxious groups performed at the same level under both conditions, but the high-anxious performed very differently: the stressed group performing at a lower level than the unstressed. Somewhat similarly, O'Neil, Spielberger and Hansen (1969) found that high trait-anxious students did better than low-anxious on the easy items in a mathematical concept task, but the low-anxious did better than the high-anxious on the difficult items.

These results indicate that trait anxiety affects performance only to the extent to which it is experienced. People low on trait anxiety will need a large 'push' before anxiety caused by the environment will be aroused to the extent that it will affect them adversely. People easily aroused to anxiety, on the other hand, only need — as these experiments show — to be told that the result is important, or to find that the items being tackled are difficult, before anxiety will inhibit performance.

When anxiety is associated with a particular set of circumstances, we speak of state anxiety. For example, *test anxiety* is associated with anxiety about doing poorly when being evaluated; *number anxiety* is associated with a fear of arithmetic. One reason why arithmetic, more than other school subjects, can create anxiety is because it is abstract and yet the answers are so definitely right or wrong. If a person is prone to anxiety, and has little grasp of number concepts, the situation is particularly threatening: one is right, or more usually wrong, for mysterious reasons that one cannot explain (Biggs, 1962). Test anxiety may be experienced when any school subject is being evaluated.

Assessment is certainly a major source of anxiety but it is not the only one. The structure of the classroom, whether formal or open in style, can affect students — and teachers — differently in terms of their emotional reactions to the teaching situation. Teachers may be affected by anxiety, particularly early in their careers and, like some students, by the style of classroom environment. It is fashionable nowadays to speak of teacher burn-out, which is certainly a reaction to stress.

In this final section, then, we look at how stress and anxiety may affect all in the classroom, teachers as well as students, and see what may be done about it, and by whom.

Test anxiety

Gaudry and Bradshaw (1970) tested Year 7 and 8 pupils in 14 Melbourne schools under two conditions of examination: *progressive assessment* (based on class assignments and informal short tests), and *terminal assessment* (based on formal examinations). They reasoned that students high in test anxiety would do better under the less pressurised progressive system than under terminal assessment, but that all test-anxious children would do less well than non-anxious whatever the method of assessment. These expectations were borne out: Gaudry and Bradshaw concluded that as terminal examinations are more potentially stressful than progressive assessment, it is unfair on test-anxious children to offer them no choice in the form of examination. Students who are not test-anxious, on the other hand, resent the continual though less severe pressure that progressive assessment brings.

Coping with test anxiety. State anxiety creates three classes of response: bodily reactions such as sweating, palpitation, discomfort; thoughts about one's inability to cope with threat; and coping styles, particularly those that have been effective in the past (Keavney and Sinclair, 1978). These responses demand awareness: one becomes *aware* of physical discomfort if it is severe enough, and also of such questions as 'What am I going to do? ... What *can* I do?' Such thoughts are irrelevant information in the sense that they will not help solve the problem; but as they are insistent, they crowd working memory and force out relevant information. On the other hand, anxiety has an activating or arousal function as well, which leads to rapid processing. If the interfering effects can be prevented, one is left with the *beneficial* effects of arousal. The clues are therefore:

1. to make the items of relevant information as stable as possible, so that they will resist the demands of irrelevant information for working-memory space;
2. to reduce the load on working memory as much as possible.

Anxious learners should train to use notes, maps, diagrams, outlines and the like wherever possible. Similarly, on first reading exam questions, they should jot down whatever points occur and then make up an outline in logical order and with subheadings. Once started, relevant information will come rushing back by association, if the material has been learned well. That relevant information will in turn crowd out such irrelevant thoughts as 'Gosh, how am I going to do this? ... I feel quite sick ... ' If this process is to work, however, there must be a solid background of well-learned relevant material. It is unlikely that such a background can be acquired in the week or two before an exam. If notes and outlines are based on just a week of rote learning, the immediate associations will be quickly exhausted with nothing to replace them.

Generic coding is the answer. A generic code is like a fishing line which has many short lines and hooks attached; and to each hook is attached another line, also with many hooks. By hauling in the main line, a great deal of richly associated material is drawn into working memory, and if it is sufficiently well learned such material will displace the feeling directly due to anxiety. The general strategy of such learning is cumulative. There are four stages:

1. *Learning.* This is the initial learning itself (a book chapter, a lecture). The basic material is read and assimilated.
2. *Elaboration.* The learner thinks about what has been learned, and relates it to relevant material already known. New material helps re-evaluate the old.
3. *Organisation.* Gradually a pattern emerges; the incident or content 'makes sense'. This process takes time, but is hastened by much note-taking during elaboration, and also during the next stage.
4. *Consolidation.* The learner starts making notes of notes, interrelating all the bits and pieces about working memory, for example, that have been picked up in the references, in discussion and in original classwork. One then makes notes of these notes, uses spatial summaries, and so on. Finally an outline of the whole course may, almost literally, be written on a bus ticket. At that point the learner is ready to rote-learn the notes-of-notes-of-notes — not to understand anything better, but simply to make sure those notes can be recalled on cue. Because of the background of learning, a particular word or pattern in the notes is like one of the hooks on the main line: it is attached by cross-referencing to so much other relevant material.

People who study according to this four-stage process can even afford to be in a state of high anxiety during an exam. Once they get going, and that is the important thing, the richly coded information will virtually take over. The student then has the advantage of working under conditions of high arousal, with a working memory dominated by relevant information.

Managing state anxiety in general. We can generalise from test anxiety to coping with all state anxiety in one-off situations. Chronic stress implicates *trait* anxiety which requires proper counselling, but when a person is faced with a single stressful situation in which it is important to function well, such as an interview, then strategies for handling the situation can be worked out.

The villain is working-memory overload: the poor performance arises because of the felt stress distracting from the important task-relevant cues. Over-learning is one means of reducing information. It is done by rehearsing the material at least as many times *again* as are needed for perfect recall. Over-learned cues are very firmly lodged and are less likely to be displaced when the arousal system is over-activated, as it is under high stress. In army training, for example, skills such as stripping, cleaning and reassembling a weapon are taught and practised over and over, long after the soldier can perform the task perfectly. The point is that the process will need to be done under battle conditions of extreme stress, and therefore the less thought needed to do the task the better. Similarly, rehearsing actors are taken over their lines, and perform certain complicated sequences many times *after* they have given a 100 per cent performance.

Over-learning thus has two effects: it *reduces the size of the chunk,* thus freeing working memory, and it makes *recall* very much easier. The first function can be achieved in other ways too, and that is where the strategies come in. When the unexpected might happen, one must have as much working memory available as possible. The following paradigm emerges:

- *Define the problem clearly.* 'The interview scares me' is too vague. What in particular about the interview is causing the worry — a tricky question? The presence of a particular individual? The unexpected?
- *Devise coping procedures to meet the defined problem.* Use hidden cue cards to prevent 'drying up' or see the individual beforehand on some pretext.
- *Over-learn those coping procedures.* Rehearse under real-life, not artificially restricted, conditions. One cannot anticipate the unexpected (by definition), so the main strategy is to keep as much working memory as free as possible to allow for any such contingencies.

In fact, one student (who we shall call Jim) devised a scheme along these lines to cope with his first supervised practice teaching lesson. (Each year we ask our students as one assignment to apply an aspect of this book to their teaching practice, and to tell us what happened.) The strategy Jim worked out, and the outcome, are described below.

How one student teacher beat practice teaching nerves. Jim was not looking forward to practice teaching. He had been a good student at both school and university. He had always been nervous about speaking in public, but he had also learned that he would get over it in time, as he had with his 'tutorial nerves' by second year. It wasn't a question of mistaking his vocation — he wanted to teach all right. It was a matter of getting through the first block practice of four weeks. What particularly worried him was being under supervision: the supervising teacher sitting in the back, making notes of his mistakes. It didn't seem fair to be judged at that time.

1.   *Defining the problem.* So far, there is nothing much to pinpoint. 'It isn't fair that I get nervous and it'll count against me': Jim could see that to dwell on that just made matters worse. His method lecturer told him he should make early contact with the school: just to find out what he *is* going to be required to do. He met his supervising subject master and class teachers. He was given a list of classes he was to teach, and details of the pupils and of the teaching program. He was also told that one of the teachers would be sitting in with him until they were reasonably sure he could handle the pupils. He asked to be shown the classrooms after school. He stood for a few minutes in each one, mentally photographing the layout: he would need those snapshots for his mental rehearsals. He now knew what the most likely problems were.

- *Content?* No, that had been covered in depth in university; he also knew the class texts and had access to plenty of reference material.
- *Method?* No. He'd done some peer teaching and microteaching, and was familiar with a range of skills, how to use the audiovisual aids, etc.
- *Discipline?* Of course, but that was unlikely to be a major problem at this stage — precisely because one of the other teachers *would* be present. More likely was some

kind of veiled insolence that would challenge him to show he recognised it as such and that he could cope. How to deal with a 'bright' remark and leave no doubt as to who was boss? He could see that his nervousness was exactly the wrong thing to show. He could also see that he would probably be the only student ending the block, still being 'babysat'. That would mean certain failure. Just thinking about *that* sent the adrenalin rushing.

- *Being centre stage?* Yes! Jim-in-the-spotlight; *that* was the problem. And in particular having to cope with the unexpected.

   2.   *Devising coping procedures*. First, he had time on his side, plenty of time to plan. Fortunately, we had covered Chapter 8 on classroom management by this stage, and that gave him a few clues.

- *Jim-in-the-spotlight?* Get out of it! No expository methods, Jim centre stage. No open-ended invitations to the class that could leave him skilfully parrying questions.
- *Afraid he'll dry up and have nothing to say?* Use materials that would cue him: handouts, transparencies, some videos, textbook as a standby.
- *Use dominant body language.* Stand straight, use frequent eye contact. Set materials up in the centre not the side. Stand centre, *look* dominant, but let the materials do most of the 'talking'. And avoid eye contact with the supervisor: that could really throw you.
- *Pupils?* Keep them busy. No gaps. Activities that will make them work, not ask questions ...
- *Routinise.* For a while he had visions of a fearfully complex and ever-changing pattern of activities that would keep his working memory working overtime. Then what about all those unexpecteds he had to cope with? No. Everything had to be as *simple as possible*. Risking an accusation of lack of imagination, he decided to follow the same lesson plan and set of routines for every lesson he could get away with: standard set of subheadings, same number of points, entry into room, diagram with name and pupil seating arrangement for each room propped on his desk in front of him, check ventilation, lighting, who was sitting where (check they haven't moved), clean chalkboard ...
- *Overlearn.* There was plenty here to overlearn — all these routines in the context of his mental photographs, and the by-now memorised lists of names. So, with his cat and budgie as understudies for those names, he rehearsed all the routines. He found the odd joke occurring to him — *quick write that down, memorise it* (you never know when that might defuse a tense moment).

   3.   *Outcome*. It worked. As he walked in with the first lesson with his class teacher, he noticed the pupils appraising him. This was going to be a problem all right, he thought. Just as he was being introduced by the class teacher, he discovered his opening line had dried up. She continued the introduction skilfully into a review of the previous lesson — which led directly into Jim's topic, and the printed sheets he was ready to distribute. He was into the lesson before he knew it.

There was the odd blip. Announcements over the PA, and visitors, sometimes disrupted his flow but the routines took over. His confidence grew. In fact by the end of the second week, he found all that over-learned material rushing to get out: at one stage he found himself talking *too* much. The supervising teacher withdrew at the beginning of the third week, apparently satisfied now that he could manage. He *did* make a crack about varying the routine: 'Just a little, old son. Keep that up for the next 40 years and you'll die of boredom ...'

Anxious teacher, anxious child?

Sellinger (quoted in Coates and Thoreson, 1976) found that pupils of teachers who were themselves highly anxious were not anxious if taught in closed, formal classrooms, but were very anxious if taught in open classrooms. This fits with Gaudrey and Spielberger's suggestion that the anxious child 'is likely to become upset if suddenly plunged into unstructured situations where he must rely on his own resources' (1971, p. 81).

On the other hand, informal and open classrooms are advocated as stress-free environments in which the child is not under strong pressure, and as such would be expected to be recommended for anxious children. What is the explanation for this apparent contradiction?

Anxiety and open classrooms. Cronbach and Snow (1977) reviewed a large number of studies concerned with teaching method and 'anxiety' — which includes neuroticism, self-deprecation, expecting to fail — and found some results that supported Gaudry and Spielberger's suggestion that anxious or neurotic students are more comfortable in highly structured environments. However, their major conclusion was that 'two decades of thinking about anxiety arousal have not yet brought the phenomenon under control so that effects can be predicted and replicated'.

The situation is indeed complex. A study in England by Bennett (1976) has been quoted widely as supporting the view that formal classrooms not only produce better students (i.e. they can read, write and calculate more effectively than students from informal classrooms), but that formally taught students are less anxious.

Barclay (1978) came up with similar results in the United States. In general, he found that the traditional (formal) approach fostered the most positive social and affective growth, but that the open approach did favour children who were 'introverted and individualistic'.

Rosenshine (1978) was quite critical of Bennett's study on several grounds. His most important point was that it is not good enough to categorise schools into 'formal', 'mixed', and 'informal': there are various *kinds* of formality. Rosenshine mentioned several studies which distinguished between *structured* (orderly, teacher-directed, work closely programmed) and *unstructured*; and between *warm* (friendly, supportive, teacher praises rather than blames) and *cold*. In Bennett's study, structure was confused with warmth, so that one is not sure whether his anxious children did better in formal classes because the classes were more structured, or because they were warmer, or both structured *and* warm.

This is an important point. Biggs (1962) found that high number anxiety was associated with high formality in teaching — but so were *low* feelings of anxiety. What

*Do these children look anxious
in an open classroom?*

made the difference was success in learning: successful children could handle the external pressures, and did well; unsuccessful children did not. The motivation system used in formal classrooms seems to follow Bugelski's stark advice — 'The task of the teacher is to create the necessary degree of anxiety' (1958, p. 460) — that anxiety then being reduced by success. Anxiety is thus a two-edged weapon, and if it is not accompanied by success, will remain to impede further learning.

In short, the questions of what environment students are going to find most or least stressful, and what interactions between student and teacher lead to optimal levels of anxiety that activate appropriately and do not hurt, are complex ones. As we shall see in Chapter 3, there are alternative and preferable ways of motivating students.

Before turning to how the teacher is to cope with anxiety arising from classroom stress, we should conclude with a general discussion of one very important resource person the teacher has. At some point or another — whether over an anxiety-related issue or not — the teacher will need to turn to the counsellor.

The school counsellor

Problems and difficulties that arise from personality characteristics of students are issues that must be taken up with the school counsellor. They require a great deal more specific training than the classroom teacher normally possesses, not to mention a 'licence to practise'. Most teachers will be at primary or secondary schools where there is a permanent counsellor, either exclusive to that school, or shared with a group of schools (frequently, a high school and its 'feeder' primary schools have the one counsellor).

To put it roughly, the teacher is responsible for the education of the general run of students; the counsellor is responsible (among other things) for the problem students who do not get on well with the main system. The teacher's task, then, is to recognise when to hand over those with problems (particularly emotional problems) for individual treatment.

The counsellor may handle several kinds of problem.

1.   Individual students. This is the most common case. Reasons for referral are ones that the teacher would normally come across in class, and could include:

- learning difficulties, particularly sudden changes (which might indicate emotional disturbance);
- study difficulties, lack of study skills or facilities;
- behaviour problems, such as delinquency, difficulties in management;
- 'crisis' intervention, where a child gives evidence of emotional upset, or drug usage;
- social problems, such as bullying or being bullied, sexual difficulties;
- home problems, which come to the teacher's attention and seem to require liaison or consultation with the school.

Many of these problems are ones that the teacher cannot handle, but someone should. Usually, the teacher is the intermediary, but counsellors also make it known to students how they may be contacted directly.

2.   Coping with discipline problems. This overlaps the above role, except that often it is not so much that the child needs psychological help as that the teacher might need some professional advice. In such an event, the counsellor is probably the best person to turn to.

3.   Vocational and career guidance. Vocational guidance is available through each State (independent of the education departments), and at some schools through a careers adviser. However, it may also be convenient and appropriate for a counsellor to provide initial testing and guidance for students.

4.   Educational resource person. There is a place in many (especially large) schools for a resource person on more general educational problems. For example, a teacher or group of teachers might wish to set up a program of behaviour modification or mastery learning, or to teach a section of the curriculum in terms of behavioural objectives. The counsellor may be a good person to advise on such matters. However, the counsellor's role is already a large one and, under present conditions of supply and training, the resource role is likely to remain a relatively minor one compared with other functions in the school.

Teacher anxiety

Like their pupils, both beginning and experienced teachers experience state anxiety which has a detrimental effect on both teacher effectiveness and personal happiness (Coates and Thoreson, 1976; Telfer, 1979a, 1981, 1982). Common sources of anxiety among beginning teachers are classroom management and pupil discipline, conflicts with supervisors, popularity with pupils, and their own expertise in terms of content knowledge and teaching skills. More experienced teachers mention discipline as a problem less frequently, being more concerned with their adequacy to handle specific student needs, and with industrial issues.

Keavney and Sinclair (1978) summarised evidence which suggested that teacher anxiety adversely affects the quality of the classroom atmosphere. Compared with non-anxious teachers, anxious teachers tend to:

- create higher student anxiety;
- teach more dogmatically and rigidly;
- behave in a less friendly manner towards students;
- use negative and critical feedback for poor student performance and behaviour rather than praise for work well done;
- have more rowdy classes;
- award lower grades for the same quality of work than non-anxious teachers.

Keavney and Sinclair suggested that one way anxious teachers cope is to become dogmatic in their teaching and interaction with students. Anxious teachers, for example, defend themselves against a sense of inadequacy:

> ... by excessive self-aggrandisement. Perhaps such teachers would be likely to dominate the classroom speaking time, only allowing students to regurgitate what they have said or to express agreement (Keavney and Sinclair, p. 287).

These authors reviewed the effects of this kind of teacher behaviour on classroom interaction (dogmatism is revealed, for example, in such statements as 'Two times three is six because it is, and that's that'). There is evidence that student teachers tend to become more dogmatic than their co-operating teachers after their first round of practice teaching. It seems likely that this is due to anxiety, a 'no questions' approach being an easy defence to adopt. It is not known at what point, and why, beginning teachers learn to be more flexible.

Teacher stress in the classroom.

'Monday morning! Ironic that the sun shines brighter as soon as the weekend's over. Oh hell! 9E's exam papers. Due back today — and they're still in the brief case with the Year 7 assignments that were overdue last week. And today's lessons have not been prepared.'

'Another school policy committee meeting at lunch time — pupil pastoral care. There's another twist for you. What about teacher pastoral care? Last period Friday with 9E was almost World War Three — and one that was adjourned, to be continued, until Monday first period. Today — in two hours' time ... I can't handle this, I'm going to take a sickie.'

The pressure on this teacher is obvious. Let's leave solutions aside, and focus on the results. What happens when teachers are under stress? Your heart starts to pound as its rate and blood pressure increases; adrenal hormones are being discharged and muscles prepare themselves for 'fight or flight' (Selye, 1974). Your ability to maintain this state of readiness is limited: you are pushing your 'twang factor' (Vivian, 1984).

Or what of the plight of Ronald, longest serving staff member, who gains promotion to deputy when only four years off retirement? Ron has lived in the school district all his life and has a friend-of-the-family role with members of the community and the school pupils. Abruptly, Ron finds that the expectations of his colleagues and pupils have changed. Staff who are experiencing problems with the pupils he knows so well expect him to take disciplinary action on their behalf. Ron feels a growing conflict between his personality and his job.

You and Ron are prime subjects for teacher 'burn-out'.

Teacher burn-out. 'Burn-out' is a syndrome of physical and psychological reactions involving a marked *change in attitude* towards recipients or clients. It is an occupational hazard of those whose work is primarily in *interaction with other people,* and is a response to *excessive job-related demands.* Teachers, like many in the helping professions, are particularly susceptible to burn-out (Mandaglio, 1984). Box 2.2 gives a few hints on how to counteract burn-out.

We have already mentioned Ron's conflict between his established role and his new role. Teachers generally are uncertain of their roles (such as the extent to which they are responsible for colleagues, subordinates or pupils' safety). Other job-related contributions are poor working conditions (such as working in demountable classrooms); job overload, school activities interfering with a teacher's personal life and family relationships or routine; questions about mobility for promotion or transfer if both partners in a family are working; and 'staffroom politics' which are seen to affect participation in decisions or restrict teachers in some way.

A real problem is that the top of the salary scale for a classroom teacher comes early in one's teaching career, leaving two-thirds of working life without a rise — unless promotion is gained, but that in turn leads to less time in teaching and more in administration. Good teachers are not rewarded (financially) if they choose to continue to do what they are best at — teaching. Career re-assessment by Australian teachers occurs after about 10 years of teaching (Newman, 1985). Just as their students daydream, dawdle and are inattentive when they regard the classroom alternative as unpalatable, so teachers arrive late for lessons or simply take a 'sickie' (Sylvester, 1983). Miller (1985) found staff absenteeism in a Brisbane high school greatest for those in their first 10 years of teaching.

Those teachers most susceptible to burn-out when teaching loses its challenge are

BOX 2.2   COUNTERING BURN-OUT

1. Accept the need for taking action about the stressors.
2. Evaluate the dissatisfactions, isolating those that can be remedied.
3. Look for new possibilities to find fresh solutions for problems. Your friends and colleagues may be able to help with such difficulties as finding time for marking and preparation. Other ways of reducing specific teaching anxieties are based on the idea of simulation games. Here, problems are defined and discussed, and solutions tried out in the 'safe' context of a game. Turney and Ryan (1978), for example, used this approach to build up the skill and confidence of beginning teachers in Australian inner-city schools.
4. Examine your total workload and learn to say 'no' in an assertive but non-aggressive response to suggestions that you take on additional roles without dropping some. Can you delegate some responsibilities?
5. Critically assess your out-of-school lifestyle, hobbies, sport and leisure. Physical work and sport provide a release.
6. Can your workplace be improved? You may be able to effect simple changes which improve lighting, ventilation or lay-out of classroom and staff room. Are you meeting only the same small group of teachers at school? Break the routine. You could also try scheduling yourself some private time.
7. The bottom line calls for professional help and/or strategic withdrawal from the most extreme situations. Teachers with dual qualifications could change teaching subjects from, say, history to English, maths to science, or English to library. A transfer to another school, new staff and new pupils is another alternative.

Source: Adapted from Pines, Aronson and Kafry, 1981.

those who have mostly taught in schools with large pupil enrolments and correspondingly large staff complements. This feeling of stifled initiative is compounded when administrators do not offer professional recognition and there are no opportunities for promotion. Miller's study showed that teachers with *added* responsibilities had 35 per cent fewer absences than classroom teachers. This raises the question whether the problem is really burn-out or 'rust-out'. Burn-out is a chronic state and cannot be managed by simple working memory management strategies.

SUMMARY

Directing attention. Two general strategies of getting students to pay attention rely on presentation and on content. *Variation of presentation* capitalises on the orienting response — voice dynamics, media of presentation, teaching methods, methods of interacting with students. All should be continually varied, with an element of surprise maintained wherever possible.

The other strategy relates to *content,* the problem being rather different when the student selects the task than when the teacher does: in the latter case, there is a selling job to do. One cognitive way of directing attention is by the use of embedded questions and overviews, before, during and after instruction as appropriate.

Optimising the use of working memory. The limited capacity of working memory is the major constraint on learning. It is important that what space there is, is used for important rather than trivial aspects of the task. Major ways of freeing working memory are by the use of notes, crutches and other devices and by automatising learning so that material is chunked into smaller units. The latter is important to enable students to operate efficiently under stress.

Encouraging meaningful learning. Two general ways of maximising meaning in line with the generative model are: defining *generic* rather than surface codes for particular tasks and focusing on them in teaching, and using multiple embodiment of a topic. In the latter, a given meaning or content is presented in varying modalities, so that the material is cross-classified in many ways. Examples included the use of strips and squares to solve quadratic functions and a geography excursion: the principle is highly generalisable.

Improving memorising. The present model of learning emphasises the importance of what goes in: incorrect encoding can be very hard to eradicate. Teachers need therefore to be careful how they present material in the first instance. When material has been encoded incorrectly, the remediation requires recoding rather than simply correction.

Another input structuring that is useful for certain tasks that need to be retained exactly, such as names, dates and formulae, is that which makes use of mnemonics. The trouble with mnemonics is that they are arbitrary: they maximise accuracy of output, but do not enhance understanding at all.

Anxiety. Anxiety affects both students and teachers. Test anxiety, incurred over assessment concerns, is particularly common in students, but aspects of it are under some measure of teacher control while students can learn coping techniques based on generic coding and over-learning. Classroom atmosphere affects different students differently. Anxious students coupled with anxious teachers in open classrooms do not work together optimally: anxiety often requires structure, even formality, to help the individuals cope. The school counsellor is a resource to whom the teacher may need to refer students with anxiety or other problems. The role of the counsellor is outlined.

Anxiety afflicts beginning and experienced teachers, but in different forms. Classroom control and relations with students concern beginning teachers most, but with 'socialisation' and experience teachers become subject to a variety of stresses: teaching is in fact a profession in which the stress reaction, 'burn-out', is relatively common. Burn-out occurs when teachers can no longer cope with frustrations induced by the peculiarly conflicting demands of teaching; ways of combating burn-out are suggested.

FURTHER READING

On attention and working memory

D. P. Ausubel, *Educational Psychology: A Cognitive View,* Holt, Rinehart & Winston, New York, 1968. Chapters 2, 3 and 4 are on meaningful and rote learning.

R. Case, *Cognitive Development,* Academic Press, New York, 1985. Chapters 14, 15 and 16 are a comprehensive review of the nature of working memory and its relation to higher order processes.

D. A. Norman, *Memory and Attention,* Wiley, New York, 1976. Chapters 2-6 provide a good basic account of selective attention, coding and rehearsal.

On long-term memory

A. D. Baddeley, *The Psychology of Memory,* Basic Books, New York, 1976. This is a very comprehensive account of recent memory research.

D. A. Norman, 1976. Chapters 7 and 8 are on mnemonics and long-term organisation.

M. C. Wittrock (ed.), *The Human Brain,* Prentice-Hall, Englewood Cliffs, N.J., 1977. See Wittrock's own chapter 'The Generative Processes of Memory', which particularly emphasises educational implications.

On arousal theory and motivation

D. O. Hebb, 'Drives and the CNS (conceptual nervous system)', *Psychological Review,* **62,** 1955, pp. 245–54. This is a classic article and is not difficult to read; a rarity on this topic.

M. Humphreys and W. Revelle, 'Personality, Motivation, and Performance: A theory of the Relationship between Individual Differences and Information Processing', *Psychological Review* **91,** 1984, pp. 153–84. This is a rather technical article which brings the reader up to date with research into effects of arousal on working memory and performance.

QUESTIONS

Questions for self-testing

1. If the cognitive process is considered as a system, which of the following are input processes, output processes or activating processes: paying attention; recalling; storing information; memorising?

2. Distinguish between the attending, processing and storing stages of the learning process.

3. Sketch a diagram representing the sensory register, working memory and long-term memory. Show the input from the environment; precoding; the path of the selected and processed input through consciousness; and the place of the plan.

4. Give three reasons why a pupil would choose to pay attention in class.

5. Give an example of a 'communication gap' (or lack of precoding priorities) between a teacher and pupil.

6. What is a typical digit span for 10-year-olds and adults?
7. When student pilots who drive a car learn to taxi aircraft they usually attempt to turn an aircraft off the runway by turning the control column like a steering wheel. In fact, they usually need to use only foot pedals. This is, of course, associative interference. But is it retroactive or proactive inhibition?
8. In this chapter seven dimensions along which dismembering may occur are discussed. Name five of these, with a brief example of each. How do they suggest that remembering might be improved?
9. Clarify how arousal can both energise and interfere with the ongoing performance.
10. Suggest three methods which can be used to organise the content of this chapter into small, manageable chunks.
11. Distinguish between trait anxiety and state anxiety.
12. Describe five strategies a teacher can use to influence a pupil's mental set to learn.
13. Three basic means of varying instruction were described in this chapter.
    List the three and provide examples of each.
14. Distinguish between a generic and a surface code.
15. Derive a mnemonic to enable you to recall the answer to question 13 above.
16. What are the main factors contributing to teacher burn-out?

Questions for discussion

1. What are some of the implications of digit span findings for your teaching?
2. Think back over your own schooling. What is the earliest lesson you can recall? Why do you think this episode has been retained in your long-term memory?
3. You are given an opportunity to express your preferences to the school timetable committee. Will you choose to have your lesson before or after the class goes to physical education? What psychological justification do you have for your decision?
4. What is the best approach, in your opinion, to avoiding nervousness when you teach your first class?
5. Your Year 12 students are about to sit for their tertiary entrance examination and are obviously feeling the strain. What advice can you offer to enable them to reduce their exam-room stress?
6. This book has been written with questions and overviews at the beginning and end of each chapter, with advance organisers for each part. Take those for this chapter and part in particular: did they achieve the effect *on you* that the content of this chapter and that of Chapter 4 (when you have read it) would have led you to expect? If not, why not?

3

Motivating academic learning

OVERVIEW

Why are you reading this book? From interest? Because you have been asked to do so? Merely to pass an examination, or to obtain as high a grade as possible? Because it is a necessary hurdle to jump in order to get your job qualifications?

Your answers to these questions represent some of the motivations for academic learning explored in this chapter. In particular, we look at competitiveness, which produces high need-achievement in pupils; and intrinsic interest, which flourishes under quite different conditions in school. In doing so, we consider answers to the following questions:

- Does competition work for all students?
- Do rewards kill intrinsic interest?
- Are some students actually turned off by too much success?
- How important is the self-concept to motivation?
- To whom (or what) do we attribute our successes and failures? Why?
- Can students learn to be helpless?
- How is student motivation affected by such factors as:
  - financial reward
  - others' expectations
  - school climate
  - consequences of failure?
- How effective is punishment in reducing pupil misbehaviour?
- What type of reinforcement do poker machine players receive when gambling?
- Who do school pupils use as their behavioural models?

When you have finished this chapter you should be able to do the following:

1. Show how achievement motivation is related to success and failure.
2. List three classroom conditions under which a sense of competition would be fostered.
3. Give three characteristics of intrinsic motivation.
4. Explain how a teacher can facilitate intrinsic motivation.
5. Explain how a teacher can depress intrinsic motivation.
6. Distinguish between 'pawns' and 'origins'.
7. Explain what is meant by 'self-efficacy'.
8. Argue for and against the practice of ability-grouping in schools.
9. Distinguish between norm-referenced and criterion-referenced evaluation.
10. Give an example of operant conditioning in the way children interact with parents.
11. Apply the Premack Principle to pupil motivation.
12. Describe a behaviour modification program to improve pupil behaviour in a classroom.
13. List two behaviours which are easily modelled.

SECTION A

WHY DO STUDENTS LEARN?

Students have all sorts of motives for learning, but it is convenient to group them into four categories. At one extreme is the kind of motivation we call *intrinsic*: it is based on wanting to learn because the student is interested or curious about the task itself. Such motivation is entirely task-centred. All other forms of motivation involve features that are more or less extrinsic to the task. Such features refer to the context in which the task is placed, to the other people who may be involved in the task, or to the pay-offs that follow from doing or not doing the task satisfactorily. These last motives are therefore called *extrinsic*. We can arrange these motives in ascending order of task-centredness:

1. *Instrumental motivation.* When students are motivated instrumentally, they perform the task because of the consequences that may follow, either in obtaining a material reward, or in avoiding a punishment or other unpleasant result. Instrumental motivation is purely extrinsic: it is learning by bribes (positive reinforcement) or blackmail (negative reinforcement).
2. *Social motivation.* Students learn in order to please people whose opinions are important to them. Motivation is less materialistic, with the possibility of more identification with the task.
3. *Achievement motivation.* Students may learn in order to enhance their egos by competing against other students and beating them: it makes them feel good about themselves and the task. There is more involvement with the task, but the end game is strictly speaking centred on the ego, not on the task.
4. *Intrinsic motivation.* Here there are no outside trappings necessary to make the students feel good. They learn because they want to.

The increasing task-centredness is evident. An instrumental reward is something that happens to be at the end of the learning trail, often because the teacher has decided to put it there (hence the reference to bribes), while under social achievement and intrinsic motivation, the student is progressively more able to become personally involved and say 'This is *me!*'

Students may nevertheless operate from a mixture, and a continually changing mixture, of these motives. You can work at a task because you are good at it and think you're likely to beat everyone else, thereby deriving the heady pleasures of the ego trip; and at the same time, know that you'll be pleasing other people important to you, winning a cash prize, and finding it all extremely interesting to boot. Such a package is, however, for the lucky few. Many students do not find their school tasks particularly interesting, or feel sufficiently self-confident to compete for the highest grades, and so teachers usually find that they have to work with students' more extrinsic motives.

This is important because of the relationship between students' motives for learning and the quality of their learning: the more intrinsic or task-centred the motivation, the better, the more complex and the more satisfying is the learning itself. Learning that is instrumentally motivated easily leads to cutting corners; the important thing becomes gaining the reward or avoiding the punishment. The learning task here is only a hurdle along the way, so attention is focused on maximising the pay-offs and minimising the costs in time and effort. If you are learning in order to satisfy curiosity, on the other hand, it makes little sense to cut corners: curiosity is not likely to be satisfied that way.

This relationship between motivation and learning quality is dealt with at length in Chapter 4. Here the point is simply that if high quality learning is more likely to come from intrinsically motivated learners, it becomes an educationally important goal to help students operate from intrinsic motivation. But if students are not already curious or interested, what then? Teachers can do many things to encourage intrinsic motivation — and they can avoid doing even more things that would strongly discourage intrinsic motivation. An important theme in this chapter is to discuss what these practices may be. First, however, it is necessary to say more about the four kinds or categories of motivation.

INSTRUMENTAL MOTIVATION

Instrumental motivation is based on what was once called trial-and-error learning by Thorndike (1898), instrumental learning by Hull (1943) and operant conditioning by Skinner (1965). Although the term 'learning' is used, in fact the experimental animals often did not learn to do anything they had not done before. They did, however, become more *motivated* to do one thing more than another. This now becomes very similar to the central problem of teaching: to get the students to sit down and learn, rather than to walk around, chatter, kick the furniture or scream.

The nature of operant conditioning

The principle of operant conditioning is simplicity itself, well known by wise parents and teachers. If you want people to do something, you make it worth their while. If you want them to stop doing it, you cease to make it worth their while, or you make it worth their while to do something else. Not a very noble message, but an effective one if it is followed through consistently. Frequently, however, we are not consistent, as the quite true example in Box 3.1 indicates.

Let us break the situation down into its components. For practical purposes, we may classify behaviour as either desirable or undesirable. Desirable behaviour is that which we wish to encourage: our objective is to increase its frequency in a given context. Undesirable behaviour is that which we wish to discourage: our objective is to decrease its frequency.

BOX 3.1   HOW TO ENCOURAGE WHAT WE LIKE LEAST

A mother was sorely pressed by her four-year-old's behaviour. He grizzled and whined for biscuits between meals, got them, and consequently wasn't hungry at mealtime. The following is a typical scene:

Tony: (entering kitchen) Mummy, wanna bickie.
Mrs Jones: Not now, Tony, it's nearly tea-time.
Tony: But I wanna (sob, sob) bickie *now*.
Mrs Jones: C'mon, don't be difficult. Run away and play with Cheryl for a while.
Tony: BUT I'M HUNGRY ...
Mrs Jones: (harassed and unthinking) OK, OK! Here's a bickie. Now take it, and go away until tea-time.

But peace cannot be bought this way. This behaviour was causing endless worry to Mrs Jones, and potential malnutrition in Tony. And Tony's whining was being reinforced several times a day, every day. Tony was learning that if he created a fuss, then he got a biscuit — it was as simple as that. The first step, then, is to make sure that Tony *never* gets biscuits by whining.

Table 3.1 illustrates the effects of different consequences on behaviour. According to this table, we can see that if we wish to increase their frequency, desirable behaviours should lead to some kind of reward. Rewards may involve gaining something pleasant (positive reinforcement) or avoiding something unpleasant (negative reinforcement). Both processes, however, are reinforcement: they strengthen the likelihood that the behaviour will be repeated. For example, one can make children say 'please' whenever they ask for something — either by rewarding them if they do or by threatening them with punishment if they don't.

If, on the other hand, our objective is to reduce the frequency of an undesired behaviour, we again have two options: either to ignore the behaviour so that it has no apparent consequences, or to make the consequences clearly unpleasant. The first involves the process called extinction, and the second, punishment. Both tend to lead to a weakening of the response, extinction more reliably than punishment.

A *behaviour modification* program involves the careful orchestration of the consequences of different behaviours so that the desired changes in a person's or a class's behaviour are brought about. The practical steps in setting up such a program are discussed in Chapter 8: here we are concerned with the basic principles.

Positive reinforcement. There are several types of positive reinforcer.

   1.   Consumables. These include food, drink, sweets etc. There are two good reasons why such reinforcers are not ideal in the classroom: they rapidly lose their

Table 3.1   The effects of different consequences on behaviour

Behaviour	Consequence	Process	Result
Desirable	Gain pleasant	Positive reinforcement (reward)	More likely to occur in future
Desirable	Avoid unpleasant	Negative reinforcement (reward)	More likely to occur in future
Undesirable	None	Extinction	Less likely to occur in future
Undesirable	Unpleasant	Punishment	Unpredictable except in special circumstances

reinforcing value (the forty-ninth Smartie is not as rewarding as the first); and health-conscious parents don't like them.

2.   *Money.* This is desirable to most people, although with young children, money — like consumables — quickly loses its appeal. There are also limits to which teachers can or will use direct payment.

3.   *Social reinforcers.* Essentially, social reinforcers — whether verbal or non-verbal — convey the information that the last response emitted is approved by the reinforcing agent. Phrases like 'That's great' and 'You're doing fine' are examples of verbal reinforcers; non-verbal reinforcers include admiring glances, proximity, touching, the appearance of paying attention, listening closely, etc. As Mehrabian (1970) pointed out, non-verbal reinforcers can be even more powerful than verbal ones.

4.   *Preferred activities.* Premack (1959) stated 'The Premack Principle': if behaviour A is more probable than behaviour B, behaviour B can be increased by making behaviour A a consequence of it. Say a child has reading difficulties, and is encouraged to read at home, but will not do it. Suppose, too, that the most frequent occupation is watching television. Then we simply make the rule that there is to be no television until some stated amount of reading is done.

5.   *Tokens.* It may be highly inconvenient, however, if not impossible, to allow children to carry out their desired behaviour immediately. This difficulty may be met by the use of token reinforcers. A token is generally some symbol object (e.g. a card, button or tally) that can be exchanged later for the real reinforcer. A 'token economy' in the classroom can be very versatile. A token can stand for a reinforcer for any child, once the 'currency' for each individual child has been established. A token can be given on the spot, making reinforcement immediate, which is a considerable advantage when the child's desired activity is, for example, a trip to a football match. Likewise, if the final reinforcement is large and expensive (e.g. a bicycle) then tokens can serve the function of 'filling in': one very powerful but remote reinforcer is transformed into a steady supply of 'reminders'.

All these positive reinforcers have their uses. For classroom purposes, the first two — foodstuffs and money — have their practical drawbacks, although parents might often find them convenient. Social reinforcements can be effective, but their value depends on the relationship between student and teacher. If the student neither likes nor respects the teacher, then praise may be seen as unpleasant and patronising rather than rewarding.

Negative reinforcement. Negative reinforcement does not mean punishment, as is so commonly assumed, but rather the avoidance of punishment. Negative reinforcement is where the consequences of the desired response remove distress, so in that sense it is rewarding, not punishing. Positive reinforcement is rewarding because the consequence is desirable for its own sake; negative reinforcement is rewarding because the consequence eliminates something that is undesirable.

The difference is essentially between doing something because we *want* a particular outcome, and doing it because otherwise we continue to receive something we do not want.

One of the most widespread negative reinforcers is anxiety, generated by the threat of punishment. The reward is the alleviation of the anxiety when the appropriate response is carried out and the threat is averted. On the other hand, use of negative reinforcement could associate anxiety with the learning context through the process of classical conditioning (see below). The full implications of negative reinforcement are best discussed in conjunction with punishment.

Extinction. Whereas reinforcement (positive or negative) increases response strength, no reinforcement extinguishes the response. Extinction (e.g. by ignoring the response) may be extremely difficult to achieve. The point is well made in an example from Haring and Whelan (1966) who were using operant techniques with a boy having difficulty with spelling:

> One subject, when asked to spell a word which he had previously studied, would make faces, mumble and pause...Even though the teacher was making extra time and effort available to the boy, spelling behaviour did not improve... (p. 286).

The psychologists reasoned that the attention the boy was receiving might be reinforcing the bad behaviour. Accordingly, they instructed the teacher to ignore the clowning and mumbling, and instead to give the boy attention when he spelled a word correctly. Lo and behold:

> After a month of exposure to this technique, the frequency of the undesirable responses decreased to near zero and the boy continued to make academic progress.

The gap between theory and practice is astonishingly wide — as the example of Tony and the biscuits also illustrates. We tend to ignore good behaviour and pay attention only to the bad.

Extinction, then, is a very good way of decreasing the strength of an unwanted response. Unfortunately, it is not only difficult to ignore a blatant piece of wrongdoing, but teachers often do not have control over all the competing sources of reinforcement. For example, you can learn to ignore the 'funny' remarks called out by the class comedian, but the source of the reinforcement is twofold: the teacher's expressions of annoyance and the amusement of the rest of the class. Even if you can remove reinforcement from the first source, you cannot from the second: thus the behaviour is maintained.

Punishment. Some writers define a reinforcer as any consequence of behaviour that increases the future rate of that behaviour, and punishment as any consequence that results in a decrease (Axelrod, 1977; Johnston, 1972). Such a definition, however, leads to special difficulties for practitioners, who tend to think of punishment as a particular kind of consequence: sarcasm, a slap or deprivation of some right. Here, then, we define punishment as an unpleasant consequence to a particular behaviour, which is perceived as being administered by another person.

Glasser (1969) distinguished between punishment and discipline. Discipline involves pain as a 'natural and realistic consequence of a person's behaviour', while punishment involves pain caused by someone else's disapproval. In the first case, the onus is on the student ('I knew I'd fail if I didn't work: I blew it!'); but in the second, it is on the punisher ('He's got it in for me!'). Future behaviour is obviously going to differ radically depending on whether the situation is read as involving discipline ('My fault') or punishment ('Teacher's spite').

What is the evidence for the effectiveness of punishment in diminishing unwanted behaviour? Following is a summary of the common findings.

1.   The initial intensity of punishment should be as great as possible, and this intensity should be maintained. This principle, is, in practice, almost always violated. The 'first offence' tends to be punished more leniently than the second and following offences: 'Well, I should punish you as I promised but I'll let you off this time. But don't let it happen again!' However humane this may be, it is not effective psychology: the child simply learns that the 'punishment' isn't so bad after all.

2.   Punishment must be administered each time it is warranted. This principle follows from the first: the negative consequences must be seen as far outweighing the positive ones. If it is at all possible to take a chance on those negative consequences not occurring, the wrongdoer will take that chance.

These two points together make the successful application of punishment somewhat impractical, and most of the successful applications have been in the specialised area of therapy (Baer, 1971). In this case it is often possible to obtain the permission of the client to administer what might appear to be unacceptably severe punishment; or the condition itself might be so severe that extreme methods are permissible. Such conditions are not attainable in the classroom: not only would the severity of the punishment be unacceptable, but teachers simply cannot guarantee 100 per cent effectiveness in policing deviant behaviour.

3.   Punishment is more effective when it is combined with reward. Here, punishment is not used alone. There are two sets of consequences: desired behaviour leading to reward, deviant behaviour leading to punishment. Students can see that although they were punished, there was also an attractive alternative open to them at the time, and that it will continue to be open. Nevertheless, the evidence is not clear-cut (Hanley, 1970). The important thing is how the situation is 'sold' to the students, and how they accept it, as we see below.

4.   *Punishment increases arousal; punished people become emotional.* The emotion created by punishment may be directed outwards or inwards. *Extrapunitive* people attribute the blame to the punisher: this is the reaction Glasser saw as the common one to punishment. 'Teacher's got it in for me!' — and the reaction to that is to retaliate. A defiant replay of the same act is a good way of retaliation. That makes teachers furious. *Intropunitive* people act as Glasser's disciplined student: they turn the blame onto themselves. The punishment is seen as a consequence of their own actions — and they are less likely to repeat the offending behaviour. Unfortunately, it is the extrapunitive child who is most likely to be punished, especially physically: the aggressive child, always blaming others, 'just asks for it — that's the language that type understands...'

5.   *Punishment makes people dislike the whole context of learning.* Punishment is unpleasant. Punishment takes place in connection with work, class, teachers, school. Therefore work, class, teachers, school become unpleasant too. That little emotional syllogism is an example of classical conditioning (see below). We learn not to like the people and situations that cause us pain. To punish by giving *added schoolwork* is a kind of educational treason.

6.   *Punishment suppresses behaviour; it may not eliminate it.* Through punishment, children learn when *not* to carry out the undesirable behaviour, and that is when they are likely to be caught. When the behaviour is only undesirable in *context*, like talking to a neighbour, punishment may be useful. But when the behaviour is *intrinsically* undesirable and may occur at any time, like hitting a neighbour, punishment will only teach the aggressor to be more cunning about doing it in future.

7.   *Punishment is ineffective as a means of moral education.* As the previous paragraph makes clear, the suppression of behaviour is in response to external conditions. Morality is a matter of internal control (see Chapter 7). Punishment endorses an external orientation: 'Punishment is the price for doing something. I want to do what you don't want me to do, so if I think the pain is worth my pleasure, your price has been paid. I'm free to do it again if I think it's worth it, or if I think that I can get away with it.' That's not what most people mean by morality.

8.   *Punishment works until it is administered.* Children fear the prospect of punishment more than the punishment itself: that is a matter of negative reinforcement and until punishment is administered it often deters. But once administered, the ice has been broken, and then it becomes self-defeating. This is particularly true of corporal punishment. As a glance in a punishment book will show, the *same names* keep cropping up.

Some aspects of reinforcement

Timing. The reinforcement should follow the response as soon as possible: any delay results in progressively weakened effectiveness of the reinforcer. One of the values of the token economy is that reinforcement tokens can be given out immediately. It is very easy to understand — and to forget — how important this principle is. If, for example, a student has just solved a very difficult problem for the first time and the teacher ignores the cries of triumph until next day — 'Oh, by the way, Kathy, that was very good the way you solved that problem yesterday' — the approval is stale. Saving up the assignments to mark at the weekend is not good psychology.

Continual versus partial reinforcement. Should the reinforcement follow every single response? Oddly enough, no, except (a) in the early stages of behaviour modification, and (b) when learners believe they have control over the consequences of their behaviour (Rotter, 1971). Otherwise the most effective program is partial reinforcement: reinforcements follow actions on a probable basis, not as a matter of certainty. What this means in practical terms is that once the response has been established, it is reinforced only every so often.

Say we have an agreement with a student to read so many pages a day, for which a reinforcement of one cent per page is negotiated. We might pay one cent after every page at first, but later it is preferable to make the payment 20 cents after 20 pages. We might then pay on a random basis: the second after 35 pages, the third after 70, the fourth after 85, and the fifth after 100. The total value received is the same, but the effects on the learner are different. First, the size of the reinforcement is reasonably substantial each time. Second, this procedure seems to help students internalise more effectively. They are on their own for much longer and learn to delay gratification — a very necessary fact of life. The aim is that the behaviours being reinforced will lead to desirable consequences on their own, and thus maintain themselves. This is much more likely to happen under a partial reinforcement schedule than under a constant one.

Partial reinforcement may be fixed or variable. If fixed, the reinforcement follows a given number of responses on what is called a ratio schedule; or, after a given time period of correct responding, on an interval schedule. A variable schedule means that while we may reinforce a particular number of responses, the reinforcement is random — the example of five 20-cent pieces spread over 100 pages is a variable schedule. Variable scheduling usually leads to more stable behaviour than fixed scheduling; the learners are never quite sure just when the reward is coming so they keep hard at it, just in case. This resistance to extinction can be seen in gambling. If someone strikes the jackpot first time on a poker machine, that person can quickly become hooked. Although receiving, more often than not, far less than the outgoings, the reinforcements come back in substantial amounts in comparison to the cost of each pull, and on a partial schedule.

Natural reinforcement. Ideally, there is a gradual process in which continual reinforcement changes to partial reinforcement. Finally, the reinforcement schedule is removed because naturally occurring contingencies maintain the desired behaviour.

Take the case of a child with a behaviour problem. At first, behaviour modification might be both arbitrary and extrinsically motivated, but once conditioned into socially acceptable behaviour, the child may discover that 'being good' is far preferable to being naughty. When this desired state occurs, further behaviour modification is unnecessary and should cease. For example, Gronert (1970) used behaviour modification, within the context of Glasser's reality therapy, on Jane:

> Jane, eleven and a half, had had two years of ineffective psychological counselling concerning her grossly inappropriate, hyperactive classroom behaviour with little or no results. Her behaviour was so gross that the school psychologist said that any method that would cure this problem would be a rare accomplishment in psychological case studies ... Jane's five teachers approached me at the point of complete exasperation and stated their

feelings that she should be sent away ... With reservations, however, they agreed to work with me in a behavioural approach (p. 106).

This, then, was the problem, and an obviously difficult one. Gronert applied behaviour-modification techniques, mainly by the use of a 'time out' procedure (that is, when Jane misbehaved in class, she was removed to a small bare room) whereby Jane's attention-getting behaviours would of course be totally ineffective. It was made clear that inappropriate behaviour would result in time out, while appropriate behaviour would be reinforced (mainly by social approval). Thus, 'the choice of appropriate versus inappropriate behaviours is hers alone'. After one week, with only two time outs, 'the teachers were delighted with the modification of Jane's behaviour ... More importantly, Jane realised this herself, so her self-concept began to improve. Her peers began to accept her and teasing diminished' (p. 108). Perhaps the most telling point made is one of Jane's own comments, one month later: 'How come the teachers are being nice to me?'

A major purpose of behaviour modifications is to change the child's world into one where appropriate behaviours are naturally reinforced. The teacher needs to intervene at first, but once the world has been changed, the situation should ideally be self-reinforcing: 'It is easier to act yourself into a new way of thinking than to think yourself into a new way of acting' (Mehrabian, 1970; p. 143).

Motivation by association

Another form of motivation, also based on conditioning, belongs in the category of instrumental motivation. A task becomes pleasant (and is therefore approached) or unpleasant (and is therefore avoided) by association with pleasant or unpleasant stimuli. Technically, this process is called *classical conditioning*: its general outline may be seen in *A Clockwork Orange* (see Box 3.2).

This form of conditioning was first studied systematically by the Russian physiologist, Pavlov. He noted that when his laboratory dogs were being fed, one of the doors leading to the lab squeaked and that the dogs salivated soon after hearing the squeak of the door, before they saw the food itself. Rather unremarkable, one might think, but Pavlov thought it remarkable enough to devote many years of research to the phenomenon.

First, there is a basic reflex: a stimulus (food) is presented and a reflex response (salivation) occurs *unconditionally*. Hence the food is called an *unconditioned stimulus* (US) and the salivation an *unconditioned response* (UR). Now a new stimulus occurs, say the sound of a buzzer (which is what is usually used in the laboratory rather than squeaking doors) just before the presentation of food (a little under half a second has been found to be an effective interval). This sequence, buzzer-food, is repeated several times. The dog at this stage is salivating in response to the food. It is found, however, that it salivates sooner and sooner, and that if the food is not presented at all it will still salivate to the buzzer. The buzzer has become a *conditioned stimulus* (CS) and the premature

---

BOX 3.2   CLASSICAL CONDITIONING IN A CLOCKWORK ORANGE

Alex, the young antihero of Anthony Burgess's novel and film is deeply committed to three things: violence, sex and classical music. After a particularly nasty escapade involving the first two of his commitments, he is arrested and sent to a reformatory. It is decided he will be used as a guinea pig in an experiment on behavioural reform. He is forced to watch films of Nazi atrocities while he is being shudderingly ill as a result of the prior injection of a particularly effective emetic. His behaviour thereafter is gentle and considerate: even thinking about violence or sex makes him ill. Unfortunately, the same is true of the music: the experimenters had overlooked the fact that Beethoven's *Ninth Symphony* was used as background music to the film.

---

salivation a *conditioned response* (CR) to the CS. If the buzzer is presented continually, without being backed up or reinforced by food, the salivation response fades or extinguishes.

The essential points of this process are reproduced in Figure 3.1.

Some theorists, such as Watson (1924) and Guthrie (1952), originally hoped that this basic model of conditioning might explain the whole of human learning. This we now know not to be possible, but it does help explain some aspects of human motivation.

Figure 3.1   Acquisition and extinction of a classically conditioned response

1.   An unconditioned stimulus (US) elicits the unconditioned response (UR):

US (food) ⟶ UR (salivation)

2.   A conditioned stimulus (CS) is introduced just prior to the US:

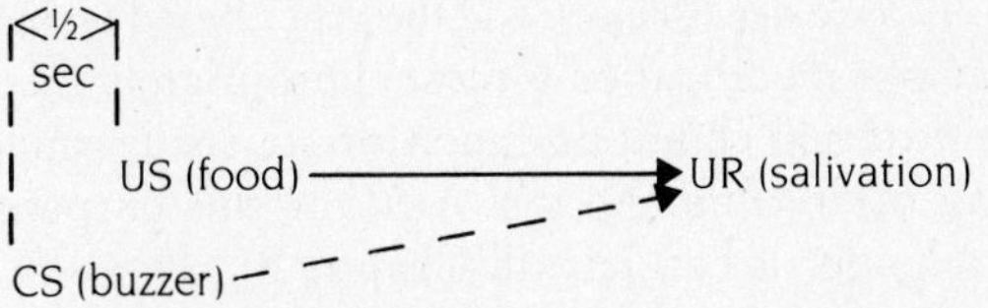

US (food) ⟶ UR (salivation)

CS (buzzer)

3.   US is omitted, CS now elicits a conditioned response (CR), which resembles a weak UR:

CS (buzzer) ⟶ CR (salivation)

4.   CS is presented continually. Without reinforcement of occasional US, extinction occurs:

CS (buzzer) (⟶)0

Parents use the process when they train children to avoid dangerous objects; when, for instance, a mother stiffens and shows great fear herself at the sight of a spider or snake. The evidence of parental fear is an excellent US for the child's fear (UR), which then becomes conditioned to the source of the parent's fear (e.g. the sight of the snake). Therapists use the same process with the Antabuse treatment for alcoholism. Antabuse is a drug that elicits a UR of violent, shuddering nausea; when mixed with alcohol, it produces (after very few trials) a CR of intense aversion to alcohol in general. The same principle is used in treating sexual deviates with electric shocks, not as punishment but simply so that the patient reacts to the previously attractive but socially unacceptable stimulus with aversion. In *A Clockwork Orange*, of course, Alex was the subject of aversive conditioning to violence, but as a second CS — the music of Beethoven — was present too, his aesthetic life also underwent a profound change.

As far as education is concerned, the application of these principles is clear. We need to make sure that a particular stimulus is associated with an appropriate emotion. Punishing a child with extra maths, for instance, is clearly poor psychology. Associating maths with punishment results in an intensified dislike of mathematics.

Classical conditioning provides a useful model for understanding how various features in the environment can become sources of what an outsider might think are 'irrational' reasons for powerful feelings of like and dislike. It is not really surprising that some children dislike school (or particular teachers, or the subjects that particular teachers have taught) if schoolwork has been associated with sarcasm, shame, discomfort, written impositions, and the sharp physical pain that is the unconditioned response to corporal punishment.

Summary

In this section, we have been discussing the most extrinsic kinds of motivation, where the task is arbitrarily linked to certain consequences or to certain emotions. Both cases involve conditioning, and psychologists have used the principles of conditioning to change behaviour and feelings by means of the technology of behaviour modification.

There are two kinds of behaviour modification: one based on classical conditioning (as in *A Clockwork Orange*), and the other based on instrumental or operant conditioning. Behaviour modification is most appropriately used for setting the stage — for making the external conditions appropriate for learning — rather than for controlling learning itself (although it is used for this purpose too) and so further discussion of this technique is best left till Chapter 8.

SOCIAL MOTIVATION

One of the most powerful influences on a person's behaviour is another person. We do things because it is important to us that we appear favourably in the eyes of significant others, whether those others be peer group, neighbourhood, boss, spouse, authorities, or whoever. A person who is immune to this kind of influence is called a sociopath.

We have already come across the social dimension of motivation in the point made above about social reinforcement. Social reinforcement is in fact quite different from material reinforcement in that the 'reward' is non-material: its value depends on the relationship between student and teacher (or other reinforcing agent). Praise from someone admired by the student helps the student internalise, to feel proprietorial about learning ('Gee, I must be good if Miss Jones says so!'). Material reinforcement, on the other hand, is impersonal, and has less effect on the student's feelings of competence.

A key concept in social motivation is modelling (Bandura, 1969). Modelling refers to the reliable tendency of people to imitate each other in the absence of direct reinforcement (that is, there is no reward for imitating others). Perhaps the best way of understanding the process is in terms of 'feeling good inside': it bolsters the self-concept to do what other important people do.

Bandura originally used the term 'imitation' to refer to this process, but he decided this was too narrow, implying a direct copy of the model's actions. Modelling occurs throughout life, although the particular model changes. At first, the young baby imitates movements, facial expressions and sounds made by the mother; later both parents are models; later still, other significant people including the peer group, the teacher, the boss, and so on, are models. It is a fundamental process for society.

Who are likely to be chosen as models? Models tend to be those most liked or respected; we model on those we like to resemble, and can identify with. Typically, different people occupy the role, often in a conflicting way. Thus, adolescents like to resemble their own peers, and consequently will model the current fads, fashions and pop heroes. Simultaneously, however, they may want to resemble an admired adult who behaves in quite a different manner. This phenomenon reflects the identity problems of adolescents, and their behaviour swings accordingly, depending, among other things, on who is currently serving as model.

In an academically oriented high school, a minority of children might model some aspects of their behaviour on an admired teacher, but this is unlikely to be true of the majority. Many students stay on until Year 12 not because they are particularly interested in schoolwork, but because there is no real alternative. For these students, teachers playing heavy 'academic' roles will not act as effective models. It is also possible that the way authority in high schools is linked to position in the hierarchy encourages teacher behaviour that is not only unlikely to be modelled by students, but also to be actively resisted. Much teacher behaviour is determined by organisational demands, and that is unlikely to be perceived by students to be relevant to themselves.

Certain behaviours are more easily modelled than others. Non-verbal behaviour is more easily modelled than verbal, so teachers have a psychological as well as a moral responsibility to practise what they preach. A colleague some years ago saw a teacher caning a boy for smoking — with a cigarette hanging out of the teacher's mouth.

Aggressive behaviours are more easily modelled than non-aggressive. Liebert and Caron (1972) showed that, after watching television programs with aggressive content, children behaved aggressively towards each other. They did not, however, tend to model loving or co-operative behaviours. Kounin and Gump (1961) observed children in the playground after lessons with punitive or non-punitive teachers. Aggression was markedly higher in the playtime activities of children who had just come from classes taught by teachers who were sarcastic, emphasised negative sanctions and punishment, and who blamed for wrongdoing rather than praised for good behaviour. These aggressive behaviours appeared to have rubbed off on the children, and as most people would agree, this is not desirable; sarcasm and punishment, generally, are therefore not good teaching techniques.

The effects of social motivation on subsequent intrinsic motivation are probably much greater than was previously thought. Whereas instrumental motivation, even using positive reinforcement under many conditions (Deci, 1975), may not develop intrinsic motivation, the beginnings of our interest in many intrinsically motivated activities — fads, crazes, intensely pursued hobbies, even lifelong obsessions — can be traced to what someone we admired at the time said or did.

Social motivation marks the first move away from what simply happened to be associated with the task, to a more personal kind of commitment to the task. The beginnings of such a commitment are more likely to occur when it is perceived that other people, particularly those who may be admired or seen as role models, are themselves committed to the task.

ACHIEVEMENT MOTIVATION

The next step along the road to full personal commitment to a task is to show that one is better than other people at doing the task. The motivation here is based upon the ego boost that comes about through social competition. Social competition is a motive that is particularly apparent in Western society: it refers to a basic need, greater in some people than in others, to achieve and attain success for its own sake. The rewards are mainly in the struggle to get to the top of the heap, beating others in open competition — it is not so important to gain material rewards as such (although that helps). Neither is it important what the task is; it can be selling cars, winning votes, publishing papers, whatever.

Achievement motivation, as this is called, was first described by McClelland, Atkinson, Clark and Howell (1953), but Atkinson later became particularly interested in applying it to the situation:

> ...when an individual knows that his performance will be evaluated (by himself or by others) in terms of some standard of excellence and that the consequences of his actions will be either a favourable evaluation (*success*) or an unfavourable evaluation (*failure*) (Atkinson, 1964, pp. 240–1; italics supplied).

Atkinson is concerned with situations in which people (a) see themselves as responsible for the outcome; and (b) know that they will be evaluated on their performance. The motivational pay-off, whether positive or negative, is a matter of whether the person's self-concept is enhanced or diminished by the outcome.

This is a fairly accurate representation of many school learning situations. Students are evaluated — by their teachers, their peers and their parents — in terms of success and failure defined by comparison with other students, and in tasks that reflect their competence. The theory of achievement motivation has important implications for teaching and evaluation strategy, which will be examined in due course. First, we should examine the theory itself.

Are you motivated to achieve success or to avoid failure?

Two major motives are involved. First, there is the motive to *achieve success*; in particular, the ego enhancement that success brings. The second motive is to *avoid failure*, which involves the fear of losing face. Test anxiety (see Chapter 2) is an example of the fear of failure.

In some people, achieving success is a stronger motive than is avoiding failure. People with this pattern of motives, regardless of their actual abilities, are called *high need-achievers*. For them, the greatest glory in winning comes when the chances are about fifty-fifty. If the probability of success is greater than 50 per cent (e.g. 90 per cent), it is like an Olympic athlete competing with the local Under-16s: the ego benefits are slight. If, on the other hand, the probability of success is low (e.g. around 10 per cent), there is not much point in wasting time as you are unlikely to win.

People in whom the motive to avoid failure is stronger than the motive to achieve success are called *low need-achievers*. The relationship between persistence and probability of success is exactly the reverse of that for need-achievers. Those who fear failure will happily blow their chance of winning, as long as they preserve face: a fifty-fifty chance is thus the most threatening, not the most appealing. When the fear of failure is paramount, it is either better to win cheaply by competing against someone who is certain to be beaten, *or* to fail gloriously by competing when the odds are hopeless.

These points are illustrated in Figure 3.2. High need-achievers are represented on the top graph (solid line). When the chances of success are *either* high or low, they are turned off. They are more likely to avoid the task than to engage it (unless there are other reasons why they might, such as extrinsic rewards). When, on the other hand, the chances of success are fifty-fifty (i.e. in the 'competition zone') then high need-achievers are most turned on: that is where they gain the most self-esteem by winning.

Low need-achievers are represented on the bottom graph (broken line). They are too defensive to put their heads on the block in the competition zone, so they avoid engagement when the odds are fifty-fifty. They feel least defensive in two contexts: when the odds are extremely favourable, and when they are so unfavourable that failure is fairly certain. In the first case success may be relied on; and in the second, failure is blameless ('Plucky little devil — at least he tried!').

Thus, we are considering two motivating tendencies in people: those who thrive on competition, and those who adopt any tactic to avoid it. Tasks with high success rates (like programmed instruction and mastery learning) bore high need-achievers, but are very suitable for low need-achievers, if that success is rewarded. It is important to note that the difference here reflects people's motives, not their ability. As Maehr and Sjogren (1971) pointed out, many studies have reported non-existent or very low correlations between IQ and achievement motivation.

Figure 3.2   Probability of success, motive predominance and task involvement

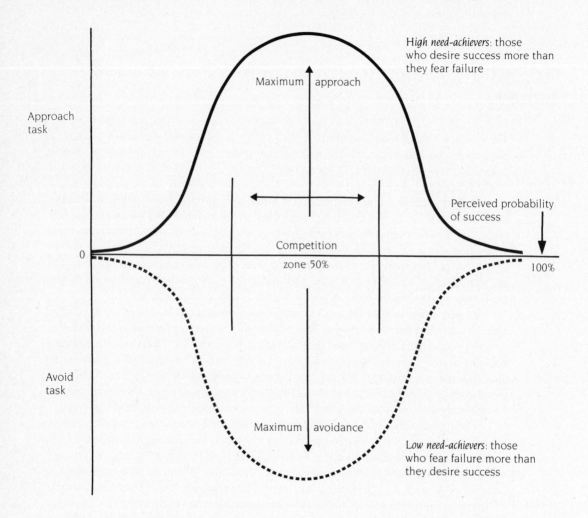

This theory has two important aspects: persistence in the course of a task, and the development of achievement motivation.

Persistence in the course of a task. The probability of success in handling a task —as estimated by the learner — changes with progress. Take first the case of high need-achievers. They approach the task, judge it to be easy, but fail. They are now more likely to judge their chances at 50 per cent, which is where they are most motivated. High need-achievers thus tend to be encouraged after failure.

Low need-achievers, on the other hand, behave quite differently (Moulton, 1969). Take the case of an easy task which is failed. The chances of success next time approach 50 per cent: the task is now perceived as less than 'easy', with the chances of success nearer 50 per cent — which is where these students are least motivated. Now take the case of a difficult task which is handled successfully. Again, future estimates of success revert to 50 per cent — so the student gives up, despite having succeeded when it was seen as being more difficult than it is now.

High need-achievers behave 'logically': they set the direction of their aspirations in accordance with their prior success. The more they succeed, the more they tend to engage in more difficult and more challenging tasks. This kind of behaviour is eminently reasonable, and it is assumed by many teachers to be the kind of motivational model that works for all children. In fact, however, it works only for people who are successfully competitive. Individuals who are afraid of competition tend to give up after they succeed; and sometimes to persist after failure against all the odds, and continue to fail.

Development of achievement motivation. Need-achievement results from interaction between personality factors and environmental influences that emphasise competition. Competition generally occurs under the following conditions:

1. A goal or reward is desired by a number of people.
2. The goal or reward is limited, and unequally available.
3. The individual's share of the reward is evaluated in relation to others, and the results are public knowledge.

Veroff (1969) and Madsen (1971) reviewed research on the effect of cultural factors on competitive behaviour and achievement motivation, and found that there are strong cross-cultural and sub-cultural differences. For example, white Americans tend to be more competitive than black Americans, and both are more competitive than Mexicans. Boys are more competitive than girls, though earlier evidence that girls actually 'fear success' and deliberately or unconsciously hold back from winning (Horner, 1968) may not be applicable today. Middle-class children tend to be more competitive than those from the working class, depending on both age and the context. Children tend to become more competitive with age until they reach nine, after which competitiveness varies according to task.

Schools adopt many practices that nurture competition between students, simply by defining goals ('being top', winning scholarships, prizes and other awards) and limiting access to them (only one person can be 'top'). However, things can be much more subtle than this. Let us illustrate the point here with two examples of classroom interaction.

> Boris had trouble reducing $\frac{12}{16}$ to the lowest terms, and could only get as far as $\frac{6}{8}$. The teacher asked him quietly if that was as far as he could reduce it. She suggested he 'think'. Much heaving up and down and waving of hands by the other children, all frantic to correct him. Boris pretty unhappy, probably mentally paralysed. The teacher, quiet, patient, ignores the others and concentrates with look and voice on Boris. She says, 'Is there a bigger number than two you can divide into the two parts of the fraction?' After a minute or two she becomes more urgent, but there is no response from Boris. She then turns to the class and says, 'Well, who can tell Boris what the number is?' A forest of hands appears, and the teacher calls Peggy. Peggy says that four may be divided into the numerator and denominator.

*There can only be one winner
in a competitive situation.*

Boris's failure has made it possible for Peggy to succeed; his depression is the price of her exhilaration; his misery the cause for her rejoicing. To a Zuni, Hopi or Dakota Indian, Peggy's performance would seem cruel beyond belief, for competition, the wringing of success from somebody's failure, is a form of torture foreign to those non-competitive redskins (Henry, 1972, pp. 243–4).

This example makes it fairly clear that the real lesson is how to encourage and cope with competition. If the lesson was in fact to teach fractions, then the teacher was singularly inept: no better way of ensuring Boris's ignorance on the subject could be devised. If it was to teach a lesson in survival values, however, then it was probably quite successful. The observation comes from the anthropologist, Jules Henry, touring American classrooms in the 1960s; the above passage comes from a chapter appropriately entitled 'Golden Rule Days: American Schoolrooms'.

The same result may be obtained in other ways. In a Canadian study of reading, Browne (1971) was concerned with the development of reading difficulties in the early grades and was studying in particular the interaction between teacher and child. She concentrated on two groups of students — good readers and poor readers — and scored the number of positive social reinforcements that the teacher gave children when they read aloud in class. Bill, a high need-achiever in Grade 1, read out the sentence 'The boy saw the dog'. *'Good'* came the quick response from the teacher. Bob, a low need-achiever, read: 'The, boy, saw, a ...' 'The' 'Er, *the*, dog'. *'Good'* came the response, but as Browne pointed out, it is clear that although Bob got 'Good' finally, he was publicly evaluated in midstream. It is fairly sure that Bob would see the correction as a hidden 'You're wrong'.

When Browne re-examined these same children in Grade 3, the hidden criticisms (quick, midstream corrections) of the original poor readers had increased manifold, whereas the criticisms of the good readers had significantly decreased. It seemed that the poor readers had learned to avoid grappling with the task; if they did try, they would simply get more and more of those subtle 'You're wrong'. It is not difficult to guess which students became motivated by fear of failure rather than by competitiveness. It should also be mentioned that when these findings were pointed out to the teachers, they were quite unaware of what they had been doing.

Thus family, peer group, mass media, and community lay the foundations for competitiveness in the total culture, particularly, perhaps, home background. Thereafter, practices in school play upon those motives so that the successful participants end up with a high need-achievement. The unsuccessful ones, however, acquire an incapacitating fear of failure, and will avoid situations that are likely to cost them more and more of their self-esteem.

INTRINSIC MOTIVATION

The distinction between extrinsic and intrinsic motivation is nicely illustrated in an experiment reported by Harlow (1953). He had rhesus monkeys performing puzzles in which they had to find out how various wire pieces interlocked to form a unit. The rhesus monkey has a storage pouch in its cheek, in which it stores peanuts or other food. From time to time it taps the pouch with its paw, pushes a nut into its mouth and chews and swallows it. In Harlow's experiment the monkeys stuffed their cheek pouches and then settled down to work with the puzzles. It was noted that whenever the monkeys made a false move and could not fit a piece into place, they would make a gesture of impatience, tap their cheek-pouches and promptly chew and swallow a nut. When they made a correct response they would simply move on to the next problem. The monkeys were regularly and reliably 'reinforcing' themselves for each *wrong* response they made — and yet they learned the puzzles! Obviously, the 'reward' was entirely irrelevant. What maintained the problem-solving behaviour was simply the fact that the monkeys *liked* them and found them *interesting*.

A need to build up competence. According to White (1959), humans have an intrinsic need to build up competence in dealing with the environment. Biologically, we are built in such a way that behaviours which maximise competence are self-rewarding. Take, for example, the case of a toddler beginning to walk, who stands, totters, falls, stands up again, walks a step or two, falls, back up, same again. Such behaviour is incomprehensible in terms of extrinsic motivation. Children practise walking and all they do is fall over and hurt themselves! Nevertheless they do walk: they just seem programmed to do so. At that critical stage of development, walking is *self-motivated*.

Berlyne (1966) suggested that the curiosity displayed by healthy animals and humans in a new situation is an inbuilt device for incorporating the means of dealing with novelty into cognitive structure, thus bringing about cognitive change and growth.

Degree of mismatch and motivation. Self-motivated competencies occur when the conflict or mismatch between environmental demands and developing cognitive structures is just right for recoding to occur (see Chapter 2). When such mismatch is optimal, positive intrinsic motivation occurs.

Where mismatch is minimal, so that the environment can be handled without too much internal change, there is no challenge and the task is boring. Where mismatch is too great, the challenge is overwhelming, and negative intrinsic motivation results.

The general cognitive processes presumed to underlie intrinsic motivation are summarised in Table 3.2.

Table 3.2   Relation between cognitive processes involving recoding and intrinsic motivation

Mismatch between input and codes	Extent of recoding	Motivational result
None: good match	None	Boredom
Slight	Optimal	Positive
Extensive	Attempted only	Negative
Very wide or total	None	Irrelevance

Positive intrinsic motivation, then, takes place when individuals are placed in a slightly 'difficult' situation involving conflict between what they know already, and what they are currently learning. Clearly, that critical level of mismatch will differ enormously between people. A flexible person, for example, can handle a larger mismatch than a rigid person; a person with a rich knowledge base will see more potential connections; low need-achievers find a gap threatening that a high need- would find challenging. The difficulties for the teacher are obvious: the process is 'internal', and different for each student in the class.

Hebb's (1946) experiments illustrate negative intrinsic motivation. He placed a headless chimp torso in a cage containing live chimps, who immediately backed away to the furthest corners of the cage, chattering and squealing with terror. An innate fear of death perhaps? No, because precisely the same result was obtained when two of their well-known and well-liked keepers appeared, dressed in each other's jackets! The conflict between the expected and the observed was too extreme.

Many school phobias belong in this category. We have noted that children who are motivated by the desire to avoid failure rather than to achieve success will get by on task-avoidant strategies. These solve the immediate problem of not failing (in the student's eyes), but deprive them of the opportunity of acquiring any task-relevant codes. There comes a time when they realise that they have no idea about what they should be doing; the conflict is too great and they become strongly negatively motivated.

Creating optimum conflict. Too great a gap between input and code structure leads to avoidance; too narrow a gap, to lack of interest. Berlyne (1966) discussed several teaching techniques that can help create the degree of conceptual conflict that leads to positive intrinsic motivation. One of these is the exploitation of *surprise*.

We have already seen that extrinsic surprise — such as the *Playboy* centrefolds (see Chapter 2) — can be used to grab attention. Here, however, we want surprise that is *intrinsic* to the content. For example, Suchman (1961) used intrinsic surprise in the teaching of science. In a lesson on the expansion of metals, the teacher begins by taking a bimetallic strip and holding it over a low flame, whereupon the strip sags downwards. Students are then invited to suggest why this occurs, and the teacher responds with 'Yes' or 'No'. Usually the class agrees that the heat has melted the strip and it sags with gravity. At that point the teacher holds the strip the other way and heats it: and of course it 'sags' towards the ceiling. Further question-and-answer produces various hypotheses, until one or two only remain under the evidence. The issue may be settled by introducing the ball-and-ring apparatus, and finally the class comes to the conclusion that metals expand when heated, some metals more than others. It is clear how conflict is used to motivate the resolution of the problem.

Conflict may be particularly appropriate in mathematics teaching. Take, for example, the general rule that any large number, the sum of whose digits is divisible by 3, is itself divisible by 3. It sounds too easy to be true — but after many inductive examples of trying-and-seeing, the students will agree that it does indeed seem to work. Very well, *why* does it work? In this way, the students may be led into a formal proof.

Other techniques involve *perplexity* ('Which alternative do I choose?'); *bafflement* ('There are no alternatives to choose — but there must be'); and *contradiction* ('But this contradicts what we just learned'). Mosston (1972) used *questions* to create and maintain intrinsic interest: the teacher who supplies more than three facts per lesson should, in his view, be fired.

Conflicts produced by these methods use the very information that is to be learned, whereas intrinsic surprise (like the centrefolds) achieves the effect by a deliberate 'ring-in'. For that reason, extrinsic surprise is probably not as effective a means of creating motivation as intrinsic surprise, but often it is just not possible to create intrinsic conflicts that are internal to the content.

To summarise this section, we may make the following generalisations.

1.   *Intrinsic motivation signals high-quality involvement.* The input has a structure that relates to, but is currently beyond, the existing codes of the learner. If the cognitive conflict is too great, the result is negative; but if the conflict is potentially within the competence of the individual, the result is positive. Where the situation requires low-quality involvement (i.e. the input is largely redundant but does need to be learned) intrinsic motivation is non-existent.

2.   *Intrinsic motivation has emotional or affective accompaniments.* Positive intrinsic motivation involves feelings of pleasure; negative intrinsic strong feelings of fear or tension. Low-quality involvement is affectively neutral.

3.   *Intrinsic motivation is self-maintaining, or self-terminating if negative.* External reasons (rewards) are not necessary to explain the behaviour.

What can the teacher do to facilitate intrinsic motivation?

The one word which sums up this problem is *involvement*. Students cannot become intrinsically motivated until they become involved in the task to the point where recoding is taking place. Involvement requires:

1. attending to the task in the first instance;
2. having or obtaining the sufficient background knowledge (existing codes) to permit involvement;
3. having the freedom to pursue involvement at the learner's own pace (not that of the teacher);
4. being sufficiently 'motivated' to want to become more involved.

The last point focuses on the teacher's main problem: how to maintain the student who is not yet intrinsically motivated on the task in such a way that the onset of intrinsic motivation is not jeopardised.

This is shown in diagram form in Figure 3.3. The shaded portion of the graph represents intrinsic motivation proper; the unshaded portion all other forms, including extrinsic, social and achievement motivation. Task involvement increases along the bottom line, progressing from left to right. As task involvement progresses, there are at first fairly slight increases in intrinsic motivation (the shaded area rises). At point 1 there is only a slight degree of intrinsic motivation; the learner is performing the task only because of the quite large proportion of extrinsic and other forms of motivation. There is then a fairly sudden 'take-off' (point X), after which intrinsic motivation increases sharply ('This is more interesting than I thought!'), until finally towards the end of the task (point 2) relatively little extrinsic and other forms of motivation are necessary. The learner is hooked. It may be that point X is never reached. In that case, the student does the task, if at all, entirely because of the non-intrinsic pay-offs. On the other hand, the student may be deeply interested all the time: in that case Figure 3.3 would be completely shaded-in and there would be nothing to discuss here.

In Figure 3.3 we are looking at the case where the student is not initially interested in the task, but becomes so with increasing involvement in the task.

The question is: how does the teacher get the student to point X? How, in other words, can the student be seduced into learning? Theoretically, there are several options (and their combinations):

1. positive and negative reinforcement (instrumental motivation);

Figure 3.3   Intrinsic motivation, task involvement and other forms of motivation

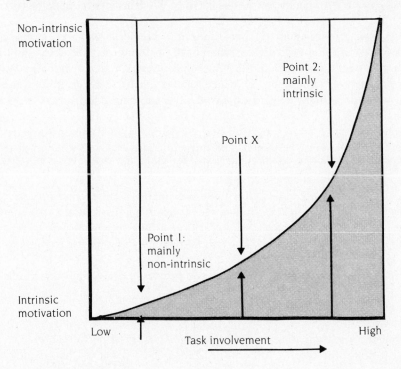

2. social modelling;
3. achievement motivation.

We can dismiss negative reinforcement straight away. Threats of punishment if the task is not tackled may result in its being carried out, but the child is not likely to feel very positive towards the task and situation (Condry, 1977). Positive reinforcement does, however, appear to be a possibility.

Social modelling is a very likely candidate, but it is rather unpredictable (like intrinsic motivation itself) and all too often works the other way: the most salient models for upper-primary and high-school students are their peers, who usually do not provide academic models.

Achievement motivation is a distinct possibility, although the focus is on winning rather than the process of getting there, which is what intrinsic motivation is all about. In any case, many students do not see themselves as competitors in the academic stakes.

For the general run of students, then, we are left with positive reinforcement, which may mean informal and ad hoc rewards for particular tasks, or a fully blown behaviour modification program. Having said that, we now enter a very controversial area.

Does extrinsic reward kill intrinsic motivation? It was suggested earlier in this chapter that extrinsic reward, particularly in the form of token economies or other behaviour modification programs, could motivate students to learn. The question is:

what happens when the reinforcements are stopped, as they must be eventually, and 'naturally occurring' reinforcers do *not* take over? Does bribery result in the corruption of pure learning?

Many writers are emphatic that it does. A. S. Neill, for instance, claimed that 'to offer a prize for doing a deed is tantamount to declaring that the deed is not worth doing for its own sake' (1960, p. 162). As if to demonstrate that very point, Festinger (1968) reported an experiment in which some students were given an excessively boring task to do; some were paid quite well, others nothing. Those who were paid said later that they didn't enjoy the task, but those who received nothing at all reported that they found it 'quite interesting'! Festinger argues that the unpaid students 'over-justified' to themselves why they had permitted themselves to be bored to their socks: they rationalised, and probably even ended up believing they enjoyed it. The paid students could afford to be more honest.

This study may not in fact have to do with intrinsic motivation as much as with how people delude themselves to save face (which is not irrelevant to some school learning problems). However, it did spark off a long line of research that is very relevant to our current problem. The best known research on these studies is by Deci (1971; 1972).

He had his subjects (undergraduates) do puzzles under various conditions:

1. payment for correct solutions;
2. no payment;
3. payment for participating, irrespective of the quality of performance;
4. verbal praise for correct solutions ('That's good — you're doing well') but no payment;
5. verbal praise *and* payment for correct solutions.

He then observed the subjects to see how long they would continue working with the puzzles after the experiment had 'officially' terminated — he argued that the longer a person continued, the more intrinsically motivated he or she was. He found that those who were paid for correct solutions only (condition 1) continued the least, but those who received verbal praise continued the longest (4). Those who were unpaid (2), *and* those who were both praised and paid (5), continued for nearly as long as those who just received verbal praise. Those who were paid regardless of their performance (3) came next.

Deci argued that payment for results did dampen interest in the task. It was as if his subjects said to themselves, 'I'll do this for you if you do this for me — and that's it. Don't expect any "overtime" from me.' Social reinforcement, however, seemed to have quite a different effect: 'If he says I am good at this, I must be. That makes me feel good about these puzzles; I like them.' The other conditions fall in between these two. This result seems to support the arguments by White and De Charms: evidence of particular competence in a task makes one feel good and is intrinsically motivating. We like those things that we are good at — or more to the point, we like those things that we are *led to believe* we are good at.

It is however, quite a jump from college students performing puzzles to school students learning socially valued tasks such as reading. Subsequent studies add

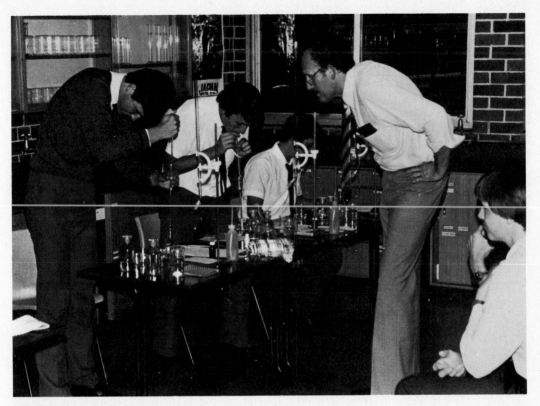

*Supervision is necessary — at what point
does it inhibit student motivation?*

considerably to the Deci findings. Calder and Staw (1975), for instance, found that
Deci's results were obtained only when the task was interesting in itself: when the task
was uninteresting, payment for good results *increased* subsequent intrinsic motivation.
Kruglanski et al. (1975) found that the nature of the task is important. If it is in the
nature of the task to receive payment (e.g. in 'Monopoly' or coin-tossing games), then
payment greatly increased enjoyment, whereas with tasks that did not naturally lead to
payment (such as Deci's) payment decreased subsequent interest.

Lepper and his associates (Lepper, Greene and Nisbett, 1973; Lepper and Greene,
1975) worked with nursery children doing interesting tasks (drawing from numbers).
They found that intrinsic motivation decreased with an expected reward, but was
highest when a reward was unexpected. Intrinsic motivation was also depressed when
children knew they were under surveillance: Lepper pointed out that watching over
someone is a signal that he or she is not trusted, an awareness that is not likely to make
the person feel good, or intrinsically motivated. This observation certainly has
implications for fostering intrinsic motivation in schools. Simply, students are unlikely
to feel intrinsically motivated if a baleful eye is glaring over their shoulder while they
are performing. They attribute the fact that they are working at all to their lack of
choice in the matter, not to any interest they might have.

Molloy and Pierce (1980), on the other hand, found intrinsic motivation was unaffected by reward, whether expected or unexpected. They worked with preschool children on a drawing task, and had two 'expected' reward conditions and one unexpected. The important difference they found was that, whether by token economy or by agreement, children who expected a reward did *better quality* drawings than those children who obtained a reward unexpectedly. They conclude that the 'widespread assumption that token economies undermine intrinsic motivation is at present unjustified' (p. 7): expected rewards make little difference to motivation, but increase the quality of output.

Conditions affecting intrinsic motivation

There have been many other studies of the conditions under which intrinsic motivation might be fostered or impaired (reviewed by Bates, 1979; Morgan, 1984). It is possible to summarise the findings of all the work done thus far as follows:

Promoting intrinsic motivation.

- positive associations of pleasure;
- social reinforcement (praise) and the example of admired figures (modelling);
- freedom to make own choice of an activity; freedom to proceed at own pace;
- reward, under certain conditions: when the activity is disliked to start with, and when the reward is used subtly, with no implication that the person is being 'bought', but is an *index of competence*.

These are conditions under which reward *may* build intrinsic motivation. In a disliked task, there is little to lose — and if it has to be performed, then reward is the best way of ensuring that it is. The chances are, particularly if the reward is unexpected and is a sign that the learner is good at the task, that the learner will end up liking the task. Reward may be an index of competence; when it is, it *enhances* intrinsic motivation.

Depressing intrinsic motivation.

- negative reinforcement (threats of punishment);
- surveillance (supervising the learner);
- unpleasant associations;
- reward, when it is diminished by poor performance or failure, it is unrelated to the task and at a rate set by an outsider, or the task is already well liked.

Reward, in essence, changes the nature of the game. Reward is directed towards results, while intrinsic motivation is concerned with the process. If attention is directed too forcefully to the end result — by high rewards on a stated piece-rate basis — then the person tends to cut corners. In one study of students tutoring other students,

Garbarino (1975) compared paid tutors with unpaid. Paid tutors were more critical and impatient, and made more demands — and their learners made more errors. Unpaid tutors produced a better learning atmosphere and achieved better results.

This study makes it obvious that one cannot generalise from short-term experiments to earning a living, for it would follow that people who like their jobs ought to be paid less or they will start disliking their job and working less well! Obviously, real life imposes quite different strictures on the effects of reward on intrinsic interest than do the conditions prevailing in laboratories or even in school.

How, then, do we make sense out of all these findings? As Morgan (1984) puts it, the *perspective of the recipient* determines the effects that rewards have on intrinsic motivation. Rewards that are seen by the recipient as a symbol of success enhance intrinsic motivation: the locus of control becomes inward, the learner performs the task in order to feel competent and self-determining. Rewards that are seen as instrumental, or based on an external justification, inhibit the development of intrinsic motivation: the locus of control becomes externalised, so that the learner can justify performing the task because of the 'going rate'.

Belief in self-efficacy

The key to this whole question is *how students see themselves*. Self-concept theory has been around for a long time (e.g. Purkey, 1970): as Dale Carnegie emphasised with profit, convincing oneself of one's competence was a good first step towards acting competently (and profitably).

The link between self-concept and intrinsic motivation was clarified by De Charms (1968). He called the intrinsically motivated person an 'origin'. Origins see themselves as the cause of their own behaviour; they are self-determining. People who see themselves as being directed by other people, more powerful than themselves, or at the mercy of external events, he called 'pawns'. Pawns are not self-determining, and are not easily intrinsically motivated. The resemblance between this concept of pawns and origins and that of external and internal locus of control (Rotter, 1966) is obvious. De Charms' particular version is, however, specifically linked to intrinsic motivation.

He worked with students in a large inner-city high school in the American mid-west, and concluded that students saw themselves as pawns as a result of the demands made upon them from outside. Both their social backgrounds and their school had a cumulative effect such that most saw themselves as very little cogs in a very large machine. De Charms relaxed these strictures and found that, as more and more aspects of their life were decided by the students themselves, the more like origins and the less like pawns they felt — and the more intrinsically motivated they became. Box 3.3 gives an example of the opposite: the creation of super-pawns.

This is an example of self-concept theory, according to which people do things well or poorly according to the image or concept they have of themselves, and according to their self-esteem (Purkey, 1970). While this is undoubtedly true, care needs to be taken. Self-concept theory can be very simplistic, a fact that advertisers use to extremes. Feel good about yourself (by cleaning your teeth with Fang-Foam) and

BOX 3.3   HOW TO PRODUCE SUPER-PAWNS: A SIMULATED
PRISON AT UNSW

Paid volunteers (previously screened for medical and psychological health)
were randomly allocated as 'warders' or 'prisoners' for a period of four days, in
three different prison conditions: *standard custodial*, which modelled procedures
(including warders' uniforms, method of address, food, etc.) in Australian
medium-high security prisons: *individual custodial*, similar to standard, except
that some respect was accorded prisoners (e.g. recognised by name instead of
number); *participatory*, which used joint decision-making by warders and
prisoners.

There were, even in the short space of four days, tremendous differences
in the 'pawnship' of all participants, both warders and prisoners. Each filled
the role the setting created for him. For example, in obtaining action from
prisoners the warders could *command*, *request* or *seek* agreement. In the standard
custodial regime, 95 per cent of all attempts to obtain action were by
command; none by agreement. In the individual custodial, 42 per cent were by
command and 55 per cent by request. In the participatory prison, there were
no commands, 52 per cent requests, and 48 per cent agreements.

Source: Lovibond, Mithiran and Adams (1979).

you can have your choice of jobs, lovers, bank-loan terms, whatever. Little better than
this is the 'amateur counsellor' comment such as: 'No wonder Bill's not doing well at
school. He's got such a poor self-concept.' The implication is that if Bill goes jogging,
learns macrame, does *something* particularly well, then 'He'll get some confidence in
himself...'; and that this will improve his schoolwork, his social relations, and wherever
else he is performing below his potential.

The world, however, is not that simple. It does not follow that feelings of
competence in one area will generalise to another. How many shy school teachers are
told: 'Oh, you can't be shy. You stand in front of a class, and talk to other people all day
long!'? Talking to students in a formal context is simply a different activity from
talking to adults in a social context. It depends what one *feels* one is good at that will
influence intrinsic motivation.

Bandura (1977) proposed a very specific form of self-concept theory: *self-efficacy*.
When people approach a task, they form two sets of expectations: efficacy
expectations and outcome expectations. The first set focuses on the question 'How
effectively will I be able to carry out this behaviour?' For example, a student is given an
assignment to do. Her first concern is the efficacy expectation: 'How well can I do
this?' Outcome expectations would revolve around grade level, the teacher's opinion
of her and so on: they tell her how important the task will be. However, her immediate
concern is with efficacy — and unless that question is resolved, the outcome may not be
an issue. In other words, the outcome sets the general context (doing or not doing), but

the actual involvement with the task, and the issue of intrinsic motivation, revolves around perceived self-efficacy. Efficacy, in other words, determines the effort and persistence the student will put into the task.

Bandura's theory differs from simple self-concept theory in the *generality* of the individual's beliefs. The child who believes that she failed in her first encounter with arithmetic may or may not believe that the same will apply to reading. After many discouraging encounters with one subject, she might well generalise to reading and to the remainder of her school work: if she does, there will be a very serious block to her school learning and a large portion of her self-concept will suffer. However, it need not be like this. A student can hug an area to himself and feel good about that. He can accept philosophically that he's 'no good' at maths, cricket and football — but he can write poetry of a special sort which is uniquely 'his', or he might be able to lose the rest of the field on a long-distance jog. Beliefs about self-efficacy are closely tied to particular tasks, which is very fortunate for the self-concepts of many students.

ATTRIBUTION THEORY

In forming efficacy beliefs, it is important that individuals attribute the success or failure of previous performance to causes that will positively motivate future performance, and not to ones that will discourage further involvement.

Let us look at such attributions in relation to the effects of extrinsic reward on intrinsic motivation. De Charms, as we have seen, strongly believed that reward shifts the locus of control from inside to outside: from 'I am doing this because I have chosen to' to 'I am doing this because someone has decided to make it worth my while if I do'. Hence, he argues, intrinsic interest declines after reward. Glasser (1969), on the other hand, used a version of behaviour modification (he calls it 'reality therapy') precisely to increase the individual's feeling of control: they can choose which of the — albeit limited — options are availble. Jane, as we saw earlier, could choose between misbehaving in class and 'time out'. De Charms assumed that in these circumstances Jane would always make an external attribution; Glasser assumed she might attribute her behaviour to her own choice (see Box 3.4).

BOX 3.4   ME ORIGIN; YOU PAWN

Rat, after being trained to press a lever for a pellet of Rat Chow: 'Boy! Have I got this psychologist conditioned... every time I press the lever he slips me some food!'

Anon

- Is this rat intrinsically or extrinsically motivated?
- Is the psychologist intrinsically or extrinsically motivated?
- Does thinking about either make you intrinsically or extrinsically motivated?

Attribution theory (Bar-Tal, 1978; Weiner, 1972, 1977) is a theory of motivation that brings together all the points we have been discussing about extrinsic motivation, social motivation, achievement and intrinsic motivation. In particular, it helps us to understand the relationship between extrinsic and intrinsic, and more important still, it suggests ways in which teachers can enhance intrinsic motivation.

We said earlier that the girl who believed she was unsuccessful in arithmetic because of the criticisms of her teacher would probably not be intrinsically motivated in future. How strongly that effect works depends on what she attributes her lack of success to. If it is to something that is unstable, then that factor may not occur in future, and may therefore not affect her motivation. *Luck* is such a factor: 'Just my luck to get Miss Smith! It was all her fault; at least I won't get her next year'. *Insufficient effort* is another factor that may not be too damaging: 'My fault: didn't try hard enough. Next year I will though.'

An internal attribution to something stable — like *ability* — is likely to affect future motivations: 'I'm just not good enough at arithmetic. Never was, never will be'. With that last attribution, future failure and lack of interest is highly predictable.

Similar effects occur for the attribution of success. If success is attributed to luck, the clear implication is that fortune will turn: failure is then the likely prospect. If success is attributed to ability, then intrinsic motivation — ownership — is likely to take over: 'I'm good at this! This is my thing.'

It is important, then, that teachers try to influence students' attributions in the most effective direction: failure should be attributed to lack of effort and success to ability. That way, the student may be led to believe that something that may be controlled can counter the failure, while the success can be attributed to ability and ownership. Failure need not be a hopeless devastation; success, the glint of fool's gold. Clearly teachers should try to structure things so that the most hopeful attribution will be made in the events of success and failure.

Thus, as Deci's work shows, praise ('social reinforcement') convinced subjects that they were good at the puzzles. Other people thus can greatly affect people's beliefs in their own ability, both positively and negatively (see Box 3.5).

Several personality factors have been shown to relate to different attributions (Bar-Tal, 1978). Females tend more than males to attribute their success to luck rather than to ability, and to rate their ability lower. Individuals with low self-esteem tend to make internal attributions (low ability) following failure. As might be expected, high need-achievers attribute their success to internal factors — ability and effort, to which greatest pride is attached — and their failures either to external factors, or to lack of effort (but not lack of ability). Low need-achievers, on the other hand, attribute their failure to lack of ability and their success to luck or an easy task.

Learned helplessness. Seligman (1975) observed that when rats are given an electric shock, and are trained to turn the shock off (e.g. by pressing a bar), they rarely show signs of distress after they have learned the procedure. However, if the bar is suddenly disconnected and the shocks come at unpredictable times, the rats become very upset, finally lapsing into a comatose state (and in extreme cases may die). When they learn that they have no control over their environment, they become helpless.

Such a state of 'learned helplessness' has been observed in humans when they *believe* they have no control over unpleasant things that happen to them. Voodoo deaths,

BOX 3.5   RESTORE A BELIEF IN SELF-EFFICACY, AND
ATTRIBUTE FAILURE TO LACK OF PERSISTENCE...

'I'd already had several children before coming to Uni, and I wasn't sure how I could handle it. I was really interested in psychology, but when we got to the psych. I lectures, the stats lecturer said 'Anyone who can't follow this isn't fit to be at University...' That was the first message I got. I *was* having difficulty with stats and so I thought maybe he's right, maybe Uni isn't for me. I liked the rest of psych. but couldn't handle the stats and had to withdraw.

Next year, funny thing, I did maths I, and we came to probability theory — much the same stuff that I had bombed out in last year. But the lecturer there was a woman and maybe she understood better the difficulties many women have, or anyone come to that, and she said: 'Probability is quite hard really; you'll need to work at it. You're welcome to come to me for help if you really need it...'

It was like a blinding light. It wasn't *me* after all! This stuff really was *hard*, but if I tried it might just work. That year I got a credit in that part of the subject.'

for example, are explained in this way. Miller and Norman (1979) distinguished three features of learned helplessness in humans:

- reduced *motivation* to control events;
- impaired *ability to learn* how to control the situation;
- strong fear, which rapidly leads to *deep depression*.

Miller and Norman explained learned helplessness in terms of attribution theory, although they also added a general–specific dimension to Weiner's stable–unstable and internal–external patterns. The worst kind of learned helplessness is attributed to internal, stable and general causes. Some kinds of learned helplessness, however, remain limited to specific events.

It is the more specific kind of helplessness that is important in the treatment of learning disabilities in school (Thomas, 1979). The under-achiever shows all the signs of learned helplessness: persistent failure, lack of motivation to avoid further failure, inability to learn remedial material, and apathy bordering on depression. Fortunately, this helplessness is in most cases specific to school: such children often blossom in the workforce, if they are lucky enough to get into it. If they are not, precisely the same symptoms remain; this time, it is helplessness about obtaining employment that is the self-perpetuating problem.

This pattern of helplessness, however, can be broken by changing the attributions. Helplessness results from the attribution of failure to stable internal causes (lack of ability), and of success either to an easy task or to luck. Neither of these attributions is likely to motivate further effort or to lead to a belief in one's ability. Dweck (1975) selected students who exhibited 'helpless' behaviour, that is, those who simply gave up apathetically after failure. She had their teachers attribute their failure to lack of effort, and success to ability — and to try to convince the students of this. As a result, the students improved rapidly, and indeed made more gains than a group based on a behaviour modification (success only) program. Likewise, Heckhausen (1975) had failing students, through teacher encouragement, attribute their failure to lack of effort, not lack of ability, with marked improvements in subsequent performance. In other words, the experience of failure was necessary so that the students could learn that their failure arose through lack of effort, not through lack of ability.

The general implications are clear. Belief in self-efficacy, and appropriate attributions of success to ability, and of failure to lack of effort, are likely to motivate the individual to future achievement. Attributions of success to luck or to an easy task, and failure to lack of ability, are likely to kill subsequent interest in the tasks that led to those attributions.

In attribution theory, we can see an explanation for the sometimes confusing findings about the effects of reward on intrinsic motivation. *It depends upon what the learners make of it*: specifically, what they attributed their performance to. Attributions that detract from one's own personal investment are not likely to lead to much interest in the task itself. Thus, the question for teachers is not so much whether to reward or not to reward, but to present the task in a context that will give students the opportunity to develop a belief in their own efficacy. Even a rat in a Skinner Box may believe it is controlling the controller.

SUMMARY

In this section, we have been concerned with one of the teacher's main tasks: motivating academic learning. We have noted a progression in terms of task-centredness from the entirely extrinsic forms of instrumental motivation, through social and achievement motivation with their increasing self-involvement, to the completely self-determined state of intrinsic motivation. The best learning takes place when it is intrinsically motivated; this type of learning is comparatively rare in school, especially in the early stage of learning a subject. It is first necessary to 'bait' the task with extrinsic rewards, social modelling and (for those who operate in this way) by achievement motivation and the heady joys of competition.

Instrumental motivation. This most extrinsic form of motivation is based on arbitrary associations between the task and its consequences or with feelings associated with the task. The manipulation of these associations gives rise to the technology of behaviour modification, which can be a powerful tool for controlling both student learning and student behaviour.

Nevertheless, there is a general belief that the use of instrumental motivational techniques is damaging to the development of intrinsic motivation, and there is some evidence for this belief. It is, however, simplistic to regard all extrinsically motivated learning as inimical to the development of intrinsic interest: the crucial question is how the learner perceives the reward system. If rewards in fact enhance the learner's belief in self-efficacy, the use of rewards can facilitate the later development of intrinsic motivation.

The important thing for the teacher, then, is to make sure that the rewards for learning are placed in an appropriate context, and that the desired task is always placed in as pleasant a context as possible so that it *feels* good.

Social motivation. The first step towards internalisation is through other people: probably the first basis of all human learning is social. We do things in order to please, or see ourselves as being like other people whom we particularly admire or respect. Social motivation is very powerful, then, but is also extraordinarily complex: different people become models for different kinds of learning at different stages throughout life. In school, social models often work in opposition: conformity to peer models is likely to tug in quite the opposite direction to identifying with a particular adult model.

Some general principles, however, can offer guidance in making appropriate use of social motivation. Teachers themselves automatically become models for some purposes for some children at different times, a responsible role that calls for much teacher self-awareness.

Achievement motivation. High need-achievers like competition; they attribute success to ability, and failure to lack of effort. Such people can be led into intrinsically motivated activity by competition in the first instance; but although the attributions are right, the focus is not. The result (winning or losing) is important to the high need-achievers, whereas the process is the issue in intrinsic motivation. Low need-achievers have the worst set of attributions for intrinsic motivation: success to external causes (luck or ease of task) and failure to lack of ability.

Intrinsic motivation. When positive intrinsic motivation does occur, it signals high quality involvement in the task; the task is enjoyable in itself, and performance is maintained with no other incentives. Intrinsic motivation takes place when input optimally mismatches existing coded knowledge; it is therefore hard to create the necessary conditions externally. For intrinsic motivation to occur, learners need some prior knowledge of or involvement in the task, freedom to pace their own continuing involvement, and positive associations with the task and its context. In this way, the task is approached with feelings of curiosity, challenge, self-efficacy, mastery and something approaching a proprietorial attitude — 'This is my particular thing': the trappings, in short, of Theory Y. It is also important to consider the factors that inhibit intrinsic motivation, and which should therefore be avoided: negative feelings and associations, surveillance, contractual rewards (especially when tied to competence) — in fact, the trappings of Theory X. These points are conveniently summarised in self-efficacy and attribution theories.

Two final points need to be made: intrinsic motivation is highly specific to its target. Despite all the appropriate attributions, the student may end up intensely interested in Coleridge but not in Wordsworth. The most likely explanation may involve what the student knows about each poet; on the other hand, it may have something to do with the perceived preferences of an admired teacher. Whatever the reason, attribution theory will not guarantee motivation; it will simply set the stage.

The second point concerns those other tasks, uninteresting and unloved, that must still be performed. What about those students who cannot be intrinsically motivated to any school work? Positive reinforcement by material reward is a good procedure in such cases. And if the task is really unpleasant — it just has to be done and it doesn't matter what the learner thinks of it all afterwards — then negative reinforcement (with punishment for failure as a necessary corollary) would be indicated. But when this final option is considered in terms of psychological effects, it can be seen as truly a last resort.

Attribution theory. To what do people attribute their successes and failures? The answer they derive to this question has a profound effect on future intrinsic motivation. Attributing success to external factors such as luck, and failure to internal factors such as lack of ability, are quite damaging attributions to make. These particular ones are typical of low achievers.

High achievers, on the other hand, attribute success to internal factors that are unlikely to change — such as their high ability, or to a good self image ('I'm good at this') — and failure to a transitory external cause such as luck. If students are making maladaptive or unhelpful attributions, the teacher should present material and advice in such a way as to challenge those unhelpful attributions: for example by making failure be seen as due to insufficient effort (a situation which the student can change) rather than to insufficient ability (over which the student has no control).

SECTION B

We shall leave applications of instrumental motivation to Chapter 8, where we discuss behaviour modification programs in the context of classroom management. Here we concentrate on the questions of school and classroom climate, some particular classroom procedures and their effects on intrinsic motivation, and evaluation.

THE CLIMATE OF THE SCHOOL

A University of New South Wales' study of volunteers' reactions to three kinds of prison atmosphere (Box 3.3) serves as a healthy reminder that rules and procedures can exert a very powerful effect on an individual's sense of identity and motivational disposition. In the context of school, we refer to these as the 'second set of three Rs' —rules, routines and regulations — which affect the student's sense of selfhood. De Charms's own work (1968) analysed the relationships between school climate, selfhood (pawn or origin) and student motivation.

Australian research by Rees (1977) indicated that the odds here favour a decidedly pawnish school climate. Rees analysed the 'learning environment' of 85 New South Wales secondary schools through the questionnaire responses of over 4,000 students.

He found that students saw themselves as being under pressure from 10 sources: home, community, principal, staff, facilities, courses, rules, personal aspirations, extra-curricular activities and peers. Note that only one of the listed pressures — personal aspirations — comes from an internal locus of control. A situation in which most felt pressures have an external locus is one which is unlikely to encourage intrinsic motivation.

Some typical school procedures illustrate their externality. Consider the school assembly routine; the segregation of boys and girls into single-sex schools; compulsory school uniforms; emphasis on the formal status of staff ('Sir!'); compulsory subjects of study; 'put-down' remarks from staff to student (even if they are facetious, they have their effect); compulsory education for all Australians between the ages of six and 15; the interlocking levels of schooling (infants/primary/secondary/tertiary), and the universal progression by age.

While individual rules might have some practical point, the cumulative effect on students is to emphasise the extent to which they are externally controlled. Such an effect must be alienating.

Involvement is the key to intrinsic motivation. Decision-making in Australian schools tends not to involve students, or even their parents. There are, however, signs of change, in terms of school initiatives and the role of individuals in education systems (see also Chapter 8).

Nevertheless, Australian education has for many years been criticised by many overseas observers for excessive centralisation of authority (Butts, 1955; Cramer, 1936; Elliott, 1936; Jackson, 1961; Kandel, 1960). The point was finally taken in Australia as late as 1973, with the appearance of the Karmel Report. The Karmel Committee (1973) made many recommendations designed to break down the massive centralised control of schools by State governments, so that all participants — teachers, students and parents — could feel that they, too, had a stake in the proceedings; that they could, in De Charms's terms, feel more like origins than pawns. Among the many recommendations were the following:

- the establishment of a Schools Commission, with autonomously funded programs;
- the Disadvantaged Schools program, whereby schools with particular difficulties could seek funds to counter what they saw as their major problems;
- the Innovations program, whereby teachers with good innovative ideas could seek financial support (if their ideas were viable) to implement them;
- community involvement, whereby parents (and, in some States, students) *could* become involved and effective in creating schools and programs suited to local conditions;
- regionalisation of control, particularly important in large States such as New South Wales.

Inevitably, these ideas become politicised, in the real sense of the word: they involved the devolution of power from central bureaucracies to the local grass roots. It was inevitable that those with power were reluctant in many cases to give it up. What was less understandable was that those without power were almost as reluctant to accept it when it was offered to them (Biggs, 1979a). As the prison studies of Lovibond et al. suggested, the system makes pawns of us all.

The case of community involvement in New South Wales State schools is a classic instance. Community involvement, with parental decision-making through 'school councils', was mooted in New South Wales in 1973. The proposal was rejected by teachers and parents, and by 1986 no formal progress had been made. Although constructive initiatives have occurred in isolated instances, the *system* remains unchanged. Why? One reason stems from a general pawnishness:

> On the issue of community involvement, then, all participants suffer from a feeling of powerlessness. The system is too big, too many people feel threatened, to allow for a genuine involvement that includes parental responsibility ... Given the superstructure, the reward systems, and the feelings of threat that all must feel under such a superstructure, it is unreal to abolish it and say, 'Now, work it out on your own'. People who feel powerless and alienated simply can't handle that (Biggs, 1979a, pp. 4-5).

There are ways in which teachers, students, parents, administrators and the community at large can be made to feel more like origins and less like pawns. And when that happens in the school context, learning is more likely to be attributed to one's own efforts, and become enjoyable for its own sake. The following suggestions increase internal–stable attributions:

- Relate promotion to teaching and/or administrative ability, not seniority (self-efficacy; origin).
- Appoint teachers to schools by school-based appointment committees, not central directives. A teacher may then say 'They chose me: I must have something to offer' (origin), not 'So I'm next on the list for subject master ... ' (pawn).
- Let representative local committees decide on the flavour of the school: 'We want this sort of program for our children' (origin).
- Allow parents and students to choose their kind of school within an area (origin), not zone schools by area (pawn).

It is possible to make far greater use of community inputs to create a healthier school climate with the system as it is. One example is a commissioned study by a New South Wales mid-coast high school, conducted under the Participation and Equity Program (Telfer, 1984). The aim was to look at school organisation and community relations in ways that might encourage retention of potential Year 10 and 11 students. Interviews and questionnaires covered 53 teachers, 207 Year 10 and 11 students, and over 350 parents. Emerging recommendations are listed in Box 3.6.

Perhaps the most important thing emerging from this study is not so much the specific points that were changed, but the fact that the school brought in an outside consultant who was open to *everyone's* view: parents, administration, students, teachers, office staff and canteen staff.

We haven't dwelt on the State bureaucracies themselves. In the larger ones, it may still be true that teachers remain pawns 'within some strange Czarist bureaucracy, remote and faceless, but with tentacles reaching to the remotest corner of the State' (Connors, 1978). In the smaller States, bureaucracies are smaller and interaction between administration and teachers is more personal, more open to change. The

BOX 3.6   CREATING A HEALTHIER SCHOOL CLIMATE:
RECOMMENDATIONS FROM A PEP STUDY OF A
NSW HIGH SCHOOL

Interface with community:

- consultation, interaction, on 'aims of school': conflict on vocationalism;
- reports when problem arises, regular newsletters, use of school facilities (out of hours);
- produce a school service directory giving information to public about facilities, equipment, resources and expertise at the school;
- a map and visitors' guide;
- parental volunteers offering expertise in Year 11 electives;
- work experience outside school, and studies accredited at other institutions such as TAFE;
- parental interviews in a common room — not a formal office, not the long queues and public discussion of parent-teacher nights.

Student facilities:

- a sealed carpark for students;
- shade trees, seats and tables in the playground;
- a sit-down cafeteria, with student notice-board prominent.

Student interaction with staff and decision-making:

- students be involved in choice of library books, texts and equipment such as micros;
- staff accessibility out-of-class at specified times;
- staff–student socials, sporting and hobby clubs, and competitions;
- school counsellor to convene teacher-student discussion groups, to start with the topic 'school discipline';
- student preferences for programs and electives to be canvassed, in relation to each providing a rationale for each subject in 'Why am I teaching this lesson, and this subject?';
- provision for free study periods;
- peer support: senior students acting as specific mentors to juniors.

Source: Telfer, 1985.

bureaucracies should be flexible enough to allow internal attributions by their staff, so that teachers in turn can transmit that freedom to their classrooms.

Let us look, then, at what may go on inside the classroom. We see that classroom climate is determined much more by the teacher's personality.

CLASSROOM PROCEDURES

Teacher–student interaction

Let us look at two brief examples:

Scene 1   A Year 11 history classroom

Teacher: Settle down. Come on, Jonesy, let's get with it. Wakey, wakey, Tony. No sleeping in *my* time! Right ... I guess we're as ready as will be ... excluding Smith and the other back-row morons.

Today's big question: has 11A done the homework? You recognise the word, I assume. You may remember that yesterday we looked at the achievements of Napoleon, and finished up with the section in the textbook which said 'He organised France'. For those of you for whom this is startling information, you might also remember that your job was to investigate the claim and come along this morning ready to justify it. Stand up any who haven't a written summary in front of them. Right, you people see me here at one o'clock and you can do it then. The rest of you make sure I have it before I leave here. Now, who's to be the sacrificial lamb? Yes, you, Thomas ... let's see what your summary is like ... it wouldn't have to be much good to be better than that last effort you had to rewrite.

Thomas: Well, he ...

Teacher: He? Who?

Thomas: *Napoleon.* He set up a new government and he ...

Teacher: Oh, come on, now. That's just not good enough. Is this Year 11 or Year 7? 'A new government'... that's so vague it's useless. Facts, specific facts, that's what I'm after. Weak effort, Thomas.

Let's take another ticket in the lottery. What's your story, Julie? You seem to have plenty to say. Try saying something useful for a change.

Julie: Napoleon organised France through, ah, a reform, no, reforms, under a new constitution he ...

Teacher: A bit closer than Thomas, but still a long way from what I need. Where are the *facts*? *Specific facts*? What reforms? What government? You were asked to read your textbook, underline the key words and phrases, then use the textbook's subheadings to organise your summary: which should be in front of you on the desk. We all can read, can't we, Smith? No, don't answer that: let me live on in Fantasyland. Read *your* summary, Joanne. You appear to at least have your textbook (covered, too, unlike a couple I can see) ...

Scene 2   Another Year 11 history classroom

Teacher: This morning you'll need textbooks, notebooks, and the results of your reading assignment examining the claim that 'Napoleon organised France'. You'll remember, too, that in one of his less restrained moments Tony suggested that Napoleon was a megalomaniac. Perhaps your reading might have provided some insight into this claim. Just to start things moving — did it appear to you that Napoleon's motives were personal or national?

Tony: I still think I'm right.

Joanne: But how do you know ... and how do we know ... that you are? Those reforms of the Consulate were France's gain, not Napoleon's.

Tony: But how much power did Napoleon give the other Consuls? Hardly any. He made sure he stayed on top.

Teacher: Well, some evidence each way. Let's look at these reforms and the so-called organisation of France. What were the reforms?

Several There were those Codes ...

students: What about the Concordat with the Pope ...?

Local Government was reorganised too ...

There was a whole range of reforms ...

Teacher: We're not going to make much progress that way. Let's get organised in our approach. If there was a wide range of reforms, can't we make our approach more systematic by grouping the reforms? As a matter of fact, isn't this the way Lambert approaches the topic in your textbook? *(Pause)* I didn't exactly expect a roar of confirmation, but could someone provide one or more of the categories we could use to group the reforms?

Julie: Oh, you mean legal reforms, and, ah, religious reforms and so on.

Teacher: That's it. Now what else do we need? Don't use your notes. Let's see if we can work out a classification. We have two groups of reforms: legal and religious. What other groups will be needed?

Teacher–student interaction can be analysed in terms of the influence a teacher extends (Flanders, 1967). Teacher criticism of a student is an example of direct influence; seeking and using a student's ideas is indirect. Our scenarios (adapted from actual observations) of the history lessons for Year 11 demonstrate these two forms of influence.

Their relative effects on student motivation are obvious:

- direct influence emphasises an external locus of control;
- indirect influence uses student-initiated content which produces feelings of competence, which lead in turn to intrinsic motivation (see Box 3.7).

The different roles teachers play in school organisations enable them to take a genuine interest in their students as individuals. Teachers are coaches of football, basketball, athletics, swimming, drama, chess, and so on; they act as advisers for careers and student clubs; they are supervisors of playgrounds, bus queues, excursions, camps and school visits. The opportunity for indirect influence, student initiation and intrinsic motivation is obviously greater when the teacher's interaction with students is related to an academic area. However, all interactions are opportunities for supportive teacher feedback to students for their achievements. They are also opportunities for teachers to provide models of those who have a genuine regard for learning.

BOX 3.7   EDUCATION FAILS TO GIVE CONFIDENCE, SAYS ALUMNUS. RESEARCH SHOWS NEGATIVE MESSAGES AFFECT CHILDREN

Dr Mary Fahey is surprised that education in Australia fails to build self-esteem and confidence in our children. 'While education in this country has progressed in many ways, teachers and parents can be extremely negative in their messages to children, with serious consequences,' she says. 'Many of our children have difficulty believing in themselves and in their abilities; they are prone to depression and have trouble reaching goals, even daily ones.'

Fahey completed a Ph.D. thesis in self-concept in 1983 and is continuing to research the area.

'There are no signs that Australian children are more confident than in the past. In comparison with American children, who are constantly reinforced and in many cases, over-confident, our children are rarely praised by their teachers and parents. We like to tell them what they are doing wrong, not what they are doing right.'

Research shows that affirmative, or positive messages, used with a person's name, eventually build a positive self-regard in another, says Fahey. It means noticing positive aspects in a child on a regular basis.

'Even when a child is very naughty, we can include a positive message for them. Suppose, for example, that Johnny throws a rock at another child. Instead of telling him how very naughty he is, we can separate the action from his own worth as a person: "I am very distressed to see such an intelligent boy as yourself, Johnny, act in so stupid a manner." This kind of message is helping Johnny realise he is a worthwhile person and has a choice.'

'When I begin working with parents and teachers, I first ask them to write down on a piece of paper six things they like about themselves. It is surprising how very hard this is for most people.' Fahey says it is important for parents and teachers to first become aware of themselves and accept both their good points and their limitations.

Many parents and teachers have poor self-esteem, as a result of their own negative conditioning, says Fahey. 'I believe 99 per cent of people are frightened of looking at themselves: they don't want to be cut down again. While it is not easy to break out of a negative self-concept, it can be done.'

'If parents and teachers genuinely want to contribute to their child's growth, and most do, they must build their own self-esteem. This means learning how to build on our positive attributes and work on our less strong points. it means learning how to cope with stress, increasing one's assertiveness and understanding the theory behind affirmations.'

Source: Alumni Papers **2** (4), 26 February 1986, University of New South Wales.

Preparing and presenting learning experiences

Julius Sumner Miller exemplifies teaching by curiosity-through-conflict. Typically, he introduces the unit of instruction by presenting an apparent mismatch between rationality and reality, or by describing a simple but baffling situation. For example, to introduce the issue of heat transfer in liquids he showed two cups: one was three-quarters full of hot coffee, the other a quarter full of cold milk. Which way, he asked, could he obtain the hottest cup of milk coffee: by adding the milk to the coffee, or the coffee to the milk?

He explained his approach (Miller, 1979) by arguing that we teach neither students nor subjects. If we are successful, we stir interest in the subject and fire the student's imagination. While not many teachers are equipped (largely because of their own teachers) to handle this approach, enthusiasm is probably more important than competence. He continues:

> Teachers must, I say, recite less facts, ask more questions, give fewer answers. The drama and beauty and aesthetic of the subject must be pointed up. The intellectual process must be stirred. A feeling for knowledge for its own sake must be engendered. Learning will then be an exciting adventure which few can escape, nor will many wish to. And it will bring the spirit to a great awakening which can likely last for the lifetime. Some of us have seen it (p.51).

Ability grouping or streaming

We refer here to the practice of teaching students in streamed or homogeneous ability groups as opposed to groups in which the students are of mixed ability. Two arguments are used for the practice of streaming (the term 'setting' is sometimes used when streaming is applied only to particular subjects, as is the case in many high schools). The first is that streamed groups are much easier to teach: the students are all likely to be working at much the same pace, and so the teacher can be confident that all, or most, students will be 'with' him or her. This is a compelling argument from the teacher's point of view, but it is valid only in so far as the teacher uses whole-class methods. The argument does not apply, for instance, with most methods used in open-plan schools.

The second argument is that the students are more comfortable: the bright child is less likely to be bored, or the dull child lost. Again, this argument applies only when whole-class methods are used. A more subtle argument for streaming is that the dull child is likely to become discouraged on seeing how far ahead the brighter ones in the class are.

An argument against streaming is that the low need-achiever is most turned off when competing against peers of the same level of ability. Streaming means that many more students are likely to perceive their individual probability of success as being near fifty-fifty — in the 'competition zone' (see Figure 3.2). As we saw in Section A, however, this situation suits the high need-achiever, but is quite unsuited for the low need-achiever.

Attribution theory would also predict streaming to be particularly bad for the poorer student. Whether the streams are called 'possums', 'emus' and 'wallabies', or 'As', 'Bs' and 'Cs', the students will quickly discover that the label contains an evaluative judgment. Those in the bottom streams will naturally see themselves as having been officially labelled 'stupid': they have been denied the one attribution — an internal-stable one of ability — that is known to relate most to subsequent intrinsic motivation. While those in the higher streams may benefit from such attributions, the lower ones will not.

These expectations, based on achievement motivation and attribution theory, are that high-ability students will improve under streaming, but that low-ability students will get worse. This is, in fact, the most usual finding in the research literature on streaming (e.g. Biggs, 1966, pp. 84–6; Weiner, 1967).

A survey of 67 New South Wales primary schools showed that 24 (36 per cent) had adopted a streamed (or graded) class organisation, and 15 (22 per cent) used parallel classes of mixed ability. The remaining schools used either a combination of streamed and parallel classes (9 per cent) or a pupil enrolment which was so small that only one class existed per year (33 per cent) (Waymouth, 1983). Waymouth reviewed 33 studies of streaming and its effect on academic attainment. Sixteen studies (48 per cent) provide evidence which supports streaming; the results of 18 (55 per cent) oppose streaming; and 10 (30 per cent) found no significant difference (with 33 per cent interpretable as favouring either). When Waymouth looked at the effects of streaming, he found that streamed classes were characterised by friction; unstreamed classes by satisfaction, cohesiveness and positive attitudes to learning and to schooling in general.

EVALUATION

The evaluation of student learning is a very complex issue, and we will consider it in more detail in Chapter 10. It is appropriate, however, to consider some aspects here, as they bear directly on student motivation. It is often assumed, for example, that students 'won't work' on a topic unless 'it's in the exam'. Like many pieces of conventional wisdom, however, this is only partly true. It is particularly true of high need-achievers: to them, the exam is the medium by which they can express their excellence, particularly when the exam is conducted in a competitive atmosphere. It is quite untrue of low need-achievers — the test-anxious who, as we have seen, are likely to perform at a level lower than their optimum. It is irrelevant to those who are intrinsically motivated, who might be expected to perform anyway. However, the hassle of formal examinations may simply remind them that the outcome of their learning is externally controlled. As we have also seen, external attributions of success and failure are likely to diminish intrinsic interest.

Campbell (1975) carried out a study involving all Year 6 students in seven Brisbane primary schools, specifically to address the question 'Do tests motivate pupils?' She found that the answer was a modified 'Yes' if the task was novel (anagrams). However, if the task was standard (spelling), the introduction of testing reinforced a fear of failure in girls and encouraged impulsive risk-taking in boys. This suggests that if a task is a new one, testing may satisfy the individual's curiosity about performance, but if the task is a familiar one, the evaluation of performance is more a direct threat to self-esteem. In any event, Campbell's results do not support the view that tests improve motivation generally. They do support the kind of predictions we have been suggesting here on the basis of attribution theory.

Two particular aspects of evaluation are relevant to the question of student motivation. We need to distinguish between *norm-referenced* evaluation and *criterion-referenced* evaluation. In *norm-referenced* evaluation, the final grade — indexing the quality of learning — is determined by how well the student compares with other students in the class. The simplest example of this is *ranking*: John came top, Betty was second, Phil third ... and poor old Fred was last. Such a grade does not give any specific information about *what* John did, only that, whatever it was, it was better than anyone else. Here there is no absolute standard: the standard shifts according to the performance of the class as a whole. Such scores may of course be useful, particularly in order to select the best of the group (for prizes, scholarships, university places and, especially today, jobs), but they turn the situation into a *competitive* one.

In *criterion-referenced* evaluation, on the other hand, the final grade does give some information about absolute standards. Criterion-referenced grades are not rationed: whoever reaches the required standard obtains the award. Mastery learning, behavioural objectives, and writing a research thesis are all examples of criterion-referenced evaluation. One needs only to demonstrate competence against a standard, not against one's competitors.

Now, what implications do these two forms of evaluation have for motivation? Briefly, norm-referenced evaluation emphasises competiton. The self-esteem of the winners is undoubtedly enhanced, but at the cost of that of the losers, who by definition are the majority. The latter are likely to attribute their failure (relatively speaking) to external causes: they couldn't help it if they landed up in the same class as 'teacher's pet', or 'the school brain'. As a result, their intrinsic motivation is likely to be lower.

Criterion-referenced evaluation emphasises individual competence — an internal attribution. Given that the pre-set standards were not too high, attributions here are likely to be internal which, as we have seen, tends to increase a sense of self-efficacy and intrinsic motivation.

SUMMARY

The climate of the school. De Charms's terms 'pawns' and 'origins' are good ones for capturing the climate of the school, and in particular the kind of climate that is likely to engender intrinsic motivation. Australian schools are decidedly pawnish in orientation, more so in the larger States because of the administrative difficulties associated with size and bureaucracy. Conditions in many schools work against intrinsic motivation:

there is often excessive emphasis upon rules, routines and regulations; some are necessary in the interests of the smooth running of the schools, but others are petty and oppressive. One crucial factor is that of parent–student involvement in decision-making; the history of such involvement in Australian schools is not altogether encouraging, with our traditional emphasis on highly centralised control of schools.

Things are better than they were even five years ago. With decentralisation, some schools are taking up the challenge. A case study of one high school was encouraging in that all participants in the school — teachers, students, parents, other staff — were approached for their views on how things were going in the school and what might reasonably be changed, with a view to greater all-round participation.

Classroom procedures. Teacher–student interaction is the backdrop, whatever particular method or procedure is being played out in the classroom. Styles of teacher–student interaction vary enormously. Sarcasm, put-downs, petty appeals to authority, insistence on trivial rules and procedures are arbitrary and demeaning. Nobody can reasonably expect such a form of interaction to lead to intrinsic motivation. In the following chapter, we allude to the student's view of these rules and forms of authority.

Other practices refer to teaching methods: questioning and enquiry techniques, mixed-ability grouping, mastery learning (where it is applicable, as in basic skills), and open education generally, are all likely to foster intrinsic motivation for some students, in their various ways.

Evaluation. Evaluation methods have an important effect on motivation. Norm-referenced methods are likely to work only for the successful need-achievers; criterion-referenced methods seem likely to be most beneficial for most students. Certainly, the traditional belief that 'tests motivate students' cannot be taken to be generally (or even frequently) true.

FURTHER READING

On achievement motivation
J. W. Atkinson, 'Mainsprings of Achievement Oriented Activity', in J. D. Krumbolz (ed.), *Learning and the Educational Process*, Rand McNally, Chicago, Ill., 1966.
M. Maehr and D. Sjogren, 'Atkinson's Theory of Achievement Motivation: First Steps Towards a Theory of Academic Motivation?', *Review of Educational Research* **41**, 1971, 143–61.

Atkinson's own account of his theory is clear and straightforward. Maehr and Sjogren's article is more concerned with educational applications. The advantage of the Atkinson article is that it is included in the collection by Krumbolz that also contains an excellent paper by Berlyne on intrinsic motivation (see below).

On intrinsic motivation
D. E. Berlyne, 'Curiosity and Education', in J. D. Krumbolz, 1966.

E. L. Deci, *Intrinsic Motivation*, Plenum Press, New York, 1975.

M. Morgan, 'Reward-induced Decrements and Increments in Intrinsic Motivation', *Review of Educational Research* **54**, 1984, 5–30.

The first two references discuss the basic theory of optimal mismatch and intrinsic motivation and how to create these conditions in the classroom. Deci is also quite strongly against the use of extrinsic rewards. That point might be matched with Morgan's paper, which is an up-to-date review of studies in this area.

On classroom climate

B. J. Fraser, *Learning Environment in Curriculum Evaluation: A Review*, Evaluation in Education Series, (Pergamon, London, 1981).

This is a valuable review of classroom climate research, covering three areas:

- classroom climate descriptors and instruments which have been developed and used internationally;
- Australian normative and validation data for instruments suitable for use in our classrooms;
- a review of Australian research into classroom climate.

QUESTIONS

Questions for self-testing

1. Match each of the following motives with its appropriate description:
   Motives: intrinsic; social; instrumental; achievement.
   Description:
   (a) learning to please others whose opinion is important;
   (b) enhancing one's ego by competing and winning;
   (c) learning because one wants to;
   (d) performing the task because of the consequences;
   (e) recognition of the rewards of upward mobility.
2. Which type of motivation is based on the learnings analysed by Thorndike (1898), Hull (1943) and Skinner (1953)?
3. List five types of positive reinforcement.
4. How does negative reinforcement differ from punishment?
5. In which two instances should reinforcement follow every response?
6. Give an experimental or filmed example of classical conditioning.
7. How is modelling more than mere imitation?
8. Which of the following pairs is more easily modelled:
   - verbal or non-verbal behaviours?
   - aggressive or non-aggressive behaviours?
9. Explain what is meant by vicarious reinforcement.

10. List three conditions under which competition generally occurs.
11. In Harlow's study, how did the rhesus monkeys show the difference between extrinsic and intrinsic motivation?
12. Does extrinsic reward undermine intrinsic motivation?
13. List four ways of promoting intrinsic motivation.
14. In your own words, distinguish between a pawn and an origin.
15. Describe an example of learned helplessness.

Questions for discussion

1. List your most important interests, such as hobbies, sports, leisure pastimes or career. Can you now identify who prompted your interest in each? Next to each interest write the name of the person. What does this tell you about social motivation?
2. Should corporal punishment have been abolished in schools?
3. Why is behaviour modification more popular in North American schools than it is in Australia?
4. When you visit a school for the first time, what indicators do you use to tell you something of the school climate?
5. What is your teaching field? Primary? Secondary? Imagine that you have entered the classroom and have introduced your planned lesson. A pupil politely enquires: 'Why do we have to learn this? Why do you teach this?' Produce an answer suitable for the pupil.

4

Student approaches to learning

OVERVIEW

Do you watch yourself when you are learning? Do you learn from your mistakes? Do you work out in advance what you want out of that learning? If you can answer 'yes' to these questions you are being metacognitive about your learning. You probably adopt a *deep* approach to learning. This chapter is about the learner's-eye-view of school, of academic tasks and of learning itself: it explains how that view affects the way students approach their learning. In it, the following kinds of questions are answered:

- How do learning tactics and learning strategies differ from each other?
- Can heuristics help people to learn more effectively?
- What are three common approaches to learning?
- Do schools and universities necessarily improve students' approaches to their learning?
- Can we measure the structural complexity of learning as opposed to the mass of detail learned?

When you have reflected on this chapter, you should be able to:

1. Explain how the material in this chapter could be used to make you a better learner.
2. Think of yourself when learning and decide to what extent you use surface, deep and achieving approaches to learning.
3. Take any lesson and restructure it so that the pupils will become more metacognitive.
4. Devise a heuristic to facilitate preparing a three-course dinner.
5. List some important aspects about your school and class policies that (a) put *pressure* on students, and (b) encourage students to be *cynical* about school.
6. Classify the SOLO levels of students' explanations of why a particular joke is funny.

SECTION A

WATCHERS OVER OUR LEARNING

One of the interesting characteristics of people is that they not only behave, but can watch themselves behaving, and believe that they can exert a certain amount of control over how they behave. People are ... active agents who can be aware that things are or are not going as intended, who can deliberately optimise their performance, and who can learn from having become aware of their mistakes (Robinson, 1983 p. 106).

The picture given so far of the learner in school might suggest a passive 'information cruncher' who precodes, encodes, recodes, dismembers and remembers on cue. That picture, which is valid as far as it goes, describes the cognitive functions referred to in Chapter 2. But the learner is more than a bundle of cognitive processes: learners learn in a context of *personal significance*. Learners actively choose to pay attention to some aspects of that context and to ignore others; more importantly, they may become aware of their own learning processes, and of how well or how poorly they are doing and may choose to alter their approach to a task in order to do it better. Learners, in short, can be *metacognitive* about their learning, as well as cognitive.

While the basic processes of learning and motivation discussed in Chapters 2 and 3 are important for understanding the sort of learning that goes on in school, they are only part of the story. It is vital that two further aspects are taken into consideration:

1. Schools have a very powerful formal structure, which provides a characteristic and influential *context* for learning.
2. Humans, as Robinson points out in the above quotation, are *watchers over their own learning*; in particular, the context of schooling is crucial in shaping the perceptions that students have of their learning.

This *institutionalisation* of learning, coupled with the *metacognitive* nature of the human learner, together create a fresh dimension to research into student learning which is full of implications for teachers and practitioners. Over the last 10 years, a body of research into student learning has grown up giving a clear shape to this line of enquiry (as reviewed for example by Entwistle and Ramsden, 1983; Marton, Hounsell and Entwistle, 1984; Ramsden, 1985; Wilson, 1981). At the same time, research into children's metacognition has also been developing rapidly (Brown, Bransford, Ferrara and Campione, 1983; Lawson, 1984; Robinson, 1983). In this chapter, we bring these two lines of enquiry together.

METACOGNITION: REFLECTIVE SELF-AWARENESS AND RESPONSIBLE SELF-DIRECTION

Flavell (1976) was one of the first writers to use the term 'metacognition', defining it as 'one's knowledge concerning one's cognitive processes and products ... [and] refers to the active monitoring and consequential regulation of those processes' (p. 232). Since then, he and others have conducted many studies on how children and adults make use of their observations of and reflection on their own thought processes. Much of this work is directly relevant to education.

In Chapter 1, it was emphasised that the aims of education include process learning, or helping students towards 'responsible self-direction', as the New South Wales State department puts it. Such an aim is explicitly metacognitive and metacognitive studies ought therefore to shed a new and important light on how this aim might be achieved. Let us take a few examples of metacognitive approaches to learning in order to see the implications.

Reading, writing and problem solving

Paris describes his own work on *reading* with primary children in the following way:

> The central tenet of our approach is that reading strategies can be explained directly to children. If they perceive the strategies as sensible and useful courses of action, we would expect children to use them appropriately and spontaneously in their subsequent reading. Our emphasis is thus upon how children's awareness about reading, or metacognition, can facilitate intentional use of particular strategies... Strategic readers combine knowledge about the task with motivation to act accordingly. Their plans are self-generated and their actions self-directed. Otherwise, students are only following directions and they may not transfer the action to other tasks and settings when they are unsupervised ... (Paris, 1984, pp. 2–3).

Another example of metacognition in action is *reflective writing*; that is, writing that explains and clarifies a complex thought or argument. Reflective writing is contrasted to 'knowledge-telling' (Scardamalia, Bereiter and Steinbach, 1982), which uses writing simply as a means of emptying the skull. In reflective writing, on the other hand, we externalise our thoughts on paper (or on CRT), and *think about our thoughts* — and then possibly redraft them. In this way, we often discover what our thoughts really are.

Drafting and redrafting an essay or other writing involves such metacognitive questions as these:

- Is this really what I mean?
- How else could it be put?
- As my reader is unlikely to know what I know, is this section likely to be misunderstood?
- Would my message be clearer if I left that bit out entirely?

Depending on the answers to such questions, we recompose what we have written. Non-metacognitive writers, who do not ask these questions, do not see the need for drafting. That is the defect in almost all beginning, and many mature, writers: they do not examine what they have written. What came out first time is near enough, give or take some spelling, grammar, and a word or two. If writing is used only for saying what they know already, then it *is* near enough. Getting students to see that writing is itself a tool for creative thought (and hence the need for drafting) is the major challenge in the teaching and use of writing in the classroom (see Chapter 6).

Heuristics for improving *problem solving* are another long-standing example of metacognition. A well-known one is Polya's *How to Solve It* (1945) (see Box 4.1). His heuristic was meant to apply to mathematical problems in the first instance but, as he says, the general steps he recommends apply to a wide range of problems. In Section B we examine how Polya's famous *How to Solve It* paradigm was adapted to teach library skills to primary school children in Perth (Kurzeja, 1986).

We have of course come across metacognitive processes in the previous chapter, although we did not use the term there. Attribution theory is essentially a

BOX 4.1   HOW TO SOLVE IT: A HEURISTIC FOR PROBLEM SOLVING

Understanding the problem

First. You have to understand the problem.

What is the unknown? What are the data? What is the condition? Is the condition sufficient to determine the unknown? Or is it insufficient? Or redundant? Or contradictory? Draw a figure. Introduce suitable notation. Separate the various parts of the condition. Can you write them down?

Devising a plan

Second. Find the connection between the data and the the unknown. You may be obliged to consider auxiliary problems if an immediate connection cannot be found. You should obtain eventually a plan of the solution.

Have you seen it before? Or have you seen the same problem in a slightly different form? Do you know a theorem that could be useful? Look at the unknown! And try to think of a familiar problem having the same or a similar unknown. Here is a problem related to yours and solved before. Could you use it? Could you use its result? Could you use its method? Should you introduce some auxiliary element in order to make its use possible? Could you restate the problem? Could you restate it still differently? Go back to definitions.

If you cannot solve the proposed problem try to solve first some related problem. Could you imagine a more accessible related problem? A more general problem? A more special problem? An analogous problem? Could you solve a part of the problem? Keep only a part of the condition, drop the other part; how far is the unknown then determined, how can it vary? Could you derive something useful from the data? Could you think of other data appropriate to determine the unknown? Could you change the unknown or the data, or both if necessary, so that the new unknown and the new data are nearer to each other? Did you use all the data? Did you use the whole condition? Have you taken into account all essential notions involved in the problem?

Carrying out the plan

Third.
Carry out your plan.

Carrying out your plan of the solution, check each step. Can you see clearly that the step is correct? Can you prove that it is correct?

Looking back

Fourth.
Examine the solution obtained.

Can you check the result? Can you check the argument? Can you derive the result differently? Can you see it at a glance? Can you use the result, or the method, for some other problem?

Source: Polya, 1945.

metacognitive theory: the student is aware of success or failure, and attributes causes to both. It would be a superior level of metacognition that went, 'Now, if I make myself believe my failure was due to bad luck, and my success to my superior ability, which of course it was ... well then, I'm in great shape for next time!'

In sum, all that metacognition means is that we *reflect critically* on what we are doing; it enters into quality performance of all kinds.

Strategies and tactics

A useful distinction to be made at this stage is between strategies and tactics (Snowman, in press). *Tactics* are (as suggested by the military reference) short-term manoeuvres during learning; they are like orders to be followed whether or not you understand them. *Strategies*, on the other hand, involve long-term planning prior to learning, and they need to be monitored constantly. If they appear not to be working, some redrafting, as in reflective writing, is called for.

An algorithm in mathematics is an example of what is meant by a tactic: a set procedure is laid down that will produce the correct answer if followed precisely. An heuristic, on the other hand, is an example of a strategy; one needs to be deliberately aware of the whole context, of the general nature of the problem, and of one's place in it, and then to predict the effects of one's actions with respect to the long-term goal.

The same item of behaviour could be either tactical or strategic. It would be a tactic if followed blindly, or a strategy if worked out by self-conscious reflection. Many study skills, for example, have this ambiguous nature. Students can read ahead and underline all the key words in a passage because they are instructed to do so, as this is a 'good' study habit (but in this case it probably is not); or because it is seen that this will enable them to construct the overall sense of the passage first, so that the detail can be linked to it on a second run through (in which case it probably is a 'good' thing to do).

The particular issue of teaching study skills is taken up in Section B. The point to be made here is that a metacognitive approach to teaching is one that emphasises heuristics and strategies, not algorithms and tactics, useful though the latter can be for quick answer-getting devices, or as crutches for students in trouble.

It is sufficiently clear that learning to watch over our own learning is deeply involved in helping students towards responsible self-direction. Two general conclusions emerge: there are things that teachers can do to encourage or to discourage metacognitive activity in students; therefore teachers should themselves reflect on what they are doing.

These two issues are explicit throughout this chapter, and implicit (at least) throughout the rest of this book. We now need to develop the picture from the student's perspective — that is what metacognition involves.

METALEARNING

Metacognition applied to student learning may be called *metalearning* (Novak and Gowin, 1984; Biggs, 1985). As a result of metalearning, students derive their ways of handling the problem of learning in institutions like schools and universities. Taylor (1984) refers to a *personal study contract* that students make with themselves: 'This is what I want. In order to obtain it, I shall have to do this, that or the other. If I don't, I would be breaking my contract with myself and I lose.' For example: 'I want a good time and a piece of paper at the end. That means doing just enough to pass'; or 'I want to really see if mathematics is for me. I'd like that, as I'm really interested in it, so I've got to be prepared to work on problems and assignments to the best of my ability.' Of course, priorities may change as students find out more about themselves and the task.

At its simplest, this contract means: 'What do I want out of this?' (What are my *motives*?) 'O.K., then, how do I propose going about getting there?' (What are my *strategies*?)

Answers to both questions call out all the dimensions of metalearning, and we shall describe these throughout this chapter.

Conceptions of learning

What do you mean when you say you 'learn' something? Students enter classrooms with reasonably fixed ideas about the answer to that question, and that answer will determine how learning is approached, and what the outcome will be. Marton and Saljo (1984) refer to five such conceptions of learning:

1. Learning means 'knowing more' in some vague way.
2. Learning means memorising or learning by heart.
3. Learning means acquiring facts and skills that can be retained and used when necessary.
4. Learning means finding out what something really means and is understood.
5. Learning means constructing a personal philosophy or world view.

It is possible to make other distinctions, but it is clear that people are going to expect different things from school, or any other context of learning, depending on what they think academic learning is all about.

Quantitative and qualitative conceptions of learning. The first three levels offer a *quantitative* view of knowledge: a good scholar is someone who knows more than other people. This view of knowing is hugely rewarded in quiz shows like *Sale of the Century*; it clearly has a fascination as is seen in the popularity of 'Trivial Pursuit'. It is also what many people think schools should be about: back to basics, drill students in the basic skills and learn lots of unrelated facts. If arithmetic is doing sums, then higher mathematics is doing very long and difficult sums. One of the present authors spent his first year 'out' in an industrial suburb. One Year 8 lad brought a note from an enthusiastic parent, thanking him for giving the boy some homework, and urging him to 'continue to stuff the gen into him'. Learning was having a head stuffed full of facts; the more the better.

The last two conceptions of learning reflect a *qualitative* view of learning. Most 'official' statements about schools (cf. Chapter 1) refer to meaning and realisation of potential; that by the end of school, students should be able to understand society, their place in it, be able to clarify and talk about their own values; in short, to hold an explicit philosophy of some sort. These two levels of conception of course feed each other: to read something with understanding may in fact change the way a person sees the world. This is reflected institutionally when we talk about 'a scientist's way' of seeing things; most students when they graduate do see the world differently and not just because they are older. What they have studied has shaped a 'paradigmatic' way of thinking (Bruner, 1985).

The quantitative view is not opposed to the qualitative; it is part of it. Knowing facts and how to do things is part of the means for understanding the world, but people who hold that view stop at that point: rote learning becomes an end, the purpose of learning, rather than as a means towards proper learning. It is necessary to rote learn scientific formulae, as part of learning to think like a scientist; the mistake is to conclude that that is the way scientists think.

Absolutist and relativistic conceptions of learning. This attitude still persists at university. Perry (1970) refers to nine levels of intellectual development which characterise students, ranging from a right/wrong *absolutist* position to a *relativistic* view which requires the student to make some sort of commitment by virtue of a worked out philosophy of knowledge. Not all students reach the highest level, and some already enter university with a relativistic view, but generally Perry found that students leave high school and enter university expecting to be given the correct interpretation of the subject matter by an authority. Then, when the student sees that so-called authorities differ, it must either be because they are confused, or because they are deliberately setting it up 'so we can learn to find The Answer for ourselves'. Even the 'frontiers of knowledge' view is absolutist: knowledge is 'there', waiting to be discovered by white-coated scientists. Many people never get beyond this position. At Perry's higher levels, students see that knowledge is simply one way of interrelating a set of data, and that other ways may be more useful for certain purposes. Which way to interpret is often a matter of commitment to a theoretical position.

The conception of learning a person holds determines *how* and *what* is learned: rehearsal-based strategies for reproducing facts, data or skills, or coding-based strategies for understanding the meaning of what is being done (cf. Chapter 2, on surface and generic coding). Another common conception *institutionalises* learning: learning has occurred when a course has been passed, so that getting good marks indicates good learning. This last conception leads to quite a different set of strategies, based on maximising marks.

These three conceptions of learning lead to three basic approaches to learning: *surface, deep* and *achieving*.

Approaches to learning

When students read a passage of text, they start with the intention either of focusing on the *words used*, or on what they think is the author's *meaning* (Marton, 1975). Their level of processing the text is then referred to as 'surface', if focused on memorising at the word/sentence level, or 'deep', if focused on understanding the semantic content. An *approach to learning* comprises this mixture of intention and congruent strategy. A surface approach leads to learning that emphasises the reproduction of words and phrases used by the author, while a deep approach leads to structured arguments describing what the text is about (Marton and Saljo, 1976a, 1976b).

The notions of surface and deep approaches to learning have been found to have a very high generality; instances may be found at primary school or at university, in particular tasks (such as essay writing, reading or problem solving) or a student's typical approach to academic learning in general.

Such an approach, whether towards schooling in general or one specific task in particular, comprises the motive(s) for undertaking the task, and the combination of strategies adopted. A student's motive(s) provide(s) the major *direction* that learning will take: a student's strategies will be assembled to pursue that general direction.

The *surface approach* is based on extrinsic motivation, with the student learning only in order to obtain some other goal. Learning then becomes a balancing act between failing and not working too hard, and is usually associated with a quantitative conception of learning. The appropriate strategy in this case is to find the most important topics and reproduce them with reasonable accuracy, using rehearsal-based procedures. The surface approach is encouraged, then, when the student sees the task as a demand to be met if some other goal is to be undertaken. The task is typically handled in discrete units that are linked together more or less arbitrarily. The student does not see the task as a whole, but as a series of unrelated sub-tasks to be performed; personal meanings and associations are avoided. The surface approach is directed towards surface codes.

The *deep approach* is based on intrinsic interest in the task or subject matter, and the logical strategy that flows from that is to satisfy one's curiosity by finding out as much as one can and understanding it. Depending on the task, this means that the student will relate the task to generic codes or to some personally meaningful context, theorising about the task, forming hypotheses about what might happen, and so on. The deep approach is involving, and leads to complex and emotionally satisfying outcomes. The surface approach, even when successful, is alienating, and leaves the student anxious about the outcome and resentful of the time taken.

The achieving approach is based on achievement motivation and is different in kind from the other two. Whereas the surface and deep strategies incorporate the basic cognitive processes of rehearsal and coding, respectively, the achieving strategies are to do with the *context*, making the best use of time and working space. The sorts of strategies that are included here are such things as systematically making clear notes, making schedules (so much time for this subject, so much for that; spacing assignments to avoid a last minute rush), and what are generally referred to as 'study skills'. In fact, many 'good' students do not use these things — they can get 'good' results on the basis of the deep approach alone — and other students practise the skills unsuccessfully. Teaching study skills to underachieving or poorly motivated students is unlikely to work: one has to *want* good results to go to all the trouble of setting up schedules, planning ahead, and so on. This important question of teaching study skills is taken up in Section B.

The surface and deep approaches are in some senses mutually exclusive. Focusing on the actual words used in order to reproduce them precludes us from attending to their meaning. These tasks can, however, be done sequentially. Actors learn their lines verbatim; then they think about how they will convey their meaning most effectively. Similarly, at any given moment, students use either a deep approach or a surface approach, depending on the task, what they want out of it, and on their predilections.

An achieving approach can be linked to *either* surface or deep: one can rote-learn systematically or in a disorganised way, or seek meaning in an organised or disorganised way. Students use composite approaches — surface-achieving or deep-achieving — as well as straight approaches. In fact, deep-achieving is associated with better grades than a straight deep approach, but surface-achieving is not usually effective (Biggs, 1986a).

PRESAGE, PROCESS AND PRODUCT IN STUDENT LEARNING: THE 3P MODEL

A typical learning situation involves presage, process and product stages.

Presage

Presage factors are independent of the immediate context and are of two kinds: factors that are brought in by the student, and factors that already exist in the situation.

The *person* factors include such things as abilities, previous knowledge about the subject matter or topic, motivation, relevant personality characteristics and in particular locus of control (pawns and origins), age and experiences. Most important is the extent to which students are spontaneously metacognitive about their learning, and what conception of learning they already have.

The *situation* factors are mostly those that are set up by the institutional context: the time available for learning, the method of teaching the topic (e.g. availability of multimodal ways of presentation or reliance on verbal/symbolic modes), the method of evaluating or grading the learning, the difficulty of the task, the nature of the task content, the structure of the course (whether it is compulsory or elective for example), and the general formal characteristics of the institution.

Process

The process factors refer to the *approaches to learning* used by the student, and have been discussed in the previous section.

Product

The product refers to the *learning outcomes* and in particular to those that formally or informally index the 'success' of the learning. Success (or its opposite) is usually objectified by the institution in the form of grading procedures which make more or less use of cognitive and affective outcomes. Formal evaluation of learning outcomes is complex and is the subject of Chapter 10. Cognitively, success can be gauged in terms of the structural complexity of the learning and/or the extent and accuracy of recall of the data learned. Affectively, it can be said that learning is successful if the student enjoys it, and feels a sense of accomplishment (whether or not that sense is justified is, of course, another matter). For the present, then, we shall refer to learning outcomes in terms of cognitive and affective dimensions.

Cognitive. *The structure–data (S–D) ratio.* All academic performances can be described in terms of the extent to which it is important that the data to be learned (skills, factual detail, etc.) are correctly reproduced or are appropriately structured. The first kind of performance, where the accurate reproduction of details is paramount, has a low S–D ratio, and the second, where appropriate structuring is paramount, has a high S–D ratio. Surface codes are low, and generic codes high on S–D ratio. For example, learning a list of spellings or scientific formulae are tasks with a low S–D ratio: the important thing is that the spellings and formulae be correctly reproduced. Learning the periodic table of elements is a high S–D task, because the point about such learning is its usability and transfer: if the structure of the table has not been grasped then there has been no point in learning it.

Learning low S–D tasks can easily be assessed by traditional means (e.g. number correctly reproduced), while high S–D tasks are more difficult. For the most part, high S–D tasks have been assessed by subjective ratings by teachers, for example 'Not well argued here, Jen!', and Jen may or may not know what the teacher means by that comment. The SOLO taxonomy (Biggs and Collis, 1982) was designed as a more systematic and objective way of categorising a learning outcome so that the manner in which data and structure are interrelated can be gauged. It is outlined in Section B.

Subjective. The cognitive outcomes of learning can also be assessed subjectively, from the student's perspective. One aspect of subjective success is how students see their performance in relation to their peers: this may be an important component of their academic self-concept ('I am best in the class at maths', or 'I blew it again: that's me.').

Another way of looking at the subjective outcomes from the student's perspective is in terms of the prevailing conception of learning, and how it might have changed as a result of an experience of learning (Martin and Ramsden, 1985). Perry's work on students progressing from an absolutist to a more relativistic level of intellectual development is another example. In these two cases, person variables are treated as outcomes of learning.

Affective outcomes. Whatever the cognitive characteristics of the outcome of learning, learning could be said to be successful if the student holds positive feelings towards the task, and unsuccessful if the student feels alienated or bored. It is difficult to assess affective outcomes formally and objectively, although all State departments acknowledge their importance, and have their own ways of incorporating teacher ratings into formal grading measures. Such outcomes are of course very important, as they determine the course of future engagements with similar learning tasks. Affective outcomes also relate to academic self-concept in the way a student *feels* about learning (successful, creative, a plodder, good at this but not at that aspect ...).

These two dimensions of learning outcome are conceptually distinct but related in practice. As learning outcomes become more structurally complex, so students enjoy them more, and feel better towards them (if they are successful). It is very difficult to feel accomplishment over learning trivial masses of unrelated detail (but then how about the popularity of 'Trivial Pursuit'? That is a problem worth thinking over, as we do in the discussion points at the end of this chapter).

The link between complexity and enjoyment takes us back to the principle of optimal mismatch: what one student finds structurally complex, another will find uninvolving. This problem of equating complexity across educational levels is addressed by looking at the structure of a learning outcome within tasks of similar levels of abstraction (see Section B).

The 3P model

We are now able to see how these three sets of variables interrelate (see Figure 4.1).

We see that the personal characteristics of the students and the situational constraints determine performance by two different routes: directly (the white arrows), and as mediated by the student's approaches to learning processes (the shaded arrows). The direct routes have been understood for years. On the person side, high ability students perform better than low ability students and having the prerequisite knowledge makes a crucial difference to whether or not a problem will be solved. On the situational side, the time allowed on a task has a crucial effect on how well it is done

Figure 4.1   The 3P model of student learning

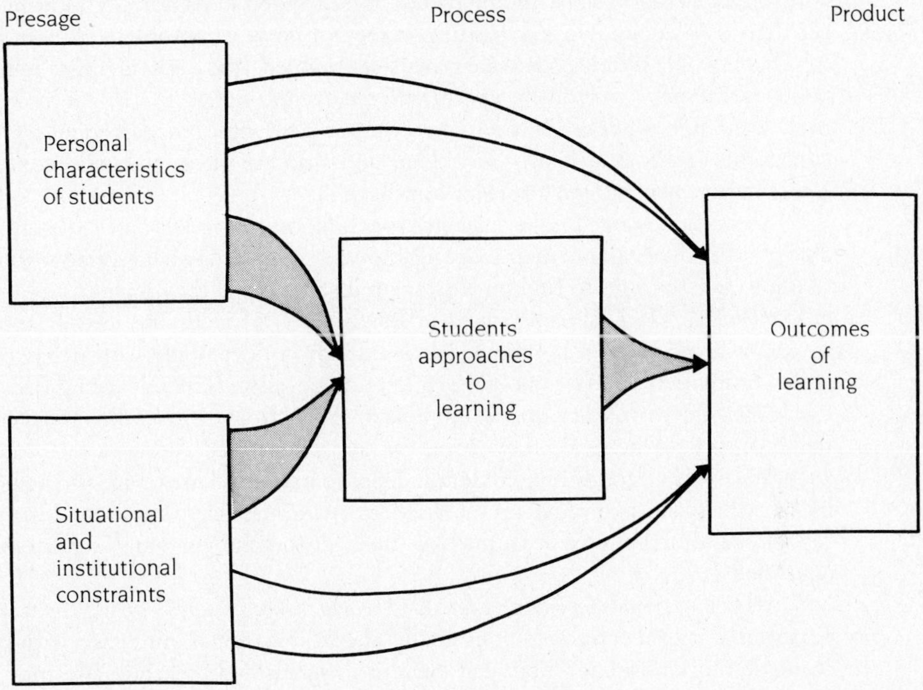

Presage   Process   Product

and again some teaching methods are better than others. Our interest in this chapter is not in these direct effects, but in the indirect ones.

What goes on if we follow the shaded route? Whole series of questions are implicit, some quite general, others specific to particular tasks. To the extent that the student (and teacher) faces those questions and attempts to answer them, metalearning is involved. Some students ask few, if any, of those questions, while others address most or all. Those students who do face these questions shape a planned strategy of attack on the task. In general, a great deal of metalearning activity indicates a deep approach towards the task in question, while little such activity indicates a surface approach.

So let us follow through.

Motives: 'What's a person like me doing in a place like this?' Some students reply, 'Nothing. I'll do as little as possible and try and keep out of trouble.' The result is adult illiteracy after 10 years of 'schooling'. More usually, though, we are reduced to our three basic motives: 'I want to do enough to just pass and keep out of trouble' (surface motive); 'I want to find out as much about this subject as possible' (deep motive); 'I want to get higher grades than anyone else' (achieving motive).

Goals: 'But what will it look like when I've got there?' Once the general direction of learning has been shaped by students' motives, it is necessary to define the end-state that is acceptable to each person.

Resources: 'What resources do I have at my disposal: What do I need in order to get there?' Planning a line of attack requires the student to consider what human and material resources are available.

Constraints: 'What stipulations or limitations must I contend with?' Institutional constraints include: 'the assignment has to be handed in tomorrow morning, clearly written on A4, all linework to be ruled in red', or 'solve this problem without reference to Theorem 4'. Often constraints are self-imposed (the student mistakenly or not believes that only a certain viewpoint will receive the highest marks). Some constraints may challenge students into a deeper approach, but more frequently extrinsic constraints (such as a heavy workload and little time or obsessive concern with 'presentation') encourage a surface approach.

Knowledge update: 'Is what I already know sufficient for handling this?' Students must be able to critically evaluate their existing knowledge, as it may bear upon a problem, and to know where to go to find out further relevant data if they have to.

Abilities: 'Do I have the ability to handle this? What are my relevant strengths and weaknesses?' Accurate self-knowledge is critical in developing a strategy; over- and under-estimation of what one is capable of doing distorts metalearning decisions.

Strategy: 'Given all that, how do I go about it?' Specific strategies will vary according to the task, but in general, they come in the three basic categories — surface, to accurately reproduce unrelated detail; deep, to maximise meaning; and achieving, to make sure space and time are so used to maximise the formal or institutionally recognised outcomes of learning (or their deep-achieving and surface-achieving equivalents).

Monitoring: 'How am I doing so far? Do I need to change strategy?' While the task is being performed, it is necessary to continually check provisional outcomes with goals and strategies: any mismatch between current progress and the end-state may indicate some revision of plans and strategy.

Finalising: 'Mission accomplished.' At some stage the student has to decide that the end-state has been reached (finalising); or has not been reached; but is good enough as far as the student is concerned, but may or may not be acceptable to the teacher (satisficing); or has not and never will be reached (capitulating).

The answers to these questions make up a complicated network from which an approach to learning emerges, and which mediates between presage, process and product.

THE 3P MODEL IN ACTION

In order to understand the 3P model in action, it would help to take each of the three major links in turn, person-to-approach, situation-to-approach, and approach-to-outcome (see shaded arrows in Figure 4.1).

Person-to-approach

While time and other pressures can force students into using a surface approach for a particular task, in general people tend to be fairly consistent in their use of an approach in formal learning contexts. Several person factors appear to relate to consistency of use of particular approaches.

Conceptions of learning. The link between a person's beliefs about what learning is, and how that person will engage a task, is a strong one. Van Rossum and Schenk (1984), for instance, found that surface learners overwhelmingly held a level 1 or 2 conception of learning, while deep learners held conceptions 4 or 5. This link is perfectly reasonable: to see learning as the accurate retention of detail obliges the student to concentrate on the details of a task rather than the structure. To change a student's approach it is thus necessary to induce an appreciation of higher conceptions of learning.

Abilities. Students of lower intelligence tend to use the surface approach rather than the others, but use of the deep approach is not particularly associated with either high or low verbal ability (Biggs, 1986a). The deep approach is not then the prerogative of only the brighter students. This is important as it means it is possible to encourage a deep approach across all except the very lowest ability levels. It has also been found (Biggs 1986a) that by Year 11, it is the average and below student, rather than the above average, who uses the achieving approach: being systematic and organised is what the less than brilliant but ambitious student does in order to get on. Ability, then, has some bearing on the use of different approaches, but it is not the most important person characteristic relating to approach.

Locus of control. Assuming control over oneself is basically what is involved in metalearning; an internal locus of control is in fact a logical prerequisite to metalearning activity. Much evidence suggests that approach to learning is affected more by locus of control than by other variables (Biggs, 1986a), as may be seen for example in the graphs in Figure 4.2.

Experiential background. Certain kinds of experience are particularly effective in bringing people to reflect on what they are doing; these experiences are in effect inducing an internal locus of control. One such set of experiences is known as simply 'growing up in the school of hard knocks'. Lawrence, Dodds and Volet (1983) for example found that a group of highly intelligent Year 12 scholarship girls performed much worse at a planning task, which involved a high degree of metacognitive activity, than a group of mature age mothers of average ability.

Learning institutions, in fact, even appear counter-productive. In a national survey of Australian high school students, it was found that on average the use of a surface approach decreased from Year 8 to Year 11, but so, too, did use of a deep–achieving approach, and in boys far more than in girls (Biggs, 1986a). The same occurs at tertiary level. Several writers have found that, except for academically oriented students intent on pursuing a research degree, ordinary undergraduates drop deep and achieving approaches alarmingly, in science more than in arts, and in colleges of advanced education more than in universities (Biggs, 1986a; Watkins and Hattie, 1985). The quotation in Box 4.2 gives some insight into this.

On the other hand, mature age students report increasing use of achieving, and especially deep, approaches the older they are when they enter university or college. This could be due to self-selection — the emotional cost of taking up studies, even part-time, is greater for older students — but it is also likely that they have learned something about themselves and their learning that school-leavers have not yet learned.

BOX 4.2   WHAT AN INSTITUTION MAY DO TO A DEEP
          APPROACH

Most of all I write what 'they' like me to ...when I get the piece of paper with BA
(Hons) then I will write the way I want using MY ideas ...

Source: An Arts undergraduate (Watkins and Hattie, 1985, p. 137).

Another group of students who show signs of high metalearning activity are
students for whom English is a second language (Biggs, 1986a). Continually monitoring
the meaning of what others are saying, and being very careful about how one expresses
oneself and checking others for signs of misunderstanding, is an extremely metacognitive thing to have to do. Thus, these students, at both secondary and tertiary levels and

Figure 4.2   Effects of ability, locus of control and achieving approaches on HSC
             aggregate

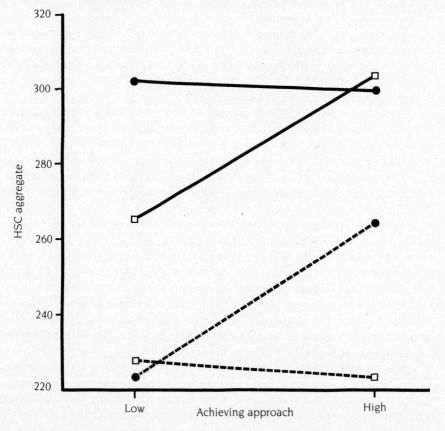

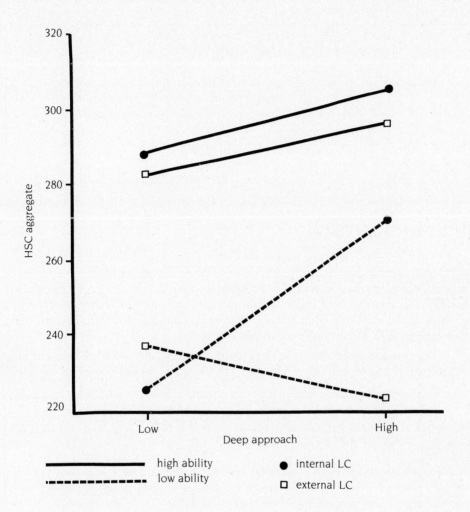

independently of country of origin, show more metacognitive awareness of their approaches to learning than do native English speakers, although their actual performance is likely to be inferior (if tested in English).

These reflective experiences thus seem to be richer outside the classroom than inside, and it is easy to see why this is so: the outside world is *much more important* to most students than inside a classroom. It is so much easier to be metacognitive about activities that have an immediate and comprehensible bearing on one's life, and a high cost if one capitulates, than in a classroom which is usually (but not quite inevitably) divorced from the action of life, and where the content is experienced second hand. The challenge is to make the classroom a place where, if they are to survive, students must learn to reflect: hopefully not like the students in Box 4.3. With that drastic proposition, we come to the link between situation and approach.

BOX 4.3   HOW METACOGNITIVE ARE YOU?

Psychology lecturer: 'To show you understand what cognitive theorists mean by it, give me a sentence containing the term "metacognitive".'

Student: 'But I've never met a cognitive theorist I could understand.'

Lecturer: 'Near enough'.

Source: Anon.

Situation-to-approach

A student's approach to learning thus depends critically on the kinds of experiences undergone and in what context. The problem is twofold: matching what the student perceives as important with what the institutional managers of learning perceive as important; and matching what teachers *do* in managing students' learning with what they believe to be important (see excerpts in Box 4.4).

The example of the physics student illustrates a fundamental point that is lacking in the case of the psychology student. In the first case, formal content is explicitly

---

BOX 4.4   TEACHER AND STUDENT PRIORITIES: PERFECT AND IMPERFECT MATCHES

Matching what the student thinks is important with what the teacher thinks is important
'Recently we were doing Fourier analysis, and the lecturer mentioned in passing that it was something which they used when they transmit moon pictures back to earth ... that makes a lot of difference, you can see it being used ... Another example he quoted was about why when you bang a drum you get lots of different sounds rather than when you, say, play a violin you just get the one note ... he said, if you look at this you can see why — and he was right, you could see why; it did make sense.'

Source: A physics student (Ramsden, 1984, p. 145).

Matching what teachers require students to do with what anybody could think is important
'I hate to say it, but what you have got to do is have a list of "facts"; you write down the important points and memorise those, then you'll do all right in the test ... if you can give a bit of factual information — so and so did that, and concluded that — for two sides of writing, then you'll get a good mark.'

Source: A psychology student (Ramsden, 1984, p. 144).

related to something in the student's experience; in the second case, to a series of unrelated points whose only importance is that they are to be formally tested. One involves a level 5 conception of learning, the other a level 2 — yet we are discussing *tertiary* level examples. The case for matching formal and experiential learning at primary and secondary school is more powerful still.

Another point that arises from the quotation from the psychology student is that *assessment*, rather than the method of teaching, or clarity of the texts or lectures, dominates her approach to learning. While assessment is not the only factor, many writers would agree that it is probably the major one:

> While it may appear obvious that assessment methods should be so designed that they encourage (and test) deep approaches, the reality revealed in the studies of student learning is very different ... assessment procedures provide crucial messages to students about the kinds of learning they are expected to carry out. (Ramsden, 1985 p. 59).

It is therefore vital that teachers match what they do with what they see as important. One of the present authors, for instance, found that when some students gave a fairly literal replay of lecture material, their essay grades were higher than expected: even when the course was in educational psychology, and the exact opposite had been said (and intended) in class (Biggs, 1973b). Clearly, in rating those essays, that teacher was not practising what he genuinely thought he was preaching. It is not only important, then, that the assessment (and other instructional) procedures be structured to encourage deeper rather than surface approaches but that the teacher be metacognitive enough to obtain, and be willing to accept, feedback on those procedures.

Thomas and Bain (1984) found that open-end assessment was more likely to evoke deep approaches to learning, and objective formats surface approaches, but this varied across subject areas. There was also a tendency for some students to maintain a degree of consistency in their approach, whatever the mode of assessment.

Unfortunately it is in general easier to call out surface approaches than deep, and one of the most effective ways of doing so is to embed assessment, or any other instructional procedure, in a context that *students* will perceive as threatening, whatever the good intentions of the teacher (Fransson, 1977). Such a threat can emanate from informal interactions with particular individuals — sarcasm, perceived unfairness, and so on — or from formal structures used in the management and evaluation of learning.

Approach-to-outcome

How, and to what extent, do approaches to learning influence performance? There would be little point in trying to change students' approaches if the 'straight through' effects of intelligence, prior knowledge, or teaching method overwhelmingly determined student performance (see Figure 4.1). It therefore needs to be remembered when interpreting approach–outcome relationships that the approach refers to the *way* of going about the task, not directly to *how well* or *efficiently* either deep or surface learning is carried out. For example, it is easily possible to imagine a brilliant surface learner getting better marks than a plodding deep; or an involved deep burrowing away at something that is simply irrelevant from the teacher's point of view.

It is, then, important to distinguish between several aspects of performance. The cognitive and affective dimensions can be related easily and directly to approach, while grades reflect various 'officially approved' mixes of structure and data, and possibly affect.

Let us look first at HSC performance. A surface approach usually relates to low marks, and deep and achieving to high marks, but the direct correlations are low (around –.25 for surface and .30 for deep and achieving). A similar picture holds at the tertiary level, with some faculty differences (e.g. Watkins and Hattie, 1981).

To give an example of how complicated the picture is, Figure 4.2 presents some relationships between deep and achieving approaches to learning and HSC aggregate in students of differing verbal ability and locus of control.

Although the students' approaches to learning were assessed in Year 11, 14 months before they sat for the HSC, there are nevertheless quite strong relationships in some students, but not in others (there were 320 students in the total group studied). The greatest gains associated with the use of the deep approach are to be found in the internally controlled group of below average verbal ability (but remember that 'below average' is relative to those sitting for the HSC) who rise 52 aggregate points, from 225 to 277. In the case of the achieving approach, two groups show similar gains: the high ability externals, and the low ability internals again, gaining 47 and 46 aggregate points respectively. Locus of control is clearly an important variable.

Now whatever the explanation for these figures — and metalearning offers one — the effect on examination performance of an approach to learning is different for different people (which is why the *overall* correlations between approach and performance are fairly low). The importance for particular students, however, may be quite considerable.

Let us look now at cognitive outcomes. There is strong evidence that a deep approach produces outcomes that are structurally complex at both secondary (Kirby and Biggs, 1981) and tertiary (Biggs, 1979b; Marton and Saljo, 1976a, 1976b; Van Rossum and Schenk, 1984; Watkins, 1983) levels. A surface approach is, however, effective for recall of unrelated detail (Biggs, 1979b). In the last study, education students were asked to read reports of research and to be prepared either to be examined for correct recall of the facts and details, or for understanding the purpose of the experiment; they were then tested on both recall and understanding. Students scoring high on surface approach, and instructed to learn the detail, obtained very high scores on a factual recall test, which they retained over two weeks. When asked to write about the purpose of the experiment, however, they did so at a very low level; most had missed the point. The opposite results were found for students using a deep approach; they recalled fewer details, but understood the purpose of the experiment. There seemed to be a 'pay-off' between the structural complexity of learning and attention to detail.

As for affective outcomes, the evidence is similar. The interview material reported throughout the chapters of Marton, Hounsell and Entwistle (1984) consistently reiterates that students using a surface approach feel variously bored, alienated, anxious or resentful; while students using a deep approach feel exhilarated, satisfied, challenged or intrigued. In surveying thousands of secondary and tertiary students, Biggs (1986a) found that students who rated themselves on a surface approach saw themselves as performing poorly in comparison to their peers, and expressed a high degree of dissatisfaction with their performance, while the opposite results were obtained with those who rated themselves as using deep and deep-achieving approaches.

The one simple generalisation derived from all these studies is that quality of learning outcome is directly related to the level of metalearning activity of the student. We address that issue in Section B, together with the question of assessing high S–D learning outcomes.

SUMMARY

Reflective self-awareness and responsible self-direction. In this chapter we look at the world of learning from the context of the student. Our point of departure is that human learners are able to become aware *that* they are learning, as well as *what* they are learning. There is much evidence that such knowledge can be used, increasingly as students grow older and more experienced, to monitor, control and improve learning. Although educators advocate aims such as 'responsible self-direction', implications for structuring teaching strategy are more radical than have been recognised. The conjunction of recent research on metacognition and on student learning helps highlight those implications.

A good example of metacognitive activity is redrafting something one has just written: our thought has been externalised (written down) so that it can be examined against whatever criteria we think are appropriate, and then redrafted until we are satisfied. In fact, most of what we do might usefully go through a similar reflective process of review-and-revise: it therefore seems to be a very useful paradigm to establish across the curriculum, and to be the sort of activity that teachers might apply to their own teaching.

Metalearning. The activity of deliberately becoming aware of, monitoring, and controlling our learning is called metalearning. One aspect of metalearning is an awareness of what learning is. Several different conceptions of learning may be distinguished, grouped for convenience as quantitative or qualitative conceptions. Many individuals — students, parents, and even teachers — have a basically quantitative view: good learning occurs when most material is retained with a high degree of accuracy. Qualitative conceptions emphasise the complexity of meaning gained from a learning act, and how that meaning may bring significance to an individual. These conceptions of learning are pervasive. They affect how individuals approach learning tasks, which in turn affect the outcomes of learning.

Metalearning integrates what happens at the three stages of presage (factors existing prior to the learning but which affect it), process (occurring during learning) and product (the outcome of learning). These are linked in the 3P model:

1.   *Presage.* The individual has a conception of what learning is, a set of interests, abilities, existing skills, personality characteristics and an existing predilection for metalearning; the situational context defines the parameters and sets the task.

2.   *Process.* As a result of the amount and quality of metalearning, the individual constructs an approach to the task (long-term or short-term) that in some sense satisfies all the constraints. Three main approaches can be distinguished: surface, deep and achieving. The surface approach is constructed around an extrinsic motive, leading to reproductive strategies based on rote rehearsal; the deep approach around intrinsic motivation and strategies based on coding for meaning; and the achieving approach around achievement motivation and planned organising. The specifics of each approach vary, leading to three groups of strategies, variously constructed according to task.

3.   *Product.* Cognitive outcomes of learning may be described in terms of their structure–data (S–D) ratio. In low level outcomes much unrelated detail is recalled; in high level outcomes the detail is embedded in a complex and relevant structure. Affective outcomes refer to how the student feels about the task, and this can range from aversion to high enthusiasm. Formal or institutional outcomes refer to how learning has been graded formally as a measure of its success, and may comprise whatever mix of structure and data recall the teacher deems appropriate. Affective outcomes are incorporated into grading procedures with difficulty.

Metalearning activity brings these three stages into a logical sequence incorporating implicit questioning of: motives, goals, resources, constraints, relevant knowledge, abilities, strategies, monitoring and finalising. The teaching implications of this model are discussed in Section B.

SECTION B

WHO IS RESPONSIBLE FOR SELF-DIRECTION?

'He wants to teach, doesn't he? That's what he's trained for. If we don't learn he might stop and take a look at what he's doing' (Adrienne, a Year 6 girl, quoted in Davies, 1982, p. 128). Adrienne takes a typical child's view of institutionalised learning: it is entirely the teacher's responsibility if no learning takes place. However, if that view of the responsibility for learning goes unchallenged, what of responsible self-direction? Adrienne, too, needs to take 'a good look at what she's doing'. Nevertheless, she is right in that the only place to start is with the teacher.

It is not, however, going to be easy for teachers to persuade children to have a look at themselves and accept more responsibility for their own learning. Davies, in her study of the ecology of classrooms in a rural school experimenting with open planning, uncovered the 'double world' of children: the world shared with other children on equal terms, and the world shared with adults on unequal (but acceptably unequal) terms. The problem with open classrooms, she says, is that they violate children's expectations about how adults and children should behave.

So how do we go about getting students to be more metacognitive in the face of opinions like Adrienne's? The problem almost certainly is not a developmental one. Certainly some sophisticated forms of metacognition may not appear until adolescence (see Chapter 5) but, like intelligence itself, metacognition is evident in some form or another from birth onwards (Robinson, 1983).

The problem, then, does not reside in serious personal limitations in the student, but in the environment of schooling. Indeed, as Adrienne's comment suggests, and as suggested too in the evidence reviewed in the last section, classrooms are structured in ways that *discourage* students from being metacognitive about their learning.

There are two ways in which matters may be improved: by *removing* or easing off those factors that *discourage* metalearning, and by *creating* or emphasising situations that *encourage* metalearning.

As far as *person*-related factors are concerned, there is probably not much teachers themselves can do. Most of the factors that appear to influence metalearning — such as upbringing, age and experience, ability and locus of control — belong in the counsellor's domain rather than in the teacher's. Teachers can benefit from knowing about the influence of these factors, but with one exception they cannot do very much about them. The exception is that by action and example, they can *demonstrate* the higher qualitative conceptions of learning in action by their teaching, assessment and interaction with students.

Discouraging surface approaches

The *situation* factors are easier to influence. The first focus is those factors that are detrimental to metacognition. In the last section it was noted that Ramsden and others working in the tertiary sector saw assessment as the arch-villain in encouraging surface approaches to learning. The same is true at secondary level, where the adverse effects of assessment have to be countered. One school known to the authors runs a very good writing program, emphasising reflective revision and redrafting. Teachers here simply inform the English/History Year 12 classes: 'This is HSC year: forget what we did in the writing program until after the exams. Those of you going on to uni can pick it up again there, where you'll find what we did in Year 11 will be useful.'

Even more pervasive than the final examination pressure is time pressure caused by unco-ordinated setting of assignments. Ironically, many individual teachers, in a genuine bid to relieve pressure, may allow students extensions to assignments to the point when there is a monumental build-up towards the end of the term. Teachers can ease that sort of pressure by planning more effectively.

The fact that learning takes place in schools, colleges and universities means that rules, routines and regulations (the 'second set of 3 Rs') are necessary to help to make things run smoothly. Sometimes, however, the tail wags the dog. Systems for marking, examining and grading are one major example of where the institutional need to establish credentials often gets in the way of educational needs. But pressure from assessment is not the only source. As we saw in the previous chapter, other factors also affect metacognition, hence motivation and approach to learning. For example, take:

- 'dragginess', that is, insisting on trivia ('Come on now! Sit up straight! Pencils pointing over your shoulder!') (Kounin, 1967);
- sarcasm and intimidation;
- closed government, where students are kept in the dark about decisions that affect them.

While pressure is probably the major factor that induces surface learning, it is not the only one arising out of institutional procedures. The last item, closed government, not only stresses students, it makes them *cynical*. Cynicism thoroughly degrades learning: it invites students to beat the system. Their personal study contracts are now in a debased currency; they will bargain for the lowest rates they can get away with. Complicated rules and routines, pedantic insistence on trivia, hypocrisy, defensiveness and pretence of any kind on matters affecting students send messages that invite replies at surface rates.

Metateaching

Every decision a teacher or an administrator makes has two sides: the *functional* side, what it is supposed to achieve (what *you* see it achieves); and the *impact* side, how it affects students (what *students* are likely to see that it does to them).

If the cost of the impact is greater than the benefit of the function, *then it is a bad decision*. Of course, costs and benefits cannot always be assessed accurately, and some decisions have a completely unpredictable impact. As far as possible *teachers should be metacognitive about their teaching*, just as much as we are arguing that they should help students become more metacognitive about their learning.

As a general strategy to counter surface learning, then, teachers should ask the following questions about every conscious decision they take:

- What sorts of pressures will this place on students? Are the pressures reasonable and realistic?
- How are the students likely to perceive it? Will they see my intended function, or are they more likely to see something else; me playing games, for instance?

Then they should take steps to find out what the students do make of it.

This dimension applies in particular to classroom management decisions, and we return to the issue in Chapter 8.

SITUATIONS THAT ENHANCE METALEARNING

The general thrust of all the techniques mentioned below is to encourage students to think about what they are doing and to use that knowledge to improve their learning. That is of course what good teaching has always meant. Some teaching techniques seem particularly effective in inducing reflective learning and they deserve highlighting.

The first few techniques mentioned spring out of teaching itself. Good teaching is *naturally* a metacognitive act: explaining something to someone requires one to analyse one's own knowledge, and how best to rearrange and present it.

Think-aloud modelling. The first technique simply starts at that point, with the teacher thinking out loud while doing the task the students are to learn. The teacher is doing the self-analysis and reflection, but is setting the students up so that eventually they take it over themselves. Writing is a particularly easy example of this technique, and is used widely in workshops. For example, a writer may bring in several stages of drafting which 'freeze' the writer's thinking at various stages in its development. The author can then discuss the various versions, why they were changed, what effect is being sought, and in the course of that, demonstrate the purposes of the various techniques and devices that professional writers use. In this way, students are brought to think about processes and possibilities that they themselves would be unlikely to think of, let alone think about.

At a recent writing conference, a curriculum expert, Garth Boomer, was asked to give a talk to a large group of Year 12 students and teachers on essay composition. The scenario, freely adapted, went something like this:

Mr Boomer enters the assembly hall of a large city school, where he finds 250 Year 12 students and the teachers from several city schools.

'Well, I'll let you have the bad news first. We're here for a talk on essay writing ...' (groans from audience) ... 'The good news is that we're going to change places. I'm going to do the writing and you're going to give me the topic ...' (instant reaction of pleased surprise).

'OK, then, what's the topic?' ... Mr Boomer stands in front of overhead projector, light showing a large blank area behind him, felt pen poised in hand. Suggestions for essay topics, mostly facetious, some quite funny, are shouted out.

The first one mentioned is chosen because 'you students don't always get to choose your topic so neither do I'. *Why is a banana bent?* is written on the transparency.

'Good. We've got the topic. Now I go into what I call "incubation". Let's all do it. For the next five minutes you write down all the things that occur to you that you think might — don't have to, just *might* — go into the final essay, and I'll do the same. Then we'll swap notes.'

Mr Boomer switches off the O/H and in the next five minutes jots down some thoughts on the bentness of bananas. He then confers with the group, discussing what might go in and what might go out. A structure for the essay begins to emerge.

'Right. Don't know about you, but I'm ready to have a go at the first paragraph ...', and thinking aloud, he writes down the first few sentences, with some misspellings (deliberate). 'First to get something down. We'll clean it up later.' He then goes back and edits it out loud, slashing here, adding there, changing the tense of one sentence, leaving spelling corrections and punctuation until last because 'we don't want to derail our train of thought with mechanical stuff like that'. All redrafting, editing and correcting is done aloud, explaining the thinking behind each change.

After the first paragraph is done, the students are asked to 'predict' each sentence by writing down their own. They find as they go through the essay, that their 'predictions' begin to foreshadow Mr Boomer's composed sentences more closely ... they are beginning to model their writing on what 'real' writers do.

Afterwards, several students told him that was the first time they had realised what good writers do. They thought text came out clean, in finished form, the first time; if it didn't it couldn't be any good. The idea of using paper as a means of examining their thinking, to see what they really *did* think about the topic, had never occurred to them. Afterwards, too, some wryly amused (and a few not-so-amused) teachers came up to him: 'What *have* you let us in for!!?'

The technique can be used in almost any pencil-and-paper task, such as writing, solving maths problems — most of the tasks set in school. The advantage of overhead projectors is of course that every move, including every mistake, can be seen by a large class simultaneously, while the teacher maintains eye contact and interaction with the class. Many teachers think aloud for their students automatically, but many do not. Some because they have not thought of it, some because they do not see the point ('after all, the students have got to learn to do these things for themselves'), but perhaps most because they see, as did Mr Boomer's not-so-amused teachers, that it could be a very threatening thing for them to have to do ('What if I got a block! I'd be a laughing stock and that wouldn't do any of us any good').

Peer teaching. If teaching induces people to reflect on their own thinking, then an obvious technique is to get the students to teach others.

This may seem like quite an innovation. In fact, as a method of instruction it dates back to 1791, when Andrew Bell devised a system for coping with a very difficult school for soldiers' children in Madras. He arranged that an older child taught younger ones, both on a one-to-one basis and in large classes, with the help of younger assistants. Not only did this system provide successful instruction, it also brought about a marked improvement in the students' behaviour. As Bell commented: 'For months together it has not been found necessary to inflict a single punishment' (quoted in Allen, 1976).

What became known as the Bell–Lancaster system was widespread in Britain in the early nineteenth century. This system died out paradoxically with the growth of professionalism among teachers: 'A self-conscious teaching profession is likely to look with disdain upon the idea that untrained young children can perform the skilled functions of a teacher' (Allen, 1976, p. 17).

Peer teaching was also used in one-teacher schools, once very common in country areas, where the same classroom might contain 30 or so children ranging anywhere from Years 1 to 6. Under those circumstances, it was natural that older children would take some sort of responsibility for the younger ones and teach them what they had learned, while the teacher was busy with another group.

In the sixties and seventies, peer tutoring became subject to much experimenta- tion in the United States where an older student (the tutor) was paired with a younger student (the tutee), mainly for social rather than academic reasons. The tutor frequently was a student who was disadvantaged in some way, or was a discipline problem. The most common finding from this work is that the tutor benefits academically more than the tutee and, while increased social skills and attitudes to school and self have been reported, the academic gains are the most reliable ones

(Allen, 1976). Gains for the tutor have been reported in reading and writing skills, mathematics and grade point average, while gains for the tutee are not usually so marked, depending partly on the skill and the age differential between tutor and tutee. A typical finding is that reported by Cloward on his work with disadvantaged New York adolescents, for which he offers what we can now see is a metacognitive explanation:

> The findings from the Mobilisation study indicated that the tutor was the major beneficiary of the tutorial experience. In attempting to help his low-achieving elementary school pupil, the tutor greatly improved his own reading ability. The reason for this is not entirely clear, but the result deserves our serious attention. It may be an example of what every beginning teacher discovers: that one must relearn one's subject in order to teach it, that one has to reanalyze what he knows and how he learns in order to promote similar knowlege and learning in others (Cloward, 1976, p. 227).

Benware and Deci (1984) actually argue that 'The process of learning is *different* when one learns material to teach it rather than for some other reason' (p. 756, italics supplied). They contrast learning undertaken for *teaching* purposes with learning undertaken for *testing* purposes. What they come up with is that the former is associated with *deep* processing, and the latter with *surface*. As the difference between deep and surface processing is in the amount of metacognitive activity involved, we keep coming back to the same proposition. Teaching enhances learning because it induces students to become metacognitive about their learning, and hence to encourage deep, rather than surface processing.

Palincsar and Brown (1984) specifically built on the metacognitive nature of teaching to improve the reading skills of grade seven students. They call their method 'reciprocal teaching'. They based a dialogue between teacher and students around four important reading strategies:

1. summarising, or identifying the gist of a passage;
2. formulating test questions on the content;
3. clarifying the meaning in unclear passages;
4. predicting what is going to come up next in the text.

The procedure then followed on from the teacher's think-aloud. The teacher first generated a question to which the group responded, and summarised their response for the group to elaborate; suggested a test item; suggested where the content was unclear; then predicted what might come up next in the text and supported the prediction. The students then took the teacher's role as they became familiar with the task. Thus the skills were learned in context, and the teacher prompted the students' metacognising by acting as model and then withdrawing. The results showed that students' reading comprehension scores were greatly increased.

There is thus very strong evidence that placing students in the role of teacher improves their performance, almost certainly because it forces them to be more metacognitive about their own learning. The new role suddenly shifts the responsibility, so that the student is now in a situation where publicly accountable decision-making and action is required: the classroom is no longer a place where students like Adrienne sit back passively to allow adults to go through their rituals, saving her involvement for the world of childhood.

The Bell–Lancaster system, and the very many variations that can be made with it, has an enormous potential. Given its many advantages — including its low cost — it is surprising that peer teaching is not used more widely.

Reflective teaching. Cruickshank (1985b) argues that we have been uncritically socialised into schooling and teaching from a very young age: reflective teaching aims to release student teachers from the trap of teaching as they themselves were taught. Unless teachers early in their careers become metacognitive about their own teaching, they will repeat their initial experiences over and over; an experience which has strong links with our discussion of burn-out.

Typically, reflective teaching is practised by dividing a group of student teachers into subgroups of four to six. One of each group is appointed to teach a nominated lesson. Each teacher can teach the same lesson in any way, but is told that the outcomes to be evaluated are learner achievement and satisfaction.

The lessons are carefully chosen (see Cruickshank, 1981) so that they are interesting to teach and learn; have content which will not be treated in other units of a teacher education program; can be taught in no more than 15 minutes; and result in a measurable outcome. The teaching can occur in the same large space (groups may be seated on the floor around a chart or overhead projector or at desks in a mini classroom lay-out; sometimes adjacent corridor space or other rooms are used). All lessons begin and end simultaneously so that the distribution and collection of post-tests (which take three to five minutes to complete) also occur at about the same time. Using specially devised questions intended to raise the cognitive level of thought about teaching and learning, the group considers the lesson for about 15 minutes. Then all the sub-groups rejoin to form the original large group of students so that the lecturer leads a discussion based on another set of prepared questions.

The *Origami Task* is an example of the reflective teaching lesson (see Box 4.5).

Studies have shown that reflective teaching enables participants to produce proportionally more analytic statements about teaching and learning than members of a control group; and that participants were 'less frightened, less anxious' and 'more confident' on semantic differential items (Cruickshank et al., 1981). Participants also

---

BOX 4.5   AN EXAMPLE OF REFLECTIVE TEACHING

The origami task
Origami is the Japanese art of paper folding.

Your objective
Your goal is to get as many of your learners as possible to make a butterfly from paper using the technique of origami, as shown below. You will have 15 minutes in which to accomplish your goal.

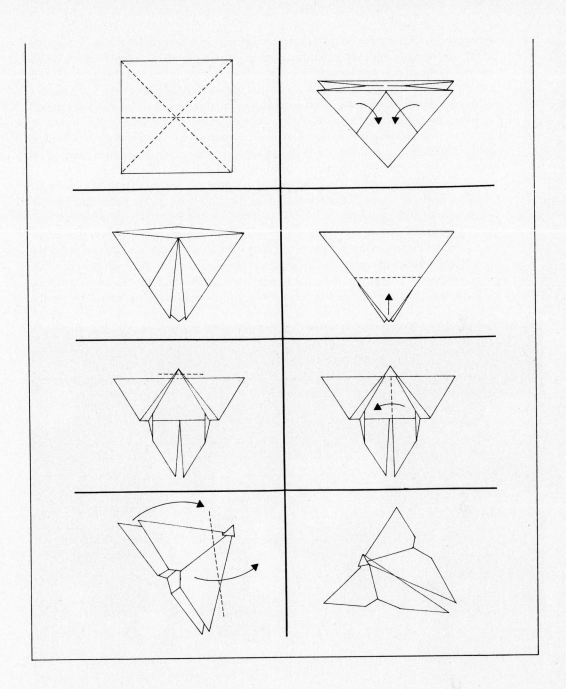

differed from control groups in terms of clarity when teaching (Cruickshank et al., 1985a). Reflective teaching, unlike peer teaching, is not concerned with being metacognitive about learning the content taught, but about the teaching process itself. It is a technique for *metateaching*, not metalearning.

Peer groups. A variation on the peer teaching theme is where students learn from each other in small groups. This technique is standard in higher education where tutorials are regularly used to supplement lectures, and to develop in students higher level and especially critical thinking skills. At least that has been the aim, but tutorials typically do not do what they are intended to do: students 'are often silent and often ill-prepared, and the tutor often finds himself giving a lecture' (Collier, 1985, p. 7). Two kinds of group have been designed to overcome these problems and specifically to encourage students to take responsibility for their own progress: these are the groups designed by Johnson Abercrombie (1969) and the syndicate methods of Collier (1983).

Johnson Abercrombie (1969) devised a small group technique that combines think-aloud and peer teaching. She worked with medical students, on the following theory:

> My hypothesis is that we may learn to make better judgments if we can become aware of some of the factors that influence their formation ... the student learns by comparing his observations with ten or so of his peers. He compares not only the results, but how the results were arrived at ... What the student learns, it is hoped, is not only how we make a more correct response when he is confronted with a similar problem, but more generally

Intensive peer group interaction helps students learn about themselves.

to gain firmer control of his behaviour by understanding better his own ways of working (pp. 18–19).

Her groups consisted of 10 or so students, and the task was diagnosis, mostly using X-ray plates as content. While that is a highly specialised content area, the principle is applicable to any situation where students are learning to make judgments, and where there is likely to be a strong difference of opinion. Essentially, we are constructing a hypothesis, where the data are insufficient to enable us to reach an unambiguous conclusion. What happens is that different individuals seize on different aspects of the data, or use the same data to draw different conclusions. The shock at finding themselves at loggerheads with others equally convinced of their own correctness can be extremely powerful, and forces students to examine closely the basis of their judging process. It was found that students taught in this way made better diagnoses, based more firmly on evidence, and they were less dogmatic, being more open to consider alternative possibilities.

In Collier's method, syndicate groups are formed out of a large class of 30 or so into four to eight students each. Each group has an assignment to work on, and the heart of the technique is the intensive debate that is meant to go on in the syndicates. The assignments are designed to draw on selected sources as well as on students' first-hand experiences, so that everyone has something to say. The syndicates then report back to plenary sessions led by the teacher to consolidate the conceptual structures that have emerged from each group. Collier reports that student motivation is very high, and particularly that the higher level skills are enhanced. However, he does point out that unless assessment is *obviously* directed towards these higher skills, the method fails. Again we see that inappropriate or over-obvious assessment can kill the highest level processes, and students simply learn what they think will assist them best in passing the examination.

Although both these discussion-based groups were designed for use with university students, the same principles apply at primary and secondary levels. The important feature of any such group is that the students have sufficient background to contribute, either because they have read or otherwise studied enough to have an informed discussion, or because the topic is directly relatable to personal experience. Above all, the group leader needs to be able to create the right sort of atmosphere so that students can discuss uninhibitedly: this is a role that many teachers find hard to adopt. The teacher must not correct a student, or be seen in any sense as an arbiter in the discussion: otherwise, the situation reverts immediately to the 'mini-lecture'. Values clarification is an obvious example where this approach works in school, but it could easily be extended to science, history, literary criticism — any area where the students have to come to a decision about something, and where there is room for differences in opinion. The important thing is that they learn how they work themselves, by being confronted with how other students work.

Using learning theory. If a student is asked: 'How did you learn that?', the reply is likely to be a list of the various sub-topics that together comprise the topic in question. In other words, they say *what* has been learned, not *how* it has been learned. What is needed is a 'process language', which psychology could provide. Does teaching students about learning actually help them manage their own learning any better? There has been surprisingly little research into using psychology in this way and all of it has so far been restricted to university students, where psychology is taught as a subject.

Johnson Abercrombie found it helpful to teach her students some psychology, so that they could discuss their own learning processes. Without such a language, it is difficult to distinguish discussion of the learning *process* from discussion of the *content*. McKeachie et al. (1984) taught several psychology classes how to use the content of learning theory to make sense out of their own learning, and to derive proper study strategies for themselves. Their approaches to learning were shown to have improved, and in the case of bright and highly anxious students, so did their overall grade point average.

The teaching of psychology in secondary school is fairly common in Britain and the United States, but it has not been tackled seriously in Australia so far. School psychology is usually taught either academically, as experimental psychology in a science elective group, or as humanistic psychology in a personal development context. Valuable though both may be, neither use is really relevant to the present purpose which would be to provide a language so that students can think about and talk about their own learning: the nearest to that are courses in study skills.

Teaching study skills. It has long been assumed that training in 'good' study skills will improve students' performance. The research evidence is, however, indecisive, and almost all of it has been conducted in college and university contexts.

Basically we can distinguish between training that is 'blind', in the sense that the students are not told why it was important to carry out the skill, and metacognitive training (Brown et al., 1983). Blind training works where the students have major learning disabilities or where certain algorithms are taught simply to provide the answer. In the case of study skills, we are not usually in a closed situation where algorithms or other tactics are appropriate: the situation usually requires planning a strategy, with monitoring and checking to see if the strategy is working or not.

Study skills then may be taught blind, as *tactics*, or metacognitively as *strategies*. That is, students can be taught to carry out certain actions ('underline the key word in each sentence'; 'keep your notes in alphabetical order within each subject'; 'set up a time schedule so that most time is spent on the more important subjects') with or without metacognitive awareness of the purpose behind those actions, and whether anyone checks that the purpose is or is not being realised. Teaching study tactics may initially lower anxiety, but performance rarely changes, and usually the tactics are rejected. A survey of several thousand British Sixth Form students who had been provided with courses in study skills produced very mixed results (Tabberer, 1984). Few students responded positively in the long term. Most paid initial lip service or were unaffected, giving as reasons that they already had established 'their' ways of working that were familiar to them, or rationalised that the advice was already familiar but had been found not to work 'for them'.

Martin and Ramsden (1985) organised two study skills classes for first year history students at a British university. One class was given a traditional series of lectures and exercises on study skills (note taking, examinations, writing essays, etc.). The other group was taught in a metacognitive framework developed by Gibbs (1981), in which students in pairs and larger groups compared their work, deriving insight into how they went about their assignments. The 'tactical' class reacted much more enthusiastically at first, but by the end of the second term were not performing particularly well and for the most part had by now rejected the skills taught them, with much the same kinds of rationalisations that Tabberer talked about. The metacognitively taught class started slowly but by the end of the term they had changed their approaches to learning, as gauged from student interviews; they performed better in their assignments and, even more interestingly, they had raised their conceptions of learning, the majority holding level 4 or 5 conceptions, as opposed to level 3 for the 'tactical' class.

Edwards (1986) conducted a study with two Hunter Valley Year 11 classes, using the Study Habits Evaluation and Instruction Kit (SHEIK) (Jackson, Reid and Croft, 1980), and a control class who continued with normal lessons. The experimental classes completed an evaluation of study habits questionnaire which told the students how they were going about study, in comparison to others; they then individually discussed the possible need for change, and how they might go about that. There were then seven sessions, one per week, which in effect presented students with the possible ways of changing their approach in the following areas: place of study, planning times of study, organisation of study, reading skills, taking notes, studying for examinations and examination technique. The ground was thus prepared: self-evaluation led to a perceived need for change, and then help with how to do that was provided. The students were all intending to go on to the HSC the following year and so were well motivated to change. Edwards assessed the students' approaches to learning on the Learning Process Questionnaire (see Chapter 10) before and after the intervention, and later followed up the HSC performance of both groups. She found that the SHEIK groups both improved their deep and achieving approaches to learning, while the surface approach remained unchanged (see Figure 4.3A): and that their HSC performance was an average of 35 aggregate marks higher, in comparison to the control group.

An interesting comparison to this study is one conducted by Biggs and Rihn (1984) in the quite different context of Stanford University, where two cohorts of 55 and 58 students were followed through a course called 'Effective Learning Skills', which brought in metacognitive processes through self-monitoring, peer tutoring and encounter groups; an ordinary study skills text (Pauk, 1974) was provided as one source of activities to be metacognitive about. The results were similar to Edwards', except that in this case surface motives and strategies significantly declined as well (the students were already excessively surface oriented, and academically 'at risk', unlike Edwards' Year 11s who were unselected HSC candidates. Deep approach and achieving strategy significantly increased and grade point average significantly increased from between C and D average before the course, to between A and B up to two terms afterwards (see Figure 4.3B).

The importance of these studies is that they emphasise the need to change the students' *approach* to learning and, through that, performance, rather than improving performance per se by simply telling them what to do. It is not a matter of teaching a new set of skills which are metacognitive, so much as *teaching cognitive skills metacognitively*.

In all the group sessions mentioned above, students brought problems and subject content from their ordinary studies as examples: learning is always about content. No

Figure 4.3   **Changes in approach to learning after encouraging metacognition**

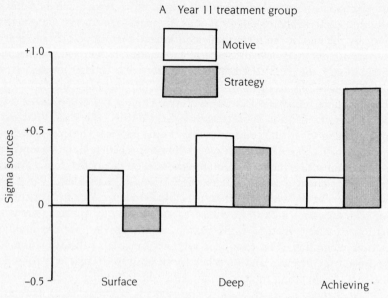

A   Year 11 treatment group

Source: Adapted from Edwards, 1986.

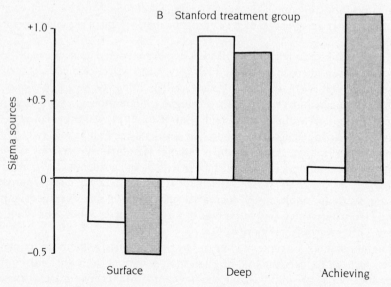

B   Stanford treatment group

Source: Adapted from Biggs and Rihn, 1984.

matter how much we encourage metacognition, there must be valid and ongoing learning to be metacognitive about.

Self-questioning. Changing students' general approaches to learning from surface towards deep-achieving is training them to be metacognitive on a broad front: 'What do I really want out of this? What will I settle for? Given my resources, what's my best way of proceeding?' Heuristics are set questions that learners may use to give themselves a nudge at crucial points, and that help structure these questions with respect to particular tasks. The classic heuristic is Polya's *How to Solve It* (see Box 4.1) which was developed for mathematics at tertiary level, but the idea can be applied to all sorts of tasks.

Kurzeja (1986), for example, adapted the *How to Solve It* paradigm for use with teaching library skills to 52 Year 3 children in a West Australian inner city primary school. She devised a 'Copy Cat' game whereby she thought aloud at each step of the heuristic about what she might do and the children imitated her: she then gradually withdrew, leaving the children verbalising the steps to themselves with each new problem. The children modelling the steps were able to use the library more successfully than non-metacognitively taught children: they were able to solve more difficult transfer problems, and were (naturally enough) more able to talk about the steps in solving library problems.

Another general problem solver is Bransford and Stein's (1984) IDEAL:

I — Identify the problem.
D — Define what it is by representing it in some way.
E — Explore possible strategies for solving it.
A — Act on selected strategies.
L — Look back over solution and evaluate it.

Such strategies do not describe any *particular* actions, and are in no sense a substitute for content knowledge. What they do is help people put whatever content knowledge they have to better use by nudging them at the crucial parts of any problem to stop and take stock of what they are doing and why. Not to do so is like a motorist who is unsure of the way, but waits for the end of the road before finding out if it is the right one or not. Some learners similarly learn algorithmically: they automatically run through the procedure before checking that it is the right one.

In this same category of 'self-nudging devices' is the SQ3R method of studying: 'the Australian crawl of study methods' (Robinson, 1946). The student is taught to:

Survey — the headings and summaries of a chapter before reading it.
Question — what questions do you think will be answered by the content?
Read — find out whether the content does answer the questions.
Recite — the question–answer combinations until you 'know' them.
Review — from time to time to see that you still remember the answers.

Again, the evidence is that it does work, given sufficient dedication by the student to do these things. One danger here is that the questions can be misleadingly put, and pitched at too factual a level.

SQ3R is a self-directed reading strategy aimed basically — but not necessarily — at tertiary students. Paris (Paris, Cross and Lipson, 1984; Paris and Oka, in press) aimed at beginning and primary level readers, not by teaching them such a formalised system as SQ3R, but by teaching them to understand what good reading strategies are for. This program he called Informed Strategies for Learning, and it is described in Chapter 6.

In Paris's case, as with Kurzeja, the self-nudges were built into and designed to suit the task being taught. The procedure is widely generalisable: probably most tasks that students will eventually need to carry out by themselves could be taught in this way. The teacher needs to work out at what point nudges would be most helpful, and, according to the task, what form they should take. Public modelling is strongly advised, as that way students will themselves discuss the points at which they have difficulty. An adult thinking aloud in private is likely to miss aspects that novices might need to be nudged about.

An ambitious program for teaching science in a Melbourne High School in Years 9 and 11 sets out as its first objective: 'Increased knowledge of the elements of metacognition' (Baird, in press; Baird and White, 1984). The specific point of departure is a question-asking checklist and evaluation and recording materials used by the student. The checklist is based on a series of heuristic-like questions that students might systematically ask themselves, and the students then evaluated themselves on an evaluation card.

The study was 'action research' conducted as a case study, without a control group or pre- and post-tests. Students were closely monitored by observation, their self-evaluations and notebooks, interviews with students and the teacher, video and audio recordings of lessons in progress, and so forth. Success for the method was judged on the change in the way students went about their learning. Students were initially dependent and receptive, with the teacher dominant, but over the 23 weeks of the intervention, students came to exert greater control over their learning, although the teacher was still dominant ('he still talks a lot ... doesn't allow students to battle with the work and generate their own questions ...'). Nevertheless, evaluation cards showed that the students made more decisions and understood more often, and at higher levels, why they did particular things. This led to carry-over into other areas: the Geography teacher was impressed that 'the students now asked, unprompted, many questions of an insightful nature'. The work is still in progress but it is an interesting example of how a metacognitive approach can be built into a traditional curriculum. The problems and difficulties arise mainly in the way in which, like Johnson Abercrombie's groups, the teacher's role shifts in ways that some teachers find hard to adapt to.

Wong (1985) reviews some 27 studies using self-questioning techniques in reading comprehension, ranging from learning disabled primary school students to college and university level, and finds uniform success: the only failure of the technique has been through inadequate time or training in question generation.

ASSESSING LEARNING OUTCOMES QUALITATIVELY

How can we assess the more complex learning outcomes; the so-called S–D ratio referred to above? There are two dimensions to be considered: the level of the data (whether we are dealing with motor skills, concrete facts, concepts or high order principles); and how well put together those data are. The first point refers to the *mode* of operation; the teacher needs to be clear about the target mode of the content to be learned. The second point refers to the *level of structural complexity* the student achieves within that mode. This structure was first observed in learning outcomes in school tasks, and may be used as a method of systematically classifying student progress: hence the SOLO taxonomy.

The SOLO taxonomy

Biggs and Collis (1982) showed that over a large variety of mainly school-based tasks, there is a consistent sequence in the way aspects of the task become related together. Although this sequence resembles the kind of developmental sequence that Piaget noted over childhood and early adolescence (see Chapter 5), it is not limited to particular stages of cognitive development: it is a *learning cycle* that applies over several developmental stages. The cycle has five general levels as in Table 4.1.

Table 4.1   Modes and levels in the SOLO taxonomy

Mode		*Structural level* (SOLO)
Previous	1.	*Prestructural.* The task is engaged, but the learner is distracted or misled by an irrelevant aspect belonging to a previous stage or mode.
	2.	*Unistructural.* The learner focuses on the relevant domain, and picks up one aspect to work with.
Target	3.	*Multistructural.* The learner picks up more and more correct or relevant features, but does not integrate them together.
	4.	*Relational.* The learner now integrates the parts with each other, so that the whole has a coherent structure and meaning.
Next	5.	*Extended abstract.* The learner now generalises the structure to take in new and more abstract features, representing a higher mode of operation.

The focus of the learning cycle is on what happens within the target mode, at levels 2, 3 and 4. The progression through levels is not necessarily hard and fast or at a fixed pace. Some learners in some tasks skip quickly through the unistructural level, quickly picking up the many features of a task, but then may take a long time to construct a way of integrating them, if at all. In other tasks, integration may be proceeding from the early stages in some aspects but not in others. These cycles then simply provide a language for describing what seems to happen: they are not prescriptions that must be followed. Let us look at an example.

A geographical example. A lesson has been given on the formation of rain, and the question is asked: 'Why is the side of a mountain that faces the coast usually wetter than the inland side?' The following responses are given by students:

1. 'Because it rains more on the side facing the sea.'
2. 'The sea breeze hits the coastal side first.'
3. 'Well, the sea breezes pick up moisture from the sea and as they hit the coastal side first, they drop their moisture so that when they cross to the other side there's no rain left for the inland side.'
4. 'Because the prevailing winds are from the sea and when they blow across they pick up water vapour, and continuing, hit the coastal ranges. They are then forced upwards and in so doing get colder so that the moisture condenses forming rain. By the time they cross the mountains the winds are dry.'
5. 'Only if the prevailing winds are from the sea, which is likely to be the case. When this is so, the winds pick up water vapour evaporated from the sea, where it is carried to the coastal slopes, rises and is deposited in the form of rain. Not only is the wind now dryer, but as it is carried up the mountain further it is compressed, which has a warming effect so is relatively much less saturated than before. The effect is similar to the "Chinooks" or warm spells experienced on the eastern slopes of the Canadian Rockies in winter. However, all these effects assume certain wind and temperature conditions. If these changed, then so would the energy exchanges and the effects would then be different.'

It can be seen that these five responses correspond, in ascending order, to the five points in the SOLO learning cycle. **1.** is not incorrect, but has nothing to do with the lesson content or what the teacher intends to elicit. It is a tautology created by reflecting or reaffirming the question. **2, 3** and **4** are all within the target mode: the facts and details the teacher gave are addressed skimpily in **2**, with more elaboration in **3**, but even **3** does not give a causal explanation; the student strings together events whose interrelationship is not made clear and hence those details lack any real meaning. **4** does show evidence that their meaning has been understood: temperature change is related to the picking up and deposition of moisture. **5** makes use of a higher order principle of heat exchange, which explains not only the particular problem of coastal rain, but related phenomena such as the Canadian Chinooks. This generalisation thus brings in a whole new and broader set of issues, and typically lacks 'closure' in that all sorts of possibilities emerge.

Clarifying the target mode. This last response raises a very important educational question. Is higher up the taxonomy necessarily better? It could be well imagined that some teachers would react with irritation to **5**. The lesson was not about Chinooks: the student is padding the answer with irrelevancies, possibly only showing off. Other teachers might be pleased that the student did see the generalisation. In fact, response **5** did not come from the class but was made up in order to illustrate an extended abstract response to the coastal rain question. Nevertheless, the question it raises is an important one; and the answer is that in instructional design the *target* mode is the operative one, not the next higher mode of an extended abstract response. Thus, the relational level, showing that the data have been meaningfully integrated within that mode, is normally the level aimed at as indicating that the quality of learning is adequate. It might well be that learning particular facts or items will be useful sub-goals along the way for some tasks and some students, but the ultimate goal is surely the integration of these components in a way that makes sense to the students and is consistent with the content taught. An extended abstract response is either a bonus or an irrelevance as far as the target mode is concerned, although of course that level of abstraction may become a target mode in *subsequent* instruction. Had this example been a genuine one, it would have indicated that that student was placed at an inappropriately low level.

It is therefore important to define the target mode quite clearly, and to operate within it. Students may bring their own frames of reference to bear. For example, a poem *The Man in the Ocelot Suit* by Christopher Brookhouse was given separately to some Year 9 and mature age students to read, and then they were asked to write a reply to the question 'What does this poem mean to you?' (Biggs and Collis, 1982a, pp. 96ff). The poem is a surrealistic story about a man who dresses up in an ocelot suit to frighten the neighbour's dog. Two responses were:

(a) 'Nothing very much I'm afraid but it does seem like a new style of writing' (from a 14-year-old Year 9 student).
(b) 'Life must contain some eccentricities' (from a 35-year-old mature age student).

What is the SOLO level of each response?

(a) seems clearly to be unistructural: the student does not understand the content, but recalls something from poetry lessons about writing style and suggests that that is an appropriate way of looking at the poem. It is not much, but it is an aspect deriving from the target mode. (b) is in fact quite abstract: the student has thought about the whole story and generalised it to a comment (albeit a banal one) on life itself. Both are, however, classified as unistructural: (a) as unistructural within the target mode of the lesson, (b) as unistructural within the target mode imposed by an adult reader. One could, however, classify the latter as extended abstract in terms of the first target mode (and depending on what the lessons were about).

The nature of target modes varies considerably of course from primary, through secondary, to tertiary levels of education, but the unistructural–multistructural–relational cycle repeats itself within all modes, with the prestructural and extended abstract levels indicating that the target mode has been missed in the former case and surpassed in the latter. This raises a very important curriculum issue: by carefully defining modes, one can then rationalise desirable curriculum objectives at school, college or university according to SOLO level within the modes appropriate to the institution (Collis and Biggs, 1983). This matter is however best discussed in the context of Chapter 5.

Evaluation. The SOLO taxonomy might be regarded as a criterion-referenced measure (see Chapter 10) of learning quality where quality rather than quantity (x problems correct) is the criterion. As responses become more and more complex, ascending the taxonomy, they become more abstract, incorporate more features or dimensions, increase the use of organising principles, become more consistent and encourage slower closure.

Criterion-referenced learning is particularly valuable because it provides immediate and visible feedback to both teacher and student. A student, for example, might seize upon the first or most striking thing in the text, and close on that before seeing that there are other relevant points to be made; the unistructural responses are evidence to both teacher and student that the latter's strategy is inappropriate. SOLO provides the teacher with both a structure and a vocabulary to express to the student some important features of good learning. For example, two students could easily make the same points in an essay, but whereas one student interrelates them and reaches a relational level (hence say a 'credit'), the other simply lists them, and thus gives a typical multistructural response (which might be coded simply a 'pass'). The scheme makes the marking system explicit.

These considerations raise the matter of intelligent question-setting on the part of the teacher. The question 'What are the main factors that led to the Franco-Prussian War?' can be answered perfectly by a multistructural listing of the points: the student is not asked to interrelate, to compare and contrast with another war, to speculate on what might have happened if Bismarck had died or been ill, and so on. If a listing is what the teacher really wanted and expected, then fair enough; if not, then the students should not be penalised for producing multistructural answers to a multistructural question.

The main point about the design and use of SOLO items to be made here is that SOLO level directly refers to the structure–data ratio, particularly at the interface between multistructural and relational levels: multistructural responses are data rich but lacking in structure, while relational responses emphasise the structural relations that give meaning to the data. Some relations will be better than others, of course; that is for the teacher to judge as appropriate to the subject matter in question. SOLO simply provides a yardstick for judging the extent to which relational concepts are used at all.

Conceptions, approaches and outcomes. Finally, we might use SOLO as a relational concept to integrate the 3P theme to this chapter. If we turn back to the five levels of conception of learning discussed earlier, we see that they too fit the SOLO structure:

1. Learning is 'knowing more'. Like the prestructural coastal rain example, this conception is little more than tautology; it does not specify what it means to know more.

2. Memorising by heart certainly specifies one relevant aspect of learning but it is limited, and represents a unistructural way of looking at learning.
3. Acquiring facts and skills to be used when necessary is multistructural, with the stress on the number of facts and skills, rather than on their meaning.
4. Finding out what something means is another way of saying that in learning we find a relating concept or idea that links unrelated facts and details, making them into a meaningful whole.
5. Constructing a personal philosophy or world view is extending meanings obtained from a particular learning context into a new and broader context.

As described in Section A, these conceptions fall into two broad categories: quantitative views of learning (levels 1–3) and qualitative (levels 4 and 5). Like learning outcomes, then, conceptions split at the multistructural and relational interface. Further, the quantitative conception links with a surface approach to learning, and the qualitative with deep (achieving may be associated with either); while surface approaches lead to multistructural outcomes or lower, and deep to relational and extended abstract (Van Rossum and Schenk, 1984; Watkins, 1983).

There is then a constantly recurring dualism throughout presage, process and product stages of learning. The individual brings a conception of what learning is into the current context, which determines the approach used, which in turn produces a congruent outcome (see Figure 4.4).

In the quantitative view, learning is an activity that involves surface processing of data as accurately as possible, to yield pre- or unistructural outcomes (irrelevant or impoverished learning) or multistructural outcomes (good learning). In the qualitative view, learning is an activity that gives meaning to known data in relational outcomes, and becomes incorporated in the student's world view in extended abstract outcomes.

The quantity/quality split reflects two fundamentally different views of education, whether held by teacher or learner, and there is hardly any educational decision that is unaffected by where one stands on the issue. Teaching decisions with respect to curriculum objectives, methods of instruction and evaluation all communicate a message that affects a student's conception of learning: the best message is one that emphasises structure and quality, not sheer quantity.

Figure 4.4   The dualism in conceptions, approaches and outcomes of learning

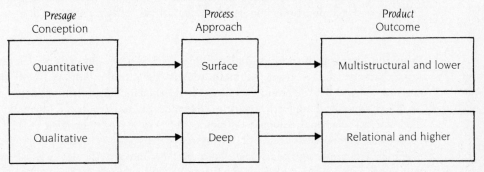

SUMMARY

Who is responsible for self-direction? Children are often reluctant to accept responsibility for directing their own learning: they believe that that is the school's responsibility. Much about the school environment reinforces that view. The problem becomes twofold:

1. *Remove factors that encourage a surface approach.* Two sets of factors encourage students to surface learn, and both spring from the management structures that are necessary to administer schools and other institutions. These structures can be the source of *pressure* on students, creating anxiety and stress; so that learning simply becomes a means of avoiding the anxiety; and they can be the source of *cynicism*, which encourages students to bargain, and to beat the system.

2. *Create situations that encourage metalearning.* Several techniques may be used to encourage metalearning. Some are more suitable for certain subjects than others, but most can be adapted to suit many lessons:

- *Think-aloud modelling*, where the teacher thinks out loud while performing a task, preferably with a (public) A/V aid like an overhead, and requires the students to contribute.
- *Peer teaching* is an old but most effective device, which relies on the fact that teaching others requires one to be metacognitive about one's own learning.
- *Reflective teaching* requires students to peer-teach exotic content so that they reflect on the teaching process itself.
- *Peer groups* make use of the fact that it is easier to become aware of our own processes when, in performing a common task or discussing a common topic, we interact closely with others like us.
- *Using learning theory* as a language for discussing learning processes in peer groups has been used to help students define their own processes more clearly.
- *Teaching study skills* can be effective if they are taught strategically or metacognitively, rather than 'blind' or tactically. They particularly address achieving strategies, organising and planning, and require high motivation.
- *Self-questioning* involves learning heuristics that require the student to stop at critical phases and ask questions about direction, course, effectiveness to date, possible options, etc.

Assessing learning outcomes qualitatively. The SOLO taxonomy is a hierarchical coding scheme that allows judgment of the structural complexity of learning outcomes. Typically, the learner acquires a little, then increasingly more detail, until it can be restructured under a relating concept: this unistructural, through multi-structural, to relational sequence defines a *learning cycle* while the *target mode* of a task refers to the level of abstraction of, or nature of, the contents. Irrelevant or immature responses are prestructural, while those that go beyond the level of abstraction required for the target are extended abstract. Multistructural responses have a low

S–D ratio, relational responses a high S–D ratio. Deep learning is concerned with constructing effective relational, and later extended abstract, responses and belongs with a qualitative conception of learning. Surface learning is concerned with accruing multistructural responses, and belongs with a quantitative conception of learning.

In this section, then, we have looked at ways in which the teacher can operationalise all facets of learning from presage, through process, to product stages. The challenge to teachers is to induce metacognitive processes in students when there are so many factors that tend to work in the opposite direction.

FURTHER READING

On student learning in general
J. Biggs, *Student Approaches to Learning and Studying*, Australian Council for Educational Research, Hawthorn, Victoria, 1986.
F. Marton, D. Hounsell and N. Entwistle (eds), *The Experience of Learning*, Scottish Academic Press, Edinburgh, 1984.
J. Wilson, *Student Learning in Higher Education*, London, Croom Helm, 1981.

The first book describes research carried out in Australian high schools, colleges and universities leading up to the 3P model and the development of two questionnaires of study skills. *The Experience of Learning* is a collection of papers by some of the leading European workers in this field. Particular attention is drawn to chapters by Entwistle, Marton and Saljo, Ramsden and Hounsell. Most of the examples are tertiary level, but the relevance to other levels is clear. Wilson's book summarises the field of student learning, and refers to a number of researchers.

On the use of heuristics
J. Bransford and B. Stein, *The IDEAL Problem Solver*, W. H. Freeman. New York, 1984.
G. Polya, *How to Solve it*, Princeton University Press, 1945.

Polya's book, which has been through many editions since the original, describes the use of heuristics to undergraduate mathematics learning, and how they may be extended to problems in general. The IDEAL system is much simpler and more generalised.

On assessing the structure of learning outcomes
J. Biggs and K. Collis, *Evaluating the Quality of Learning: The SOLO Taxonomy*, Academic Press, New York, 1982.

The major source for the SOLO Taxonomy, describing how open-end responses can be classified into the five basic SOLO levels. Examples are drawn from the subjects of English, reading, mathematics, geography, modern languages and history.

On study skills
G. Gibbs, *Teaching Students to Learn*, Open University Press, Milton Keynes, 1981.
P. Jackson, N. Reid and A. Croft, *Study Habits Evaluation and Instruction Kit (SHEIK)*, Australian Council for Educational Research, Hawthorn, Victoria, 1980.

Two approaches to study skills: Gibbs' highly student-centred and non-directive, SHEIK, rather structured but can be used metacognitively.

On using groups for metacognitive learning

Johnson Abercrombie, *The Anatomy of Judgment*, Penguin Books, Harmondsworth, Middlesex, 1969.

G. Collier, *The Management of Peer-group Learning*, Society for Research in Higher Education, Guildford, Surrey, 1983.

D. Johnson and F. Johnson, *Joining Together: Group Theory and Group Skills*, Prentice-Hall, Englewood Cliffs, 1975.

Johnson Abercrombie and Collier are concerned with tertiary level group work (described in this chapter); Johnson and Johnson, any age, with 'structured exercises' inviting reflection by group participants.

QUESTIONS

Questions for self-testing

1. Use your own words to explain what is meant by the term 'metacognition'.
2. Give an example of metacognition in reading, writing and problem solving.
3. Is a mathematics algorithm a strategy or a tactic?
4. Provide five conceptions of learning.
5. Distinguish between qualitative and quantitative conceptions of learning.
6. Identify three approaches to learning and distinguish between them.
7. Match the three learning situations — presage, process, product — with one of the following descriptions: approaches to learning; factors brought in by the student or in the classroom; outcomes of learning; feedback from learning; prior experience.
8. Distinguish between cognitive and affective learning outcomes.
9. How can teachers encourage students to be metacognitive about their learning?
10. What do the initials of the problem solver acronym IDEAL stand for?
11. Match the following levels of the SOLO taxonomy to previous, target, next modes: extended abstract, multistructural, prestructural, relational, unistructural.
12. Distinguish between surface and deep learning.

Questions for discussion

1. What effect on learning would *this chapter* lead you to expect from the use of questions and overviews? Is this effect any different from that which you expected after reading Chapter 2? Did either effect occur for your learning of these chapters?

2. 'It is very difficult to feel accomplishment over learning trivial masses of unrelated detail ...' Why, then, is 'Trivial Pursuit' so popular?

3. In your experience as a student, what do you remember about the classroom structure which may have discouraged you from being metacognitive about your learning?

4. During in-school experience or practice teaching, try to make an opportunity to sit-in when a friend is teaching, and ask one or more peers to observe your teaching. You could try some team teaching, perhaps. After the lesson, conduct a metacognitive discussion about the teaching.

5. Your senior secondary class asks you to give them a talk on study skills. What will you say?

Part 3

Individual development in the context of society: Developmental and social processes

According to the fifth and highest conception of learning, content learning in school subjects is only the beginning. Each individual, in varying ways and with varying success, tries to *make sense* out of experience. Cognitive and social development describe how we try to make increasingly better sense out of our experience of the physical world, and out of our interactions with other people.

What, then, are the ways in which people make sense out of things? Bruner (1985) draws attention to two, the way of the *scientist* and the way of the *storyteller*. The picture that each paints is quite distinct, and each is valid for its own purposes. We can use them to complement each other, or use one to exclude the other. We can use either one effectively or poorly.

Bruner calls the way of the scientist *paradigmatic* — following the paradigms of science, dealing with general causes. It establishes that we 'know' by reference to objective fact, and that we judge in accordance with an accepted framework of knowledge based on formal procedures, empirical evidence and logical argument. The knowledge so 'accepted' underpins society, and this way of thinking runs technology, business, politics and establishments. Many terms describe the paradigmatic way: logical, based on fact, rational, convergent, linear, unbiased, verifiable by anyone who follows the rules, (dubiously) left hemisphere and (by now aging storytellers) 'headshit'. Paradigmatic knowledge, and the frame of mind best accommodated to it, is what is expected and encouraged in schools.

The way of the storyteller is the way of *narrative*. It is not concerned with fact or truth, but truth-likeness (or verisimilitude). It leads to good stories, gripping drama, believable historical accounts, and the understanding of human affairs. The way of narrative is less well regarded in our society. The arts have a lower value than technology; to appreciate and value something for its own sake is seen as less important than using knowledge to predict, control and create wealth. Our society does not, as do some others, make functional use of narrative knowledge within society. The corresponding terms here are: intuitive, based on feeling, divergent lateral, creative, subjective, value-laden and (again, with reservation) right hemisphere. This kind of knowledge is dealt with in schools, but many would say trivially or inappropriately.

As we grow older, we increasingly come to make sense of the world by using the paradigmatic way, the narrative way, or both. Even educational researchers use both. Some use the paradigms of science, others the narrative descriptions of ethnography and phenomenology. Marton (1985), for example, says researchers should try to discover what the child's conception of the world currently is and, when that is understood, we shall be better able to help see what is wrong with it, and lead the child towards more adequate conceptions. In Chapter 5, we see what 'alternative frameworks' children have constructed to make sense of their world, and how teachers might use that knowledge; in Chapter 7, Davies (1982) describes how children perceive their social world and how it relates to the world of school. Chapters 2 and 3, on the other hand, were based on the paradigmatic way of knowing.

Young children take to the narrative way of knowing quickly and naturally as they interpret their world in terms of myth, fantasy and fairy tale. The paradigmatic way is acquired painfully and through formal instruction. That both exist, and develop at different rates, contributes towards the fact that the course of cognitive growth is uneven.

We continue at first with the individual perspective on development. Chapter 5 traces how knowledge develops both 'horizontally' and 'vertically': in extent and in depth of understanding. From birth until early adulthood, the level of abstraction of the preferred mode of thinking increases.

Development throughout adulthood is mainly concerned with meta-cognitive aspects. Children's alternative frameworks involve an organisation and a level of abstraction below that needed for understanding the accepted frameworks of paradigmatic knowledge. This chapter addresses the question of what are suitable exit levels of understanding at various stages of secondary and tertiary education, with particular but not exclusive reference to the science curriculum.

Chapter 6 is concerned with language development, both oral and written. Implications for the teaching of reading and writing are discussed. Written language is particularly useful for helping students reflect on their thinking, whatever the content area. Unfortunately, essays and other written modes are used for assessing learning, which often diminishes rather than enhances learning. The question of second language learning is raised, in particular how multicultural and assimilation models affect ESL students and their learning.

Chapter 7 deals with socialisation: acquiring the values and frameworks that are socially determined. Children form their own worlds; these may conflict with, or complement, the adult world. As metacognition underpins 'responsible self-direction', so does social learning and moral development underpin 'moral autonomy'. We see a conflict between stated aims and practice in the second area corresponding to that already noted with the first: conformity is the surface learning of the affective domain.

Chapter 8 deals with the single issue that gives most beginning teachers most concern: classroom management. Despite the disjunction between stated aims and actual practice, we see a confluence evolving between shifts in society and in-school developments, which gives considerable hope that we will arrive at viable methods of management. The classroom context provides a meeting ground where teacher and students may 'negotiate' a collaborative network within which it is possible for both parties to realise at least some of their goals. That need not be a bad deal at all. It calls for managerial skills of a kind parallel to those required outside the classroom, rather than a discipline imposed by sheer force of personality.

5

Cognitive development

OVERVIEW

The chapter explains how children develop competence at handling and understanding the physical world; how, in Bruner's terms explained in the introduction to Part 3, they increasingly take on the way of the scientist. How do we explain that progression? What course does it take? These and the following questions are answered:

- What kinds of things do children typically do at different ages?
- Do children operate evenly across school subjects according to their stage of development?
- What role does physiology play in cognitive development?
- How can we distinguish between learning and developmental phenomena?
- What aspects of Piagetian theory are useful for educators, and what are actually misleading?
- Can a simple logical test be administered to see if a child is 'ready' to be taught arithmetic?
- What sort of cognitive development goes on into and through adulthood?
- How can we tie cognitive development to curriculum objectives at different levels of schooling?
- What are some 'alternative frameworks' that children use at different ages to explain natural phenomena?
- What lessons does adult and continuing education hold for ordinary schooling?

By the end of this chapter, you should be able to:

1. Take a topic and show how it may be structured in concrete–symbolic and formal–1 modes of thinking.
2. Distinguish between the accretion, the structuring and the generalising of knowledge.
3. Devise a demonstration of some physical phenomenon, and show how children's explanations fall short of a scientifically acceptable explanation.
4. Explain how children may be helped to progress from one developmental mode to the next.
5. Design curriculum objectives in a topic of your choice, structuring them using the SOLO taxonomy to suit a generalist Year 10, an academic Year 10 and an academic Year 12 student.
6. Explain how, in terms of cognitive sophistication, science fiction is different from science fantasy.
7. Diagnose the symptoms of a budding midlife crisis.
8. Explain how adults improve with age in their cognitive abilities, despite supposed loss of brain cells from early adulthood onwards.
9. Use children's 'alternative' knowledge for teaching them a topic in the science curriculum in a way that brings them closer to 'accepted' knowledge.

SECTION A

THE COURSE OF COGNITIVE GROWTH

The thinking of educators and developmental psychologists has been dominated by the notion of *stages*. There are two reasons for this. First, stages are very convenient ways of looking at children's growth. By and large in Western society, we find that there are key periods during which most children learn to do some very important things. In infancy, children learn to co-ordinate their movements in relation to their physical environment. At two, all but the handicapped are learning to speak. At six years, most children are on the way to learning how to read and then to write. And by adolescence, most children are beginning to theorise about their world: to think abstractly in terms of the possible, and how their world might otherwise be. Here, then, we have a sequence of increasingly abstract activities — making co-ordinated movements, learning language then other symbol systems, and theorising — which all children (in our society) seem to go through at approximately similar ages. Further, we have designed social rites and institutions, such as schools and universities, at least to endorse and hopefully to promote, these developments.

Second, philosophers and psychologists, of whom Piaget was the most significant, tried to explain the structure and genesis of human knowledge. The highest and most complex human thinking in adults can be described by symbolic logic, which Piaget (1950) took to be the goal towards which cognitive development was directed. He therefore studied how children solved tight logical problems, starting with extremely simple ones (hiding objects in the romper room with varying degrees of subtlety), through to formal logical and mathematical problems in adolescence. He found that the tasks were solved in steps — little progress for a long time and then a fairly rapid solution for several tasks of the same logical structure. The steps were associated with an extra logical dimension, and the ages at which they occurred corresponded moderately well with the ages mentioned in the previous section.

Piaget then proposed that thinking developed in stages, and each stage had its own logical integrity (a 'structured whole' as Piaget called it). To use a computing analogy, it was as if a master program was called out at each stage to control all cognitive processes — and not only those used to structure the physical world. The social world, as well as moral judgment, would be subject to the same program (Kohlberg, 1969). In particular, students would react 'evenly' towards school tasks, and in a way determined by their current stage.

For several years the Piagetian model governed 'progressive' educational thought (Furth, 1970; Ginsburg and Opper, 1979; Lovell, 1961) but it now appears that the straight Piagetian model is too simplistic. Children do not consistently approach tasks in the way their developmental stage says they 'should' (Fischer and Sylvan, 1985); this is particularly noticed in school tasks, where students use different approaches in different subject areas, and even in the same subject from one day to the next (Biggs and Collis, 1982a). Finally it is becoming clear that late adolescence is not, as Piaget thought, the peak of cognitive development (Knox, 1977; Levinson et al., 1978).

In this chapter, we look at a 'neo-Piagetian' theory of development which takes into account much of what Piaget discovered, and also a considerable amount of work done by others, and which allows for the kinds of unevenness that characterises so much school learning. There is also an important and still rapidly developing body of research in the 'alternative frameworks' that children use to help them make sense of their world. This work is particularly relevant to science teaching at primary and high school. We also take a quick look at developments throughout adulthood, and the implications for continuing education.

DEVELOPMENT AND LEARNING

The key to understanding cognitive development, and what teachers might do about it, is contained in the two concepts *optimal level* and *skill acquisition* (Fischer and Pipp, 1984). Optimal level refers to the undisputed fact that there are upper limits to the level of complexity that a person can handle, and that these upper limits are at least partially age-related. Skill acquisition refers to the way skills or competencies grow up until they reach their optimal level.

The two questions thus become: *What* develops? *How?* 'What' is concerned with *development,* 'how' with *learning.* As we have already discussed, learning has both quantitative and qualitative aspects; it is associated with how much, how well (and perhaps how quickly) a particular task is mastered. Development refers more to the *nature* of the task that can be handled at various ages.

What develops?

Whether or not we agree with a stage theory as such, it is obvious that the *kinds of things* that people are able to do are limited by their age. Babies can learn to find things that are hidden from them, but they cannot use words to wonder about where they might have been hidden. Seven-year-olds can learn to make marks on paper to say what they would like for Christmas instead of telling someone else, but they cannot use symbols to prove an argument is incorrect. No doubt this is partly a matter of learning to walk before running — learning how to write is prerequisite to demonstrating a logical proof — but not entirely. Many people learn to write and are never able to learn logic no matter how hard they try. In short, some kinds of tasks are easier to learn than others.

The Piagetian stages in fact give a strong clue to what is happening: not because logical programs are masterminding how children perform during these stages, but simply because we see that children progressively do different sorts of things. What changes with age is that the task content — the *target mode* of learning referred to in Chapter 4 — becomes progressively more abstract.

What changes in development, then, are the modes of thinking: we are able to handle progressively more abstract content.

Some common modes of thought

What common modes are there? Opinions differ, but reasonable consensus would be found about the following (the ages are when at least *one* significant task is *typically* handled in that mode):

1.   *Sensori-motor* (from birth). The most concrete way of acting towards the world is by *doing something,* giving a motor response, to a sensory stimulus. For the first 18 months, learning becomes very complex, but the content is concerned with co-ordinating actions with each other in increasingly complex patterns, and with the environment. Learning motor skills is something we continue to do well into adulthood but during infancy it is the only form of learning available.

2.   *Ikonic* (from 18 months). To make an action more abstract, it must be represented internally; Piaget himself defined thought as 'the internalisation of action'. The simplest internal representation of an action is to image it, to form an internal picture or 'ikon', as Bruner terms it. The extended abstract version of the sensori-motor mode is therefore called *ikonic,* which begins to occur after the first year and which generalises, with the help of language, after 18 months.

3.   *Concrete–symbolic* (from five years). The next mode deals in concepts and operations, which are linked directly to *concrete* experience by *symbols.* Number operations can be carried out symbolically, yet relate uniquely to real world happenings. There is logic and order between symbols and the world they directly refer to.

4.   *Formal–1 (first order)* (from 12 years). To understand that concepts can relate to other concepts is to talk 'in *principle*'. Principles are more abstract than concepts: concepts relate to concrete happenings, principles to hypothetical happenings. The order to be found in abstractions allows thinking about logical possibilities.

5.   *Formal–2 (second order)* (from 18 years). Principles may relate to other principles and thus form academic *disciplines.* To study, and then to question and reshape these disciplines as is done in research, is to become very abstract indeed.

What goes on *within* these modes is a matter of learning. Given time, motivation, and so on, the optimal level of complexity and competence obtained within modes can be very high, but it may be unrelated to the highest *level of abstraction* a person can handle. A person can have amazing skill in craft, but be quite incapable of understanding the simplest logical arguments. That observation, and the fair degree of universality surrounding the ages at which the first three modes especially appear, suggests that like adolescence itself, physical maturation may be involved.

Does physiology determine when modes may be used? 'Certainly' at the first two modes, then with decreasing certainty at the last, but there the verdict would still be 'very likely'. Precisely *how* physiology affects our ability to handle abstract tasks has, however, received little systematic research (Fischer and Bullock, 1984).

Certain brain functions such as size changes, brain wave patterns and sleep cycles appear to undergo periodic and regular changes that on average seem to parallel the ages at which Piaget's modal changes typically occur. In particular, Epstein (1978) reports large scale studies of rapid growth in brain areas (measured by skull circumference) at the key ages, but these are group averages. When these physical growth spurts are correlated with growth spurts on cognitive tests *within the same individual,* there is no relation. Marsh (1985) reanalysed Epstein's own data and found that spurts did exist, but not in the regular intervals suggested by Epstein.

Case (1985) refers to 'waves of myelinisation' also occurring at the crucial age periods (which would not show up in skull circumference) and says that 'these waves take place in neurological systems which serve different psychological functions' (p. 380). The myelin sheath is a fatty protective coating that improves the efficiency of neural transmission, and these sheaths grow fairly suddenly in different brain areas throughout childhood, the last such wave of myelinisation occurring between 18 and 25 years. Multiple sclerosis is the reverse process, where the sheaths are progressively destroyed, leading to sensori-motor degeneration first, then progressively higher. When these sheaths grow, they protect neurones from interfering with each other, resulting in more rapid and efficient operation. It could easily be the case that progressively higher order (more abstract) thinking becomes possible as more and more areas of the brain start interacting with more efficiency. Whatever the actual mechanism, the idea is quite plausible.

Any physiological explanation is, however, only part of the story. To put it crudely, physiology may determine the 'stuff' out of which codes are made, but it is experience — not input — that forms the content of the codes, and particularly input that *mismatches* existing codes and induces recoding at the higher order level. But it can only go to the higher order level if the 'right stuff' is there to make it from.

This kind of explanation does not require the evenness of performance demanded by stage theory. A person will reach the higher modes only with sufficient and appropriate *experience* in the relevant content: and with a great deal of experience (e.g. with formal writing and schoolwork) that mode may become the preferred option. Thus early in our acquisition of a task there will be a preference for working in a more concrete mode, but later, with experience, we come to operate more efficiently in the most abstract modes. Some say that is the trouble with many academics: they prefer talking about it to actually doing it.

THE MODES WE LEARN WITHIN

Learning has been described as skill acquisition within a mode. There are several aspects to this: the content area, its structure, the amount learned, and the speed or efficiency of learning. And then there is the teacher's role. Broad content areas refer to knowledge of the physical world, language, knowledge of people, and to feelings about them. The particular content to be learned is internalised by rehearsal and coding, as discussed in Chapter 2, while the outcome of those processes was discussed in Chapter 4. Content is accumulated in increasing quantities and, early or late, is coded into meaningful units: the general sequence is that one, then several, relevant aspects are acquired through uni- and multistructural levels until a relational structure integrates them. Developmental change is imminent when, for the first time in an individual's history, an extended abstract response indicates a breakthrough to the next higher mode.

The sensori-motor mode

The infant is born with a few basic reflexes, such as sucking, and an extraordinary degree of plasticity. For the first two months nothing very much seems to be happening from the outside, then the first social reactions occur: reacting to the parent's face, to others, reaching out for objects, following movements with the eyes. The reflex is a hangover, vitally necessary to be sure, from a purely 'biological' phase of existence. The first genuine smile of recognition (and not just wind) is evidence that the first unistructural co-ordination between movements and an outside stimulus has occurred. Now is the time for mobiles to dangle enticingly, for rattles to shake, for Teddies to be clutched; and those actions are what give the objects their meaning. If the rattle is taken away, it will be missed only if it was removed while the baby was shaking it. The action of shaking is what the rattle means. If the baby is doing something else, the rattle is not missed.

Next, at around eight months, objects can be handled in a variety of ways: rattles are thrown, sucked, shaken, as are other objects. It is as though a repertoire of actions is being tried out to see which is best for what. Two or more objects will be used together. For instance, Piaget found that at this level, the baby will miss a stolen rattle and, if it was seen being hidden under a cushion, will crawl there to find it. At the unistructural level that search does not occur. If, however, the rattle is then transferred to another hiding place, and the baby watches the transfer, it still seeks under the *first* hiding place. It is as though the perception of the transfer has not been read in and co-ordinated. That happens in the relational level of sensori-motor functioning, where perceptions and motor action are co-ordinated: what is *seen* becomes the basis for *action*.

The limitations of this final stage are evident if the object is removed when the baby is not looking. When the infant finds that the rattle is not where it is expected to be it gives up, baffled, although the transfer game has been played before. To solve this problem, the transfer has to be imagined; *possible* hiding places have to be checked out. This problem involves the use of an early but genuine form of *hypothesis:* one has to think about what might happen to things in their absence. This, of course, requires something more abstract than a percept or an action to go on. It requires an *internal representation* of the action, or as Bruner puts it, an *ikon*.

The ikonic mode

The ikon is the first and simplest form of internal representation. In a sense it may be regarded as an image, or 'photocopy' of reality, although that conveys too visual and too cognitive a picture. In fact, the distinction between cognition and affect, what is thought and what is felt, is rather unclear, as is the distinction between one emotion and another. As these distinctions become clearer — indeed perhaps to help make them clearer — the child thinks in polarities of good–evil, nice–nasty, like it–hate it.

Naming. Internalisation makes language itself possible. Unless there is some form of inner representation of an object, there is no way the object can be referred to in its absence, because the name is attached to the inner representation, not the object. The ikonic form of inner representation has its limitations; in particular, this global, holistic mix of affect and image, gives it a rigid and unidimensional character.

The single dimension around which the ikon is organised may be *perceptual* or *emotional* in character. In either case, the dimension is often associated with a name or label of some kind: and because the dimension is not analysed, it becomes attached to the name in a very powerful and special way. Thus, naming an object to young children somehow 'explains' all about it to them. If we tell them that a strange new object is a gudgeon-trundler they are satisfied: they have the total percept of the object and now they have its name. Only later will they be full of questions about its use, manufacture, and so on.

Egocentricity. Another aspect of this unidimensionality results in an *egocentric* flavour to ikonic thought. Piaget first used this term in his earlier work (1926), meaning the literal, rather than the moral, sense of 'egocentric'.

Piaget presented four- and five-year-olds with a papier-mâché model of a mountain scene, with a peak on the left and a tree on the right of the model. He asked the children to draw what they saw, and they produced recognisable pictures. He then asked them to draw what someone would see from the *opposite* side of the table. Children before about age seven drew exactly the same picture: they appeared unable to see that their view of the scene was not the only one. Similarly, if young children are asked who is standing to the left of someone in a photograph, they will invariably indicate the person standing on the right (i.e. to their own left). More recently, however, others (e.g. Donaldson, 1978; Borke, 1978) have found that when more familiar situations are used — what a police officer would see at a traffic intersection, or a teddy bear looking behind objects —even three-year-olds can see the other point of view.

Piaget also collected data on what he termed egocentric speech, in which the speaker does not take into account the knowledge and perspective of the listener. He closely observed two six-year-old boys, and noted that 40 per cent of their conversation was entirely self-focused: what appeared to be conversation between them was simply monologue-in-turn, each speaker referring back to where he left off, not to where his conversation partner did. This is not, of course, limited to children: many situation comedies have been written around precisely this scenario. The following exchange illustrates the egocentric viewpoint:

Interviewer:	Do you have any brothers or sisters?
Child:	A sister.
Interviewer:	Any brothers?
Child:	No.
Interviewer:	Does your sister have any brothers then?
Child:	No.

Flavell and his colleagues (1968) carried out several experiments on the ability of young children to take on roles and give information. In one test, two children are separated by a screen, each having the same array of pictures in front of him. One child tells the other which picture he has chosen, and his partner points to a picture in front of him and says, 'This one?' — to which the first child replies 'Yes' (although unable to see which one is being referred to).

Emotion. Unidimensionality extends to the *emotions*. Fischer and Bullock (1984) describe several studies indicating that preschool children are incapable of seeing themselves as experiencing more than one emotion at a time, for example, that a little girl was both happy at receiving a bike for her birthday but sad that it was only a three-speed and not a 10-speed. In another study, a five-year-old was told a story about another little girl who acted both nastily and nicely to another girl. When asked to retell the story afterwards, the child turned it into two separate stories. She told one story about a girl who acted nastily, who 'a long time later', and in quite a different story, acted nicely.

The mythic stage. Where only sensori-motor and ikonic modes are available, and thought is egocentric and emotions are simple, children structure reality by using what is best known and familiar to them: themselves. Not only do they assume that other people think and feel as they do, but so do animals, plants and inanimate features such as rocks. There is an early stage when children believe that animals speak to them, that Teddy is hurt when he is smacked, or that trees get tired as they wave around to make wind. Later, they may know these things are not *really* true, but it is certainly a lot easier making sense out of the world if they assume that they are. Even in primary school, children classify natural phenomena that move, such as clouds, as 'living', although they could classify plants and animals (Angus, 1981): which, as White and Tisher (1983) comment, indicates how difficult it is to eradicate features used to interpret the world before formal instruction commences.

How does a child make best sense out of this — the world of chattering animals, tired trees, inexplicable happenings and simplistic emotions? The paradigmatic way of knowing is not available as the concepts and operations basic to that way are not in the repertoire yet. The other way is by narrative: myths, fables, legends and fairy stories which, as Egan (1984) points out, are what engage young children's minds most powerfully (and indeed also those minds that in other cultures make little use of the paradigmatic way). Fairy stories derive their power, Egan says, because they reflect so accurately the characteristics endemic to the ikonic mode. The characters portray one or two outstanding characteristics (big and bad, poor but honest): meaning is always clear, so is who is to be disapproved of, and the resolution (good will be rewarded). The context is remote ('once upon a time ...') but the time-line linear and inevitable ('... and they lived happily ever after'). Because of this close interweaving of story and psychology, Egan calls childhood the *mythic* stage, while the fascination of high fantasy continues right through primary school and beyond. He argues that the emotional power of myths, and later of romances, should be used to help structure the social science curriculum, engaging children's minds with what they understand best, and react to with meaning.

In fact, the hold that miraculous happenings, the triumph of good over evil, and emotional simplicity has over people extends well into adulthood. These are precisely the ingredients of TV soapies, professional wrestling, and political and religious fundamentalism: even very experienced and powerful people play with the image of an evil empire. What this shows, of course, is that lower level modes are accessible to people who more usually operate within higher and more abstract modes. However, as propagandists and public relations experts know, if you want to influence the maximum number of people, go for those modes that are available to everybody. In the case of communication, that means the ikonic mode because that is the earliest one in which language is viable; lots of pictures, loud repetitive slogans, little written language. It is also that mode in which there is greatest emotional investment and least criticism.

The concrete-symbolic mode

The relational units in the ikonic mode may become very rich, complex and emotionally compelling. The problem is that they do not help run a culture that is ultimately based on the paradigmatic way of knowing. Trees do not talk back; evil does not always get its comeuppance. Time and space have an inevitability that eventually defies wishful thinking.

Aspects, symbols and operations. To illustrate the difference between ikonic and concrete-symbolic units of thought, let us look at one of Piaget's experiments. Three coloured marbles (R for red, Y for yellow, B for blue) are placed in one end of an opaque tube. The tube is tilted, and the child is asked to predict the order in which the marbles will emerge the other end when the tube is rotated. The simplest case is no rotations, and children using the ikonic mode can predict that easily: the ikon or picture-image R-Y-B that comes out is the same as that which went in.

The tube is then rotated one half-turn, which reverses the order. A preschooler will still predict the original order, R-Y-B, and will be very surprised when B-Y-R emerges: so turning makes it backwards! We repeat the trial. This time the correct response is given; it is still fairly easy to read an ikon backwards. We then give *two* half-turns. The reasoning goes: he's still turning, so it's still backwards. Or maybe an extra turn really messes up the order. We may then elicit two replies to this one: B-Y-R (backwards again) or Y-B-R or B-R-Y (really messed up). No: R-Y-B again! Ikons are clumsy and global: there is not all that much you can do with them and they do not predict the physical world very well at all.

In order to handle this little problem effectively, we need to *abstract* or disembed the salient features, and *link* them to some kind of symbol system. The salient features are: that there are only two aspects of the colours to be considered, reverse order and same order, and that the number of turns determines whether the outcome is reverse or same. These features, then, are abstracted elements from the ikon, and make it possible to operate in the concrete-symbolic mode, correctly shadowing the world with symbolic representations, appropriately linked.

The unistructural response is simply to take these two abstractions and co-ordinate them mentally. This breaks down fairly quickly, but if a third element is brought in — *keep count* — the problem is manageable, if clumsy. The multistructural way of handling the problem is, then: one gives reverse, two gives same, three gives reverse, four gives same; keep count of the number of turns actually given.

The relational response is to code the number of turns as an *odd* or an *even* number. All you have to do is to count the number of turns and note if that is odd or even.

What we see developing through the concrete-symbolic mode, then, is:

- use of *aspects* or dimensions of the problem;
- *a symbol system* to represent them;
- a set of appropriate *operations* to perform on the symbols.

This means that the individual is working at one step removed from reality, but still firmly linked with what is given and present in the situation. There are no hypotheticals, or what-ifs.

Conservation. The essence of the concrete-symbolic mode is finding a co-ordinating relationship that gives stability to the task in question. The classic examples Piaget used were on conservation. Lemonade is poured into two identical glasses to the same height. The child agrees that both are the same. One glass is then poured into a tall thin glass so that the lemonade reaches a higher level. If the ikonic mode is used, as it typically is until around five years, the tall glass is chosen 'because there's more'. 'Why?' 'Because it's taller.' When the tall glass is poured into a squat broad glass, the child now prefers the original, because 'it's now taller and there's more in it'.

In the ikonic mode, judgments are based on appearance and total impressions. 'Conservation' demands that appearances be ignored in favour of the co-ordinating relationship: nothing has been added or taken away, so the result remains constant. This point applies whatever the context or however familiar the task; yet Piaget showed that (rather against his own theory then) conservation in the lemonade-and-glass experiments was obtained a year or so earlier than conservation of weight. In the latter experiment, two identical balls of plasticine are placed one in each pan of a balance, and the child agrees that they weigh the same. But if one ball is rolled into a long thin sausage, the child will now state that the sausage weighs more than the ball. Conservation of volume is obtained even later, nearer 11 or 12 years: here the balls of plasticine are each placed into a graduated cylinder already half-filled with water. It is noticed that the water level rises equally in both cases. One of the balls is taken out of its cylinder and rolled into a long thin sausage: the child now predicts that it will displace more water than the ball.

Exactly the same logic can explain all three cases of conservation — quantity, mass and volume —yet the lemonade case is resolved much earlier and more readily than the displacement case. As with early childhood, thinking in middle childhood is still tied to particular situations rather than to general principles. Those situations that are most familiar (lemonade) are grasped much earlier than less familiar ones (displacing water).

Readiness. This sort of result led many to argue that teaching should be withheld until the child was 'ready'; this usually meant until conservation tasks could be successfully completed (e.g. Biggs, 1959; Furth, 1970; Lovell, 1961). If the amount of lemonade in a glass keeps changing when it is poured from one different shaped glass to another, then it would appear that the child has not grasped the idea that unless something has been added or taken away, the net result must remain the same. And in that case, they are not yet 'ready' for arithmetic: five objects are still five in number, whether they are packed together in a close array or spread out in a long line.

That line of argument assumes that the logician's concept of number is what children use, and it is now clear that they do not (Brainerd, 1975). As in other aspects of reality, children construct their own ways of handling particular tasks. Even when they grasped the key point in conservation — that if nothing has been added or taken away the result is the same — for one task, as we have seen, it does not follow that they will see that same point for another task. It is totally unjustified to withhold instruction in an area on the basis of a result on a test that *appears* to involve the same logical principle.

The first order formal mode: Formal–1

Somewhere after beginning high school, some students will show that they can operate in the formal mode, with many giving formal responses by Year 11 and onwards. These responses are, however, more common in the paradigmatic subjects like maths and science. They are *context-free*, which means that they often lack closure or a definite conclusion. Like the extended abstract response on coastal rain, responses in the formal mode often contain phrases like 'Only if ... which is likely to be the case ... the effect is similar to ... all these effects assume ... If these changed, then...' The appreciation of general principle ushers in the world of the possible, of what *might* be the case.

Exhausting what might be the case: the pendulum problem. Let us look at the pendulum problem (Piaget and Inhelder, 1958). The problem is to find the relationships between factors influencing the swing (or period) of a pendulum. The child is supplied with string of varying lengths, a ruler, and a light and a heavy weight. A weight is attached to the string; the resulting pendulum is suspended and pushed. The child then times the period of swing and reports the result. Ikonic children tend to have the firm idea that the strength of the push determines how fast the pendulum swings. Accordingly, they attend to just that; they duly 'observe' and note this finding. Their preconceptions, in other words, govern what they actually see. In fact, the amount of push has nothing to do with the period of the swing.

Children operating in the concrete-symbolic mode are able to observe this point quite accurately. They then examine other factors. Does the heaviness of the weight have an effect? Or the length of the string? To test these ideas, they might first tie a light weight to a short string and time that. The first one went faster: therefore the swing depends upon both weight and the length of the string. Wrong: the experiment was not properly controlled; not all the possibilities were examined.

In order to arrive unequivocally at the correct answer, it is necessary to control for weight independently of length, and for length independently of weight — to see that there are *four* possibilities, not two (working-memory space again). The question is not heavy-long versus light-short; but heavy-long versus heavy-short versus light-long versus light-short. Thus, the following table can be set up and the results noted for each alternative:

Weight	Length	Result
Heavy	Long	Slow
Heavy	Short	Fast
Light	Long	Slow
Light	Short	Fast

It is now seen clearly that weight has no effect at all: with a heavy weight, the period may be slow or fast. Altering the length, however, has an immediate effect on periodicity: whatever the weight, a short string produces a fast period and a long string a slow period. Experimental control in scientific research means working out the possibilities and then ruling them out, one by one.

To think in the formal mode is to conceive reality not only in terms of what is, but also in terms of what might be. In formal thinking, dimensions of the problem are abstracted and looked at simultaneously. Thus, formal thought is more flexible: if one solution does not work, look at plausible alternatives and try them out.

Verbalising in the formal mode. Thought in the formal mode is not limited to mathematical and scientific thinking. The symptoms of the formal mode in ordinary conversation refer to this openness of thinking; for example, 'It depends on what you mean by party policy. If you mean what was said before the last election by the leader of the party, then ... But if on the other hand you look at trends in policy since 1975 ...' Questioning-the-question is another example of this. The formal mode recognises that other questions might better have been asked. 'So what we *should* be addressing is not party policy at all. It's whether New Zealand is correct *in principle* to ban peanut imports from Queensland ...'

As we saw in Chapter 4, one needs to be very careful about such 'open' responses. HSC examiners just may not take kindly to a papers that begins: 'This question is misleading. What the examiner should be asking, if I read the intent correctly, is...' On the other hand, some examiners might be hugely delighted with some originality for a change. It is a high risk strategy; perhaps justifiably so, as it is easy to do a 'snow-job' with the trappings of the formal mode to conceal substantive ignorance.

The appreciation of political cartoons is essentially a formal task (Elkind, 1968). The point is the metaphor that is hidden in the cartoon and it requires the formal mode to decode it. Many cartoons involve the principle of the *reductio ad absurdum*, in which the logical implications of a situation are played out to a ludicrous end — but to get the joke, you have to abstract the implied principle. For example, in an article 'How good is your sense of humor?' (*Weekend Magazine*, 10 July 1971), 10 jokes were listed, with four punch-lines given for each: one had to pick the best and funniest line, and then match one's choice with the punch-line selected by the 'panel of experts'. As we hope you will see (Box 5.1), the 'best' punch-line is the formal one.

Metacognition in the formal mode. Adolescent thought deals with a world of *possibilities*. These possibilities are generated by the laws and principles that govern social systems and the physical world.

There is a truth about the world and that world includes oneself. And that latter realisation is itself a moment of truth; it dominates adolescent thinking, to the point where they think and behave in a very egocentric way.

BOX 5.1   AT WHAT LEVEL OF DEVELOPMENT IS YOUR
            SENSE OF HUMOUR?

A man with an unpronounceable European name changed it to McGillicuddy.
Three months later he changed it once more, this time to MacDonald. When
asked why he had done this, he replied:

1. I liked the MacDonald tartan better than the McGillicuddy one.
2. I decided I'd rather be a Mac than a Mick.
3. Every time I met someone, he would ask me what my name was
    before I changed it.
4. We Scots like to have change.

It's not difficult to see which is the superior choice: **1, 2** and **4** all involve a
simple extension of the original joke, structured by fact or preference; whereas
3 involves an extension of the joke in terms of intrinsic logical structure. The
latter is embedded abstractly in the joke, the rest are given fairly directly and
obviously. Try it out on children of different ages and see what they say.

Source: Weekend Magazine, 10 July 1971.

    The egocentrism of adolescence is however quite different from that of early
childhood (Elkind, 1967). Thinkers in the ikonic mode, typically preschoolers, are
unselfconscious in their egocentrism: there simply is no other perspective but their
own. Adolescents discriminate all too easily between their world and other people's —
and cringe at the comparison. Other people have a view too — and it includes — *me!*
Hence the swagger and pretension of adolescence, and the flip-side, morbid self-
examination and sensitive, bruised egos.

    The awareness both of self and of the fact that human behaviour, including your
own, is rule-governed brings a new meaning to metacognition. Metacognition is like
intelligence: there is always some there (otherwise we would not be human) but it gets
better as we grow older. The Flavell and Wellman (1977) memory experiments, and
Paris's work on strategies in Year 3, show that pre-adolescents are able to monitor their
activities: they can be aware of doing this and not that, and that if they did something
else the result might be better. They do not, however, see themselves from another's
point of view, in Piaget's (1932) sence of *allocentric* (as opposed to egocentric).
Allocentric thought enables individuals to see others, and themselves, in the same light
(as in the Golden Rule). A good non-moral example of that is what professional writers
call a sense of audience: evaluating your own text from how the reader is likely to see
it. Burtis et al. (1984) found that audience sense did not unequivocally appear in
children's writing (under normal conditions) until Year 11/12, in that writers could *talk
about* what they were going to say from the point of view of the presumed reader.

    Allocentrism, then, opens a new dimension to metacognition. To be able to think
about ourselves in the formal mode means that there are so many more possibilities and
contexts that we can weave into our plans about ourselves, and which enable us for the

first time to really compare ourselves with others on standardised dimensions. This means too that the foundations are there for a realistic self-concept, not one based on wish-fulfilment or evaluations relected from others.

All that, however, takes time: it certainly does not fall into place by the end of adolescence, and in many people never does. As is discussed later in this chapter, metacognition is one of the areas that continues to develop into middle age. In late adolescence, most individuals are still too impressed (one way or the other) with their discovery of self to give it a realistic place in its relation to the rest of the world.

The second order formal mode: Formal–2

In formal-1, principle is used to explain the world and to order the behaviour of people. It enables us to deduce what might happen in particular circumstances that we have not yet actually experienced, to conclude that the world is a stable and ordered place, to solve equations with two unknown variables, to apply the four rules of number meaningfully to indeterminate quantities, to vote for a political party whose policies are against our own personal interests, to define the formal characteristics of an Agatha Christie novel...

The formal modes in higher education. In each of these content areas, we come with more experience to be able to define more and more of these principles, and after a while we see them beginning to interrelate. When that happens we can say that we are beginning to appreciate an *academic discipline:* physics, biology, mathematics, literary criticism, and so on. And that is the progress followed by students at university: they enter with a smattering of principles, which they continue to acquire systematically until the time comes when they have an overview, a grasp, of established knowledge in that discipline. That is the relational level of thinking in the first order mode. A bachelor's degree is official recognition that that level has, in the opinion of the academic department concerned, been attained (Collis and Biggs, 1983).

Degree structures at university are hierarchical. The student reads a 'major' subject, progressing from first through second to third year; by the end of third year thinking should be relational. The student should be thinking like a physicist about physical science matters, or like a historian about history. This hierarchy is sometimes hard to find in some Arts subjects. First year History, for example, might concentrate on British and European history, second year on Australian, third on American or Asian. The years are not cumulatively more difficult or detailed, or the content of one prerequisite to being able adequately to follow the next year's work; rather, they are just *different* contents. How then can one say they are ever integrated in the sense meant by relational thinking within a discipline?

The integration in these cases refers to the *way of thinking* about content, not integrating the content itself. The content is simply the medium in which that way of thinking is cultivated. In the case of history, that way of thinking is part paradigmatic, largely narrative, that enables one to understand and interpret the development of societies in time periods, and to estimate the role played by powerful individuals in shaping that development. Because historical paradigms are loose and the room for individual interpretation of historical narrative expansive, there is no one way of thinking historically. *Schools* of thought exist and, as with literary criticism and other disciplines, they vie for dominance as academic fashions. Nevertheless, at any moment there is a conventional wisdom, an orthodoxy.

So let's 'do a formal' on that, and question *that* question. What if the orthodoxy has assumed something that ought not to be assumed? What if parallel lines *do* meet? What if the 'Mahogany Ship' had grounded in Sydney Cove, not in the Bight; and that its cargo comprised Portuguese convicts, its captain searching for prison space? What if the dinosaurs had not been exterminated 63 million years ago: would not egg-laying *Saurus sapiens,* its hatching unfettered by birth canal limitations on cranial capacity, be vastly more intelligent than *Homo sapiens*?

These are *second order* formal questions. They give rise to research on the one hand, science fiction on the other. They speak not of the ordered and principled world that we know and can predict within, but of the world that might be. And gradually, in the case of research, that world becomes the disciplined world; and in the case of science fiction a disciplined thrill. The first is the paradigmatic way; the second the way of narrative.

The nature of research. To return to the campus, then, the extended abstract breakthrough comes when the established orthodoxy is questioned: the theory does not explain this phenomenon; these results are inconsistent; there is a flaw in this experiment. Whereas Perry's (1970) more sophisticated levels of absolutism will do for undergraduates, second order thinking *must* be relativistic. In a research higher degree, the student in a sense questions established authority: as with formal–1 thinking with respect to concrete thought, the matter is not closed. A bachelor graduate goes into the world to practise this or that profession with a reasonably clear idea of what the state of the art is in the relevant discipline. A researcher is more interested in what the discipline is not, and what it might become.

Not all research enters the second order mode. Historical research frequently does not question the orthodoxy, it simply extends it; the research applies the prevailing historiography to the events that occurred in a particular district between certain times that nobody else happens to have covered previously. Much scientific research, too, simply establishes boiling points, melting points, conductivities, and all the other traditional parameters of substances that happen to have escaped the net so far. This is formal–1 research, no more *abstract* than first year studies.

University studies thus have a discipline-oriented degree structure from undergraduate to postgraduate levels. Undergraduate studies show the unistructural-multistructural-relational learning cycle in the first order formal mode, with the learning cycle extending into the second order formal mode in the case of some research-oriented higher degrees.

The narrative way of formal thought. Formal-2 thinking is involved whenever we question orthodoxies in terms of principles still wider than those comprising the orthodoxy. But when is that questioning more *abstract* and when simply *different,* and not necessarily more abstract? Questioning questions involves more than just modes of thinking; processes of thinking are also involved, particularly *divergent* ('creative') thought (see Chapter 9 for further discussion of this point).

Science fiction authors create their own context within a consistent set of principles of their own making. *The Amtrak Wars,* by Patrick Tilley, illustrates the point very topically for this chapter. The nuclear holocaust occurred. Those in underground bunkers survived relatively unscathed physically and, millennia later, formed the paradigmatically obsessed 'Federation'. Those few surface dwellers who survived suffered massive genetic damage; their descendants become the degenerate and sub-human 'Mutes'. Thus far we are within extrapolations from the known, within the paradigmatic way. But then we apply the narrative way, as the Mute 'wordsmiths' do to make sense out of their own experience. We find then that Mutes are degenerate only when weighed in the Federation's paradigmatic scales. In fact, they know a narrative-based trick or two ...

Another variation on the same theme is Russell Hoban's *Riddley Walker.* What would the psychology of a subsistence level post-holocaust society look like through the semi-literate writing of an adolescent boy, confused but obsessed by the ikonic narratives confabulated by his own forefathers to explain their miserable situation? The reader has to pick up a new dialect and a second order alternative framework in order to find out.

How many formal modes? If formal-2, why not formal-3 or formal-4? We have seen that even second order, formal-2, tends to tilt over towards the simply different: higher orders still would probably become the horizontal scrub of the formal mode: impenetrable, and in the wrong direction. Or is that perception because these writers can themselves see no higher? The distinction between formal-1 and formal-2 is not to be found in many textbooks. We think it is justified because it is possible to describe a more abstract logical structure than the first order mode, as in our distinction between undergraduate and postgraduate work; and that there is discontinuity of performance between the two levels. Students who do well in pass degree work do not necessarily do well at basic research, while students who do not do particularly well at their first degree may become outstanding researchers (Einstein being the most extreme example). That implies a modal barrier between the two levels, which is certainly compatible with what we know of the physiology. It is thus convenient for educators to presuppose two formal modes — but like all orthodoxies, this one too is open to question.

THE PROCESSES OF DEVELOPMENTAL GROWTH

What is seen as the growth of complexity in thinking and learning across the school-age years is associated with growth at two levels: *within-modes,* seen in the learning cycles from unistructural through to relational in particular tasks, and *across-modes,* seen in the shift to a new level of abstraction in the nature of the task. While physiological changes most likely make the latter shifts *possible,* they do not guarantee them. For that to happen, other conditions are necessary:

1. organised and consolidated prior knowledge obtained by building up a number of related tasks to relational level in the previous mode;
2. confrontation or challenge: the perception that the existing repertoire of lower level relational modes is inadequate to handle a new problem. This has two aspects: cognitive, defining the problem, and affective, providing motivation through optimal mismatch;
3. social support, which again has both cognitive and motivational aspects.

Let us take these points in turn.

Relational level prior knowledge in the previous mode

The first prerequisite, then, is to build a significant number of related tasks up to relational level. This is essentially a two-stage process: assembling the contents through uni- to multistructural levels, then integrating by a relating concept. The essence of the relating concept is that it incorporates what may be construed as *common* to the multistructural aspects of the task, so that they are no longer disconnected. In building up prior knowledge to relational level, then, two general processes are involved: concepts and operations are acquired and become familiar through use; they are then reorganised into a new unit, by some relating or integrating concept. The first is a 'horizontal' process, involving the acquisition and automatisation of material; and the second is a 'vertical' one, bringing these familiarised chunks under the same conceptual umbrella. Working memory plays an important part in this.

The role of working memory. Several writers have emphasised the role of working memory in learning and development (e.g. Case, 1985). The fact that working memory is of fixed capacity can be used to explain the progression of learning cycles. In coming across something for the first time there is a lot of 'noise': we are not sure what is important and what can be ignored. Hence, at the unistructural level, we tend to grasp hold of only one aspect of the task at a time. Then, with increasing familiarity (or what Case calls *automatisation)* we learn what to ignore and what to retain about the task. Thus, with familiarisation there is more working memory available for the relevant aspects of the task: we free space by learning to ignore the noise. Hence the multistructural level of operation: we can handle more aspects of the task within the same working memory. This uni- to multistructural movement, then, is the *horizontal* aspect of learning.

When enough aspects of the task have been assembled, and sufficiently familiarised to free even more working memory, the time is ripe to relate them all together: that is the *vertical* aspect of learning. It evolves through recoding the construction of a superordinate concept; for example, a causal explanation linking up the events or *whats* that happened with one *why*. That 'why' then 'contains' all the preceding data. Take the coastal rain example (Chapter 4). The relating concept subordinating all the facts is 'get colder so that the moisture condenses forming rain': once that is understood all the multistructural bits and pieces fall into place (winds from the sea, pick up water vapour, etc.).

This is not intended to mean, however, that knowledge is acquired uncoded and unrelated to anything else, and then held in a multistructural limbo until the relational stage. It is expected that all students (with varying success) will structure knowledge as they acquire it. As their knowledge grows, however, the existing structures will be partial and improperly integrated: this is in fact what the multistructural stage is. The relational stage occurs when it is seen that all the parts now make up a new whole, which is a matter of structuring or recoding what is already there.

In short, then, working memory limitations constrain us to focus on the relevant aspects of the task, and knowledge gradually (sometimes suddenly, depending on how easy the task is) grows horizontally. When enough is known to make an abstraction, *and* is familiar enough to allow the space, knowledge reorganises vertically, subsumed under an integrating, superordinate, concept.

Transition: Extending into the abstract. When a number of relating superordinate concepts has been assembled the next question is to explain *those.* To see what they have in common involves another vertical shift, an extension into a more abstract mode. Physiology has — somehow — made it possible in principle to recode using the more abstract 'raw material' of the higher order; the student will need much familiarity with the content to free working memory sufficiently to allow the search for a higher order principle. The actual abstraction and generalisation, however, occur much as before.

Whatever the actual mechanisms, the conditions are clear enough: *physiological maturity is* positively indicated, for example, if the individual has reached that mode in some *other* task area; and *familiarity* in related topics at the relational level in the preceding mode.

The second condition explains why students do not move wholesale into a new mode: they only do, if they do at all, in those areas in which they have experience and expertise.

Confrontation and challenge. Why should the student try and recode at a higher level? For the same reason as applies within modes: there is mismatch between what is known, and what is needed to be known. And as we have seen in Chapters 2 and 3, such a mismatch may be very motivating. We are seekers after meaning and, given our limited capacity working memories, we have to interrelate things as much as possible in order to make sense out of a large, complex and changing environment. We are simply built that way.

In making extended abstract responses, then, *sufficient prior knowledge*, and *confrontation with a problem* that requires us to use and reorganise that knowledge, are both necessary. Do we then call these new principles and extended abstract constructions out of thin air? Hardly; and that is where the next condition comes in.

Social support. Vygotsky (1978, but writing in 1934) referred to 'zones of proximal development' by which he means that children become increasingly ready to shift into a more abstract mode. When a child is within that zone, appropriate social support from parent or teacher may enable the child to operate at the higher level when it would have been impossible without that support. In other words, interaction with other people hastens development.

Fischer and Bullock (1984) talk of *scaffolded* mental states. A common form of scaffolding is in language learning when parents (in particular) provide supportive structures in close one-to-one (dyadic) interaction with their child. This is described as *embedded* teaching, as opposed to *formal* teaching, of the kind dealt with in schools. In embedded teaching, the child receives a flow of information that is deliberately related to the child's ongoing and self-initiated activity, and is continually adjusted to suit, in nature and rate of flow, the child's immediate behaviour. In formal teaching, on the other hand, such closely interwoven interaction is rare, and the child has to set up the structures unaided: the result — as we saw in Chapter 4 — is that much that is learned in school is not deeply integrated with existing knowledge but is accumulated on the side, in isolation from what the child perceives as important knowledge.

Embedded teaching is, however, only one mechanism by which other people influence cognitive development. Another important factor is modelling, both by peers and by teachers. Other people provide examples of what can be done, and the social motivation to provide the push: to be as good as others, to be like someone who is admired by doing the same things, to be better than others. We also saw in Chapter 4 that peers in particular play an important role in developing metacognitive processes, so that self-awareness, planning for realistic goals, are likely to encourage cognitive growth.

Finally, peers and especially teachers play the most important role of providing the *content* that will help the child structure experience vertically. Where do we obtain most of those integrating, superordinate concepts that create relational and extended abstract structures? From other people, wiser than us! We do not reinvent the wheel all the time: we try to understand what others are saying and use that as best we may.

The role of the school in promoting growth. Extended abstract thinking may be promoted in three main ways, assuming the prerequisite biological hardware to be in place:

- establishing well-structured prior knowledge (to relational level) in a number of tasks and problems related to a content area;
- providing challenging problems, at the appropriate level of abstraction, to produce optimal mismatch;
- providing social support both of peers and of adults to scaffold thinking, to provide helpful content and to motivate.

The school of course may make a contribution in all three ways. Much school learning in primary and secondary will be concerned with horizontal and vertical processes within the concrete mode as target (in academic learning — obviously not in PE or drama). From middle secondary school, however, and increasingly thereafter, the formal mode for an increasing number of students becomes the target.

This discussion, then, focuses the school's task onto three processes:

1. the *accretion of relevant knowledge* (a horizontal process), and familiarisation with it;
2. the *structuring of knowledge* (a vertical process);
3. the extension and *generalisation of knowledge* (a vertical process across modes).

It is likely that enhancing each of these processes will raise different issues for curriculum, teaching method and assessment. These issues are addressed in Section B.

CHILDREN'S SCIENCE: ALTERNATIVE FRAMEWORKS FOR CONSTRUING REALITY

The first scientifically acceptable *explanations* of natural phenomena occur at the relational level in the concrete mode. That level of responding is typically observed in mid-secondary, rarely in primary, school (see Section B). How then do children explain things in the meantime?

It must first be understood that an 'explanation' for a young child is not what scientists mean. The first 'why' questions are to seek reassurance, which parents frequently give: 'Why have all the lights gone out?' 'Because we are having a blackout.' (Solomon, 1985). Another form of explanation Solomon mentions is 'reaffirmation' (a form of tautology) which persists until high school:

Question: 'Gold can be found as the pure metal in the earth's crust. Iron cannot be found as a pure metal. Why is this?'

Answer: 'Because iron is not found in the earth's crust.'

The Year 9 student on coastal rain reaffirmed the question when she replied, 'Because it rains more on the coastal side.' Better explanations come when children explain by substituting one word for another. 'Vinegar protects food from going bad because it pickles them' may or may not be suggesting that vinegar is one example of a superordinate class of pickling fluids (Solomon, 1985).

Causality in the accepted sense is relational in structure; children however will accept much looser explanations and be satisfied with them. The educational challenge is to make children see that their explanations really will not do at all.

The first explanations are couched in narrative, which results in animism (Piaget, 1926). Children use the ikonic mode to explain things, as do preliterate societies, by projecting human characteristics onto animals, plants and inanimate objects, and weaving stories around them. Then, particularly if assisted by interaction with adults, it is seen that these animistic explanations do not make sense: they lead to too many contradictions. For example, an early explanation for wind imputes some sort of intentionality to trees, and is constructed by putting together quite correct observations: that when there is a wind, the trees wave around. When I wave my hand there is a wind: so it is the trees that wave when they want to make a wind.

In between the use of frank animism and myth to explain the world, and the first working models in high school, children create their own science as best they can (Gilbert, Osborne and Fensham, 1982), forming what are now referred to as *alternative frameworks* (Driver and Easley, 1978; Driver, 1981). Rather like the wind explanation, which is based on true observation, children focus on aspects of a phenomenon that are close to their own experience. There are several interesting features about these explanations:

1. They are remarkably similar to each other.
2. They are also similar to explanations used in the history of science, progressing from

Aristotelian and pre-Newtonian, through Newtonian, to currently accepted frameworks.

3. Some are remarkably resistant to change. Even university physics students (who should 'know better') act out their lives on Newtonian assumptions about force, energy and motion — but pass exams on the accepted wisdom (Gunstone and White, 1981; Marton, 1981).

In forming these explanations, students seize on aspects that are striking, and what strikes one student is likely to strike another. That does not however quite explain the similarity in (1), or the resistance to science teaching in (3), above.

The social construction of children's science

When children play and talk together, they rarely *argue* when they discuss experiences they have shared, such as a TV program. They *reconstruct* the event (Solomon, 1984). They establish this particular piece of world knowledge by sharing perspectives on it and, when they agree, *that* is what goes down as what is to be made of the program. The meaning is not validated by logical argument but by consensus. Even adults deal with inconsistency by arriving at a shared perspective: 'I know what you mean', and having said that we have obviated the need to analyse differences any further. Social approval accommodates contradictory views.

Children then in story, discussion, play and finally consensus, construct accounts of what the world is about. Consensus can however work for the accepted frameworks as well as for the alternative frameworks:

A Second Year (Year 8/9) group was discussing the nature of energy. Asked if a piece of bread lying on the bench had energy, Mark volunteered the opinion that it could not because 'it couldn't jump around'. This meaning of energy was familiar to most of the others who leapt eagerly into the fray using the same argument against petrol having energy. Errol [is] trying to disagree but his view is ignored ...

Two years later, when these pupils were about to start their first course on energy, the same question was put to them. At once Mark staked out his previous claim that food could not have energy but this time his was the view that was to be ignored. Errol offered the idea that the energy was contained in the food but that it was stored, and the others agreed with him. One week later, in the next discussion on energy, Mark changed his mind and came into line with the rest of the class (Solomon, 1984, p. 8).

It will be noted that by the time Errol's view has become the consensus, we are now into Year 9 or Year 10. In the meantime, and in fact throughout primary and secondary schooling to that time, mistaken conceptions of the world have dominated the children's thinking. This makes the learning of science peculiarly difficult, as might be imagined.

Some common alternative frameworks

Clough and Driver (1984) set out to determine the extent to which adolescents used the same or similar alternative frameworks to explain the same situation; and the extent to which the same framework was used across different situations. They gave a series of tasks to groups of students aged 12, 14 and 16; they were to explain what happened. The tasks illustrated movement of fluids from regions of higher to lower pressure, and included: drinking from a straw; placing a syringe under water and withdrawing the plunger; and placing hot glasses upside down on a soapy sink. Another concept was the conduction of heat energy through solids; and these three tasks were: plastic, wooden and metal spoons standing in a cup of hot water —explain why the metal spoon felt hotter than the other spoons; explain why a metal plate felt colder than a plastic plate; and explain why, on a cold day, the handlebars of a bicycle felt colder than the plastic grips.

In the straw task, the way the question was put suggested that the students use the idea of atmospheric pressure; at all three ages, the majority response echoed this concept ('the air pressure forces it up'). With the other two tasks, however, with no leading questions, about half the respondents used the concept that 'the vacuum actively sucks' rather than that the atmospheric pressure stabilises the difference. At age 16, substantially more students used the atmospheric difference concept, but the most popular response at all three levels was a 'sucking vacuum'.

In the heat energy problems, the spoons question attracted the accepted framework (heat energy travels through different materials at different rates) much more readily than did the plates and handlebars questions. The latter task especially was put in the framework that metal attracts coldness, that is, that cold is a property just like heat. Again, older students increasingly used the accepted framework (heat energy travels through different materials at different rates).

The results suggested that the accepted framework is more stable across tasks, and less susceptible to influence by wording of the question. Nevertheless, some tasks with which the students were familiar (like the bicycle handlebars) had stable frameworks (metal conducts/attracts coldness) which contradict the accepted framework. Clough and Driver conclude: 'Unfortunately, there is evidence that many incorrect scientific conceptualisations are resistant to instruction, even when the teaching has been deliberately structured to incorporate or confront children's ideas' (p. 21).

Frameworks that become part of folklore, matters to do with health and hygiene for example, receive massive social (and not infrequently media) support: 'sugar gives you energy', 'if milk is good for babies it's got to be good for everyone', and so on. These are even more difficult to counter. What frequently happens is isolation: we *talk* the accepted framework and *act on* the alternative framework. We 'sort of know about electrons' but actually operate on a hydraulic framework: electricity 'flows' through the wires so that some, like Thurber's aunt, leave dead light bulbs in their sockets so that electricity doesn't leak into the room.

The 'schizophrenic' world in which many students seem to live is illustrated by Gunstone and White (1981), who found that physics students entering Monash University — the 'successful fraction from 13 years of (mainly Victorian) schooling'

—had quite serious misunderstandings about gravity. 'Students know a lot about physics but do not relate it to the everyday world ... much more attention may have to be given to integrating the knowledge acquired in school to general knowledge' (p. 298). These students had passed their HSC in physics, but kept it apart from their experiencing: they observed what they predicted would happen when it did not, and 'some even managed not to observe at all and gave mathematical equations when asked what they had seen'.

To sum up, then, alternative frameworks are constructions that stand in for 'true' (accepted framework) explanations, which involve at least relational thinking in the concrete-symbolic mode. Alternative frameworks may be constructed around one, few or several aspects relevant to the final concept, or around quite irrelevant aspects.

Different ways of teaching science arise out of alternative frameworks and children's science. We return to this matter in Section B.

THE COURSE OF COGNITIVE GROWTH IN ADULTHOOD

Reference has been made to studies of adult development in which stage-like regularities have been found and related to ages. In particular, these studies show changes (for the better) in adult thinking long after adolescence.

Tested intelligence and brain deterioration

First, what are the physiological facts of the lifespan? For some years it was believed that intelligence reached a peak in the early twenties, then slowly declined thereafter, with increasing rapidity from age 60 or so. These conclusions were based on norming data for IQ test items (Wechsler, 1955). IQ data are, however, obtained cross-sectionally (that is, they are *averages* of samples aged 20, 30, 40, 50 etc.); and many of Wechsler's items reflected the effects of schooling. As people in the older samples had less schooling than those in the 20 year sample, they scored lower on these items and therefore obtained lower IQs. When people are followed through *longitudinally* (their own performance is compared to what they themselves did earlier), the decline is evident in some, disappears in others, and reverses in still others (Knox, 1977; Schaie, 1979). What determines whether or not there is a decline in earlier years are *lifestyle* factors. People who leave school early, and get jobs that do not require the sorts of things sampled in IQ tests, start dropping in performance in their twenties. Others in professions in which they have to 'use their brains' do not decline until much later. Retirement often signals massive deterioration, the cause being withdrawal from involvement and activity, not physiological deterioration.

The later drop-off in performance towards the end of the lifespan strongly implies brain deterioration, resulting in senility, a premature form of which is Alzheimer's disease. In fact, it is true that the brain changes that occur after the early twenties *are* detrimental: brain cells die off and are not replaced, a process which is markedly hastened by drugs (alcohol being the most significant in our society), and factors affecting oxygen supply (such as smoking and sleep apnea), and some chemicals (such as aluminium) (Horne, 1984). Because of lifestyle variations and heredity, there are enormous differences in the rate at which the brain deteriorates, and when manifest signs of senility occur. *Consistent* deterioration in test scores after early adulthood occurs only in items involving sensori-motor co-ordination, especially when per-formance is timed.

On the other hand, tested IQ continues rising for many people for a long time; and in everyday life, we value 'maturity of judgment', 'experience' and other positive indices of cognitive improvement. What improves? Certainly older people *know* more: they are more worldly-wise. They score higher on test items measuring what Cattell (1971) calls 'crystallised intelligence', that is, test items such as formal reasoning, vocabulary and the use of language generally (Knox, 1977). Experience also helps people to discriminate better, to learn to plan ahead, to watch themselves so that they do not make the same mistake again: in short, to be more *metacognitive*.

Lawrence, Dodds and Volet (1983) showed that adults of average intelligence were far superior to highly intelligent scholarship girls in solving problems that required planning and co-ordinating one's activities. Similarly, Biggs (1986a) showed that scores of mature age tertiary students were higher on deep and achieving motives and strategies than those of regular students of the same academic year, and that there was a linear increase with age: the older the student, the clearer they were about their motives, the relevance of their learning to their own lives, and the need for planning and organisation. Paradoxically, mature age learners are more likely to *feel* that they lack study skills, and have 'forgotten how to learn'. That says more about their perceptions of institutional expectations, and perhaps their use of language, than it does about their presumed lack of learning ability.

Stages through the lifespan?

The notion of stages and process in adulthood came first from post-Freudian psychoanalysts in treating adult patients with coping problems. The two most influential today are Erikson (1959), with his eight stages covering the entire lifespan, and Jung (1956), who concentrated on problems associated with the middle adult years, and whose work is now being resurrected with reference to the so-called 'midlife crisis'. Levinson et al. (1978) studied 40 adult males in depth, and was impressed by the evidence for 'seasons' or regular stages, which required facing prototypical problems. The restriction to males was, he says, due to logistics not choice; but apart from smaller studies by Viney (1980) and Sheehy (1976), Levinson's study of males is the best recent work we have to go on.

Metacognition is the key to understanding Levinson's stages or seasons. His point is that Western society offers *choices* that must be faced; if a choice is incorrect or inappropriate, there will be a price to pay at the next choice period. These periods of self-evaluation, choice and commitment occur in the early twenties, at 40 and at 60 years of age.

After leaving school or university, young people (Levinson claims the same principles apply to women) have to make two commitments in order to show competence in the two areas in which Freud (1905) said mature adults have to do well: love and work. This involves forming a 'dream' of the kind of life they want as adults, and much depends on how realistic the dream is, both in real-world terms and in the sense of being true to oneself. Next, a mentor appears who gives significant support towards realising the dream. The mentor is usually a teacher or older colleague who forms a very special relationship with the individual that is in some respects not unlike a love relationship (it is intense, possessive and usually ends traumatically). An occupation is then 'formed' (rather than chosen) and likewise marriage and family. The balancing act is between the priorities to love and to work. If the balance is wrong, this will come out in the mid-stage review around age 30 (a divorce prime time, according to Levinson). This review is to see how on course things are; basically there is no questioning of the general course itself. That more major review occurs at the end of the thirties, ushering in the so-called 'midlife transition'. This is a time of moderate to severe crisis, evoking 'tumultuous struggles' within the self and the external world.

At 40 is what Jung called the 'noonhour of life'. Before then, all has gone into realising the dream, at the expense of other important aspects of the self that now, to be a real, integrated person, need to be expressed. Usually by 40, a person will either have achieved the dream, or will know that it never will be. The individual now turns to the neglected aspects of self: women tend to become more aggressive and 'masculine', men more nurturant and 'feminine'. Some people really cut loose. Not all change overnight from a timid bourgeois bank clerk to paint and make love in exotic places, as did Paul Gauguin, but something along those lines. Thoughts of death and impermanence enter consciousness, followed swiftly by their presumed antidotes; jogging, dieting and giving up smoking. Life is seen to have an end; there is more to be done with it yet. Towards the end of the forties, or later, some kind of equilibrium is reached; Jung himself referred to *individuation*, a state of integration that has strong religious overtones, which may be achieved by some.

Adult development and the teacher

It is obviously inappropriate to expand on these periods in adult thinking, and to review alternative models and the evidence for them. It is however important for teachers to recognise that both the quality and the quantity of thinking develop progressively after leaving school. One important feature of adult thought is its increased *metacognitive* character. The wild idealism of adolescence becomes tempered with self-knowledge, as with world-knowledge. That makes a difference in approach to adult education (Knowles, 1978; Knox, 1977), as we see in Section B.

Levinson draws attention to some of the tasks that young people face on entering adult life. Teachers and counsellors could help school-leavers enter their novitiate more effectively if the tasks of the general kind outlined by Levinson were better understood, although the world has changed rather critically since the mid-seventies when Levinson's work was undertaken. Studies are urgently needed for Australia; in particular that apply to both sexes, and that take into account the difficulties many young people have, not only in forming an occupation, but in coping with the prospect of being denied the opportunity of even making the attempt. Finally, the application of adult studies to teachers themselves is an interesting area: 'burn out' usually occurs rather earlier than Levinson's 'midlife-transition' period, but the parallel indicates further study.

SUMMARY

The course of cognitive growth. Does children's thinking about the world develop in stages that are fixed by their age? There is some evidence that this is so. Children do appear to be able to do whole classes of increasingly abstract tasks at typical age levels. Psychologists, in particular Piaget, have tested children with 'tight' logical tasks and found that there were typical ages at which certain logical structures appeared to be solved. This led to a view of stage that dominated educational thought for some years; according to it, children were expected to perform in similar ways across the whole range of school tasks. The evidence is, however, that they do not. It is now clear that what changes with age is the *abstractness* of the task that can be handled, not its logical structure. There had been a confusion between what develops and what is learned.

Development and learning. What *develops* is an ability to handle tasks of increasing abstractness, which opens out higher level *target modes* for learning as children grow older. What is *learned* is the amount of data acquired within a target mode, and its organisation within various stages of the learning cycle. One of the factors that seems to permit (but not guarantee) the emergence of a new mode is physiological, possibly related to successive waves of myelinisation within the brain and nervous system. The modes we learn within the unistructural–multistructural–relational learning cycle can be described within each of the modes.

    Sensori-motor. The sensori-motor mode runs from birth to around 18 months. At the end of that learning cycle, the infant can co-ordinate action to take into account information gained directly through the senses, but is unable to imagine or represent reality internally, for example, to suppose that a toy has been hidden if the transfer has not been actually witnessed.

    Ikonic. The first internal representation is based on a perceptual picture or an emotion or a mixture of both. The ikon is rigid and unidimensional, but it makes oral language possible, and may persist into adult life. A frequent way of integrating ikonic thought relationally is through narrative: hence, the 'mythic stage', where reality is perceived as explained in terms of stories with clear stereotypical characters and obvious morals and plots.

    Concrete-symbolic. Thinking in the concrete mode begins to emerge around five or six years of age, and with it the realisation that the world is ordered and predictable. One of the most powerful tools children learn over the years of schooling is the second order symbol system of written language and signs. Operations are performed on symbols standing for the important aspects of events and objects in the real world. The relational level of thinking is attained according to the child's interest in and experience of the task in question, and has no bearing on how apparently similar tasks might be performed. 'Readiness tests' are based on the false assumption that such a relationship between tasks does exist.

First order formal. Formal-1 thinking commences in early adolescence. It transcends what is given; the *logic* of a situation is used to construct what might be the case. Formal thought thus has an open character: 'it depends what you mean by ... ' The world is run on principles, not the concrete and specific relations of the former mode. These principles apply to people and to oneself. Metacognition takes a deeper turn when the self can be examined in the same light and from the same perspective as one examines others. The relational level of first order formal thought involves the integration of principles into self-consistent disciplines. Understanding that integration is the basis of undergraduate study at university.

Second order formal. Questioning the formal mode itself opens out a whole new range of possibilities, and is the basis of research on the one hand, or science fiction on the other. Formal-2 thinking is less well studied than the others, and is relatively uncommon. Professional practice itself works from formal-1 thinking.

The processes of developmental growth. While physiology makes a change into a higher mode possible, it does not guarantee it. Three further components are necessary: organisation of relevant prior knowledge to relational level in the previous mode, confrontation or challenge, and social support. Prior knowledge is acquired through *horizontal* processes, so that knowledge is accumulated to form a rich multistructural base; and reorganised through *vertical* processes by means of which an appropriate superordinate concept or operation subsumes the multistructural content. The further change into a higher mode occurs when relational concepts are themselves subsumed under a higher order principle. Challenging problems and social support providing modelling, feedback and motivation are important for both levels of vertical process. These three processes, the *accretion, structuring* and *generalisation* of knowledge, are ones in which the school has an important role to play.

Children's science: Alternative frameworks for constructing reality. Alternative frameworks are particular explanations children use for understanding natural phenomena that are not those 'accepted' by science, which themselves involve at least relational level thinking in the concrete mode. Prior to that level, children take one or more relevant, or irrelevant but striking, aspects of a situation and, frequently with the help of wishful thinking, folklore and consensus, construct a framework using those aspects. Frameworks usually have some aspects that are true, so that they tend to be seen as 'obvious' and self-validating: they thus stand in the way of learning accepted frameworks. Frequently, students learn the accepted framework at a surface level, but conduct their own lives well into adulthood on the assumption that the alternative is the valid framework. Teaching strategies vary from *confrontation* (to prove the alternative is wrong), or *reconstruction* (starting where the alternative is right).

The course of cognitive growth in adults. An alternative framework that has persisted in the last few decades in Western society is that intelligence peaks in the early twenties and deteriorates from there. This is found to be true of only a restricted range of cognitive performances, particularly those that are timed and that emphasise speed of performance. Competence otherwise tends to grow, depending on lifestyle, until middle to late middle age. Lifespan studies emphasise that adults have to face common problems at different age periods, which give a typical flavour to their decision-making during the period in question. Metacognition seems to play an increasingly important role in adult life and learning.

SECTION B

Developmental psychology has implications for educational practice in several areas. We shall consider here implications for curriculum design, teaching method, science teaching and alternative frameworks, and lifespan education.

CURRICULUM DESIGN

'If one were to design an organism that had to be ready for formal school by the age of five to seven years, it would be hard to imagine how one could improve on the design that nature had already created' (Case, 1985, p. 180).

As Case goes on to point out, all the competencies are in place by this age: following commands, counting and the use of symbolism. Actually, we tend to think the boot is on the other foot. With the emergence of the possibility of carrying out tasks in the concrete mode, it seemed to our forefathers that six or so was probably a suitable age to commence formal teaching. But the trouble many students have with learning to read, write and do arithmetic seems to indicate that nature might not have done such a perfect job after all: as suggested in Chapter 1, a few thousand more generations of natural selection might help matters.

It is nevertheless true that the appearance of new modes of thought at the beginning and towards the end of the age span covering the years of compulsory schooling has important implications for curriculum. First, one should try and avoid 'the stages trap': that because children *typically* become capable of handling more abstract content around a certain age, that all their learning should be geared towards that new level of abstraction; or that the new level is one in which they are even comfortable. We would not teach the most intelligent of our friends how to play bridge just by explaining the formal rules: we would always illustrate with practice hands. Likewise in teaching students, at whatever level. The modes define *upper limits*.

What are appropriate curriculum objectives?

In discussing the content of the curriculum, there are two matters to be decided once we have designated the subject matter itself: the target mode and the SOLO level within that mode. Subjects involving motor skills (such as PE, fine arts, home economics or industrial arts) involve mixed modes; some tasks are defined in the sensori-motor mode, and other tasks in the ikonic and concrete-symbolic or formal modes. In the 'academic' subjects (mathematics, science, language, history, etc., which mostly concern us here) the target mode would be *concrete-symbolic* for most school years, entering formal-1 only beyond Year 10 (except perhaps for particularly advanced students) and remaining at that level throughout the undergraduate years.

In teaching a particular topic to a particular year level, then, the issue is to decide what level in the SOLO learning cycle the students might reasonably be expected to attain. The 'natural' end-point of the learning cycle, when the most relevant features of the task have been sorted from the less relevant and are functionally tied up with each other, is *relational*, and ultimately that is the appropriate objective. Some tasks however take years to do satisfactorily, and meantime one makes do with uni- and multistructural objectives. Many students might reasonably leave school just 'knowing something about' certain scientific topics studied. To see what these levels look like in curriculum form, Table 5.1 illustrates some topics (adapted from Shayer and Adey, 1981) from the science curriculum.

The first thing to establish after determining the mode, then, is whether you are primarily aiming at horizontal (to multistructural) or vertical (relational) levels of knowing. In many instances, it is possible that both processes are going on simultaneously, or are difficult to distinguish between. For example, in extending horizontally what we know about something, we often come across (or construct ourselves) an idea that links the details in a new and illuminating way. What starts as a quantitative enrichment becomes a qualitative shift in meaning; all those data are now collected under a different heading. Mostly, though, we would start out quite differently, depending on the teacher's and learner's intentions. The selection of content, tasks, problems and activities depends on whether the aim is to *increase knowledge* or to *deepen understanding*.

What levels are appropriate to various stages of schooling? One way of answering this is to look at what levels are typically attained under current conditions. As noted in Section A, a scientific explanation is at least at relational level, and alternative frameworks are still flourishing by the middle of secondary school. Collis and Davey (1984) surveyed Year 7 and Year 9 students in five Tasmanian high schools using 19 concepts from biology, chemistry, physics and geology selected from the State Education Department Science Guidelines. These were graded into tasks representing all levels in the concrete mode learning cycle. Table 5.2 shows their findings.

As can be seen, the most common level of successful responding in Year 7 is unistructural, and by Year 9 multistructural. Nevertheless, 38 per cent of the Year 9s are still finding multistructural too difficult, and the chances of the majority of students reaching the relational level by Year 10 Collis and Davey see as 'remote'. These data thus raise the question of what are reasonable goals; Collis and Davey point out that if a multistructural level of understanding is considered adequate for a general education, the problem is reduced. In mathematics on the other hand, Collis (1975) found considerable variation in levels attained according to the topic taught. In several topics, what we would now describe as relational thinking was common in 15-year-olds, and first order formal thinking by age 17.

It seems likely that most students are *capable* of relational thinking in the concrete

Table 5.1 Learning cycles and modes for some science curriculum topics

Topic	Concrete-symbolic mode				First order formal mode	
	Unistructural	*Multistructural*	*Relational*	*Prestructural*	*Unistructural*	*Extended abstract*
Kinetic theory	Discrete items of information: for example 'solid turns to water'; 'liquid turns to gas'.	Change of state reversible ice-to-water; water-to-steam by *heating*; steam-to-water, water-to-ice by *cooling*.	Energy speeds particles. All matter might exist as solid liquid or gas depending on particle state.			Melting and vapourisation, equilibrium processes. Latent heat the energy required to change state.
Experimental design	To see if something produces an effect, try it. No attempt to compare across situations, only before–after.	Sees need for a comparison but satisfied with one with and one without' design. Ignores other variables when testing for one.	Controls obvious variables, but not for possible ones that are not present.			Sees system as a whole and controls for all possible combinations. Sees variables may interact: need for sampling to control natural variation.
Velocity and acceleration	Speed and relative position undifferentiated: faster object is the one ahead. Acceleration not differentiated.	Speed relation between distance and time (kph). Intuitive notion of acceleration (push in back).	Acceleration is rate of change of velocity. Can equations involving acceleration as algorithm ($S = ut + \frac{1}{2}at^2$)			Acceleration is the limiting value of: $\dfrac{\Delta v}{\Delta t}$
Acids and alkalis	'Acids' are substances with properties (turn litmus paper red, sour taste, attack metals) that work one at a time.	Acids and bases are opposites: neutralise each other in same quantities if teacher makes equivalent solutions. Metal oxides are alkaline; non-metal oxides are acidic.	Base + acid = salt + water because H^+ in acid + OH^- = H_2O. Nothing is lost during neutralisation.			Acid-base reactions due to disturbance of equilibrium between H^+ and OH^- ions in water. Use of quantities for finding equation of reaction.

Source: Adapted from Shayer and Adey, 1981.

Table 5.2   Percentage of students successfully completing science items at various levels

Mode	Ikonic		Concrete-symbolic		Formal
Level	Pre-	Uni-	Multi-	Relational	Extended abstract
Year 7	24	34	22	16	4
Year 9	15	23	32	23	7

Source: Collis and Davey, 1984.

mode by middle high school. Whether or not that *should* be the goal in all subjects and all topics within those subjects is, however, quite another question.

Pallett (1985), in recommending the use of SOLO items to Tasmanian science teachers, suggests: 'The object should be to raise the level of all children at grade 10 to the relational level. There should also be provision for a small percentage to attain the extended abstract level' (p. 3). In other words, by the end of compulsory schooling, all students should have understood the accepted frameworks for explaining the physical world: the average citizen should have a basic understanding of the physical world and the technology in everyday use.

Maybe so, but it seems on the Collis and Davey figures that, while this is a reasonable ideal, it would be impractical to achieve this for all the topics in the curriculum. Clearly, educators will need to form their own priorities; perhaps most school-leavers only need to 'know something about' acids and alkalis, but to 'understand how' the human body works (at a concrete level of course). Table 5.1 suggests strongly that the relational level in all topics represents a large investment of teaching time and effort.

In determining exit levels for the school curriculum, then, we should obviously be guided by the relative importance of the topics, and by the requirements of the next stage, whether that is employment or a new level of education.

Primary school. The primary years operate horizontally. Students acquire skills and knowledge which are essentially broadened throughout the primary years. The basic tools — reading, writing and operating the four rules of number — are acquired and deployed over increasingly diverse subject matter. The knowledge so gained should parallel students' observation, experiences and activities at first hand. The parallel between these tools and symbols and personal experience is the essence of the concrete-symbolic mode, but the evidence suggests that relational levels of thought are attained after primary school. For the most part, then, Year 6 would not go beyond multistructural response levels. Some students do reach relational levels of responding in some familiar tasks (especially in mathematics), but typically this would not be expected.

In short, the primary curriculum is directed towards horizontal rather than vertical processes, and multistructural responding in most subjects would be the reasonable expectation.

Secondary school. In secondary school, vertical processes forming relational responses should become a major focus in many topics towards Years 9 and 10. By the time they are ready to leave school and enter the workforce, students should not only know about their world but also understand some of the more important aspects of it. They should have mastered the basic mathematical techniques and operations, and know how to use them in solving the kinds of problems they are likely to meet, such as fencing a block of land, painting a house, estimating the volume of a swimming pool, calculating tax, and so forth. This is not a matter of knowing how to do different sorts of sums (which is multistructural), but how to interlock number operations with the structure of the problem. Again, in a subject like history, it seems reasonable to expect that students should be able to do more than list events; they should be able to *interpret* important events to form a point of view. Events like the Bicentennial re-enactments, films and TV mini-series such as *A Fortunate Life, Breaker Morant, Gallipoli,* etc. provide opportunities for students to relate historical narrative and time scales from texts to meaningful frameworks.

Curriculum objectives for Year 10 should then be providing for the *relational* structuring of knowledge. Curriculum statements should include such terms as 'understanding', 'appreciating', 'interpreting', 'forming an opinion about', 'applying' as well as 'listing', 'knowing about'. There will inevitably be unevenness across subjects and between students, but relational thinking for most students in the more important topics in most subjects seems a reasonable objective.

The goals for Year 12 are now mixed. The traditional track which still exists is for students going on to tertiary studies, and who have to show evidence of extended abstract (formal) thinking in at least their specialist subjects. Curriculum statements, then, should reflect formal mode thinking: for example, 'understand the principle of supply and demand', 'hypothesise', 'critically evaluate', 'generalise', etc. Not all topics in a subject would be treated at this level, but students need to show that they are at least *capable* of operating in the formal mode.

Second, there are now many students in Years 11 and 12 who do not intend to operate formally, and in fact many cannot. These years thus provide a useful opportunity to establish relational thinking in those topics not successfully dealt with by Year 10.

In sum, then, by the end of Year 10, relational thinking should be established in the more important topics, and multistructural in the remainder; while by the end of Year 12, all thinking should be vertically structured, extended abstract for academic subjects, and relational for the remainder.

Technical and further education. TAFE curriculum goals are strongly skill-based, academic content rarely exceeding relational. Technicians need to know enough about electricity, properties of metals, mechanics, etc. to be able to understand what to do within given concrete contexts. TAFE should not therefore attempt teaching content in the formal mode. The highest level of abstraction is a relational symbolic statement like Ohm's Law, or a mathematical equation, which simply puts all the relevant parameters together in their proper relationship for solving certain kinds of problem. A technician simply needs to be able to identify and measure the parameters, know where the equation applies or does not apply, and carry out the operations accurately. One difficulty with TAFE is that teachers in trade courses are often appointed solely for their practical experience and, if they lack a relational level of understanding themselves, their students will face grave difficulties in achieving the appropriate blend of skill and understanding. Killen (1983), for example, shows how the 'magic triangle' mnemonic for Ohm's Law (see Box 5.2), then becomes an impediment to the students' understanding. Killen found a high proportion of uni- and multistructural responses in trade students.

Advanced education. Advanced education at degree and diploma level addresses professional preparation. Professionals operate with an espoused theory, constructed by the individual by the study of some subjects in the formal-1 mode, and others in the concrete-symbolic mode. For example, it is not necessary for a market researcher to study mathematics at the formal level in order to understand and carry out statistical operations: statistics in that sense are simply a set of techniques for getting a job done. It would, however, be necessary to understand some aspects of psychology, sociology, and economics at a formal level in order to conceptualise a situation so that one could decide when statistical analysis is necessary in order to solve a market research problem.

The ultimate goal in professional education is therefore relational, with the theory and the practice integrated. This integration is done by the individual; the components are presented in a multistructural fashion and it is likely that their integration is a gradual process that takes a considerable amount of time and experience in the field.

University. Universities currently pursue two functions: professional education and education in particular disciplines. The professional model is different from that used in advanced education in that it usually involves the study in depth of one or few disciplines, with very much less emphasis on practical experience, although the difference is less obvious on closer analysis. Is 'medicine' a discipline, or a multistructural conglomerate of biochemistry, anatomy, pharmacology, etc.? Is education a discipline? Some say that it is, some say that it is not. In either event, the typical university mode of teacher education is a subject degree followed by a one-year

---

BOX 5.2   THE MAGIC TRIANGLE FOR OHM's LAW — E = IR

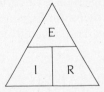

Cover the symbol for the unknown quantity and the triangle tells you whether to multiply or divide the two known quantities. (Note: E = Voltage; I = Current; and R = Resistance.)

Source: Killen, 1983.

diploma, which is a short length of time in which to integrate that content with theories of human nature, of curriculum and of society.

The real difference between universities and CAEs in professional education is rather a matter of emphasis; on the one hand building up an espoused theory by studying relatively few disciplines in the formal mode but in depth, and on the other studying a broader range of subject matter in less depth but with more practical experience. The first suggests a relational level of theory, with practical expertise developing in the field beyond the university (and basically none of the latter's business); the second suggests multistructural understanding in the formal mode, the practicum being the medium for helping the student to develop a relational integration between theory and practice.

The other function of universities is studying disciplines, which leads in the undergraduate years also to a relational level of thinking (like a historian, like a physicist ...); and in the postgraduate years to the second order formal mode. Questioning the orthodoxy is what basic research is all about, likewise, extending the questioning into disciplines. Asking if education is a discipline leads into second order formal thinking.

Summary

Figure 5.1 summarises these relationships between development stage, learning cycle and curriculum.

Ages are given at which the modes, and levels within modes, typically emerge for school-related subjects. The build-up is cumulative so that by age five to 10 years, relational levels are available in sensori-motor and ikonic modes, and uni- and multistructural in the concrete mode. The optimal target mode is concrete, with multistructural levels in the learning cycle of curriculum topics being the appropriate level for Year 6 curriculum objectives.

Relational levels in the concrete mode are appropriate for important Year 10, TAFE and some Year 12 subjects, with multistructural formal mode exit levels for 'academic' Year 12 subjects and for some CAE subjects, and relational exit levels for university degrees.

It must be stressed that Figure 5.1 refers to 'important' curriculum topics. It would be unrealistic to apply the suggested exit levels to all subjects taught in school. Nevertheless, these levels are useful for helping teachers structure their teaching as curriculum gets to be more and more school based.

INSTRUCTIONAL APPROACH

The material reviewed in this chapter has led to two major approaches to teaching —low structure and high structure. Paradoxically, Case (1985), who in many respects

Figure 5.1   Optimal targets and processes at various levels of schooling

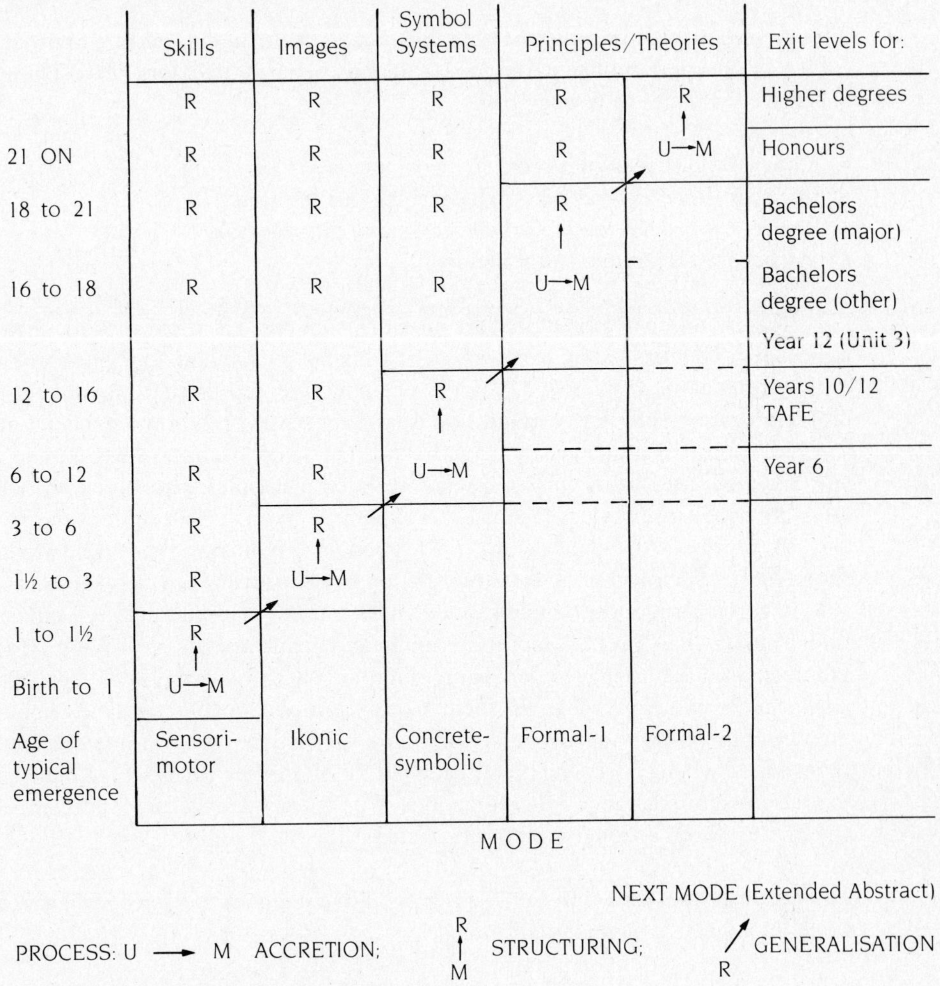

	Skills	Images	Symbol Systems	Principles/Theories		Exit levels for:
	R	R	R	R	R ↑	Higher degrees
21 ON	R	R	R	R	U→M	Honours
18 to 21	R	R	R	R ↑		Bachelors degree (major)
16 to 18	R	R	R	U→M		Bachelors degree (other)
						Year 12 (Unit 3)
12 to 16	R	R	R ↑			Years 10/12 TAFE
6 to 12	R	R	U→M			Year 6
3 to 6	R	R ↑				
1½ to 3	R	U→M				
1 to 1½	R ↑					
Birth to 1	U→M					
Age of typical emergence	Sensori-motor	Ikonic	Concrete-symbolic	Formal-1	Formal-2	

M O D E

NEXT MODE (Extended Abstract)

PROCESS: U → M ACCRETION;   R↑M STRUCTURING;   / GENERALISATION (R→)

U: unistructural level in learning cycle
M: multistructural level in learning cycle
R: relational level in learning cycle

is closest to Piaget's own position on the question of stages, himself generates a high structure teaching program, while Piaget became the guru of the advocates of the open classroom. High structure approaches take a specified curriculum objective, order all the prerequisite knowledge and teach it carefully and systematically. Low structure approaches take the point at which the students are currently, and arrange their experience so that they are likely themselves to reconstruct their knowledge more acceptably.

High structure approaches

The expert-novice paradigm. One illustration of the high structure approach bases itself on the expert-novice paradigm (Chipman, Segal and Glaser, 1984). This model is deceptively simple. In essence one:

- takes a problem-solving task;
- finds out what experts do when carrying out the task;
- finds out what novices do when they carry out the task;
- teaches the difference to the novices.

Glaser and his team studied all sorts of problems, from chess to mechanics and radiology. The first step in problem-solving is to 'understand' the problem by representing it in some way. Novices use concrete representations, aspects of the problem that are explicitly given, whereas experts use relational concepts that are derived from their much greater experience. They know what is relevant and what is not, and they infer from what is given to related principles that can be brought in to solve the problem. Novices take what is explicitly given in the problem and try to use that to represent it. This work thus strongly implicates prior knowledge and experience: which rather slows down the progression from novice to expert.

In curriculum design, such detailed analysis is very helpful, and particularly with adult subjects can greatly facilitate teaching particular topics. Taylor (1986), for example, used the novice-expert paradigm to teach 26 industrial sales representatives sufficient metallurgy to enable them to talk knowledgeably to their clients in an average of three-and-a-half hours' study time. He analysed what frameworks and cues experts used when classifying metals, and put this material into tapes and diagrams that could be used in a distance education mode. The technique was most successful and far superior to the traditional methods of training the salespeople.

The Case curriculum. Case (1985) proposes a five stage teaching program based on his model of cognitive development:

1. *Specify the topics to be taught.* This involves listing the major topics to be contained in the curriculum.
2. *Analyse how adults already handle these topics.* This is equivalent to finding out how the 'experts' (adults in the case of curriculum materials) go about these tasks.
3. *Find out the steps children use typically at different ages in getting there.* This step would incorporate all the information (and much more...) in Section A about what are the most common ways children move towards mature handling of tasks. Each task has its own sequential analysis.
4. *Design educational activities* that maximise the chance that each individual child will be able to engage the task and progress towards higher levels, allowing much practice for consolidation.
5. *Implementation*, judging the amount of task simplification necessary for each student; the need for group or individual activity, and so forth.

Case's own view: 'If such an approach were implemented ... the majority of children would reach a vectorial level of functioning [i.e. in the formal mode] in the majority of subjects areas' (p. 395). Teaching the concept of ratio with his method, eight out of nine students reached the criterion of 65 per cent of all problems correct, compared with three out of nine in the 'standard' school curriculum.

A major difficulty with his method is that the prior research needed to establish all the prerequisite knowledge for each task, and the effort needed to design individually tailored educational experiences, are both prodigious. Further, the method assumed 'that a universal developmental sequence will be found to underlie the attainment of any adult structure' (p. 394). For some concepts in the curriculum this might be a reasonable assumption, but much of the work reviewed in Section A suggests that with many concepts, children establish quite diverse frameworks that persist in different ways and at different levels — and often simultaneously. It is likely that for most topics, there is no *single* universal sequence to the final adult stage.

Low structure

Dealing with alternative frameworks. Establishing a framework for making sense of the world is something that the *learner* does spontaneously (Driver and Bell, 1985). If a teacher insists on a view that does not evidently make sense to the learner — and why should it when it is contrary to what the learner already knows is 'true'? — the learner will simply surface learn, using the symbols of the accepted framework, while living in a world interpreted by the alternative framework. Driver and Bell insist that students need to *reconstruct* their frameworks, not simply correct them. To do that, they need to be first convinced of the *need* to do so, although as the following study shows, this is by no means easy.

Gunstone, Champagne and Klopfer (1981) worked intensively with 12 Year 7 and Year 8 students, *specially selected* for their interest and ability in science, for one day a week for eight weeks. They first found out what the students believed about force and motion and then provided a rich program of activities, including a computer simulation of Aristotelian and Newtonian worlds, that challenged those beliefs. They seemed to be successful, for the students appeared to have adopted the accepted frameworks. However, on retesting with a new set of demonstrations, most retained their Aristotelian frameworks — *alongside* the newly acquired Newtonian knowledge.

In the face of such rigidity, and in such ideal circumstances, what can the science teacher do? There are three basic strategies:

1.   *Nothing.* If ideas work, why change them? As Driver and Bell (1985) point out, builders operate effectively in their calculations of conductivity of materials in terms of a flow model of heat. This is a 'bottom line' argument. With some concepts, and some students, it is hard to disagree, but it is unacceptable in general. If it is a matter of teaching or endorsing survival strategies it probably is not a bad idea, but one would have to be very selective about the alternative frameworks that are given institutional blessing.

2.   *Build on what is there.* Bruner, in an oft-quoted and deeply misunderstood phrase, once said: 'Any subject can be taught in some intellectually honest form to any child in any stage of development' (1960, p. 33). He was referring to what Driver and Bell (1985) call the 'spiral curriculum', Carmi (1981) the 'onion principle'. Alternative frameworks make do at the time: they enable the child to make some sort of sense of things. They aren't *wrong* so much as *incomplete.* Carmi suggests that many concepts can be used and built on. Cognitive development involves the *gradual* widening of that range of applicability until it finally results in a context-free handling of the concept:

> In my Israeli work I teach 'qualitative physics' in kindergarten and grade one, 'gradative physics' in grades two and three, etc. Each such stratum of physics is a self-contained science, with its own experiments, definitions, etc. and is in no sense 'less rigorous' a discipline than fully fledged quantitative physics (Carmi, 1981, p. 48).

He has designed a spiral curriculum that progressively develops these views.

3.   *Confront.* One of the problems noted by many writers is that students distort their observations to fit their existing frameworks. Several of Gunstone and White's physics students 'observed' what did not happen. Driver and Bell (1985) mention a 14-year-old boy who was asked to observe Brownian movement through a microscope: he reported 'smooth' particle movement. When asked to have another look, and observed 'smooth' movement once again — he shrugged 'Oh well, everyone sees different things I guess' — and then wrote 'jerky' in his lab report, because that was what he was 'supposed' to observe. Clearly, that boy did not see any need to revise his ideas at all, only to be careful that what he wrote down was the official version. Confrontation must *challenge* the student's own construction and create a *perceived need* for change. The above 14-year-old's perceived need was to be seen to be putting down the correct answer.

There is undoubtedly room for all three strategies. There may well be some alternative frameworks that work sufficiently well for some people for some purposes; and if one is very selective the curriculum could be adjusted accordingly. Using the onion principle is also sound, where it can be done. A spiral curriculum however needs to be carefully researched and developed for each topic, just as do Case's recommendations for setting up his developmental sequences for each task.

The real trouble with both (1) and (2) is that they sanction incorrect frameworks. In (2), the moment of truth must be faced at each twist in the spiral: the student has to be persuaded of the need to give up the prevailing conception. Otherwise it will continue to prevail. How then is (3) to be most effectively implemented? The following strategies are recommended (derived from Driver and Bell, 1985; Fensham, 1980; Gilbert and Watts, 1983; Watts and Bentley, 1984).

1.   *Find out what common alternative frameworks exist.* Table 5.3 lists some references that present common frameworks for some basic topics in the science curriculum. Science teachers should be aware of these.

Table 5.3   Some sources for alternative frameworks on various topics

Force: Watts (1983), Driver (1985), Watts and Zylbursztajn (1981)
Heat: Clough and Driver (1985a)
Pressure in fluids: Clough and Driver (1985b)
Energy conservation: Driver and Warrington (1985)
Mechanics: Driver (1985), Gilbert, Watts and Osborne (1982)
Evaporation: Beveridge (1985)
Children's Learning in Science Project (CLISP), Centre for Studies in Science and Mathematics Education, University of Leeds, LS2 9JT, has collected material for teaching and curriculum development based on alternative frameworks about: particles, heat, plant nutrition, energy and chemistry.

2.   *Find out what your own students think.* This is usually done with a demonstration of some phenomenon with a built-in 'surprise', occasioned by showing a situation and asking for a prediction of what is going to happen and why.

3.   *Present them with events that challenge these ideas.* Now knowing what they think, design a demonstration that *does not* happen according to prediction, and ask them to explain *that*. The explanation then elicits the students' frameworks for interpreting the event. For example, Gunstone and White (1981) for one of their situations used a bicycle wheel mounted as a pulley, and a bucket of sand connected by a cord to a block of wood, of the same mass as the sand. The cord was placed over the pulley, with the bucket much higher than the block: Question 1: 'How does the weight of the bucket compare with the weight of the block?' (27 per cent said the block was heavier). Question 2: 'Now predict what will happen if this small spoon of sand is added to the bucket'. (Only 54 per cent said the bucket would accelerate smoothly to the floor.)

4.   *Encourage hypothesising and the generation of explanations to replace those that have just been demonstrated to be inadequate.* While the discovery that one has predicted incorrectly may be challenging, it is also threatening (Watts and Gilbert, 1983; Watts and Bentley, 1984; Driver and Bell, 1985). Students can easily be made to look foolish by these demonstrations. They therefore 'clam up', and do defensive things, such as the 14-year-old boy who simply complied with expectations, or Gunstone and White's students who 'observed' mathematical equations. The environment for these elaborations, and explorations of alternatives, must therefore be non-threatening. Students have to be able to admit their mistakes without shame, and explore alternatives without inhibition.

5.   *Allow many opportunities to use new ideas in a wide range of situations* so that the utility of the newer conceptions, and their superiority to the old, can be tested and confirmed on a large scale. Fensham (1980) refers to 'scientism', when students play scientists with a variety of natural phenomena and items of technology, systematically identifying and labelling features.

6.   *Point out where scientific definitions conflict with those in common use.*

7.   *Explain scientific method.* Scientists *oversimplify*: they invent idealised solutions and concepts, such as absolute zero or a perfect vacuum. Like Glaser's 'experts', they use abstract principles that are not observed in the situation to explain why, for

instance, pieces of paper are attracted to a plastic comb that has been whisked briskly through a dry head of hair. Children, like 'novices' generally, use what they see: 'the rubbing makes the paper stick'. Electrons and fields aren't visible. As students realise what scientists *do* — that in many respects it is not so different from what they do — scientific explanations may become more acceptable.

Open classrooms. The kind of approach arising out of the alternative frameworks research is low structure and student-centred, in that the *students themselves* need to reconstruct their thinking in terms of the accepted framework.

This approach fits well with the philosophy behind open classrooms in general, and with which Piaget's psychology has been frequently associated. McNally (1975) regards the *integrated day* as 'the greatest practical expression to Piaget's ideas' (p. 96). The integrated day combines Years 1 to 6 (usually this program is implemented in primary schools but it can be made to work equally in secondary). There is minimal timetabling, no rigid division into subjects; activities are problem-centred, and draw on several subjects. Classes are of mixed ability and mixed age, older students mentoring younger ones (as proposed by Andrew Bell in 1791, see Chapter 4).

Tasks and activities are usually built around integrated subject areas, while the development of individual skills (e.g. in reading, spelling or mathematics) is approached on an individual mastery basis. Group and individual work is carried out in music, craft, oral expression, debates, and so on. Evaluation may be carried out by teachers and pupils in consultation, with little emphasis on marks or competitive grading systems. McNally considers that this type of scheme illustrates Piagetian theory in four ways:

1. Generalised experiences, self-regulatory behaviour and cognitive match. Piaget insisted on self-chosen spontaneous activity in a structured environment that provides a variety of tasks appropriate to particular stages of cognitive development. In his view, the optimal mismatch leading to recoding (accommodation) is most likely to occur under such conditions and much less likely when the choice and pace of learning is forced upon the child.

2. Motivation. These conditions of optimal mismatch are, as we have seen in Chapter 3, associated with intrinsic motivation. The elimination of marks and competition also agrees with the points made in Chapter 3 about the conditions favouring intrinsic motivation: a sense of competence and mastery (being an 'origin'), with little room for fear of failure.

3. Interpersonal interaction. Piaget emphasised interpersonal interaction and co-operation as a means of reducing egocentrism in thought and prompting allocentrism. The ideas of small-group work, and making older students responsible for mentoring younger ones, are clearly compatible with this aspect. They are also highly compatible with the points in Chapter 4 on peer-tutoring and the development of metacognition.

4. Activity and discovery. Piaget believed in the importance of the child's own activity leading to discoveries and concept formation. Again, this is a common theme, emphasised by Driver and Bell and others working with alternative frameworks.

These are generalisations to which many educators (progressive) would give rousing assent: and to which other educators (traditional) would voice equally strong disagreement. They do not, however, tell the educator *how* to teach a child along 'Piagetian' lines. Such generalisations relate to values or philosophy, not established techniques or psychology.

Further, Piaget was not the first to expound such a philosophy. The Rousseauian tradition is a long one, and has already had several representatives this century — Dewey, Montessori, Isaacs, Neill, and many others. In Britain, which has long had a tradition of progressive primary school education, Piaget's terminology and rationale was eagerly used to support what was already established practice.

The open classroom in general represents this 'progressive' movement in Australian schools. They follow the general rationale of the integrated day. If they are perhaps less stringent on matters of timetabling, the spirit is similar, and certainly the integrated day and open classrooms in general require different teaching styles from traditional classes.

The most notable research into open schools in Australia has been carried out by the Australian Open Area Schools Project (Angus, 1979), which warned that teachers should be very cautious in drawing inferences about specific situations from the general results. For example, while *average* school scores for reading and mathematics were higher for pupils from conventional schools than those from open schools, there were of course a number of open schools that performed better than conventional schools.

A special test was used to gather data on self-esteem. It was found that the relationship between school design and pupil self-concept varied across different social levels. Conventionally designed schools seemed to benefit pupils of low social status; pupils of high and middle social status seemed better suited to open-plan schools. On a test of general intellectual ability, the children in conventional schools scored significantly higher than those in open schools. On several tests no significant differences could be found, despite the bias against open schools that standardised testing is bound to have.

Pickens (1980) argues that there are two clear findings from research into open classrooms:

1. No consistent differences have been found in the academic achievement of pupils in open-plan and traditional classrooms.
2. Children in open classrooms have, however, been found to rate more highly on tests of motivation, peer relations, attitudes to school, self-concept and similar characteristics, than children in traditional classrooms.

LIFESPAN EDUCATION

The model of schooling that prevails today was designed on four broad assumptions:

1. The best time for learning is through childhood and up to the early twenties. Thereafter, people decline in learning ability, especially after the forties.
2. People need to have their learning environments highly structured for them (as to what, where, when and how to learn) if learning is to take place. Following from this, learning is not 'real' unless accredited by an institution.

3. Society is sufficiently stable to enable us to predict both the nature and extent of employment opportunities.

4. The knowledge needed to carry out particular jobs is already available or may easily become available. That knowledge is changing slowly enough so that it is sensible to teach in anticipation of society's needs 10, 20, even 30 years hence.

The model of schooling that derives from such assumptions is that formal schooling should be provided during their 'learning years' so that people may then go out and perform to their best advantage during their 'earning years', or, to change the metaphor, fill-up-the-tanks to permit the long journey ahead along the road of life. That model is the *basis* of today's schooling, although we are finding out that it leaves much to be desired, particularly for older people. In fact, of course, these assumptions are wrong on all four counts:

1. While cognitive abilities change through the lifespan, they do not significantly decline *in the aspects that matter* until old age. There is a slowdown in some sensori-motor skills, but in healthy individuals reasoning and memory are relatively unimpaired, while some aspects of learning and particularly metacognition abilities are much superior.

2. If the learning environment is too highly structured, surface rather than deep learning occurs. Accreditation procedures can induce cynicism and game-playing.

3. Youth can no longer look forward to almost certain employment in the area of their choice upon leaving school, as they once could. Today, many adults face significant changes in job area about every 10 years; leisure time is much increased.

4. Knowledge requirements for certain jobs cannot be predicted with any certainty at all. The fastest growing employment area is currently in high technology; market potential is growing faster than the knowledge base while job opportunities are drastically in excess of the number of educated professionals higher education can produce (Le Fevre, 1985). Universities and CAEs are hopelessly behind both in knowledge production and in supply of professionals in certain key areas.

On the institutional front, then, we clearly need to look at the educational needs of adults. As far as non-accredited learning is concerned, Tough (1971) found that North American adults spent an average of 700 hours each a year in what he called 'learning projects', where people sought instruction in such topics as business management, history, psychology, gardening, etc. That was over 15 years ago. That figure would be much higher today with increased leisure opportunities. When we add in formal provisions for sport and recreation, inservice courses for teachers and other professionals, retraining, TAFE, WEA classes, and the fact that formal enrolments of mature age students in all tertiary sectors has been rising dramatically since 1980, the whole area of providing for the needs of adult learners becomes enormous. We cannot devote to this topic the attention it deserves, but in view of its importance we should address two broad issues: Do adult learners differ sufficiently from younger learners to warrant different instructional methods? What implications are there in adult learning for the educational system?

Do adult learners differ from younger learners?

The question for anyone associated with the formal provision of adult learning programs is whether adults are sufficiently different *as learners* from child and adolescent learners to warrant different ways of teaching, instruction and evaluation.

Knowles (1978) thought so: he called the adult learner a 'neglected species' and proposed *androgogy* as the science of instruction suited to the adult, as *pedagogy* is that suited to the child. Knowles lists some of the more important features of the adult learner:

1. Adults are motivated to learn particular topics because their life situation has defined *a need to know,* or because they have developed an *interest* in a topic. They rarely study something because they have been told it will be important to them one day: it already is important, now.
2. What adults learn is thus based in an experienced situation. Genuine problems define what is important to learn, not the fact that the topic belongs in a particular subject area.
3. Adults usually come to a topic with a *background of experience* in the area that can be considerable, and often a high degree of *success*.
4. Adults are strongly oriented towards *self-direction* in their learning, whereas younger students react to a learning situation directed by others (teachers).
5. Individual differences between learners, in their knowledge, styles and competencies, increase with age, so that older students are much *more diverse* in their learning than younger students.

As Tough's work made clear, adults are frequently highly self-directed, defining for themselves what they want to know, where to go to find out, and when their requirements for that learning have been met. On the other hand, they often have a belief in credentials — in the need for formal qualifications. Also, as adults have a higher personal stake, both literally and in their self-esteem, success and failure are much more important to them. When institutional learning is structured too heavily, adults can go overboard in struggling for high grades and in being competitive. Mature age learners often feel unfairly disadvantaged when in the same class as younger through-the-system students: but see Box 5.3. In fact, the advantages pointed out by Knowles, and the additional experience and metacognitive abilities referred to in Section A, far more than outweigh the disadvantages. Records of mature age external students' progress, as compared to younger internals, invariably show that while drop-out rates are higher, externals who stay in the system achieve considerably better results than younger, internal students.

Ultra-competitiveness and feelings of insecurity are the dark side of adult learning. They arise precisely because the institution takes over directing matters, whereas adults have been doing this for themselves during their non-school lives. Table 5.4 contrasts institutional with mature adult learning decisions.

It is not necessarily the case that the institutional mode of learning is better for younger students, and the self-directed mode better for older ones. Chapter 4 would suggest that the latter best suits both, with variations according to differential experience, maturity etc. The problem of reconciling self-direction, institutional direction, and the effect on the quality of learning, exists at all ages. We disagree with Knowles that the difference is so great that it creates a new (and neglected) 'species' of learner.

While adults are highly self-directed,
they frequently seek
formal qualifications.

BOX 5.3   REFLECTIONS OF A MAS

Mr Ted Miller's reason for coming to university was an awareness of impending early retirement. He says his first days as a MAS (mature age student) were horrific.

'When one walked towards the first lecture or tutorial after half a lifetime spent out in the marketplace, humility was the dominant mood! In this new and strange environment, you were unsure of what responses were expected of you, wondering what that turbulent sea of young students thought of you, but more importantly what your tutor thought of this strange, too well-dressed, middle-aged creature who was trying too visibly hard to blend into the group. You had to learn a new jargon', Mr Miller says, 'new parking regulations and most importantly you had to learn all over again how to listen and analyse what was being said. One had to mimic the proverbial duck: serene on the surface but paddling like hell underneath!'

Experience urged Mr Miller to be a 'joiner' — joining in with literary clubs, extracurricular societies, lunch-time seminars, philosophy lectures and even creative writing. This is the only arena where students can meet and mingle socially without any unspoken competitive pressure inhibiting conversation. Here is where the aged MAS eventually finds out that his or her paranoid generation gap exists only in the imagination; that he or she is simply accepted for personality and intellect.

The remainder of their undergraduate years completes the meta-morphosis of the mature student, Mr Miller says. 'We learn that the library is the sanctum sanctorum and the very nerve centre of the University and that spending many hours there, reading and writing, does pay off in higher grades. We probably have less distractions. We place a great deal of emphasis on organising our time and our study material, and we gradually, but inexorably, are being made aware of our own intellectual limitations. Perhaps this latter self-knowledge is the single most important step.'

'However coming to university is not a denial of our mortality; but like the noted writer, who, when in his seventies, took up his first piano lessons, it is an affirmation of how much we value life.'

(Mr Miller, aged 58, is an Arts Honours student who is working on Classical Renaissance Epic Poetry. He had a long successful working life as a manager in Philips Industries Ltd. He presented his 'reflections of a mature age graduate' at a conference of Arts Deans at the University of Newcastle.)

Source: *The Gazette*, University of Newcastle, 17 December 1985.

Table 5.4   Decisions about learning and who makes them

Decision	Institutional response	Mature adult response
What to learn	As set out in the official syllabus, usually defined in self-contained subject areas.	As suggested by the experience of the problem situation, but help often needed to know where to go.
How to go about learning	As directed by the teacher who plans activities and exercises.	By reading, asking others, being metacognitively resourceful.
What resources to use	What the institution makes available; what teacher says to use.	What the situation turns up.
How will learning be evaluated; when to stop	As laid down, by exam, test, by institution; fail or continue if successful.	When personally satisfied or when problem is solved; topic 'learned' because it works. No formal testing.

What forms of learning best suit adults?

Problem-based learning. This mode of learning has been around for many years, but it is only relatively recently that it has become 'institutionalised' (e.g. Boud, 1985a). One of the pioneers was the McMaster Medical School in Ontario, Canada. This model of medical education inspired the University of Newcastle Faculty of Medicine, and has since spread to Newcastle CAE Paramedical School, to Tocal Agricultural College and to the University of Newcastle Faculty of Education, among others. In the Faculty of Medicine, the first year undergraduate is presented within weeks with a genuine patient. To understand the case, it is necessary to find out a lot of information: from experts in the faculty, from prepared audiovisual resources, from group seminars including local doctors, etc. Each student covers five or six very carefully selected patients a year, so that over the full extent of the course, the required anatomical, biochemical, pharmaceutical and other technical knowledge and skills — that would have been formally taught in traditional fill-the-tanks-first coursework — have been covered. The difference is that the coverage is in a real and obviously highly meaningful context (they *are* real patients): the context defines what the students need to know. The skill is in selecting the situations and problems so that what would otherwise be called 'the relevant syllabus' is covered. The evidence is that this approach is much superior to traditional coursework in terms of student motivation and depth of learning (Clarke and Newble, in press).

Here, a leaf has been taken out of the adult educator's book and applied to a real situation. Much adult learning, retraining, inservice courses, etc. follow this mode, if in a less obvious or spectacular fashion. Why does a teacher go to an inservice course? To find out more about how to handle a particular kind of problem. And who takes the

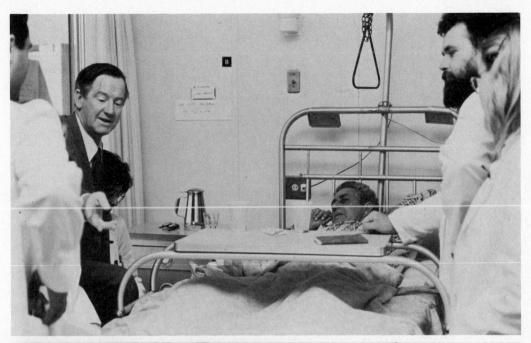

Problem-based learning:
To understand the case, it is
necessary to find out and
analyse a lot of information.

course? Somebody who in real life has successfully handled that problem, usually a colleague, but possibly a visitor or a faculty member of a local institution who has done research on the topic. The whole context is problem-based and experiential: the learning has a self-defined problem and the teacher is simply a fellow-learner who is just a little farther down the track.

Workshopping. The workshop is simply one popular way of handling a problem. The leader (the fellow-learner-who-is-farther-down-the-same-track) provides experiences that crystallise the points to be learned. Everything is in context: any expository talk directly addresses the materials and problems to be handled.

Contracting. Knowles (1978) suggests that contracts be negotiated between adult learner and a learning consultant, in which the particular points addressed in Table 5.4 are covered: what to learn, when to know it has been learned, etc. That way an adult-mode businesslike arrangement has been set up between two partners in a concern of mutual interest. Contracting is advocated in schools too (see Chapter 8): all that says is that the adult mode may be used with non-adults as well as with adults. Certainly it is more realistic in preparing children for living in an adult world to use adult modes of interaction in helping them get there, than it is to use highly directive (or childish) modes of learning; and particularly to use them for adults in helping them cope with different adult-world problems!

Will lifelong education pre-empt the need for schools?

To return to the point where we came in, if the assumptions about learners, society and knowledge that underlie the present fill-up-the-tanks model of school are all wrong, shouldn't schools be disbanded in favour of periodic lifelong/low-structure/inservice/problem-based/contracted/workshops for learning? Certainly Illich (1971) thought so. He would have deschooled society in favour of marketplace 'learning exchanges' — and that too was over 15 years ago. It is unlikely, however, that schools will suddenly vanish, for all the reasons implicit here (see also Cropley, 1976). What seems more likely is that schools will remain; that leaving ages may even rise (perhaps for social and economic reasons rather than for educational ones); but that schools will more and more take on adult modes of learning, and an adult climate, emphasising hands-on experience and self-direction in all aspects of curriculum, approach to learning and instruction, and evaluation. These general themes have been addressed in Chapter 4 especially, and will be addressed again in Chapters 10 (evaluation) and 11 (the future).

Our study of lifespan development, and the burden of this chapter, indicate that the worlds of childhood and adulthood are closer together than we thought, and the learning that takes place in each will increasingly share each other's ways, problems and management structures.

SUMMARY

The study of cognitive development reveals how children come to make sense out of their physical world, and how their ways of knowing become more sophisticated. This knowledge is helpful in considering the nature and structure of educational objectives at different levels of schooling, and in considering approaches to instruction and to science teaching in particular. When we extend our study across the lifespan, as has been done only fairly recently, a commonality emerges that is helpful both for continuing and for normal patterns of education.

Curriculum design. To suggest that developmental psychology provides a useful framework for considering curriculum design, and particularly the exit levels of performance at various stages of schooling, is not to fall into the 'stages trap'. Because certain higher level modes of response typically occur at certain ages, it does not follow that all learning after those ages should be at the new level. In arriving at exit levels, we ask what *function* the learning is to achieve in the next phase (whether that is the next level of schooling; or employment; or leisure); and what levels seem to be *achieved already* in school (and hopefully we would not find too much disparity between these two criteria). We then specify the *target mode* and the *level in the learning cycle*. Sensori-motor and ikonic modes would be well established, so for fine arts, drama, PE, etc. the exit is always relational. In 'academic' subjects we specify the optimal mode. On these grounds, the following exit levels seem appropriate:

- *Year 6 or end of primary schooling:* multistructural in concrete-symbolic mode;
- *Year 10 for school-leavers:* relational level in the concrete-symbolic mode in important subjects, or important topics within those subjects; multistructural in the rest. Perhaps some formal mode responses (i.e. extended abstract conrete) for academically oriented students;
- *Year 12:* formal mode (uni- and multistructural) in some topics for academic students and concrete-symbolic (relational) in the remainder of subjects; and relational for all other students and subjects;
- *Technical and further education:* relational level in the concrete-symbolic mode for academic subjects, and for linking academic knowledge with skill knowledge;
- *Higher education:* mixture of concrete-symbolic and formal modes. Relational level (concrete) for some service subjects, but multistructural (first order formal) in most others, reaching to relational (formal) in major subject of university degree. Second order formal mode is not used until honours and postgraduate study.

Instructional approach. The material reviewed here can be interpreted, depending on subject matter and educational philosophy, within high and low structure approaches to learning.

The *expert-novice* paradigm is an example of a high structure approach, involving detailed analysis, task by task, of what constitutes expert performance in that task, and designing instruction around that analysis. Case's curriculum is an example of this approach in a developmental context. The approach works where there is a common if not universal sequence leading to expert performance, and where the quite considerable research and development has been done in advance.

The analysis of children's *alternative frameworks* for explaining natural phenomena emphasises that students enter the classroom with their own (often quite unexpected) models of explanation already in place. Teachers need to know what these models or frameworks are, to work with them where appropriate, but to confront the student with evidence of the need to change when necessary. Low structure applications are designed to encourage students to form their own reconstructions along the lines established by science, and to make use of the spontaneous learnings that they already have.

The *open classroom,* and its variant the integrated day, are low structure environments for teaching generally, in the 'progressive' philosophy. Piaget's theory of cognitive development has been used in the past by progressive educators as an espoused theory, but there are problems with his theory of stages. Other aspects of the open classroom — self-direction, intrinsic motivation, social and especially peer interaction — are however very compatible with modern theories of optimal cognitive growth.

Lifespan education. The theme of responsible self-direction recurs when we look at how adults differ from younger learners, and at the structure of education. The model of schooling that is most common today was based on assumptions about learning and cognitive development, the growth of knowledge, societal change and employment prospects that no longer apply, whatever their truth years ago.

Adult educators have long emphasised the need to take context, prior knowledge, self-defined objectives and prior experience into account in the design of instruction: such models as problem-based learning, workshops and contracts are examples of adult models of instruction. These models, however, appear to work well for both mature and younger learners. The distinctions between school and continuing education that once prevailed may well have reflected the needs and served the purposes of a more static and predictable society. Today, it seems that we are moving towards a model of schooling that presents much less contrast between children's and adults' learning. The differences are not as great as we once might have thought. Schools will continue to exist, but they will look a lot more like other structures in society, and the modes and contents of school learning will reflect the problems and concerns of society.

FURTHER READING

On cognitive development

R. Case, *Cognitive Development,* Academic Press, New York, 1985.

M. Donaldson, *Children's Minds,* Fontana, London, 1978.

K. Fischer and D. Bullock, 'Cognitive Development in School-age Children: Conclusions and New Directions', in W. Collins (ed.), *Development during Middle Childhood,* National Academy of Sciences Press, Washington, DC, 1984.

H. Ginsburg and S. Opper, *Piaget's Theory of Intellectual Development,* Prentice-Hall, Englewood Cliffs, NJ, 1979.

G. S. Halford, *The Development of Thought,* Laurence Erlbaum, Hillsdale, NJ.

Case and Halford present neo-Piagetian theories, with an emphasis on the influence of stages appearing at regular intervals. Case is more concerned with educational implications; Donaldson, and Fischer and Bullock, are rather more eclectic in their review, with less of a Piagetian orientation. Ginsburg and Opper present an orthodox and clear account of Piaget, with a final chapter devoted to educational implications. Donaldson's book is a very clear but more controversial discussion of development. In particular, she criticises some of Piaget's crucial experiments. To fully understand the points about 'stages' made in this chapter, both Ginsburg and Opper, and Donaldson, should be read: neither is hard work.

On alternative frameworks

R. Driver, 'Pupils' Alternative Frameworks in Science', *European Journal of Science Education* **3**, 1981, 93-101.

R. Driver, *The Pupil as Scientist,* The Open University Press, Milton Keynes, 1983.

R. Gunstone and R. White, Understanding of gravity. *Science Education,* **65**, 1981, 291-9.

Driver's 1981 article fixed the term 'alternative framework'; the 1983 book enlarges on the concept and the implications for teaching. Gunstone and White's paper is interesting as it shows the effect teaching doesn't have on how students perceive scientific phenomena.

On the lifespan

M. Knowles, *The Adult Learner: A Neglected Species,* Gulf Press, Houston, 1978.

D. Levinson et al., *The Seasons of a Man's Life,* Knopf, New York, 1978.

G. Sheehy, *Passages*, Dutton, New York, 1976.

L. Viney, *Transitions,* Cassell Australia, Melbourne, 1980.

It is nice being reminded that life is not all downhill from late adolescence onwards (as an uncritical reading of most developmental psychologists, including Piaget, might suggest). Levinson's work is the more scholarly; Sheehy's is a popularised version; Viney's work applies lifespan psychology to the role of women in Australian society. Knowles is concerned with the provision of educational programs for the adult.

On problem-based learning

D. Boud (ed.), *Problem-based Learning in Education for the Professions,* Higher Education Research and Development Society of Australasia, Sydney, 1985.

This book is a collection of papers by leading practitioners of problem-based learning throughout universities and colleges in Australia. The theory, design, implementation and evaluation of this approach is documented, with reference to many professional education areas. While the orientation here is tertiary, there are lessons to be learned at primary and secondary levels.

QUESTIONS

Questions for self-testing

1. List five characteristics of the developmental stages according to the Piagetian view.
2. What is meant by 'optimal level' when referring to cognitive development?
3. List five modes of thinking, briefly describing each.
4. What three components have to be added to physical growth to ensure developmental progression?
5. What is an 'alternative framework'? Give an example.
6. Briefly show how developmental psychology has implications for educational practice in:
    (a) curriculum design;
    (b) teaching method;
    (c) science teaching;
    (d) alternative frameworks;
    (e) lifespan education.
7. Why shouldn't the child's understanding of the conservation of number be used to determine whether that child is yet ready to be taught arithmetic?
8. What happens during:
    - the accretion of knowledge;
    - the structuring of knowledge;
    - the generalisation of knowledge?
    Give an example of each on a school-based topic.
9. Why is science fiction in a second order formal mode, whereas science fantasy is not?
10. What aspects of cognitive performance quite unequivocally decline by middle adulthood?

Questions for discussion

1. Apply the Case five-stage teaching program to a topic from your teaching syllabus. Does the time taken to obtain the required information justify the advantage in pupil gains?
2. Do you accept Bruner's claim that any subject can be taught 'in some intellectually honest form' to any pupil? Justify your view.
3. Take a curriculum topic and devise a set of objectives for that topic which go through unistructural, multistructural and relational stages in the concrete mode, and an extended abstract version in the formal mode. Does that give you any ideas about teaching the topic?

4. Find out an alternative framework not mentioned in this chapter that children use to understand some natural phenomena. What is *wrong* with the framework? What is right about it? How would you use this knowledge to teach students the accepted framework?
5. From your knowledge of adult learning, analyse some aspects of teaching curriculum and assessment in your present course of study. Do you conclude it is a good compromise between institutional and psychological needs?
6. Describe an alternative framework you remember having as a child. Where did you get it from?

6

Language development

OVERVIEW

This chapter examines the development of the uniquely human ability to communicate in spoken and written ways. This development is linked to what occurs in the home, the school and society itself. Skill in spoken language (oracy) is developed in the home, but literacy skills in both reading and writing are the special concern of the school. Social class and ethnic differences provide special problems for schooling, and these are given further attention in Section B of the chapter. Questions answered by this chapter include the following:

- Do babies learn to speak by imitation?
- How is a child's make-believe world related to language development?
- Do children learn a second language more easily than adults?
- How can reading be taught?
- Should immigrants be taught English as a second language in special classes?
- Do Australian babies learn their language in the same way as babies in other cultures?
- How do heredity and context affect language development?
- How can young pupils be helped to become more metacognitive about their comprehension?
- Why does egocentrism persist longer in children's written language than it does in spoken language?
- How can a student attempt to deceive an examiner into perceiving a cohesive argument in an examination essay?
- What variations in language use exist between social classes?
- Which children learn a second language more easily?

When you have finished this chapter, you should be able to understand or do the following:

1. How children use different features of text to aid their understanding.
2. How young pupils can be helped to become more metacognitive about their comprehension.
3. How student comprehension of text can be maximised.
4. Distinguish the assimilation and multicultural models of migrant education and argue a case for the adoption of one of them.
5. Distinguish between the processes involved in learning phonemes and syntax.
6. How deep and surface approaches to writing are distinguished.
7. How the work of good and poor writers can be differentiated.
8. How conferencing helps teachers of writing.
9. Describe the advantages of word processors in teaching writing skills.
10. Convince a sceptic that an ESL student will learn *English* better by concentrating on his or her *original* language as well as on English.

SECTION A

LANGUAGE AND BEING HUMAN

Language is the most outstandingly *human* of all our behavioural and cognitive attributes. Its importance cannot be over-emphasised. Language makes it possible to live together in society; language greatly facilitates inventive problem-solving; and certainly, without written language, it would not be possible to perpetuate the culture of which such inventions are just one small part.

In this chapter, we shall briefly consider the following aspects of language development and usage:

- the development of spoken language (*oracy*);
- the psychology of reading;
- the psychology of writing;
- language and social class; the function of language within society;
- second-language learning, with special reference to learning English as a second language.

The study of the ability to communicate through language is necessary in any study of human psychology, simply because it is such a unique and significant function. In educational psychology this study becomes even more important because school is the institution that has been charged by society to develop the skills, particularly written, of communication. However, we shall see that this leads to particular problems for teachers — or, rather, for some students — because the school has its own vested interests in language, and these interests are shared with those of some social classes or groupings, but not with others. The school's investment in language may even be seen as a political question. Children whose parents occupy underprivileged positions in society come to acquire a functional need for language that is quite different from those children who are privileged. Migrant and Aboriginal children in particular face special problems of language.

The first question is: how does language develop?

THE DEVELOPMENT OF SPOKEN LANGUAGE

Despite the enormous differences in adult language in different cultures in the world — such that even speakers of related languages, such as French and Italian, cannot converse without translation — the development of language proficiency is remarkably constant.

The unit of spoken language is called the *phoneme*: it is the smallest sound-unit that indicates a change of meaning. The words 'sex' and 'six' are remarkably similar in structure, length and sound — but there is a critical difference that is contained in the middle phonemes (written /e/ and /i/). Some phonemes are used in some languages but not in others: /bh/ appears in Hindi but not in English, while the Japanese make no distinction between /l/ and /r/. New Zealanders, as it happens, make little distinction between /e/ and /i/. Yet the course of development in oracy is remarkably similar across cultures — until that point (usually around 18 months) when the child's own particular language develops. Thereafter, the specifics of the language become more and more firmly embedded, although not until puberty is there a virtual point-of-no-return with respect to the pronounced language. Prior to puberty, the child's voice production is still malleable, and can blend with local accents unselfconsciously and convincingly. After puberty, such adaptability is rare and, when it does take place, it is by self-conscious effort.

Learning phonemes

What is responsible for the production of phonemes peculiar to a language and an accent? Babies in all cultures commence their careers in oracy with cooing and babbling, which begins spontaneously at about three to four months, and continues until nine to 12 months. *Babbling* consists of sentence-like strings of sounds, which may rise and fall in intonation like conversation but cannot be interpreted by an outsider, even a parent. Analysis has shown that the sounds emitted cover all known phonemes, and that the babbling of English, Chinese or Aboriginal children is identical.

This phase reaches its strongest around nine months and then ceases; sometimes abruptly, sometimes overlapping the formation of the first genuine words. 'Genuine' words are those which have a definite outside referent (object referred to), such as 'Mama' or 'Dadda'. It is interesting that even children who are profoundly deaf commence and cease babbling at the same time as other children, even though they do not go on to produce words.

Babbling is obviously an important stage and is largely internally controlled: it makes little difference precisely what, if anything, the children actually hear, they will babble just the same. Nevertheless, hearing is obviously closely related to the *next* stage, that of forming true words. Some writers have suggested (e.g. Skinner, 1957) that language learning is simply a matter of imitation, with parents rewarding or withholding reward according to how well the infant imitates them. This is true to an extent. Parents do smile and cuddle their baby when the right sounds are produced. In the natural setting, when the baby says something meaningful, immediate notice is taken, whereas something indistinct is likely to be ignored. This does indeed seem to fit Skinner's model of operant conditioning (see Chapter 3). However, it cannot be the full story or even the most important part of it.

Once children have started to form words, the locus of control over the formation of words swings back internally. The De Villiers (1979) tell of their son Nicholas who at 15 months responded with a clear and correct 'turtle' to the various toy turtles that were floating in his bath. At 18 months, however, his very proper 'turtle' had become 'kurka' and stayed that way for some months. The change from 'turtle' to 'kurka' is a typical transformation: children seem to abstract a rule about how things 'should' be pronounced. Until they refine their articulation, they operate according to their internalised rule rather than what they actually see and hear. For example, it is common to find that voiced consonants (e.g. /b/, /g/) change places with unvoiced ones (e.g. /p/, /k/) at the beginning and ends of words. Thus, 'pussy' becomes 'bussy', 'Bob' becomes 'Bop'; and 'frog', 'frok': what might originally have been learned and imitated correctly is transformed into a version that assuredly has *not* been learned by imitation.

Learning syntax

Exactly the same principle applies in the learning of syntax. If children learned by imitation, they would not come out with such words as 'wented', 'goodest', 'breaked', and so on, with such regularity. Children also quickly learn the difference between a proper noun (e.g. their own name) and a pronoun. For example, a parent may say 'Tommy come to Mummy' and the child, on repeating it, will say 'Tommy come to Mummy'. However, if she says 'You come to Mummy', he will not repeat the 'you' if it refers to himself. The only exception to this appears to be with autistic children, who have been noted to use 'you' for the first person, and, perhaps more significantly, 'he' or 'she' for self-reference. But these errors reveal one of the pathologies of the autistic child: the inability to see oneself and others in a personal light.

Just as babbling is the first step towards the controlled and meaningful emission of sounds, there is a period that lays the groundrules for conversation. Games like build-and-bust require, first, a party carrying out the activity (building), while the other is passive; then the roles are reversed. The previously passive party now busts the tower the other has built. This is the pattern for conversational interaction. As with the formation of words, the rules here are not just learned. Infants seek eye contact when they initiate a verbal exchange, from a very early age; they seem 'primed' with the basic rules of personal interaction. Some psychologists believe that human beings have an inborn set of rules — a generative transformational grammar as Chomsky (1957) called it — that guides the growth of linguistic ability independently of intelligence, race or experience. Lenneberg (1969), for example, noted that speech development parallels physical development, even in retarded children. According to Lenneberg, there is a critical period of development during which oral language structures are acquired. If they are not — as in the case of deaf children whose first experience with language is at school age — the native-language syntax is learned as if it were a second ('foreign') language, so that such children are placed at a severe disadvantage. In other words, oral language is highly prepared, biologically speaking.

The context of communication

If heredity provides the structure, experience provides the content and context of language. Let us look at context. In any exchange between two people who know each other well, but particularly between parent and young child, much of what is said is unnecessary or redundant. For example:

Mother:	Now darling, let's put the doggy in his housie.
Child:	Doggy in housie. Mummy, doggy in there.
Mother:	Yes, darling. Where did doggy go?
Child:	Doggy in there.
Mother:	Yes, doggy's in there, isn't he?
Child:	Doggy in there ...

Clearly, something more than the whereabouts of the doggy is at issue; indeed the verbal (as opposed to the non-verbal) conversation is mostly unnecessary. Here, we have seen *too much* spelling out of detail. The opposite also occurs in intimate conversation in the form of *exophoric reference*: the use of pronouns such as 'it', 'he' and 'she', when it is not clear to an outsider what or who 'it', 'he' and 'she' refer to. Such conversation has 'in-group' references that make interpretation almost impossible outside that context.

Language, in short, is learned in a very supportive context which reflects the intimacy and shared experience of the participants. Language is just as embedded as is reasoning: and in both cases, developmental growth is indicated by the increasing ability of the child to operate in *disembedded* contexts. The role of the school is crucial here. The traditional disciplines — history, science, mathematics, economics, etc. —are all *public* bodies of knowledge in the sense that anyone who can 'crack the code' is able to understand them. This is not true of the intimate and highly embedded language of the four-year-old. Hence, one of the tasks of the school is to teach the child how to use language in an increasingly disembedded or public manner (Donaldson, 1978).

Two critical characteristics of adult speech, lacking in the pre-school child, grow gradually but firmly during middle childhood. Both refer to an aspect of disembeddedness.

Expanding contexts. A pre-school child's language is limited in its reference to immediate experience. Children at first name objects only in their presence — as if the word, and the first thing referred to, must occur together (as of course they do, in the *initial* learning of language). However, it is the very power of language that it comes to transcend this one-to-one relationship with the real world.

Until the age of six there is a steady increase in ability to transcend context. Until the age of three, time references are to the past but not yet the future. Future references occur fairly soon after age three — as, for example, when the three-year-old states 'I'll eat you!'. More remote future events, such as 'tomorrow' and 'next week', are not understood until a year or so later. Causality ('If you put out your tooth, the tooth fairy will come') seems to be understood quite well by three-and-a-half or four. Hypothetical sentences, on the other hand, although they appear to follow the same pattern, in fact depend partly on future reference and on events outside the child's control and are not really understood until the age of five or so. A statement such as 'If it stops raining, we'll go for a walk this afternoon' is interpreted by a four-year-old in a reward/punishment sense; the five-year-old, however, will see this as a logical sequence of events that depends on the weather. A more complex form of the hypothetical — make-believe — is not established until six years or so.

Make-believe is, in fact, the first real disembedding of the word from its referents. The six-year-old child can use words, communicate them to a playmate, and pretend that what is referred to is really happening. This is the middle-childhood version of the formal mode. While the six-year-old's 'hypotheses' are constructed on the basis of wish-fulfilment and fantasy, not on that of abstract principle (which happens later), they do represent a functional separation of language and reality which is in the child's control. This is the thin edge of the wedge. It is now a good time for the school to intervene, to begin play with word symbols themselves — reading, writing, spelling — so that this process of disembedding can be furthered.

Awareness of language. Separating words from their referents has a further consequence: words can become their own referents. This is something that pre-school children cannot understand; they cannot talk *about* words. Such a child will judge 'house' to be a big word, but 'mouse' a little word.

Much children's humour in the early primary years is about word-play yet many children fail to see the point of the joke and laugh for other reasons. As recounted by the De Villiers (1979, p. 93), children, in retelling a joke, often wreck it:

Why is the man in the fish market stingy? Because his job makes him sell fish.

thus becomes:

Why is the man in the fish market stingy? Because he sells fish.

One of the authors recalls how he first heard the joke as '... because he sells shellfish'. He never did see what the joke was supposed to be until he read De Villiers' account of it!

Metalinguistic awareness develops from about four to five years of age, and has profound effects on language and cognitive development generally (Tunmer, Pratt and Herrtman, 1984). The emergence may be seen in the way children begin to use language as a *tool*, adapting it so that it may perform its various functions. Even at five years of age, children's talk refers more on balance to the listener's activities than to the speaker's which is not quite as egocentrically oriented as Piaget indicated. Thus, five-year-olds give more information to a blindfolded listener than to a listener who can watch the speaker (Paris and Lindauer, 1982).

Oral language becomes truly disembedded in early adolescence, when children may become strategic and use language for particular purposes with highly differentiated audiences. For example, Pengilley refers to a Year 7 girl: 'Oh yeah! I always talk high and fast when I'm arguing with Mum. She hates it and gives in' (in Flynn and Savage, 1980, p. 19). Such a correspondingly skilful use of *written* language — referred to as a 'sense of audience' — is not usually well developed until much later.

THE DEVELOPMENT OF WRITTEN LANGUAGE

The preceding discussion has been mainly concerned with the development of oral language ability in embedded contexts. The major progressions are typical of all races and social classes: almost all people acquire reasonable skills in oracy, and differences can be put down to personality characteristics (e.g. shyness) rather than ability as such.

What a difference when we come to disembedded and, particularly, written language! As soon as school takes over, so it seems, the trouble starts. Reading is so easy for some children that they are reading fluently before even going to school; others find it so difficult that, 10 years of schooling later, they are still barely literate, although they may have excellent speech skills.

The trouble is that written language is not speech transcribed. Writing is a *special form* of language: it emphasises the logical and conceptual components, whereas spoken language emphasises the interpersonal and rhetorical. The rules are so different that skill in the mother tongue is often unrelated to skill in expressive writing. It is even probable that different parts of the brain are involved in the functions of literacy and oracy. As was suggested in Chapter 1, natural selection has had some part to play in the development of oral ability, so that most people are well endowed in this respect. But selection has had little to do with modifying the structures controlling literacy skills, hence the wide differences teachers find in students in their ability to learn to read and to write.

Traditionally, it has been usual to treat the psychology and teaching of reading and that of writing separately as if they were quite unrelated activities. Yet both are 'applied cognition'. If reading is a process of 'thought-getting' (Huey, 1968), writing is one of thought clarification. Both involve processing second order symbolic information in a limited capacity system, and with metacognitive awareness: 'the thoughtful reader ... reads as if she were a writer composing a text for yet another reader who lives within her' (Pearson and Tierney, 1984, p. 144). And while it was once thought that reading was a prerequisite to writing, educators today teach reading *through* writing (Graves, 1983; Kamler and Klarr, 1984).

On the other hand, there are clear differences between the two processes and, historically, each has attracted a rather different body of research. For convenience, then, we treat the development of text processing (reading) and text production (writing) separately. The two processes are, however, closely intertwined, and should be treated in the classroom as two sides of the same coin.

The psychology of reading

The teaching of reading has been riddled with controversy for over a hundred years. Essentially, it comes down to what we would today call 'look-and-say' versus 'phonics'. In the first, the meaning of the word is emphasised: it is a matter of recognising the whole word in context, and requires a heavier memory load on the reader (each word has to be remembered and distinguished from every other word). Phonics involves a phoneme-by-phoneme analysis of the word so that recognition of the sound of the full word may follow, and with it the meaning. Teachers tended to espouse these approaches with something like religious fervour: progressives going for look-and-say, and traditionalists for phonics.

The trouble with English is that the rules for decoding are not as regular as they are in various other languages. In Italian and Welsh, for example, consonants and vowels are sounded according to regular rules: there are no vagaries such as the 'ough' in English (as in 'cough', 'bough', 'bought'). The fact of irregularities in English has led some to propose that reading be taught using a modified, phonetic alphabet. The best-known of these proposals is that of Pitman (who invented shorthand): the *initial teaching alphabet* (ITA). Many studies have shown, however (e.g. Bond and Dykstra, 1967), that teaching by the ITA makes little difference; there is also the problem, after two years on ITA, of switching to the conventional alphabet. The controversy involves a confusion over what is best done at three quite distinct phases of reading:

1. *Pre-reading.* This phase is before reading proper takes place. It involves an orientation to text and its context whenever the reader gets into the *right relation* to the text. Text is not analysed: it is a stimulus for the young 'reader' to role play. The text is 'read' upside down, right side up; pictures and any other marks on the page are 'read'. Graves suggests that this is the time to start teaching both reading and writing. The child realises, in global terms, what the marks on the page are for.
2. *Decoding.* This is an analytic phase, in which the child begins to 'crack the code', to learn the *particular associations* between visual symbols and sounds.
3. *Comprehending.* In this phase, the reader *synthesises meaning* from the clues in both text and context.

Each phase requires a different way of processing text, so to insist that *all* teaching be carried out according to the way of processing of just one phase will of course be unbalanced. Total reliance on whole words not only places an enormous memory load on readers but leaves them without the means of tackling new or strange words, while total reliance on phonetic analysis misses the *meaning of* the words.

The pre-reading phase. The child has a problem that adults in their long-held competence forget. Try to read the following paragraph without rotating the page:

Children come to school with a level of oral competence in their mother-tongue only to be confronted with an exemplar of written text, the reader, which is an autonomous representation of meaning. Ideally, the printed reader depends on no cues other than linguistic ones; it represents no intentions other than those already represented in the text; it is addressed to no one in particular; its author is essentially anonymous; and its meaning is precisely that pre-presented by the sentence meaning. As a result when children are taught to read, they are learning both to read and to treat language as a text. Children familiar with the use of text-like language through hearing printed stories obviously confront less of a hurdle than those for whom both reading and form of language are

novel (Olson, 1977, p. 276).

As the passage indicates, this is really a *very* simplified version of what we expect a young child to accomplish. As soon as we can say, 'Ah! Got it! It's upside down and back-to-front', it is a fairly routine job of applying transformation rules: start at bottom right instead of top left, and rotate each letter 180°.

The young beginner has a similar problem, but it is worse. Smith (1971) pointed out that the young reader has to acquire two further, and brand-new, insights in learning to read. Unlike the reader having to decode the upside-down passage, the child has first to understand that print is meaningful, and second that written language is different from speech.

In decoding the above passage, the reader knew both these things: the only trick was to find out what the rule was, and then to apply it. In other words, the child has to appreciate what the game itself is all about. When that is understood, the search begins for some rule or rules — decoding rules, as they are usually called — to translate a meaningless jumble into sense (i.e. into something already known). But this is a *new* game.

As Olson says in the inverted passage, the child acquires spoken language in the rich and personally meaningful context of family — with all the repetitious words and the non-verbal supports such as smiles, eye contact, hand gestures and body language. The notion that words can mean anything outside the spoken context is quite foreign to some children. How are they to supply to the written word the rich embeddings that verbal expression automatically gives?

The cold, black text thus presents a new ball-game: except that many children simply do not understand what it is. What are the rules of this new game, upon which so much appears to depend?

Reading processes

It is usual to distinguish *decoding* (translating orthographics, or marks on paper, into words) from *comprehension* (translating words into meanings). It is, however, more helpful to see reading as a total process. 'Reading' is extracting meaning from text, for immediate or long-term purposes. The term 'comprehension' refers to the extraction of meaning simultaneous with the act of reading, 'studying' to the extraction of meaning for future use (Paris and Lindauer, 1982).

As in studying itself, it is useful to distinguish between cognitive and metacognitive processes. Kirby (in press) refers to reading *skills*, which are existing cognitive routines often carried out automatically, and reading *strategies*, which involve redesigning existing routines, or selecting routines for particular purposes, which are carried out with conscious deliberation.

In all reading processes, there are several levels at which attention may be focused. Kirby distinguishes eight such levels:

1. *features*, such as the loops, lines and curves that make up letters;
2. *letters* themselves;
3. *sounds*, which are associated with letters and letter combinations;
4. *words*, encoded both visually and phonemically (not one or the other);
5. *chunks*, or combinations of words into meaningful phrases which give a unit of sense. A sentence may comprise eleven words, say, but only three chunks: '/The three fat men // entered the room // and gaped in astonishment /';
6. *ideas*, a statement of meaning at the sentence level. For the first time, the level of meaning is not a direct association of what is on the page, but an *abstraction* and a *synthesis*;

7. *main ideas*, which are a distillation of what the text has to say: the gist, which is constructed out of all the ideas in the passage;
8. *the theme*, which is inferred, going beyond the main ideas and generalising them to a new level of the abstraction.

Within the concrete mode, with 'meaning' as the target, *words* and *chunks*, as single units of meaning, are unistructural; *ideas*, comprising several units, are multistructural; *main ideas*, the integration of several ideas, are relational; and *themes*, which convey deeper message, and may not occur in simple, context-bound texts, are extended abstract.

All these processes now fit into place (see Figure 6.1).

Decoding. Decoding may be done at two levels, phonological or visual. Phonological decoding links features to letters and letters to sound. This seems to be a basic skill that is missing in poor readers. Pflaum et al. (1980) analysed over 90 studies of reading, which agreed on two very clear points:

• Experimental programs of whatever kind were better than none at all. This undoubtedly reflects the fact that innovative teachers (those willing to experiment with new methods) are likely to be both more careful and more enthusiastic than teachers who cannot be bothered to change.
• One aspect of one analysis, sound–symbol blending (/b/, /a/, /d/ forms /bad/), consistently turned up in the superior methods and was the only aspect of teaching that did.

However, we have to go from sounds to words, and that is the target of visual (whole word) decoding. With practice, children frequently do this themselves: they simply learn to recognise words. When they come across a new word, they can go back to phonological analysis to see if they recognise the sound they synthesise. Yet as Paris and Lindauer (1982) say: 'Perhaps the most fundamental paradox in reading disabilities is that some children can pronounce words but show little understanding of what they read' (p. 338). These children have a conception of reading that does not include the extraction of meaning. It is therefore important when teaching phonetics to convey the idea that 'barking' correctly at print is *not* what the game is all about. 'Do I recognise that sound? What word does it make? Does that word make sense here?' As soon as we ask questions like that, we have shifted across to *comprehension*.

Comprehension. Comprehension starts at the word level, from where decoding synthesises or recalls the word. In other words, word identification is *both* a 'top-down' *and* a 'bottom-up' process, not one or the other (as was once insisted in the great reading debates). Readers approach text with their expectations, like a writer's composing processes (Pearson and Tierney, 1984), but their composing cannot be *too* creative, or they will miss the author's intended meaning. The interface between visual and phonological analysis ('bottom-up'), and the expectations of the reader created by the meanings synthesis so far ('top-down'), is the written word (Kirby, in press). Even at the level of word identification, then, strategies for comprehension are important and *complement* decoding skills, whether the latter are phonological or visual (see Figure 6.2).

Figure 6.1 Decoding, comprehending and studying aspects of the reading process and level of textual unit processed

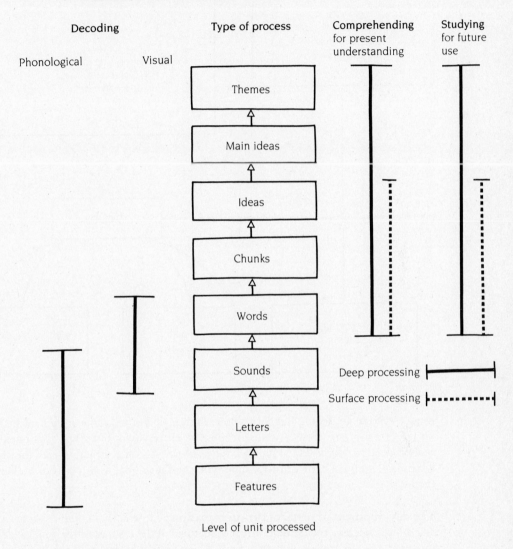

Level of unit processed

Source: Kirby, in press.

Meaning becomes more involved as higher and higher levels of unit are processed. It is at the sentence level (ideas) that one can distinguish between surface and deep approaches to reading and studying. Readers, whether for immediate understanding or for future reference, who focus on the surface features of the text — the words, phrases and sentences used by the author — process in the words-chunks-ideas range, and are

Figure 6.2   'Top-down' and 'bottom-up' processes in word identification

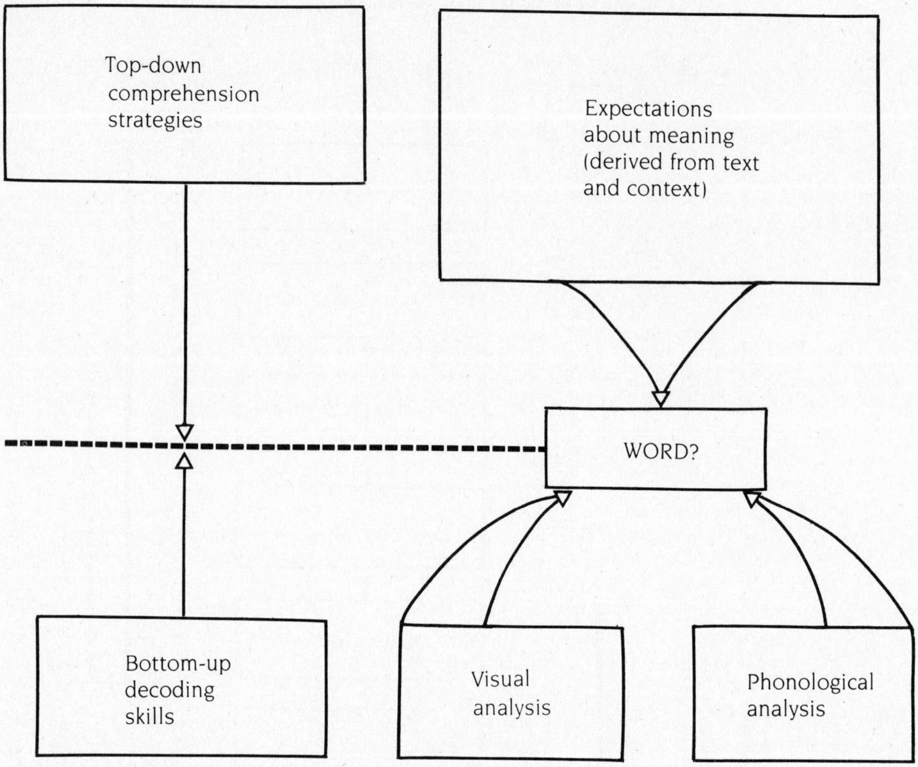

```
┌─────────────────┐              ┌──────────────────────┐
│ Top-down        │              │                      │
│ comprehension   │              │  Expectations        │
│ strategies      │              │  about meaning       │
│                 │              │  (derived from text  │
└────────┬────────┘              │  and context)        │
         │                       │                      │
         │                       └──────────┬───────────┘
         │                                  │
         ▽                                  ▽
- - - - -△- - - - - - - - - - - - - - ┌─────────────┐
         △                            │   WORD?     │
         │                            └──△───────△──┘
┌────────┴────────┐      ┌──────────┐      ┌─────────────┐
│ Bottom-up       │      │ Visual   │      │ Phonological│
│ decoding        │      │ analysis │      │ analysis    │
│ skills          │      │          │      │             │
└─────────────────┘      └──────────┘      └─────────────┘
```

using a surface approach. Readers who are interested in what the author means focus on larger and more abstract units. It must be emphasised, however, that even deep readers need to *range widely*: if they are too concerned with abstract themes, they might well miss significant lower order inputs that in fact signal a different or a changing theme (Kirby, in press).

The development of metacognition in reading. How early in their reading careers do children become aware that different features of the text, or of their knowledge of the topic, can affect their understanding? When do they make use of this knowledge to enhance their comprehension?

Myers and Paris (1978) found that children in second grade were aware that their knowledge of a topic and their interest in it affected their comprehension when reading about it (for example, reading about a place they had visited as opposed to a place they had not). Children are also aware by grade four that the context may be used in finding the meaning of a word (as in the 'cloze' procedure in which a gap in a sentence is filled with a word generated by the meaning of the passage). Moore and Kirby (1981) found, however, that that knowledge was counterproductive in Year 4 — their performance was actually *worse* when they tried to use context — yet by Year 6 reading performance was greatly enhanced by using context. Kirby (1984) explains this apparent contradiction by suggesting that working memory limitations prevented concentration on *both* decoding skills and meaning; but once the former were in place, by Year 6, students could bring their full attention to bear on meaning.

Findings such as this prompt a three-stage model of comprehension (Kirby and Moore, in press): (a) letter decoding, (b) comprehending semantic meaning, (c) metacognitive 'amplification' of (b). In other words, as students develop their knowledge of word meanings, and the ideas of a context and main idea, *then* they may develop metacognitive comprehension strategies that become entirely focused on the real purpose of reading: to extract maximum meaning from the text. This last stage, however, does not appear to develop spontaneously until Year 6.

The big question is this: can students be encouraged to be more metacognitive about their comprehension strategies *earlier* than Year 6, and thus enhance their reading and studying?

An interesting series of American studies demonstrates that they can, from around Year 3 level onwards (Paris, in press; Paris, Cross and Lipson, 1984). We see how in Section B.

Limitations in working memory: The 'double-whammy' in reading. One basic point to remember when promoting comprehension is that working memory is limited: if decoding skills are slow and unsure, words slip from working memory before the contextual relationship with other words can be understood. Slow reading, in other words, inevitably leads to poor comprehension. Perfetti and Lesgold (1979) referred to this as the 'double whammy' in reading: without rapid and accurate decoding skills, comprehension suffers. The poor reader suffers both ways; and, not surprisingly, the difference between good and poor readers tends to become greater and greater throughout the school years.

In essence, moving upwards in Figure 6.1 requires readers to be *strategic*. As working memory is limited, the processes lower down than the level at which you are working need to be automatised. Ideally, then, the reader focuses on one transformation at a time (from words to chunks, from ideas to the main idea) and that is the immediate task, to be handled metacognitively with the best strategies available. All tasks *below* that level should be automatic skills: for example, you cannot think about meaning if you are busy working out how the word sounds.

Skilled readers, aiming high up the scale, do not therefore pay attention to lower level units. Are *you* aware of the particular words used when you are reading this? Probably not: or if you are, as *by now* you probably are, you will not be relating the main ideas being expressed. Proof-readers do not tune themselves to be receptive to meaning, only to letters, features and words. As we shall see in the writing section, reviewing text for orthographics (spelling, punctuation) is best carried out *separately* from reviewing for clarity of meaning (in fact, to make that distinction clear, it is better to use the word 'editing' for the former task: and we shall do so in future).

In the teaching of reading, then, it is important to encourage *both* top-down and bottom-up processes. Old-fashioned texts with carefully composed sentences, phono-logically speaking, like 'the fat cat that ate the rat on the mat' have little meaning children can relate to, so they identify reading with making the right noises, not with getting involved with text: so too, on the other side, the success of 'organic reading' (see Box 6.1).

The psychology of writing

The ability to decode written text with speed, accuracy and comprehension develops earlier and, typically, reaches maximum efficiency much more quickly than its counterpart, the *creation* of written text. It is unlikely, for instance, that adults spontaneously improve their reading skills very much after adolescence; writing skill, on the other hand, continues to develop, and in some professional writers never ceases to develop.

Writing is very much more complex than reading. It involves a large number of independent skills: handwriting, spelling, punctuation, word choice, syntax, textual connections, purpose, organisation, clarity and reader characteristics (Scardamalia, 1980). Given the limited capacity of working memory, it is clearly impossible to devote

---

BOX 6.1   ORGANIC READING

Children have two visions, the inner and the outer. Of the two the inner vision is brighter.

I hear that in other infant rooms widespread illustration is used to introduce the reading vocabulary to a five-year-old, a vocabulary chosen by adult educationists. I use pictures, too, to introduce the reading vocabulary, but they are pictures of the inner vision and the captions are chosen by the children themselves. True, the picture of the outer, adult-chosen visions can be meaningful and delightful to children; but it is the captions of the mind pictures that have the power and the light. For whereas the illustrations perceived by the outer eye cannot be other than interesting, the illustrations seen by the inner eye are organic, and it is the captioning of these that I call the 'Key Vocabulary' ...

Back to these first words. To these first books. They must be made out of the stuff of the child itself. I reach a hand into the mind of the child, bring out a handful of the stuff I find there, and use that as our first working material. Whether it is good or bad stuff, violent or placid stuff, coloured or dun. To effect an unbroken beginning. And in this dynamic material, within the familiarity and security of it, the Maori finds that words have intense meaning to him, from which cannot help but arise a love of reading. For it's here, right in this first word, that the love of reading is born, and the longer his reading is organic the stronger it becomes, until by the time he arrives at the books of the new culture, he receives them as another joy rather than as a labour. I know all this because I've done it.

Source: Sylvia Ashton-Warner, 1980, pp. 32–4.

conscious attention to all of these features at the same time. Whereas skilled writers often find that expressing their thoughts in writing not only clarifies but significantly enhances their thinking, beginners (and this implies virtually all students even well into high school) are so weighed down by the technicalities that their thinking is diminished; they explain things orally much better than they can put them into writing.

Nevertheless, although writing is more complex than reading, development of writing skill follows a similar course: the disembedding of higher levels of meaning from text. Two views on this distinction are expressed in Box 6.2: the young writer sees the function of writing as recording thoughts that are already worked out, the professionals as a means of working out what those thoughts might be.

What then, are the main ways in which unskilled writers differ from skilled?

> Texts produced by younger children often seem choppy and ill-structured, as if sentences go down on the page in the exact form and in the same order they come to the child's mind, with little transition between one and the next. Older children's texts begin to 'flow' more smoothly, and sentences in the text seem better related and organised (McCutchen, 1985, pp. 1, 12).

Unskilled writing that begins to communicate, and is not simply incoherent, has a simple unistructural character, referred to variously as 'associative' (Bereiter, 1980), 'linear' (Biggs and Collis, 1982b) or 'bed-to-bed' (Graves, 1983). In such writing, content is presented in the order it is received by the writer: when narrating events, for example, children start with getting up in the morning, go through the events of the day (which include the point of the story) and finish ('and so we had tea and went to bed'). The point of the story is buried.

As McCutchen says, young children focus 'on what they know *they* mean, rather than on what the *reader* will think they mean' (p. 12). Unskilled writers write prose that is 'writer-based' not 'reader-based' (Flower, 1980); it is a form of egocentrism, not taking the perspective of the other person in the communication act into account.

Growth in writing skill thus involves a shift in the writer's concerns: from 'emptying the skull' onto paper, to using text in such a way that others will understand most clearly. The latter becomes a *metacognitive* activity: a sense of audience requires

---

BOX 6.2   THE PROBLEM WITH WRITING: TWO VIEWS

With writing, you've got to think before you print it on paper. But if you speak it out, you sort of don't have to think about what you're going to say.

Source: A Year 10 boy explaining his difficulties about writing in Elizabeth Stelzer, 'Writing about Writing', *Language in Education*, No. 1, Tasmanian Department of Education, 1975, p. 39.

The basic problem in writing is discovering what one wishes to say, not simply how best to present ideas that already exist.

Source: Cooper and Odell, 1978, p. xi.

close examination of your own thoughts and, in doing that, writing becomes the *act of discovery* referred to by Cooper and Odell; and by E. M. Forster when he said, 'How can I know what I think until I see what I say?'

Scardamalia and Bereiter (1982), in referring to student essays, distinguish between 'knowledge-telling' and 'reflective' writing. Knowledge-telling is a writer-based strategy which consists of reducing the essay to a list of topics, and then simply telling what one knows about each topic. The concerns of the writer are what to say next, and how to put that in suitable language. Knowledge-telling is a sentence-by-sentence routine that 'does' for most of the writing tasks that are demanded in high school, even in senior years. Applebee (1984) claims that high school almost exclusively uses writing to convey already organised content to an audience better informed than the writer — a gross undersell of the power of writing. Whereas knowledge-telling is one-way, reflective writing is cyclical. The text produced becomes the object of further reflection:

- Is what I have written what I want to say?
- Is the reader likely to understand it?
- How can I make the point more clearly?
- What new insights does my reshaped thought now lead me to?

Knowledge-telling and reflective writing are surface and deep approaches to writing, respectively. They are contrasted in Figure 6.3.

Reflective writing presupposes a very complex and high level set of metacognitive processes, focused on the meaning of the text as a whole, not just on the idea expressed in a single sentence. To convert 'What I have written' into reader-based text requires planning, monitored composing, reviewing with many complex criteria in mind, recomposing and editing. We now turn to some of these activities.

Aspects of writing

Let us distinguish the following aspects of the writing process:

- *intentional:* the motives, intentions and conceptions of writing that guide a student's thinking about the task before it is actually undertaken;
- *parawriting:* the processes to do with a particular writing task (such as planning) that are distinguishable from actually writing or creating text;
- *writing:* the activities focused on the text itself.

The model of writing we are going to look at here is applicable to any genre, but, to keep it in the academic context, we shall take the essay assignment as the prototypical example for discussion.

Figure 6.3   Surface and deep approaches to writing: knowledge-telling and reflective writing

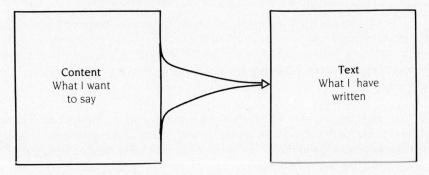

(a) Knowledge-telling

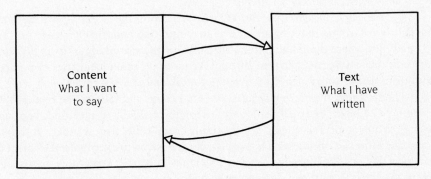

(b) Reflective writing

Intentional aspects. These refer to the motives students have for writing, their conceptions of writing and their feelings about it. As we have seen, conceptions of learning or of reading help shape outcomes. If a child thinks that reading is only being able to make the right noises at print, comprehension will be inhibited. Thus, students who think that an essay is 'the presentation of relevant facts and ideas in an ordered form' (i.e. knowledge-telling), as opposed to 'an integrated argument', write accordingly (Hounsell, 1984).

Students may be variously motivated by an essay assignment. They may view a particular essay as an opportunity for personal learning and expression, as a hurdle to be cleared with as little trouble as possible, or as a means of maintaining a high grade-point average. We are on familiar ground here, as these are the deep, surface and achieving motives, respectively. Students who want to use the essay as a means of finding out something about a topic and forming their viewpoint on it, or clarifying one they already hold, will adopt a deep approach. Students who see the essay as a make-work device or who feel pressured, cynical or fearful about the essay, will adopt a surface approach. Students who are motivated to getting the highest marks for an essay will adopt achieving strategies: organising, 'sussing out' favoured viewpoints, adhering lovingly to prescriptions as to presentation, etc.

The intentional aspects of writing orient the writer towards parawriting and writing activities.

Parawriting activities: planning and composing. Planning an essay involves several activities:

1.   *Forming global intentions.* The essay question is read and interpreted. The student has then to decide the broad way to go: 'I intend to handle the question in this way and to make the general point that ... but in the meantime, I don't know enough about X, Y and Z ... and had better find out ...'

2.   *Knowledge update.* Students may then turn to several sources to update their knowledge: books, other people, audiovisual resources, etc. This stage is common to both knowledge-tellers and reflective writers. The crucial point is how the knowledge is *structured* while, or after, it is being acquired.

3.   *Forming a structure.* (See Box 6.3.) Emma claims she 'doesn't plan anything' — she only 'goes around thinking about it all the time'. She finds that her ideas just 'spring to mind'. Jim, more disciplined, similarly finds 'a structure emerges' from his personal focus. Both are reflective writers. Bill and Anne, on the other hand, use other people to help them decide what bits of knowledge to tell, and in what order.

The structure thus formed shapes the final essay, and follows the familiar SOLO pattern. Structures are usually either multistructural, which result from a knowledge-telling strategy, or relational, which result from reflective writing. A relational structure addresses the question appropriately and is said to exemplify the correct *genre* for the essay or other piece of writing. Extended abstract structures may adapt the genre for better effect, or reinterpret the question.

4.   *Opportunistic planning.* This refers to the willingness of the student to tolerate deviation or to be led into hitherto unplanned directions: surface writers are usually unwilling to allow this to happen: 'No, I ignore sudden inspirations. That'd make things too messy. I'd get right off the track' (Biggs, in press, d).

5.   *Monitoring criteria.* During planning and again during reviewing, writers may adopt several criteria for monitoring their activity. These criteria, which may include 'mechanics' (spelling, punctuation), word choice (appropriate, best meaning) and sticking to the question, are at the heart of the writing exercise. We devote more space to this aspect below.

6.   *Forming focal intentions.* The culmination is 'shaping at the point of utterance' (Britton et al., 1975). Somewhere around 'forming a structure' (3, above), planning takes on a specific edge that makes the word 'composing' more appropriate. This process is at its most intense as inner thoughts become frozen as marks on paper. Perhaps the best that can be said about what is happening at this point was said by the novelist Saul Bellow: 'Well I don't know exactly how it's done. I let it alone a good deal' (quoted in Salgado, 1980, p. 70).

BOX 6.3   THERE'S PLANNING AND PLANNING ...

... enthusiasm

E*mma*: As soon as I get the assignment I read what I can find. Race down to the library the minute the lecture finishes and get there first to get all the stuff and then read it and then I just think about it while I'm going about whatever I'm going about. And then I leave it as long as I can before I write anything except for the odd thought that I have ... so you see, I don't plan anything. I just go around thinking about it all the time when I'm driving my car and in the garden and thoughts just spring to mind ... you know, the light bulb flashes and I think, ah yes, that's great. I keep these little exercise books and I write down thoughts that may be useful when I come to the essay.

... a personal focus

Jim: Obviously notes and books are important. Then there are the critics in the various journals. That gives a broad outline and you can always agree with them or disagree; it gives a starting point from where to work ... I always try to include at least one reference I've dug out for myself; it's nice to have that as a focus. It's more 'mine'. Then I mull it all over until a structure emerges.

... class-based

B*ill*: The lecturer tells us the basic points are in the lecture notes. Then it's a matter of matching those up with selections from one or two of the recommended critiques. I go on from there.

... my old English teacher

Anne: I try to plan but I usually go straight into it. As soon as I think of an idea I write it down. I write bits and pieces ... just sit there grabbing ideas here and there, trying to see what I can do with them ... If I have a lot of trouble I go to my old English teacher. She helps me get my ideas together.

Source: From interviews with first year English students, Biggs, in press, d.

Writing activities.

1.   *Transcribing*. Transcription is the physical act of writing words. The medium of transcription — writing with a pencil or typewriter, dictating or using a word processor — is *in itself* probably not very important. McCutchen (1985), for example, found that when elementary and junior high school students dictated their essays, their texts were longer than when written, but not better constructed. What is important is how the medium interferes with or facilitates particular writing activities; for example, the word processor makes revision much easier.

2.   *Reviewing.* Beginning writers see transcription as the end of writing: when the marks are there the job is done. Skilled writers see the first marks as the beginning of writing. The questions of when to review, how much text to review at a time and what things to look out for while reviewing, are matters of critical importance. So too is what to do after reviewing.

3.   *Revising.* It is important to recompose unsatisfactory text. This can involve revising any or all of the parawriting and writing activities mentioned above.

4.   *Editing.* The minimum thing one can do is attend to 'mechanics': neatness of layout, legibility, spelling, punctuation, etc. Editing focuses on low level surface features; revising on the impact of the whole text. It is important to distinguish these two activities from each other, so we call alterations to mechanical or surface features of the text 'editing' and alterations that significantly affect meaning 'revising'.

Levels of focus in writing processes. The distinction between editing and revising brings us back to Kirby's (in press) model of levels of textual processing, derived for reading processes. Apart from the 'sounds' level, which is less an issue in the present context, the remaining seven levels have an important relationship to the writer's focus (Table 6.1).

Table 6.1   Focus of writer on mechanical and meaning aspects of text, and level of textual unit being processed

Level of textual unit	Focus of writer	
	Mechanical	Meaning
Theme	—	Generalisations, alternative constructions
Main idea	Discourse structure, cohesive devices (across sentence)	Answers essay question
Ideas	Sentence grammar (within sentence)	Sentence meaning
Chunks	Punctuation	Phrase, meaning
Words	Spelling	Lexicon, word meaning
Letters	Legibility	—
Features	Typeface, font	—

Writers have two concerns: with *mechanics* (orthographics, grammar, style and other formal features) and with *meaning*. While ultimately efficient communication of meaning involves mastery of the mechanics, it is necessary — working memory being limited — that writers focus on only one domain at a time. One of the major sources of 'writer's block' is caused by frequent review while writing (e.g. correcting spelling or punctuation on the run) (Rose, 1984). Text is most efficiently reviewed in *large units* (i.e. pages, rather than sentences), and *separately* for meaning and for mechanics. Otherwise writers simply lose track of what they are thinking.

With processing at high textual levels, the two domains get closer and closer. Poorly shaped letters have little relation to meaning but spelling has, as do punctuation and within-sentence grammar; while at the level of main ideas, a relational level of meaning cannot be expressed without mastery of cohesive devices. The reverse side of that last coin is the student trick of using phrases that indicate textual cohesion and, by implication, logical coherence, when in fact the ideas expressed are unrelated or not understood. 'It therefore follows that ...', 'accordingly, this writer would suggest ...', 'thus', 'then', 'on the other hand', etc., liberally sprinkled throughout a text, can give a quick and busy marker the firm impression that the writer has an integrated message and has carefully orchestrated the argument. Essay *markers* must pay attention to the meaning domain too.

As in reading, the difference between surface and deep approaches to text revolves around the level of textual unit being processed. A deep approach involves reflective writing, during which the main focus of attention is on the level of *main ideas*, with occasional and discrete shifts to the word–sentence level. A surface approach, involving knowledge-telling, concentrates at or below the *sentence* level.

Given these foci of attention, then, we can set up a parallel to Figure 6.4 showing how writing and parawriting processes relate to the level of textual units processed, except that here we construe mainly from the top down rather than from the lower to higher units as in Figure 6.4. That is, whereas in general a reader constructs meaning from the marks upwards, the writer in general constructs text from the intended meaning downwards. We have emphasised 'in general' twice here because that last sentence is a kind of oversimplification. Just as reading must be seen as involving both top-down and bottom-up procedures, so must writing. As McCutchen (1985) discovered in her case study of a professional wine columnist, the feel or 'cadence' of a particular word often provided the writer with a new insight or a new angle on the main idea. Always, the constraints of working memory make it strategic for the writer to focus on only a limited range of textual units at a time. As with reading and studying, then, we can distinguish deep and surface strategies in writing by the range of units scanned over the entire act of text production.

The focal points of revision. Writers may monitor both parawriting and writing activities: during planning and composing, and before anything appears on paper, or when reviewing after text has been created. The *focus* of this monitoring activity varies. In general, experienced and skilled writers think of the total message and the overall discourse structure for much of composing and reviewing, saving the review of the focal mechanics (editing) for a final one-off operation. The sudden realisation that a word has been misspelled during writing should be ignored at the time — those details can always be picked up later, but a thread of ideas can be lost forever.

What criteria are variously at the back and the front of a writer's mind?

1. *Compatibility with global intentions.* Composing must be within constraints and, once the global intentions have been decided, all further idea generation goes on within those self-defined limits — unless the writer is prepared to be opportunistic, and try a new tack if it seems promising. While that leads to original and creative work, it obviously cannot be tolerated too much, otherwise the text would roam in all directions.

Figure 6.4 Approaches to writing and parawriting processes, and level of textual unit processed

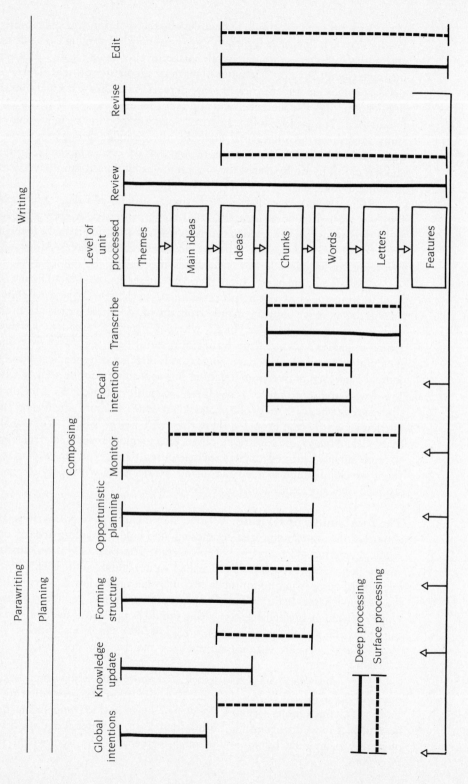

2. *Genre.* A more restricted way of putting this is the extent to which the writer sticks to the established genre rules. This need not be as formally and deliberately conscious as may appear. A compare-and-contrast essay, for example, has different genre rules than a causal explanation essay. Usually genre takes care of itself if the question is answered appropriately. In other words, the student should think about the *substance* of what is being written, rather than be concerned with conformity to a rule structure. Professional writers often have to be more self-consciously concerned with genre.

3. *Coherence.* The coherence of a text refers to its logical integrity, and usually this is reflected by *cohesive devices* or connectives that link adjacent and remote sentences. Again, attention to meaning tends to take care of the syntactic issues involved. Different genres call out different cohesive devices. Multistructural writing such as knowledge-telling makes much use of conjunctions such as 'and', 'so', 'then', whereas relational writing uses cohesive devices that reflect the logical coherence of the main idea ('therefore', 'an interesting exception ...').

4. *Sense of audience.* This is all-important throughout all writing: attention to what Britton et al. refer to as 'the face beneath the page'. Being able to monitor one's composing and completed text from the point of view of the likely reader is a form of allocentrism. The question of who is the audience for a student essay is an excellent one to ponder — yourself, the community of scholars, the individual you happen to know will be marking it? Some answers are given in Box 6.4.

5. *Style.* In essays a sense of style is perhaps not as important as in creative writing where aesthetic considerations are part of the whole purpose. Technical

---

BOX 6.4   WHO IS THE AUDIENCE?

Emma: Funny, I've never thought of an audience. The whole process of writing seems to me to be such a strangely personal one that it's not as if it's for an audience. Now philosophy essays are much more for an audience because with them I have to keep telling myself, well, this is what he wants ... it's an important way of being able to even write the wretched thing.

Margaret: I'm my own audience. I write it as if it's making sense to me to reread to myself. It's different to writing speeches because they are for a specific audience but you don't know who you are writing for in essays.

Anne: I've got to look at it from the lecturer's point of view because it seems that what the lecturer thinks is the most important thing rather than what you think ... You really try to make it really sophisticated and complicated because you think you will be impressing the lecturer. It's what the lecturer thinks is what matters. I've found that if you don't give back what you've been given it's not accepted.

Source: From interviews with first year English students, Biggs, in press, d.

writers should, however, master the appropriate 'grapholect', the written equivalent of dialect (Hausen, 1968). That is, certain conventions, vocabulary, usages, etc. mark literary criticism (as text) from historical analysis or sociological description. Each discipline has its grapholect that students need to master: a process usually acquired by unconscious imitation — a sort of osmosis — rather than through formal instruction. Some student views on style are given in Box 6.5.

6.   *Lexicon.* Is this exactly the word I want? If not, and I am still composing, then it will do. The time to change it to something better is during review, when I can afford to spend time thinking about it, looking up a thesaurus or a dictionary.

7.   *Within-sentence grammar.* Again, this is best left to the edit stage; grammar should not be handled during composing or transcription. Attention to sense often fixes grammatical problems but not always: knowledge of formal grammar is definitely helpful in working out which clauses are dependent or which verbs agree with what subjects.

8.   *Orthographics and presentation.* Spelling (word level) and punctuation (chunk and sentence level) are matters left for later editing. Legibility of writing, typeface, margins and all matters of presentation are for final one-off concern.

The development of revision on drafting strategies. The difference between unskilled and professional level writing is captured by the extent to which, and what, textual levels are focused on during planning and reviewing. As noted at the beginning of this section, unskilled text is 'choppy' and incoherent, in the sense that segments of text are unrelated by cohesive devices. This is knowledge-telling in the most basic form and without any sense of audience, and no evidence of monitoring at either planning or review. At first, then, young writers do not redraft at all: the first draft is the final text.

After that stage, we can trace a progressively more sophisticated set of strategies for redrafting which usually unfolds in the order outlined below. It is, however,

---

BOX 6.5   WHAT TWO ENGLISH STUDENTS THINK ABOUT
                  STYLE

Emma: Another thing I don't like about philosophy essays is that there isn't any joy in creating a lovely essay. They don't really care if it's a clumsy sentence as long as the point you are making comes across. So the crafting of an essay for itself alone doesn't have the enjoyment that I get from English ones. I am not able to look at a beautiful sentence and find some lovely words to go into it that are really expressive of the right feeling and exactly the right sort of emotion ... I think philosophy is so boring having to do away with things like beauty, joy and pleasure.

Bill: No, I don't worry about style. I write to say what I think is wanted, what they're looking for. I'm not a poet (laughs).

Source: From interviews with first year English students, Biggs, in press, d.

impossible to tie these stages to typical age levels; they reflect a sequence in which writing skill is acquired rather than a developmentally based pattern. So much depends on the genre, the individual's interest in the text and the writing context. Many people regard drafting as high cost: the marks on paper are there permanently, and it is a real chore to create them in a new form and destroy the old. Many students seem to think that only bad writing should be redrafted: 'good' writers do not need to redraft. That attitude is very much more easily corrected with the word processor, because the ephemeral nature of the words on the screen emphasises their impermanence: they can easily be erased and better arrangements of words substituted. Further, Graves (1983) showed that by the technique of 'conferencing' (see Section B), even very young beginning writers can be trained to redraft. For all these reasons, then, we cannot be dogmatic about ages. The sequence itself, however, runs as follows.

The first feature that receives attention is *physical presentation*. The most basic form of sense of audience is awareness that the text is or is not legible. Following that, the writer attends to other aspects of presentation: that the stipulations for margins, neatness, no dirty marks, etc. have been met. The unistructural level of redrafting, then, is simply rewriting the text to make it look neat.

The next stage of redrafting concentrates on *words*, *chunks* and *sentences*; this is as far as writers who use a surface approach go in reviewing and redrafting. In the mechanics domain, they look at spelling, punctuation and within-sentence grammar; as far as meaning is concerned they look little further than the single idea in a sentence. Semantically, then, the structure is no more than multistructural: telling this bit of knowledge, then that, then another. Writers who operate at this level will replace individual words with better ones and *add* sentences in subsequent drafts, but they will not *delete* sentences they have already written or substantially alter the *order* of sentences. This is because the last two operations, deletion and reordering, require focusing on the main idea and the total discourse structure. To see that something is superfluous presupposes a clear idea of what the big picture is, but that overall picture is not necessary if you simply keep adding single ideas.

When the focus is on the *main idea*, writing becomes reflective and drafting is at the relational level. All the sentences now interrelate to form a composite: some will be seen to be not contributing to that main idea and will need changing or deleting; other ideas will need to be added to balance the picture or to sharpen a point. When meaning has been satisfactorily addressed, the genre for that piece of writing, or for the essay-type, will have been realised. At this stage, the writer's attention is primarily on the main idea; adding, deleting, cut-and-paste and recomposing text will all be guided by it. At this stage, most skilled writers make a clear separation between revising and editing, leaving the latter process until last. Of course, editing too can sharpen meaning, but the main idea has to be in place first.

Redrafting strategies do not usually develop beyond this point, although logically we could extrapolate an extended abstract form of drafting. This would transcend the genre; for example, an idea occurring during any part of the process that would be better addressed by a different or more generalised question. (We see an example of this in Section B with Syd's essay.) In the case of creative writing, extended abstract revision would involve experimenting with the genre itself.

We thus see a clear development from no drafting at all to successively more complex forms — from unistructural, to multistructural, to relational — as drafting strategies are built around successively higher levels of textual unit as they become the major focus of the writer's attention.

In sum, the flow from unskilled to skilled writing can be charted along fairly simple lines. The real issues focus on the transition from writer-based to reader-based prose — the development of a sense of audience; and the transition from disconnected sentences to smoothly flowing sentences that interrelate and address one main idea.

In Section B we look at two case studies of writers who adopt a surface and a deep approach to writing, and at the implications for teaching that these considerations have, both in the teaching of particular subjects and in the teaching of writing itself.

THE SOCIAL CONTEXT OF LANGUAGE IN SCHOOL AND SOCIETY

We now turn to a much broader question. We have looked at the development of oral language up to school level, and then the development of the specific skills of reading and writing. All this presupposes that the mother tongue exists out there, to be assimilated orally, then decoded from script and transformed from intention into writing.

In this section, we deal with this *social* context of language. The two main issues are:

- language differences within the mother tongue;
- learning a second language.

Standard and non-standard English

Within any given language, such as English or French, there are different *kinds* of language — specifically, the variations of language found between social classes. One of the first studies to draw attention to this phenomenon was carried out by Schatzman and Strauss (1955). They studied the interviews of 10 working-class and 10 middle-class people whose town had been devastated by a tornado. The two sets of accounts were strikingly different. We can use the concept of disembedding again to capture the difference. The working-class reports tended to be unorganised, describing events as they happened to the interviewee: they failed to take into account the fact that the *listener* had not shared those experiences. There was a great deal of exophoric reference: applying words like 'it' and 'he' to events and people out of the immediate context and hence unknown to the listener.

Elaborated and restricted codes. Bernstein (1961, 1965) formalised these observations into a theory of *elaborated* and *restricted* codes, which were used by the middle- and working-classes, respectively. Essentially, an elaborated code bridges the gap between speaker and listener by explicit speech, governed by public rules and referents; a restricted code presupposes a common context or background of shared experiences and is, consequently, less subject to the rules of formal grammar, less abstract, and dependent on the context. Another way of looking at a similar distinction is to refer to *standard* and *non-standard* English (Bernard and Delbridge, 1980). Standard English is that used by the 'establishment'; non-standard English is some dialectical variant, such as Cockney, Southern USA or Strine.

As originally formulated, Bernstein's theory was an oversimplification: society does not form itself so neatly into two distinct classes. Nevertheless, Poole (1971) showed that the general correlations between class and speech did exist in Australia; even in such a selected group as university students. She categorised students into middle- and working-classes (on the basis of father's occupation), interviewed 40 of each, and analysed their speech. The middle-class students used more complex syntax, more uncommon adjectives and adverbs, more first-person references, and fewer fragmented or repetitious sequences. To illustrate, in a different context, let us look at two sets of participants. The scene is a bus.

Mother 1:	Now sit down darling, the bus will start in a moment.
Child 1:	Why?
Mother 1:	Because the bus will start in a moment and you might fall over and hurt yourself.
Child 1:	Why?
Mother 1:	Do as I say, and don't worry Mummy any more.

Now take the other pair:

Mother 2:	Siddown.
Child 2:	Why?
Mother 2:	Because I say so. Now siddown.
Child 2:	Why?
Mother 2:	Siddown or you'll get a smack.

The example is fictitious, but it illustrates two important techniques of child control which use language in quite different ways. Mother 1 hopes to control her child's behaviour by appealing to reasons the child will understand (hopefully), implying consideration for others and self-control as an ultimate end ('I will not do this because I can see that ...'). Mother 2 uses external methods of control, in particular conformity to rules imposed by authority (in this case herself), backed up by the most external sanction of all: punishment.

The reasons why these different codes arise in sections of society reflect the differing roles that parents see themselves and their children occupying (Edwards, 1976). As Western society is presently structured, working-class parents tend to perceive their role as subservient, and accordingly they train their children to follow instructions, not to question matters they scarcely understand. Middle-class parents, on the other hand, see themselves (and, in time, their children) as the givers of instructions and as the providers of reasons for those instructions. Bernstein argued that working-class children learn to look to adults as the source of directives, and not to question the reasons behind them. They are not used to having their motives probed, to responding to indirect commands, to exploring alternatives to those given, or to solving problems where the solutions are diverse or uncertain.

This implies that restricted codes (or non-standard English) are substandard or deficient versions of the language. It is a small step from there to suggest that non-standard English is related to cognitive impairment — that non-standard speakers are less able to solve complex problems which require a fine language structure, Bernstein (1970) himself seemed to regret this implication in his earlier work, and warned that the distinction between elaborated and restricted codes 'has sometimes led to the erroneous conception that a restricted code can be directly equated with linguistic deprivation, linguistic deficiency, or being nonverbal' (p. 26).

Nevertheless, many educators have adopted the deficit model, seeing it as one of their roles to get their charges to 'talk proper'. The point is, of course, that the language of schooling is that of the elaborated code of standard English: a disembedded public language. One of the major functions of school, as we saw in Chapter 1, is to pass on the cultural traditions and accumulated knowledge of society, which is necessarily expressed in a language that assumes a lack of both shared personal experience and non-verbal supports between communicator and learner. This puts the educator in a real dilemma, for there are two related problems:

1. Is the difference between non-standard and standard English one of deficit or difference? Do speakers of non-standard English genuinely lack (acquired) abilities to cope with society? Or is it simply that they have learned a different grammar and vocabulary that serve their functions just as well as the elaborated code serves its own?

2. Whether or not it is a question of deficit or difference, the more practical question is what the school should do about it. If the aim is, for instance, to teach children to read, then it would follow from the discussion earlier in this chapter that successful decoding of print is most likely to occur when the child can relate meaningfully to the context — which, in the case of subcultural groups (such as users of non-standard English, whether they are working-class groups or immigrant minorities) is not likely to be standard English contexts.

Non-standard English: difference or deficit? Probably the most common reaction to non-standard English is that the speaker is deficient in a most important aspect of socialisation. Accordingly, it is argued that a primary function of school is to remedy that deficit. As Bernard and Delbridge (1980) said:

> The children of low socio-economic groups do not do well at school and they have a language which is different from those from homes more advantaged in socio-economic terms. It has occurred to some that their language must be the cause of their difficulty and that their language must be 'inferior' (p. 268).

The argument has two aspects. The most extreme interpretation is that the actual *cognitive structure* of children of low socio-economic status is impoverished by a lifetime of using a restricted — and restricting — code. The more moderate approach is that the road to social advancement requires fluency in the elaborated code — standard English — and that it is therefore in the child's own interests to be educated in standard English; to supplement the familiar non-standard variant, if not replace it.

Bereiter and Engelmann (1966) were firm advocates of the first view. They saw non-standard English as 'not merely an underdeveloped version of standard English, but ... a basically non-logical mode of expressive behavior'. Their solution was, as Shuy (1973) put it, 'to train children to proceed as though the children have no language at all and to train children to speak in fully explicit formal language' (p. 32).

There are two major objections to such an approach. Linguists object strongly to the notion that any language, standard or not, is 'inferior' to any other (Labov, 1970). A language within a cultural or subcultural group develops to allow communication within that group; one cannot apply the rules of one group to claim that usage in another group is 'wrong'. Shuy cited the example where teachers call Black American children 'wrong' who say *desses* for the plural of 'desk'. In fact, the child who says *desses* has shown mastery of the rules of pluralisation — given that the singular is pronounced *dess*, the correct phonemic suffix *is* /es/ and not /s/.

As Di Vesta and Palermo (1974) said:

> Linguistically, nonstandard English is as well developed, as structured, and as grammatical as any other language. The kinds of grammatical difference between it and standard English are no more indicative of defects in communication potential than are the differences between standard English and languages like French, German or Russian ...
>
> ... In general, it must be concluded that the apparent poor performance of children who use nonstandard English is a reflection of situational (testing) constraints and the demands of a particular language, rather than an indication of linguistic capabilities (p. 92).

The second objection is more philosophical. 'Children who speak the regional and social dialects of their home communities cannot be considered pathological ... A child speaks the language that he hears and reveres' (Shuy, 1973, p. 25). To treat such children as if they have no language at all is deeply insulting to them and to the community or group with which they identify. To tell people that they will have to change their manner of speaking 'if they want to get on in the world' is to criticise them for what they are now. Of course, many working-class children do possess strong ambitions to 'get on' but, as the English writer Hoggart (1959) pointed out, the cost was high in personal terms: grammar (selective) school children in Britain acquired two dialects —standard English for school and outside, non-standard for home. However, the strain told, and the net result was commonly for children to grow away from their cultural and familial roots.

What should the school do about non-standard English? The dilemma is revealed in the following small example. Johnny is asked to read aloud the words 'And then he came home'. He reads ''n then 'e come 'ome'. Johnny has achieved two tasks to perfection: he has correctly decoded the script, and he has translated equally correctly into the dialect of his community. Many teachers, however, would consider his reading wrong, on both lexical (reading *a* for *o*) and phonetic (/e/ for /he/) grounds, with the result that he becomes bewildered ('wrong' when he thought he understood) and insulted. He learns very quickly that school is not 'for the likes of 'im'.

According to Bernard and Delbridge (1980), on the other hand:

> It is just not possible to see nonstandard English as the language of literature or scholarship ... Accordingly, the school should do as it has always done and try to give its pupils command of the standard form as the tool to their own advancement. If it has not been as successful with some groups in the past as it would like, the reason may lie less with matters of technique than of attitude and in particular with a complete refusal to give any honour at all to nonstandard forms (p. 269).

The rather general advice here is to teach solidly for standard usage from the outset, but to avoid denigration or sarcasm. The suggestion seems to be that *regular correction* of the non-standard form be avoided, as this approach has its own implicit curriculum.

Di Vesta and Palermo (1974) advocated a different approach, on the basis of work done particularly with Black non-standard (American) English. The non-standard version should be accommodated in the curriculum so that the pupils learn first through their own language system. Then:

> Subsequent instruction might be directed towards teaching the pupil the standard form without the risk of rejecting loyalty to his own language, self-incrimination because of the language he uses, or negative evaluation from others because he uses a nonstandard language form. Out of such instructional systems may eventually emerge still another bicultural model which provides for dual socialisation simultaneously in the mainstream culture and in the subculture (p. 93).

Non-standard English does not indicate deficiency, but simply that different vocabulary and rules of syntax and pronunciation have been learned. This does not alter the fact, however, that ultimately non-standard English is an inappropriate tool for educational growth, and that at some stage the student will need to acquire standard English to reach higher educational goals.

The school, then, does have a responsibility in helping students acquire the standard form. The question is: how may that best be achieved?

- The *difference* model: instruct first in the non-standard version, then fade out.
- The *deficit* model: concentrate throughout on the standard version. Basically the same alternatives arise when the non-standard version is not another dialect of English or the majority language, but another language. Let us now look at this second case.

Learning a second language

An important issue in language development is the learning of a second language (symbolised as L2) after the individuals have gained some sort of fluency with their first

— native or mother — language (L1). There are two different aspects to this. The first is where (in an English-speaking culture) a native English speaker learns a foreign language at school. The second, and much more complex, case is where a non-English speaker migrates to an English-speaking country, and has to acquire English as a second language. While there are certain factors common to both cases, the second involves many additional problems, some of which are not unlike those already mentioned in connection with non-standard and standard English. In the present section we shall deal with some common issues in second-language learning, with special reference to the case of English as a second language.

What sort of children learn a second language easily? There appear to be few specific factors involved. In an early but comprehensive review, Pimsleur, Mosberg and Morrison (1962) found that general intelligence (IQ) and verbal ability (as measured in L1) were closely related to L2 learning, as too were affective factors such as interest and motivation. Factors like pitch discrimination and personality were not important. In other words, and not very surprisingly perhaps, a bright child, with good competence in L1 and an interest in L2, is likely to be good at learning L2.

The next question is: do children learn a second language more easily than adults? Di Vesta and Palermo (1974) reviewed the evidence then available, and suggested the following conclusions:

- Pronunciation is learned more easily by children.
- Vocabulary is learned more easily by adults.
- Grammar is learned equally by both children and adults.
- There are marked differences between children in the ease with which they acquire a second language, even when they are equally bright in other ways.

Immersion or submersion? Cummins (1979) reviewed a great deal of research relating to L2 learning in 'immersion' programs (i.e. where L2 is the only language used for all communications). He was attempting to account for the common finding that learning L2 by middle-class majority-language children usually results in *better* language competence and academic achievement generally, but learning a second language by minority-language children usually results in *poor* competence in both the mother tongue and the second language.

In other words, a bright native-English speaker in an English-speaking country *benefits* on all fronts from learning French, German or any other language by immersion. However, a Greek speaker in an English-speaking country, for example, is often apparently disadvantaged by attempts to teach English as a second language. Why the difference?

In the case of the bright English-speaking child learning French by immersion, L1 (English) is not denigrated by the teacher. In fact, its importance is recognised by the fact that it becomes a school subject in its own right, whereas the migrant child's L1 becomes so only rarely. For example, Australia has many migrants from Greece, Italy, Yugoslavia, Lebanon, and non-German-speaking Europe, but very few from France or Germany. Yet the high school language subjects (after English) are: French, German, Indonesian and Japanese. Migrant students might see a hidden curriculum in that.

In short, although all immersion programs are technically the same (L2 learned without recourse to L1), their contexts are entirely different. In particular, a complex

*Establishing mastery in the first
language is essential for subsequent
learning in either language.*

of attitudes and value judgments favour the English-speaker learning French by
immersion, but inhibit the Greek-speaker learning English. The latter learns by
submersion rather than by immersion, a frequent result being impaired learning in both
L1 and L2.

But this is not the full explanation. The effectiveness of L2 learning also depends on *competence in L1*, on the stage of development in L1 before exposure to L2. According to a common alternative framework on language learning, there is a trade-off between L1 and L2 — the better you learn L2, the less you remember of L1. To become moderately proficient in a second language means impaired efficiency in both. There is, however, strong evidence (Cummins, 1979) for a 'threshold effect' which works in precisely the *opposite* way:

1. If a person is *already competent* in two languages, further learning in any one language will enhance that person's general competence even further.
2. If a person is competent in only one language, second-language learning will have no marked effect on either, until the point when bilingualism is reached in the second language (as in point 1.)
3. If a person is minimally competent in L1, further learning in L2 will have *negative* effects on both L1 and L2, *and* on competence in general cognitive tasks.

In case 3, the negative effects become general because L2 is usually the language of instruction. This is the unfortunate situation in which many migrant children find themselves. *It suggests strongly that basic instruction should continue in L1 (the native tongue) until sufficient competence is reached that it will not suffer when L2 learning begins.*

Skutnabb-Kangas and Toukomaa, in a series of studies conducted in Scandinavia (reported in Cummins), found that Finnish children of average (non-verbal) ability who migrated to Sweden at the age of 10 maintained a level of Finnish (L1) comparable to that of Finnish students who remained at home. They *also* achieved a level of competence in Swedish (L2) comparable to that of native-born Swedes, and surpassed the competence in Swedish of *Swedish-born* children of Finnish migrant families. In fact, the ability of these students in Finnish (which they maintained) was a better predictor of mathematics achievement than Swedish; although the mathematics exam was in Swedish! Children whose families migrated to Sweden when they were younger not only learned to speak Swedish poorly but also lost competence in Finnish.

Results similar to these have been found in the case of Spanish-speaking immigrants to the United States, and Canadian Indians (whose L1 was Cree) and French Canadians learning English. In rather a different study, Dulay and Burt (1974) analysed the sorts of errors that Spanish-speaking children made when learning English. The first sort were *developmental* errors which are typically made by all children whether native English-speaking or not. The second sort of errors were *interference* errors, which are caused by imposing Spanish (L1) structures on to learning English. For example, for the sentence 'The dog ate it', a developmental error would be 'The dog eat it' (all English-speaking children tend to make this error); and an interference error, 'The dog it ate' (which directly reflects Spanish structure). Of all the errors made, 87 per cent were developmental, and only 5 per cent were attributable to the interfering effect of L1. Dulay and Burt argued that these results indicate *common processes* between L1 and L2 learning, so that as children spontaneously improve their competence in L1, they will also develop in their L2 competence if allowed to do so by immersion. These findings are very compatible with Cummins' suggestion that L2 acquisition is *enhanced* by improving L1 competence, in the immersion context.

Collectively, this research strongly suggests that the child's mother tongue is the basic tool for developing strategies for scholastic and general intellectual achievement. Reading skill is a good case in point — if gained sufficiently well in L1, it is transferred readily to L2. If, however, reading skills are not well developed in L1 — to the point, say, where the child can read fluently in the mother tongue — total immersion in L2 will be likely to damage what reading skills have been developed in L1, and make it extremely difficult to learn reading in L2. The child loses on all fronts. Existing skill in the mother tongue is lost and progress in the adoptive tongue severely hampered.

Such findings suggest that migrant children should continue to be taught in their mother tongue to a fairly high level of literary competence before immersion in L2. It would undoubtedly be unwise to ignore L2; it needs to be taught alongside L1 but not to replace it. There is a threshold of competence in L1 which is *necessary* for cognitive survival if immigrant children are immersed in L2. For many migrants, however, 'immersion' rapidly becomes 'submersion', to the detriment of both L1 and L2.

These interactions are also dependent on motivational factors, as we noted earlier in this section. A child may be strongly motivated to learn L2; or, after some unpleasant experiences, such as 'wog-calling', strongly resist attempts to learn L2 (see Box 6.6).

There are in fact four ways migrant children can react:

1. Identify positively with both L1 and L2 cultures (the most desirable).
2. Identify with L2 culture but reject their native culture.
3. Reject L2 culture but identify strongly with L1.
4. Reject both (the least desirable and most alienating).

Clearly the reaction to L2, particularly in the immersion context, depends on how students perceive their own identity, as well as on actual cognitive abilities.

Educationally speaking, then, the most important factors that emerge in L2 learning, particularly in the 'immersion' context, in which virtually all migrant children find themselves placed, are:

- positive motivational attitudes to the L2 language and culture;
- developed competence in their own language.

These conclusions are not unlike those reached in the case of non-standard English speakers; to a certain extent, non-standard and standard English may be regarded as examples of L1 and L2.

SUMMARY

The development of spoken language. Spoken language develops from soon after the first year of age and, by school-age, most children have begun to *disembed* language from its context and to see it as an object in its own right. This enables children to *manipulate* language to achieve their own ends and, in particular, to use a new symbol

BOX 6.6   WOG BOY

An autobiography

Wog Boy
sits in a crowded bus
close to his old mother
clad all in black.
His face is one of embarrassment,
why he knows not.
But he can feel
them all,
watching him,
fifty pairs of eyes
eagerly plotting
his mental destruction.
And their laughter
is like a hot knife;
and his feelings are but butter;
and they are cutting
those feelings to nothing.
Sounds,
are all magnified
one hundred times over
and the walls
of that old bus
are starting to move,
intent on crushing
him to death.
He feels terribly confined;
no room
in which to cry out,
to cry out for mercy
from some two-bob god
who has pre-plotted his destiny.
And he looks for some way out.
There's no one to turn to
but his old mother
clad all in black.

Ali Eyian,
Form 6,
University High School, Melbourne

By permission of the author.

system to handle language. The printed word is the ultimate in disembedding language and meaning from context, but it is many years yet before individuals demonstrate mastery over the creation of their own texts.

The development of written language. Several stages may be distinguished in the growth of *reading* skill, from orienting to marks on paper, decoding what letter-sound combinations make what words, comprehending their meaning and using metacognitive skills in extracting maximum meaning from text.

Controversy in the teaching of reading has raged around the relative importance that should be placed on the skills and strategies that are best used at each stage. The point is that all are important at various times. Reading involves about eight levels of text, and each may be the unit focused on during reading. These levels range from physical features and letter shapes, through words, phrases and sentences, to underlying themes. Working memory limitations force the reader to concentrate on one or a few levels to the exclusion of the others. Effective reading thus requires both teacher and reader to be smart about what is best to concentrate on at what particular point and with what skills and strategies. 'Reading comprehension' refers to the extraction of meaning at the present time for optimal understanding of the text; 'studying' refers to optimal ways of extracting meaning for *future* use.

The same general principles that apply to comprehending text apply to creating text. The latter is, however, a more complex process, and different strategies apply at the various levels of textual unit. Not surprisingly, the development of writing skill shows a progression from the *writer's* concern with conveying meaning to the *reader's* concern with using textual clues to extract meaning: a shift from 'knowledge-telling' to reflective writing.

Three aspects of writing are distinguished: *intentional*, that shape the general approach to the task; *parawriting* activities, that include planning and composing; and *writing* activities, that include transcribing, reviewing, revising and editing. During all these activities the writer's focus needs to incorporate both mechanical and meaning aspects of the text. Unskilled writers, like unskilled readers, focus on the lower levels of text; skilled writers focus on the highest levels during planning, composing and reviewing, that is, on the main ideas and the theme, and keep until last attention to mechanics. There is nevertheless an interaction between mechanics and meaning —the one affects the other — but the appropriate way to handle this interaction is to concentrate on meaning. Traditional approaches to reading and writing concentrated on the mechanics, to the detriment of both.

Writing progresses, then, from disjointed sentences that show no sense of audience or awareness of the reader's problems, to smoothly flowing sentences that individually contribute to an overall theme.

The social context. We then looked at the social context of language and differences in the use of standard and non-standard English. The problem is that schooling is carried out in standard English, which places a double burden on the non-standard speaker; who has both to learn the new code itself and to learn the content that the code is conveying. Two models of teaching have been suggested: deficit and difference. According to the first, non-standard English should be stamped out and the student drilled in standard English. According to the difference model, instruction should be continued in the non-standard version until the student has picked up sufficient competence in standard English to make the transfer without pain. Contemporary American research favours the latter model, although the former is in fact the most widespread.

Learning a second language. The above problem is a less extreme version of that faced by non-English-speaking migrants, and we looked at the acquisition of second language (L2) learning within that context. Available research suggests that L2 should not become the medium of instruction until the child has acquired good competence (e.g. ability to read and write) in L1.

The principles discussed in this section have obvious practical application, and we turn to this in Section B.

SECTION B

We now turn to some of the practical implications of material reviewed in Section A. Topics refer to teaching strategies to increase reading comprehension, students' approaches to essay writing, a consideration of the teaching of writing in schools, and the difference/deficit problem as it relates to dealing with non-standard language in schools and the teaching of English as a second language.

MAXIMISING READING COMPREHENSION: INFORMED STRATEGIES FOR LEARNING

A question we left in Section A asked if students can be encouraged to be more metacognitive about their reading comprehension strategies earlier than Year 6, which is typically when students seem to use these strategies effectively for themselves.

Paris, at the University of Michigan, with the help of 40 grade-three and grade-five teachers and over 800 students in local schools, showed that students can, gaining as much as two years on some comprehension tests (Paris, in press; Paris, Cross and Lipson, 1984). His program, Informed Strategies for Learning (ISL), begins with the assumption that reading strategies can be explained directly to children and, if that is done effectively, they will then use them correctly and spontaneously in subsequent reading. There are several aspects of ISL:

1. *Informed teaching.* If teachers are to tell students *what* a strategy is, *how* it operates, and *when* and *why* it should be used, the teachers had better know themselves. Although this knowledge is simple enough, it does not appear in any teachers' manuals. For example, many people do not really understand what 'skimming' is, or what it is

best used for. Many students think skimming is reading the first and last words of sentences, reading very fast, missing out the long words, and so forth. Some think it is something that only poor readers do. The idea that it is a quick way of finding out what a story is about, and instruction in how to do it, is very simple. It is just that teachers do not specifically think about strategies such as skimming, summarising, rephrasing in one's own words, and so on.

2.   *Use of metaphors.* In order to cue students to use these strategies, vivid, concrete directions are needed. Paris uses various metaphors and analogies to do this, pasting each in bright colours on a bulletin board:

- Prereading — 'Plan your reading trip.' (See Box 6.7.)
- Summarising — 'Round up your ideas.'
- Identifying the main idea — 'Be a sleuth. Track down the main idea.'

3.   *Group discussion.* Students need the opportunity to express their confusion, distress — or pride. Discussion enables students to share with others ways they have developed that seem to work for them; this works in a way very similar to the discussion groups used by Johnson Abercrombie (see Chapter 4, Section B). Paris notes that teachers are often surprised both at the naivete, and at the understanding, manifested by some young readers in their approach to text.

4.   *Guided practice.* Each lesson requires students to read and apply the strategy they are currently learning, and then they discuss again immediately afterwards: Did it work? How did it work?

BOX 6.7   PLAN YOUR READING TRIP (GRADE THREE)
(A SAMPLE SET OF INSTRUCTIONS FOR ISL
TEACHERS)

On the analogy of taking a trip away for a holiday, children discuss questions such as the following:

- How do you prepare for your holidays? What sorts of things do you have to think about?
- How is planning to read like planning a trip?
- Would you read in a different way if you wanted to learn lots of details or just the general idea?

Construct a worksheet around a short passage that puts up road signs throughout. The students must obey these signs:

- STOP!   Say the meaning in your own words.
- DEAD END   Go back and reread the parts you didn't understand.
- SLOW   Lower your reading speed.

Source: Adapted and abbreviated from Paris, in press.

5. *Bridging to content area.* One of the problems of teaching students to read with a prepared text is that students may learn to do the appropriate thing in that context, but not see it as something you do outside 'reading class'. Science, history and all normal class content is used with each strategy to show that they should be applied to all their class work.

Paris has developed 20 modules, five grouped around each theme:

- planning for reading;
- identifying meaning;
- reasoning while reading;
- maintaining comprehension.

DEEP AND SURFACE APPROACHES TO WRITING A HISTORY ESSAY: TWO CASE STUDIES

In Section A, surface and deep approaches to the various aspects of writing and parawriting were described (see Figure 6.4) in terms primarily of the level of textual unit focused on. What does this mean in terms of what the writer actually does? And what might we be able to learn from this in terms of improving students' approaches to writing? Let us look at a couple of case studies.

The two examples reported here were part of a larger study (Biggs, in press d), in which students were interviewed about what they did when they planned and wrote essays. These findings were related to their general approaches to learning and studying on the one hand, and to the quality of the essays on the other. In particular, the interest was on defining a surface and a deep approach, and how each produced different outcomes, particularly with respect to the structure of the essay in relation to the question.

Geoff and Syd (the names are fictitious) were studying Australian History in an Open Foundations Course, which is designed for mature age students who do not possess the HSC. Students who pass two OFC subjects in a year of study qualify for university entry into certain faculties. The essay in question was the second and final assignment in the course. The students were interviewed after the essay had been marked and handed back. The question was: *Identify the basic causes of the Eureka Stockade, and try to establish which were the most important. Explain whether you think that this revolt was inevitable.*

Geoff: A surface approach

Geoff, 34 years old, left school nearly 20 years previously, having completed his Intermediate Certificate (Year 9). He was currently a clerk, and wanted to discover his capacity for university work. His SPQ profile* (ranging in deciles from 1–10) was:

---

* The Study Process Questionnaire (SPQ) assesses the approaches to learning described in Chapter 4, and is fully described in Chapter 10.

surface approach, 8; deep approach 1; achieving approach, 3. In general approach to studying, then, he is well above average in surface learning, and well below on achieving approach and especially on deep. In general, he thought writing 'an involved process', which he did not usually enjoy. How did he approach this particular writing task?

Parawriting activities. On *interpreting the question*, his immediate response was to 'present the facts ... just cover the whole story right through and say why I think it happened'. Immediately, then, he was committed to knowledge-telling. This was unfortunate, as he was disappointed with his result for his first essay: the marker then commented that it read 'more like a narrative than a historical analysis' but Geoff took that simply to be a comment on his 'style', not on his understanding of what historical analysis is: *structurally*, the difference is between multistructural and relational or higher.

This multistructural view of history then led him to read the three recommended texts: his *knowledge update* was to ensure that he had all the recognised causes and the information associated with each, so that he could 'cover the whole story'.

Composing involved taking all the jottings and quotes from the main readings and making a precis of each around each of the 'causes': the introduction of the licence fee, the harassing tactics of the police, the acquittal of Bentley for killing a digger, and so on. Where the sources 'did a couple of paragraphs, I try and combine them together, just with a couple of sentences ... bring in my own words and I did a paragraph on each point'. As for *sense of audience*, he was aware who was going to mark it but 'I just try and present my own sort of version. I didn't really have anyone in mind reading it'. There was no evidence of any *opportunistic planning*.

Writing activities. *Transcription* thus amounted to rewriting and reducing his sources. He made six drafts, *reviewing* each for spelling and grammar and to make sure he did not use the same words all the time. He changed the structure a couple of times because he thought a few paragraphs were out of sequence.

A heavily abbreviated version, to give an idea of the flavour and structure, is produced in Box 6.8.

Analysis. The approach Geoff used is apparent in the essay: he is telling a story with a wealth of often irrelevant detail, in a multistructural framework. His focus is on a sequence of ideas, expressed around the word-phrase-sentence level, which basically precludes him from answering the question using a causal explanation genre. This focus was again reflected in the marker's comment, 'You did not have to give an account of the rebellion, merely discuss its causes' and again resulted in a bare pass. The word-structure focus guides his reviewing and revising: although he attempted six whole drafts (which is a lot) he edited for spelling and grammar *each time*, while his restructuring was only within a time frame, not a logical or causal frame. His attempts at making 'his' version were not based on the whole viewpoint, but only on the words used in expressing the storyline. It is not surprising, then, that he 'found the first and last paragraphs the hardest ... the middle part was covering the topic, which I found easy'.

BOX 6.8   EXCERPTS FROM GEOFF'S ESSAY

There were several basic causes of the Eureka Stockade. These included the payment of a licence fee, the purchase of squatters' land and the right to vote ... the way government officials and police administered the law on the goldfields ... mistreated the diggers who already had to overcome difficult conditions to mine the deep leads of Ballarat ... the acquittal by a local magistrate of the murderer of a miner accelerated a confrontation between the diggers and the government ...

To reach the deep leads the diggers had to overcome many problems. Initially they formed into small syndicates of four or six men to cope with the heavy workload and to help with the high cost of supplies. While digging the shaft the miners had to contend with water flooding and shifting sand. If the water became too heavy men from other shafts had to help bale water out by order of the gold commissioner or they would forfeit their claim ...

The Government was worried by this campaign especially when the diggers on some fields offered only ten shillings for their licences in September 1853. Governor La Trobe then waived the fee but a week later it had returned in a different form. The licence fees were reduced to £1 for the month, £2 for three months, £4 for six months and £8 for twelve months. Soon after the diggers held meetings to discuss the new regulations. At one meeting on 21 November 1853, A. H. M. (Manning) CLARK stated in 'A HISTORY OF AUSTRALIA IV' that a huge number gathered at Eureka on the Ballarat field to hear Dr Carr tell them that the new regulations would lead to armed rebellion ...

... All that was needed was one incident to accelerate their inevitable confrontation. That incident occurred on the night of the 6 October 1884, when a miner named Scobie was murdered outside the Eureka Hotel. James Bentley, an ex convict who owned the hotel, his wife Hanacea and John Farrell were tried and acquitted of the murder charge.

... The next day saw the government deliberately looking for trouble by organising a general licence hunt. It was a hot windy day and diggers began to rebel ...

The dedicated men moved to the Eureka Section of the hill fields where they built a rough stockade. There they marched, drilled and reinforced the stockade ...

The most important causes of the Eureka Stockade were the introduction of the licence fee and how the government officials and police enforced it without any consideration for the diggers of the Ballarat goldfields. I think that this revolt was inevitable because the diggers after years of petitioning, protesting and voicing their grievances to the authorities without result had no alternative left for them except rebellion.

(Total: 1500 words)

Syd: A deep approach

Syd, aged 57, left school over 40 years previously, also after completing the Intermediate examination. He was currently unemployed, and his previous employment included clerical and industrial (foreman) experience. He was taking the course for personal satisfaction. He claimed to have no difficulties with essay writing, and had in fact written book reviews for the local newspaper: 'I write to produce something I like.'

His SPQ profile was a striking deep-achieving: surface approach, 1; deep approach, 10; achieving approach, 10.

Parawriting activities. Syd said that in general he likes to read a lot around an essay topic: 'Various points of view all differ to some extent ... sometimes that slight difference can be the interesting twist you can put into the essay ... as soon as this topic came up, I had in mind that the slant would be that it was part of the rise of the middle class in the nineteenth century.'

In one hit, *interpreting the question*, Syd had determined *knowledge update, opportunistic planning* (which normally comes later in his reading to give him his 'twist', but he recognised immediately what his twist was to be) and *structure*. By placing this event within a superordinate framework — the rise of the middle classes with their liberal/democratic psychology — he has used a formal principle to explain the causes and to give the essay its structure (which is extended abstract compared to Geoff's).

In this case, Syd read the three recommended texts and five others, from which he took notes that helped back up the case he was making:

> My first draft is done by collating the rough notes and what else I want to say. Once I have the outline, based on my own twist, the rough draft didn't take long to do. The rise of the middle classes in the nineteenth century is how I started. The Eureka Stockade is just part of that: that was my case, my twist. I then selected the reference notes to support that, the details etc.

As for *sense of audience*, he said that he really writes to suit himself, but it is a bit of a compromise: 'You have to take into account your own point of view and what is actually being sought by the person setting the essay'.

Writing activities. Once Syd had worked out his structure, the writing was surprisingly rapid: a rough outline from the notes, then the first draft, which was reviewed 'to keep it coherent, logical and orderly as possible'. Also at that time he changed the weighting he gave to one issue. He then edited the final draft from that: 'spelling mistakes, badly expressed things, verbosity, if it's convoluted, repetition — none of that sort of thing. I try to keep it as straightforward as possible and as direct as possible.'

Excerpts illustrating the flavour and the structure of Syd's writing are reproduced in Box 6.9.

BOX 6.9   EXCERPTS FROM SYD'S ESSAY

The eighteenth century is regarded as the Age of Enlightenment, a period that brought the flowering of new scientific and philosophical thought and a stronger concept of individual freedom for the common man ...

The nineteenth century saw the tide of liberalism and democracy fostered largely by the growing middle class ... It was from this background of stirring ideas and emotions that many of those who took part in the gold rushes, came ... or would-be small capitalists and their main aim was to improve their own lot ... It was these middle class elements among the diggers that gave impetus to the reform movements in the gold fields ...

... The Master and Servant Act having proved ineffectual in stemming this loss, the expensive Gold Licence was introduced (originally in New South Wales) ... so that the licence fee of thirty Shillings per month became a heavy burden (Ward.) ...

... as the gold tended to be concentrated in small, rich pockets, a few struck it very rich, while most made little or nothing. Also, the alluvial gold, which was what was being sought, was quite deeply buried in old, over-lain stream beds and this necessitated 'deep' mining with its' increased and strenuous work, its attendant risks of cave-ins and problems with both gases and water ...

While it seems obvious from this that the majority of the diggers as a whole, were more concerned with social and political reform than with the irritant of the Gold Licence, it was, none the less, the Gold Licence that became the fuse to the powder keg.

The spark that lit the fuse was undoubtedly the riot that led to the burning down of Bentleys' hotel after he had been acquitted, by magistrate D'ewes, of the murder of Scobie ...

Hotham failed to appreciate that he was no longer on the quarter-deck of a man-of-war and that the diggers were not prepared to be treated as surly lower deck ratings. In this, he displayed a failing noticeable among other naval officers who became Colonial Governors ...

... Eureka Stockade, the Australian revolution that never really got off the ground, faded quickly into memories shortly after the event as other rushes carried the diggers to new fields and dispersed them across the continent. It has never been completely forgotten and lingers uneasily in the folk-memory even today. It has become a symbol, of sorts, to the mild mannered left of Australian politics and to the trendy, if tepid, would-be republicans.

(Total: 2100 words)

Analysis. The essay is very much 'top-down', reflecting his focus on the theme. In fact, the theme possibly dominates too much: he does not really address the Eureka

Stockade until after three long paragraphs into the essay. That reflects the potential danger of extended abstract responses: unless the case is put extremely well, it may be seen as irrelevant to the particular point at issue. In this case, however, the marker commented, 'You are perhaps the only student who is capable of fitting both (events and causes) into a broad political/historical framework', and marked the essay accordingly.

Syd only did two drafts after the outline, compared with Geoff's six, yet Syd shows much more evidence of reflective writing, using writing to test a hypothesis (does Eureka fit the European pattern?). In planning, outlining and drafting, his focus is on the theme and main idea, switching to words and sentence levels only at the final draft.

IMPLICATIONS FOR THE TEACHING OF WRITING

What do these case studies and the material reviewed in Section A generally have to tell us about who are good writers, and how they get that way? That good writers know more, and so students should read more? Or that students should make more drafts?

In many ways, Geoff went to more trouble than did Syd: he spent longer at the task, did more drafts and, although he only read the set texts, he seemed from the final text to *know more* about Eureka (the changes in the licence fees, names of individuals, depth of shafts, etc.). On the other hand, Syd seemed to know more about European history and politics.

The point is not who knew more, but the *level* of knowledge. Syd's knowledge provided him with a context: it was wider ranging and more abstract than Geoff's knowledge. The difference strongly recalls Glaser's (1984) expert-novice differences. The first feature that emerges then is that good essay writers need a background structured in increasing levels of abstraction: from ideas, to main ideas, to a theme.

The second feature is that writing is *reflective*: it turns back on itself to lead the writer to refine the emerging ideas, perhaps to discover new ideas. We saw little evidence of that in Syd's case, as it happened, because his hypothesis was well-formed from the outset, but this feature was represented in his approach. What-has-been-written is *provisional*: the knowledge has not only not yet all been told, it may not even have been structured. Applebee (1984) argues that reflective writing enhances a person's reasoning ability: externalising thought, and 'freezing' it out there, enables the writer to have second thoughts, to experiment with new combinations of ideas. Writing also forces the writer to try to be clear and precise in thinking a topic through; it is not possible to give the reader a nudge or a wink to reinforce meaning.

In that case, writing should not only be widely used across the curriculum in schools in order to sharpen thinking, whatever the content area, but be used *reflectively*. As Applebee points out, however, this is not the case. Writing is used either as a means of *storing* and prompting knowledge that is already in existence — for example note-taking, which captures ideas only at the sentence level at most — or for *testing* purposes, where the writer communicates second-hand content to someone who always knows more about the topic than does the writer. In neither case is writing used reflectively: the knowledge is never shaped by the writer, simply reported back. Further, the testing function of the essay or short answer introduces all the pressures and challenges that promote cynicism and anxiety and which in turn promote a surface approach to learning.

The teaching of writing is typically seen to be a function of the English department. Further, if 'writing' is to be taught as a generalised, content-free 'subject', it means that how-to-write courses can only concentrate on spelling, grammar, orthographics and vague all-purpose 'structures'. To teach 'content-free' writing techniques automatically draws attention away from main ideas and themes, focusing it on mechanics. Mechanics are obviously important, but their importance derives from the fact that they help to convey meaning efficiently. Without the content, mechanics are not only meaningless themselves, but concentration on them is dangerous because they divert attention away from the fundamental problem of writing (see Box 6.2). At least in the early stages of writing, mechanics are best learned in context: how this may be done is illustrated below.

As far as implications for teaching are concerned, then, the following points crystallise:

- Writing should be used for much more than testing and jogging the memory.
- Writing should be dealt with in the content areas in which it is used, and for purposes requiring the writer to focus on main ideas and themes, rather than on disjointed ideas, facts and points.
- Markers of essays and exams should therefore focus on the main ideas and themes, rather than on mechanics. When mechanics *are* singled out for attention, it should be pointed out that the misspelling (or the sentence construction or the placement of the comma) interferes with the *meaning*.
- Emphasis should be placed on the cyclical, reflective, nature of writing rather than on the one-way transcription of preformed thoughts.

Adequate treatment of all these issues is beyond our present scope, but two matters stand out for attention: the level of the writer's focus and the question of review and revision. Two recent developments specifically address these issues.

Conferencing

Conferencing is the term used to describe the 'process' approach to writing developed by Donald Graves, which is currently being widely used in Australian schools (Graves, 1983; Turbill, 1982). As Turbill says, what is new about this approach is that the child, rather than the teacher, is given control or 'ownership' over the what, when and how of writing. The teacher's role is to assist the child in these decisions in a one-to-one 'conference', in which the activities of writing and parawriting (selecting a topic, updating knowledge, working out a structure, monitoring, attending to mechanics, redrafting, etc.) are discussed as the need arises. In a class of 25 children or so, all writing at once, this sounds impossible but as Graves points out a single 'conference' can last as little as 12 seconds; with different children at different stages and some conferencing with each other, it is in fact quite easy to arrange. Turbill, who used the method with 27 primary teachers in New South Wales, confirms that this is so.

In her view (p. 6) the features of this approach are:

- the program is completely individualised;
- the child makes responsible decisions about what to write;
- there is daily time to 'learn to write by writing';
- the child can discover his or her unique way or 'process' of writing;
- there is time to talk individually with the teacher in conference;
- the conference attends to making the writing better.

There are no teacher assigned tasks beyond providing at least half an hour a day for writing. The teacher is encouraged to keep a list of each child's interests and any significant events that may have happened, so that the child may be helped towards a topic during early conferences. The provisional nature of writing is constantly emphasised: each piece of writing is introduced as a draft, and some run up to six or more drafts before all agree that it is 'finished'. All finished works go into each child's 'Writing Folder', from which each child is encouraged to select one or more 'books' for 'publication'. When this happens, children are eager to make sure that presentation is correct and neat, spelling is such that everyone can read it (i.e. is correct), and so forth. Each class has its library of books made by students within the class, and they are read by the others just as eagerly as are trade books.

Emphasis throughout the drafting stages is on 'flow'. Writing is seen as one of many forms of communication: talking, drawing, drama, role play. These activities are used — children talking to themselves, to others or to the teacher — to help them plan their topics and their drafts. Graves points out that children have yet to internalise their thoughts — as adults do with their 'inner speech' when they compose — so that talking is an important part of planning, composing and revising.

'Flow' also requires that thoughts get down as soon as possible: stopping to check on spelling stops the flow. Graves therefore encourages *invented spelling*: 'John began composing when he wrote: "SSTK (This is a truck)". Fifteen minutes later John couldn't read the message. There were too few cues. Nevertheless he had the idea that the letters written had to correspond to sounds ... he is learning to write the way he learned to speak' (Graves, 1983, p. 183).

Gradually, the children stabilise with the standard spellings. Graves kept records of individual children's invented spellings and their evolution. For example, Toni in grade one spelt 'and' in the following ways, from October to December: D D ND AD ND LA ANE AND ND AND AND AND. From 8 December, 'and' remained constant. Graves claims that *all* mechanics can be taught in the conference as the need arises, and that when learned in this way they are retained and used accurately.

Most of the published work on conferencing refers to the beginning years, where writing and reading arise out of precisely the same activities, and thereafter develop in parallel. The specific technique of conferencing may, however, be used at any level: Graves runs workshops for professional writers using essentially the same techniques. The essence is that the conference situation enables writers to talk about, hence think about and focus on, the higher level units of meaning: what the text is all *about*. The emphasis on redrafting enables them to have another think — and another.

Word processing

The use of the personal computer in education has yet to be properly assessed. It is, however, appropriate to say something here about its application to writing because it *appears* to address directly some of the central issues: in particular that of review and revise, level of focus and mechanics. Events are happening too fast for anyone to come up with properly conducted research, but there is no shortage of opinions about micros. As soon as new software or hardware emerges, the game changes: this is happening all the time. For example, at the time of writing, one megabyte of random access memory (RAM) has recently become easily available (i.e. 1,000K, when 64K was considered more than adequate three years ago!). This development has opened up all sorts of possibilities: for example, text can be simultaneously checked for mechanics as it is being produced. There is enough 'memory' to store a thesaurus, a dictionary and a grammar checker, so that the writer simply may never need to worry about synonyms, spelling, grammar etc., thus leaving attention focused exclusively on higher level meanings. The 'talking screen' is another 'gee-whiz' innovation, where writers can have the machine speak back what has been written so that they can hear what it sounds like, or how a particular word is pronounced (Watt, 1984).

For present purposes, however, the pertinent feature of micros is the way they make revising and redrafting — the very features that distinguish reflective writing from knowledge-telling — so much easier. Several factors have hitherto strongly discouraged students from redrafting:

*Revision is so much easier
on the word processor.*

- the belief that redrafting is what has to be done as a 'punishment' for not planning properly first time round;
- the high cost in terms of effort in rephrasing a section, or inserting material. One small alteration to a six-page paper means the whole lot has to be rewritten;
- a reluctance to change what is already fixed in print.

Word processors, on the other hand, allow alterations to be made at a very *low* cost, and the appearance of a word on a screen emphasises its *impermanence*. The words on the screen can be changed instantly and neatly. If a word has been consistently misspelled throughout a 200-page document, the correct spelling has only to be typed in once with a simple instruction. If four lines are to be deleted from the middle of a page this may be carried out in seconds, and the printout reads as if it had always been written this way.

Schwartz (1982) claims the following advantages of the word processor which she has found when using them in her writing classes:

- It reduces the initial fear students have of making their mistakes, and hence decreases writers' block.
- Students are much more willing to fully explore what they might mean.
- Writers are less defensive about taking advice — changes can be made instantly without tedious recopying.
- Writers are able to read clean drafts (without erasures, over-writing, arrows, etc.), which allows them to revise more efficiently and more objectively.

There may however be some disadvantages, too. The greater legibility and presentation of material arouse the danger of 'smokescreen revision': by sprinkling cohesive devices through the text (such as 'It therefore follows that ...') the reader may be deceived into thinking the content is better than it is.

The second problem is perhaps more serious, and certainly requires research. The very feature that permits low-cost revision — the monitor — is itself of limited capacity: the writer cannot view the whole text at once. The view is usually limited to a few sentences at a time, which may not be enough to keep the main idea in focus. The writer should therefore revise on the basis of the *complete text* before the final printout.

In general, though, the careful classroom use of the word processor has enormous potential to encourage writers to be more reflective, and to use language in a way that more closely reflects and reshapes their thinking.

THE SOCIAL CONTEXT OF LANGUAGE

In Section A, we saw that minority group language differences occurred in two contexts: where the minority group used a non-standard *version* of the main language, and where the minority group used a *different* language, so that the main language, in this case English, had to be learned as a second language. Each context could be approached with either a *difference* model of teaching or a *deficit* model. According to the first, the minority language is seen as a valid language form: that recognition is used to *bridge the difference* between the minority and majority languages. According to the second, the minority language is seen to be an inferior form of language: the standard version of the majority language is taught rigorously to *replace* the minority language or version.

Complex social as well as linguistic questions are at issue here. In this chapter we focus as far as possible on the linguistic questions: some social issues are discussed in Chapter 7.

Standard versus non-standard English

The teacher has two possible approaches to the non-standard English problem described in Section A: the difference and the deficit models.

The difference model. Di Vesta and Palermo (1974) recommended use of the difference model to assist non-standard English speakers. This approach concentrates initially on learning through the *student's* (non-standard) language. Standard English would then be introduced in the manner described below for learning a second language. An approach based on this model does not however appear to have been attempted in Australia. It is one which presupposes a qualitative difference between non-standard and standard English like that separating L1 and L2 learning. In this country standard English is possibly sufficiently familiar to non-standard speakers for it to be focused on directly. We turn, then, to the deficit model.

The deficit model. Based on the work of Bereiter and Engelmann (1966), who emphasised the need to lift language development by changing pupils' attitudes, values and behaviours to those of middle-class children, an outback pre-school project has been quite successful. A team of educational psychologists undertook the project — called 'Enrichment of Childhood' — at Bourke, New South Wales (de Lacey, 1974). Two concurrent programs were run with matched groups of children. One was typical of those offered in New South Wales kindergartens, the other based on the Bereiter drill techniques. A teacher was appointed to communicate directly with parents in their homes, and to explain homework tasks. In sustained sessions, the pupils provided chorus answers when asked to identify objects and sentence responses. The 20-minute sessions were varied only by free play or songs which reinforced the language skills. At Bourke, where Aboriginal people constituted 25 per cent of the population and spoke what de Lacey termed 'a variation of low-income rural English', the Bereiter-Engelmann group showed 'spectacular gains of an order seldom encountered in educational research'. These gains were still in evidence two years later.

The Bourke approach exemplifies 'closed' instruction based on the *deficit* model of non-standard English. The problem is seen as a lack of skill in standard English, and direct instructions and drills are thus used to build up competence in standard English as quickly as possible.

An 'open' alternative has been suggested by Evans, Georgeff and Poole (1980). These writers argued that working-class (particularly immigrant) children do not use standard (or elaborated-code) English because their environment is full of non-verbal communication clues and so they do not have to. They placed children in a discovery-learning situation which offered no facial or bodily clues: they were forced to use the public, elaborated code if they were to communicate at all. Pupils were grouped into four or six, and then subgrouped by means of a physical partition between groups so that all non-verbal communication was prevented. Four tasks were set:

1. Speakers and listeners were given identical sets of six to eight items such as plastic shapes or pictures. Speakers were then asked to describe specified objects so that listeners could correctly identify them.
2. Listeners had the task of building a pattern of shapes identical to that of the speaker.
3. Listeners were required to carry out an everyday task (such as fitting a baby's nappy) on the instructions of the speaker.
4. More general activities included a game in which a blindfolded child had to be verbally directed past obstacles, or drawings were reproduced.

The results strongly favoured the experimental approach, with children significantly improving their language skills and ability to communicate.

In sum, then, we find that, in Australia, the problem of non-standard English has been addressed in terms of the deficit model, perhaps because the minority/majority gap is not so wide that the direct approach does not represent too great a mismatch, with the major exception of Aboriginal languages. Aboriginal education is, however, an issue that requires separate treatment (see next chapter).

Teaching English as a second language

This problem is very complex but, as far as the language issues are concerned, the material reviewed in Section A suggests a clear message: by the time children have started to read, proficiency in the minority language (L1) is a prerequisite for proficiency in the majority language (L2, in this case English). Otherwise, performance suffers on most fronts. This seems clearly to rule out the deficit model which suggests concentrating on L2: yet for years, Australia's policy was assimilation, a version of the deficit model. What is the scope of the problem?

Immigration, language and school performance. Australia, contrary to common stereotypes, is one of the most cosmopolitan societies in the world, containing people of 140 ethnic backgrounds speaking 80 languages, and practising more than 80 religions. Twenty-two per cent of the population in 1986 had been born overseas. Earlier migrant groups were mainly British, Italian, Greek and Yugoslav, but today the Southern European immigration has slowed, and that from South East Asia has increased (Callan, 1986).

How do migrants, particularly from non-English-speaking backgrounds, fare in the classroom? A number of surveys in the 1970s provided evidence of the academic achievements of migrant children in Australian schools. The evidence comes primarily from Victoria (surveys in 1970 and 1974 reported by Elliot and Margitta, 1975; and by

Cox et al., 1978); New South Wales (two surveys reported in 1971 by the Department of Education); across both States (Australian Department of Education, 1975); and national (ACER studies by de Lemos (1975)), and Bourke and Keeves (1977). In brief, these were the findings:

- About one-third of the school migrant population in New South Wales was being impeded because of language difficulties, primary pupils more than secondary students.
- Of the 47,000 migrant children surveyed in Victoria, over 10,000 required special tuition in English. All had lived for at least six years in Australia.
- The most common problem of 188 Melbourne migrant children who were seeking professional educational assistance was 'learning differences/educational retardation' exacerbated by 'language factors'.
- Non-English-speaking pupils did better in non-verbal and arithmetic tests than in literacy tests. Indeed, in the ACER reading test there was no significant difference for 10-year-old migrant and Australian pupils on the numeracy test.

In the average Australian classroom, there are five or six students from a non-English-speaking background, and in particular areas, that figure may rise to as high as 90 per cent. The evidence suggests that their best chance of survival is to have a good foundation in their L1 before bridging to L2.

Approaches to language problems of migrant students. As it happens, this country has tried policies based on both difference and deficit models. The deficit model was used until the seventies. The policy was called *assimilation* and meant that officially the cultural diversity of immigrants was not recognised: all new arrivals were expected to assimilate to prevailing Australian Anglo-Celtic norms. This policy was based 'on the myth of the homogeneous Australian' (Grassby, 1978).

The second policy, introduced in the early seventies and officially labelled *multiculturalism*, encourages immigrant groups to retain their cultural identity. Such an approach is highly compatible with the difference model of the majority/minority gap and, although there has been some quite strident criticism of the model (e.g. Chipman, 1980), it is that towards which we are working today. Some ambivalence still exists among teachers: while 84 per cent feel that migrant children should be given opportunities to learn their community language, 44 per cent saw these opportunities should be given *outside* school hours (Callan, 1986). In other words, there is official support for a view that the general school community has not quite caught up with —this is a familiar phenomenon and we return to it again in Chapter 8.

Nonetheless, we should still ask what a multicultural classroom would look like. It would be based on the principle that L1 should be learned and preserved, and an immediate implication is that L1 should be used extensively in the classroom. For this to be feasible, it implies that classrooms be homogeneous with respect to the particular minority language (teacher as well as students) at least for regular and particular lessons. In many schools, this would mean cross-age grouping, and scheduling such classes for different ethnic groups. Within each class, teachers would use relevant materials such as books, drama, SBS videos, other films, etc.

*Learning a second language
using language masters.*

The Saturday or ethnic school has recently been granted governmental support: they are officially seen as 'taking a legitimate role in teaching community language and cultural traditions' (Callan, p. 88).

Nikko: a case study. (Adapted from McQuinn, 1979.) Nikko is the first-born of a family who arrived from Greece some six years before his birth. Nikko's parents have taken out Australian citizenship but remain essentially Greek in language and customs. Thus Nikko spent his first five years surrounded by things Greek. The language Nikko hears and learns has a different phonology, syntax and rhythm. His vocabulary usage is equivalent to that of his English-speaking peers, but most words are Greek; his few English words have come from television and contact with Australian neighbours.

On his first day at school Nikko receives a shock. He is not the articulate child known to his parents, but a bewildered pupil trying to make sense out of what he hears. He cannot rely on his experience and use those five years of stored linguistic information. Competence and performance are no longer allied, but become two disparate factors.

For Nikko, the possibility is that the school will now regard him in the same light as a native-English-speaking child who has failed to reach a satisfactory level of competence and performance. His ability to communicate with other Greek speakers is irrelevant: he is labelled a linguistic failure. There are now three options open to Nikko and his parents:

1.   *They decide that Nikko cannot allow his language to be discarded.* They enrol him in a school which has a bilingual program with Greek as the alternative. This program values Nikko's language and extends his fluency. A program of English is structured on Nikko's Greek lessons, thus he gains literacy through his use of Greek. Nikko's reading of English requires him to learn a new set of phonemes and syntax. As with his Greek, this reading is based on a newly gained fluency. By the time Nikko is in Year 6, he can be both bilingual and literate. He has progressed beyond the period of interlanguage.

2.   *Nikko attends a school which provides an ESL program (immersion).* He is recognised as a child who can communicate with his own group, but not effectively with the mainstream population. He is placed in a special class and led through a carefully structured program in which he may acquire fluency in English without unnecessary impediment to his normal school program. Skills in literacy and numeracy are, however, acquired in his L2 (English) — in which he is not yet proficient. He does not receive any instruction in learning to read in Greek.

There remains an element of risk, for Nikko may be regarded by his peers as a person apart. He is, after all, separated from them for extended periods (shades of the 'spazzo' class). If Nikko's ESL program were part of normal school activity, he would not be withdrawn from his peers' class or group activities. If special lessons are needed for Nikko, these could occur when the rest of the class also undertakes elective or specialist activities.

3.   *Nikko attends a school which does not provide language assistance (submersion).* Despite the claim that he will learn English naturally, Nikko is isolated: there is nothing 'natural' in being subjected to a barrage of incomprehensible language which requires responses. Nikko learns to survive in the classroom by following the leads of others and keeping out of the teacher's range of vision when questions are asked. Play and social interaction enable language to be acquired informally — sufficiently for his teachers to presume that Nikko is coping with the English language. As each academic year passes, the gap between Nikko's receptive and functional language widens. He remains in the interlanguage period and may be assigned to the remedial class.

Should the school have enrolled Nikko? Were his parents aware of the other two alternatives? Nikko may be the one student required to make the difference between retaining or losing a teacher. There may be a school policy based on neighbourhood groups: but this mainstreaming policy ignores Nikko's language.

This example substantiates the conclusions that L1 should be well established, and that the stage of development in L1 is crucial before L2 is attempted. It can easily be seen that neither conclusion is applicable to the last two alternatives facing Nikko: immersion and submersion. Even in the case of the school with the ESL program, L1 is regarded as irrelevant, with L2 being shored up as quickly as possible so that it can bear the weight of the instructional burden it is to carry. That solution is analogous to the Bereiter–Engelmann program in the case of the standard/non-standard English problem. On the assumption that the non-standard version is a deficient one, the only logical alternative is to work hard on the standard. This solution may succeed when the difference between standard and non-standard is not great, but when the difference amounts to a whole language, the child's competence in standard English (L2) is simply not great enough to carry sole responsibility for the medium of learning; and both L1 and L2 suffer.

SUMMARY

Maximising reading comprehension. It is usually not until Year 6 that students spontaneously use context and other metacognitive strategies for maximising their comprehension of text. An American program, Informed Strategies for Learning (ISL), deliberately teaches younger children how to be strategic about reading by training them in the use of strategies such as skimming, planning, checking comprehension using context, and so forth.

ISL is fairly direct; these strategies are ones that are not usually formally taught and so the first step is to make sure the teachers know what different comprehension strategies are, how they are best used and for what purposes. Group discussions, simulated games and exercises are used to supplement teaching. Students readily adopt the strategies and use them in subject content about two years earlier than they would otherwise use them had they been left alone.

Deep and surface approaches to writing. The approaches to writing a history essay used by two mature age students were studied, and related on the one hand to their general approach to learning, and to the quality of the particular product on the other. Geoff, who used a surface approach in general, concentrated on the level of words and sentences when writing his essay: he had the view that an essay should 'cover the whole story' and that his job was to give all the salient facts about each possible 'cause' of the historical event (the Eureka Stockade).

Syd immediately saw the topic as an opportunity to test a hypothesis, and constructed his essay and arranged his parawriting and writing activities around that. His essay showed evidence of his deep approach — he kept his concentration on the level of main ideas and the theme, correcting mechanics and low level aspects at the final draft.

Implications for the teaching of writing. Two main points distinguish good writers from poor. Good writers have main ideas and a theme as their major concentration, with mechanical features and presentation being only a subsequent and distinct concern; text is regarded as provisional and continually available for revision. Poor writers concentrate at or below the sentence level, and continually monitor for mechanical correctness; text is regarded as final. Good writers plan at a high level of abstraction, and update their knowledge selectively; poor writers operate at low levels of abstraction, and do not discriminate between fact and principle.

Two recent techniques in the teaching of writing address these points: *conferencing* is a 'process' approach to teaching writing. The teacher enters into a one-to-one conference with the (usually beginning or young) writer to help with the writing and parawriting activities and maintaining attention on content. Mechanics are addressed only incidentally as they arise, and drafting is encouraged.

Word processors are technically ideal for removing the high physical and psychological cost of making multiple drafts. It is possible, however, that they restrict the level of focus, as the whole text is not visible at any one time unless positive steps are taken to make it so. This is a very new and developing area, however, and much research remains to be done on how word processors will most effectively develop writing skill.

The social context of language. Two groups of students face the common problem of being instructed in a linguistic code which is different from their native code. The first group consists of those who learn at home to speak a non-standard version of English (described by Bernstein as a 'restricted code') and then have to cope with instruction which is given in standard English (an 'elaborated code').

In the deficit model, instruction is aimed to increase competence in the standard English; in the difference model, instruction is modified to suit the non-standard version. Two examples of the former strategy have been used in the Australian context: building up standard English in one case by exercises and drill, and in the other by a discovery-learning technique. Both were successful. There have been no attempts to use the second model in Australia, possibly because non-standard and standard English are more similar here than they are in the United States or Britain.

The second group of disadvantaged students are migrants from non-English-speaking countries. Until quite recently, migrants were simply expected to conform to Australian language and cultural usage. That model failed badly. The current alternative is the multicultural model, which recognises all ethnic differences as valid. In the multicultural model, special attention would be given to teaching L1 alongside English as a second language (ESL), so that the migrant student could maintain competence in L1. Instruction would be in the most appropriate language; a Greek student could, for example, do the HSC in the Greek language, while at the same time studying English as a second language, in much the same way as an Anglo-Australian would study German as a second language. The latter model is being implemented in some States, and it is certainly the one that is in most accord with the theory and research findings outlined in Section A.

FURTHER READING

On the development of oracy
P. A. and J. S. De Villiers, *Early Language*, Harvard University Press, Cambridge, Mass., 1979.

This book is a straightforward account of the development of language up to school age.

On reading

J. Kirby, 'Style, Strategy and Skill in Reading', in R. R. Schmeck (ed.), *Learning Styles and Learning Strategies*, Plenum, New York, in press.

S. Paris, 'Teaching Children to Guide their Reading and Learning', in T. Raphael and L. Reynolds (eds), *Contexts of Literacy*, Longman, New York, 1985.

Kirby's chapter outlines a model of reading that integrates decoding, comprehension and metacognition. In Paris, the ISL program is described.

On writing

J. Turbill (ed.), *No Better Way to Teach Writing!* Primary English Teaching Association, Rozelle, NSW, 1982.

D. Graves, *Writing: Teachers and Children at Work*, Heinemann Educational, Exeter, New Hampshire, 1983.

J. Biggs, 'Approaches to Learning and to Essay Writing', in R. R. Schmeck (ed.), *Learning Examples and Learning Strategies*, Plenum, New York, in press.

The first book gives an account of the conferencing approach in 27 New South Wales schools; the second gives a much more detailed and highly practical account of how to implement the approach.

Biggs' chapter in Schmeck's book looks at essay writing at the upper secondary and tertiary levels. Fuller details are given on Syd and Geoff, and other students' approaches at various stages of writing.

On standard and non-standard English

J. Bernard and A. Delbridge, *Introduction to Linguistics: An Australian Perspective*, Prentice-Hall of Australia, Sydney, 1980.

Rather technical, but valuable for the student who particularly wishes to pursue the question of Bernstein's work in the Australian context, and to study a linguist's analysis of Australian English.

On English as a second language

L. Lippman, *The Aim is Understanding: Educational Techniques for a Multi-Cultural Society* Australia and New Zealand Book Co, Sydney, 1977.

M. Poole, P. De Lacey and B. Randhawa, *Australia in Transition*, Harcourt Brace Jovanovich Group, North Ryde, 1985.

The appendix of Lippman's book lists resource materials available for education related to Aboriginal students; race relations and racism; immigrants in Australia; other cultures; world religions; audiovisual aids; and games. Teaching techniques for primary, secondary, youth and adult groups are provided. Poole et al. is an up-to-date and comprehensive coverage of the changing patterns in Australian society, from monoculturalism to pluralism.

Curriculum Development Centre (authors not given), PO Box 34, Woden, ACT, 2606, offers:

- *Language and Learning*, a practical guide to strategies for teaching second-language students in the mainstream classroom — strategies to assist ESL students across the primary and secondary curriculum, in English, maths, social science, science, creative arts and practical subjects.
- *Teaching in the Multilingual Classroom*, a handbook offering both theoretical and practical

information on bilingual learning and teaching — how to develop multilingual materials, syllabus and methodology. The book reviews personnel, resources and action needed to teach effectively in the multilingual classroom.

QUESTIONS

Questions for self-testing

1. What is the first step towards controlled and meaningful emission of sounds?
2. What is meant by Chomsky's 'generative transformational grammar'?
3. In what ways can writing be seen as a special form of language?
4. Identify three phases of reading.
5. How can decoding be distinguished from comprehension?
6. Name eight levels of textual unit on which attention may be focused during reading.
7. Name three processes that may be associated with word identification in reading.
8. From the process of writing, distinguish between intentional, parawriting and writing aspects.
9. Identify seven focal points when revising an essay.
10. What are elaborated and restricted codes?
11. What is the so-called 'threshold' effect in learning a second language?

Questions for discussion

1. Oracy has developed strongly by the time children start school, while mastery of written language is rudimentary. It is reasonable, then, that schools concentrate on treatment of the written word in reading and writing. Has the school any significant part to play in oracy education? Discuss the sorts of things an oracy program should address.
2. The principal of your local primary school has asked you to provide a brief talk to parents on 'The best way to teach children to read'. What will you say?
3. What should a teacher do about non-standard English in the classroom? Why?
4. Your colleague, a science teacher, complains to you of the standard of writing of the lab reports and field trip reports, saying that 'the English department isn't teaching the kids to write properly'. What do you, an English teacher, say to that? Can you explain, using the nature of thought and language, why science teachers should teach written language in science?
5. Explore the relationship between reflective writing and creative writing, using the model outlined in this chapter. How might it help you teach creative writing?

7

Social development: Acculturation *and* moral development

OVERVIEW

In this chapter we look at how people interact, in particular at how they understand and act on the *rules* of interpersonal conduct, that is, what is meant by *morality*. Schools have a dual role to play: enabling students to grow in moral sophistication, and going about their other business like any social institution. This ambivalence causes conflicts and inconsistencies. We shall discuss answers to the following questions:

- Is the essence of morality in behaviour, or in the reasons behind behaviour?
- What do young children see as constituting a naughty act?
- If you were asked to electrocute a stranger, would you be likely to?
- Why do so few people in a crowded place help another in trouble?
- Does a high level of moral reasoning imply that behaviour will be moral?
- Do very young children spontaneously help others?
- Can encounter groups be used in education?
- How can 'neutral' schools teach specific values?
- Should schools require obedience or moral autonomy from pupils?
- What are process approaches to values education?
- How can a teacher provide the conditions leading to students' moral development?
- How far should teachers try to encourage moral development?
- Do Australian teachers have professional autonomy?
- Is there a second set of three Rs in a school curriculum?
- How is sexism shown in a school organisation?
- Can a school textbook be racist?
- What is an Aboriginal view of Aboriginal education?
- Can schools help ethnic minorities preserve their culture and at the same time perpetuate an Australian culture?

When you have finished this chapter, you should be able to do the following:

1. Outline the main stages of moral development according to cognitive psychologists.
2. Distinguish between 'egocentricity' in childhood and in adolescence.
3. Hear a student explain what would be the 'right' thing to do in a situation involving moral choice, and classify response in terms of Kohlberg's stages.
4. Distinguish between a content and a process approach to values education.
5. Explain how the hidden curriculum may impede moral growth.
6. Use the Piaget–Kohlberg psychology of moral development to provide a suitable response to a student boycott of school socials because 'outsiders' are refused admission.
7. Distinguish between the roles of a teacher as an agent of moral maintenance and as an agent of moral growth.
8. Identify the content of the hidden curriculum and describe how it would be transmitted.
9. Detect bias in textbooks, school organisation and classroom practices.
10. Complete a checklist on sexist teaching practices.

SECTION A

INDIVIDUAL DEVELOPMENT, THE CONTEXT OF SOCIETY AND THE ROLE OF THE SCHOOL

That the school has a responsibility for and a role to play in affective issues such as interpersonal feelings, moral values and the norms prevailing in both minority and majority cultures, is clear. It is not quite so clear what that role is. It is certainly different from that assumed last century: even different from that assumed only recently. In relation to societal norms and moral values, the school has moved:

- from actually teaching 'the principles of morality... to avoid idleness, profanity and falsehood' (1886 Public Instruction Act, see Box 7.1);
- to the 'neutral grounds for rational discourse' position, as long as the rational discourse excludes 'any issue on which the community is divided' (the Buggie directive, see Box 7.2);
- to encouraging minority students to maintain their cultural diversity, and majority students to *value* that diversity (the multicultural position; the 'official' policy of the eighties).

We seem to have come quite a distance since the horse-and-buggy days. The 1973 New South Wales statement of aims — promoting 'individual development in the context of society' towards 'responsible self-direction and moral autonomy' — is an excellent summary of the process-oriented, multicultural position, yet it was published exactly two years *before* the quite incompatible statement appearing in Box 7.2! The tension between individual and society, between self-fulfilment and social conformity, exists at all levels and has not been adequately resolved.

The whole issue of individuals developing in the context of society is enormously complex. A first complication is that the term 'acculturation' in the title of this chapter incorporates two distinct but related processes: the process of socialising or 'taming' individuals to conform to what is socially acceptable; and the process of interaction between minority and majority cultures within society (as in multiculturalism) (cf. *Macquarie Dictionary*, 1982). We are interested here in both: in the social context as it impinges on individuals, and on minorities *vis à vis* the majority culture. (The purely linguistic aspects of the latter process have already been alluded to in the previous chapter.)

A second complication is the tension between individual development and conformity to cultural norms. How *can* people be morally autonomous in the context of society? 'What right has one to place one's principles above the laws and agreements of one's group?' ask Wallach and Wallach (1983) in a book intriguingly entitled *Psychology's Sanction for Selfishness*. In addressing this particular problem, Gibbs and

BOX 7.1   NINETEENTH CENTURY VIEWS OF THE
INVOLVEMENT OF SCHOOLS IN MORAL
EDUCATION — AND WHY

... to impress upon the minds of their pupils the principles of morality,
truth, justice and patriotism; to teach them to avoid idleness, profanity
and falsehood; to instruct them in the principles of free Government;
and to train them up to a true comprehension of the rights, duties, and
dignity of citizenship.

Source: New South Wales Public Instruction Act 1886, quoted in Bessant and Spaull, 1976,
pp. 1–2.

And are these 'the principles of morality' referred to in the Act?

I have never considered mere knowledge ... as the only advantage
derived from a good Common School education ... [Workers with more
education possess] a higher and better stage of morals, are more orderly
and respectful in their deportment, and more ready to comply with the
wholesome and necessary regulations of an establishment...In times of
agitation, on account of some change in regulations or wages, I have
always looked to the most intelligent, best educated and the most moral
for support. The ignorant and uneducated I have generally found the
most turbulent and troublesome, acting under the impulse of excited
passion and jealousy.

Source: A manufacturer writing to the Massachusetts State Board of Education in 1841, quoted in
Katz, 1968, p. 83.

Schnell (1985) point out that the 'let's be morally autonomous' school of thought
emphasises how individuals develop their moral *reasoning* (cognitive), while socialisation
theorists emphasise shared values and interpersonal *feelings* (affective). Both are
important and are considered in the chapter. Specifically, we address the following
issues:

- the development of moral reasoning: how individuals come to think the way they do
  about what is right and what is wrong;
- acculturation: the development of socially acceptable values and feelings towards
  others, both as regards individuals in society, and minority groups in a majority
  society;
- the expression of interpersonal feelings on an individual basis, as seen by humanist
  psychologists;
- the place of the school in all this.

BOX 7.2   WHAT ONE AUSTRALIAN DIRECTOR-GENERAL
THOUGHT ABOUT THE NEUTRALITY OF SCHOOLS
AND THE AUTONOMY OF TEACHERS

Schools are neutral grounds for rational discourse and objective study
and should not become arenas for opposing politics or other ideologies
... The teacher's personal view should not intrude into discussions of
controversial subjects ... [These controversies] would include politics,
sex education, high rise development, open spaces, media bias or any
other issue on which the community is divided ... We're saying implicitly
that the teacher is not an autonomous person.

Source: J. Buggie, reported in The Australian, 18 November 1975; from a letter addressed to all
schools in New South Wales. (Note the date: There was an interesting election campaign in full
swing!)

Discussion point
• Has the role of schools and teachers changed significantly since 1975?

THE DEVELOPMENT OF MORAL REASONING

One of the pioneers of the study of how moral reasoning develops was Piaget (1932) (in
his earlier phase, before he attempted to describe thinking in terms of logical systems).
He defined 'morality' simply as the tendency to accept and follow a system of rules
governing interpersonal behaviour. He was interested in how children come to accept
and understand those rules, and thought that the pattern of their development would be
the same, whatever the behaviours referred to. He studied the game of marbles, which
was pretty much the rage in the streets of Geneva in the late twenties, and asked
children of various ages where the rules came from, why they had to obey them, and so
on. He then asked more obviously 'moral' questions, such as 'Why is telling lies
wrong?'; and asked children his famous moral dilemma stories.

In a moral dilemma, two stories may be presented about how two children
behaved; for example, Mary, to give her mother a nice surprise, did the washing-up for
her, but in so doing broke 16 cups. Jane was forced to do the washing-up, so she showed
her resentment by deliberately breaking one cup. The child is then asked who was the
naughtiest and why. In another form, a person is presented with two courses of action:
one that leads to personal gain, the other to an altruistic choice that leads to personal
cost (and someone else's gain).

The assumption here is that there must be some sort of *intention* behind an action if
it is to be deemed moral: the *fact* of lying is not as important as the intentions leading to
the lie. To lie in order to gain ('I lost that wallet you found') is morally different from
lying in order to protect someone else ('Sorry she was late: it was my fault for
forgetting the time').

Note that morality in this view refers not to the action itself, but to the reasons behind it, and that the thrust concerns what people *think* about behaviour rather than what they *do*.

First, then, we trace the development of moral reasoning along the general lines established in Chapter 5. Second, as the structure of individual thinking is only part of the story, we look at acculturation to the particular values and norms held by the society, and the feelings people have towards those norms and towards each other.

The sensori-motor mode: Amorality

Behaviour in the sensori-motor mode can only be *amoral*. As it is concerned only with doing, intentions are excluded.

Control over behaviour is at this level quite external. Hot things burn, so the infant acquires a 'don't touch hot things' rule. From this basic start, we move through a process of simple conditioning to a general rule of 'no-nos'. Thus the infant's first glimmerings of *social* control — as opposed to physical control, as in the case of hot objects — come about through the use of arbitrarily assigned rewards and punishments: some things, like hitting baby brother, are no-nos. There is little generality of the kind required in the normal meaning of a rule: the no-no characteristic begins and ends with each action. 'Morality' at this level is thus entirely a matter of consequences (rewards and punishments) designed by some powerful other.

The ikonic mode: Egocentric morality

We have seen the main characteristics of ikonic thinking in Chapter 5: rigid unidimensional thinking based on a strong precept, emotion or fusion of the two, with strong self-reference or *egocentrism*.

In the case of playing marbles, Piaget observed that two little boys did not understand the rules and were actually playing according to different rules. They were mimicking what they thought older children were doing. Yet their rules were absolute, laid down by quite unimpeachable authorities: 'God', 'the Mayor of Geneva' and 'Daddy' were variously quoted as the sources of their rules.

Morality at this stage is thus quite rule-bound, the strict letter of the law: what Piaget calls the morality of *unilateral respect*. Rules in ikonic law demand instant obedience: they are sacred, infallible and unchangeable.

In egocentric thinking the point of view of another cannot be taken into account, so that rules out intentions. Naughtiness can then only be judged either by whether or not a rule has been broken, or who did most damage. In the washing-up story, no rule appeared to be involved — but Mary broke 16 cups and Jane only broke one. Naughty Mary.

The same argument applies to lying. Lies are wrong, because they are 'naughty words'. Similarly, the word 'fool' is regarded as a lie because that, too, is naughty. In later childhood, a lie is naughty because it does not correspond to objective fact. It is only in adolescence that a lie is wrong because it is *intended to mislead*. In one of Piaget's stories, a little boy came racing home to say that he had received good marks in school when in fact he had done badly; another to say that he had seen a dog as big as a cow. Children aged around eight years regarded the second boy as telling the worse lie: dogs as big as cows just do not exist, so that was very naughty. The first child, on the other hand, *might* have got good grades, so his was not so bad a lie.

How do children react to punishment? Piaget distinguished between two kinds of punishment: *expiatory* and *reciprocal*. In the first view, wrongdoing demands a natural price, the currency of which is pain. Up to about 10 years of age, children tend to regard the fairest punishment as the most severe, which is consistent with their morality-by-consequences. Paradoxically, they accept punishment for lying long before they understand the nature of a lie, or even before they know they are lying. After 10 or so, however, children tend to regard wrongdoing as a reversible sequence: if the punishment involves the wrongdoer in putting himself out to make good any damage caused, it is a better punishment than one that merely hurts. Some adults retain the more primitive expiatory view of punishment: as a glance at letters to the editor of the local paper will show, many literate members of the general public demand to bring back flogging, and to make prisons as unpleasant as possible, simply to 'teach a lesson'. It is only very recently that countries have introduced the notion of *reciprocity*: that the victim of an aggressive act against person or property should be compensated with money earned by agressors during their prison term.

Finally, we come to the effect of childrearing on morality. When the parent issues contradictory rules, and then punishes for the inevitable violations, Piaget claimed that the 'egocentric morality is guaranteed'. On the other hand, operating on a democratic let's-discuss-this-together basis with the five- or six-year-old just does not work. Piaget tried precisely this, but his daughter came back with the old ikonic slogans 'But you can't do that; that's not right'. In expressing his disappointment about this, Piaget also expressed a hope that, given time and the opportunity to strike when appropriate on a reciprocal morality basis, the stage may be shed that much sooner.

An authoritarian parent who lays down the law and regularly responds to 'why?' questions with 'Because I say so, that's why!' is quite clearly encouraging a morality of unilateral respect. If the parent also punishes on the grounds of extent of material damage, then the child is being encouraged to remain at the egocentric stage: to evaluate right and wrong in terms of results not intentions, and to regard the law as arbitrary, immutable, imposed from outside. Personal responsibility is pre-empted.

The concrete-symbolic mode: Sociocentric morality

During this period, rules and codes are assembled to cover particular contexts and situations, eventually to cover society itself, with the relational system of law-and-order. On the way, sets of rules govern particular contexts — family, peer group, school, neighbourhood — each set sitting multistructurally alongside the other. There are different codes for playground, home, school, the beach, the footie, church.

Inconsistencies between those codes tend to be resolved in favour of the source of most perceived pressure: usually that is the peer group.

Concrete-symbolic morality differs from ikonic morality in the generality of the rules, not in their felt power to command obedience. Egocentrism diminishes but is replaced with *sociocentrism*, vestiges of which carry over into adulthood as *ethnocentrism* (Piaget and Weil, 1951): that is, the rules apply equally to all members of the peer or reference group. Whereas earlier the adult was the authority who commanded obedience, now it is the peer group. Although children must obviously live with adult authority in most homes and schools, this is just an inconvenient fact of life: their major loyalty is to their group. Parents will recognise many instances of behaviour typical of this level. Typically, a rule evolves, say to cope with biscuit-eating: if one gets a biscuit, then all get a biscuit. Such rules can lead to such 'democratic' lengths that a biscuit is refused on the grounds that it would mean '*he'd* get an extra one'. One in, all in.

This general trend is healthy. It means that sheer egocentrism is breaking down. But before reaching the highest stage of moral development — where the individual can see the *purpose* of the rules (e.g. to make life tolerable for everybody) — the specific rules are first extended only to include the immediate group, but without exception and with rigid uniformity.

Hess (1970) pointed out that while there are social-class differences in the *rate* of moral development — as would be expected on the basis of the more frequent use of external control techniques in lower-class homes — these differences tend to disappear when children join clubs and organisations. Such memberships tend to encourage a new perspective whereby behaviour is considered from different points of view and thus egocentric orientation begins to be broken down. Similarly, children's experiences in the larger community at school teach them that the ways things are at home do not apply to everyone. Other children, other parents, have different rules. They believe different things; they do or do not go to church, they allow their children to stay up later or go to bed earlier, and so on. But all this takes time, and during middle to later childhood the child develops codes and rules that govern interaction with other children, within the overall constraint of adult authority. The 'democratic' neo-fascism of the 10-year-old should thus be a passing phase, beginning to die down by the age of 12 and increasingly thereafter.

The formal mode: Allocentric morality

What makes a rule a rule? We can question the question here as we could in Chapter 5. Justice is not the letter of the law — if you get a biscuit then I get a biscuit — but the *spirit* of the law. For each to be served equally in principle, justice might better be served by inequality in practice. This is recognised by, for example, the notion of diminished responsibility: it was specifically not recognised by the good citizens of Erwin, Tennessee (see Box 7.3).

The application of principle requires *allocentric* thought: the ability to place oneself in the position of another, a notion already introduced in Chapter 5. The obverse is that self may be viewed as if you were another.

BOX 7.3   THE CRUEL DEATH OF 'FIVE-TON MARY'

There are ancient records of the hangings of bulls and oxen, but there is only one known case of the hanging of an elephant — it happened in Erwin, Tennessee, on 13 September 1916. The Sparks Circus was stationed in Kingsport, Tennessee, when Mary, a veteran circus elephant, was being ridden to water by an inexperienced trainer, Walter Eldridge. On the way, Mary spotted a watermelon rind and headed for this snack. When Eldridge jerked hard on her head with a spear-tipped stick, Mary let out a loud trumpet, reached behind her with her trunk, and yanked the trainer off her back. Mary dashed Eldridge against a soft-drink stand and then walked over and stepped on his head. A Kingsport resident came running and fired five pistol shots into the huge animal. Mary groaned and shook but didn't die — in fact, she performed in that night's show. The next day the circus moved to Erwin, where 'authorities' (no one is sure who) decreed that Mary should die on the gallows, to the great sorrow of her friends in the circus. She was taken to the Clinchfield railroad yards, where a large crowd was gathered. A ⅞-inch chain was slung around her neck, and a 100-ton derrick hoisted her 5 feet in the air. The chain broke. The next chain held, and Mary died quickly. Her five-ton corpse was buried with a steam shovel.

Source: Wallace, Wallechinsky and Wallace, 1984, pp. 67–9.

A sociocentric thinker would say that Australians and Americans have directly opposed traffic systems: an Australian drives on the left, an American on the right. On the other hand, the allocentric thinker would realise that the *principle* is the same: to establish a coherent system whereby drivers can reasonably assume that all the other drivers on their side of the road will be going in the same direction, and that each is driving from a position of maximum visibility, in the seat nearest the middle of the road. From this point of view, the Australian and American systems are similar, not different.

Formal thought permits people to think in terms of the possible: what might be, rather than what is. Thinking adolescents and adults can see that society can be different, and should be different and, if they care enough, will try to *make* things different. Sociocentric thinkers (which of course may include adults) tend to take a conformist line on social issues. If an elected government has decided that it is in the corporate interest to clearfell a large section of a national park for woodchipping, so be it: it is a government's job to make those decisions, even if you personally disagree. Allocentrics and egocentrics would challenge that decision if they disagreed: allocentrics because of a stand on principle, egocentrics if they personally stood to gain or lose.

At the highest level of moral judgment, then, there may well be times when it is right to challenge law and order, even to disobey the law of the land. It is that point which rouses the fury of so many sociocentrics; likewise when it is suggested that the role of the schools is to develop 'moral autonomy'. But that is moral autonomy within 'the context of society', remember.

We are back to the same tension between individuals and conformity we noted at the beginning of this chapter. Teachers, who are both individual and society's professional managers of learning, have to resolve that tension to suit their own lights — or is it to suit society's?

Kohlberg's stages of moral development

The most influential and thoroughly worked out version of Piaget's developmental approach to moral reasoning is that of Lawrence Kohlberg (1969). He distinguished two stages within each of the egocentric, sociocentric and allocentric levels. He takes the middle level, what he calls 'conventional', as the point of departure (see Table 7.1).

Table 7.1   Comparison of Piaget's and Kohlberg's stages of moral development

Piaget's stages	Judgment		Kohlberg's stages
Egocentric	Pre-conventional		1. Punishment
			2. Reward
Sociocentric	Conventional		3. Conformity
			4. Law and order
Allocentric	Post-conventional		5. Contract
			6. Autonomy

Kohlberg, like Piaget, examined these levels of morality primarily by means of moral dilemmas. In one example, Hans has a very sick wife who can be cured only by a certain drug which has been developed by the local pharmacist. The latter, however, requires an enormous sum of money for the drug (although it is cheap to produce) and Hans does not have this amount available. What should he do?

Kohlberg was careful to point out that there is no 'right' decision: any decision can be justified. The interesting thing is *how* the subject justifies it. Kohlberg classified the replies he obtained (mainly from a sample of 78 boys studied over a period of 12 years) in terms of his six stages. He maintained that 50 per cent of a person's replies could be classified as belonging to one stage (the rest being above and below); this he regarded as the individual's *stage of moral development*.

*Is an allocentric level of development
necessary to be altruistic?*

Pre-conventional morality. This general level is said to characterise children's thinking up to 10 years of age, after which most people move on to the conventional level. Good and bad are defined on the basis of *actual consequences* — in particular, whether they are rewarding or punishing for the individual — rather than in terms of more general standards of right and wrong. It is thus egocentric in nature.

Stage 1:   Punishment. In Stage 1, the *likelihood of punishment* determines whether a thing is wrong or not. The Stage 1 delinquent believes that the crime is being caught. In terms of the Hans story, a typical Stage 1 reply would be that 'Hans should steal the drug because his father-in-law might punish him if he let her die'. People act in this way when they break what is to them a trivial law: for example, crossing a street against a red light. They would be Stage 1 in their moral development if they *usually* behaved in this way: if you can get away with it, do it.

Stage 2:   Reward. An element of reciprocity enters into Stage 2's judgments. Stage 2 acts because of individual advantage, but may often modify this because of an immediately valid claim by someone else. This might best be summarised in the phrase: 'I'll scratch your back if you'll scratch mine.' Hans would steal the drug and save his wife because she'd then render him many wifely services, which would make it worth his while. On the other hand, he might not steal it because that would render him *persona non grata* with the pharmacist, whose services he might well need in the future. Stage 2 goes beyond Stage 1 in that immediate physical consequences are somewhat tempered by considering the interests of others, but essentially the Stage 2 individual is a self-seeking opportunist.

Conventional morality. This is essentially a sociocentric view of morality, with some reciprocity and the recognition that objective standards apply both to oneself and to others. Other people dictate what is right and what is wrong. One's own views are unimportant.

Stage 3:   Conformity. Stage 3 is 'being good'. Morality is very much in accordance with the slogans appropriate to one's role. Hans, in this view, 'would do what any *decent husband* would do — protect his wife even if that meant breaking the law'. His not to reason why, his but to do and die. This kind of reasoning is typical of the bureaucrat whose job is to carry out orders (an extreme example is that of Adolf Eichmann, whose orders included genocide). Stage 3s do not question the morality of their orders — that is the responsibility of those who issue them. The only moral question is whether they were successful or not. As Lieutenant William Calley said on reporting back to base after the infamous My Lai massacre during the Vietnam War: 'I did my duty, Sir.'

Stage 4:   Law and order. The morality of Stage 4 is still other-directed, but it is rather more sophisticated than Stage 3. Stage 4 would demand to know what is the lawful authority, wherever a conflict exists between two lines of apparent duty. In the Hans story, Stage 4 might reply that he should steal the drug, because not to do so would endanger the institution of marriage, which is the fabric of society. Or he might answer that he should *not* steal the drug: that the pharmacist is operating according to the established precepts of our society (he has used his creativity and genius to invent the drug, and is practising free enterprise in charging what the market will take). It is unfortunate for Hans, but the general law is greater than the individual.

Post-conventional morality. Stages 3 and 4 do not question the law: post-conventionals do. Using the formal mode, they see that there are higher principles applying.

Stage 5:   Contract. Stage 5 recognises that the rules of any particular society are arbitrary; behind each rule system are general principles of justice, love and humanity that transcend the particular. Stage 5 people tend to see society in terms of a legal contract between various factions, the particular clauses of which are open to change by virtue of the arbitrary nature of particular rules. This is analogous to Piaget's adolescents who would happily invent new rules for a game and modify them as experience suggested. In the Hans story, the Stage 5 person would argue that Hans and his wife committed themselves to each other for better or for worse, and this is a contract that overrides the social-legal contract of payment. The pharmacist is being unreasonable in terms of natural law, and thus the existing law is wrong and Hans must stand by his greater obligations.

A judge trying a case would ideally be operating at Stage 5. The particular case may well have extenuating circumstances that make the literal application of the law as it stands unfair. The judge, mindful that the ruling will create a precedent for future cases, has to weigh up all these alternatives and make a judgment that may both involve an example acceptable to society and be in keeping with very abstract principles of justice.

Stage 6:   Autonomy. Stage 6 represents the highest level of morality, which few reach: it may be regarded as a formal–2 mode, in which the individual recognises that there may be principles higher than those that underlie society itself. Thus, Stage 6 would recommend that Hans steal the drug, but publicly. In that way he would be saving his wife, and also making the point that the free enterprise system may be destructive of human relations (if that's the point driving Stage 6) and therefore should be changed.

The difference between Stages 5 and 6 is nicely illustrated in the famous exchange (quoted in Feigelson, 1970, p. 146) between the two friends, Thoreau and Emerson. Thoreau was a radical and idealist; Emerson a famous jurist and poet. On this occasion, Emerson was being conducted through a new prison and saw his old friend locked up. Shocked, he asked the jailed Thoreau: 'Why David, what are you doing in there?' To which Thoreau replied: 'Why Ralph, what are you doing out there?' A modern example is in Box 7.4.

An evaluation of the cognitivist position

In considering Kohlberg's position on moral development, some rather obvious questions emerge:

- Do people go through the stages as outlined, and make judgments over a variety of situations according to their current stage?

BOX 7.4   DO INDIVIDUALS HAVE THE RIGHT TO PLACE
THEIR OWN PRINCIPLES ABOVE THE LAW?
STAGE 6s THINK THAT THEY HAVE

The peaceful arrests climaxed a week of tension at Farmhouse Creek where a timber company plans to build an access road past the creek that Dr Brown calls a wilderness gateway.

During the week, more than 60 forest workers dragged conservationists away from the paths of earthmovers, and two shots were fired toward Dr Brown.

These two incidents contributed to heated responses from members of a lunchtime crowd that spilled over the lawn in front of State Parliament in Hobart yesterday.

The crowd was estimated by police at 2,000, and by the Wilderness Society at 5,000.

It cheered Dr Brown as he said: 'When the law is wrong, the only place for a true citizen to be is in jail.'

Source: The Newcastle Herald, 14 March 1986.

- Are there gender differences in these stages?
- Do people *actually behave* according to the way they say others 'should'?

The question of stage. We saw in Chapter 5 that when handling cognitive tasks in school, students tend to operate 'unevenly': they handle tasks at different levels of sophistication according to their interest in the task, their previous experience, and so forth. Variation in moral judgment is even more notable across situations. The stage of moral reasoning based on an individual's responses to one story may have little or no correlation with the stage of the same individual based on another story, contrary to Kohlberg's claim that 50 per cent of a person's responses will fall at the one stage (Kurtines and Greif, 1974). In order to meet these criticisms, Kohlberg changed his method of scoring (Tomlinson, 1980), but Phillips and Nicolayev (1978) claimed that this was done arbitrarily in order to force the appearance of stages; by scoring responses in an open-ended way, it is frequently possible to find evidence of *all six* stages in a person's responses.

In other words, the way a person thinks about a situation depends on the *situation*, as much as on a person's 'stage of moral development'; in particular, it depends on the *costs* for acting in a certain way, or for saying one thing or another. As we shall see in the next section, a number of contextual factors influence both what people say and what they actually do.

Moral development in females. It is possible to interpret Kohlberg as implying that the moral thinking of adult women is constrained to Stage 3: conformity to avoid disapproval and the dislike of others (Gilligan, 1982). Gilligan points out that Kohlberg's data were obtained from an all-male sample, and that the post-conventional levels for female moral development were simply not examined: for example, the 'network of caring' through which girls and women make sense of their lives. Davies (1984a) shows that the frameworks girls use to construe their relationships with other children, teachers, parents and adults in general are *different* from those used by boys.

Davies then argues that not only do females differ from males in their frameworks, but children differ from adults not by any deficit of cognitive functioning, 'nor through an inability to act on the basis of moral principles where these are relevant' (p. 291). They define themselves as children, and are aware of adults' definitions of them as children, but are equally willing and able to interact with adults on their own terms too, if they wish. The difference Davies is drawing attention to here is like that in standard or non-standard English: it is not a deficit conceived in vertical terms, but a difference, conceived horizontally.

Suzie, age 10, fullblown 'sociocentric' comments:

> Some people tease Aborigines, well for instance, a long time ago Sherryl Grimes was at school and there was a lot of people teasing her and this Aborigine Susy she used to go around with ... and that's what happened to a lot of Aborigines at D school, and that's why I feel sorry for them and I let them play with us, cos they were always being teased (Davies, 1984a, p. 290).

Egocentrism, sociocentrism, peer pressure: these are not the inevitable springs to action that cognitive developmental theory would lead one to expect at first sight. *Feelings* matter: and it is pretty clear from the evidence of Davies and Gilligan that feelings guide female morality — both thought and action — differently from the way male morality is guided and from the way children's morality is different from that of adults.

From judgment to action. Do people act in the way they say others should in these moral dilemmas? Or are we simply talking about a cognitive test, which may say something about how complex their thinking is, but next to nothing about morality or otherwise of their behaviour?

Delinquents are consistently found to respond at the lowest levels on the Kohlberg dilemmas. Ewanyk (1973), for instance, found that 82 per cent of referred 16-year-old delinquent boys typically gave Stage 1 and Stage 2 (pre-conventional) responses, the remainder being at Stage 3 ('good boys' conforming to a sociocentric norm established by bad boys). Indeed, it makes sense that people who so consistently judge self-interested behaviour as 'right' are likely to behave in a delinquent manner.

Moral levels are also related to behaviour in a series of studies on conformity. Students who successfully resisted conforming to peer group pressure in judging the length of lines, or to authority pressure to inflict punishment on someone else (in the Asch and Milgram experiments described later), were at higher Kohlberg levels than those who did conform. On the other hand, in other situations — such as cheating in examinations and helping others — little or no relationship exists between moral judgment and moral behaviour. In the case of helping others, Blasi (1980) reports a striking difference between the actual behaviour of kindergarten children and senior high-school students, and what they said they would do. For example, 100 per cent of the 'egocentric' kindergarten children helped a student carry a large pile of books across a crowded classroom, whereas only 5 per cent of the high-school students co-operated under the same circumstances. This was despite the fact that most kindergarten children said they would not help, and most of the high-school students said that they would!

Cognitive developmental theory clearly does not cover the whole story. It is almost certainly incorrect in asserting that people behave consistently across a variety of situations according to the stage they are currently occupying. First, people do *not* make consistently similar judgments across a variety of situations. As will become clearer below, the circumstances can make an enormous difference to what people judge as right or wrong. Second, judgment is only one of several determinants of behaviour. Where the cognitive position *is* useful, is in categorising the different *kinds* of judgment that people may make. At one extreme, a person may decide in a particular situation to act out of self-interest; and in another out of a sense of either loyalty or conformity to the group; and in yet another out of conscience, in defiance of group or self-interests.

It is important to know how people think about moral situations, and what the sequence of their thinking tends to be. But if young children and delinquents can think in the same way (preconventionally or egocentrically) while delinquents act selfishly and many young children act altruistically, there is obviously more to it than the structure of their thinking. Let us look at situational factors, and the social context in general.

THE SOCIAL CONTEXT

Growth in moral autonomy does not occur in a vacuum: in fact, the idea of an individual being morally autonomous whatever the social context is nonsensical. Moral autonomy does not mean defiance of the social context, but the use of higher order principles that take context into account; only when there is an inconsistency between principle and practice may one proceed contrary to the established social order.

Cognitive factors may provide the structure and complexity of moral judgment, but the social context provides the particular values, opinions, attitudes and interpersonal feelings that lead from finely structured judgment to altruistic and even passionate action.

We have used the term 'acculturation' to describe this infusion of fire and substance into the domain of morality. As we saw, acculturation has two meanings: taming the individual into group ways — a shift from egocentric, through sociocentric, to allocentric thinking about social issues; and the interaction between two social norms, those belonging to minority groups, and those of the majority culture.

We came across the second meaning in the previous chapter when we looked at immigrants lacking the majority language, a situation in which the majority/minority conflict is at its sharpest. The assimilation model of acculturation involves the virtual annihilation of the minority culture, as its members take on the values, modes and attitudes of the majority. One multicultural concept of acculturation is the 'mosaic', where each group retains its belief and ways within the majority culture, with little modification of values (De Lacey and Poole, 1979). The mosaic is however an unstable and unrealistic model: multiculturalism leads almost inevitably to the 'melting pot', where both minority and majority cultures are mutually permeated and changed, with each retaining a core of self-identity.

Multiculturalism is official policy, and is endorsed by a majority of Australians, but with rather mixed feelings (Callan, 1986). The problems of the Aboriginal population are even more complex, in view of the hugely varying subcultures within the Aboriginal population itself, ranging from tribal groups with minimal contact, urbanised and highly articulate individuals wishing for minimal contact and returning to tribal lands to establish it, successful and established workers in majority culture trades and professions, and those on the fringes of country towns and in inner city areas, with high to total unemployment and the attending problems of drink, poverty and alienation.

Multiculturalism obviously represents an enormous challenge to educators, not only linguistically (which we touched on last chapter) but in terms of provision of services, which includes teachers familiar not only with the mother languages (L1s) but with the values, customs, folkways and mores that make multicultural education possible. Teachers intending to serve in multicultural and Aboriginal education obviously need specialised training.

Our contribution here can only be to point in Section B to some developments and sources that will be of value to general teachers.

Taming the individual

Acculturation in the sense of 'taming' is also an enormous topic: we concentrate on the school-age influences that provide growing children with their values and some of the mechanisms by which this takes place.

The first source is of course the family, particularly in the early childhood period after the development of oral language. Piaget (1932) himself emphasised the role of childrearing procedures: he thought that strict punishment for deviant behaviour delayed internalising values. Punishment emphasises the externals: that what is wrong is the *behaviour,* and that the 'wrongness' is somehow cancelled by the punishment. Attention is therefore deflected from intentions. Middle-class childrearing practices emphasise internalisation of values: by reason where possible, and by the induction of guilt otherwise. *Conscience* represents the inner operation of parental values.

By the time the child enters primary or infants school, a complex set of values, beliefs and opinions is in place. The problems take on a different shape according to whether the child comes from a family whose own values are congruent with the majority culture, or with a minority culture, but the socialising agencies start multiplying from now onwards: school, peer groups and community (such as neighbourhood friends and associations such as church groups).

Assuming that we are talking about government schooling, the school becomes the major source of the majority values, in both playground and classroom. We deal with the classroom in a later section. For the moment we look at children's friendships.

The development of children's friendships. A useful link between the previous section and the present one is provided by Selman's (1980) work on children's friendships. He took six basic issues in friendship: forming a friendship, degree of intimacy within a friendship, trust, jealousy and how that is handled, dealing with conflict and terminating a friendship. He argued that the way children understood and handled these issues in maintaining and breaking a friendship would reflect their 'social cognitive' development; and, Piagetian that he was, that children would normally show a similar level of development with respect to each issue. He postulated a five-stage sequence, from momentary playmate, through 'fairweather co-operation', to autonomous interdependence (see Table 7.2).

Table 7.2   A sequence in one aspect of children's friendships — 'Why do you need a good friend?'

SOLO *level*	*Selman's categories*	*Examples (from Schofield and Kafer, 1985)*
Prestructural	*Momentary physical playmate* Happens to be present, considers own needs only	'So they have a good friend.'
Unistructural	*One-way assistance* Can separate self from other, but only considers one aspect in common	'So they have someone to play with.'
Multistructural	*Fairweather co-operation* Sum of discontinuous individual perspectives. Context specific	'For someone to play with, to walk to school with, to let her new friends show her around, to talk to and go swimming with her. To help her and go places with.'
Relational	*Intimate, mutual sharing* Allocentrism showing: co-ordination of mutual interests with common bond	'With a good friend you can share things and have things in common. Otherwise you get tired of each other.'
Extended abstract	*Autonomous interdependence* Openness to change and growth; resolves problem of own autonomy and sharing in a relationship	None observed in primary sample.

Given the unevenness of development in cognitive areas (see Chapter 5), it seems unlikely that social development would proceed as evenly as Selman suggests. Schofield and Kafer (1985) studied 166 primary students (Years 4 to 6), and interviewed them about their friendships, but instead of using Selman's scoring system, they used the SOLO taxonomy on the individual responses. They also determined the students' popularity by asking them to nominate a friend, a work companion, and so on.

Table 7.2 shows the Selman levels classified as SOLO responses to the question 'Why do you need a good friend?'

The general structural similarity of the Selman categories to a SOLO analysis of this particular question is striking. A response to one aspect of friendship did not, however, generalise to other aspects. The Schofield-Kafer results showed that:

- children were situation-specific about their understanding of friendship;
- popular children were more advanced socially than unpopular;
- girls were more advanced socially than boys, at this age;
- 74 per cent of all responses were at the multistructural level.

A multistructural 'fairweather co-operation' seems to be the cement binding peer groups together in the upper primary groups of middle childhood. Where does 'peer group pressure' come from then? What values does the typical playground group impart? Do peer groups impede or facilitate classroom interaction? What use can the teacher make of all this?

The functions of friendships. Davies (1982, 1983, 1984b) talked with, recorded and observed pupils in a country primary school for a whole year. She concluded that children have their own valid culture, with its own values. Children recognise a wide range of appropriate and inappropriate behaviours but, truly multistructural, they are less concerned with consistency from individuals, than with consistency within *situations.* They are not bothered if a friend's home behaviour is different from the same friend's behaviour in school, or if 'friends' are unfriendly if the situation demands it. Adults are disconcerted by children's fickleness and squabbles, Davies says, because adults do not understand what is going on. Such terms as 'posing' and 'getting the snobs' may or may not be known to adults (those are very likely not the terms used by 10-year-olds in the New England Tablelands in New South Wales today, some 10 years later) but their meaning as used by children is quite precise, and their functions important to them (see Box 7.5).

The situation specificity comes out in the following extracts from Davies' interviews (the point at issue is how the same individual can behave so differently between school and home):

Linda: At home I sort of do everything, I sorta show off a bit at home ... I don't show off at school 'cos you get called ...

Terry: Poser! Poser! (said sing-song)

Linda: Yeah 'Poser! Poser!'

Davies: So what the other kids say about you at school has a big effect on what you are at school?

Suzie: Yes, see, whenever I'm being called a name or somethin' like that, I dunno what happens, but it feels horrible.

Linda: I sorta really go. I really get the snobs.

BOX 7.5   APPROPRIATE AND INAPPROPRIATE BEHAVIOURS
IN A FRIEND — AND HOW TO LET THEM KNOW

1. *Appropriate behaviours for a friend*
   Plays with you, plays properly, plays nice, takes turns.
   Helps, does things for you, is good at school work.
   Sticks up for you, is tough, tells the teacher what he or she thinks.
   Knows your feelings, shares.

Thus a friend is someone who sticks by you, who knows how to co-operate and who will share their world with you.

2. *Inappropriate behaviours for a friend.*
   Posing, showing off, being too full of yourself.
   Wanting everything your way.
   Picking on you, teasing you.
   Leaving you on your own.
   Being stupid.

Non-friends will use you to bignote themselves by putting you down. They will use you as the butt of their hard-won superiority. They will not co-operate with you over maintaining the world as a sensible place.

3. *Ways to let others know they have behaved inappropriately*
   Leave them on their own.
   Get the snobs.
   Get the cranks.
   Be piss weak, dob.

Since friendships and proper behaviour within friendship are so important, strategies for maintaining appropriate behaviour are developed, the most powerful of which is probably the first.

   Note the overlap of behaviour in 2 and 3. What are inappropriate behaviours for a friend are appropriate behaviours for friends who have behaved inappropriately.

Source: Davies, 1982.

Terry:	Yeah, me too.
Suzie:	And Betty comes up and says 'Don't get the snobs' (Davies, 1984b, p. 256).

The pressure is powerful not to pose: doubly powerful, because if you are teased and withdraw, that brings on more teasing. But when is posing posing? There are subtleties. 'Bashing up' can be seen either as posing (by the victim) or as being tough (by friends): being tough is good, posing is bad. *Circumstances* determine whether bashing up is good or bad: not the person or the act itself.

Situations throw up 'contingency friends': if there is conflict with the 'best friend', withdrawing to the contingency friend (who simply is someone who happens to be around at the time) increases bargaining power with the 'best friend':

Jane:	We were having a game with Betty's ball, and Mandy got bashed in the eye by Betty and then she's back sitting with her. It's a wonder she didn't get the huffs!
Davies comments:	Mandy can't afford to get the huffs. She and Suzie are still estranged, and Betty is her contingency friend. To get the huffs with Betty would be to force reconciliation with Suzie, since there are no further contingency friends lined up. Mandy's failure to get the huffs shows that the groundwork for reconciliation is not yet complete (1982, p. 94).

How did Davies fit into this? Didn't her presence disrupt or influence what she saw or was told? As she says:

The idea that I was there to listen to them, to write a book about children, impressed them immensely. They were very keen, therefore, that I get it right. They were interested in the process of recording their conversations, and of replaying those conversations so they could ... draw my attention to those aspects ... that were noteworthy ... teach me to see their point of view ... Subsequently, my purpose changes ... from one of understanding ... to one attempting to state what that understanding is (1980, pp. 260–1).

What was her final understanding? What is the culture of childhood like? Several generalisations may be made:

- Reciprocity (a point also mentioned by Piaget): 'I should behave to you as you behave to me.' In particular, that means negatively, as in the old law of talion ('an eye for an eye, a tooth for a tooth'). Such repayments are instant; who 'started it' rapidly becomes irrelevant. Hence fights are self-maintaining.
- There is only one account of what 'really' happened. As Solomon also said, children's talk is often negotiating a consensus view of what happened; that is then the official record. The allocentric view of participants having valid but different perspectives is beyond them.
- People are what they are because of the situation. What is true of someone today may be untrue tomorrow. You behave to people as they are now, not what they might be tomorrow.
- Children inhabit at least two cultures: their own and (partially) adult culture.

The multistructural, concrete, nature of this world is easy to see. It is a richer picture of the 'fairweather co-operation' painted by Selman, but very much the same landscape: except for one important point. Davies sees that culture as entirely valid in its own right, not an immature version of adult culture. Indeed, in a similar world of a here-and-now culture (the playground) within a one-way institutionalised culture (the school), adults would behave identically. Davies' example is the behaviour of the inmates in Kesey's *One Flew Over the Cuckoo's Nest*; the treatment, and resulting behaviour, of inmates in old people's homes is another (see Peterson, 1984).

We now need to look more closely at the interface between child and adult cultures: that is where teachers have to work.

The rules of teacher–child interaction. Children participate in two agendas: their own and the teacher's. The framework which they see as the most important and relevant is their own. Carrying out the teacher's agenda, involving the teacher's rules, is done alongside their own and more important set of rules.

At best the two agendas run alongside each other. While freedom to carry out their own more important agenda is essential, at the same time children acknowledge the importance of learning about the adult world (Davies, 1982). There is thus an uneasy balance tilted in favour of the children's agenda when conflict is imminent. How that may affect student teachers may be seen in Box 7.6.

Another complication is that two layers of rules exist. First there are the explicit stateable rules, such as those of classroom interaction; and second, the tacit, background, rules that are not clearly stated, which form the way adults behave and are learned only after long exposure to the culture. The school Davies visited was an experimental school; the principal (Mr Bell) had some traditional and some open classes. He encouraged reciprocity in interaction between children and teachers for instance, treating each with 'respect', explaining why something needed doing rather than issuing unilateral orders. Mr Bell was well-liked, until the day when in the music room he found some boys and girls listening to music under a blanket: a situation Mr Bell immediately misunderstood with all his background knowledge of what individuals of the opposite sex tend to do under blankets. He overreacted with a harsh adult–child reaction and a punishment. The children were mortified: 'Their anger was not that their teacher had punished them (they could handle that if they thought it was justified) but to the fact that he had become *unpredictable*' (1982, p. 121, italics supplied). They did not understand the *tacit* set of rules, that set of rules that made Mr Bell act 'out of character'. They did not ask the allocentric question: 'That's not like him ... how could he have seen it to act like that?'

BOX 7.6   FROM THE HORSE'S MOUTH

Question: What's the most important advice you'd give a student teacher?
Paul: Don't treat kids badly, or else they'll treat you worse than you treat them. If you treat them badly on the first day, they'll absolutely murder you.
Friend: Oh well, if they be nice to us, we'll probably be nice to them, you know, we wouldn't be naughty or anything. Any teachers that can take a joke we really like and we treat them really well.

Source: Davies, 1981, p. 172.

Mr Dance was an object of derision all the time: he was English and required the pupils to call him 'Mr Darnse' (their natural pronunciation being 'Dense'). Roddie finds it ridiculous that he be corrected:

> Poms are you know, polite, but this pom 'ere, 'e aint. You know 'e tells you to say 'Mr Darnse'. It's real stupid. Me and Warwick we was goin' into the music room yesterday before we got into trouble, and he said 'Where are youse goin'?' 'Into the music room', 'I beg your pardon?' 'Into the music room, Mr Darnse!' You've always got to call him Mr Dense (1982, p. 272).

In school, then, there are many interfaces between the stable and known childhood rules and the adult rules: the latter either keep changing from adult to adult or, as in the case of the blanket incident, the tacit rules suddenly and unpredictably surge up to make adults act 'out of situation', which behaviour is seen as unpredictable and capricious.

What are the major implications for the teacher? Basically, it is a matter of *reciprocity*. Children are naturally willing to learn an adult's particular rules and about the adult world in general; at the same time, their own rules are more salient to them. Adults must therefore show sensitivity and respect for children's rules (Davies, 1982). Teachers should therefore find out what they can about their students' rules, show that they know and respect them, make their own rules absolutely clear and explicit, and be ready to negotiate the obvious mismatches. An example is given in Box 7.7. These are, after all, basic ground rules for negotiating between any two responsible parties. If schools are to induct young people into the world of adulthood it seems appropriate, as we also concluded at the end of Chapter 5, to use the management metaphor from the world of business: teachers are managers of learning and classroom management is their profession. We explore the full implications of this in the following chapter.

Conformity

Children conform to their own peer group norms and to adult rules: the sociocentric phase is characterised by conformity. We need to say a little more about this. Obviously some people are more conformist than others, and some situations extract more conformity than others.

Conformity to the group. Conformity is 'a change in a person's behaviour or opinions as a result of real or imagined pressure from a person or a group of people' (Aronson, 1984, p. 17). The classic study of conformity is an experiment by Asch (1956). The task involved judging which one of three presented lines is closest in length to a standard. The task is extremely simple, and the correct answer is clear. In the experiment, however, the subject who is to make the judgment is required to speak last, after four others (stooges) have confidently announced the 'correct' answer to be a *different* (incorrect) line. Subjects are then asked to announce their choice publicly. Over one-third of Asch's undergraduate subjects conformed to the group judgment. It is

---

BOX 7.7   HOW ONE TEACHER ENTERED JACOB'S FRAMEWORK, CHOPPED HIM UP — AND WAS GREATLY ADMIRED

Jacob had been asked by this teacher to write out 10 times that he must not talk. Jacob wrote his lines hurriedly and in his worst possible writing. The teacher wrote across the page in perfect handwriting, 'Jacob your writing is 'orrible (just like your face, yuk, yuk)' and signed his name with a beautiful flourish. Jacob's comment was, 'He's great. He really knows how to chop people'. The teacher had corrected Jacob, shown himself very correct on the point at issue, made a joking insult (using the 'yuk yuk' to ensure it was recognised as a joke) and displayed at the same time a capacity to play the pupils' game of chopping each other up. In other words he had pursued his central purpose of teaching (in this case, how to write properly) and had at the same time revealed a knowledge about and acceptance of the pupil's perspective in which neat writing, especially the writing of lines, is an awful bore, and where being artfully chopped up is infinitely preferable to being punished ...

Source: Davies, 1982, p. 172.

---

important to note that they were not *persuaded* that they were incorrect because, when asked to make their judgments privately, the tendency to follow the group dropped markedly.

Much research has been done to see what factors influence conformity in this situation (summarised in Blasi, 1980; Aronson, 1984):

- If the subject is required to give a public commitment first, before the group give theirs, and again afterwards, the last judgment conforms less. Not surprisingly, people are more likely to stick to their first commitment, figuring that they would make even bigger fools of themselves if they then changed.
- If people are trained to believe that they are good at the task, by prior runs, they are less likely to change to the group norm opinion: their self-esteem is sufficiently strong to withstand the tendency to follow the mob.
- Subjects at post-conventional levels on the Kohlberg scale conform less.
- Whereas in earlier (pre-women's lib) experiments, women were found to be more conformist, more recent experiments show this to occur only when either the experimenter is male, or the task male-oriented (as in the Milgram task below).
- Conformity increases where the group is of higher perceived status than the subject.

Conformity to authority: Obedience. Perhaps the most stunning experiments on conformity and obedience were those initiated by Milgram (1964), which have been repeated with variations many times since. At this point, let us return to the argument presented above on Stage 3 reasoning: that many people see their role as following orders, as Eichmann and Calley claimed. The thing that shocked many people, possibly as much as the acts they committed, was the evidence given by psychiatrists at their respective trials that neither Eichmann nor Calley was sadistic or grossly unbalanced mentally. They saw themselves as *agents*: if there were any moral responsibility involved, it was borne by those who gave orders, not those who carried them out. Most individuals would imagine that they (and all right-thinking people) would refuse to carry out such orders. In fact, Milgram set out to demonstrate that there must be some basic flaw in the German race that allowed 'normal' men like Eichmann to operate in the way he did. He ran some pilot studies in America — and the results told him he need not bother going to Germany.

Milgram ran an advertisement for subjects for a 'learning experiment', at $4.50 per session. The respondents were told they were to take part in an experiment on the effects of punishment on learning. Each subject, tested individually, was to act as 'teacher' by reading out a list of words, and when the 'subject' (who was in fact a stooge of Milgram's) made an incorrect response, the 'teacher' was to throw a switch that would administer a shock. After each mistake the shock was to be increased: the 'teacher' used a switchboard that ran from an innocuous 15 volts to 450 volts, with warning signs (DANGER: SEVERE SHOCK) written at the high-voltage end. The 'subject' initially informed the 'teacher' that he had a weak heart. During the course of the experiment, the 'teacher' was requested to increase the shock after each error and to continue the experiment until either the 'subject' learned the word list or the extreme 450-volt position had been reached. After each shock, the 'subject' registered pain: at medium shock levels, the 'subject' was already screaming, groaning and begging for the experiment to terminate; at the extreme end, he lay slumped in his chair, apparently either unconscious or dead. (There were no shocks received, in actual fact.)

Milgram and his colleagues initially estimated that no more than about 5 per cent of people would continue administering the 'shocks' up to the 450-volt mark. In one study he found that 65 per cent did so: in another, 48 per cent. He was careful to point out that sadism was not the reason for these astonishing figures: his 'teachers' were clearly distressed about the situation, *but this was what they had to do and they did it*, even if this meant extreme pain and possibly death for another person. The implications with respect to Eichmann are clear enough. As Milgram (in Meyer, 1970, p. 132) said:

> If, in this study, an anonymous experimenter can successfully command adults to subdue a fifty-year-old man and force on him painful electric shocks against his protest, one can only wonder what government, with its vastly greater authority and prestige, can command of its subjects.

Meyer (1970), in commenting upon Milgram's studies, suggested that it would be even more alarming if people did *not* obey. Without this strong tendency in people, society would not function — everyone would be a law unto themselves, and total anarchy would result. This appears to be a reasonable comment, until we remember the post-conventional mode of moral reasoning. Meyer assumed that the alternatives are: (a) pre-conventional behaviour, or (b) conventional behaviour based on obedience and duty. There is, however, the post-conventional stage. The alternative to obedience in agency situations is *not* anarchy. There are higher-order principles that may make disobedience the more moral alternative.

It is thus not a question of being an agent or not being an agent; it is *when* to be an agent. We have to decide if, *in this situation*, it is right for us to carry out orders unquestioningly. The Stage 3 answer is that there are *no* situations in which it is right to disobey orders from a higher authority. Milgram's research shows that a surprising 62 per cent of people are Stage 3s in this sense: they adhere to the morality of unilateral respect to the extreme of committing severe injury or killing another person.

Yet would those 62 per cent allow themselves to be Eichmanns, willingly or unwillingly? As Aronson (1984) pointed out, there are aspects about the situation that allow us to maintain some faith in humankind. First, and most obviously, the victim had given his prior assent, and we may assume that few of the Jews or Vietnamese villagers did so. Further, the experiment was conducted by a scientist affiliated to the highly prestigious Yale University. When the experiment was repeated in a rundown commercial building in an industrial city, the figure of obedience dropped from 62 per cent to 48 per cent — but still a high figure, to be sure. When, moreover, the subject witnessed other subjects (stooges), who refused to comply, conformity appeared on the side of the angels: those who went along with the experimenter dropped to 10 per cent. And when the experimenter was out of the room, and his orders delivered by telephone, only 25 per cent actually complied, with a substantial number of these 'cheating' (i.e. they delivered lower-level 'shocks' than they were instructed to, without telling the experimenter that they had defied his orders).

In short, then, while the Milgram experiments do show that a significant number of people tend to follow a unilateral rule that 'authority is right', it is not binding for the majority. If the situation is such that they can bend that rule — to disobey with honour — many will do so.

The uninvolved bystander. In a gruesome murder in New York, a young girl, Kitti Genovese, was stabbed to death outside an apartment building. A particularly shocking thing about this was that the act took 30 minutes, the girl screaming all the time and her attacker returning three times within that period before finally murdering her — and 38 neighbours watched horror-struck from the safety of their own windows. The police were called only after the killing was completed.

Subsequent research (summarised in Aronson) has indicated that, in such situations, the more people there are around, the *less* likely it is that anyone will help, even when to do so involves little risk of personal harm. The reason apparently is twofold. First, people reason that someone else will assume responsibility if they have not done so already; the more people there are around, the less *personal* responsibility any given individual feels. Second (in situations where such an interpretation is at all feasible) people reason that if no one else is acting then the situation cannot be as serious as it looks — and few people want to see themselves made fools of, such as seeing themselves on *Candid Camera* next week. Where the victim is *known* to the witnesses, or where there is some fellow-feeling — such as a road accident in a remote country area as opposed to the city in rush-hour — the chances of help are very much higher.

Aggression and altruism

Social interaction is built on two basic feelings: aggression and altruism. Aggression refers to inflicting pain or harm on others deliberately, altruism to helping or giving pleasure to others when there is nothing in it materially for oneself. These two feelings determine whether we behave positively or negatively to others. We could be forgiven for coming to pessimistic conclusions.

Altruism seems to result from sophisticated moral judgments: sociocentric thought allows us to be altruistic to our group, and only when allocentric thought develops can we be altruistic to people in general. Altruism seems to be a late arrival on the developmental scene, impossible when thinking is mainly egocentric. Even when people do have sophisticated moral judgments, however, they may not act on them.

For example, people are just as likely *not* to act on their beliefs

- when they are under pressure to conform to someone else's, whether that is a peer group or an authority;
- when they think they can get away with it. Hartshorne and May (1928) found that student cheating was unrelated to students' expressed values or honesty, but to whether or not they thought they were under surveillance;
- when they can make themselves believe it is someone else's responsibility.

These sorts of generalisations, and the findings of Milgram and others, could lead us to believe that people secretly enjoy the pain inflicted on others, even that aggression is a natural instinct.

Some psychologists believe it is. Freud (1905) even postulated a 'death instinct': Storr (1970) described human beings as 'the cruellest and most ruthless species that has ever walked the earth'. There is some evidence that aggression is genetic in origin (e.g. Morris, 1969), but a very great deal of the aggression displayed by people towards each other can be put down to situational factors or to social learning (Aronson, 1984). Situations that induce frustration, for example, have long been known to increase aggression. Barker, Dembo and Lewin (1941) showed that children who had every expectation of playing with some attractive toys, but were prevented from doing so for some time, were very destructive when they were finally allowed to do so, whereas children who were allowed to play with the toys immediately were not. Frustration occurs when a goal seems in sight, and then one is prevented from reaching it. In such circumstances, people are likely to become aggressive. Paradoxically, when there is no hope of reaching the goal, the situation is accepted.

Nevertheless aggression is modelled only too readily. It is important, particularly in understanding the role of the media and particularly TV, to understand this. One theory — to which the media and advertising industries are naturally attracted — is that viewing aggressive content is *cathartic*. If people are 'naturally' aggressive, watching other people be aggressive to each other or indulging in violent sports, allows them to 'let off steam'. Not to ease the pressure in socially controllable ways will build up and explode in socially disastrous ways: hence, it is argued, the *positive* value of violent TV, or *Rambo* films.

The facts are otherwise. Watching violence breeds violence, particularly sexual violence, both in fantasy and in real life. Aronson (1984) reviews a variety of carefully controlled studies and comes to a very sobering conclusion (see Box 7.8).

If aggression is learned, then so is altruism — and rather more easily, and earlier, than developmental theory would lead us to expect. Pines (1979) refers to several incidents which show that young children do feel for the pain or discomfort of others:

> One woman who accidentally bit her cheek and winced reported that her daughter's face was 'an exact mirror of the pain'.
> When one woman bumped her albow and said 'Ouch', her 20-month-old son at once screwed up his face, rubbed his own elbow, and said 'Ow'. Only then did he begin to rub *her* elbow.

These observations clarify several things: the behaviour of the children was imitative — and not only of aggressive behaviour; they were clearly learning socially appropriate responses; and perhaps even more important, a new dimension of social behaviour is emerging, which was markedly absent from our discussion of cognitive-development theories — that of the individual's *feelings*. Clearly it was feelings that inspired the altruistic behaviour, not judgment or reasoning. The children felt sympathy and behaved in a way that is in anyone's definition morally (or socially) appropriate. Similarly, Rushton and Littlefield (1979) reported an experiment showing that altruism (the offering of sweets to others) increased with exposure to incidents in which models showed the altruistic behaviour. The altruistic behaviour was shown to be strongest in 11-year-olds as opposed to seven-year-olds. Basically, 'allocentrism' was a function of social learning.

Nevertheless, Pines pointed out that there are striking individual differences in the readiness of young children to display altruism. Some do so from a very early age, even before social learning and imitation might play a part, while others show little

---

BOX 7.8   WHAT THE EVIDENCE SAYS ABOUT MEDIA VIOLENCE

To sum up, the effect of violent pornography through the media seems to be remarkably similar to the effect of other violence in the media: the level of aggressiveness is increased. Viewing violence (pornographic or otherwise) does *not* serve a cathartic function but seems, rather, to stimulate aggressive behaviour. These data raise complex policy issues involving censorship and First Amendment rights which extend beyond the scope of this book. While I personally am opposed to censorship, I think that an impartial reading of the research would lead media decision-makers to exercise some prudent self-restraint.

Source: Aronson, 1984, p. 206.

altruism or even concern for the distress of others. Although such differences might in part, even a large part, be explained by childrearing and social learning, Pines suggests that genetic factors may also contribute.

HUMANIST PSYCHOLOGY

The suggestion that altruism might have genetic factors brings us to the third major group of psychologists: 'third force' or humanist psychologists referred to in Chapter 1. This school of thought (or rather school of feeling) is based firmly on Theory Y, and traces its roots back to Jean-Jacques Rousseau's notion of the 'noble savage'.

The humanist movement is not so much a theory based on scientific evidence as a set of philosophical assumptions about the essential goodness of humanity. Each one of us, it is said, has innate potential and gifts which are unique, and which become 'actualised' in an atmosphere of caring and trust. People who know and respect themselves will respect others and act morally towards them. Coming to know oneself is achieved through other people, but this requires a special atmosphere that is open and person-centred (Maslow, 1954; Rogers, 1951). Rogers developed a therapy called 'client-centred' which illustrates the general approach. The individual initiates all interaction; the therapist simply reflects, helping the client to redefine the problem, and does not intervene in any way, and particularly does not supply or suggest solutions. People must create their own solutions. Such a non-directive approach works well with some people, but others, who want the therapist to solve their problems for them, are disappointed.

These ideas are readily transferred to education (Rogers, 1983), but the result is different indeed from traditional forms of education (see Box 7.9). Teachers become resources and facilitators; they do not make judgments on students' actions or force them to do things they do not want to do. The emphasis is on *good feelings,* towards oneself and towards others; such feelings cannot be cultivated under pressure. Rogerian psychology translates into alternative and free school models.

It is practically difficult to run a whole school system on Rogerian lines, but aspects have emerged from the humanist school in general that are valuable.

One tool particularly used by humanist psychologists is the encounter group, in which communication is free and open. The ordinary rules of white lies and courtesies are dropped so that people can say what they really mean. Ideally, the group leader attempts to create an atmosphere of mutual concern between the dozen or so participants so that they can feel great trust, which lasts for many weeks after the group sessions. Sometimes, however, these efforts can come apart drastically (Ruitenbeek, 1970). A variation of this technique, called T-groups (for 'training'), has been used in industry to create an atmosphere in which hostile parties (e.g. unions and management) can achieve communication and trust and conclude negotiations that would otherwise have been impossible.

There are then three main sources from psychology that help us deal with the individual in the context of society:

• cognitive psychology and the development of moral reasoning in the individual;

BOX 7.9   ROGERS ON EDUCATION

Our educational system is, I believe, failing to meet the real needs of our society: I have said that our schools, generally, constitute the most traditional, conservative, rigid, bureaucratic institution of our time, and the institution most resistant to change. I stand by that statement, but it does not describe the whole situation. There are new developments — alternative schools, open classrooms, opportunities for independent study — all kinds of adventurous enterprises being carried on by dedicated teachers and parents. One of my purposes in bringing out this book is to encourage these new trends, these new hopes in the educational world, and to point the way to still further advances.

I would like to summarise the general aims of the book before giving a brief account of its organisation and content. Here are some of the goals that are implicit throughout its pages.

- It aims towards a climate of trust in the classroom in which curiosity and the natural desire to learn can be nourished and enhanced.
- It aims towards a participatory mode of decision-making in all aspects of learning in which students, teachers and administrators each have a part.
- It aims towards helping students to prize themselves, to build their confidence and self-esteem.
- It aims towards uncovering the excitement in intellectual and emotional discovery, which leads students to become life-long learners.
- It aims towards developing in teachers the attitudes that research has shown to be most effective in facilitating learning.
- It aims towards helping teachers to grow as persons, finding rich satisfaction in their interaction with learners.
- Even more deeply, it aims towards an awareness that, for all of us, the good life is within, not something which is dependent on outside sources.

Source: Rogers, 1983, pp. 1, 3.

- social psychology and the development of values and interpersonal feelings;
- humanist psychology and the development of individual feelings.

A large canvas indeed: it now remains to look at the one socialising agent we have not discussed so far, the school itself.

THE ROLE OF THE SCHOOL

We saw at the beginning of this chapter how the role of the school in the process of acculturation has changed. 'Teaching the principles of morality' is, in government schools at any rate, not on. Neither is 'neutrality', if by that is meant withdrawal from the field of expressing opinion. However, we did see an example of how schools operate in the incident reported by Davies of Mr Bell and the blanket: the background of *tacit* or unspoken rules that govern behaviour and that need to be learned by experience over a long period of time. Schools do, whatever the intentions of those in charge, impart values. They do so not by the explicit but by the implicit or *hidden* curriculum:

> ... every classroom really has two curriculums that the students are expected to master. The one that educators traditionally have paid most attention to might be called the official curriculum. Its core is the three Rs, and it contains all of the school subjects for which we produce study guides and workbooks and teaching materials. It is the curriculum that all the curriculum reform groups are shouting about these days.
>
> The other curriculum might be described as unofficial, or perhaps even hidden, because to date it has received scant attention from educators. This hidden curriculum can also be represented by three Rs, but not the familiar ones of reading, 'riting and 'rithmetic. It is instead the curriculum of rules, regulations and routines, of things teachers and students must learn if they are to make their way with minimum pain in the institution called the *school* (Jackson, in M. Silberman, 1971, pp. 19-20).

Another aspect of this involves the self-concept: the hidden curriculum 'teaches each student who he is in relation to others' (Bloom, 1971). Norm-referenced testing techniques, such as ranking, clearly place each student in an academic pecking order which says something positive or negative about one's feelings of self-worth. Bloom estimated that a student in school would encounter something like 200 separate learning tasks, all of which are evaluated in terms of how well the student performs the task in relation to others in the class. This is unique to the school culture — nowhere else, as worker, family member or citizen, is a person compared to others so relentlessly and unremittingly. This evaluative approach teaches a lesson which is, however vaguely, *intended* to be learned.

This brings us to the important question of the *function* of the implicit curriculum. It seems unlikely that this all-powerful 'course of study' is merely incidental — it is possible that administrators and individual teachers choose particular regulations and practices because they are seen to reflect *values* (i.e. ideas or beliefs about what is good or right). The choice of these regulations may not always be a conscious one, for educators may be unaware of their motives, but a school's implicit curriculum is recognisable as a small-scale version of society's official values. The following list of learnings and values (M. Silberman, 1971) helps to illustrate the point:

- Learning the rules, routines and regulations (the second set of three Rs) that mould individual behaviour to the requirements of institutional living. Although these rules are specific to schools, they are meant to generalise to the context of the potential adult living in society. It is this aspect that concerned Jackson. These 'three Rs' help the student adjust to a world in which authority is important. Students *should,* he suggested, learn to obey regulations when their purpose is unclear.
- Learning to live without the assurance of adult acceptance. The family is usually highly supportive; society-at-large is not. The school helps the child learn in the absence of nurturance.

- Learning to manage in a highly congested environment, in which both personal and material resources have to be shared. In school, the child cannot have the undivided attention of an adult.
- Learning to withstand continuous evaluation of words and deeds. The classroom is a place where judgments are passed publicly, before one's own friends, day after day.
- Learning to tolerate uncertainty; in particular the uncertainty of not knowing whether one's behaviour will lead to pleasurable or painful outcomes.

Some of these points today seem a little harsh, perhaps *not* so reflective of society. But it is easily seen how these school procedures 'teach' values, which in turn assist in acculturation. At best, the second set of three Rs tell us that there are *some* circumstances when automatic obedience is appropriate, as for example at a busy traffic intersection. At worst, they tell us that automatic obedience is appropriate at *all* times, even when we are ordered to administer powerful electric shocks to another. It is comforting to recall that there is evidence suggesting that those with allocentric moral systems are likely to discriminate between those occasions when conformity is appropriate, and when it is not.

There is, then, no *necessary* conflict between fostering moral autonomy and transmitting the values that uphold society. In fact, in our society there is a general belief in the value of cultural diversity and in conformity to certain basic views involving allocentrism or altruism. There is a shifting balance, to be sure, but if anything emerges from the work reviewed in this chapter, it is that the school is inextricably involved in moral education in some sense or another, and that the aims of personal autonomy, as well as of diversity in a complex community, are well served by the pursuit of *allocentrism*. We turn to what this might mean in Section B, while the delicate task of negotiating the rule world of adults and that of children has important implications for classroom management in the following chapter.

SUMMARY

Individual development, the context of society and the role of the school. Schools have become increasingly shy about teaching values. They have moved from actively teaching 'the' principles of morality, and such sociocentric values as patriotism, through 'neutrality' (where one affects to be teaching cognitive data only), to multiculturalism, where students are encouraged to tolerate and to value diversity within the community. The latter is the official position of government schools today.

Acculturation has two meanings: the 'taming' of individuals to fit into society, and the mutual interaction between minority and majority societies. Multiculturalism leads from 'mosaic' to 'melting pot': the majority society is itself different as a result of acculturation. This chapter concentrates on the first, individually oriented, meaning of acculturation, with an implied tension between individual and societal aims: what right has one to place one's own principles above those of one's group?

The development of moral reasoning. Piaget defined morality as 'the rules governing interpersonal conduct'. People have to *understand* those rules, and then to *act* upon them. Cognitivists have stressed the first aspect (understanding by the individual); social psychologists the second (internalising particular values and feelings towards others).

Understanding goes through three main stages: *egocentric,* where self is the sole point of reference; *sociocentric,* where the group is the point of reference; *allocentric,* where the point of view of people in general is the point of reference. These stages closely follow those outlined in Chapter 6 — ikonic, concrete-symbolic and formal, respectively.

An elaboration of this basic theory is provided by Kohlberg, who subdivides each stage into two, producing six stages of moral development:

1. punishment orientation
2. maximising reward   } Egocentric or preconventional
3. conformity to 'good' image
4. law and order   } Sociocentric or conventional
5. adherence to contract
6. individual conscience, irrespective of   } Allocentric or postconventional
    particular laws

Kohlberg's stage theory is probably correct in its general sequence, but people are much more affected by the particular situation than Kohlberg would seem to allow. The same point arises in children's understandings of the functions of friendship. Nevertheless post-conventional or allocentric people seem more able to resist pressure to conform to the group or to obey authority against their own judgment.

The social context. The social context acculturates both individuals and social groups. Individuals begin the acculturation process through the family: after early childhood, the agencies for socialising and transmitting the prevailing cultural values multiply. Whether the family reflects the majority value system or not greatly influences the course of acculturation. Acculturation (in both individual and group senses) is especially complicated within Aboriginal cultures.

The peer group is a particularly important influence on developing values. Within primary school, peer groups develop their own integrity, reward systems and values. The 'agenda' of children's playground and community groups is that which most affects children's behaviour. There are strict behavioural rules, based on a literal interpretation of reciprocity, about what constitutes friendly and unfriendly behaviour; people act 'in situation' rather than 'in character'. Children and adults who act unpredictably ('out of situation') cause anger and resentment. Teachers need to know the children's agenda, be sensitive to it, and be clear themselves about their own agenda.

Conformity is affected both by situation and by personal moral development. Situational factors include peer group judgments, directions from authority, the pressure of others (which inhibits altruism) and modelling. The two major social values revolve around aggression and altruism. Some psychologists and ethologists say that aggression and altruism are basically innate. While there is undoubtedly some innate component in both, the evidence is overwhelming that both altruism and aggression are affected by learning. There is a great deal of evidence that TV violence encourages people to be more violent, in thought and in deed.

Humanist psychology. Humanist psychologists base their model of moral behaviour on the way individuals feel about themselves and their relations to others. Humanists have developed techniques in non-directive therapy and in encounter groups which emphasise self-respect and 'prizing' the authenticity of others. These techniques are said to lead to moral judgment and, especially, to allocentric behaviour.

The role of the school. While the official role of schools is to teach tolerance of diversity, the facts that they are institutions, and that people are people, mean that there *is* a direct communication of values. The explicit teaching of values is not official policy today, but values are inevitably taught tacitly, through rules that are unstated and learned through long exposure to an implicit or *hidden* curriculum. These rules mostly refer to obedience — to the 'second set of three Rs' (rules, routines and regulations) — but the hidden curriculum also refers to learning about oneself in relation to others as a result of evaluational procedures.

    The impact of school on the affective domain of values is thus widespread. Official stances are sometimes contrary to practice. Teachers can do a lot, positively or negatively, about their students' moral and social development.

SECTION B

In this section we deal with several aspects of moral and social development and ways in which the school may be involved. First, we take the question of the direct teaching of values through a hidden curriculum. Then we will examine the more positive ways in which the school facilitates the process of acculturation.

THE IMPLICIT CURRICULUM

If the implicit or hidden curriculum (that educational backdrop of unspoken rules and attitudes) is to teach those values that maintain society and the individual's survival within it, how does that transmission occur? Four methods can be identified:

1. the second set of three Rs;
2. biased textbooks;
3. teacher expectations;
4. evaluation.

The second set of three Rs

C. Silberman (1970) pointed out:

> What educators must realise, moreover, is that how they teach and how they act may be more important than what they teach. The way we do things, that is to say, shapes values more directly and more effectively than the way we talk about them (p. 9).

Farber (1970, pp. 19–20) made the same point. Many school rules (e.g. as to dress, conventions of approaching an authority figure, meeting deadlines, etc.) are arbitrary for a reason: 'The very point about such rules is their pointlessness. It's not *what* you're taught that does the harm, it's *how* you're taught ... the real lesson is the method ... the method that currently prevails in schools is standardised, impersonal and coercive. What it teaches best is ... itself.' It teaches the child to obey, and obedience is a stance desired by many. It is desired, first, by those who profit most from it (i.e. high-status persons whose power derives from their ability to exact obedience). Second, a majority of the population may think that obedience, in and of itself, is *morally right:* the implicit curriculum of a rule-bound school becomes, in their view, an important lesson in morality.

In Dreeben's (1968) view, the hidden curriculum also provides an opportunity for students to learn to cope with the differing styles of authority they will unquestionably meet in later life. Dreeben did not deny that the implicit curriculum exerts a powerful effect, but he maintained that it is beneficial and desirable.

The issue here is whether the educator is committed to a process- or content-oriented view of education. Dreeben himself clearly saw the content of the values transmitted by the implicit curriculum as being an important, if not the main, function of education. This implies that such values are the same as those required for adequate living in the foreseeable future. The process-oriented educator, on the other hand, would say (a) that things will become increasingly complicated in the future, so that content *per se* is irrelevant in the domain of values, as it is for cognitive knowledge; and (b) that the focus in education should be upon the growth and sophistication of the learner. This growth is likely to be hampered by an emphasis on obedience to given values regardless of situation, and so the influence of the typical hidden curriculum cannot be beneficial.

Biased textbooks

Racism. Another way of transmitting a value system is through biased textbooks. McDiarmid and Pratt (1971), in a book appropriately entitled *Teaching Prejudice,* analysed pictorial and prose treatments in 143 social-studies texts, in use in Canada from Grades 2 to 13. They focused attention on six 'target' groups — Christians, Jews, immigrants, Moslems, Negroes and Indians — and found striking differences. Christians and Jews were dealt with favourably, in terms of number of evaluative comments, and were not different from each other. Negroes and Indians, however, were dealt with unfavourably, and indistinguishably from each other. The other groups fell in between.

Closer to home, Spalding (1974, pp. 26–9) found some interesting examples of race bias in social studies textbooks used in Australia. The following are two examples:

For secondary students:

> Over the 25,000 years during which the Australian natives occupied our land before the coming of the white man, they never advanced beyond the stone age or hunting stage of development (Sparkes et al., 1970, p. 52).

And for junior primaries:

> People who live together in tribes like the early Aborigines are called PRIMITIVE people (Lloyd, 1970, p. 49).

Sexism. A number of articles have been devoted to the assertion that children's reading material is biased because of discrimination based on gender (sexism). For example, Tibbetts (1978, p. 165), listed 18 papers published in the 1970s based on five themes in sexist content:

1. Presenting more male than female characters.
2. Portraying males in a greater number and variety of occupations.
3. Depicting most female characters in passive, subordinate, incompetent roles in contrast to most male characters being active, dominant and capable.
4. Attributing desirable traits to males and undesirable traits to females.
5. Presenting females as people to be denigrated.

How can sexist bias in textbooks be overcome? This was a question considered by a conference of school consultants on non-sexist education, who discussed the following guidelines (Foster, 1981):

- The *actions and achievement* of women should be recognised.
- Women and girls should be given the same *respect* as men and boys — and not typified as the bad driver; the cranky mother-in-law, frightened of mice, or mere followers.
- *Abilities or interests* should not be assigned on the basis of male or female stereotypes — both men and women can be frightened, poor mechanics, good decision-makers and caring childminders.
- *Sexist language* invariably has non-sexist alternatives: *The World of Man* can become simply *World History;* instead of 'Greg Norman is one of the top golfers in the world, and Jan Stephenson is one of the best women players'; 'Greg Norman and Jan Stephenson are among the best golfers in the world'.

The list in Box 7.10 provides a means of checking the extent to which sexist bias could be part of the hidden curriculum in your school.

BOX 7.10   TOWARDS NON–SEXIST EDUCATION IN SCHOOLS

School Organisation
- School uniforms need not be the same, but should enable students to comfortably participate in a variety of activities.
- Assemblies should consist of mixed groupings with female as well as male staff leading.
- School awards should be made on the basis of merit irrespective of sex.
- Sports and physical education should be equally available to all students — but contact sports (such as rugby) are not considered suitable for co-educational sports.
- Curriculum and timetable should not restrict the choices of boys or girls.
- Discipline should be similar for boys and girls.
- Careers advice/counselling should be on the basis of ability, interest and personality regardless of sex.
- School displays should maintain a reasonable balance in relation to the sexes.
- Playgrounds should be open in all areas to both boys and girls.
- Staff duties should be distributed so that both women and men are equally encouraged to undertake duties and responsibilities.
- Visiting resource people should exemplify appropriate attitudes, language and methods.

Classrooms
- Teachers should examine their own assumptions about the academic achievement, future employment and general behaviour of boys and girls.
- Teachers should be sensitive to the language and tone of voice they use with girls and boys, and their differential use of praise and criticism.
- Pupils should be encouraged to be considerate of each other as people.
- Assertiveness and independence in girls, and gentleness or caring in boys should not be discouraged.
- Sexist comments should be checked.
- Class programs should reflect a balance of interests and both sexes in language.
- Non-sexist resources should be used when possible: with attention being drawn to sexism if it exists. For example, a picture of a male airline pilot could prompt discussion of whether there are women airline pilots.
- Examples, exercises and test questions should make balanced reference to both sexes.
- Assignments should raise questions about sex-roles and sex-stereotypes in life, literature and media.
- Historical contributions of women should not be overlooked.
- Real-life situations (such as males portraying a doctor and females

portraying a nurse) should be used to investigate student attitudes and concepts.
- Visual materials should depict people in non-traditional roles.
- Boys and girls should be given opportunities to carry out similar tasks (such as decorating a room or arranging furniture).
- Sex should not be the criterion for line formations or seating plans.

Source: Adapted from NSW Department of Education, 1980.

Another claim of bias has been based on the *Situational English* textbooks used in the education of adult migrants to Australia (and children after Year 4 learning English as a second language). In Unit 15, the indefinite article (*a, an*) is taught with the help of occupations. Here are the examples (pp. 26–7):

What's his job?	*What's her job?*
He's *a* doctor	She's *a* nurse
builder	teacher
mechanic	typist
farmer.	housewife.
He's *an* engineer	She's *an* artist
actor	actress
accountant.	interpreter.

The report of the committee investigating sexism in education in New South Wales (Guthrie, 1977) saw a need for revision of the materials used in schools if 'young people are to gain a balanced view of their past and present' (p. 30). This committee found that male and female stereotypes are shown in most published school materials, especially those used in reading, mathematics and social studies. The committee drew attention to such examples as the following:

- Girls cook, sew and look on while boys climb, race and are generally adventurous.
- Women cope with washing powder, eggs and unpleasant minor disciplinary actions while men are astronauts, scientists and policemen.
- Girls jump skipping ropes, weigh flour or buy fabric while boys demonstrate to girls how to solve their technical, mathematical and mechanical difficulties.

The argument works both ways. Thus Conway (1975) saw a need for boys to have more exposure to a curriculum which emphasises sensitivity towards others and a responsiveness to cultural subjects such as art, music, history, drama and social problems. The 'biology for girls' and 'physics, chemistry and maths for boys' stereotypes need to be challenged. Conway reserved the most vigorous challenge of all for the 'iron jock-strap' syndrome of sport-obsessed boys' schools.

*Students may choose electives because
of their interest, not their sex.*

Teacher expectations

A third important means of 'teaching' the implicit curriculum is through teachers' expectations (Good and Brophy, 1973; Finn, 1972; Rosenthal, 1971; Rosenthal and Jacobson, 1968). Teachers can, by *expecting* a certain outcome, make it more likely to become a fact: if a child is expected to under-achieve, then it is more likely that failure will be the outcome. It does not take much imagination to see that a student is likely to fail when working out a sum on the blackboard before the whole class, if the teacher announces: 'I bet I can pick those who can't do it!' (C. Silberman, 1970).

The self-fulfilling prophecy can work more subtly than this. Teachers might spend more time with pupils they expect will do well. They might be more inclined to give particular pupils the benefit of the doubt, which is the kind of reinforcement that will help them try harder. They might set more trivial goals for pupils they expect little from, thus never giving them the opportunity to show how good they are. They might merely insult or ignore pupils and thus ... There are obviously many factors that may explain the phenomenon.

Values and feelings relating to pupils' self-worth may also be communicated by non-verbal gestures — by *not* calling on a student ever to make a contribution in class, by ignoring questions asked by a student, and so on. Where the student may easily be 'typed' (e.g. comes from a Commission area, is black, parents are divorced or divorcing, has a foreign accent, etc.), it is easy for the teacher to signal what may be interpreted by the student as evaluative messages.

Isaacs (1979) studied the schooling of Greek children in Sydney schools, and found that the discriminatory messages are sometimes not as subtle as this:

> Angela, Maria's sister, repeating Form 6, adds, 'In the lower forms teachers are forever telling the Australian girls how well they are doing, and denigrate the Greek girls: they refer at times to wogs and then say "I'm sorry", to the Greeks in the class' (p. 219).

The communication of teachers' expectations of failure may sometimes only have the effect of postponing the students' achievement until they are clear of the school and can handle their education in their own time:

> Steven says, 'I wanted to do medicine and I was doing well at school ... I remember one day getting 16/20 for my English essay, but because of flu I handed my work in a few days late, the teacher took off fourteen marks, and this pulled me down to a failure and when I said to the teacher she shouldn't do this, I got six cuts. This happened often. I lost marks for silly things; I had to leave school, because I was frightened that, if they provoked me enough, I'd do something stupid and I would regret it. I am working and attending evening school and I have a good chance of passing the School Certificate and I might get to medicine yet (p. 218).

Steven's account poignantly and definitely demonstrates the two curricula. He was doing well in the explicit (official) curriculum. However, at least two teachers thought there were more important things to schooling than doing well academically, such as not handing in assignments late, and not querying the decisions of a teacher. It is not made clear in this example — as it is perfectly clear in Angela's — that there is a double standard operating, one for 'old' Australians and another for 'new' Australians.

For both 'old' and 'new' Australians there can be compelling messages in teacher expectations. These range from communications which convey the lack of parity of esteem among school subjects: giving the 'academic' subjects such as English, science and mathematics ascendancy over the 'non-academics' (such as industrial arts, home economics or the arts), to further restrictions on electives. For example, industrial arts has been perceived as unfeminine, uninteresting to girls, heavy and unattractive, a male domain, messy and grimy, and non-academic. (Directorate of Special Programs, 1985b). See also Box 8.3 in the next chapter.

In other subjects where female teachers predominate, as in music, reverse messages may be interpreted. 'You don't *really* want to play the drums, do you, Jenny?' (Directorate of Special Programs, 1985b). Music teachers need to foster the idea that the full range of musical instruments is appropriate for all students — and to restrict musical discrimination to selection of students on the basis of voice range or type.

A similar sort of message could come through in a subject such as the visual arts in which there could be a teacher expectation for boys to do better at sculpture because of prior manual training ... or that boys will see art as a 'girls'' subject. (Directorate of Special Programs, 1985d). Teacher expectations are powerful media for the implicit curriculum.

Evaluation

There is considerable overlap in the sources of the hidden curriculum, giving them a stronger and more unified effect on pupils than they appear to have when considered individually. For example, there is a strong link between evaluation of pupil progress and teacher expectations, as we have discussed. In itself, though, evaluation conveys a message. For example:

- It is better to beat others in competition than to write essays for the sake of their quality and interest.
- It is not important how you do it, as long as you get an acceptable result.
- It is not what you do, but whether you beat the opposition.
- Nothing is worth learning unless it is tested.

Of course, all these things are oversimplifications, logically speaking. But the implicit curriculum is a matter of feeling and psychology rather than of logic — the hidden messages that come through from the routines of testing have their effect. No matter how rationally the teacher explains the need for testing, the students will assimilate the implicit value judgments. They may then reach the stage where they think that you don't 'really' know anything just by reading books — you have to 'do' a course and pass the exams. Such messages have a strong negative effect on academic motivation, as we have seen. Further effects of evaluation on students are dealt with in Chapter 10.

SCHOOL AND COMMUNITY

How can schools train students to handle the diversity they will encounter in the community? That is the challenge of multicultural education and bicultural education (exemplified by Aboriginal education).

Multicultural education

The problem facing teachers in multicultural education is essentially one of attaining the basic goal of schooling: to perpetuate Australian culture yet to retain the cultural identity of ethnic minority groups. As Australia has the most diverse workforce in the industrial West, excluding Israel and the OPEC Arab regions (see Chapter 6 and Callan, 1986), this dual goal is difficult to attain.

The multicultural classroom was discussed in Chapter 6, with specific reference to learning English as a second language. In this section, the focus is on more general educational issues. The relevant policy of the Commonwealth Schools Commission has two facets:

1. That schools will attempt to reflect within their curriculum the realities of the differing lives of their students, and within their organisation provide ways to support student self-esteem and confidence.
2. That schools will attempt to provide opportunities for students to broaden and enrich their lives through acquisition of at least some aspects of another culture (Education Commission of NSW, 1983).

These policies have effects on students who come from both the majority and minority cultural streams. Schools provide support for the maintenance of the minority culture while providing acculturation to the broader stream. For schools, the important questions are:

- Who should be responsible for teaching community languages, the schools or ethnic groups through such means as the Saturday schools discussed in Chapter 6?
- Who should fund ethnic schools?
- Can all Australians become bilingual?

A starting point is in higher education where the incorporation of multicultural studies in teacher education programs will be the first step in providing multicultural classrooms and multiculturalism as part of the general school curriculum.

Bicultural education: Aboriginal education

Aboriginal education has two purposes:

1. To enhance the learning and development of Aboriginal students; and,
2. To enable all students to have some knowledge, understanding and appreciation of the Aboriginal culture (Directorate of Special Programs, 1985d).

Realisation of the first of these purposes will be the more difficult, for it is apparent that Aborigines are dissatisfied with existing educational provision. Three Aboriginal communities, Dandenong and Shepparton in Victoria and Bourke in New South Wales, pointed to differences between so-called Anglo-education for Aborigines and Aboriginal education for Aborigines (Fesl, 1983). Thus the term 'Aboriginal education' needs to be used with discretion (see Box 7.11). That same point was made to a Northern Territory researcher who was told that just because schools are established in Aboriginal communities, or have Aboriginal dancing or craft as part of the curriculum, they are Aboriginal schools.

> Education in Aboriginal communities is a two-way thing. If the school wants the community to be involved in the school it must first show its attitude to the Aboriginal community. Individual teachers must set aside a time for the community to be involved in their program and bring Aboriginal people into the classroom (Davis, 1980).

Aboriginal studies focus on the history, cultures, languages and lifestyles of Aboriginal and Torres Strait Islanders, but a survey of over 1,200 schools (with 72 known to have programs in Aboriginal Studies) showed that there was uncertainty on how increased emphasis should be given to Aboriginal Studies in schools (Budby, 1982). The survey showed that most of the schools emphasised social and cultural aspects of the traditional culture and involved Aboriginal people, but that teaching is mainly undertaken on an ad hoc basis according to teacher interest.

Essentially, the approach to Aboriginal education is one of bicultural study in which cultural differences are given sensitive treatment in the classroom. In common with multicultural education is a heavy reliance on involvement of members of the community, who bring diversity into the classroom.

USING SOCIAL PROCESSES IN THE CLASSROOM

Group interaction

A number of teaching methods are designed to promote the social development of students. For example, in Chapter 4 we discussed reflective teaching as a variant of peer teaching which is itself a type of group activity contributing to social development. In small groups, students can be given a structured experience, 'an organised game-like activity designed to produce group processes that can easily be understood by participants and which can greatly assist in the development of effective group interaction' (Watson, Vallee and Mulford, 1981). An effective group has to attain its goals by completing set tasks, and at the same time it has to maintain itself internally (through human relationships) to enable it to remain effective.

BOX 7.11   INVOLVEMENT OF THE ABORIGINAL COMMUNITY
IN EDUCATION

Like faded dots of confetti strewn along a path from the altar to the car, lie the skeletal remains of a cession of Australian education programs.

The High Priest of Knowledge has watched the marriages and divorces between 'Perceived Educational Needs' and 'Social Realities' since the arrival of the First Fleet — through the early days of 'moral' education for the convicts; through the battle of the churches for control of the education system, the temporary Anglican victory (whose monuments — Geelong, Melbourne and other grammar schools — still stand); tugs-of-war between the free, compulsory and secular systems of the latter part of the Nineteenth Century; the Twentieth Century's reforms in teaching methods, curricula and schools; and now he anxiously presides as the bride approaches her latest marriage with — Multicultural Education.

Suffering far more than their white counterparts, whose own systems are still unsettled, are the Aboriginal people of Australia upon whose lifestyles and own education system have been imposed the assumed needs and experiments of the ruling classes of the white society.

The attempts at imposed Aboriginal 'Education' can be roughly summarised as follows:

- Elimination — of language and culture
- Assimilation — into Christian ideology and the white man's way of life
- Integration and acquisition — of enough literacy skills to make Aborigines useful tools of the white economy.

Successive attempts over nearly two centuries to interest Aborigines in the white education systems have failed — failed because Aborigines' interests and goals were neither sought nor contemplated.

It is hoped that the present project will contribute usefully to change long overdue; a closer involvement of Aborigines in the shaping of their own education.

Source: Introduction to Bala Bala: Some Literacy and Educational Perceptions of Three Aboriginal Communities (Australian Government Publishing Service), quoted by Fesl 1983, p. 15.

Students learn distinctive social skills in group situations when they have the opportunity to practise them and gain feedback. This learning follows a cycle in which concrete personal experiences lead to observation, reflection and examination; then comes a formulation of abstract concepts, rules or principles and, finally, a personal theory to be tested in new situations (Johnson and Johnson, 1975).

Structured experiences through group interaction are used, not only in schools, but in a number of business and service organisations to develop skills in communication, decision-making, problem-solving, leadership and team-building. A typical structured experience on communication would enable students to test both sending and receiving skills, verbal and non-verbal messages, seeking and gaining feedback, and non-evaluative paraphrasing of the content of a message and the feelings of the sender (Johnson and Johnson, 1975).

An example of a group interaction using social processes is 'The Prisoner's Dilemma', designed to explore trust between group members and the effects of betrayal of trust. The game shows the effects of interpersonal competition and the benefits of collaboration (Watson, Vallee and Mulford, 1981). Groups are told that they are going to experience the risk-taking faced by guilty prisoners being interrogated by police. Questioned separately, the prisoners are each told that the other has confessed and that if they collaborate, they will be treated more leniently. The dilemma is whether to confess when they should not, or fail to confess when they should. Teams are given time to make decisions, and coloured cards by means of which members indicate their preference in a series of rounds during which representatives of each team act as negotiators. After the final round and the totalling of points, the teams combine for the first time to discuss as a group who the winners were in the win/lose situation, what were the benefits of collaboration versus competition, and the effect of high or low trust on interpersonal relationships.

In group interactions the role of the teacher switches: no longer is teacher-student interaction the key, nor is the curriculum content or the resources used in the lesson; it is the interaction between students that is all important. While the teacher may establish objectives, provide materials and facilities, or explain the co-operative goal structure, during the group interaction itself, the teacher's principal role is that of observer, only intervening as a consultant to help a group solve problems of working together, and, finally, helping the group to evaluate the products. Such experiences help to dispel the myth that competition and individual experiences are the ways to build character and self-esteem (Johnson and Johnson, 1982).

Moral education

Content approaches. The second set of three Rs (rules, routines and regulations) teach explicitly the ways in which schools operate day to day, but implicitly certain sociocentric values. We might ask, for example, what values a student would learn from the following:

- There are only two 10 grades to be awarded in HSC English.
- His worth as a scholar (and by implication as a person) depends on how he compares with his peers, not upon what he actually knows and can do.
- She is to sit all day close to a friend, but may neither talk to nor help her.

Clearly, these practices teach the specific values that operate at the conventional level of morality (Stages 3 and 4), and a 'pawn' self-concept. Many writers regard the operation of the implicit curriculum in this way as detrimental to the child's moral growth and ethically unacceptable, simply because it is dishonest. Kohlberg (1970) noted that the hidden curriculum engages teachers in moral education without explicit and philosophical discussion of goals and methods. Gordon (1980) made a similar point, but more strongly. He argued that, since the operation of the hidden curriculum is unconscious, it violates two basic rights: to decide what to study, and to be aware of forces that influence behaviour. He placed the hidden curriculum in the same category as subliminal advertising, which is illegal in many countries, including Australia.

An opposing view is that of Dreeben (1968), for whom the hidden curriculum is simply a matter of reality: survival in society *does* require obedience to authority, and the conventional 'bag of virtues'. Peters (1963) made a similar point on psychological grounds: it is desirable for people to make reasoned moral judgments, but 'the brute facts' are that children are incapable of this and must 'enter the palace of Reason through the courtyard of Habit and Tradition'. Peters' argument was devised largely before the present preoccupation with 'moral autonomy' in schools. Do habit and tradition promote or stultify moral growth?

Process approaches. Current *official* policy in most States is that moral education should be tackled as a process issue, with allocentric or post-conventional modes of moral reasoning being the desirable goal, not conventional or sociocentric ones.

There are two ways of doing this. The first is to teach moral reasoning as a subject (albeit process-oriented) just like any other. The second approach is through what Kohlberg (1970) called 'the moral atmosphere of the school' — by which he meant that the school must be geared to post-conventional operation. Morality is something that applies 'across the curriculum', and is not learned in specific programs.

Specific programs on moral education are mostly aimed at raising the level of moral judgment from egocentric to allocentric. The important thing is that certain *modes of thinking* are more desirable (in terms of any definition of moral autonomy) than are others (Williams, 1969). Thus, in this approach, the school plays a *cognitive* role in moral education. Bailey (1979) made this quite clear when he said that moral education 'is best seen as the development of certain kinds of knowledge and reasoning rather than the cultivation of certain kinds of feeling' (p. 114). This is a view that many, particularly humanist psychologists, would reject.

Kohlberg programs. Several researchers have directly adapted programs from Kohlberg's theory. Essentially, the technique is to present a moral dilemma in group discussion: if change is to take place, there must be an element of conflict (or mismatch) that forces participants to confront their own beliefs and values. However, the timing and extent of the conflict are said to be crucial, for people will simply reject an argument if it is *too* far above their present level. Kohlberg and his colleagues (Rest, Turiel and Kohlberg, 1969; Turiel, 1966) proposed the 'Plus One' hypothesis: people are most likely to change when an argument is present at one stage above that at which they are currently operating.

According to this stategy, an argument which represents reasoning at the next stage is carefully presented to students. Preaching law and order (Stage 3 or 4) to punishment-oriented Stage 1s is likely to be ineffective; instead, one would show that it is worthwhile (Stage 2) to co-operate. Then, when they are at Stage 2, they should be presented with a 'being good' argument, not one based on abstract principles. While this seems to make good sense, there is little experimental support for Plus One (Kurtines and Grief, 1974), and further, it is impractical to monitor several individuals simultaneously and present Plus One arguments to suit each (Rest, 1974).

Schlaefli, Rest and Thoma (1985) reviewed 55 studies using a test (Defining Issues) based on Kohlberg's moral dilemmas. In the studies, the experimenters intervened by discussing dilemmas with the subjects, providing the following results:

- the intervention was successful with all subjects, but especially with subjects aged 24 years and older;
- interventions worked when they lasted three to 12 weeks, but had no effect if they were under three weeks long.

These results suggest that there are benefits in discussing moral dilemmas, but that effects will be longer and more marked with older, tertiary students. More research is needed to clarify the situation in secondary schools.

Other programs. Other programs have been advocated that are more flexible than the Kohlberg programs themselves. Often, they are included in social science courses (e.g. Newman and Oliver, 1970; Metcalfe, 1971). In New South Wales, moral education is not addressed as such, but role-playing and the clarification of values are taught in social studies (Hepworth, 1979). An important stimulus in New South Wales was the adoption of Bruner's *Man: a Course of Study* (MACOS), which was adapted by including Aboriginal content. A similar course is SEMP, which involves role-playing by students in situations involving moral dilemmas or the kinds of cultural conflicts faced by some minority ethnic groups in our culture.

Values clarification (e.g. Raths, Harmin and Simon, 1978) helps students become aware of the values they espouse. They are led to recognise what they prize, to be able to defend that choice and be prepared to act upon it. Brady (1979) presented a comprehensive program that incorporated values clarification, but built it into a cognitive-development approach. He believed that cognitive-development theory would provide a yardstick for students, enabling them to make relative ('better' or 'worse' than) judgments about values. He included a variety of approaches, including role-playing and moral dilemmas covering most aspects of modern urban life in Australia. His book is called *Feel Value Act* (see Box 7.12), and stresses valuing as only a part of the total complex, which ends in appropriate action by the student.

Once one moves away from strict moral judgment as such, and into feeling and action, the program begins to become much more *humanist* than cognitive-developmental. Essentially, humanist experiences involve *concrete activity*, whereas the cognitive approach requires training in moral reasoning and judgment. For example, it is one thing to discuss racial *prejudice* rationally: it is another to dress up as a black and tour the south (e.g. Griffin, 1961; Raucher, 1970). In one enterprising and direct experiment (Peters, 1971), the teacher designated 'niggers for the day' (on Monday, say, all blond children were to be discriminated against and called names; the next day, it was the turn of children who had brown eyes; then those who had freckles ...). The children were learning in a highly conrete way just what it *feels* like to be discriminated against. The evidence was that racial *prejudice* and, even more important, prejudiced *behaviour*, decreased markedly: but the experiment was called off because of parental protest.

Encounter groups use a similar process. Here, the group members are instructed to provide valid feedback to each other about how each person comes across to the others. Our normal roles in society prevent us from getting information about our interpersonal effectiveness, which makes it very difficult for feelings and self-concept to be firmly based in reality. Such experiences are often most beneficial when the participants are already open to change, and fairly well 'together'. Participants need to possess a stable self-concept if they are to withstand receiving information about themselves that challenges what they would *like* to think about themselves. As mentioned earlier, there are dangers in group experience, and some people cannot handle them at all.

It is a moot point how far group experience of this kind should be brought into the scope of education: with appropriate safeguards, there may be some room within the senior high school. Nevertheless, Grainger (1970) described a loosely structured group encounter for the whole class called 'The Bullring' — so-called because, as one student wrote:

> The speaker and person being spoken to are all alone, like the bull and the matador in a bullring (p. 29).

In this situation, 'bull' and 'matador' keep changing roles: the idea is that students will come to recognise their own (and others') motives and failings. As one Year 9 boy expressed it:

> Because some people dislike others they oppose them in the Bullring ... I believe that the only thing we can do is to speak to anyone we dislike and try to understand why we don't like them. Then perhaps we could discuss things without feeling we have to oppose the speaker (p. 130).

Grainger found the technique highly successful from Years 7 to 10; and, interestingly, with low-intelligent as much as with highly intelligent pupils. This last point is clear from this final quotation from pupil records:

> I have learnt that i am a bit shy to speak to, i join the noisey lot I speak to my next door nabourgh and he speak to me we have confersaisions which I dere not speak out — also I have learnt that also i throw things about and try show of a bit like going up to the teacher and pulling his ear or talking to him in a funny way also when I sujest something the group does not carry on with the confersation and that's why I dear not speak up ... (p. 140).

Evidence for the success of such programs as the above is largely impressionistic: that is, the participants enjoy them (even when they are painful) and seem to believe in their value. But 'hard data' are difficult to obtain and are often regarded by the participants as irrelevant or inappropriate. It is also obvious that such experiences need to be handled by teachers who are skilled in group dynamics.

BOX 7.12   VALUES EDUCATION: GETTING ALONG WITH PEOPLE

'We shouldn't really be doing this.' Scott looked at the other five boys who were already busy tying a rope to the tree trunk.

'But it'll help our fathers', said John. 'They've been mighty good about building this tree house for us! The least we can do is help them by moving this big tree trunk out of the way!'

The boys went on working. That is all except Scott. Help or not, he thought, they were being disobedient.

'John, your father said to keep away ... and Brett, your dad said that we should not try to do anything by ourselves.'

'We're here now!' one of the other boys said. 'Are you going to help us or not?' Some of the boys were getting cross with Scott.

So when the rope had been tied to the tree trunk, Scott helped the others pull.

'We're not moving it at all,' John said, grunting as he pulled. 'One more time,' said Brett. 'After three ... one, two, three.'

The boys pulled as hard as they could, and the tree began to move. 'Keep pulling,' John shouted. But the tree slid sideways, and began to roll down the hill. The rope was ripped from the boys' hands.

Scott didn't have time to curse the rope burn on his hands. There was a loud crash, like a cannon firing, and the tree crashed through Mrs Kelly's front fence, and came to rest against the front of the house.

For a second the boys were frozen with shock. They looked down at the mess they'd caused. Then they started, some more slowly than others, to run over the hill and out of sight.

But Scott was the last to move, and as he disappeared over the hill, he could see Mrs Kelly standing in her front doorway. She held her hands to her head, and was looking towards him.

When the boys were safely away, they met again, panting and white with shock.

'We mustn't say a thing,' said Brett. 'We mustn't own up.'

'If our fathers find out,' said another boy, 'we'll be in terrible trouble.'

'And that will be the end of the tree house,' said John.

'But I think Mrs Kelly saw me,' moaned Scott, rubbing his hands.

The boys were quiet for a while, and then Brett spoke. 'We've got to take a chance,' he said, 'We've just got to hope that Mrs Kelly didn't see anyone.' The boys all nodded.

'But what about Mrs Kelly's front fence?' Scott asked.

'We've all agreed to say nothing, Scott,' Brett said sternly. Again the boys nodded.

Scott wasn't sure what to do. He was the one who might have been seen! He felt sorry for Mrs Kelly, but the boys had said to say nothing. They'd all been disobedient, and now someone else was paying for it. People might believe that the tree had blown down in the wind ... as long as Mrs Kelly had not seen him!

What should Scott do?

Now Talk About

A If the boys owned up to their fathers, what should their fathers do?

B The boys were disobedient, but their reason was a 'good' one, that is, they wanted to help their fathers. Should this make a difference to how they are treated?

C If Scott knew he had been seen and recognised, should this make a difference to what he does?

In the story about the boys and the tree house, role play a talk between Scott and Mrs Kelly. Pretend that Scott has decided to own up.
In one role play, make Mrs Kelly kind. In another, make her very angry.

Put a tick in the column which is closest to the way you feel about each of these. You may answer: Strongly Agree (SA), Agree (A), Disagree (D), Strongly Disagree (SD).

	SA	A	D	SD
A People shouldn't ask you personal questions.				
B People shouldn't be completely honest all the time.				
C People should share everything.				
D People should be able to laugh at their own silly ways.				
E People shouldn't have to give others a turn before they have their own.				
F I want my own way most of the time.				
G I'm not shy with big groups of people.				

Discuss your answers with others.

Source: Brady, 1979.

MORAL EDUCATION ACROSS THE CURRICULUM

Kohlberg's own phrase, 'the moral atmosphere of the school', makes it quite clear that moral education pervades the total school environment. According to Hemming (1980):

> ... moral education calls for much more than competent teachers with a battery of items to dispense; it needs a civilised school community and teachers whose quality of life are models of moral feeling and intelligence (p. 75).

In Hemming's view moral education is achieved, not by preaching, but by immersing young people in open social situations where their validity can be discovered in action — across the curriculum, not in special 'values classes'.

In order to run a complex institution such as a school, it is necessary to impose structure: to set up rules, routines and regulations that make smooth running of that institution possible. That task is made very much easier by the structuring of sociocentric norms that exact their own obedience — by discouraging the questioning of rules and the reasons for them. There rapidly comes a time, however, when these rules take over: they exceed their original function, and it becomes 'morally right' to adhere to them when their function has been forgotten. The difficulty, as far as moral education is concerned, is that while official aims dictate moral autonomy or post-conventional judgment, everyday interaction requires at best conventional behaviour. If students do not accept the existing norms, attempts are then made to elicit appropriate behaviour through the manipulation of rewards and punishments — at the level of pre-conventional morality.

Take the issue of school uniforms. At a recent P & C meeting, a high school principal argued that the 'best' (i.e. fee-paying private schools) schools have strict uniform rules; therefore a (government) school that did not insist on uniforms would be settling for 'less than the best' for its own students. This argument is sociocentric. Kohlberg's 'good boy' requires that all students dress and comport themselves like good little children. Economic or egalitarian arguments are not as strong in comparison. The *zeal* with which uniform infringements are pursued makes that quite clear. In the celebrated *Woodville Case* in South Australia, the refusal of a student to wear a uniform led to a Royal Commission in 1974. This is only explicable in terms of a conflict of *values:* the rule is to be enforced and violations of the rule must be punished. Not to do so, in the eyes of a sociocentric thinker, is to promote disorder.

The problem is that schools today face a real dilemma. When sociocentric morality was widely accepted, the 'bag of virtues' could become an explicit aim of schooling with few questions asked. Today, however, the aims are for an allocentric morality, but the system that is itself to promote such aims is run on sociocentric lines. The situation is therefore inherently unstable and teachers find themselves in an unenviable position. It is very difficult to have a sociocentric set of rules for some, and (as it appears to the sociocentrics) different rules for others.

In the event, it appears that Peters' (1963) recommendations will be followed: habit and tradition will mould the behaviours of children and keep them manageable.

The lesson of this chapter, however, is that this should be done explicitly and openly, using social learning as a means of behavioural control rather than attempting to inculcate obedience and conformity for their own sake.

SUMMARY

The implicit curriculum. Four methods of transmitting the hidden curriculum were identified:

1. the second set of three Rs — school rules, routines and regulations;
2. biased textbooks which could convey racist and sexist teachings through such diverse methods as choice of examples or use of pronouns and central characters;
3. teacher expectations: self-fulfilling prophecies which relate to the pupils' self-worth and potential and relay appropriate choice of activities, topics and even school subjects;
4. evaluation: methods which convey the competitive myth: it is not what you do, it is whether you win.

School and community. To handle the diversity students will encounter in a life, schools have a responsibilty to provide multicultural and bicultural (as in Aboriginal education) studies. Both studies enable students from one cultural background to experience another; both enable reciprocal interaction between the cultures and their representatives. Movement between school and community has to be two way, with pupils going out into the community for educational experiences, and members of the community bringing expertise and experience into the classroom.

Using social processes in the classroom. Group situations enable interactions between participants, leading to the refinement of social skills through experience which has been carefully structured and monitored. Skills in communication, problem-solving, decision-making, leadership and team-building lead to important conclusions about the relative importance of aspects such as collaboration and trust. Structured interactions require a different teacher role: acting as a catalyst for pupil realisation of social insight.

Moral education was approached through content (teaching the answers) and process (how to get the answers). Programs in moral education have been derived from Kohlberg's theory, presenting moral dilemmas for discussion and a confrontation of beliefs and values. Research suggests that such techniques may be more effective with older students in tertiary institutions. Other programs such as role-playing and value clarification are more flexible.

Moral education across the curriculum. Moral education pervades the whole school environment, but it is difficult to administer a complex organisation such as a school without rules, routines and regulations — and that brings the dreaded three Rs. If habit and tradition are to mould the behaviour of pupils then the moulding should be explicit, using social learning as a means of behavioural control. Acculturation is a major intention of formal education, yet many of the means by which schools socialise students are indirect. For the teacher, the essential point is whether the acculturation that occurs is the one which was intended.

FURTHER READING

On multicultural education

V. J. Callan, *Australian Minority Groups,* Harcourt Brace Jovanovich, Sydney, 1986.
M. E. Poole, P. R. DeLacey, and B. S. Randhawa, *Australia in Transition — Culture and Life Possibilties,* Harcourt Brace Jovanovich, Sydney, 1985.

Callan argues cogently that being a minority is more than mere mathematics: it involves matters such as power, status, discrimination and exploitation. These aspects and the personal and group strategies available to redress the imbalance are discussed with reference to the Australian Aborigines; the migrant presence; the aged and the ethnic aged; women and homosexuals. Poole et al. is an enquiry into the issues and processes affecting the 100 plus ethnic groups in Australia. The four sections encompass the changing pattern of Australian society, plotting the shift from monoculturalism to pluralism; the issues of life chances; sociocultural adaptation and conflict; family, social and cultural environments; and major social questions of participation and equity in the maintenance of cultures and the emergence of a national culture. The essential theme is one of commonality as well as diversity.

On cognitive-development theory

Ḥ. Ginsburg and S. Opper, *Piaget's Theory of Intellectual Development,* Prentice-Hall, Englewood Cliffs, NJ, 1979, Chapter 3.
D. Graham, *Moral Learning and Development,* Angus & Robertson, Sydney, 1972.

Ginsburg and Opper's book is an easy-to-read summary of Piaget's theory of moral development. Graham provides a good summary of the whole field, including Kohlberg, Piaget and social-learning theory.

L. Kohlberg, 'The Child as Moral Philosopher', in *Readings in Psychology Today,* CRM books, Del Mar, Calif., 1969.
L. Kohlberg and E. Turiel, 'Moral Development and Moral Education', in G. S. Lesser (ed.), *Psychology and Educational Practice,* Scott, Foresman, Glenview, Ill., 1971.

The first is a straightforward account of his system by Kohlberg. The second particularly examines the relevance of Kohlberg's theory to education.

On social learning

E. Aronson, *The Social Animal,* W. H. Freeman, San Francisco, 1980.
H. Kaufman, *Aggression and Altruism,* Holt, Rinehart & Winston, New York, 1970.

H. J. Watson, J. M. Vallee, and W. M. Mulford, *Structured Experiences and Group Development,* Curriculum Development Centre, Canberra, 1981.

Aronson is an excellent, up-to-date and easy-to-read account of much of the social psychology relevant to such topics as obedience, conformity, self-justification, prejudice — and many other topics relevant to the present concerns. (Definitely for the social psychological view: Kohlberg and Piaget do not even rate a mention in the index.) Kaufman provides a good, if rather dated, summary of biological and social-psychological theories of aggression and altruism; comes down on the side of psychology. Watson et al. is a very useful compendium of tested structured experiences and activities relating to the processes of small groups. Three chapters aid the teacher in understanding group dynamics and how they can be used in the classroom for educational purposes, then 45 activities are presented in detail and arranged in order of stages of group development.

On the biological foundations
R. Ardrey, *The Hunting Hypothesis,* Atheneum Press, New York, 1976.
D. Morris, *The Human Zoo,* Jonathan Cape, London, 1969.
L. Tiger and R. Fox, *Man: The Imperial Animal,* Granada, London, 1974.

Perhaps not very relevant to education, but Ardrey's book is a brilliant account of social evolution: what we were, what we are now, and some of the sociobiological reasons for the change. Morris gives a challenging account of a zoologist's view of the human condition. 'Tiger' and 'Fox': the authors' names are not a spoof: the book is in fact another superbly written, marginally relevant brain-teaser.

On humanist psychology and education
W. Glasser, *Schools Without Failure,* Harper & Row, New York, 1969.
C. R. Rogers, *Freedom to Learn,* Merrill, Columbus, Ohio, 1969.

These are the best of many books in this area, describing how a whole approach to education can address feelings and moral/personal growth for students.

On moral education programs
L. Brady, *Feel Value Act: Learning about Values, Theory and Practice,* Prentice-Hall of Australia, Sydney, 1979.
D. A. Read and S. B. Simon (eds), *Humanistic Education Sourcebook,* Prentice-Hall, Englewood Cliffs, NJ, 1975.

For the practising teacher, Brady is superb. The examples are attractively laid out, their range is wide, and the theory is excellent. Read and Simon is a practical approach to moral education, which covers a wide field. Any issues of the *Journal of Moral Education* will contain relevant articles.

On teachers and social issues.
G. W. Bassett, P. Cullen and L. Logan, *Australian Primary Schools and their Principals,* Harcourt Brace Jovanovich, Sydney, 1984.

There are 20 case studies contributed by primary school principals to complement the basic approach outlined by the authors — that a school philosophy links to school programs through the organisation. The school is seen as an educative community in which participants (including parents) work co-operatively.

On hidden curriculum

Towards Non-Sexist Education — Curriculum Ideas, NSW Department of Education, Directorate of
Special Programs, 1985.

J. Whyte, R. Deem, L. Kant and M. Cruickshank (eds), *Girl Friendly Schooling,* Methuen, London,
1985.

The Directorate of Special Programs series deals with subjects such as English, industrial arts,
music and the visual arts. Developed by groups of teachers, the booklets provide sample units of
study, resources, lesson ideas, insights into body language and non-verbal communication in the
classroom, and teaching strategies. Whyte et al. ask 'What makes schooling unfriendly to
girls?', and in seeking a solution examine aspects such as the impact of the new vocationalism on
girls' educational opportunities and teacher attitudes about equal opportunities. Three kinds of
intervention are described: reversing educational processes which usually filter girls out; work
with teachers; and initiatives by regional education authorities. Implications for changes in
schooling and curriculum are discussed.

QUESTIONS

Questions for self-testing

1. What are two processes involved in acculturation?
2. How did Piaget define morality?
3. Why can behaviour in the sensori-motor mode be termed amoral?
4. How does concrete-symbolic morality differ from ikonic morality?
5. What is allocentric thought?
6. How does Kohlberg's version of a developmental approach to moral reasoning
   differ from Piaget's?
7. List the two stages in each of the following:
   - pre-conventional morality;
   - conventional morality;
   - post-conventional morality.
8. Describe the mosaic concept of acculturation.
9. Identify Selman's six basic issues in friendship.
10. Give four conclusions Davies reached about the culture of childhood.
11. Explain the application of reciprocity to teacher–pupil interaction in the
    classroom.
12. Describe an experiment which shows a person's susceptibility to:
    - conformity;
    - obedience.
13. What two basic feelings underlie social interaction?
14. Would a humanist psychologist follow Theory X or Theory Y?
15. What are the three Rs of the hidden curriculum?
16. List four methods which contribute to the transmission of the hidden curriculum.

17. Describe how teacher expectations can convey covert messages to pupils.
18. What erroneous interpretations could be placed by pupils on evaluation practices in schools?
19. What are the advantages of a Saturday school for ethnic minorities?

Questions for discussion

1. How are children socialised into traditional sex roles or attitudes towards other races? List the agencies which contribute to the process, and the ways in which they are influential, then indicate the extent to which schools can remedy the situation.
2. Do habit and tradition promote or stultify moral growth?
3. Use the non-sexist checklist provided (Box 7.13) to assess your approach to teaching, then compare your responses with those of a teacher of the opposite sex.
4. To what extent is acculturation a taming of the individual?
5. What use can the teacher make of peer groups in the classroom? Make a list and rank the uses in order of importance.
6. One characteristic of a profession is that it is altruistic. Is teaching altruistic? Argue your case.

BOX 7.13   NON-SEXIST TEACHING CHECKLIST

- Do you expect girls to do well in spelling, reading, language, arts and boys to excel in science, mechanical skills and mathematics?
- Do you ever use sex as a basis for separating students (organise boys against girls in academic or physical competition, lining up boys and girls separately)?
- Do you discuss sex typing with your students — its causes and possible effect?
- When students do classroom chores do you expect boys to run film projectors and move books and girls to keep records (or tidy, clean, wash and sweep)?
- When report cards are processed do girls usually receive higher scores? Is it true academic achievement or is it reward for more submissive and controllable behaviour (i.e. neatness in handwriting)?
- Do you expect girls to become teachers, nurses and secretaries and boys to have a wide range of occupations?
- When did you last tell a girl she was good because she was quiet?
- Do you usually analyse material to see if female characters are represented in a non-stereotyped manner?
- Have you told a boy 'Big boys don't cry'?
- Do you give more attention to boys, both disciplining and talking to them more?
- Do you tend to ignore the group of quiet, 'good' students in your classroom?

- Do you stop one sex from making demeaning comments about the other such as 'I don't want to read any dumb girl's book'?
- Would you rather have a male than a female principal?
- If your school has a segregated sports program, are more money and facilities allotted to boys (i.e. how many coaches, teams, equipment, referees and buses for trips)?
- Are boys more severely disciplined than girls for equal misdemeanours?
- Does your school allow pregnant teenage women to attend class if they wish?
- Do you have separate staffrooms for men and women?

Source: NSW Teachers Federation, 1979, p. 6.

8

Classroom management

OVERVIEW

Some teachers have an easy and effective manner with their students and seem to enjoy their teaching, while others fight to control the classroom. Teachers using extremely different management styles — one retaining full authority and directing the instruction step by step, the other allowing students to decide both lesson content and the approach they would prefer — appear to be equally effective. How can this be? Does it mean that classroom management consists of a wide range of approaches? If so, how does a teacher remain consistent in management decisions or know which reward or punishment is going to be effective? These, and the further questions listed below, are addressed in this chapter.

- Why does classroom control remain a major teaching problem both in Australia and overseas?
- How do societal factors influence the role of a teacher in the classroom?
- How is the selection and appointment of Australian principals changing?
- What enables one person, say, a teacher, to influence another, such as a pupil?
- What sorts of management decisions are needed to control a class?
- What is the difference between a teacher's intention and a pupil's interpretation of a management decision?
- If corporal punishment is no longer an option for the teacher, what alternatives are there?
- How does one set up a behaviour modification program in the classroom?

When you have finished this chapter, you should be able to do the following:

1. Distinguish between high and low structure classroom management decisions.
2. Provide a statement of personal classroom management objectives and a description of intended management style.
3. Influence pupils by means of informal methods.
4. Differentiate pupil discipline and control from classroom management.
5. Describe the classroom characteristics which make it such a complex environment for management decisions.
6. Provide a systematic sequence of activities for linking lessons.
7. Use 'direct teaching' methods.
8. Make effective use of groups in the classroom.
9. Practise overlapping, momentum, smoothness, 'withitness', the 'ripple effect' and routines in the classroom.
10. Resolve classroom conflict so that there is no loser.
11. Identify authentic student–teacher communication.
12. Set and maintain limits on pupil behaviour with questions, messages and demands.
13. Use the 'broken-record' and 'what are you doing?' management techniques.
14. Set up a formal behaviour modification program.
15. Provide at least five groups of alternatives to corporal punishment.
16. Use a checklist to ascertain preparation for classroom management.

SECTION A

THE PROBLEM OF CLASSROOM MANAGEMENT

'How on earth can I keep a full class of kids in order until the lunch bell? They'll be all over me!' This question dominates the thinking of most beginning (and some experienced) teachers. Teachers worry more about the problem of general class control than about actual teaching techniques, dealing with the occasional but very difficult student, dealing with irate parents or about assessment. That has been found repeatedly in international studies (Veenman, 1984) and in Australia (Telfer, 1979a, 1981).

The good old days

In the old days, the answer to the question was comparatively simple. Teaching was essentially a matter of providing content to be learned, using expository methods. The teacher knew the material to be taught and the pupils sat at their desks, listening and learning: very much a quantitative conception of learning. There was a two-part teaching task: keep them quiet and provide the instruction. The first part, keeping them quiet, was society's expectation, so society accordingly endorsed the teacher's use of strong measures in doing so: until very recently, for example, corporal punishment was officially sanctioned as a disciplinary option. School policies and procedures were designed to assist the teacher in maintaining order (with quietness as the criterion of success).

And today

That is no longer so. Since the seventies the task of teaching has become vastly more complicated, with expository methods only one of the wide range of techniques a teacher must master. Some demands placed on the teacher today require very high student activity, perhaps outside the classroom. For example, one geography lesson may require pupils to collect samples of vegetation. The next lesson may then be a formal one on the formation of rain, in which the pupils are required to sit quietly, as in the old days. The difference is that now the teacher has less authoritative support to enforce quietness. To maintain student interest and participation in the lesson, the teacher now is forced to rely more on personal resources, as society no longer endorses harsh methods of control. For example, a complex network of anti-discrimination laws makes harsh methods unworkable even if a teacher did try to use them. We are *not* saying that society should not have these laws, but the fact that (rightly or wrongly) they exist places a considerable strain on teachers, particularly on senior teachers who gained their experience in a different system.

To argue that the new and difficult times are due to a breakdown in discipline is to miss the point entirely. The problem is one of *management*, not of discipline. Today's teacher looks not to remedy disciplinary problems once they have occurred, but to manage events so that problems are less likely to arise in the first place. Order through obedience has been replaced by planning, management, routines and activities — by professionalism.

A teacher could once command respect by virtue of formal status and authority. Today's teacher has to earn it. Yesterday's teachers had only to know their subject and to be recognised as one who was not an easy mark. Today they have not only to know their subject, but to be able to use a range of management skills far beyond the Victorian simplicity of just being strict.

It is symptomatic of this change that the mid-eighties debate on corporal punishment in New South Wales shifted the perspective from 'punishment' to 'pastoral care'. It became a matter of 'individual development in the context of society' rather than one of teacher authority to demand obedience. Some teachers must feel disappointed with this societal switch: their job has been made tougher and, what is worse, their power to do that job has been undermined in what they would see as a vote of no-confidence. That is an unfortunate and demoralising view to adopt: and it is mistaken.

Schools, too, belong in the context of society, but today they are required by society to do a different job — not a 'tougher' job, just a *different* one. Some teachers may not have seen the implications of that, as they may still be operating with school policies that (for all sorts of reasons) are geared to the earlier roles expected of teachers. In other words, society has changed, and schools have not yet changed sufficiently. Meantime, individual teachers have a very complex task to fulfil.

Management and instruction

We should distinguish between *instructional and management issues*. We are not concerned here with the whole gamut of curriculum, teaching methods and evaluation. Our focus is on the sorts of decisions a teacher must make to be a successful manager of instruction in the here-and-now of the classroom. These decisions fall between two extremes:

1. *high-structure* decisions, which emphasise the teacher's role in setting up the learning environment, and which allow relatively few options and hence require a reactive role from the students;
2. *low-structure* decisions, which provide the pupil with many options and maximum autonomy when in the learning experience (which is not to say that the teacher does not have to work very hard to provide a low-structure environment).

In this chapter, we look at the changes in society affecting this question of classroom management. Then come options from which teachers may choose to manage classroom learning more effectively. We review material from earlier chapters, helping us to define the pupil's needs and the kinds of learning required. We then look at what teachers need to form a policy about: setting up routines, rules, interacting with students and rewarding or punishing pupil behaviour. There are some philosophical and value judgments to be made, so teachers need to be clear where they stand.

Today's classroom control is not just a matter of keeping order: it is more a matter of being an efficient manager of learning. For such a manager, 'discipline' looks after itself (see Box 8.1).

THE SCHOOL IN THE CONTEXT OF SOCIETY

The management of education in the late nineteenth century in Australia had to be cost efficient. An economic depression in the last decade of that century meant small budgets for education; it was a logical extension of those constraints that learning was seen in a quantitative way. The thinking behind the factory methods characteristic of the industrial revolution — large-scale production with minimal unit costs — was the same for the design of public instruction: large numbers of pupils per unit teacher. This

---

BOX 8.1   SHEILA: A TEACHER WHO ADAPTED

The school is not exceptionally rough, but it has problems of control. The kids walked all over her. In retrospect she is critical of her teacher training. It gave her lots of ideas for lessons, 'but I was never prepared for the discipline, at all. I think it was unreal'. Facing the classic shock of the idealistic young teacher dumped into her first classroom, she reacted in a classic way. She came down hard on the kids. She called in support from the school hierarchy, and insisted on silence and order. After a few months she got it.

But she soon came to see this as the wrong solution. She had control, all right; but the kids still were not learning anything. 'Learning doesn't necessarily happen in a dead quiet classroom with everyone jumping when you say "jump"'. So she began to put her main effort into building personal relationships with the kids in which they *would* become involved.

This has led in two directions. On the one hand it has produced lively, informal classes with a great deal of student participation. Most of the kids love it. Sheila has gone far beyond the conventional devices of debates and projects. She has adapted encounter-group techniques, and uses them as 'self-exploration' exercises in the classroom. She uses workshops, self-directed group projects, and free-floating discussions in which she is an active particpant but not the source of all wisdom. And this energy is by no means confined to the classroom. She is also involved with the school magazine and the drama program, she supervises debating, organises the school dance, goes on vacation camps with the kids.

Source: Connell, 1985, p. 14.

combination was made workable by the emphasis on moral values inculcated by explicit religious teaching and by the expectation of many and complicated rules and regulations (see Chapter 7). These rules applied to teachers, too, whose dress was a suit, collar and tie — and academic gown, no less. Teachers' tasks, as also discussed in Chapter 7, were to inculcate moral principles, truth, justice and patriotism — and to teach a proper disdain for 'idleness, profanity and falsehood' (New South Wales Public Instruction Act 1886).

Our present system of public schooling in Australia has obviously changed since those days, both with respect to class size (60 pupils per class was common at the turn of the century) and on the question of inculcating values (even if it has gone underground rather than disappeared). In other respects, however, today's schools are obvious descendants of last century's system: the remaining emphasis on formality, hierarchy, submission to authority, and the still predominant emphasis on expository methods.

The point is that schools are total institutions in the extent to which they maintain these trappings of Theory X. Schools are not philosophically in step with society as they were once. They will probably regain step (in so far as any one system can do so in a highly diversified society such as ours), and in some important matters they have moved far in the last few years (see Box 8.2). Between the first and second editions of this book, for instance, corporal punishment has been abolished in nearly all State systems (it was abolished in Polish schools in the eighteenth century, and in the British Navy in the nineteenth). What then are some of the mismatches between school and society, and how do they affect the issue of classroom management?

BOX 8.2   AND IT TOOK 15 YEARS ...

The manner in which the school deals with disorder among students, whether of a relatively trivial or serious nature, will no doubt to some extent reflect attitudes prevailing in society. It is debatable at this stage, however, whether the secondary schools are reflecting society to the extent necessary if students are to be adequately prepared for their adult roles. To what extent should the school adopt the disciplinary measures practised in society at large? ... educators may need to examine their methods and motives to determine whether the school has built up a structure of relationships and sanctions which appear artificial and negative alongside both the ideals of the school itself and the actual outside world (p. 14).

Caning should become, over a period of years, an obsolete and generally disapproved means of handling troublesome classroom situations ...

... Teachers should do all in their power to develop a sense of responsibility among students. Responsibility cannot be learnt in a climate of distrust where student behaviour is regulated by fear of punishment. Self discipline is most likely to be acquired where students are given practice in making decisions about their school life, even if occasionally they are the wrong decisions (p. 160).

Source: Dettman, 1972, p. 160.

Personal autonomy

Changes in society over the past 20 or 30 years centre around what can best be called *personal autonomy*. By this is meant a rejection of paternalism and of the formalities that emphasise status, and a movement towards self-determination. It is a shift from Theory X towards Theory Y.

In society at large, this movement can be seen in a whole host of specific issues, any one of which would have been unthinkable 30 years ago, but which only a minority would regard as unthinkable today. For example, imagine how a person waking up today after taking a long sleep in 1956 would react to: topless (even nude) bathing on public beaches; displays of homosexual affection in public; rights for ethnic minorities; having dinner in a quality restaurant without a coat and tie; a single woman obtaining a mortgage; the power of affected minority groups to influence governmental decisions; and the whole notion of community involvement. We are not saying these things are good or bad but the changes would certainly be extremely surprising. There has been an extension of the rights of individuals to be different and to determine their own destinies, far beyond the point that was earlier tolerated.

Within schools, this change has not been nearly so rapid. It has, however, in *official* positions taken on school. In 1973, the Karmel Committee commented '... In a changing world the special functions of the schools extend beyond the traditional ones to acknowledge the importance of confident self-initiated learning and of creative response'. (Report of the Interim Committee for the Australian Schools Commission, May 1973, p. 14.) This view is now reflected in the policy statements of all State Education Departments as in the one from New South Wales we keep quoting: 'moral autonomy and responsible self-direction'. It is reflected, too, in policies of school-based curriculum development and school-based assessment, and encouragement of (if little action towards) community involvement in schools. Actual within-school policy, however, has often to catch up with official positions.

Changes within the school. It has been traditional over many years for promotion to senior positions in schools to be mainly based on seniority. This meant that in large high schools, a principal on appointment would be well into his (it usually was a 'he') fifties. When society's values were fairly static, the policy determined by these individuals would not be too remote from that of his staff's own views. And when, as in the seventies, society was changing very fast, teachers who did not like the existing policies left — at an extremely high rate, so that five years after entering the profession only a relatively small proportion remained in service (Barcan, 1976). As a result, schools in the seventies were quite out of step with society in some respects: as indicated by the stand taken by many school principals on the issue of long hair. In short, the policy-makers in schools tended to be both older and more conservative than was the case in society at large.

Today that is changing. First, the exit has closed: those entering the teaching profession now do not so easily have the choice of leaving and making another career, so that any selective retention in terms of conservative social philosophy that may once have existed does so no longer. The value balance between school staff and community is slowly being redressed (see Box 8.3).

BOX 8.3   SCHOOL IN THE CONTEXT OF SOCIETY

A 15-year-old Sydney schoolgirl began a battle yesterday against the State's education system which could have national implications in high schools.

Melinda, a student at Canterbury Girls High School, says the Education Department is discriminating against her because she cannot choose as many subjects as her twin brother, who attends Canterbury Boys High School.

Her case opened at a preliminary hearing yesterday before the Equal Opportunity Tribunal in Sydney.

Melinda's solicitor said she knew that the legal process was slow and that she might not benefit from the outcome if she won. He said it was a test case which could have implications for schools throughout Australia.

Melinda, who has three more years in high school, said she could take only those subjects regarded as traditionally female, for example needlework and cooking.

But her brother could choose to study computer studies, graphics and technics.

A spokesman for the New South Wales Education Department said Melinda had been offered a transfer to another school but had refused.

Students could take electives according to resources available at individual schools, he said.

Source: *Newcastle Herald*, 25 January 1986.

A key person in setting the tone of a school is the principal. Chapman (1984) analysed the methods of selection and appointment of principals to government schools in all Australian States. He showed that while many features of the traditional system continue to exist, change is imminent. The traditional and still common features are:

- principals are appointed from teachers already employed in the system;
- they have been previously assessed to determine suitability for promotion to such a school;
- processing and selection of applications is a head office procedure;
- ratings of seniority and/or efficiency are the major criteria.

In the more recently established systems in the Australian Capital Territory and Northern Territory, however, the pattern is to meet modern management criteria: to attempt to match candidates with needs of particular positions. Signs of change are evident in South Australia and Western Australia where alternative routes to the principalship are available through special appointments and open advertisement. Victoria epitomises the transition from a centralised system to local participation on the School Council which conducts interviews and makes a short list.

Incentives. If changing attitudes towards personal autonomy have given teachers and administrators a hard time in adjustment, society has also been very hard on the question of incentives.

In times past, students, parents and employers recognised public examinations and their associated award (Intermediate Certificate, etc.) as passports to employment. There was the promise, too, of upward social mobility and an opportunity that one's parents had not enjoyed. A changed economy has destroyed the promise and the motivation. The teacher can no longer boast, 'I have my Higher School Certificate; you have yet to get yours', and expect that that would dramatically emphasise the importance of assiduous study and the resulting piece of paper.

Not many years ago, an able student could simply decide what profession to enter, then proceed to study with that end in view, and be realistically optimistic about the likelihood of getting there. Such optimism does not exist today. The HSC is not the guarantee of employment that it once was. On the other hand, the less able student has to be prepared to accept whatever job is going, or to go on the dole. Consequently, many more students are staying on after Year 10 than used to be the case, but they are not motivated academically. With the alternative being unemployment, in our classrooms are some students who have little incentive to undertake prescribed learning activities.

Nature of learning. The press for 'responsible self-direction' results in teachers having to help students to take responsibility for their own learning. Such teaching is usually group or individually based, requiring specialist techniques quite different from those of the traditional classroom. In fact, all of the aspects of teaching raised in Chapter 4, such as think-aloud modelling, heuristics and reflective teaching, require teachers to share their thoughts for genuine consideration and reflection by the students: all need to be sincere and authentic. The nature of learning in today's classroom calls for teachers who are both open and non-authoritarian.

The transmission of content prescribed by a syllabus nevertheless remains a major responsibility for the classroom teacher. Expository teaching now takes place, however, without the traditional back-up of teacher authority and the piece-of-paper syndrome. Instead, the teacher relies on a unique combination of education, development as a teacher and individual strengths and interests.

As for tomorrow's classrooms, we saw in Chapter 5 that schools in the future are likely to become more and more like other societal structures; that the notion of continuing education and use of adult modes of learning will make the learning that takes place in school more like the learning that takes place out of school. And in that event, the management of learning will resemble the management of anything else. Although we have not reached that point yet, it is clear that *management* is the central issue.

Authority of the teacher. The major issue underlying all issues of classroom management is teacher *authority* as a basis for controlling pupils. The key question for today's teachers is: 'If my authority as a teacher is weakened, or even removed, how can I influence my pupils so that they will do as I ask?'

Five bases of influence have been identified (French and Raven, 1959).

1. legitimate power (the perceived right of a person to be influential);

2. reward power (the extent to which a person is seen as having an ability to provide rewards);
3. coercive power (the extent to which a person is seen to be able to punish others);
4. expert power (the extent of knowledge and skills a person seems to have);
5. referential power (the extent to which others identify with a person).

Of these, the last two provide the most effective bases for influence and are means for a teacher to cope with the changed societal context for classroom management. At a time when a teacher's legal, reward and coercive basis for influence is diminishing, increasing importance is given to the expert and referential bases.

Reliance on being an expert and modelling espoused values, such as a belief in education and a love of learning, gives the teacher validity and authenticity. It also forces the teacher to make use of personal and professional resources, not in the sense of being a martinet, but more in the ability to defuse situations through the use of humour, knowledge of subject, compromise and discussion. The sustained need to come up with a quick solution to an impending conflict can create the stress which causes the burn-out we discussed in Chapter 2.

TOWARDS A MODEL OF CLASSROOM MANAGEMENT

In this book we have continually emphasised the development of student self-awareness and responsibility. In this chapter, we have looked at the relationship between school and society and have seen that there are some mismatches, but that we are heading towards a new equilibrium.

All this underlines our point that teachers need to derive *workable models of management* in order to cope with this complex situation. We cannot provide teachers with a finished set of prescriptions: each individual must derive a personal model through reflection on decisions about teaching. We can, however, help make that process of metateaching easier by drawing out some of the dimensions on which management decisions have to be made.

The notion of classroom management that we are putting forward here differs from traditional notions of 'good discipline' in one major aspect. Whereas discipline is aimed at preventing misbehaviour and at dealing with it when it does occur, management pervades *all* aspects of teaching. We may distinguish four major areas of management decisions:

- planning before entering the classroom;
- setting up operational procedures for running the classroom;
- teacher–pupil interaction;
- establishing a policy on rewards and punishments.

We can opt for high or low structure decisions on any aspect of any of these areas (see Figure 8.1). High-structure decisions restrict student options; low-structure decisions throw the responsibility onto students to make their own decisions. There is a continuum from high to low structure and teachers must make their decisions somewhere along that continuum to best suit their own aims and values, the students they are teaching and the nature of the learning experience. It is, however, important that teachers' choices made along this continuum are compatible both with their philosophies and with how they feel they can operate. Some teachers would be quite uncomfortable operating in a style that depended on a high degree of student self-direction; others operate very well in a low-structure environment. Of course, decisions must also be compatible with school policy in general; and perhaps most important of all, these decisions have to be compatible with each other. To make low-structure decisions on some aspects of a lesson, and high-structure decisions on others, will lead to contradictions and to the likelihood that neither set of decisions will work.

Figure 8.1   Structure in pupil management decisions

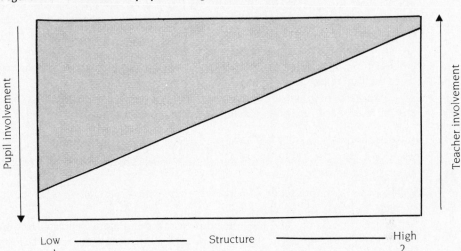

1. *Teacher*:   There are several topics we can cover next, and we should now decide which will be done, and how we are going to do it ...
2. *Teacher*:   I have decided on our next topic — explorers and exploration. I want you to make notes from the following references, and have a 1,000–word essay handed in by lunchtime Friday ...

Function and impact

A problem in teacher education about such methods is that we all have attended school, and we all have experienced teaching. Even before experiencing any teacher education we may have reached conclusions about what seems to work best. Our personal experiences with schools and teachers remains quite an influence when we start to teach, especially in times of crisis when we grasp for a solution. Regardless of the sophistication and relevance of the teacher education program, memories of earlier days compete with research evidence on effective practice. The effect can be minimised, however, by reviewing the teacher's job of classroom management in the light of our own experience in the classroom as a pupil.

Let us consider the two essential components in any classroom management decision by the teacher: *function* and *impact*. High-structure decisions are more likely (but not necessarily) to have a negative impact than low-structure. Let us say the class has been divided into groups, each working on a sub-topic of the Australian gold rush (such as the economic, demographic and political consequences). For a number of reasons, some of the groups have not worked on their tasks as well as others, and as lunchtime draws near it is obvious that two groups will not be finished.

Because the next lesson and your completion of the term's program depends on the work, you announce that the two groups will need to return in the second half of lunchtime to complete their tasks.

The functional aspect of this decision is clear: the groups had adequate time and opportunity to complete the work during lesson time; they chose not to; they should therefore complete the work in their own time. But what was the actual impact of this decision on the two groups detained? What if they consisted mainly of girls or of Greeks? What if their topics were seen to be more difficult than the others' or if they had fewer resources? The impact of management decisions is frequently quite different from the functional intention.

Being aware of the options helps teachers to avoid the more ambiguous decisions, but one really needs to evaluate them by asking the sorts of questions raised in Chapter 4:

- What is the functional aim of this decision? What am I trying to do?
- What sort of pressure will this put on the pupils? Are those pressures reasonable and realistic?
- How are the pupils likely to perceive it? As game-playing — and an invitation for them to join in on the other side?
- On the other hand, can I take the consequences of a pupil-centred decision, such as criticism for an apparent abdication of leadership; am I prepared to follow through on whatever the pupils decide?

Management decisions

Consistency in the choice of structure in management decisions can come from following a clear personal philosophy of teaching, but this is an abstract influence which the beginning teacher may lack, especially under the pressures of classroom unpredictability, complexity and immediacy. A simple and systematic solution is to use a framework of classroom activities and the surroundings in which they occur. There are four groups of instructional decisions which need to be made:

1. *Pre-instructional decisions.* These are the *planning* decisions before the lesson; details of resources, aids, materials and equipment needed; analysis of pupil needs and

determination of objectives; sequencing activities; and ensuring familiarity with the teaching techniques to be used (see Tyler, 1950; Taba, 1962; Popham, 1970).

 2.   *Setting up operational structures.* What are the ground rules for your classroom? Who decides: you, the pupils, or you and the pupils together? How do you go about that?

 3.   *Pupil-teacher interaction.* What underlies effective and efficient communication? Are you going to be assertive or empathetic? Do you know how to be either?

 4.   *Rewarding and punishing.* Should you always reward desirable behaviour? What are effective ways of punishing pupils? Should you punish pupils at all?

The range of options: Low to high structure

For each management decision, then, the possibilities fall within two extremes: the highly structured decision emanating from the teacher; and the low structure which effectively places students in a situation where they initiate their own decision. Teacher-centred methods emphasise the need for effectiveness when a teacher interacts with pupils (Gordon, 1974a), the use of classroom routines (Yinger, 1979) and methods which are presented with prescriptive detail and sequence (Berliner, 1980). In contrast, low-structure management focuses on the motivation and personal growth of the individual (Gnagey, 1975), authenticity in interactions between teachers and pupils (Berne, 1964; Lett, 1971), and clear communication (Ginott, 1971).

 Teachers managing by high or low structure need to maintain the same degree of structure over the full teaching episode — that is, through the planning and implementation stages. Management decisions thus need to be consistent in degree of structure. Confusion is sure to result if a low-structure plan is introduced (such as permitting students to make their own decision about topic and source for a project) but the operational procedures are high structure, so that student access to sources such as the library are reduced, or the time scale does not allow students the time they need to operate on their own. Fortunately, there is a range of management models of varying structure applicable to teaching episodes. These models are the focus of Section B.

 Essentially, then, each management decision has a bias towards high structure (because it comes from the teacher) or low structure (because it comes from the pupil) (see Figure 8.1). That does not mean that the teacher dominates high-structure decisions or pupils have a monopoly over all activities associated with a low-structure decision. Often, in order for pupils to have the opportunity to successfully make and implement their own decision about learning, an extraordinary amount of teacher preparation is necessary: ensuring that facilities and resources are available, monitoring the stage of decision attained by pupils and co-ordinating classroom activities.

 The basis for all management is to *know what you propose to do and to organise in advance.* This is especially important in teaching for two reasons. First, nothing is more conducive to pupil misbehaviour than gaps in the execution of a lesson because of shoddy planning. Second, the classroom is a complex environment at the best of times because it is *multidimensional* (with numerous pupil–pupil and pupil–class interactions as well as the teacher–class and teacher–pupil interactions). There is a degree of *unpredictability* to the classroom, giving an *immediacy* to teacher decisions which cannot be deliberated but are required on the spot. A final complication is the fact that events and their players have a *history* from precedents and backgrounds that colour classroom events (Yinger, 1979).

For the sake of this argument, assume that the pupil activity in your classroom is a constant. The pupils will not sit there and do nothing unless severe coercion is used. If, however, pupil activity can be aligned with the learning task, leading towards your objectives for the lesson, your job is done. In simple terms, the teacher ensures that what pupils do is relevant to the lesson by ensuring that appropriate activities are available. If the structured learning activities are not available, the pupils' efforts will be expended on something else, which is unwanted and almost certainly disruptive.

The teacher–student collaborative network: Negotiating the contract

The impression might have been given so far that classroom management involves a top-down managerial style, with the teacher making all the decisions, coolly and in advance. This is not the case: even the most unilateral business deals require the co-opera-tion of the customers. The students in the classroom are in effect the other negotiating party to the contract offered by the teacher–manager. Teachers and pupils *co-operatively construct* the-order-that-is-to-be (or not-to-be) in the classroom (Davies, 1983).

Consider what happens when that co-operation is withdrawn. Wax (1971) observed such a scene, with the comment 'never in my most anxiety-ridden professional nightmares had I imagined that a school room could be like this one' (p. 253). The students were not violent, or even aggressive in the slightest way, towards their teacher (Mrs Walker). They did more than that; they *totally ignored* her. Wax describes how Mrs Walker went on with the lesson, addressing the whole class, writing on the board, issuing materials, calling on individuals ... as if the pupils were attending, writing, responding. Instead, they were walking around the room, not once glancing at her (but as Wax notes 'two boys grin at me knowingly'), children were queuing at the noisy pencil sharpener to maintain a continual background of noise. When relative quiet descends 'it is because the pupils grow tired of their game'.

We saw in Chapter 7 that children attend to two agendas: their own, and to them the more important one; and the teacher's (or other adult, depending on context), in which they are required to participate, and are willing to do so — up to a point. *That point is negotiable*, with each teacher, in each classroom, and for each situation.

Even before the teacher enters the classroom for the first time, some of the basic ground rules are laid for the collaborative network that is to be constructed: these outlines are based on previous experience of both parties and school policy. The details are, however, negotiable between the parties.

The moment the teacher enters the room, the specifics begin to harden. The best word is *presence*, which establishes remarkably quickly the negotiating positions in terms of dominance–submission. The following are some indices of 'presence':

Preparing the students' agenda.

- body language: strides, slinks, struts, slides, sweeps or shuffles into the room;
- eye contacts students (or not) while talking;
- tone of voice: abrasive, humorous, loud, wheedling ...;
- dress: trendy, formal, quiet, gaudy ...;
- substance of what is said: commands, questions, etc.

Figure 8.2 illustrates the main features. The student agenda is set at C, a relatively low level of dominance. Usually, the teacher's agenda is placed at a higher level, at B

Figure 8.2   The teacher–student collaborative network

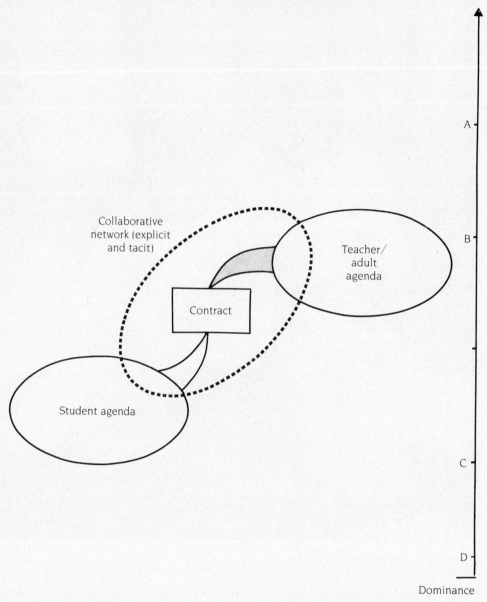

or, in the case of highly assertive teachers, at A. Occasionally, teachers attempt to enter and establish a contract as peers, at C. Very occasionally, the teacher deliberately allows the students to set the terms for negotiation, by coming in at D. Rather more often, a sort of 'gravity' takes over and the teacher slides from B to D, entering in the formally dominant position, but in time becoming functionally the submissive party.

Sometimes the students can take over the teacher's agenda because it is being played so badly. One of the authors supervised a practice teaching student who was a kind of reverse Mrs Walker: *he* ignored the *class*! He stood at the side-front of the class, and lectured solidly in a monotone, totally ignoring the students: no eye contact, no seeking for signs of incomprehension, no variation. Instead of 'absolutely murdering' him (see Box 7.6), however, the class, which consisted of senior girls in a religious school, remained silent, busily taking notes, pretending they understood — especially when the supervisor came into the room. They felt sorry for him and his obvious incompetence, and took him into their 'network of caring' (Gilligan, 1982). (Other classes, however, were not so caring.)

At all events, the teacher is usually the first to state the terms, both overtly and implicitly, at the first encounter, from the position of dominance established then. The students can accept, reject outright (as they did with Mrs Walker), or counter-offer. Or they might test the water to see what is allowable and what the consequences might be. In carrying out this negotiation, it seems helpful if the teacher knows and understands the specific frameworks in the students' agenda (see previous chapter), remembering that once a reciprocal network of agreements has been set up, it is usually in a sociocentric framework that is situation-specific and rigid to its application: one in, all in.

The explicit rules — what is acceptable, what is unacceptable, and what the formal and stated consequences are to be in each case — can be set up fairly quickly. The tacit rules, lurking in the hidden curriculum, need to be discovered over a longer period of time — and as Mr Bell found with the children under the blanket — often with surprise and resentment.

The old schoolie's advice, 'Crack down hard at first, you can always ease up later', is only partly true. In most contexts, it will be true that the teacher should enter at a point higher than C (the students' dominance level). It is also true that 'classroom gravity' will pull downwards not upwards: the teacher's position may settle lower, but it is unlikely to float higher. So one should start at a position higher than that position of dominance finally desired *vis à vis* the class: but not from a position so high that the teacher cannot maintain it authentically, or that will lock both parties into a set of negotiations neither wants.

This collaborative network builds up over a period of time around the initial contract, and is different between each teacher and each class. Management style should ideally, then, fit into the evolving collaborative network, and discipline problems will be worked out within that framework. In only a few weeks of practice teaching, one of our students, a mature age woman, negotiated a contract based essentially on her 'network of caring': mothering the students (junior high school). It worked, although her classes tended to be noisy: the noise of naughty children with a caring mother. Twice, she spoke sharply to a boy who promptly swore back at her, loudly and violently. On the second occasion, his best friend sought her out afterwards and apologised on the boy's behalf; the class were disgusted and expressed their feelings too. The sociocentric network took over and isolated the deviate: he had violated the contract. You can be naughty with mums, but you do not tell them to 'f*** off'.

Classroom climate

We have been speaking of 'negotiations' and 'management decisions' as deliberate, sometimes very complex, but essentially cognitive activities. And so they are; but they do not account for another equally important aspect of a classroom (although they may contribute towards it). That aspect is almost tangible as soon as you walk through the door of any classroom: what it *feels* like. That powerful but often elusive feeling we refer to as the *climate* of the classroom, and like its physical counterpart, it can be referred to as 'warm', 'cold', 'unpredictable' and the like.

Climate in this sense, then, is generated by the 'mental chemistry' of the participants. The initiative is usually set by the teacher, but not always, as in the example of the student teacher in the previous section. A 'warm' climate is characterised by a caring, empathetic relationship between teacher and students, and between student and student; there are strong positive feelings between participants, and they choose aspects of participants that they can value and respect. A 'cold' climate is marked by aggression, negative feelings, criticism and sarcastic exchanges between participants.

High-structure decisions may tend to elicit a cold climate, because they frequently are made on Theory X assumptions: students are basically not to be trusted, so I shall have to make all the major decisions for them and ensure that they are properly enacted. Low-structure decisions, on the other hand, give decision-making over to the students on Theory Y assumptions: students can be trusted to make good decisions. Nevertheless, it is not as simple as this. It is perfectly possible to set up a formal, high-structure classroom in an atmosphere of caring and good will. Equally, a low-structure classroom can be cold and uncaring, as it would be in a completely *laissez-faire* classroom, where a teacher may not care enough to see that the students make any sort of decisions.

The factor that sets the climate of a classroom is the *personality* of the teacher: it is the affective side of professionalism. It is true that some management decisions tend to have a coolish hidden curriculum, but those decisions too spring from the person who made them. All we are saying is that the teacher will necessarily create a climate of feeling in which the management decisions will play their part. The management decisions and climate together make the *total learning environment* in both cognitive and affective aspects.

To summarise all this, then, teachers in arriving at a management policy, are not strictly speaking dictating the terms; they are *offering* terms that are 'negotiable' in a very real sense. If the students can be open and genuine parties to the negotiations so much the better; the sense of ownership will be that much stronger, and the contract more binding. Everyone knows where each stands.

Nevertheless, teachers need to be as metacognitive about this as possible. They should enter into negotiatons knowing very clearly what sort of climate they want, what sort of policy they will settle for which will achieve their own goals, and what sort of dominance they want and can sustain without violating their authenticity as a person. They may then learn what Connell says so eloquently in Box 8.4.

BOX 8.4   WHAT IS THERE LEFT TO SAY?

Teaching depends on being able to control the kids. What seems a simple task is actually an extremely complex set of relationships involving gender, class and age, and working through pedagogy as well as policing. An antagonism is built into the structure of mass schooling; difficulties are compounded by contradictory demands from kids and from parents. Teachers have evolved a range of strategies for handling discipline, which often cut across each other. School-wide strategies are evolved but are impossible to make consistent. The elite private schools put a great deal of energy into maintaining a tighter disciplinary regime; their teachers have to police this, not always willingly. Teaching is an emotionally demanding job. Teachers necessarily work via their emotional relationships to individual pupils and whole classes. Maintaining control implies emotional strategies that form them as teachers and as people. Getting the kids to learn often means an identification with them, a willingness to care about them and commonly to like them. This risks over-involvement. Many teachers therefore restrict their commitment to the kids; some embrace it, while some work out a relationship based on mutual respect but not mutual identification. Teachers of working-class kids are under constant emotional pressure; it is likely that this has increased historically. Teaching can also be an exhilarating and joyful experience, expanding the teacher's life through skills or human relations, or both. Teaching well is a thrill.

Source: Connell, 1985, p. 127.

SUMMARY

School in the context of society. It has been argued that societal changes have forced teachers to manage classrooms, rather than discipline students, and have reduced the formal means at teachers' disposal to implement management in each stage of teaching: planning, procedures, interacting with pupils, establishing policy on rewards and punishments, and creating an appropriate classroom climate. One of the major changes has been a new emphasis on personal autonomy and self-determination and, although schools have lagged behind society in this regard, there are other indications (such as the ways in which principals are appointed) that schools too are moving now in this general direction.

    The possibility of unemployment despite educational qualification has removed one source of pupil incentive. When this is coupled with the weakening of teacher authority, teachers need to operate within a different sphere of influence: one that emphasises a marginal expertise compatible with their own personal style.

Towards a model of classroom management. A suitable model of management adjusts the amount of structure in management decisions and takes into account both the teacher's intention (function) and the pupils' perception (impact) of these decisions. Management decisions need to be made in four main areas — planning prior to instruction, setting up operational rules and procedures, rewarding and punishing, and student–teacher interaction — and it is imperative that teachers derive a management policy to help them to be consistent in all four areas. Once that has been decided in general terms, they have to enter into 'negotiations' with the class: a collaborative network of some kind will evolve, whatever happens, which will have a 'warm' or 'cold' climate of feeling. One should be as sure as possible that the evolving network is both professionally viable and personally compatible with the desired climate. How all this translates into action is considered in Section B.

SECTION B

MODELS OF CLASSROOM MANAGEMENT

In this section, models of management are analysed in terms of their structure so that teacher roles and their consequences are clarified. When teachers plan lessons, establish procedures, question students, or choose rewards and punishments, they make classroom management decisions along a continuum ranging from high to low structure. Table 8.1 shows the way these management decisions are treated, and indicates some of the examples of teachers' high- and low-structure decisions.

The management decisions in Table 8.1 are used as headings for this section, with examples of high and low structure provided for each. The total effect of these decisions for students is the classroom climate, the final topic for discussion before a case study is presented. The section concludes with a checklist for beginning teachers.

Table 8.1   Structure and classroom management decisions

Management decisions	High-structure examples	Low-structure examples
Planning	Direct teaching	Class groups
Classroom operations and procedures	Routines	Participative decision-making and consultation
Questioning	Conveying limits Assertiveness	Authentic communication
Rewarding and punishing	Behaviour modification	Pupil self-discipline

Planning

Structure in planning is difficult to completely isolate because of clear differences between planning in theory and planning in practice. Planning in theory, as presented in teacher education programs, consists of a rational process which moves from pupil needs, to aims, objectives, learning activities and an evaluation of pupil attainment. Studies of teacher planning (see Shavelson and Stern, 1981, for a comprehensive review) show that the *activity*, not the objectives, are the planning unit in classroom practice. That is, teachers in practice plan what to do in order to carry the lesson through, rather than what the students are to learn. In some cases this is because teachers think the lesson through, considering objectives, but do not write this step in their lesson plan (Morine-Dershimer, 1978–79), while in others it would suggest an inappropriately narrow focus on planning. Objectives should guide planning for action.

Regardless of whether a high- or low-structure approach is being taken, instructional planning is an integral part of classroom management, as it enables teachers to consider the potential problems in the lesson sequence and to prepare appropriate responses. An example of the preventative approach working in extremely adverse circumstances is given by Hocking (1984) who describes the Tasmanian case of alienated, disturbed and disruptive students who reject societal values and come from non-nuclear families at or below the poverty level. A planning solution was found through intervening early in primary school years with an alternate curriculum, use of support teachers, parental involvement and stronger disciplinary measures.

Whether planning for high or low structure, it is helpful to establish a planning sequence which may start with reference to a syllabus or teaching program, then a listing of relevant sources and materials, next a list of possible learning activities and experiences, and finally to a decision on the actual lesson plan — what is to be taught and how.

High structure. The type of sequence which would be followed for effective classroom management and teaching with high structure would systematically pick up new learning where the previous learning had finished.

The sequence may go like this:

- following this review with new content or skills and allowing student practice;
- checking pupils' work and understanding, giving feedback, correction or reteaching as required;
- allowing independent student practice;
- providing weekly and monthly reviews (Rosenshine, 1983).

At the same time, high-structure management approaches would be:

- establishing and maintaining clear rules and applying them consistently;
- providing limits for the physical activity of students;
- monitoring student behaviour;

- holding students responsible for their behaviour;
- when students complete their work, directing them to their next activity;
- minimising the delay in transition from one activity to the next;
- acting quickly to deal with misbehaviour when it occurs (Cruickshank, 1985a).

Another high-structure model based heavily on teacher planning has been termed 'direct teaching' because the teacher uses a no-frills approach with the whole class, concentrating on the structure of the lesson and on pupil attainment. Objectives are usually expressed in behavioural terms, then the teacher provides appropriate learning materials and carefully paces the lesson to suit the class (Berliner, 1980). This method has been seen as a reaction to the resource person/helper/facilitator role given teachers in the seventies (see Rogers, 1969) and has demonstrated effectiveness (Rosenshine, 1978; Morison, 1979). To manage a class by direct teaching methods, a teacher emphasises the task or activity by preparing worksheets or problems based on textbooks. The extent of pupil engagement on these tasks is a criterion of the effectiveness of the method. Questions are designed to give a high proportion of correct pupil responses and the teacher provides immediate feedback.

Five common direct teaching methods are employed:

- *diagnostic/prescriptive teaching*, in which pupil weaknesses are identified, enabling objectives for activities to be prescribed;
- *expository teaching*, in subjects such as mathematics or life skills;
- *modelling*, as when an industrial arts teacher instructs students in taper turning on a lathe;
- *read–review–write*, as when history students are given primary source documents and questions based on them;
- *competency based education*, in which the evaluation criteria are drawn from the objectives.

Low structure. One of the commonest low-structure planning methods is through class groups.

If the classroom is to be managed with pupils allocated to groups, special planning is required. For example, chairs and tables need to be easily moved; resources (such as instructional materials and books) have to be readily available in the required numbers; and group membership has to be decided.

Apart from the specific point about peer teaching raised in Chapter 4 with regard to metacognition, pro-social peer groups assist in classroom management in three ways (Schmuck, 1971, 1977):

1. The peer group can support individual pupils ('Gee, you did well in that test, Alfie, and you were worried that you were going to fail!').
2. They can raise self-esteem and provide new aspirations, helping to reshape students ('You used to say that you would never be any good at maths — you look like being top in the year.').
3. The group helps in introductory learning, teaching new material, values and attitudes. ('Heard about the new elective in peace studies for Year 11? Well, Grant

told me that they were looking at how much countries spend on weapons and ...'). This benefit from the group to the individual led to special group activities with delinquents by Vorrath and Brendiro (1979).

In managing through groups, the teacher emphasises collaboration and delegation of responsibility. Discussion is prevalent, with an emphasis on listening skills. Schmuck suggests that teachers occasionally ask pupils to paraphrase the previous speaker's contribution before speaking themselves.

The class as a group can provide an important aid to classroom management when it is the focus for learning activities. With the class as a whole given the responsibility for attaining a task, each student has to be ready to answer questions or to carry out a personal role. Thus, even when students are working on their own, or when one student is being given help by the teacher, the remainder are aware of the expectation that they will be working. The element of unpredictability, not knowing if and when they can be called upon to make their contribution, helps to keep the class alert (Kounin, 1967).

Unfortunately, it does not follow that extensive use of group accountability provides a commensurate increase in teacher effectiveness. It seems that teachers who use group accountability moderately are more effective than those who use it a lot, or not at all (Good and Grouws, 1977).

Setting up classroom operations and procedures

High structure. High-structure methods of setting and implementing classroom operating procedures include the use of specified teaching skills, pupil routines and school policies. The first, teaching skills, are largely derived from the two decades of classroom observational research by Kounin (1977) who emphasised the following high-structure skills:

1.   *Overlapping* enables teachers to handle more than one classroom activity simultaneously. While one pupil's work or assignment is being checked, others in the class are being given assistance or direction. The teacher can pause to promote simultaneous activities. This is in keeping with the basic principle of preventative classroom management: no 'gaps' between classroom activities. Early planning and decisive intervention keep students on task continually.

Thus, too, areas will be allocated for specific activities, equipment will be stored in accessible and recognised places, and students will be aware of expectations (Brophy, 1983). Like sporting champions, good teachers appear to devote little effort to their success in classroom management. That does not mean that an effort has not been expended beforehand, and is not being consistently used to attain high standards of pupil behaviour.

2.   *Momentum* and *smoothness* in the pace of activities avoid slowdowns or jerky transitions which unsettle students. Dislocations can occur when teachers *overdwell* (talk too much) and *fragment* lessons or procedures unnecessarily. For example, too many

pupils could be involved in a multitude of minuscule tasks rather than a few pupils participating in appropriate divisions of the activity. Teachers provide smoothness by continuously signalling *expectations* through questions, cues, eye contact, gestures and so on. Non-verbal communication is an important aspect of classroom management.

3.   Boredom (termed 'satiation' by Kounin) is avoided by challenging students with a variety of instructional groupings, activities, teaching methods and media of instruction. Later research suggests that such challenges should not be extreme as students need to be able to attain a high rate of success and complete the task (Gantt, 1981).

4.   'Withitness' is a teacher's ability to monitor what is occurring in the learning environment. This enables prompt reaction to circumstances and accurate identification of culprits. 'Withit' teachers have fewer management problems and obtain greater pupil achievement.

5.   The 'ripple effect' occurs when a teacher reprimands a student and others nearby feel and act as if they, too, have been rebuked. Younger pupils are more susceptible, older pupils being influenced only by more prestigious teachers. To avoid unwanted 'ripples' when criticising pupils, teachers need to focus on the behaviour under criticism, not the individual.

Routines are long-term teaching plans which can be applied to repetitive situations in the school (such as rainy day lunchtimes or pupils entering and leaving classrooms). Establishing routines offers several advantages. Routines reduce the need to fully plan every proposed educational activity, simplifying classroom management. They increase the students' time on task, and thus the efficient use of available school time. Finally, routines reduce student anxieties about expectations of them, because activities become predictable. Routines may seem trivial but they link instructional planning and classroom management. For example, they are helpful in the management of primary and infant school classes where special rooms (toilets, store rooms, library and washrooms) are to be used; where areas of the playground are allocated for special purposes (such as one area for football or cricket); for beginning or ending the school day (or after breaks in the day, such as recess and lunchtime). Particular applications of routines to secondary schools are unsupervised pupil movement between classrooms, beginning and ending of lessons, joining school buses and notification of pupil absence (see Evertson and Emmer, 1982).

There are three kinds of routine:

1.   Activity routines focus on the learning activity. They control and co-ordinate such aspects as where pupils go, what materials are needed and where they are placed; allocated time; and special requirements in terms of pupil behaviour. For example, art work may be done on Wednesday afternoon. Paper and paints will be distributed in the second half of lunchtime by pupils nominated for the task. All pupils will bring a smock, apron or old shirt as protective clothing when working on the potter's wheel. All art work will finish 10 minutes before the bell to allow time for clearing up. The class will not leave until the room has been cleaned up and all materials stored.

2.   Instructional routines facilitate the teacher's roles in various types of lesson. In a practical lesson in science, home economics or industrial arts, the teacher may establish a routine whereby students do not leave their places to seek assistance. To reduce traffic while practical activity is occurring with equipment around the room, the teacher may ask students to stand or raise a hand when assistance is required. Particular instructional routines will, of course, differ in various subjects.

3.   Management routines control and co-ordinate the organisation and administration of the classroom. In the activity routine example above they are evidenced in the arrangements made for the distribution and collection of materials. Other common examples are in the plans made for schools to operate in the event of a wet weather cancellation of sport, or wet weather during recess or lunchtime, preventing pupils from using outdoor areas.

Low structure. To establish classroom operations with low-structure methods, teachers can involve pupils in consultation and participative decision processes.

A method of sensitising teachers to the advantages of involving pupils in management decisions is *Teacher Effectiveness Training* (TET) (Gordon, 1974a). This low-structure alternative is based on the assumption that students cannot be physically forced to learn, and that there will usually be a minority posing some form of management problem for the teacher. Like its equivalent for parents (PET) (Gordon, 1974b), which has been provided by many Australian schools for the parents of pupils, the program works on the principle of resolving conflict so that there is no loser.

Six steps are advocated:

1. analyse the problem;
2. generate solutions;
3. evaluate each solution;
4. select the best alternative;
5. work out how the solution can be implemented;
6. assess how well the solution to the problem is working.

To avoid creating problems, teachers are advised not to be provocative in their communication; use 'I' messages instead of 'you' messages. Thus 'I can't continue to chair the debate if I am unable to hear the speaker', would be preferred to 'If you keep talking, the debate is off'. The key, according to Gordon, is the improved teacher–pupil relationship which results when teachers talk with, not at, their students. This result is also achieved by 'active listening' (also used in Schmuck's peer group approach, below). Teacher and pupils make a special effort to value others' communication to them, so that listening is elevated from a passive role.

Wider pupil participation is another low-structure alternative that extends beyond the advantages of gaining commitment and demonstrating democracy. Classroom problems may be symptoms of a school-wide malaise, meriting consideration by the school rather than the class. For example, procedures such as class movement in corridors between lessons, or policies on notification of student absences, could be involved. In such cases, there is an approach through whole-school consultation (Duke and Meckel, 1984). Typically, the procedure begins with a thorough analysis of the school organisation with an emphasis on the apparent problems of pupil discipline. Not only teachers, but students and parents are involved in the review and modification of school policy. In the interim, classroom rules are reduced to a minimum but consistently enforced.

The consistent focus in high- and low-structure analyses of classroom management is *teacher–student interaction*. This variable is critical in low-structure solutions where authentic communication and minimal game-playing are required.

Figure 8.3 provides one explanation of classroom management problems: *communication breakdown*. Berne (1964) argues that we are guided by one of three ego states — child, parent or adult. Effective communication takes place when people interact in parallel. For example, a *parent-to-child* comment ('Don't read your book at the dinner table') produces a child-to-parent acquiescence. An *adult* opening gambit ('How do you think the Aussie cricketers will go in the one-day match against India?') can produce an adult-to-adult response. Communication breaks down when the lines cross. For example, teachers in an open classroom initiated adult–adult interactions but the children responded child-to-parent (as indicated in Figure 8.3, and in Adrienne's comment in Chapter 4). Crossed communications can result in the ludicrous sorts of game-playing described by Lett (1971) in terms of teachers who seek to draw pupils to them (the obsequious, 'doormat', walk-all-over-me, child-to-child approach) or those who seek to hold pupils at a distance (the strutting academic with the continual adult-to-child communication pattern). What is your communication style to be?

Questioning

High structure. A common form of teacher–pupil interaction in the classroom is *questioning*, a vital skill in teaching. The options again fall between the two extremes of assertive or sympathetic teaching. Assertive teachers respond by showing disapproval of pupil misbehaviour and indicate what should be done (Canter and Canter, 1976). Thus 'We agreed that there would be no talking while some of the class were still completing the test', is used in preference to a non-assertive 'Please try to be a little quieter', or hostile 'Shut-up!'

The limits of acceptable pupil behaviour are conveyed by teacher–pupil interaction. The ultimate test, according to the Canters, is when a visitor arrives in the classroom. Any pupil should be able to tell the visitor exactly how the class should be behaving at the time. In teaching, limits are conveyed by *questions* ('Shouldn't you be working on your own without help?'), *messages* ('At this stage everyone should be working quietly and independently on the comprehension questions. Reading time has finished.'), *demands* ('I cannot give the group at the microcomputer any assistance while this level of noise exists.'), and by *non-verbal cues* such as eye contact, facial expressions and gestures. The Canters also suggest the use of pupil names in communication and the 'broken-record' technique:

> *Teacher:*   Julie, there is to be no pushing on the stairs.
> *Julie* gives an excuse.
> *Teacher:*   That does not matter. What matters is that you will not push on the stairs.
> *Julie* responds.
> *Teacher:*   Perhaps. But you will not push on the stairs.

Figure 8.3   The problem of crossed communication

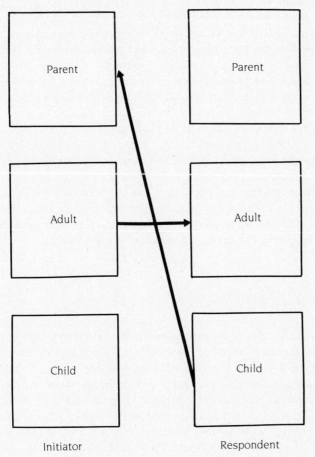

The teacher initiates adult-to-adult communication, but the pupil responds child-to-parent. The lines cross: no effective communication. For example:

Teacher: Let's work out some rules together so we all know where we stand.
Pupil: You're in charge. You're supposed to tell us what's right and wrong.

Appropriate pupil behaviour is reinforced by teacher recognition, either verbally or non-verbally. For example, if students do not behave acceptably, within the prescribed limits, offenders' names can be written on the board. A second offence earns an asterisk or underline and carries the automatic penalty of detention. A third offence means that parents are brought into the matter and another repetition invokes a mandatory conference in the principal's office. As the Canters put it 'say what you mean and mean what you say'.

Low structure. In contrast to the *assertive* teacher is the *sympathetic* teacher who invites pupil co-operation and also communicates feelings about *situations* rather than about *individuals*. Termed 'sane' messages (Ginott, 1971), these communications do not label pupils and are not sarcastic, verbal attacks.

Instead of losing their temper in verbal attacks, teachers model the behaviour they expect from their pupils. They acknowledge pupil feelings ('you appear upset because you did not do very well in the term test, Mary') and add the question, 'How can I help?'

Ginott suggests that praise should be linked to circumstances, instead of 'Good girl, Elizabeth!', say 'It was thoughtful of you to collect the art brushes before you went home yesterday, Elizabeth'. Such a comment is more finely focused on the student's behaviour and makes her feel better: she is more likely to collect the art brushes again tomorrow.

Helping students to meet such basic needs as security, belonging and esteem is another empathetic and pupil-oriented management strategy. Designing lessons so that pupils experience success and have the opportunity to heighten their expectations of themselves, taking time for personal interaction (humour, informal conversation) as well as task priorities, and providing positive feedback when possible to pupils, are some ways in which teachers can promote motivation (Gnagey, 1981).

Rewarding and punishing

We now have a rationale for classroom management: the extent to which a teacher will choose to present a high-structured or low-structured learning situation. Thus a high-structure choice would result in a teacher assessing desirable and undesirable pupil behaviours, making appropriate classroom rules and enforcing them. At the other extreme, a teacher may permit natural consequences to be the source of control.

When we think of classroom management we usually think of what teachers are to do when pupils *mis*behave. One possibility is that teachers will choose to do nothing. What happens then? And what do we do about the case when the pupils are doing just what we expect of them? Do we always comment favourably or otherwise reward them or only sometimes? Or do we ignore 'good' behaviour on the grounds that that is what they *should* be doing?

If pupils are aware of the rules and the consequences for breaking them, shouldn't they be held responsible for their actions? The principle of accountability fits easily with classroom management. For example, it has been suggested that pupil misbehaviour can come from mistaken goals such as attention seeking (Dreikurs and Cassel, 1972; Dreikurs, Grunwald and Pepper, 1971). Pupils do not have to be disruptive to seek attention: they can simply continue to make requests or seek teacher explanations or assistance. They can also seek attention by power conflicts (arguing, contradicting, lying) with the teacher, and that puts the teacher in a no-win situation. If the teacher gains the upper hand, then that tells the student that such tactics are *right*; it is power that counts, which in turn justifies revenge for the embarrassment of defeat. Or the failure could prompt a helpless withdrawal of the pupil who is now feeling inadequate.

Whatever the answers to these questions, it is vital to be consistent. A teacher, then, needs to derive a policy on this question of consequences, following through with reward and punishment. There are several sources to help formulate a policy to suit personal circumstances, but the essential choice is one of who decides rewards and punishments, thus automatically involving the matter of high or low structure.

High structure. As indicated in the scale of punishments provided below, traditional educational practice incorporates a range of high-structure punishments. Teachers decide whether to rebuke, detain, isolate or suspend pupils, for example. The advantages and disadvantages of such methods are also discussed below, after we examine behaviour modification as a high-structure option. In behaviour modification, essentially, a teacher decides whether to ignore misbehaviour and reward appropriate behaviour. In some cases, however, this optimal teacher response is impossible (for lack of time, for instance); then it is possible for the teacher to incorporate punishment.

Behaviour modification. Behaviour modification emphasises environmental factors and what happens before and after certain behaviour occurs, rather than the origins of the behaviour.

Behaviour modification, contingency management and applied behavioural analysis are all terms used to refer to the technology of changing the behaviour of another person through conditioning. The critical difference between behaviour modification (the most widely used term) and any other kind of application of psychology to personal relations centres on the word contingency: something must clearly happen after the person has committed some overt act. Behaviour modification is, in other words, based exclusively on extrinsic motivation. The contingent links between desirable and undesirable acts and various pleasant, unpleasant or natural consequences are set out in Table 3.1. In a behaviour modification scheme, unlike any other schemes of classroom management, these relationships are consistently applied. In non-contingent management, on the other hand, the aim is to get at why the student misbehaves: for example, a teacher might give a student a 'good talking to' after misbehaviour to encourage more care in future.

Setting up a formal behaviour modification program. There are a few simple steps in making a formal program:

1. *Define the target behaviours.* This is exactly like defining behavioural objectives in instruction. It is not good enough to say 'I'll reward him when he's good'. What exactly does 'good' mean in this context? What do the students have to do? Talk? Not talk? Raise hands when asking a question? Sit at desks and at least look as if working? If so, for how long? Ten seconds? Ten minutes? The unit of behaviour must be defined exactly, so that the teacher knows when to reinforce, and the students know why.

2. *Record the baseline.* Once the target behaviour has been clearly defined, it is necessary to see what the pre-treatment or baseline rate is. Do students sit at their desks for five minutes in total per lesson; 15 minutes; not at all? The importance of this step is that the rate of behaviour can be compared with the baseline during and after treatment. If this is not done, you might only have vague and subjective impressions about the success of the program.

3. *Reinforcement contingencies applied.* This stage is the heart of the program. The contingencies are applied, so that when the target behaviours occur, the chosen consequences follow. If this is done in the context of a formal program, the students themselves should be utterly clear as to what it is they are or are not supposed to be doing and what the consequences will be. Further, the rules or contingencies should be applied without exception.

4. *Measure target behaviours.* Now the reinforcement schedule has been applied, what has happened to the rate of target behaviours? Is it higher? If not, there has been an error of judgment in the appropriate reinforcer and another one should be applied. Steps 3 and 4 should be applied until there is a marked variation in 4 in the appropriate direction.

5. *Reversal.* This step is not always necessary, but the most successful behaviour-modifiers do it. Remove step 3, the reinforcement. The point of this is to demonstrate the effectiveness of the program: within a few days, the target behaviours should revert close to the baseline rate.

6. *Reapply contingencies.* The rate of responding should now return to the level at Step 4, thus confirming that the program is having the desired effect on the students' behaviour.

The essence of the procedure is in the first four steps and even then it may not be essential to be very particular about 1 and 3. After all, if the program is working it will usually be pretty clear to the teacher that, for example, the students are a lot quieter or are attending more to their work. Nevertheless, it helps to have the data available. The really tricky parts are to decide on a suitable reinforcement schedule, and to stick to it.

Figure 8.4 is a typical graph of a behaviour modification program. Here, the time on task (minutes per 40 minute lesson) is plotted for each day (based on observing a few target students for one lesson per day). Baseline is established on days 1–3: only 10–15 minutes are spent on task. Then the contingencies are applied: now 25–35 minutes are spent on task. Reversal for days 10–12 shows a typical drop: but when the contingencies are reapplied from day 13 onwards, on-task behaviour settles around 35+ minutes per lesson.

Behaviour modification in practice. A study of Packard (1970) illustrates the steps described above. He was interested in the control of classroom attention: when the child was attending and responding to a task-related stimulus (e.g. writing in a book, watching the teacher demonstrate something). Packard took normal classes (ranging from 25 to 34 students in each) from kindergarten and Grades 3, 5 and 6, and had the teachers distribute tokens for 'attending' behaviours, and to *ignore* inattention. The tokens could be exchanged for preferred activities that were discussed in advance and decided upon by each class on a contractual basis. First, he measured the baseline of target behaviours that occurred 'naturally'. Next, he set up the reinforcement conditions and then measured the proportion of target behaviours now occurring. As a check, he carried out the reversal procedure, and then the reinforcement schedule was reinstituted.

In Grades 5 and 6, he found that the percentages of time that children devoted to 'attending' behaviours during class instruction were as follows:

Grade	Baseline	Reinforcement	Reversal	Reinforcement
6	24	78	43	76
5	58	78	58	80

Similar results were found in earlier grades. In Grade 6, then, only 24 per cent of the class's time was spent on attending to the lesson during instruction; the corresponding figure in Grade 5 was 58 per cent. When the reinforcement schedule was imposed, and the tokens distributed for attending behaviours, time spent in attending jumped to 78 per cent in both grades. When the reinforcement schedule was removed, attending times tended to drop back to near baseline, but when the reinforcement contingencies were again reimposed, attention shot up again to near 80 per cent. Clearly, attention was closely related to the reinforcement schedule.

Becker et al. (1971) worked on the classes of five teachers who were instructed to:

- make the rules clear to the children;
- ignore deviant behaviours whenever possible;
- praise behaviours that facilitate learning;
- especially praise those behaviours that were incompatible with deviant ones (e.g. sitting in one's place is incompatible with running around the room, the latter being a common deviant response).

Figure 8.4   A typical record of a behaviour modification program

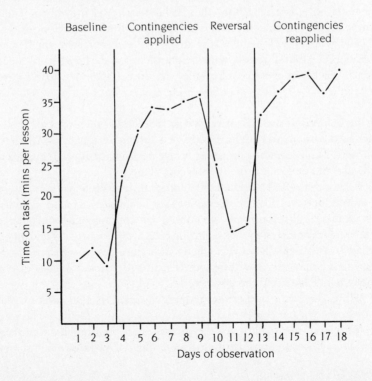

Given that the classes were initially described as disorderly, the overall results were successful: of all behaviours observed (paid observers took note of behavioural frequencies on two 'target' children from each class), 62 per cent were originally deviant. This dropped to 29 per cent a short time after the modification had been in effect, and it stayed that way for the eight weeks of observation.

Thomas, Becker and Armstrong (1968) showed the opposite effect in a class of 28 well-behaved primary school children. Their teacher typically praised and encouraged rather than scolded: they therefore asked her to change her behaviour to see what effect that had. She was asked to become more authoritarian — to decrease her praising and encouraging, and to increase the threats, punishments, etc., for bad behaviour. Authoritarians take note: the bad behaviour *increased* under threats, from an initial 9 per cent to 31 per cent at the end of eight days. When the teacher resumed her usually positive approach, the disruptive behaviours reverted to their initial rates.

Hall et al. (1968) demonstrated the effectiveness of behaviour modification where it is most needed: among beginning teachers worried about discipline, and whose only experience with controlling children had been unhappy. Three teachers were instructed to ignore deviant behaviour and to reward desired behaviours. One Grade 6 class was described as 'completely out of control': the baseline 'study rate' (time spent attending to relevant activities) was 44 per cent — this jumped to 72 per cent simply by getting the teacher to comment positively whenever a child was apparently paying attention. A reversal procedure was used, and when reinforcement ceased, the study rate approached the baseline again. It reversed again when reinforcement was imposed, this time reaching a rate of 76 per cent. A 'very noisy' Grade 7 class had a baseline of 47 per cent which jumped to 65 per cent (with verbal attention to study behaviours only, ignoring non-study behaviour), and moved to 76 per cent when negative reinforcements (threats) were imposed. Study behaviour dropped back to 50 per cent when the schedule was dropped, and reverted to 81 per cent when reintroduced. Similar results were obtained in Grade 1, where a much-liked game called Seven Up was used as a positive reinforcer together with praise ('You're all being *very* good — so let's play Seven Up ...').

Making behaviour modification work. The studies reviewed so far all suggest that a good disciplinarian does not have to have a 'strong personality'. All one has to do is to spell out the rules and be consistent, using positive, or mixed positive and negative, reinforcers but never negative reinforcers alone.

Becker et al. (1971) stipulated that ignoring deviant behaviour is quite ineffective, and indeed increases the occurrence of that behaviour. This seems reasonable, since many deviant behaviours are reinforced by contingencies unconnected with the teacher (e.g. playing it for laughs, getting class attention, etc.). Deviant behaviour does decrease considerably, however, when a desired response, which is incompatible with the deviant behaviour, is reinforced. It is not so much a matter of eliminating the negative as accentuating the positive.

Why, then, are authoritarian methods used if they are so ineffective? An authoritarian teacher comes to the classroom expecting trouble. The way to deal with that? Threaten, then follow up the threats with punishment. Result: more deviant behaviour. Obviously, too soft first time around. Thus: more punishment still. More deviant behaviour. Still too soft ... It would be difficult to convince this teacher that such 'firmness' is probably producing the unwanted results. It would be even more difficult to bring about a change of behaviour in such teachers; they have been in the habit of focusing their attention on unwanted behaviour for too long to make it easy for them to ignore such behaviour, and to concentrate on the desired responses instead. It is a matter of changing the basic orientation from 'catching them being naughty' to that of 'catching them being good' (Howe, 1970b).

If behaviour modification works so well, then, why is it not universal? One reason is that the need for consistency may make superhuman demands on the teacher-reinforcer. A flash of anger or impatience can confound the whole system of reinforcement. Or take the situation when a child sidles up to the desk to ask a question, often thereby jumping the queue for the teacher's attention. The human reaction is to forget psychology and attend to the student who is nearest. But if it is a stated rule that the only proper way to get teacher's attention is for hands to be raised and permission to speak to be granted, then the teacher should never leave a student patiently waiting with hand up because nuisance-at-the-desk is easier to attend to and get out of the way.

Another problem is that the *teacher's* behaviour is reinforceable. No one denies that a sudden yell will immediately result in what is known as a pregnant hush. This sudden transition from chaos to a deathly stillness is ecstatically reinforcing to an insecure teacher. Unfortunately, although the desired effect is immediate it is also very temporary and, in the long term, the undesirable effects of punishment predominate. Unfortunately, too, sustained shouts of rage have to be progressively louder to maintain the same shock value: children rapidly satiate on surprising events, and the teacher is then left with nothing — except a sore throat.

A beginning teacher who starts out using punitive disciplinary techniques is therefore fighting a losing battle. The effects of yelling and threatening are for the first few times so clear-cut and beautiful that one finds oneself committed to a style of discipline which is likely to work less and less effectively in the future.

Ignoring deviant behaviour instead of punishing it is quite difficult for most teachers. Supervisors, colleagues and pupils' parents can interpret such teacher behaviour as 'letting kids get away with it'. There is a moral conviction that wrong behaviour should be punished. These views may be shared by teachers, but they obstruct the establishment of an appropriate classroom atmosphere for behaviour modification.

The successful behaviour modifier starts by deciding a hierarchy of target behaviours — preferably with class participation — a list of rules, their rewards and possible penalties. Then all concerned have the same expectations.

Behaviour modification in the Australian scene. An extensive application of behaviour modification methods was made at Newcastle College of Advanced Education where school pupils requiring remedial assistance were given a program designed to increase time spent on active learning.

Behaviour modification is, however, rarely used in Australian classrooms with normal children. After a series of studies of the use of behaviour modification in open-plan primary schools in Sydney, Winkler (1976) concluded that the methods and concepts of behaviour modification were inadequate to handle the diversity found in open-plan schools. The reason for the unpopularity of behaviour modification in Australia is, however, more deep-rooted than that: it is more a question of the basic values underlying behaviour modification and the social context.

In Australia, questions of morality and value judgments about 'bribery', 'encouraging materialism', 'ignoring wrongdoing' and so on, are raised. In the United States, founded upon rugged individualism and the Puritan ethic — reward contingent upon effort — the hidden curriculum of behaviour modification finds strong compatibility (Gardner, 1976).

Punishment. Our examination of the effects of punishment (see Chapter 3) concluded that they were unpredictable: sometimes the undesirable behaviours were suppressed, sometimes they increased. The problem is that the individual being punished can react in so many different ways; from deciding the behaviour is not worthwhile (the desired effect), to deciding that he or she has found an excellent way of controlling the punisher. There is no surer way of making a teacher angry than repeating the very behaviour that led to the punishment. In order to ensure that the effects of punishment are predictable and desirable, it is necessary to punish immediately, infallibly and with maximum severity. These conditions suggest the infliction of physical pain in a way that would be both impractical and intolerable in the public education system.

A scale of punishments. Telfer and Rees (1975, pp. 46–9) listed the more common punishments used in school, with an analysis of advantages and disadvantages of each. The punishments are in ascending order of severity.

1.   *Ignoring the behaviour.* We have looked at the advantages of this in Section A. The disadvantages are that the teacher may not be the only one providing reinforcement for the behaviour; and to the pupil, this may suggest that the teacher is condoning the behaviour.

2.   *Recognition.* If, for example, the teacher pauses significantly or calls the pupil's name, the pupil cannot pretend that he or she has not gone beyond the bounds of the acceptable. On the other hand, the fact of recognition has brought the situation out of extinction into that of punishment. Except in the hands of an experienced teacher with charisma, and with whom the pause or naming can be expected to presage events of a dire nature, this tactic is likely to wear very thin.

3.   *Rebuke.* This may range from mild comment to cutting sarcasm, perhaps in either event with a request to see the teacher after the lesson. The benefit of the comment alone will depend upon the nature of the sarcasm (if used) and the reaction of the student. The advantages of seeing the student later and in private are that interruption to the lesson is minimised; that neither teacher nor student has to play a role publicly; and that the class is kept guessing as to the severity of the penalty.

4.   *Mild punishment.* (Examples are detention, isolation, loss of a privilege.) Detention raises many difficulties: no States, for instance, permit detention during recess times. Restriction of favoured activities (e.g. sport) may involve an activity the student particularly benefits from.

5.   *Send from the room.* If done naturistically (i.e. as a logical consequence of antisocial or other unacceptable behaviour), this is a sound procedure. It also leaves the

class undistracted. One obvious problem is that students may refuse to go; another is where to send them, if the school has made no special provision for this. Also, if used frequently, both students and school administrators might think that teachers are abdicating their responsibilities.

   6.   *Corporal punishment.* Tis is no longer a legal alternative in most public education systems. The last round in that debate in New South Wales is given in Box 8.5.

   7.   *Drastic consequences.* These range from arrangements for a parent interview to expulsion, which may perhaps be classified as natural consequences rather than punishments. If a child is consistently and seriously misbehaving, the problem reasonably requires consultation with parents and school counsellor.

Effects of punishment. When the Dettman Committee investigated punishment in West Australian classrooms they found an interesting link between the frequency and perceived dislike of punishment (see Table 8.2). Those students who were punished most were worried least — there has to be a message there! (See discussion Question 2.)

Table 8.2   Frequency and perceived dislike of punishment

Punishment		Frequency of visits to deputy					
		None	One	Two	Three	Four	Five+
		N = 4,065	438	200	115	53	101
		%	%	%	%	%	%
Physical punishment (e.g. with cane, ruler or hand)	It does not worry me	16	22	30	26	52	41
Suspended from school	It does not worry me	9	15	20	28	26	38
Sent out of the classroom	It does not worry me	39	49	63	69	71	66
Note from the teacher or principal to your parents	It does not worry me	8	10	16	15	16	25
Made fun of by the teacher with a sarcastic remark	It does not worry me	16	23	22	29	24	33

Source: Dettmann, 1972, pp. 143–4.

   Low structure. Inviting pupil participation in decisions about classroom management is a typical low-structure approach. For example, teachers can avoid power struggles by inviting pupils to consider such questions as 'What do you think should be done about the problem of people arriving late for this lesson?' Teachers should ignore attention seeking, but give students attention when they are not demanding it. For non-achievers, effort rather than achievement should be rewarded. Encouragement — promoting student self-satisfaction — is regarded as preferable to praise (which is

BOX 8.5   CORPORAL PUNISHMENT

The case for ...

All human beings have a natural instinct for aggression, tempered of course by the necessity to live in a civilised community.

Our children are born without any ingrained sense of right and wrong, and it is only an uncaring parent who will not lay down clear guidelines for behaviour and, at times, enforce those lines by slapping or hitting. Indeed the parent who does not use some means of coercion at some time is probably non-existent. How then is the school to cope without at least the possibility of reverting to corporal punishment when all else fails?

Teachers must cope with not only those children who are accustomed to occasional (and often justified) physical punishment, but children who, sadly, are subjected frequently and sometimes without justification, to severe punishment.

What then are the disciplinary courses open to teachers? In a case where a pupil deliberately disobeys rules, and refuses detention, ignores counselling and wilfully disrupts, when isolation fails and suspension is a long drawn-out agony, then teachers need to know that corporal punishment is available.

All human societies use some form of physical coercion, at some point: they incarcerate people, deprive them of liberty, cast them out, and our society is no exception. To pretend this is not so, or that the world is so benign as to be able to do away with physical punishment is frankly dishonest.

The time to dispense with corporal punishment in schools will be the time that our society has firmly rejected all forms of aggression and physical restraint. That time has not yet arrived. To do away with corporal punishment in schools now would be doing neither pupils nor teachers a favour.

The case against ...

When is murder justified? When one's country is officially or unofficially at war with another?

If *no one* was prepared to accept that murder was ever justifiable, would we be free of war?

How do children come to accept that physical punishment is acceptable? The answer is that children learn by the examples set before them. If physical punishment is sanctioned first by parents, and at a later age by schools, then we are teaching each generation, that ultimately, physical coercion or punishment is in some circumstances socially acceptable.

There is then considerable weight in the argument that a person who will hit or cane another in a certain situation is a person who will ultimately sanction murder, shooting, bombing and war, in order to have their rule obeyed, to defend or to be revenged.

Our world community has only a short time to rid itself of war and to do that we must explore the alternatives of discussion, communication and respect for the humanity and inviolability of our fellow humans. Schools and teachers must actively pursue those alternatives. We must accept that talking and counselling, while more time-consuming and demanding of resources, are finally better solutions.

After all, what does hitting a child prove? It simply confirms for the child that the teacher doing the hitting is stronger and more powerful. Hitting does not confirm that a certain rule is correct, but that a rule will be enforced by physical punishment. For the huge numbers of children who are regularly hit, beaten or even battered at home, the cane is an idle threat, laughed at scornfully. The most probable result for such children is that they learn disrespect for people who hit, and eventually they will strike back.

Many children become so estranged from the society which hits or batters them that aggression becomes the mode of their relationship to others.

We must use alternatives to caning now, because to continue to use corporal punishment at school is to continue to sanction the use of violence in our world community.

Source: Education, 11 February 1985, p. 5.

---

extrinsic). Logical or natural consequences, rather than punishment, follow misbehaviour. If equipment is forgotten or maliciously damaged, the pupil cannot participate in the activity requiring that equipment. To make pupils aware of their behaviour, its causes and logical consequences, Dreikurs advocates pupil–teacher conferences.

The consequences of misbehaving, when pupils are given a choice of behaving appropriately, are the focus of the management model presented by Glasser (1969, 1977). Pupils should be placed in the position of making an informed decision by being involved in formulating rules. These rules should focus on learning activities, and be subject to regular review. What happens if the rules are broken? Consider this example:

Teacher: (in an unthreatening manner) What are you doing?
Student: Nothing.
Teacher: Is that helping you or the class?
Student: I don't know.
Teacher: What could you do that would help?
Student: I don't know.
Teacher: (gives alternatives) You could get on with the set work, and fix that book tonight at home. Or you could fix the book straight away and stay back after the lesson and finish the work. If you can't repair the book, you may have to replace it.

Naturally, if the student's responses are more constructive, the teacher uses the suggestion and does not continue to supply other alternatives.

If the pupil's response remains non-committal or negative, the teacher arranges a later private discussion when the pupil is again asked:

- 'Was it against the rules?'
- 'What should you have been doing?'

Further offences lead to another private conference which produces a plan stipulating exactly what the student has to do. Any infringements lead to isolation from the group, then from the room. The last alternative is for the principal to ask the parents to come to the school.

Glasser advises teachers to focus on improving pupil self-esteem to develop responsible behaviour. Groups formed in the class can enable students to discuss concerns. Activities which ensure some students fail (such as graded report cards) are eliminated. Instead of being given an imposition, a misbehaving student would be asked to compose a plan which will result in improved behaviour. But if changing pupil behaviour is the focus, there is some highly detailed advice available.

CLASSROOM CLIMATE

Strictly speaking, the climate of the classroom is a matter that resolves itself through the interaction of the personalities of teacher and students. Nevertheless, the nature of that interaction, and the way it 'feels', will be influenced by the kinds of management decisions that are consistently chosen. Consistently choosing high-structure options will tend to produce a formal and rather cold classroom climate, unless specific steps are taken to warm things up.

It is however important to distinguish between warmth and formality. We saw in Chapter 2 that Rosenshine criticised Bennett's study of British primary schools because he did not distinguish between formality and climate, with warm formal classrooms leading to different outcomes than cold formal classrooms. Having made the managerial decisions that appear most appropriate, you, as teacher, then need to work at creating the sort of atmosphere that is consistent both with those decisions and with the sort of person that you are. How all that will work out will depend further on what sort of people the students are, and what is the outcome of your negotiations with them. Further, all of that depends in part on the school climate itself, which is based to a large degree on principal-staff relationships (Halpin, 1966), and possibly too on the students' perceptions of teacher/teacher or teacher/administrator relations.

A PRINCIPLE OF CLASSROOM MANAGEMENT — A CASE STUDY

Perhaps the best means of demonstrating the link between management decisions and climate is to examine a class situation.

It is Thursday afternoon, and the last week of term. As you walk down the corridor it is apparent that 10E is not awaiting its English literature lesson with bated breath. You have been working through the *Merchant of Venice* and it has proved a slow drag for you and them. The louvre windows of the classroom open into the corridor which funnels unrelated bursts of pupil conversation. You hear your name mentioned and the context clearly confirms your suspicion that this is not the most popular lesson of the week.

It takes time to settle the class, and to solve the inevitable incongruence between numbers of textbooks and numbers of pupils. 'Forgetting' the textbook seems to be on the increase again. Finally, roles are allocated and the reading begins at the place you had the book marked at the end of the previous period.

In halting fashion, the reading begins. Listening to the hesitancy you ponder the general paucity of reading ability in the class, and the unwillingness to tackle the simple challenges of Elizabethan English. The real problem, of course, is not reading ability. Alternate activities —conversation, note-passing and general inattention — cyclically demand your intervention. The lesson grinds on, with its periodic pauses and restarts.

The stated objectives of the English syllabus have little to do with these classroom activities. The students appear to be breaking their 'contract' with you. Or are *you* the guilty party: have you broken it with them? What will you do?

Applying the model of classroom management

The case study shows a mixture of high and low structures: on the one hand, the intent of the lesson relies on high structure — the class is to read the text of the play. On the other, the motivation for the pupils to read with interest seems to be low structure — it is expected that some intrinsic motivator will help the lesson on its way. We can apply the management model by looking at the key management areas: planning, procedures, pupil–teacher interaction, reward and punishment, and climate.

1.   Pre-instructional planning. This seems to be an appropriate place to start when looking at the classroom management problem. Insufficient preparation has been undertaken: for example, if a pupil-need analysis were undertaken, you might discover that none of 10E have actually experienced live theatre or considered the ways in which live theatre differs from television, cinema or a heavy metal rock concert. What do you really want to achieve with 10E? Sure, you know what the syllabus says, and you know that such a play has to be treated: but what are your precise objectives?

Having decided upon objectives, you can then focus your planning on the resources you will use. Why not some recordings of a modern English version of the play? Why not let pupils practise reading on tape? Why not vary your media of instruction by preparing some hand-outs, perhaps with questions based on content, plot summaries, diagrams of links between characters, and so on. Wouldn't 10E be interested in a model of the Globe Theatre? There are numerous ways in which this lesson would be strengthened by more thoughtful planning. Just more planning would be a good start.

2.   *Operation and procedures.* Despite apparent 'withitness', this teacher's lesson is not working and the class is not involved. There is no 'element of unpredictability' advocated by Kounin (1971), rather, the lesson has become tediously predictable. Variability is needed urgently, within the size of the group (either provide some individualised instruction through work sheets? Or divide into groups with each looking at a different aspect of the play?) Variations are also possible in the media of instruction (printed sheets of questions; films or videotapes of the play; seeing the play itself, etc.) and variations in the teacher's style and method. Your movement, use of aids, use of voice, use of non-verbal communication are all potential sources of variation. Those are a lot of possibilities for you to work on for the next lesson with 10E.

For example, how do Shakespearean plots apply in this century? Introduce the class to *West Side Story* and show the link to the plot of *Romeo and Juliet*. The next step could be for 10E to come up with a modern application of the *Merchant of Venice*. Shylock may become a finance company or a merchant bank.

There are opportunities for implementing routines in lessons which recur in the timetable each week. Apart from the beginning and ending of a lesson, in situations such as issuing scripts, getting out drama text and notebooks, or moving front rows of desks back to provide a stage, routines would have helped this lesson.

3.   *Pupil–teacher interaction.* The teacher's high-structure lesson is not reflected in a very low-structure approach to pupil misbehaviour. Action is taken, but in a remedial way after the offence has occurred. Does 10E know why they are expected to study the play? Teacher and pupils are not working together on the same task: their goals seem quite different. One is attempting to meet the formal demands of a program of study in return for a pay cheque, while the other is looking for ways to make the time go a little faster in a very boring lesson. It is an 'us versus them' pattern of interaction in which the intent and the impact of a teacher's actions and statements are quite different. The teacher is the adult — the pupils are the children.

4.   *Rewards and punishment.* Instead of working out what to do with the offenders, why not reward those doing the right thing? There may be insufficient time to run the whole gamut of behaviour modification, so establish clear limits and rules, praise those who follow them but ignore those who do not. A more structured alternative would be to establish rules, reward those who adhere to them and punish those who break them. In the secondary school, pupil contracts — signed by parents, pupil and teacher — may be even more appropriate.

For those seeking higher structure, precise limits on pupil behaviour can be established or re-established. The teacher should use both verbal and non-verbal means to show disapproval if the limits are breached and to indicate what is expected of pupils. This is an instance where 'the broken record', 'what are you doing?' and name-on-the-board methods can be used. If it is to be a high-structure lesson, high-structure teacher–pupil interaction needs to go with it.

5.   *Climate.* No matter how elaborate the lesson plan and how structured the relationships in the class or the system of rewards and punishment, the teacher cannot force pupils to listen. The climate is not one of collaboration and authenticity; nor is it task-oriented. It is quite possible that fear of failure has something to do with pupils' reticence to read — but whatever the reason, the climate lacks enthusiastic and warm teacher input. It would probably work wonders if you (the teacher) showed a little more enthusiasm and commitment: that is the way to raise the temperature.

A CHECKLIST FOR BEGINNING TEACHERS

A minimum set of information forms the basis for effective classroom management, regardless of whether the choice of style of management is high or low structure. This checklist is designed to provide that information.

1.   *The names of the school staff* (teaching/non-teaching) to whom you need to refer in your interaction with pupils.

2.   *The routines and school policy* which cover students who are late or sick; getting lunches from the canteen; out of bounds areas; playground supervision; detention; students leaving school early; parents asking for pupils to leave the class; 'early marks'; bell times; means of access to and maintenance of student records; recording pupil absences; calling class rolls; how to obtain teaching programs and register completed lessons. To operate efficiently you will need to know this and more. Reading a copy of the school's policy statement is a good start.

3.   *The optimal lay-out for your classroom.* Secondary teachers have to take into account the fact that a number of different classes could meet in the classroom in any one day, and thus may not have the autonomy of their primary and infants school colleagues who normally have sole use of one room. Aim to give maximum pupil *comfort* (in terms of light, ventilation, posture and visibility of focal areas such as the chalkboard or television screen); *flexibility* (so that small group activities or specific work stations can be implemented); *and ease of movement* (consider the traffic patterns).

The ways in which *pupils are arranged for instruction* is a significant factor in establishing and maintaining order in the classroom (Doyle and Rutherford, 1984). Note that there are two decisions here: (1) how to arrange the class; (2) for how long. Methods of arranging students for discussion, group work, a lecture or a debate differ in complexity and in the demands they make on teacher and pupils. For example, desks can be placed in a horseshoe pattern or clusters depending on your intentions. While desks in the traditional rows produced higher levels of on-task behaviour in a study of Grade 2 to 7 reading pupils conducted by Axelrod (1979), such a pattern would be quite inappropriate for group discussions where eye contact is important.

4.   *The names of the students in your class.* Learn them and use them as soon as possible. Don't say: 'Keep quiet! I can't talk over this noise.' Say instead: 'Jasmine, please be quiet — you are interrupting me.' That ensures she, and other deviates, are included in the contract; and they know it — Good luck!

SUMMARY

Planning. Instructional planning is integral to classroom management, and ideally follows a sequence that commences with pupil needs, establishing objectives and learning activities, and concludes with an evaluation of attainment. A typical high-structure management method is direct instruction, and an example of low structure is the use of class groups.

Setting up classroom operations and procedures. High-structure procedures include teaching skills (overlapping, momentum, smoothness, avoidance of pupil boredom, withitness and use of the 'ripple effect'); pupil routines (for activities, instruction and management); and policies for the whole school. Participative decision-making is a low-structure approach.

Consulting students. Authentic communication, conflict resolution without a loser and 'I' messages rather than 'you' messages by the teacher are possible methods, with the possibility of whole-school involvement for policy matters. Verbal (questions, messages and demands) and non-verbal (eye contact, facial expression, gesture) techniques convey limits, and the 'broken record' technique can be used to maintain them.

Rewarding and punishing. Traditional educational practice has a range of high-structure punishments, such as rebukes, detention, impositions, loss of privileges, isolation and suspension.

Behaviour modification. A behaviour modification program can be established by:

1. defining target behaviours;
2. recording a baseline rate;
3. applying reinforcement contingencies;
4. measuring target contingencies;
5. reversal;
6. reapplying contingencies.

Punishment. Teachers have a range of choices:

1. ignore pupil behaviour;
2. maintain pupil limits by verbal or non-verbal means;
3. punish (detain, isolate within or outside the room, imposition, loss of privileges, suspension, expulsion).

Evidence was presented that students punished most were affected least, alternatives being consultation with pupils about problems; pupil involvement in formulating rules; use of the question, 'what are you doing?'; and improvement of pupil self-esteem. High-structure approaches include establishing and enforcing clear rules, keeping students engaged on suitable tasks; holding them responsible for their behaviour; and acting promptly if misbehaviour occurs.

Classroom climate. Climate is an emotional atmosphere in the classroom, the affective dimension for which management decision by the teacher is the equivalent cognitive dimension. The teacher's personality makes the difference between cold and warm classroom climates.

Applying this model. A prototypical case study of an English literature class was described, and the model was used to generate possible ways of handling the situation, with high- and low- structure alternatives. Whatever alternative is used, a checklist of things a teacher needs to know was provided.

FURTHER READING

On operant conditioning
B. F. Skinner, *Science and Human Behaviour*, Free Press, New York, 1965.
B. F. Skinner, *Walden Two*, Macmillan, New York, 1949.

Both books are unusually easy to read, and explain the principles and applications of respondent and operant conditioning. The second represents Skinner's ambitions as a novelist.

On behaviour modification in education
S. Axelrod, *Behaviour Modification for the Classroom Teacher*, McGraw-Hill, New York, 1977.
C. H. and C. K. Madsen, *Teaching/Discipline*, Allyn & Bacon, Boston, 1970.
M. C. Meacham and A. E. Wiesen, *Changing Classroom Behaviour* (2nd edn). International Textbook Co., New York, 1974.

These books are oriented towards applying operant theory to education. Madsen and Madsen's book is perhaps the most practical; the others devote more space to explaining the theory. All are easy to read. There is in fact a wide literature on this subject, and most are quite good.

On classroom management (non-behaviourist)
C. Turney and L. G. Cairns, *Sydney Micro Skills Series 3: Classroom Management and Discipline*, Sydney University Press, Sydney, 1976.
D. L. Duke and M. A. Meckel, *Teachers' Guide to Classroom Management*, Random House, New York, 1984.
C. M. Charles, *Building Classroom Discipline: From Models to Practice*, (2nd edn) Longman, New York, 1985.

Turney and Cairns is a practical text, based on Kounin's model, and analysing classroom management as a teaching skill. An accompanying videotape is available. Using a rationale that the classroom teacher is in the best position to choose the optimal management strategy, Duke and Meckel provide nine alternative approaches. They then detail typical classroom problems and apply the approaches to demonstrate applicability (and limitations). Charles presents and discusses seven models of discipline, then supplements the models with practical suggestions. He concludes with sections on how to develop and implement a personal system of discipline, incorporating 20 strategies (pp. 210–12).

On corporal punishment
J. Mercurio, *Caning: Educational Ritual*, Holt, Rinehart & Winston, Sydney, 1975.
P. Newell (ed.), *A Last Resort: Corporal Punishment in the Schools*, Pelican, UK, 1972.

The first book is a sociological examination of caning in a New Zealand high school, and provides a fascinating insight into the rituals of caning. Newell's book is a well-written and balanced evaluation of corporal punishment in the United Kingdom.

QUESTIONS

Questions for self-testing

1. Distinguish between high and low structure in management decisions, and give an example of each.
2. Of the five bases for interpersonal influence, which two are advocated as a guide to classroom management?
3. Is classroom management the same as pupil discipline? If not, how can they be distinguished?
4. Provide a classroom example which shows the difference between the function and impact of a decision.
5. What are the classroom characteristics which make it such a complex environment for management decisions?
6. List three ways in which routines can be used as long-term plans to manage a class, providing an example of each way.
7. Provide five major areas of management decisions for teachers, and give an example of each.
8. List the four steps advocated by Rosenshine (1983) as a sequence to link lessons.
9. Expository teaching is one method used in direct teaching. What are four others? Give brief explanatory details of each.
10. Describe how you would set out pupil desks for a group activity lesson (assuming the class was to be divided into five groups of five pupils). You plan to include a whole class discussion: indicate whether or not the plan would need to change, and why.
11. Provide a brief example of the following teaching techniques: overlapping, momentum, overdwell, non-verbal communication, satiation, 'withitness', ripple effect, an instructional routine, an activity routine.
12. Provide the six steps to enable no-loss conflict resolution.
13. What are the three ego states which guide communication? Provide examples of how a teacher can convey pupil behaviour limits by means of: questions, messages, demands, the 'broken-record' technique, assertiveness.
14. The following are the six steps in setting up a behaviour modification program. List them in the correct sequence.

    - reversal;
    - reapply contingencies;
    - record the baseline;
    - define the target behaviours;
    - measure the target behaviours;
    - apply the reinforcement contingencies.

15. What is an advantage and a disadvantage of sending a misbehaving pupil from the classroom?
16. Distinguish between a 'warm' and 'cold' classroom climate.
17. What uses can be made of wall space to promote classroom climate?

Questions for discussion

1. A student teacher encountered problems with pupil behaviour during practice teaching, especially with Year 7 and Year 8 classes. Disappointed with the amount of the lesson devoted to class management, the student re-read this chapter and evolved the following strategy:

   - He would be quite explicit in identifying unacceptable behaviour, and involve the pupils in the development of class rules which will then form a type of contract.
   - A token economy would be established to reward good behaviour and start pupils 'feeling good about being good'. The tokens (or points) could be accumulated to enable individuals or the class to undertake a preferred learning activity from a predetermined list. Those who misbehave lose the privilege of joining in the preferred activity and, ultimately, could lead to a loss of class time on that activity. Chronic misbehavers can earn the class extra time on a desired activity by not misbehaving for a set time.
   - More time would be spent on lesson planning, to over-prepare, if necessary. This would ensure that a range of activities was available at any stage of the lesson.
   - Attention would also be given to non-verbal reinforcers such as a confident appearance, appropriate facial expressions, proximity to pupils, tone of voice and eye contact.
   - Those who behave well will be positively reinforced. The chronic misbehaver will be sent out of the room to undertake set work elsewhere, until an assurance is given that the contract will be respected.

   What do you think of this solution to classroom management during practice teaching? What advantages and disadvantages can you find in this approach?
2. Refer to the statistics in Table 8.1 (Frequency and perceived dislike of punishment). Take each set of results in turn, and say what implications you can derive for teaching practice.
3. When you take your first full-time class, how can you 'negotiate a collaborative network'? List the steps you would take.
4. Would you make use of behaviour modification methods in the classroom? Justify your response.
5. What is the ideal classroom climate? Describe it and suggest how you would attain and maintain it.
6. When do teachers plan? With a full teaching load a beginning teacher needs to manage time efficiently in order to prepare lessons thoroughly. When next at a school, make an informal survey of when teachers plan their lessons and mark student work.

Part 4

Understanding and evaluating individual differences in learning

We have dealt with cognitive, metacognitive, developmental and social aspects of the learner. Two major topics remain: differences between learners, and evaluating learning. These two chapters may not appear to sit alongside each other as well as previous ones. Both could be seen as dealing with differences between students, and with testing procedures that establish those differences. In that light, Chapter 9 would deal with ability and its measurement and Chapter 10 with attainment and its measurement. The first deals with permanent differences between students, the second with 'engineered' differences.

To put the matter like this would, however, lead to an inappropriately quantitative view of both ability and of attainment, and is certainly not the message intended by the present grouping of chapters. If, however, we talk about abilities as *processes* that help determine how students learn some tasks better than other tasks; and if the differences have been 'engineered' by the intervention called 'teaching', then we are in business.

Intelligence (IQ) tests are actuarial devices specially designed to predict school performance. They therefore minimise the role of teaching. Recent research into learning-related individual differences is, however, more concerned with looking at abilities that may be used to help design and facilitate instruction. One particularly promising model of this kind is the Das-Kirby information integration model, which can be used to construct ways of going about a task by different students, or about the same task at different stages of its learning.

One difficulty with the abilities model is that it is easy to slip into a way of thinking that implicates heredity much *beyond* the level heredity actually does affect academic performance. The information integration model, on the other hand, sets the teacher thinking about the metacognitive issues of planning, and strategic use of personal and contextual resources.

Another process distinction is between convergent and divergent abilities, a distinction closely related to the paradigmatic and narrative ways of knowing. High attainment is linked to both, even if the structures and content of schooling emphasise convergent processes.

The ways in which students can differ from each other are many; too many for teachers to be able to keep track and design instructional packages that suit each ability profile on a class basis. A medium that does lend itself to immediate adaptation to the individual — at least in pace, interaction and sequencing — is computer assisted instruction (CAI). With adequate programming, an interactive CAI package comes closest to the 'embedded teaching' that occurs in early childhood between parent and child, and when cognitive gains are greatest. It seems that this kind of conception of individualisation of instruction is most likely to lead to greater learning than matching abilities with teaching styles.

Evaluation is one of the greatest bugbears of education, yet it is really only the third 'P' in the 3P model. Early strategies of evaluation stressed norm-referencing in a context out of Theory X (and quantitatively conceived). Evaluation here is treated as an integral part of learning, and one in which students can become increasingly involved, as must be the case in a conception of process learning. Chapter 10 goes into the philosophy of evaluation in both traditional and process models of learning, and also into the media and techniques of testing and where each may most appropriately be used.

9

Individual differences in learning

OVERVIEW

Many educational decisions are made on the basis of differences between students. Affective differences have been addressed in other chapters; here we look at cognitive differences, reflected in various kinds of abilities. Some abilities are based on the content of the task, such as verbal, spatial or number problems. Other abilities are based on the processes used in handling a task. These important aspects of cognitive abilities relate to the classroom through both teacher attitudes and teacher actions.

Questions answered by this chapter include the following:

- How is pupil giftedness different from intellectual capacity and academic performance?
- Does reading involve simultaneous or successive processing? Or both?
- How do poor planners differ from good planners in game strategies?
- What are some of the important ways in which students differ?
- Does the mere fact of labelling students affect their chances of success?
- What are cognitive styles, and are they useful for educators?
- Can an educational system be based on competencies rather than abilities?
- Does being good at one thing imply being good at another?
- How did the IQ test originate?
- How can microcomputers individualise instruction?
- Is intelligence, as measured by the IQ, mainly determined genetically or by environmental influences?
- Is it useful for teachers to have access to students' IQ scores?
- Does divergent ability relate to educational achievement?
- Why do many teachers dislike divergent students?
- What can schools do to help gifted children?
- What can each teacher do to accommodate individual differences in the classroom?

The last question is the most important one. Hopefully, readers will be able to construct their own list of answers. With experience in the classroom, and further reflection on the kinds of things that have been discussed in this chapter, the list will become longer and more practicable. When you have finished this chapter, you should also be able to do the following:

1. Use knowledge about students' abilities to construct realistic expectations.
2. Differentiate the genuinely divergent student from the class nuisance.
3. Evaluate the success of a learning episode by using both convergent and divergent test items.
4. Construct a program for a group of gifted children.
5. Distinguish between content abilities and process abilities.
6. Identify three cognitive styles.
7. Describe how models of intelligence are becoming more content based.
8. Differentiate between mental retardation, specific learning disabilities and the physically and sensorily handicapped.

9. Explain what is meant by aptitude-treatment interaction (ATI).
10. Describe a variety of means which enable instruction to be individualised.

SECTION A

HOW DO STUDENTS DIFFER FROM EACH OTHER?

Every teacher's theory-in-use has something to say about differences between students, and how educational decisions should take such differences into account. A seventeenth century example is given in Box 9.1.

Earlier this century, it was thought essential that students be grouped according to prior attainment, and so promotion at the end of each year depended upon the student completing the year's work satisfactorily. In one-teacher country schools, this could lead to anomalies such as dull 14-year-olds, large and self-conscious, attempting the same tasks as bright 8-year-olds. The next move was to introduce streaming, which combines grouping by age and attainment. Under a streaming policy, the slow child is 'promoted' each year with others of the same age, and to maintain homogeneity of attainment within the class, classes are *streamed* into higher and lower levels of attainment. In recent years there have been moves, particularly in primary schools, to

---

BOX 9.1   AN EARLY LOOK AT INDIVIDUAL DIFFERENCES IN EDUCATION

Begin therefore betimes nicely to observe your Son's *Temper* ... See what are his *predominant* Passions, and *prevailing* Inclinations; whether he be Fierce or Mild, Bold or Bashful, Compassionate or Cruel, Open or Reserv'd, &c. For as these are different in him, so are your Methods to be different, and your Authority must hence take measures to apply it self different ways to him. These *native Propensities*, these Prevalencies of Constitution, are not to be cured by Rules, or a direct Contest; especially those of them that are the humbler and meaner sort, which proceed from fear, and lowness of Spirit; though with Art they may be much mended, and turned to good purposes. But this, be sure, after all is done, the Byass will always hand on that side, that Nature first place it: And if you carefully observe the Characters of his Mind, now in the first Scenes of his Life, you will ever after be able to judge which way his Thoughts lean, and what he aims at, even hereafter, when, as he grows up, the Plot thickens, and he puts on several Shapes to act it.

Source: Locke, 1699, pp. 101–2, original edition 1693.

drop grouping-by-attainment, so that in unstreamed schools promotion is carried out on age alone. In this case, of course, instruction is not given to the class as a whole or, when it is, it is not dependent on particular prior knowledge or skill. Finally, even age has been dropped in the 'family grouping' scheme used in some British primary schools, and in some Australian open-area schools.

Gender is not now used as a means of grouping students in most government schools, although both sex and religion are used as criteria for segregating students in many private schools. Segregated schooling is an interesting example of using student differences for educational decision-making. It probably has two justifications. First, in the explicit curriculum, sex segregation may be justified on the grounds that it is believed that boys and girls are interested in, and are most capable of learning, different subjects. Thus it is felt that the actual curriculum for boys should be different from that for girls. However, since such differences could easily be met by an elective system, the real reason for sex segregation is probably in the implicit curriculum. Appearing to withhold approval from social mixing between the sexes may be seen as both discouraging promiscuity and teaching an implicit curriculum based on sexism and male dominance. It is, however, females who benefit from segregated education: the self-concept and academic performance of girls is higher in segregated schools. It seems that boys usually win in the competition for formal and informal leadership in coeducational schools, leaving girls with the self-concepts of losers, and in the position of followers (Phillips, 1979).

What do *teachers* see as the more important distinctions between students as far as decision-making in their classroom is concerned? Holland (1959) found that many teachers see students in two ways: as bright-dull or co-operative-nuisance. Other characteristics tend to be merged with these two dimensions: for example, creative students tended to be lumped in the 'bright-nuisance' category, whereas ideal students are in the 'bright-co-operative' group. (The former raises an important point to which we shall return later in the chapter.) Common theories-in-use are therefore rather impoverished on the question of student differences. What student characteristics should teachers be made aware of according to espoused theory, and what would such theory say about how they should make use of those characteristics in their decision-making?

It is time to examine what espoused theory has to say about the cognitive domain of student differences.

A self-fulfilling prophecy

The cognitive domain is complex and controversial, particularly with respect to educational applications. It is an important area, however, for teachers to understand, as illustrated in a study by Beez (1970). He randomly selected students for individual tutoring by teachers. The only information the teachers were given about the students were false IQ scores and a misleading interpretation of those scores. The IQs allegedly ranged from 90 to 110, and labels were attached to the quoted IQs of children (e.g. Sue might be quoted as 'a dull, slow child with an IQ of 94', Bill as 'verbally quick, promising academically; IQ 107'). Beez then arranged for the children to be taught a simple symbol-learning task on an individual basis.

The results were staggering. Not only did the teachers produce results which matched their expectations (that Sue was dull and Bill was bright), but when the real IQs were established some quite disturbing anomalies were found. One child (labelled 'bright', but with a real IQ of 71) learned seven of the 14 symbols he was given to learn; while another child (labelled 'dull', but with a real IQ of 127) was given only five symbols, of which he learned three! The teachers may then look at these results, with their preconceptions confirmed: the 'bright' child learned seven items and the 'dull' child three. If the teachers had known more about IQ scores, they might have realised that the interpretations were inappropriate. And had they known more about the theory of intelligence, they would have realised that IQ scores are not in fact very relevant to simple symbol-learning tasks.

This study illustrates what is known as the 'self-fulfilling prophecy' or the Pygmalion Effect (Rosenthal and Jacobson, 1968); the *fact* of labelling children makes them behave in ways appropriate to the label. In their original study, Rosenthal and Jacobson supplied teachers with false information about which children were 'spurters' (i.e. on the point of making a spurt in academic progress) and which were not. Sure enough, to a slight but significant extent, the designated spurters made more academic progress by the end of the school year than the non-spurters.

Rosenthal's work has been criticised (e.g. Thorndike, 1968; Elashoff and Snow, 1971), and it is true that the original study had some methodological weaknesses. Since then more tightly controlled research has been carried out, such as Beez's study and that by Finn (1972). There appears to be little doubt that teacher expectations, for good or ill, do affect pupil performance through *goal-setting*. (As Beez shows, the 'bright' children were simply given more tasks and so achieved more.) This has the effect of reinforcing the 'bright' children with attention, and ignoring the 'dull' or giving the benefit of the doubt to the 'brights' but not to the 'dulls' when marking their work.

It is thus particularly important to look at the kinds of evidence that teachers may use in arriving at their expectations of students' performance. One of these is the IQ, and we shall pay particular attention to what it may mean *vis à vis* school performance.

CONTENT AND PROCESS ABILITIES, STYLES AND COMPETENCIES

Content abilities

Abilities are hypothetical: they are presumed traits in the individual that are invoked to explain why some obtain a correct response more quickly or solve more difficult items than others in tests involving verbal, mathematical, spatial or other types of items. Tests used to assess abilities are not intended to reflect the amount of instruction that has been given; that is the junction of *attainment* tests. General intelligence may be regarded as a tendency to do well over a wide range of ability tests. Sometimes the distinction between ability tests and intelligence tests may become blurred (psychologists often use the terms 'verbal intelligence' and 'verbal ability' interchangeably): in general, however, 'ability' has a narrower meaning than 'intelligence', and 'attainment' a narrower meaning than 'ability'.

The traditional way of distinguishing between different abilities is on the basis of *content*. Verbal ability refers to the solving of problems presented in a verbal format (i.e. such tests include vocabulary, syllogisms, analogies, and much school achievement). Spatial ability is that needed to work out mazes, copy designs, follow diagrams, do geometry, and so on. Number ability is involved in calculations.

Process abilities

The above distinctions, although they have practical use in designing tests and predicting individual performance, do not say very much about the processes used when performing on a test. Other ways of explaining test performance have therefore been suggested. Guilford (1956, 1967) proposed a complex model in which he distinguished *convergent* from *divergent* ability, on the basis of the *processes used* to arrive at an answer. A person who is high on convergent ability applies specific rules to achieve an accurate answer. This strategy is required in such tasks as working out a sum, solving verbal analogies ('Kitten is to cat as _____ is to goose'), or remembering the spelling of a word. In all these tasks, irrespective of content, there is only *one correct answer*. This feature has identified convergence with low level rote processes: Box 9.2 shows this view of convergence is mistaken.

BOX 9.2   AN EXAMPLE OF HIGH-LEVEL CONVERGENCE

Two brothers lived in a cottage situated at the fork in a road, one branch leading to Conville, the other to Diville. One brother always spoke the truth, the other brother always told lies. A traveller arrived at the fork, wanting to get to Conville but did not know which brother was the liar and which one spoke the truth. He was only allowed one question: what question could he ask *either* brother, and be sure of taking the right track to Conville?

(The answer is given below — upside down.)

Answer

'If I want to go to Conville and I asked your brother, what would he say?' When you hear the answer, take the opposite fork.

Divergence involves the opposite process. The person who is high on divergent ability generates alternatives and suggests different answers to those already given. This approach is required where several alternatives may be equally correct (which is not to say that some are not preferable to others), such as 'How else could the story have ended?'; 'Think up a different title from the one it has already'; 'How many different explanations can you find to account for the failure of that experiment?'. The relationship between divergence and creativity is evident, and we shall return to that particular point later.

Divergent and convergent abilities strongly recall the narrative and paradigmatic ways of knowing (Bruner, 1985), already referred to in the Introduction to Part 3; and it is suggested that that section be reread.

A number of writers have pointed to other process distinctions between abilities. Jensen (1973) referred to two main abilities: Level 1, which is based on memory processes; and Level 2, which is based on reasoning processes. Das, Kirby and Jarman (1979), on the other hand, used the work of the Russian neurologist Luria, whose work with brain-damaged patients led him to postulate two main kinds of processing activity: simultaneous and successive processing. We shall explain these terms, in their applications to education, later in this section.

The distinction between content and process abilities is useful because it allows us to emphasise different aspects of a performance (or potential for a performance). If we are interested in establishing how well individuals perform a task, then we would talk about content abilities, which is the usual meaning of ability. If, on the other hand, we are interested in the *way* a student typically approaches a task or problem, then we would be more interested in looking at process variables. For example, process variables are frequently of more value when matching a style of teaching to suit a student's typical processing style (called 'aptitude-treatment interaction', discussed below). Thus, individual differences in convergence may be assessed by an IQ test, and so the same measure — an IQ test result — may be regarded as either an ability measure or a process measure according to one's purpose.

Cognitive styles. Cognitive styles are consistent individual differences that reflect the style or manner in which a person perceives the world, conceptualises meanings, learns a task or solves a problem. Cognitive styles are related to process abilities, but are much more specific to the task being undertaken, and are generally designed so that they tend *not* to correlate with ability (Kogan, 1971).

In cognitive-style research, people are classified according to their performance in an experimental task or a test, and their performance is then analysed on other tasks (or in real-life, including educational, situations). A great deal of work has been done in this area, and several applications to education have been made (Kagan, 1965: Kogan, 1971; Staines, 1968; Witkin, Moore, Goodenough and Cox, 1977). Some of the more important cognitive styles are:

Field dependence-independence (Witkin et al., 1954). Field-dependent individuals are unable to separate relevant from compellingly irrelevant cues in perceptual tasks, such as perceiving a complex geometrical figure embedded in a complex background, or in judging verticality when seated in a tilted chair. Such people are said to perform poorly in low-structure environments (such as open classrooms) and to be more extrinsically motivated, but more socially competent than field-independent individuals (Witkin et al., 1977).

Reflection-impulsivity (Kagan, 1966). This style contrasts slow and accurate scanning of information (reflection) with rapid and inaccurate scanning (impulsivity). The initial 'diagnosis' is made on the Matching Familiar Figures test, in which various line drawings are checked for accuracy against a standard. Children who are classified as reflective (slow and accurate) in this task tend to be better readers than impulsive children of equal IQ (Kagan, 1965).

Cognitive complexity (Harvey, Hunt and Schroder, 1961; Kelly, 1955). This style, and a similar variable called *conceptual level* (Hunt, 1971), refers to the number of dimensions a person uses in making judgments. Conceptual level has been used by Hunt in matching children to classroom environments, with students at a high conceptual level (those using several dimensions) doing better in low-structure classrooms; and those at a low conceptual level doing better in high-structure classrooms (op. cit.).

We could go on and on. One of the writers once attempted to review all the material on cognitive styles: he had reached 18 different styles when he came across Kogan's (1971) review — which added five new ones to the list. However, not all of these styles were easily distinguishable from each other; many appeared to be the same thing with a different name. It was decided, with relief, that the review would do better service for practising educators if it remained unfinished. The work that is of value to educators can be accounted for with the more general process variables; the rest makes points that are of relatively minor import.

One overriding general point does emerge: educational performance is not always best understood in terms of some students having more or less of a particular ability than others. It is not recommended that students be classified into *types* on the basis of tests that a teacher is almost certainly not going to use in practice.

Competencies

Tyler (1978) presented a new slant on the question of abilities. Unhappy about the reliance of educators and vocational-guidance counsellors on ability testing, she suggested that people are more helpfully understood in terms of their repertoire of *competencies*. She defined a competency as 'a particular skill, something an individual knows how to do' (p. 99). To her, the basic questions are: '*Which* competencies are in an individual's repertoire?', and '*How*, out of the innumerable competencies in the total human repertoire, does an individual acquire his or her own unique assortment?'. As far as education is concerned, certain *core* competencies are required by all school leavers. In addition, there is a wide variety of *individual* competencies that may be acquired with the aid of schooling and which reflect an individual's plans, interests, lifestyle and abilities. Abilities are not used to predict what a person may or may not learn; all they do is to set broad limits, beyond which certain competencies will not easily be learned. Within those limits, the focus is on teaching the skill or knowledge that a student or teacher has decided could be usefully added to the student's repertoire.

Many school systems in the United States are already specifying core competencies in this sense (e.g. 'Read well enough to follow an instruction manual'; 'Write a letter of application using correct grammar and spelling'; 'Work out the total square footage of a room' (Tyler, 1978). Similar competencies were used in the ACER numeracy and literacy studies (Keeves, Bourke and Matthews, 1976), and in the tests Goyen (1974) used to gauge adult literacy.

Individual competencies encompass an enormous range of things that an individual may wish to acquire, from unaccompanied singing to zoo management. Tyler suggested that such a change in emphasis would have a considerable effect on public education, requiring definition of a range of individual competencies, and a different record-keeping system to keep track of an individual's successive accomplishments.

Wide-scale implementation of competency-based education is a long way off, but some aspects of this notion are gaining acceptance. At present, the emphasis is on broadly defined academic learnings that reflect the distribution of abilities in the student population. When school learning is conceived as acquiring competencies, on the other hand, a task analysis of the competency is required, and the emphasis is upon these analyses and how to teach them. Closely linked to this notion is the focus on *teaching* (over which teachers are believed to have some control) as opposed to the chance distribution of *abilities* (over which teachers have no control). It is a short step from that point to the argument that control implies responsibility, and that teachers are in some measure accountable for the learning (or lack of it) displayed by their students. Teachers' unions do not believe that such attributions are fair, whereas some politicians and business people believe that teachers should be accountable. As we shall see in this chapter, the facts permit either interpretation.

Meanwhile — and for both practical and political reasons — the quite sensible notion of competency has found application in technical, vocational and lifespan education rather than primary and secondary schooling. Our major concern here is with education in school as presently structured. We leave the competency-based notion, then, to consider the role of ability and process variables in education.

THE CONCEPT OF INTELLIGENCE

The concept of a single 'super-ability' underlying the successful performance of a wide range of tasks is a surprisingly modern one. It was the introduction of compulsory schooling at about the turn of the century, and its social consequences, that led people to ask whether finer distinctions might be made about intellectual functioning. Once schooling rather than family connections became the route to high-status occupations, it became pertinent to ask just what it was that the more successful students 'had', and whether or not it was related to more efficient performance on the job.

It was in the school context, in fact, that the first intelligence testing was carried out. Binet and Simon (1908) were asked to devise some means of determining the educability of children attending Paris schools: teachers and administrators were concerned by the fact that some children appeared to be gaining much more from their education than were others. Binet concluded, rightly, that the sorts of tasks psychologists then used (such as reaction times, and learning nonsense syllables) did not relate to the kind of thinking required in schools. Consequently, he used words and numbers as content in tasks that were not directly taught in school, like 'commonsense' reasoning tasks. Many of Binet's intuitions about the nature of thought were remarkably good; so much so that his basic items are still in use today, and one of the most widely used tests (the Stanford Binet) is a direct descendant of the original Binet-Simon test. Binet used test items that predicted school performance and agreed with teachers' ratings of 'intelligence' or educability.

Where Binet's test differs most from modern tests is only in scoring. When he had assembled a number of apparently good items, he gave them to large samples of children and found out what the 'average' performance was from four-year-olds, five-year-olds, and so on. A child performing at the level of an average six-year-old is said to have a mental age of six; if the actual chronological age is eight, then that is *below* average. The *intelligence quotient,* or IQ, is found by dividing mental age by chronological age and multiplying by 100 (to get rid of decimals). This child's IQ is thus: $\frac{6}{8} \times 100 = 75$. If a four-year-old passed the items expected of a six-year-old, that child's IQ would be $\frac{6}{4} \times 100 = 150$.

The notion of an IQ was very convenient, but it had one fundamental difficulty. After the age of 16, mental age tends to remain constant: on this formula, a 'normal' 32-year-old would automatically have an IQ of 50. This problem is now overcome by the use of *deviation* IQ scores, based on normalised scores rather than the ratio of mental to chronological age.

But all this is a matter of how the IQ is scored. What is important is the *meaning* of the intelligence: it is an aggregate or global estimate (Wechsler, 1949) of an individual's capacity for schooling, relative to age peers in the normal population. The tests themselves were selected because they predicted school performance; they were not based so much on a theory about how intelligence 'works'. We are now much more interested in this last question.

Over the years, indeed very rapidly after Binet's work and perhaps particularly as a result of massive testing of American army draftees in World War I, it was found that racial and cultural groups differed widely in performance on IQ tests (e.g. Kamin, 1974). As a result, IQ scores came to be seen as a measure of an individual's *innate capacity* for intellectual functioning (i.e. one which had a biological foundation and was largely determined by heredity). This shift in meaning — from an empirical instrument predicting educability to a biological entity — resulted in many misunderstandings, which are still rife today. Trying to clear up this misunderstanding, Hebb (1949) distinguished *Intelligence A,* which refers to the biological capacity and is *never* measured directly, from *Intelligence B,* which is capacity for *acting intelligently* as a result of the interaction between innate capacity and specific learnings. To this, only half-seriously, Vernon (1969) added *Intelligence C,* that is, what intelligence tests measure. Intelligence C is derived from a highly specific subsample of test situations and is two steps removed from innate capacity. Nevertheless, this clarification did not prevent an enormous amount of controversy about the role of genetic factors in intelligence-test scores, and we shall briefly examine the controversy later in this section.

For the moment, let us look at the question of the *structure* of intelligence, and its relationship to particular abilities. How many aspects are there to 'intelligence'? Is being good at arithmetic a sign that one is probably good at music, history, business management, car-driving, motherhood ... and so on?

THE STRUCTURE OF INTELLECTUAL ABILITIES

In 1922, Terman, a psychologist at Stanford University, selected 1,400 Californian children with IQs of 130+ and followed them through their school years and subsequently (Terman, 1954). The members of that group are now retired, and although Terman himself has since died, they are still being monitored by Stanford psychologists Robert and Pauline Sears. Some more recent findings are reviewed by Goleman (1980). The important point is that Terman noted that these highly intelligent people were superior in a variety of ways: longevity, low rate of physical and mental illness, sporting ability, even happiness and marital harmony. Nature does not appear to distribute its favours evenly.

Terman, of course, was dealing with a highly selected group of people, and the general principle seems to be that people who are superior in some ways tend to be superior in others. But what about the general run of the population? What happens within more 'normal' limits? There has been a tremendous amount of research into this question, and a useful summary may be found in Vernon (1979). If a battery of tests on such activities as memorising, reasoning, following instructions to make patterns, and so on — all of which relate to 'educability' — is given to a randomly selected group of normal people educated in the Western tradition, a fairly consistent pattern emerges. Data such as these present a complex statistical problem, which is usually solved by *factor analysis*. If 20 interrelated tests are presented to a large sample of people, the problem is to find the smallest number of factors or abilities involved. If four tests (e.g. adding, subtracting, multiplying and dividing) produce exactly the same results, then one factor, based on what we might call 'number ability', underlies any or all of the tests. Real-life tests give similar (although rarely identical) results. Factor analysis is thus a way of finding the most economical solution to an array of test results.

No single factor can be discovered to account equally for all tests, but one factor can account for some variability in many tests. This factor was called *g* ('general intelligence') by Spearman (1927), and was regarded by Jensen (1969) as the best estimate we have of intelligence: in process terms, it involves what might best be called *reasoning*. However, factor analysis also shows that other factors or abilities are involved in such wide-ranging tests, and there is a great deal of controversy about what the 'real' abilities might be. Vernon (1950) advocated a *hierarchical* model of intelligence:

1. A general *g* factor, which is a component of all tests but is most prominent in tests involving reasoning.
2. *Major* group factors, of which there are two, *v:ed* (verbal, educational) and *k:m* (spatial, practical).
3. *Minor* group factors, which are subdivisions of *v:ed* (verbal understanding and fluency, numerical ability — factors that are mostly involved in formal education) and of *k:m* (spatial ability, mechanical information and manual ability).
4. Several highly *specific* factors that Vernon does not consider to be important.

In Vernon's view, then, a particular verbal or perceptual-motor task will first require some of the *g* factor, then a less general verbal or practical factor, then more particular types of verbal or practical ability, and finally abilities specific to the task.

Other writers emphasise the *independence* of the various abilities that supposedly comprise intelligence. Guilford's (1967) 'structure of the intellect' model is the most complex, consisting of the independent components defined by five operations (including convergent and divergent productions), four contents and six products: a total of 120 separate complexes of abilities. This approach is somewhat impractical, however logical it might be. A more influential approach from the practical point of view is Thurstone's (1938) theory of *primary mental abilities,* which he claimed to be equal and independent of each other. These are:

1. *N,* the number factor: the ability to use numbers with speed and accuracy;
2. *V,* the verbal factor: the ability to use and manipulate words with understanding;
3. *S,* the spatial factor: the ability to think in spatial terms;
4. *W,* the word fluency factor: the ability to think of unrelated words rapidly;
5. *R,* the reasoning factor: inductive and deductive abilities;
6. *M,* the rote-memory factor: ability to memorise rapidly and accurately.

As a matter of fact, this list is rather similar to Vernon's: *R,* or reasoning, is very like the concept of *g,* and the rest recall his minor group factors. Indeed Vernon (1979) later pointed out that the (g + group factor) solution, and the Thurstone multiple-abilities model were mathematically equivalent, so that one's choice between the hierarchical and Thurstonian models is 'a matter of taste' (McKenzie, 1980).

Another theory is that put forward by Cattell (1971) and Horn (1968), who distinguished between *fluid* (g_f) and *crystallised* (g_c) intelligence. Fluid intelligence is 'pure' potential, which is highest at birth and declines with ageing and brain damage (e.g. through alcohol or drugs). With learning experience, it 'crystallises' into g_c, which increases with acculturation and particularly schooling. Crystallised intelligence, which becomes increasingly important in everyday decision-making, continues to develop until old age (see Chapter 6). The two abilities thus interact, together with motivational and individual style factors, in any task or test situation. Different tests are presumed to tap relatively different proportions of g_f and g_c: good g_f tests requiring spatial ability, and good g_c tests verbal ability (Snow, 1976). This brings us back, by a devious route, to the basic content distinctions between verbal and non-verbal intelligence.

This account is necessarily oversimplified, but we hope to have given a feel for both the complexity of the field and its underlying simplicity. We may conclude that:

- There is a 'bright-dull' dimension that underlies the performance of many intellectual tasks.
- Psychologists call this dimension g, or general intelligence.
- Task content does, however, call out further distinctions, particularly between verbal and non-verbal (spatial) ability.
- Intelligence tests have little or nothing to say on the issue of metacognition.

SOME PROCESS VERSIONS OF INTELLIGENCE

Kirby (1980) argued that general measures such as *g* 'do not serve as effective bases for understanding intelligence, or for the design of educational or remedial programs' (p. 120). Instead, he proposed that intelligent behaviour be analysed and measured in terms of the *cognitive processes* leading to that behaviour. Knowledge of those processes can lead to an analysis of the *instructional* processes that might best key in to the cognitive ones.

Information integration theory: Simultaneous and successive processing

Das, Kirby and Jarman (1979), following Luria's (1966) model, proposed two modes of information-processing. In the first, *successive synthesis,* information is held in working memory for processing when there is no interrelationship between the data other than their sequence (i.e. we rote-learn on the basis of which item follows what). This is very close to what happens during rote memorising and acquiring skills. Obviously, successive synthesis is involved in understanding spoken or written sentences, but it is also necessary at the same time to transform the original word units into a single meaning unit.

This transformation is achieved by *simultaneous synthesis,* the second mode of information-processing. Simultaneous synthesis is an ability to hold two or more items in mind simultaneously, while attempting to find a relationship between them. Reasoning, such as the verbal item 'Cat is to kitten as _____ ...', etc., is just one example of such a process. Luria located these two processes in different parts of the brain, and has shown how inadequate successive or simultaneous functioning in patients may be related to injury in the appropriate brain areas.

Simultaneous and successive synthesis are processes that are involved — either one or both — in virtually every cognitive task. In doing anything, we have either to follow through one step after the other, or to react simultaneously to the aspects that are presented; sometimes each process is involved at different stages of the same task. The horizontal processes described in Chapter 5 are primarily successive; the vertical processes that involve understanding have a strong simultaneous bias.

We can talk about these processes as 'abilities' when we measure them and see *how well* people perform in simultaneous or successive tasks with respect to a particular content domain. Thus, an individual may be measured on performance in verbal tests, and it is usually found (as we saw above) that good performance at one or other process generalises across several verbal tests. It may seem that we are back into dealing with fixed abilities again, but there is a difference: now we are looking at how well people go about a group of tasks in a *particular way* or approach. Are they good at handling the simultaneous aspects, the successive aspects, or equally good at both? As many tasks may be approached with either a simultaneous bias or a successive bias, this model provides a way of generating alternative approaches to a particular task.

The key to the use of either, and when the right mix of process is best for the task in question, is the concept of *planning* — which brings us back to the metacognitive domain once again.

Planning. Plans are analogous to computer programs (Kirby, 1984b): they mastermind the use of particular simultaneous or successive strategies which are appropriate for the task in question. The word 'mastermind' is used advisedly: one of the tests of planning ability is in fact the game 'Master Mind', in which one has to match a hidden array of coloured pegs in as few moves as possible on the basis of feedback provided on the correctness of the guesses so far. Poor planners use superstition ('Red seems to be working for me today so I'll use that'), and they tend to ignore feedback, replaying a colour they should know to be wrong. Good planners use their prior knowledge to work out their strategy (for instance, do they change their strategy if they know the opponent consistently selects colours systematically or randomly?); they vary few variables at a time; they take a logical set of alternatives and exhaust that before trying a different set.

Other planning tasks include searching for targets in a large visual array, planning composition and connecting up letters and figures systematically (Ashman and Das, 1980). A variety of possible tasks can be used, but they have in common: systematic and reasoned forethought before making a move; making use of feedback as one progresses and use of other relevant prior knowledge; a concern to be economical or 'elegant' in solution, and so forth. These are all features that have been discusssed in Chapter 4: this is highly metacognitive territory.

Planning may operate, as we saw in the case of planning for an essay (Chapter 6), at different levels of generality: 'macroplans' are focused on generalised aspects (e.g. the main ideas or theme of an essay) and 'microplans' on detail (e.g. sentence construction). Strategies may be regarded as components of a plan, or subplans, that are set up to handle a particular kind of task (Kirby, 1984c). Unfortunately, as Kirby points out, it is harder to change a person's macroplans than more narrowly focused plans: unfortunate, because there is obviously more educational mileage to be gained from changing the way a person will approach a variety of tasks, than from changing particular approaches to a narrow range of tasks or to specific aspects of the one task. Nevertheless, as the work on heuristics training showed (see Chapter 4), it can be done. Planning obviously represents a good target for educational intervention.

What is the relationship between planning and intelligence? What we are describing here seems clearly to be closely related to what we mean by 'intelligent' behaviour: yet 'traditional tests of intelligence appear to minimise the input of planning, in that they do not assess how the subject solves the task, only how well' (Kirby, 1984, p. 85). The information integration model, then, adds an important dimension to the concept of intelligence. Planning is in fact a form of self-instruction, and thus provides a paradigm for designing instruction, as illustrated in Figure 9.1. Figure 9.1 outlines a very general schema for three tasks:

- Task 1 requires a predominantly simultaneous approach (e.g. memorising a visual pattern).
- Task 2 requires both simultaneous and successive approaches for best solution (e.g. reading a moderately difficult text and taking notes).

- Task 3 requires a predominantly successive approach (e.g. debugging a simple computer program).

In planning an approach for any of these tasks, the learner needs to take into account:

- what the intentions are with respect to the task and what constitutes a solution;
- what the learner already knows that is relevant for systematic and reasoned forethought;
- the nature of the task; what operations would see a solution through;
- use of feedback while the task is being performed; being ready to alter the strategy package if the first one is not working.

The simultaneous and successive repertoires refer to the abilities the learner already has with respect to these two processes, and which should be regarded as general potentialities. The 'strategy packages' are what actually engage each task, and these will differ according to individual preference, ability profile and what the task demands.

Here we see that three strategy packages have been assembled: a simultaneous one for Task 1, a successive one for Task 3 and a mixed package for Task 2. The bottom row indicates that effective planning and operating will require feedback from each task as it is being performed.

Information integration and reading. As an example of applying the model to an instructional task, let us look at the case of reading. The early stages of decoding involve letter-sound blending, which is an essentially successive task: letters are taken in one after the other and run together to make a sound. Then with practice, word identification becomes more a matter of recognising the whole word: the letters are taken as a simultaneous whole that is instantly identifiable as a known word.

Both simultaneous and successive processes are involved with comprehension, and differently at different stages of reading skill development. A young child comprehending a sentence relies heavily on tracing word by word and then holding the gists of individual words and phrases in mind at once to see what their collective meaning is. A practised reader who is focusing on a main idea, on the other hand, holds that in mind simultaneously with the sentence meanings as they are rapidly processed. Meaning is thus added to or clarified simultaneously.

Successive processes thus tend to precede simultaneous, in both word identification and in comprehension, and this is important information for teachers of reading: clearly strategies of approach should reflect the balance of simultaneous and successive processes required currently. For example, Krywaniuk (1974) found that Canadian Cree Indian children were higher on simultaneous processing and lower on successive than Caucasians, a difference reflecting the way they were brought up to respond to their environment. A similar imbalance exists with Australian Aboriginal children, and undoubtedly for the same reasons (Klich and Davidson, 1984). The Cree children (again like Aboriginals) tended to score very poorly on early reading tests. Could it be that the failure to learn to read was due to a simultaneous-biased attack on a task that at this stage required a successive approach? Krywaniuk thought so: and in that event, the

Figure 9.1   The information integration model applied to three tasks

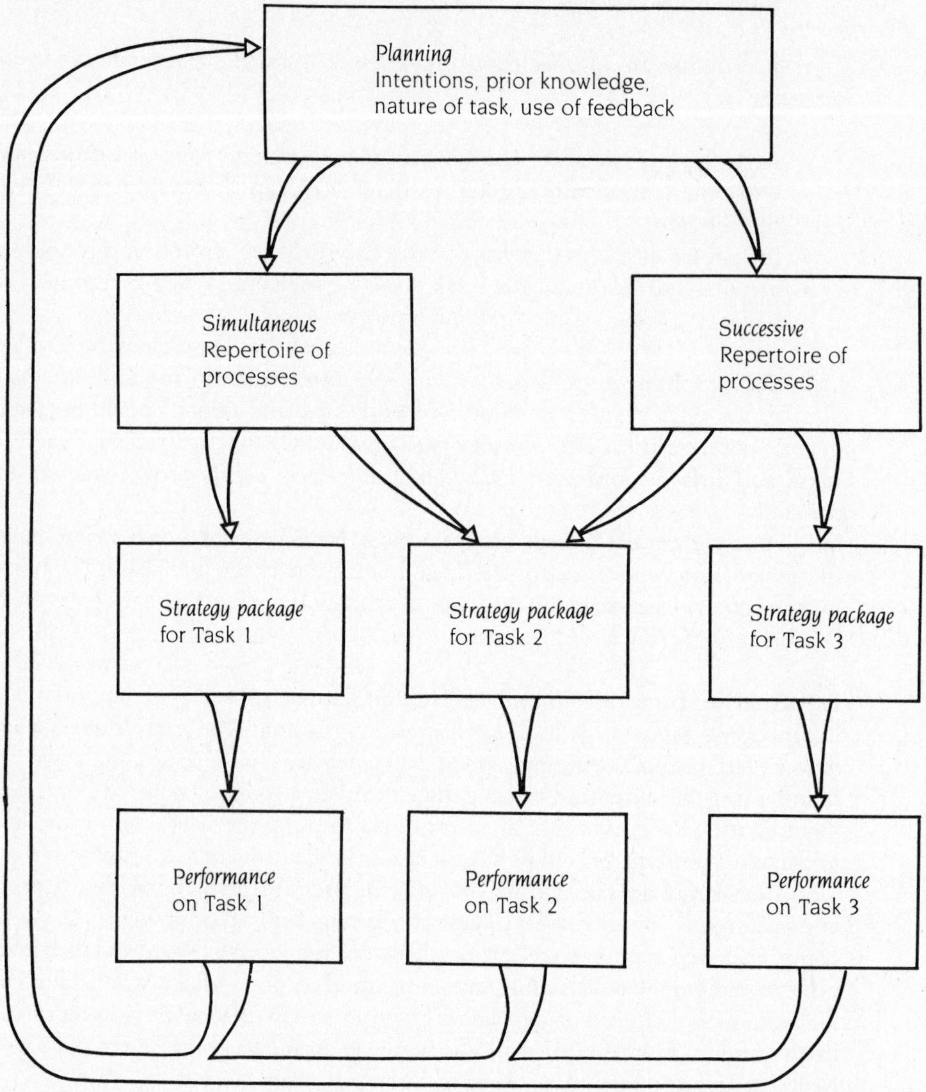

appropriate strategy was to build up successive processing by providing practice on a variety of sucessive tasks, which Cree children in their normal habitat do not experience but European children do. The tasks and activities were built into games, such as laying out toys in series. It was found that after such practice, the children began to adopt more appropriate successive-based approaches to word identification, and their reading skills improved accordingly.

A parallel study does not yet appear to have been attempted in this country, but the potential is clearly there. The general paradigm for the design of instruction, then, is to match the approach to the appropriate balance of simultaneous and successive processing that is required for the level of skill demanded at that point.

Level 1 and Level 2 abilities

Jensen's (1969, 1970) theory of Level 1 and Level 2 abilities is a much more traditional theory of process abilities. He takes the processes of memory and reasoning and identifies them as fixed abilities that are mostly innate. Level 1 ability is the ability to read in input and reproduce it exactly: rote memory is the prototypical example. Level 2 ability involves transformation between input and output: that is a process that involves reasoning. He regards Raven's progressive matrices as a good test of reasoning (which Cattell regards as a good test of g_f and Das of simultaneous processing). In an item in this test, a series of line diagrams is presented, the subject has to abstract the rule (e.g. a 90° clockwise turn) from the examples given, and then pick the next example in the series from a set of alternatives. This can become very complex when several rules are to be combined simultaneously, and such an ability is, in Jensen's view, one of the best all-round predictors of academic progress.

Two further points should be noted about Level 1 and Level 2 abilities. First, their relationship is hierarchical: Level 2 ability depends on a substantial degree of Level 1 ability, but Level 1 ability is independent of Level 2. A person with little Level 1 ability will have little Level 2 ability; but someone with high Level 1 ability may (or may not) have a high degree of Level 2. Whether he or she does or not depends on the second point, the *genetic inheritance* of both abilities. This point has caused much controversy —among not only psychologists and educators, but also the general public — for it implies that both memory and reasoning abilities are mostly inherited (Jensen put the figure of 80 per cent on the proportion of IQ test variance that can be attributed to heredity). He went further to state that there are racial differences in Level 2 ability, whites inheriting more reasoning ability than blacks. The trouble that this statement caused is now part of history. (For a review, see the list of suggested readings at the end of this chapter.)

Jensen stated further that lower-class children have less inherited reasoning ability than middle-class children. This, in his view, explains why lower-class children typically do less well in school than middle-class children; and also why attempts at compensatory education, such as the Head Start program, have mostly failed (this argument is most clearly stated in the 1969 paper). While both these statements are substantially true, many psychologists (e.g. Coleman, 1966) would explain them on grounds of impoverished environment rather than of genetic endowment. Jensen argued that children who are born with high Level 2 ability in lower social groups tend to be upwardly mobile. Through the medium of education — which Jensen believed to involve Level 2 rather than Level 1 abilities — the 'bright' lower-class children join the professional ranks, intermarry within their new social class, and thus pass on to their own children (now middle-class) their own Level 2 ability. The general effect is thus for the lower-class 'gene pool' to be depleted and the middle, professional classes to be enriched.

In discussing the implication of his theory for remedial education, Jensen (1970) distinguished between primary retardation (Level 1 *and* Level 2 deficient) and secondary retardation (Level 2 deficient only). The majority of retardates of IQ 70-85 are secondary retardates, and almost all come from lower-class homes. Their Level 1 abilities are 'quite normal', yet their under-achievement in school is staggering. Jensen believed this to be due to the fact that teachers encourage and reward Level 2 performances ('Tell it in your own words'), and strongly recommended that secondary retardates be taught instead by rote-associative methods. This is, of course, a highly controversial conclusion; the interested reader should turn to the original paper.

Jensen's theory is in some respects similar to that of Das and Kirby: each refers to two processes, and at least one of the processes is usually measured by the same test (Raven's progressive matrices). The differences are, however, even more important. Jensen interprets a person's score on a test as a measure of that person's 'power' with respect to the ability in question; and that power is fixed. Das and Kirby refer to a test score as indicating the *way of processing* information: the 'power' in the Das–Kirby model comes rather from planning, a metacognitive rather than a cognitive aspect. In effect, Jensen uses the model to tell the teacher what is or is not possible; the Das–Kirby model, on the other hand, tells the teacher what seems to be a fruitful way of organising instruction for a particular task. The first model is pessimistic: it tells the teacher where *not* to go. The second is optimistic: it tells the teacher where to go and what might be done about it.

The IQ and teaching practice: Conclusions

We started this chapter by reviewing a study that carried a clear warning about the use of IQs by teachers. What do the contents of this chapter so far add to this warning?

First, it is true that the single most effective predictor of academic achievement is the IQ. This is not, however, because the IQ in some mysterious way measures an individual's innate potential: our review has shown that IQ tests predict school performance for the very simple reason that they are designed to do so. IQ is a comprehensive and global index of performance, deliberately constructed to make no concessions to stylistic or qualitative differences in students' learning styles, or to show any sensitivity to different methods of teaching or to task structures. An across-the-board index of general ability is intended to refer to all students and to all teaching situations. The only differences that do tend to stand out are content ones, variously referred to as fluid and crystallised, or spatial and verbal, abilities. IQ, particularly verbal IQ, is a good strong single measure that predicts school performance in the main.

In the excitement of carrying out factor analysis, and calculating heritability indices, the cart came to be placed before the horse. IQ became the basic capacity the child 'had' in varying degrees, that more than any other single factor accounted for educability. IQ began to *set* the educational goals. Children whose performance in school deviated from the limits thought to be set by nature were *labelled*: as 'over-achievers' if their achievement was higher than their IQ suggested it 'should' be; and as 'under-achievers' if their achievement was lower than that predicted by their IQs. Only under-achievers were given remedial work, as the over-achievers were working *beyond* their theoretical capacity. In actual fact, both might need help.

In the development of the IQ test and testing theory, then, a confusion between causes and effects was created and perpetuated. The IQ was developed for purely practical reasons: it predicted school performance. Then somehow it became the criterion for *setting* school performance. Such a turn-around is illogical.

Models of intelligence are nowadays becoming more *process* based: the previous comparison between the Level 1 and Level 2 model of Jensen, and the information integration model of Das et al., shows the general direction in which we are heading. A very similar approach to the Das-Kirby model is Sternberg's (1980), who postulates higher order control processes, knowledge-acquisition components and performance components. His performance components are rather broader than simultaneous and successive processes, and he refers to the need for acquiring a knowledge base specific to the task, but these are only different ways of reallocating the planning strategies suggested by Das et al.

After an extensive review of models of intellectual functioning, Wagner and Sternberg (1984) conclude that educational programs must be:

- based on tasks drawn from the everyday world — including but not limited to the world of school.
- directed towards the metacognitive: 'There is ample evidence that training programs that omit metacognitive skills training have effects highly specific to the training task and situation' (p. 213).

That is a message that is becoming increasingly familiar (cf. Chapters 4 and 6). It also rather plays down the importance of a topic that dominated the thinking of psychologists and educators who for so many years worked on the assumptions of an ability model of intelligence that did not allow for metacognitive processes. That issue is nevertheless one we should refer to: the nature-nurture controversy. Are people born intelligent? Can they be made to become more intelligent than they already are?

THE NATURE–NURTURE CONTROVERSY

We have already referred several times to the question of the relative effects of heredity and environment upon intelligence. This is a very difficult issue to review dispassionately — and not only because it is so complex a field. It is an issue which, perhaps more than any other in psychology, relates closely to political and philosophical theories about equality. Whatever stance one adopts on the issue predetermines one's further views on the social structures (including schooling) best suited to realising those theories. Emphasis on the importance of genetic differences is called *jensenism,* which Jensen himself defined as: 'a biological and genetical view of human kind and of human differences ... [and] the bringing to bear of this genetic viewpoint upon understanding some of the problems of education' (1973, p. 7).

There are two major components in the jensenist argument:

1. IQ scores reflect the basic biological substratum of intelligence.
2. Environmental influences remain constant.

Evidence for both aspects is obtainable from data which express the relationship between the IQ scores of individuals who are related by blood. It is also possible to estimate what this relationship would be if genetic factors alone were operating. Jensen (1969) collected the median value for these correlations, obtained over a number of studies, some examples of which are given in Table 9.1. The theoretical value (genetic factors alone) for unrelated individuals is 0.00, whether or not they live together. Thus, the fact that the correlations between individuals who live together are higher than zero shows that environment exerts some effect on IQ scores. On the other hand, as the degree of kinship increases from, for example, cousins to identical twins (whose genetic make-up is the same), so the correlations rise — from .16 for second cousins to .75 for identical twins reared apart, and .87 for identical twins reared together. These last figures are, however, mainly derived from studies carried out by Burt (the latest being in 1966), and there is reasonable evidence that the data were faked (Hearnshaw, 1979; Kamin, 1974). The *heritability* of intelligence which, when multiplied by 100, is the percentage variance in IQ scores that can be *directly attributed* to genetic factors, and may be calculated from these correlations (assuming they can be trusted). Jensen gave the figure .82, or 82 per cent; other estimates for the Binet IQ range from .53 to .72 (summarised by Jensen, 1972, p. 300). Pezzullo, Thorsen and Madaus (1972) confirmed Jensen's findings with respect to Level 1 (.54) and Level 2 (.85) abilities, but found the heritability of divergent thinking to be zero.

Table 9.1   Obtained and theoretical correlations for IQs of people of varying kinship

Correlations between	1 Obtained median relationship	2 Theoretical value of relationship
Unrelated people		
Children reared apart	-.01	0.00
Foster parent and child	+.20	0.00
Children reared together	+.24	0.00
Related people		
Second cousins	+.16	+.14
First cousins	+.26	+.18
Uncle/aunt and nephew/niece	+.34	+.31
Siblings reared apart	+.47	+.52
Siblings reared together	+.55	+.52
Fraternal twins (different sex)	+.49	+.50
Fraternal twins (same sex)	+.56	+.54
Identical twins reared apart	+.75	+1.00
Identical twins reared together	+.87	+1.00

Note: Column 1 refers to the *obtained* median of all observed correlations. Column 2 refers to the *theoretical* value of the correlation on a genetic theory (i.e. if genetics explained the relationship totally, this is what the correlation *should* be).

Source: Jensen, 1969.

Vernon (1979), in a balanced discussion of the issue, put the heritability of intelligence at .6, but warned that such an estimate must be tentative, not only because of the *assumed* relationship between IQ score (Intelligence C) and basic innate potential

(Intelligence A), but also because such estimates are necessarily based on cultural and environmental effects as they exist *currently*.

To put this matter into perspective, let us look at the heritability of achievement. Estimates range from .15 to .41 for general achievement; and in particular subjects, from .04 to .57 (reading) and from .23 to .74 (arithmetic). Such ranges are enormous, and probably reflect (apart from the unreliability of the data), the genuine variation in environmental effects. If teaching were totally ineffective, arithmetic or reading would only be acquired to the extent that students taught themselves (i.e. the smart ones would end up knowing these subjects well, and the not-so-smart would not). If, on the other hand, teaching were totally effective, then heritability would drop to zero: no matter how dull the student, good teaching would result in good attainment. These different estimates tell us, then, not so much about genetics as about the effectiveness of teaching (i.e. environmental effects).

Thus a heritability estimate, whether for achievement or for IQ, is relative to the environmental conditions prevailing in the sample tested. In Western society, environment is relatively constant in that few children experience drastically impoverished environments and virtually all attend school for a minimum of nine to 10 years. Thus the effect of environment is underestimated because it is moderately constant. However, even in these conditions, individuals may experience drastic changes, and IQ can change accordingly. This was found to be the case in Newman, Freeman and Holzinger's classic study (1937): one of a pair of identical twin girls was reared by a relative in the country, the other in the city. The city twin's IQ was over 20 points higher than her country sister's.

Other writers adopt a more aggressive environmentalist stance. Kamin (1974) took the researchers on at their own game, claiming that if one starts with the 'null hypothesis' (that there are *no* genetic effects on IQ) then there has not been one study to date that can unequivocally disprove that hypothesis. The fact that no one has yet adopted such a research strategy in this area, whereas it is widely used on other areas, is, Kamin said, because it lets educators off the hook. In his view, the situation in this respect is no different from that earlier this century, when it was pointed out that the IQs of Northern European immigrants to the United States were superior to those of Southern European immigrants to the United States, thus proving the genetic superiority of the Nordic races. In fact, the difference was entirely accountable for in terms of the number of years of residence in the United States!

Kamin was really asking for the perfect study to be carried out; and that is inherently unlikely. Vernon's position is probably the most reasonable. On balance, under present circumstances, it seems that approximately half, possibly a little more, of the variation in IQ scores can be attributed to genetic factors, operating both directly and in interaction with the environment. (By 'interaction' is meant that bright children are likely to influence their own environment: for example, by interacting with intelligent rather than dull people who do not challenge them intellectually.) This position allows plenty of scope for schooling effects, while allowing for the likelihood that some students will be more adept learners than others. Indeed, the heritability estimates for achievement itself are low. If .3 is accepted as a general estimate, that means that schooling may have over *twice* the effect on determining a reading or arithmetic score than heredity. Kamin need not have worried: heritability arguments do *not* let educators off the hook!

General estimates of heritability are of course applicable to populations, not to individuals or to special subgroups. For example, the rural twin's IQ (in Newman et al.'s study) was clearly less influenced by environment than was that of the city twin. For this reason, among others, it is dangerous to generalise about racial groups or other minorities. Tests that measure certain proportions of environmental and genetic components in a standard white population are unlikely to measure the same proportions in other racial or cultural groups.

DIVERGENT ABILITY

Some years ago, Bartlett (1958) distinguished between open-system and closed-system thinking. Closed-system thinking is paradigmatic; as in convergence, effort is devoted towards obtaining the single answer that best fits the constraints of the problem. All the above conceptions of intelligence were of this closed, paradigmatic nature.

Many problems, however, have no unique or existing solutions. The solver's task is to invent some, and find out those that are most suitable for the particular purpose —and then the notion of 'best' may only be a matter of taste or circumstance. This is open-system thinking, or what Guilford (1967) called divergent productions. Beethoven could (and very nearly did) write several Ninth Symphonies: it is clearly absurd to say that the one that came down to us is the only one that he could have written, or that it is more 'correct' than the possible alternatives.

This second kind of thinking raises many problems when we try to measure the ability that is supposed to underlie it. When, as in convergent thought, there is one correct answer, measurement is in principle fairly easy and straightforward. But when the product of thought is novel, measurement in terms of products (the correct answer) becomes extremely difficult; in fact we have to assess the process itself.

Measurement of divergence

The pioneer work in this area was carried out by Guilford. In the Uses of Objects Test, for example, common objects are mentioned one at a time and subjects have to think up as many different uses for it as they can. For example, given *brick*, one person might list: to build a factory, to build a house, to build a garage, to build a wall, to throw at people, to throw at stray cats, to drop on spiders. Another person may list: to build houses, to use as a weapon, to grind into powder to make paint, to make a tombstone for a mouse, to put into cisterns to save water, to use as a paperweight, to stand on to gain extra height. The total number of *responses* (the fluency score) is the same in both cases, but the total number of *categories* is clearly different. The first person has listed only two categories (building and missile), whereas the second person has produced seven different categories (building, missile, paint, tombstone, displacement, weight, height). Accordingly, the latter is considered to be more *spontaneously flexible*, having given an example of each of many different properties, while the former has concentrated on only two properties. Although these differences between fluency and category-scoring are important theoretically, in actual practice the two scores correlate highly (Biggs, 1970). Box 9.3 lists two sets of responses.

Another method of scoring the uses test is to calculate the *originality* of the responses. This involves finding out the frequency of each response in the sample tested, and then weighting each individual response according to its uniqueness. This is, unfortunately, quite a tedious procedure. Many people, for instance, do not readily think of the 'tombstone' response, so that would be given a higher originality score than 'build a house' (which is mentioned by almost everyone). Originality scores correlate with fluency and flexibility, but they appear to get at a different aspect of divergence: all aspects are related to *creativity*.

A different technique of measuring divergence is to require subjects to complete a half-finished story, or to invent witty titles for given stories. Guilford, with regrettable disregard for the spirit of Box 9.3, mentions the following:

BOX 9.3   SOME RESPONSES TO THE USES TEST

'Think of as many uses for a paper clip as you can'

High Divergent	Low Divergent
To hold papers and stuff together	To fasten letter and papers with
To mend fuses with	A bookmark
To make wire sculpture	A missile
To unbend and poke at people you don't like	To hold photos in an album
To pick locks	
To join several up and make a necklace	
To use as weights on science beam balance	
To heat red-hot and drop down lower-class backs	
To perform operations with (e.g. cauterising diseased genitals)	
A frame for a mouse's sailboat	
To hold glued surfaces together to dry	
A clothes peg for dwarf's washday	
A stick for iced lollies	
For clamping the flapmouths of psychologists shut ...	

(*At this point the subject stopped writing*)

A man had a wife who had been injured and was unable to speak. He found a surgeon who restored her power of speech. Then the man's peace was shattered by his wife's incessant talking. He solved the problem by having a doctor perform an operation on him so that, although she talked endlessly, he was unable to hear a thing she said (Guilford, 1967, p. 156).

Non-witty titles, from low divergers, include 'Medicine triumphs', 'Never satisfied'. Witty titles, indicating high divergence, are 'Anything for a quiet wife'; 'A matter of wife and deaf'. There is clearly some degree of subjectivity involved in deciding whether one title is wittier than another — scorers of the test ought not to be low on divergence themselves — but usually there is a fair degree of reliability between judges on this.

Humour, cleverness and wit are thus also characteristic of the diverger. Hudson (1966) pointed out that when he gave the uses test, the great majority of humorous replies came from the high divergers. He also pointed out that divergers express high aggressive content. One of the present authors, for example, obtained the following response as a use for a paper clip: 'To heat red-hot and drop down lower-class backs' (see Box 9.3). Freud, in his celebrated essay 'Wit and its Relation to the Unconscious', mentioned the story of a Roman emperor noted for his rather indiscriminate sexual athleticism, who was leading a parade through Rome with the populace lining in the streets to cheer the procession. The emperor at one point noticed a man in the crowd, many years his junior, who bore a striking resemblance to himself. He stopped the procession, leaned toward the man and asked: 'You there! Was your mother ever at court?', to which the man immediately replied, 'Nay Sire, my father'. Freud interpreted this story in psychoanalytical terms; the present point is that it reveals the wit, aggression, unexpectedness and appropriateness of the high diverger.

Tests of divergent ability need not be verbal. One of Guilford's tests involved presenting an incomplete line drawing reproduced 20 times on a page: the task is to complete as many recognisable but different drawings on each outline as possible. This test, like the uses test, thus requires producing several appropriate responses rather than a single correct one.

We could go on listing further types of test, but enough has been said to gain some idea of what is meant by divergent ability. The general features are:

1. *Fluency.* The production of many responses, as opposed to settling on any one.
2. *Flexibility.* The production of many *categories* of response. These categories do, however, have to be minimally relevant: a random list of uses would hardly classify as divergent.
3. *Originality.* Being different is a further characteristic of divergence; this is often displayed as wit, delighting in the unexpected.

The dynamics of divergence thus come from the interplay of these components. To be divergent one has to produce fluent responses, an aspect that Thurstone called a primary mental ability. Cognitive flexibility is another component: the readiness to change categories, to explore different trains of thought. Finally, divergers are original: they create novel responses rather than settle for existing ones.

Factors producing divergence

In relation to home background, Getzels and Jackson (1962) found that highly creative (which in this context means divergent) children came from 'bohemian' homes, in which the rules were few and the children were encouraged to express themselves. One major component in their plan was 'Have a go' rather than 'Oh, maybe I'd better not'. High convergers, on the other hand, tended to say 'Better stick the rules out than your neck', which is a general life-plan readily acquired in the typical high converger's home, where the rules were strict and conformity enforced. Achievement, in these homes, was regarded in terms of the Puritan ethic: it was an all-important goal that was attainable through effort and doing the right thing.

Anderson and Cropley (1966) suggested that divergent children are unwilling to internalise 'stop-rules' in their plans, in particular those which say 'Don't take risks'. Thus the humorous and aggressive content of divergers' responses; the low diverger, on the other hand, may be afraid to risk offending the person giving the test. The findings concerning home background are clearly highly compatible with this theory.

Anderson and Cropley also found that boys were more original than girls; girls needed a much higher level of risk-taking to achieve the same originality scores as the boys. This also makes sense, in view of the greater caution and restriction surrounding girls' upbringing in our culture at that time: the traditional feminine virtues did not include non-conformity and risk-taking. Oddly, there is no current research on this that we could find.

Divergence involves a balance between *relevance* and *originality*. The high diverger has to make sure that unusual responses are also appropriate: there are limits to flexibility, and the stop-rule must be applied somewhere. This would appear to require a generic, easy-access, code system, which would also appear to be a prerequisite to high-level *convergent* functioning. Indeed there does tend to be a general positive relationship between convergent and divergent ability (Biggs, Fitzgerald and Atkinson, 1971; Cropley, 1966). However, the relationship is not simple, being closer at average and low IQ levels than at superior levels of intelligence (Yamamoto, 1965). The *threshold theory* states that a person cannot be properly divergent until functioning adequately as a *converger*: convergent ability may not be a sufficient foundation for divergence, but it is probably a *necessary* one.

Divergent ability and creativity

The description of divergence as involving fluency, originality, flexibility, intelligence, wit and humour seems to be describing what many people would refer to as 'creativity'. Indeed, in many early studies, the terms 'divergent' and 'creative' could be used interchangeably (e.g. Getzels and Jackson, 1962; Torrance, 1963; Cropley, 1967). This equation is, however, ill-advised. The very word creativity has strong value overtones: to be creative is to be sensitive, artistic, beautiful, free, unconventional and all the rest of it — all the things that progressive educators simply *must* be. Such thinking is one-dimensional and categoric: it puts convergent thought down as a polar opposite to creativity. Two things may be said of this:

- divergence and convergence are not opposite ends of the same dimension, but are two separate dimensions which, as noted already, correlate positively. To be highly divergent does not preclude one from being highly convergent; rather, the high diverger is likely to be both.
- divergence refers to a *characteristic* of thinking, which all people display to some extent (just as all people are intelligent to some extent — what would a person with *no* intelligence be like?). Creativity, on the other hand, is in some sense an all-or-nothing state, because there is a new product at the end of the process.

Creativity, in other words, always refers to a particular product within a particular area (painting, music, mathematics, etc.) whereas divergence is a process variable that applies across areas and is possessed to some extent by all students. Creativity appears to have the following components:

1. Divergent thought. This may subdivide into at least flexibility, originality and fluency.
2. Convergent thought, to some 'threshold' point. The person must be at least moderately bright in the normal (convergent) sense.
3. Total immersion in a particular area. Both 1 and 2 apply to general processes that are content-free: a creative *work*, however, is a particular product in an area in which the individual has considerable prior experience and expertise. The old gag about '90 per cent perspiration and 10 per cent inspiration' is to the point — a potter, for example, cannot be unaware of the work of other artists, ignorant of the properties of various clays and their optimum firing temperatures, or of various glazing techniques.
4. As a corollary of 3 the creative person is highly intrinsically motivated. Given expertise (which presupposes convergent ability), motivation, plus the bonus of divergent ability, *then* we might begin to talk about creativity
5. Finally, the world plays a large part in defining whether or not a work is genuinely creative. Someone who is mad could pass tests 1–4: unless there is the test of expert opinion, we should still withhold the appellation 'creative'. This is obviously a tricky question. Beethoven *was* conceived to be a madman by his contemporaries. Schubert was virtually ignored, Cherubini was a public idol. These judgments are all reversed today. But however one resolves this question, it is an aesthetic not a psychological issue.

In summary, teachers should not confuse the process and the product. For example, training children in divergent thinking (process) *might* make it more likely that they will be creative (product) later on, but not necessarily. We ought not to confuse the creation of products with modifying an intellectual process. Thus, discovery methods are not useful because students are likely to make substantive discoveries, they almost certainly are not. They are useful because the *backwash* from discovery methods — the means used, the processes employed — may be of considerable value in developing the cognitive processes of the learner.

*Divergence is a process which
may be developed by all students.*

SUMMARY

In this section, we have attempted to summarise some of the more important aspects of cognitive abilities as they relate to the classroom. Teachers believe that one of the most important, if not *the* most important, way in which students differ from each other is in terms of 'brightness'. Further, what they believe about a student's brightness will exert a profound effect on their interactions with that student, even if the belief is wrong.

Content and process abilities, styles and competencies. Ability is usually conceived in terms of either the *content* referred to (e.g. spatial or verbal abilities) or the *processes* used (e.g. convergent and divergent ability). Other ways of looking at this complex issue are in terms of cognitive styles and of competencies. Style, however, is too variable to be of much practical value to educators; the main contribution is a conceptual one, namely that the *way* of handling a problem is often of more educational value than the *power* of problem-solving. Competencies are based on particular skills and have a strong potential for influencing educational practice, particularly in vocational and post-compulsory schooling. Our main focus at the compulsory stage of schooling is on the concept of ability.

The structure of intellectual abilities. Intelligence can be seen as the group of abilities that underlie successful performance in school. The IQ test was in fact devised to predict educability. Three main theories about the structure of intelligence were reviewed: Vernon's hierarchical theory of *g*, or general intelligence, and several group factors; Thurstone's six primary mental abilities; and the theory of fluid and crystallised intelligence put forward by Cattell and Horn. Despite apparent differences, however, there is in fact a good deal of consensus about intelligence. There are *general* abilities that underlie the performance of most tasks, but there is some specialisation too, particularly in terms of the content. Verbal performance is often separated from spatial performance in a way that recalls the Cattell distinction between fluid and crystallised intelligence.

Some process versions of intelligence. The Das-Kirby model of information integration emphasises that the *way* people approach a task is important in defining what might be 'intelligent' behaviour. Although these authors use the same tests as traditional psychologists, they interpret them differently, using the scores as indicating a simultaneous or a successive 'bias' in deploying strategies for handling particular tasks. The important thrust of this theory is to emphasise planning, a metacognitive function, which is something lacking in the traditional psychometric model of intelligence. The latter model has (apart from testing which is itself now looked at askance by many educators) actually given little to education.

The difference between psychometric and true process models emerged in a comparison between the Jensen two-factor model of reasoning (Level 2) and memory (Level 1) abilities. Level 1 and Level 2 abilities are seen as fixed and limiting: their use in education is *actuarial*, indicating the probabilities of particular students performing or not performing in the desired ways. Such a view does not exploit the potential power of educational intervention.

The nature–nurture controversy. The question of the heritability of intelligence was looked at briefly, but the scene is confusing and politicised. While there is evidence that both hereditary and environmental factors affect intellectual functioning, it is not usually possible to establish the extent of this in any particular circumstance, for the very simple reason that the proportions keep changing. It is enough for educators to note that both factors *do* operate, and that educational strategies need to be designed with this in mind.

Divergent ability. All of the above was concerned with convergent ability. Divergent ability is less well understood, although it also has a strong effect on educational achievement. Divergence was seen to involve the criteria of fluency, flexibility and originality; which, with sufficient motivation and convergent ability, comprise creativity. Divergence was related to different childrearing practices and, when compared to convergence abilities, has a low heritability. It appears to involve the creation of novelty by bright people who are prepared, by personality and upbringing, to take risks. We should now turn to the educational implications of our discussion on convergent and divergent abilities.

SECTION B

CONVERGENT AND DIVERGENT ABILITIES IN THE CLASSROOM

Attainment

It has been noted that most subjects at school are taught and evaluated in a convergent manner (i.e. with emphasis on mastery of existing skills and knowledge, with correct application of known rules, and with evaluation emphasising the one-correct-answer principle). However, one of the more important findings of Getzels and Jackson (1962) was that divergent abilities do seem to relate to ordinary achievement in school. They found a difference of over 20 IQ points between their high-convergent and high-divergent (they used the term 'creative') groups, yet the overall performance in school of these groups was the same. Torrance (1960), and Hasan and Butcher (1966), reported many studies using samples from primary school to university, and two generalisations emerge. First, divergent ability contributes to academic attainment over and above the contribution from convergent ability, but more so in verbal than in numerical subjects. Second, this contribution is greater in the more permissive schools.

These data have important implications for the phenomenon of under-achievement, which is defined in terms of the *actual* achievement of the student compared with that *predicted* by an IQ test. High converger/low divergers will *appear* as under-achievers because they are not doing as well as high converger/high divergers. They have the same IQs, so they should reach the same level of attainment. Because divergence *is* relevant to school achievement, the high-IQ/low-divergent students show up badly in comparison.

The higher the academic ladder the student ascends, the more important divergent abilities seem to become. Wallach and Wing (1969) showed that Scholastic Aptitude Test (SAT) scores (which are convergent), and fluency and originality scores on five tests (divergent) were all related to attainment, the divergence measures more strongly linked to university than to high-school attainment. One or other (or both) of the divergence measures were also related to the following extracurricular activities, while convergence was related to none: leadership of student societies, art interests, social service, writing and science. Strangely, no measures related to music and drama activities. These data show clearly that, whatever is measured by normal scholastic tests, *it begins and ends with formal grades.* Divergence, on the other hand, relates to both formal grades and activities pursued out of interest — even in science, where the activity itself may require convergent thought.

Hudson (1968) showed that the full power of divergent thinking is more likely to emerge at the end of undergraduate, and during graduate, days: students who were so-so in their first year at university, but who were high divergers, emerged finally as significantly ahead of very able convergers. In his earlier work (1966), Hudson also presented evidence suggesting that students specialising in arts get relatively higher scores on divergent tests than on convergent ones, while those specialising in science are more convergently biased. Areas such as languages and classics fall somewhere in between, as 'ambivergent'. His findings have been supported by Cropley and Field (1968), Mackay and Cameron (1968) and Field and Poole (1970). It is possible that these and similar results may be explained by the study strategies the student typically uses: the high diverger using strategies that are more appropriate to arts, and the high converger strategies more appropriate for science (Biggs, 1970).

Divergent methods of evaluation

It should not be assumed that if objective tests maximise convergent processes, then essays (being 'open-ended', in theory) favour divergers. While Biggs (1973b) found that an objective format favoured students with some convergent characteristics (a tendency to rote-learning and teacher-dependence), those who did well in the essay format were not notably divergent.

Measures that emphasise divergent ability have an open-ended format (e.g. 'Think of as many —— as you can', the blank being filled with instruction appropriate to the subject). The responses can be scored according to fluency, flexibility or originality, although busy classroom teachers might find it convenient to score only according to the total number of responses (fluency). The inserted instructions might refer to maths (problems and calculations required in building a garage); English (synonyms or antonyms for supplied words); science (uses of a galvanometer in a school lab; improving the design of ...; things that might happen if water froze at -5°); and so on. The general strategy is that the one-correct-answer restriction be removed so that students are free to structure their responses.

Very little work has been done on the reliability and validity of these techniques. Usually they have been used for the purpose of assessing divergence in general, not for allowing divergers to express themselves comfortably in given content areas, which is what educational evaluation is concerned with. As indicated above, there is great potential for incorporating divergently structured tests into courses — and given the domination of convergent instruments in this area, the effects on teaching technique and student contact could be considerable.

Student–teacher interaction

Given the humour and playfulness, yet good attainment, of the high diverger, one might think that divergers would in general be popular with teachers. However, consider the following exchange:

Teacher: And now can anyone tell me what infinity means? (*Silence*) What is infinity?
Billy: (*Pause*) Uh, I think it's like a box of Cream of Wheat.
Teacher: Billy, don't be silly! (Jones, 1968, p.72)

Getzels and Jackson reported, and others have subsequently confirmed many times, that high divergers are *not liked* by their teachers. They are regarded as a little bit *too* clever — non-conformists, rebels, nuisances, troublemakers, cheap comedians, and so on — despite the fact that their actual attainment is as good as and often better than that of high-IQ students.

It is understandable that teachers should react in this way. As we have seen, divergers are highly original, and so are bound to raise issues and possibilities that may not occur to anyone else in the class (including the teacher). Divergers are likely to upset the lesson if their comments and suggestions are taken seriously. They will lead the train of thought into directions that the teacher simply had not anticipated. The teacher who is anxious to cover a set number of topics in a given time and in a given order is bound to be irritated by someone who would, if permitted, make this impossible.

Further, it can readily be seen that if the teacher is insecure, the high diverger poses a serious threat. If whacky comments are actually sound — as is Billy's Cream-of-Wheat answer (the packaging has a picture of a man holding a Cream of Wheat box, on which there is depicted a man holding a Cream of Wheat box ... etc.) — then the teacher has to be constantly on guard. The point of many remarks may not be seen immediately, and they *might* happen to be good ones. A simpler alternative is to deride whatever the high diverger comes out with, as either insolent or just plain foolish: the high diverger is typecast as the class nuisance, the class clown, or both. Torrance (1965b, pp. 51–2) quoted one example where a boy regarded by both his parents and pediatrician as gifted, was actually classified by his teacher as retarded — mostly because he did not accept the tasks he was assigned and was consequently awarded failing grades.

Getzels and Jackson used a 'desirable as pupil' rating and found that the high divergers were consistently regarded as 'undesirable', while high convergers were regarded as 'highly desirable' by teachers. Similar findings have also been reported by Hasan and Butcher (1966) and by Torrance (1963).

Let us look at teacher-pupil interaction in a wider context. Holland (1959) intercorrelated teacher ratings of pupils on 12 separate traits, and found that achievement, persistence and 'leadership' were the most valued qualities of students: hardly, Holland noted, a picture of the creative person, but rather that of the conforming and conventional one.

Add to this general picture the finding by Getzels and Jackson, that the achievement-oriented middle-class home tends to breed the high converger, and one would expect to find that teachers as a group would *tend* to be more convergently biased than the general run of the population, including their pupils. The converger-teacher and diverger-student interaction is relatively common; it also thus represents a basic clash of values. The tendency is for the non-conforming, divergent student to be regarded as something of a subversive and a threat to the established order, rather than as someone who is clever and amusing and who one day will go far.

There is an obvious paradox involved here. Most teachers would undoubtedly claim that 'creativity', independence, capacity for intrinsic motivation, flexibility and originality are worthwhile educational goals. Yet most (not all, of course) teachers tend to regard children who manifest these qualities as 'undesirable'. This suggests that teacher education should be much more effective than it is about the recognition and encouragement of quality, and specifically the particular quality of performance that stems from divergent ability. Thus Biggs, Fitzgerald and Atkinson (1971) found that teachers rated both high convergers and high divergers positively on such attitudes as 'conceptual approach to problem-solving', 'independence' and 'asks questions'. Whether they *liked* the divergent children was regarded as a separate issue. As for what creative *students* see as desirable in *teachers,* see Box 9.4.

In terms of coping with individual differences, then, it seems most important to stress that divergence is a source of behaviours that may be confused with sheer nasty-mindedness in the child — even, as Torrance pointed out, with mental retardation. We need only recall the self-fulfilling prophecy to point out that if a teacher does decide that highly divergent Johnny is a stupid and evil-minded little boy, Johnny may before long become just that — at least with that particular teacher. So next time the teacher tells the class to draw a human head, and one bright spark pipes up 'From the inside or the outside, Miss?' (Cropley, 1967), it may be worth considering the possibility that a genuine question is being asked.

We would expect, from the above discussion, that convergent children would do better and feel happier with a convergent teacher, and vice versa. Yamamoto (1963) showed that with IQ held constant, low divergers did better on Grade 5 arithmetic than high divergers when taught by low-divergent teachers, while the opposite was true with high-divergent teachers. It seems that the divergent-teacher/divergent-student match meant that the teachers and students were all on the same wavelength, which facilitated the educational process.

However, this raises the important question as to whether this kind of match is in the long term the most *desirable* one. Perhaps divergent children *should* be exposed to other people who are convergent, as they certainly will be when they leave school. And similarly, should not convergent children see how the other half lives — acquire tolerance for divergent behaviours and perhaps even become more flexible and spontaneous themselves? It is possible that this is indeed the case, but there is little research reported that speaks directly to the question, and the issue of who to match with whom remains at this stage rather a matter of opinion.

BOX 9.4   WHAT CREATIVE STUDENTS SEE AS DESIRABLE QUALITIES IN TEACHERS

'They need patience, that's for sure. I guess they would have to have a very creative mind and an ability to judge because for a teacher to go home and mark 32 pieces of writing is not the thing that most people would want to do. So they've got to be able to judge whether it's good, but they've got to keep an open mind about it because they can't just say — well that piece of writing it's no good because ... it's written in some other form than everybody else's.' (Student 8, M, Yr 9)

'... my teacher last year used to always read out my writing because he thought it was good, and that really made me mad ... I didn't mind it when it was fiction but when it was something that said my feelings about something I didn't like that ... He didn't have any right to tell everyone in the world how I felt ...' (Student 12, F, Yr 8)

'Someone who can persuade other people to express themselves, someone who can, yes, bring out the creativity in the kids. Because I think probably everyone's got creativity they don't use, and I think it's how good the teacher is that they can show that creativity to the person and persuade them to use it.' (Student 34, F, Yr 11)

'... the ultimate thing ... is the ability and the willingness to sit down and talk to students, because you find some English teachers (they're in a minority, thank God) aren't willing to talk to their students on a level ... you get people who talk down ... which is the worst thing possible for the writing of English because you need to be able to discuss things absolutely straight.' (Student 35, F, Yr 11)

The quality most mentioned by students (15 responses; 43 per cent) was that English teachers more than anything else should be 'tolerant', 'fair' or accepting of individual points of view, styles and opinions:

'It's so important to know that whatever you say will be listened to and considered. I think an English teacher should be willing to put aside their own point of view and consider somebody else's point of view solely on its own merits.' (Student 35, F, Yr 11)

'Just being cheerful and fairly funny, or doing little things that probably other teachers wouldn't do ...' (Student 5, F, Yr 8)

'Being able to be different — all maths teachers are the same, and all science teachers are the same — but all English teachers are different — they've got their own character and personality ...' (Student 28, M, Yr 11)

Source: O'Neill and Reid, 1985, pp. 131–3.

Training in divergent and convergent abilities

Part of the answer to the question about the most desirable kind of match lies in the extent to which these two abilities are in fact *modifiable* by experience. Modifiability of divergence is of course presupposed in attempts to 'teach for creativity'.

The first point to emphasise is that no amount of permissiveness and child-centredness will result in creativity for all. Such training can only have as a reasonable goal the modification of the divergent *style*. Further, it is too simplistic to argue that, because certain teaching environments are associated with more frequent responses on the Guilford Uses Test, a deep-seated change in the creativity potential of the person has therefore been effected. Hudson (1968), for instance, showed that scores on the uses test could be boosted considerably simply by *instructing* the students to be as 'original' as possible (on one occasion, Hudsons's subjects gave more divergent responses when he threw a tantrum while administering the test!). As Anderson and Anderson (1963) likewise pointed out, training can produce high-divergence scores but there is often little or no transfer to other divergence tests. Such manipulated changes in originality are trivial, from the educational point of view.

Bearing these warnings in mind, there are nevertheless some studies that are relevant to the school environment. Torrance (1961, 1965) has shown that divergent thinking abilities, as measured by *several* independent tests, may be affected by the nature of the school environment. In one study, he classified the teachers in a primary school as being basically 'creativity-motivated' or 'power-motivated' in their teaching. The first group emphasised flexibility in problem-solving, were keen to have children produce their own solutions, and so on; the second emphasised adherence to rules, firm discipline, and had no tolerance for distracting or time-wasting questions. He found that at kindergarten and Grades 1–3, divergence increased in the children taught by the 'creativity-motivated' teachers, but decreased in the 'power-taught' children.

Haddon and Lytton (1968, 1971) predicted that a highly formal, authoritarian school atmosphere would inhibit divergence in pupils, but that an informal atmosphere which emphasised self-directed learning experiences would permit expression of divergent qualities. They selected from schools representing both formal and informal atmospheres, and found that the informally taught children were significantly more divergent on five out of six measures of divergence. They also found the threshold effect referred to earlier: the emergence of divergent thought was most pronounced among the more *convergently* able children. In a follow-up study four years later, they traced most of the sample of about 200 children in various secondary schools and found that, after verbal ability, the most important factor affecting the *current* level of divergence was whether they had attended formal or informal primary schools; the effect of their current secondary school was negligible. Haddon and Lytton concluded that formal education fails to develop divergent thinking abilities in the most able children, and that this effect is critically important in the primary school years.

These studies collectively suggest the 'releasing' of divergence: the school environment may not be *making* children divergent so much as making it possible for them to *manifest* their existing divergence. If school can release divergence, then we might also expect that the school atmosphere may *suppress* it. Cropley (1967) summarised several teaching practices that inhibit divergent abilities.

1. *Emphasis upon being right.* Naturally enough, where insistence is upon one correct answer, divergent children are not capitalising on their abilities.

2. *External evaluation.* 'Being right' implies an external criterion of truth (i.e. what the teacher or the textbook lays down as truth). Such an approach encourages the learner to adopt a pawn-like stance which is inimical to personal involvement and the development of intrinsic motivation (see also Chapter 3). It is likely that excessive reliance on external sources of truth will make it more difficult to cope later when such sources do not exist.

3. *Impatience with wasting time.* When teachers are anxious to get on with the lesson and to cover the set curriculum, they will be disinclined to allow time to follow up the novel suggestions or interpretations that are thrown into the ring by the high divergers. Some of these may be worth following up, others may not; but if they are not pursued, then obviously the diverger will be increasingly discouraged. This frustration may well lead them to sabotage the lesson by falling into the role of class clown (in which the diverger may have already been typecast.)

4. *Conformity pressures.* It is clear by now that one major attribute of divergent thought is originality, a tendency which is obviously discouraged where there are strong pressures to conform to the established standards. If divergers persist in such a situation, they are likely to be defined as rebels, which may well become a self-fulfilling prophecy with respect to nuisance value.

5. *Distinction between work and play.* Another notable characteristic of divergent thought is humour, wit and playfulness. If work is maintained as solid and serious, with play treated as a separate area where frivolity is permitted, the play-work amalgam so characteristic of divergent processes is never permitted adequate expression. The Puritan ethic provides poor soil for growing divergence.

Torrance (1965b) believed that the teacher can take more positive steps than simply avoiding techniques that inhibit divergence. He referred to what he called 'guided self-evaluation', which embodies the principles we have been discussing: a cognitive *acceptance* of the child's efforts, and an affective *approval* of them. When children offer solutions to problems or write stories, teachers would not dismiss them out of hand or vigorously correct them, even if they can see glaring faults in terms of whether they work or not. Rather they would indicate that they welcome the fact that the child has tried, praise the effort, and then turn the evaluation back on to the child (hence the term *self*-evaluation): 'Do you think this would work? ... Are there other ways you can think of that might improve your idea? ... Try it out and see what happens ...', etc. (see Box 9.5).

Thus, it is clearly evident that schools affect the expression of divergence, and that the major effect is in the primary grades (or even earlier) rather than later on. We have insufficient details of the process to be very specific, beyond a few commonsense words of advice about creating an environment that is congenial to divergent production. A child may have been brought up to believe that every question does have a correct answer, whether the question is about a maths problem, the nature of the universe, or the choice of a spouse. It would be a strange and unsettling experience to then land in a class where all these ideas and, more importantly, the values behind them, are open to question. Brainstorming and other group techniques are all useful methods of bringing the message home that ideas are free and that their 'correctness' is relative.

BOX 9.5   SOME QUALITIES OF CREATIVE TEACHING

E. Paul Torrance and R. E. Myers studied examples of teaching situations which produced 'creative' or good divergent responses from students. They suggest the following factors as coming through most strongly in the examples they looked at:

- Recognising some heretofore unrecognised potential.
- Respecting a child's need to work alone.
- Inhibiting the teacher's censorship role long enough to permit a creative response to occur.
- Allowing or encouraging a child to go ahead and achieve success in an area of interest in a way possible for him or her.
- Permitting the curriculum to be different for different children.
- Giving concrete embodiment to the creative ideas of children.
- Giving a chance to develop responsibility and to make a contribution to the welfare of the group.
- Encouraging deep involvement and permitting self-initiated projects.
- Reducing pressure, providing a relatively non-punitive environment.
- Approving the pupil's work in one area to provide courage to try the others.
- Voicing the beauty of individual differences.
- Respecting the potential of low achievers.
- Showing enthusiasm for the pupil's ideas.
- Supporting the pupil against peer pressures to conformity.
- Placing an unproductive child in contact with a productive, creative child.
- Using fantasy ability to establish contacts with reality.
- Capitalising on hobbies, special interests and enthusiasms.
- Tolerating complexity and disorder, at least for a period.
- Permitting oneself to become involved with pupils.
- Communicating that the teacher is 'for' rather than 'against' the child.
- Giving stimulating or provocative examinations.

Study the list carefully. See if you can add to it, from your own experience as either teacher or learner.

Source: Torrance and Myers, 1970, p. 35.

Divergent teachers would no doubt find it easy to think up their own flexibility exercises. One famous physicist developed a technique for improving his tolerance for novel ideas, by writing on cards as many physical principles as he could think of — one per card — and placing the cards in a goldfish bowl by his front door. When he left for work each morning, he would shake the bowl, extract three cards at random, and spend the first hour of the morning thinking up ways in which the three principles could be interrelated.

EXCEPTIONAL CHILDREN

So far, we have been discussing divergent and convergent *processes* in the classroom. We should now return to the other aspect, that of divergent and convergent *abilities*. While teachers will most commonly deal with children in the normal range of abilities, they may alse encounter students who exceed these limits (whether above or below).

Exceptional children may indeed require a 'special' education. Teachers who want to deal with exceptional children are therefore usually required to undergo additional training, with particular reference to the kind of exceptionality they want to specialise in. Common areas of special education include the following:

Mental retardation is often classified as 'mild' (around 55 to 75 IQ) and 'severe' (below 55). Mildly mentally retarded children usually attend ordinary schools, and may either be streamed into 'opportunity' classes, or mainstreamed with their age peers. Severely retarded children are more usually sent to separate schools or sheltered workshops.

Specific learning disabilities is a term that covers an enormous range of problems, related to particular impairments rather than general lack of ability. It refers to *under-achievement*, in either one or a few subjects, or throughout the curriculum. The causes of specific learning disabilities may be purely educational (e.g. missing a crucial experience such as learning to read) or extend to presumed brain injury or malfunction. Other learning disabilities might be due to behaviour problems such as hyperactivity, or to emotional problems, neither of which directly cause cognitive impairment but which are likely to lead to poor learning. Learning disabilities may also be culturally or economically based, such as those experienced by some minority children: migrants, Aborigines, or those from severely impoverished circumstances.

Physically and sensorily handicapped children may have no cognitive impairments, but because of their handicap (e.g. quadriplegia, spina bifida, blindness or deafness) need specific resources and teaching techniques that cannot be provided in the normal classroom.

Giftedness, the other end of the exceptionality scale, is an area that is increasingly recognised as requiring special assistance, either within the mainstream or in special classes.

The whole area of exceptionality is thus enormously complex. So, too, are the procedures schools use to deal with exceptional children. The official policy across Australia today is to avoid special placement, either by class (beyond normal streaming or setting) or by school, except in those cases where the sheer logistics of teaching exceptional children demand such treatment. The GA class or its equivalent persists in practice, often as a frank survival tactic. Indeed, the official policy is becoming more viable with the increasing numbers of school counsellors, and with the more specialised and extended training that counsellors are now receiving. If learning, behavioural or emotional disabilities are displayed in the normal classroom, the appropriate procedure is to refer the student to the school counsellor.

There is, however, an area of exceptionality that is becoming the focus of increasing concern, which is not the domain of the counsellor, and for which teachers (as yet) receive minimal in-service training. This is the problem of the gifted child which, in view of our discussion of convergent and divergent abilities, it is appropriate to discuss now.

The gifted child

A decade or so ago, in the days of selective schooling, exceptionally able children would find themselves in the top stream of selective high schools. Most schools in most States are now non-selective, or comprehensive: a situation that has led many parents and educators to become increasingly worried that the potential of the gifted child is not being stretched, with the result that able children are becoming lazy, bored with schooling, and dropping out of formal education prematurely.

This problem was faced many years ago in the United States, where comprehensive schooling has been the mode for most of this century. Alternatives adopted in that country vary from special 'greenhouse' schools for the gifted to extracurricular enrichment programs within the normal system. An example of the former is Calasanctius School in Buffalo, New York (named after a Roman poet), where the students face a prodigious curriculum including eight modern languages (for five- and six-year-olds), and very high-powered seminars in which students' ideas are analysed and criticised in public by the other students (Gerencser, 1979). More commonly, however, students with special gifts undergo enrichment programs that are additional to their normal schooling, often involving attendance at university classes in their subject of special interest.

Before we speak of provision for the gifted, however, we should decide who 'the gifted' are. As we have seen above, Terman in 1922 defined 'genius' (which was far too strong a word for his sample) on the basis of an IQ of 130+. However, IQ is a measure of convergent ability; and by any definition, giftedness must include divergent ability. Further, many think of giftedness in terms of a particular and exceptional talent, as displayed by a musical or a mathematical prodigy. Any definition must also include an affective component: deep personal involvement, dedication or intrinsic motivation in a particular topic. Today, then, the term is 'gifted and talented' (Braggett, 1984), which may include outstanding ability in a wide array of areas: intellectual, academic, creative, leadership and psychomotor skills.

What are the family backgrounds of gifted children? It is not surprising — whether one argues from nature or nurture — that 'gifted children tend to come from smaller, middle class or upper-middle class families in which the quality of parental involvement is particularly noticeable and in which intellectual stimulation is strongly apparent' (Braggett, 1983, p. 74). In attempting to follow this up more explicitly, Braggett interviewed the families of 25 gifted children and found:

- Language activities were stressed by parents (books, songs, stories, etc.).
- Each home provided a wide range of toys and construction materials, although Braggett notes 'a surprisingly rigid sex-role pattern'.
- TV viewing was 2.6 hours a day — less than average, and programs were monitored by parents.

- Over 80 per cent of the parents had consciously taken their children on 'educational' excursions (zoo, bushwalks, art gallery, museum, etc.).
- Social development was considered particularly important by parents.

Clearly, these children were brought up in an environment that stressed achievement, as well as the opportunity for diverse learnings as such.

There are various kinds of provision for gifted children in Australia (see Box 9.6): mostly, this provision is within the mainstream, rather than in the provision of 'greenhouses' on the Calasanctius model. Whatever the specific framework, a successful program is that proposed by Renzulli (1978), who proposed a three-stage program for gifted children:

1. enrichment, which provides an experiential background for the children to draw on in stage 2;
2. strategy development, for handling the enrichment information and breaking new ground by recombining information to ask novel questions;
3. independence, which involves coping on one's own, in particular by applying the learned strategies to novel situations.

The general approach is to take a topic which has particular local relevance, such as the effects and problems of coal-mining, and in the enrichment phase take the students to a mine and experience all stages of coal production. Students with literary talents would then write a poem (or musicians a piece of music) to capture the experience. They are then asked to pose questions: Is mining particularly unpleasant or dangerous? Should miners be paid more money? What moral problems are involved (e.g. in ecological or human terms)? They then look at ways of resolving the questions. Finally, students work on their own to pose similar questions to *other* problems. This last aspect recalls the physicist and his goldfish bowl of items — forcing relatedness on to initially independent issues. In another project, the topic was 'The effects of living in cities': the departments of architecture, drama, community programs and medicine were used as resources to provide their particular expertise on aesthetic, health and community aspects of this problem.

Clearly, such a program requires from the children a high level of both convergent and divergent abilities, the educational skills to cope with the reading, writing and mathematical tasks required and, not least, a high degree of motivational commitment. Also pretty clearly, such a program requires that teachers must be of a special kind. If they are to survive at all, they would have to be themselves expert in various areas, and be prepared to act as intellectual and creative models to the children. Special training in handling programs for the gifted is clearly very important (see Box 9.6).

INDIVIDUALISING INSTRUCTION

Any systematic study of individual differences between learners raises the question for educators of how to suit instruction to pupils. Earlier chapters have already discussed

BOX 9.6   PROVISION FOR GIFTED/TALENTED STUDENTS

There are six different forms of curriculum provision for gifted/talented students across Australia.

1. **Enrichment:** the school provides experiences beyond those which form part of the regular curriculum; allows for wider interests to be fostered, specific in-depth interests to be cultivated, the regular curriculum to be extended, and process skills to be developed. May be combined with out-of-school camps.

2. **Cluster groups:** a number of schools in the same locality provide specialised programs at a central point; talented students from each school attend specific courses (often half a day a week for eight to 10 weeks). Permits the rationalisation of resources across State, Catholic and other independent schools at primary and secondary levels.

3. **Special classes/schools:** children attend a full-time class in a primary or secondary school, having been selected on specific intellectual, performance and/or other criteria. Enrichment and extension activities form an integral part of the curriculum and a compacted program of core studies is frequently introduced.

4. **Special interest secondary centres:** a department within a comprehensive secondary school is developed as a highly specialised unit (e.g. music, art, drama, languages) and provides quality courses for students with specific talents. Students are usually highly selected and allowed to specialise in their area of expertise in addition to pursuing a regular secondary curriculum.

5. **Acceleration:** students may be accelerated in their studies through:

   - grade skipping;
   - subject acceleration;
   - individual rate of progression;
   - a special program which permits selected students to pursue a specially devised curriculum over a shortened period of time, for example, a six years secondary course in four years.

6. **Mentor programs:** individual students with specialised abilities are matched with adult mentors who have similar interests and abilities. An individual program is devised for each student.

Source: Braggett, 1985.

both differences and appropriate teaching practices, and this chapter raises the educational problems of pupils with exceptionally high or low abilities, and of those who adopt divergent processes in the normally convergently oriented classroom.

The simplest and most widely used is streaming: separating high ability and low ability students and teaching accordingly. We have reviewed the research evidence here earlier, with regard to both motivational and academic outcomes (see Chapter 3). Other methods are outlined below.

Aptitude-treatment interaction (ATI) is when one treatment or method works well with the children high on a particular aptitude and poorly with those low on that aptitude, but with another treatment the picture is reversed. Theoretically, then, all children work under conditions that are ideal for their own sets of aptitudes. Later, Cronbach and Snow (1977) reviewed many studies of ATI and found some consistent results: for example, anxious children perform better in high-structure classrooms, whereas non-anxious do better in low-structure informal classes.

To fully implement the results of ATI research in practical situations requires that students be *identified* as being high or low on a particular aptitude, and then placed in classes where each one is *taught consistently* in a manner appropriate to that aptitude. There are many theoretical and practical reasons why this procedure is unlikely to be adopted:

1. As in the case of cognitive styles, the number of potentially usable aptitudes is large: including anxiety, g_f, g_c, achievement motivation, internality, convergence/divergence, Level 1/Level 2, simultaneous/successive processing, and so on. A case can be made for any or all of these as suitable aptitudes. Which ones does the educator choose?
2. The measurement of most, if not all, these aptitudes is not so exact that misdiagnosing can be avoided. Further, many of the tests used are not those to which teachers have ready access.
3. Should students be *matched* or *mismatched*? As Watson (1971) asks: 'How much does society really want to commit itself to the accentuation of differences in cognitive style, or to other individual differences, by individualising techniques that cater to these differences?' (p. 84). While *achievement* may be maximised when the treatment fits the style of the child, the style itself is likely to be even more entrenched. We have already faced this issue when discussing Yamamoto's (1963) study of convergence-divergence. It is not an empirical question, to which there is a right or wrong answer: it depends upon one's educational aims.
4. The prevailing view in Australian schools is, as we have seen, away from placing students into homogeneous groups, unless there are very strong logistic or humane reasons for doing so.

For these reasons, the ATI model is not really a practical way of individualising instruction (Lesser, 1971). Indeed, it is now mostly used for experimental research into learning processes themselves (e.g. Pask and Scott, 1972; Snow, 1977).

The smorgasbord. A very neat way of handling this problem is to offer a diversity of schooling styles. Hunt (1971), for example, presented a 'smorgasbord' of styles in five senior high schools in Toronto, ranging from very high to low structure. The students were given a trial of three weeks to sample the styles, and could then opt for the style in which they felt most comfortable. In this way the problem of identifying and measuring a particular aptitude was entirely obviated, while catering for individual differences: unlike the animal school (Box 9.7).

BOX 9.7   THE PROCESS OF SCHOOLING OR CATERING FOR
                INDIVIDUAL DIFFERENCES

Many moons ago, Australian animals faced the problem of changing times by opening a school. The curriculum consisted of four activities: running, climbing, swimming and flying. The school was for all animals, so, naturally, all subjects were compulsory.

Individual differences emerged, though. The duck topped the class in swimming; just scraped a pass in flying, but failed running. To take remedial running, he had to withdraw from swimming. Attempts to modify his running behaviour ultimately led to worn webs which then detracted from his swimming performance. Despite this, the duck was still able to gain a pass: and that's the main thing.

The rabbit topped the first running test, but the pressures of remedial swimming seemed to affect his outlook. Some thought it was because his parents were migrants. The possum was classified by some teachers as a gifted pupil because of her climbing achievements. When she was forced to demonstrate flying from the ground, instead of the top of the gum tree, she tended to put on temper tantrums. This hysteria soon affected her climbing (bare pass) and running (fail).

The chicken hawk was a classroom control problem and needed close supervision. A real troublemaker, that one. First in climbing, but refused to go up the trunk like all the others.

At prize-giving night, it was a rather malformed galah who had topped the class by gaining the highest average in all subjects.

When the Department of Education would not add digging and burrowing to the curriculum, wombats refused to allow their children to attend. Emus, dingoes and kangaroos subsequently joined the wombats to set up a successful independent system.

Source: Freely adapted from Reavis, 1968.

An important point here is that diversity is defined on educational grounds, not in terms of a score on a psychological test that measures some hypothetical aptitude. This particular solution of Hunt's is unlikely to gain popular support, however, for obvious practical reasons. Nevertheless, some Australian States have moved in this direction by allowing parents the option of open and traditional school within the same general areas (in the Australian Capital Territory, South Australia and, to an extent, Queensland). Other States, such as New South Wales, have zoning rules that make it difficult for parents to send their children to a government school that is outside their residential zone.

The adoption of self-paced instructional strategies. These include mastery learning, programmed instruction and independent study. In such systems, the 'individualising' is mainly in terms of rate of learning: students work through the programs at their own pace, not that enforced by the whole class. The supreme example of self-pacing is of course computer assisted instruction (CAI), to which we return below.

Extracurricular activities. As with those reviewed for gifted children, students follow basically the same course as the others in school; their particular talents and curiosities are exercised out of school.

Informal teacher–student interaction. For most intents and purposes, the more formal options (altering the composition of classes and teaching accordingly) are not viable. The most important way in which teachers can individualise their instruction to suit the vast array of individual differences they will meet in their classrooms is in their everyday interaction with students.

Computer assisted instruction

We have already referred to the use of microcomputers in the teaching of writing, and in the next chapter we also refer to their use for individualised testing. Computers can also be used for managing instruction (CMI), which involves the administrative aspects of instruction rather than giving instruction (such as establishing data bases on students, processing performance data, generating reports, etc.). We are concerned here with their use in individualising instruction.

Computer assisted instruction (CAI) is in fact characterised by the individualised nature of the instruction (Thomas, 1979). Of all teaching media, it can, if used properly, come closest to the embedded teaching between parent and child, when cognitive gains are so rapid (Fischer and Bullock, 1984). That is, the learner's response is the cue (with good software) for a finely tuned reply, as in one-to-one conversation. These conditions are ideally suited for optimal mismatch and the generation of intrinsic motivation, and in fact Clements and Gullo (1984) found that 12 weeks training in LOGO programming increased a group of 18 six-year-olds' divergent ability, metacognitive ability, and ability to follow directions.

The problem is not the process but the content. The evidence for that can be seen whenever a child sits down to a reasonably complex computer game. The pity of it is that so much of the software that is available, and that has this potential for so engrossing the learner, is so trivial or even obnoxious in content (what better way of teaching sociocentric values than a game requiring the player to kill as many of the 'not-us' group as possible?). Undoubtedly we shall see the development of software packages that will be specifically designed for educational purposes. At present all too frequently unprepared teachers use whatever software is readily available from commercial suppliers. This is a complex and rapidly developing area: some guidelines for the design of educational software are given in Box 9.8.

The important thing is that the software is *interactive*, that is, it responds to the last move made by the student, inviting or challenging a further response. An excellent

BOX 9.8   GUIDELINES FOR THE DESIGN OF SOFTWARE

These guidelines were developed by Ryba and Chapman (1983) after a review of relevant theory. It is interesting to note the application of the guidelines to the pre-electronic classroom, too.

Guidelines	Example
1. **Maximise student control.** Ensure that students can direct the program at several points with decisions such as to advance, quit, repeat, review, etc.	'Did you understand this module?' 'Would you like to review again?'
2. **Personalise internal feedback.** Use messages that reinforce the student's personal effectiveness.	'You learned this work really well.' 'Congratulations on achieving a higher score than last time. This was a difficult assignment and you did a fine job.'
3. **Self-evaluation.** Provide opportunities for the student to rate his/her own progress.	'Did you have any difficulty with this?' 'What should you do now? 1. Study some more? 2. Try harder? 3. Go to the next module?'
4. **Goal setting.** Provide opportunities for the student to set personal goals.	'Last time you had five correct answers. How many will you get this time?'
5. **Evaluation of goals.** Ensure that the student assesses his or her performance on the basis of previously set goals.	'Did you reach your goal? Was your goal: 1. Too high? 2. Just right? 3. Too low?'
6. **Personally meaningful rewards.** Provide an opportunity for the student to contract for type of reward and conditions for achieving reward. Note that this behaviour contract could be negotiated directly between student and teacher as well.	'Set your contract here: ... 'How many points earn reward (minimum is 10)? Select type of reward: 1. Game; 2. Free period; 3. Extra computer time.

7. **Stress relevant concepts.** Ensure that the program clearly displays essential information. Use prompts to focus students' attention on important elements.

Use colour coding to highlight grammatical terms.
Avoid excessive use of graphics unless they are relevant for learning a specific operation.

8. **Encourage self commentaries.** Research has shown that overt verbalisation can help mediate many kinds of problem solving. Collaborative learning could be encouraged by assigning teams of children to each computer.

'Now you say this number.'
'Say what colour this is.'
'Show another student how you solved this problem.'

example of this is Webster's (1986) Interactive Video (IV) system, which went a stage further and incorporated a home video unit to provide visual input into the program (usually this is a very expensive option available only on laserdisc). Webster then compared this system with a small group taught personally, and a passive video system, which used exactly the same input as the IV system. He thus had three groups: IV, small group and passive video, and in each taught 24 students a soldering unit from a TAFE course. The IV group was consistently equal to or better than the small group method, with the passive video group consistently last. This study makes it very clear that it is not the stimulus material itself that matters, but the way in which it is used.

CAI may be used in many different ways, from straight drill with fixed pacing (which makes it no better than the simplest forms of programmed instruction) to highly adaptive software that truly 'converses' with the user. Some of the uses of CAI are listed below (for further details, see Probert, 1985; Thomas and McClain, 1983; Spuck and Atkinson, 1984):

1.   *Drill and practice* does not provide new information, but reinforces what has been learned previously by pupils. The material is presented repetitively until the student demonstrates attainment of specific criteria as in mathematical calculations, spelling, historical dates, parts of the anatomy, etc. This procedure is basically similar to the 'flash-card' method common in infants and primary schools.

2.   *Tutorials* introduce new material, in the same way as programmed instruction. The content is divided into discrete components which are then sequentially linked as mastery is attained on each. These can be characterised as instruction in 'paragraph' form.

3.   *Dialogue* with the computer is demanding both on the programmer and the computer capacity. Ideally, it enables the user to question the computer which will demonstrate a wide tolerance in the range of terms it can understand. For example, a computer can question a student to elicit progressively finer responses so a difficulty in mathematics, say, can be diagnosed: suitable drills and exercises can then be prescribed.

Interactive CAI is ideal for generating
optimal mismatch and intrinsic motivation.

4.   *Simulations* are already in widespread use in medical education (a simulated patient interview in the surgery) and in pilot training. Some simulations represent reality to such a high degree of fidelity that airline pilots can convert to new models almost entirely by computer-based simulation in replicas of the flight deck. Classroom simulations enable students to experience decision-making in situations normally unavailable. Time can be compressed to enable study of inflation in an economy or erosion in farmland.

5.   *Problem solving* is of course the basis for many existing commercial games: the extension into all subject areas, especially science and mathematics, will soon be made.

6.   *Data banks can be used for inquiry lessons.* For example, the details of the passengers on the First Fleet can be used for student research: what can be concluded about the social, geographical, economic, religious and political backgrounds of those sent to the penal colony?

Such a list is endless, and in this rapidly moving area is being extended daily. One thing is sure, however: this is the way that individualised instruction will go.

SUMMARY

Convergent and divergent abilities in the classroom. Although schooling generally favours convergent processes, divergent abilities contribute to school performance as well as convergent. This contribution from divergent abilities is more evident

- in verbal rather than numerical subject areas;
- the higher up the academic ladder one goes, being greatest in postgraduate areas;
- in informal and more permissive environments.

This contribution from divergent processes has generally not been recognised in evaluation and testing procedures. It would undoubtedly be greater still if open-ended formats were used more often in assessing student learning.

The convergent bias of classroom instruction becomes evident when studying teacher-student interaction. Managing a classroom is generally (and depending on teaching style) a convergent business: keeping on track, not wasting time, arriving at the predetermined goals for the lesson, correcting students as right or wrong in their responses. Teachers therefore do not take kindly to students whose divergence leads them to ask unexpected questions, show unwillingness to accept a simple right answer, or who give logical but unexpected and complex alternatives. It is an interesting and important question whether teachers and students should be matched or mismatched on their cognitive biases. Should students be reinforced in their strengths or learn to make the best of their weaknesses?

Where possible, classroom teachers should organise their structure flexibly to permit divergence to be expressed.

1. Methods of evaluation should allow the expression of divergent products as well as purely convergent ones.
2. Teachers need to be able to *recognise* divergent ability; more difficult, to *tolerate* it; and even more difficult, to *foster* it.
3. Divergence is suppressed by many traditional classroom procedures (emphasis on being right, impatience with wasting time, insistence on conformity), and enhanced by others (low structure, approval, emphasis on independence).

Exceptional children. Exceptionality refers to those who are so different from other children that some special sort of provision is necessary for them. This differentness may be in terms of learning disability, physical handicap, or at the other end of the scale, giftedness. Exceptional children of whatever kind can be treated within or outside the mainstream. Present Australian policy is to incorporate exceptional children within the mainstream wherever possible, although it is well recognised that the learning and physically disabled need specially trained teachers and special resources. The gifted and talented, however, have tended to have been neglected in normal schools, although they tend strongly to come from 'privileged' backgrounds. Nevertheless, their needs are real, and some provisions that are now being made were outlined.

Individualising instruction. The whole question of individualising instruction is changing. Previous attempts at individualisation really amounted to grouping students, mainly according to ability, and teaching different curricula and different levels, either on a group basis within a class or by streaming the whole class. Such methods are complex, and depend critically on teaching style: they tend thus to sort themselves out according to other teaching decisions.

Individualising now is coming to mean what the term really says: instructing on an individual basis. Independent study is one way of doing this, but the method that is really taking off is computer assisted instruction (CAI), which with appropriate adaptive software can be extremely powerful in engaging the student in carefully tuned 'conversations'. We are undoubtedly on the threshold of an important change; more and more schools are obtaining viable numbers of micros, and software will inevitably be produced by dedicated educators rather than by those whose interests are predominantly commercial.

The question underlying all teaching, whatever the particular mode, is: How can I allow in my teaching for the fact that different children will react to my teaching in different ways?

FURTHER READING

On intelligence

P. E. Vernon, *Intelligence: Heredity and Environment,* W. H. Freeman, San Francisco, Calif., 1979.

J. R. Kirby (ed.), *Cognitive Strategies and Educational Performance,* Academic Press, New York, 1984.

A. R. Jensen, 'How Much can we Boost IQ and Scholastic Achievement?', *Harvard Educational Review,* 39, 1969, 1–123.

L. Kamin, *The Science and Politics of IQ,* Lawrence Erlbaum, Potomac, Ill., 1974.

Vernon presents the history of the concept of intelligence, its basic structure and the interrelation of abilities, and a balanced up-to-date appraisal of the nature-nurture issue. The only aspect worthy of correction is that Hearnshaw's (1979) results, effectively implying fraudulence in Burt's results, were not available to Vernon and so he gives too much credence to Burt's position. Kirby gives an account of a conference held at the University of Newcastle, in which the information integration theory of Das-Kirby is the main focus. Issues discussed include the nature of planning, remedial education and learning disability, motivation and student learning, and Aboriginal cognition. Jensen's article caused a tremendous furore when it appeared, with its implications for the nature-nurture issue. Kamin makes a determined attack on the hereditarian position, first setting the historical perspective and then covering the present protagonists such as Jensen, with a detailed analysis of the weaknesses in Burt's data.

On creativity

A. J. Cropley, *Creativity,* Longmans Green, London, 1967.

J. Getzels and P. Jackson, *Creativity and Intelligence,* Wiley, New York, 1962.

M. Gilchrist, *The Psychology of Creativity,* Melbourne University Press, Melbourne, 1972.

The first is a concise and clearly written account of creativity and divergent thought, with educational implications to the forefront. Getzels and Jackson is the book that really established the issue of creativity (divergence) and its educational implications. Should be read, especially the case studies and empirical work. The last is a small, easy-to-read but comprehensive coverage of the psychology of creativity. It is not addressed directly to educators, but is relevant none the less.

On CAI
E. R. Steinberg, *Teaching Computers to Teach,* Lawrence Erlbaum, Hillsdale, NJ, 1984.
'Goodbye, Little Red Schoolhouse', *Creative Computing,* April 1985, 64–76.

Steinberg emphasises the centrality of the learner, not the medium. The computer is 'merely a vehicle of instruction'. In exposition of CAI, consideration is given to interactive dialogue between the computer and pupils. 'Goodbye, Little Red Schoolhouse' provides an overview of the educational software market. Although US oriented, the survey refers to products distributed in Australia. Sixty-odd manufacturers' addresses are incorporated, for direct contact; together with details of their main products and the systems on which they can be used.

On giftedness
C. P. Clendening and R. A. Davies, *Creating Programs for the Gifted: A Guide for Teachers, Librarians and Students,* Bowker, UK, 1980.
Free to Be, Talented and Gifted Children Curriculum Committee, Curriculum Branch, Education Department of Victoria, 1984.
M. O'Neill and J. Reid, *Educational and Psychological Characteristics of Students Gifted in English,* Commonwealth Schools Commission, Canberra, 1985.

Clendening and Davies identify the gifted and talented, then discuss independent study methods, curriculum modifications and instructional methods, model programs, guidelines for program development and a directory of resources. *Free to Be* provides details on the themes of needs, design, implementation and resources for curriculum for gifted and talented children, working with parents and the value of a mentor program. O'Neill and Reid's study assists in the provision of programs for students gifted in English, and the direct quotations from students on the nature and function of literature and language, and the patterns and processes of writing are good value for all teachers.

QUESTIONS

Questions for self-testing

1. Distinguish pupil giftedness from academic performance.
2. Describe what is meant by cognitive style.
3. Name and describe three cognitive styles.
4. Briefly describe what is meant by aptitude-treatment interaction (ATI).
5. What is meant by the 'Pygmalion Effect'?

6. Distinguish between process and content abilities.
7. Define intelligence.
8. Describe Vernon's hierarchical model of intelligence.
9. What were the primary mental abilities described by Thurstone?
10. Distinguish between successive and simultaneous synthesis.
11. Jensen described Level 1 and Level 2 abilities. How did they differ?
12. Describe one way of measuring divergence.
13. List five components of creativity.
14. What are five teaching practices that inhibit divergent abilities?
15. Describe six ways of catering for the needs of gifted and talented children.
16. Provide four ways in which a micro can be used to individualise instruction.

Questions for discussion

1. Should teachers have access to pupil IQ scores? Give arguments for and against, then provide your own view.
2. What answers did you reach after considering the question at the end of this chapter ('How can I allow for the fact that children will react to my teaching in different ways?')? In your response, ensure that you explicitly refer to ways of catering for the divergent pupil.
3. It is suggested in this chapter that, apart from the use of CAI, formal methods of grouping students according to ability are not recommended. Using evidence from this chapter, and from previous chapters (see especially Chapter 3), discuss this proposition with respect to your own teaching subject. Take into account: curriculum objectives, the methods of teaching and of evaluation you would propose, the size of the class, teacher–student interaction.
4. In an interview (quoted in Psychology Today, July 1980, p. 41), Piaget was asked about the aim of education. The following exchange took place:

Piaget: Education, for most people, means trying to lead the child to resemble the typical adult of his society. For me, education means making creators, even if there aren't many of them, even if the creations of one are limited by comparison with those of another. But you have to make inventors, innovators, not conformists.

Interviewer: Do you think that every individual can be a creator?

Piaget: In varying degrees, of course; there is always a field in which he can be one.

Do you agree with Piaget? What implications would that have for your teaching?
5. Assume you were either an expert programmer or had access to one. Outline the sort of software package you would design to suit a particular topic you are teaching. What would you have it do that cannot be done by ordinary classroom teaching?

10

Evaluating learning

OVERVIEW

This chapter discusses the question of evaluating the outcomes of learning. Evaluation is one of the issues of greatest concern to teachers, parents and students. It is of special interest to the latter because the results of evaluation will often determine the course of the rest of their lives. Educational evaluation relies heavily on a technology that itself may be complex, and in some cases mystifying. Here, we elucidate some of the more important concepts and techniques of evaluation, and then examine some of the more important issues concerning evaluation that teachers will face in the classroom. Questions answered in the chapter include:

- What is a 'test'?
- How do attainment tests differ from ability tests?
- What does 'grading on the curve' mean?
- Do tests make students more competitive?
- How is the validity of a test established?
- What does test reliability mean?
- How are various forms of test constructed?
- Do essays assess more significant learnings than objective tests?
- How can the results of different tests be combined to allow decisions about final grades?
- What is 'moderation' and is it effective as a method of replacing external exams?
- Can students assess their own learning?

When you have finished this chapter you should be able to:

1. Take a distribution of scores on a Year 7 maths tests and determine final grades in letter grades.
2. Construct a norm-referenced objective test in your teaching subject and determine its reliability and validity.
3. Show how you can mark a series of essays in such a way as to minimise unreliability.
4. Argue what method(s) of examining would best suit a particular class and subject you are teaching.
5. Construct a criterion-referenced test in your teaching area.
6. Argue the pros and cons of moderated assessment.
7. Describe how to evaluate students' learning processes in a specific task in your teaching area.
8. Convert a collection of marks obtained from tests and assignments throughout the year into a final grade.
9. Design a system of evaluating a course you are teaching that incorporates students' assessments of their own work.
10. Explain to another teacher the advantages of the Rasch model of evaluation.

SECTION A

LEARNING AND EVALUATION: TWO SIDES, SAME COIN

We have deliberately used the word 'evaluation' in this chapter: not 'assessment', 'measurement', 'testing', 'marking' or 'grading'. These terms variously suggest a quantitative, one-off exercise which is used to label or to sort students. Evaluation is much more than that.

Evaluation requires making a *judgment*, in terms of *criteria*, as to what constitutes good or poor learning. The 3P — presage-process-product — model of learning suggests three stages where critical monitoring should take place:

- at presage: are the *curricular aims* appropriate?
- at process: is the student *approaching the task* appropriately?
- at product: are the *outcomes* satisfactory? Do they meet the initial objectives?

Initially the teacher evaluates at these three levels, but if there is anything in the notion of responsible self-direction, clearly the *student* should increasingly take over. Almost every autonomous act of creation — writing a letter to the editor, designing a fernery, getting a novel published — involves the same three stages:

- setting up intentions — and *judging* them to be realistic and appropriate;
- deciding how to go about it — and *judging* what procedure is likely to be successful;
- deciding when the task is finished — and *judging* that the product is satisfactory.

Despite the obvious interdependence of learning and evaluation, attitudes to evaluation do diverge along Theory X/Theory Y lines.

The hard-nosed approach sees evaluation in the form of *quantitative assessment*, to be done frequently and making use of the quite complicated technology of educational measurement that has developed. Teachers taking this approach believe that elaborate testing is necessary either to *motivate* students: ('They won't work unless it's in the exam' — Theory X) or for *credentialling*, to provide the data necessary for career and placement decisions, or for both purposes. A fair and State-wide grading system is necessary in order to maintain standards, and to sort out students for employment or for further education. All very bothersome, and sometimes individuals do suffer, and sometimes teaching is stultified — but there is no real alternative. We looked at the mixed truth contained in the motivational assumption in Chapter 3.

At the other extreme are those who point to the damage that frequent, mindless and inappropriate testing can do: such as student stress and alienation, suppression of intrinsic motivation and the growth of cynicism, trivialising learning to those aspects that are easily measured, 'labelling' students as failures or incompetents when those labels promptly bring about their own fruition, and unfairness due to culture or other bias. These teachers (and parents and students) would claim that the most important learning is not easily measured no matter how elaborate the technology. Do not pressurise by testing, labelling and grading: then students might really learn (Theory Y).

In Australia, because of the way things have been structured in the past and because of the otherwise commendable obsession with 'fairness' throughout our State systems, State-wide curriculum and examining boards have had a tremendous influence on school practice, and on attitudes to examining and evaluation. Now schools are being handed more and more responsibility for curriculum design, and the corresponding responsibility for assessment. Not all teachers are looking forward to accepting either responsibility, yet most are happy about the loosening of State control. Undoubtedly, when we have moved as far as the United States with regard to school-based assessment, opinions in school will change. Box 10.1 shows the results of a recent survey of over 500 Wyoming teachers — the results are said to be typical of similar surveys in California and South Dakota. Will Australian schools be devoting six hours a week over all years to testing? Will 82 per cent of all Australian teachers in future be seeking out courses (pre-service or in-service) in measurement and evaluation?

It seems unlikely. It is, however, certain that teachers will in future need to understand evaluation and how it links with learning more thoroughly than previously. In particular, it will be increasingly important to dispel the notions that evaluation is something that happens *after* learning, that it is necessarily highly quantitative, and that it is necessarily linked with trivial aspects of learning. If we are beyond a quantitative

---

BOX 10.1   THE SHAPE OF THINGS TO COME?
HOW WIDESPREAD IS THE USE OF TESTS IN
SCHOOLS?

In a survey of 555 Wyoming teachers, covering Grades 1 to 12, it was found that:

- six hours a week were spent on testing in schools;
- 55 per cent of the tests were made by the teachers themselves;
- 40 per cent of student grades were based on tests;
- 82 per cent of teachers had at least one complete course on measurement;
- teachers with courses in measurement liked tests and used them more often;
- male teachers used more tests than female teachers;
- criterion-referenced tests were preferred to norm-referenced tests;
- micros were used infrequently for testing purposes.

What would a similar survey in Australia show?

Source: Green and Stager, 1985.

conception of learning ourselves, our conception of evaluation will accordingly be qualitative, linking curriculum, process and outcome.

Evaluation and the 3P model

Evaluation may be associated with all three of the presage, process and product stages of learning.

Presage: Curriculum evaluation. This aspect suddenly becomes important when it is realised that schools (and regions) will be developing their own curricula. There are two aspects: curriculum development and the evaluation of that *curriculum* to see how good it is; and the evaluation of *students* in terms of the objectives in that curriculum. The first aspect is beyond our present concern; it is an issue in its own right, with a massive literature in each content area, to which the reader's attention will no doubt be drawn in other coursework.

The second issue is the important one for present purposes. When the State departments set the curricula, they in effect told teachers what should be tested — and until fairly recently, those departments themselves did the testing at the end of Years 10 and 12. Now teachers will have to decide what to teach , and hence what to evaluate. While this throws a larger responsibility onto teachers, it also greatly frees up the instructional process, putting learning and its monitoring side by side with decisions as to what to learn, how to go about it and how to decide when it has been learned sufficiently well. Such a holistic conception of education is much more appropriate than the old externally imposed model, with its artificial distinctions between curriculum and testing, and the resultant over-emphasis on testing and grading. Further, bringing the whole process in-house enables the *student* to participate in ways that were simply not possible under the external model.

The specific question of what to put into the curriculum is a matter for curriculum development. Once it is there, however, the teacher needs to judge how best students' learning of each objective or aspect may be evaluated. This chapter will provide some concepts that will be helpful in achieving that.

Process evaluation. Evaluation usually refers (a) to how well the learning outcomes match the curriculum (criterion-referenced), or (b) to how students compare with each other with respect to some measure of outcome (norm-referenced; see below, 'How are tests calibrated?'). Both kinds of evaluation miss what many would consider to be an extremely important result of learning: *how the student has been changed by the learning experience*. The outcome of a study skills course, for example, is hopefully that the students are more strategic and more skilful about the way they go about studying in future (see Chapter 4, the Edwards and the Stanford studies). Likewise, we saw that one of the hoped-for outcomes of open schooling is that students change in self-concept, in the ability to direct their own learning, and so forth. Paris' Informed Strategies for Learning (ISL) program aims to change the way young readers approach text, of which the outcome measure of improved comprehension is only one index.

There are so many examples. The British 'public' school for instance insisted on the classics as part of the basic curriculum, not because upper classes *needed* Latin in their future lives (except to scatter classical allusions throughout their conversation), but because rigorous study of such formal disciplines as Latin and Greek was thought to be 'character building': not a content but a process outcome. Helping students become more self-aware of their learning processes, and the aims of responsible self-direction and moral autonomy, refer of course to process outcomes. Writers become better writers by doing different things — for example, by reviewing in larger units than they did before — and while the adoption of the appropriate process may (and assuredly will in the long term) result in a better product, that is not the particular point at the time of teaching.

Hand in hand with curriculum development, then, goes another task for the teacher: to specify how the student is to approach the task in question, and then to evaluate how well the student does so. This will involve a task analysis — as we saw in reading comprehension and writing, for example, we need to see what it is that good readers do and what good writers do. The same can be said of good mathematicians and scientists, although it must be said that awareness of process has been rather keener in the science disciplines than it has in the humanities. Some examples of more process evaluation are given in Section B.

Product: Outcome evaluation. As we saw in Chapter 4, outcomes may be either cognitive or affective: how students *think* after a learning experience, and what they *feel* about that experience. The latter aspect obviously says something important about the quality of the learning experience, and it also is likely to have a profound influence on how the task or related tasks are likely to be handled in future. Bloom, Krathwohl and Masia (1960) attempted a taxonomy of affective objectives, but with distinctly less success than Bloom and his colleagues had with their more famous taxonomy of cognitive objectives (see below). Today, there is renewed interest in affective outcomes, and we look at some aspects of this in Section B.

Cognitive outcomes have been described in Chapter 4 in terms of the S–D (structure-to-data) ratio, thus emphasising that outcomes are not only quantitative but qualitative. Quantitative outcomes are 'horizontal', referring to the *accretion* of knowledge; qualitative outcomes are 'vertical', referring to *understanding*. Curriculum objectives thus need to specify both the kinds of structuring (multistructural or relational), and the level of abstraction in the target mode.

White (1984) says that school tests measure understanding only in terms of problem solving, a conception that rapidly becomes quantitative: the more problems addressing a topic the student can solve, the more that student 'understands' the topic. As White points out, however, concepts, whole disciplines, single elements of knowledge, extensive communications, situations, and people, are all 'understood' differently; entirely different methods of seeing that we do 'understand' the domain in question are used. For example, understanding situations (e.g. those in the alternative frameworks research) is often done by interview, asking the students to predict, observe and explain the demonstration. The point is simply that teachers need to decide what is to be understood, and to be creative about designing the most appropriate methods of evaluating understanding in each context.

Quantitative evaluation, then, focuses on accretion of knowledge in a multi-structural framework. As we saw in Chapter 5, that is often valid for an educational outcome. Quantitative evaluation is comparatively easy to carry out. The teacher wants to know how many points the student can recall, the number of words spelt, the number of problems solved correctly, the number of grammatical rules applied and so on. There is an elaborate technology to help the teacher evaluate quantitatively.

Quantitative evaluation is evident when we look at the use of multiple-choice tests, which are based on the number of items correctly answered. Even essay marking has a quantitative bias in practice: the almost universal procedure in marking open-ended essay responses is to award a mark for each relevant point made, and convert the ratio of actual marks to possible marks into some kind of number. The teacher then adjusts the final mark for overall quality, so that a final grade (A, B or D, or Pass, Fail, Distinction) is arrived at. While everyone would agree that quality is important, that final adjustment for quality is usually quite subjective. These terms are rarely spelt out for the student to understand and benefit from. Even in essay marking, then, 'how much' tends to call the grading tune more than 'how well'.

One method of introducing qualitative differences in item selection in tests is the Bloom taxonomy (Bloom et al. 1956), which outlines six levels of response, ordered in increasing levels of quality:

1. *knowledge:* rote reproduction of the correct response;
2. *comprehension:* explaining the response in the student's words;
3. *application:* applying the knowledge to a practical situation;
4. *analysis:* isolating crucial components of the knowledge;
5. *synthesis:* recombining elements to yield new knowledge;
6. *evaluation:* applying higher order principles to test the worth of the new knowledge.

The Bloom taxonomy has mainly been used to guide the selection of items for a test; it is not suitable for evaluating the quality of a response to an open-ended item. Second, it is not easy, in practice, to devise items to draw out levels of response quality much above comprehension (Anderson, 1972).

We concentrate in this chapter on methods of evaluation that address both quantitative and qualitative aspects, although there is a more extensive literature on the first aspect. We are concerned to convey a balanced view of evaluation and to point to the need for both kinds of evaluation, and to the techniques that already exist and that may be helpful.

SOME BASIC CONCEPTS IN EVALUATION

In this section, we take a non-technical look at some of the assumptions and distinctions involved in the relationship between evaluation and learning.

What is a test?

A test is an instrument for measuring educational outcomes. It may consist of one or several items, and it may be in one of several forms (e.g. multiple-choice, essay, practicum, and so on). A test may yield a numerical score or a qualitative category, and the teacher has then to make a reasonable decision on the basis of this information. The use of test information is based on the kinds of distinctions considered below.

Tests can be used to measure abilities, school achievement, personality and attitudes. 'Cognitive' tests, with which this chapter is concerned, can be either instruction-dependent or instruction-free. Instruction-free tests are so called because they measure performances that are relatively free from the effects of instruction: they are ability tests that characterise the *person*, and include measures of general abilities such as IQ, spatial ability, verbal reasoning or divergent ability. Instruction-dependent tests evaluate how well students have learned particular bodies of knowledge or skills which have been the subject of instruction. These are called *attainment* or *achievement* tests, and are usually constructed by the teacher, although several commercial tests are available — and with school-based assessment, these sources of tests (e.g. the Australian Council for Educational Research) will no doubt become more widely used.

A test, then, is simply an instrument or a situation that provides information about the learner's progress.

Functions of evaluation

Scriven (1967) distinguished between *formative* and *summative* evaluation. Formative evaluation provides feedback to both teacher and learner, and is used *during* the teaching process; summative evaluation indicates how well material has been learned *after* teaching is completed. 'Grading' is virtually a synonym for individual summative evaluation: every professional certificate, diploma or degree is a summative statement that a person has successfully completed certain requirements.

While summative evaluation tells the student, teacher and potential customer how well the course has been completed, formative evaluation tells the student and teacher how well the course is being learned at any given stage in the learner's development. Formative evaluation is intended simply to give information to the participants — not to punish, grade, inform the public or award scholarships. Thus, formative evaluation is continuous, diagnostic and remedial; while summative is terminal, finite and descriptive.

As techniques of formative and summative evaluation are quite different, teachers must be clear as to what they are trying to do when administering a test. Is it to find out how well students are taking to the material? Is it to find out if there are any misunderstandings so far; if the teaching is aimed at the right level? Or is it to gain information for grading purposes? Will the test data appear on final reports? The answers to these questions point to the different tests needed.

How are tests calibrated?

Everyone used to understand what a 'mark' was: it was something 'out of a hundred' and called a 'per cent' and 'the pass' was 50 of them. Tests in the good old days had a remarkable stability, and a common currency, which enabled one to compare student with student and subject with subject; determining grades was simplicity itself. Of course, all those qualities were in the eye of the beholder: certainly they did not inhere in the test.

There are much better ways of calibrating tests than decreeing that the scores are in percentages: the most suitable way for any particular occasion will depend on how the score is to be used.

There are three main ways of calibrating tests.

Norm-referencing. Norm-referenced measures are interpreted according to the performance of an individual in relation to others (see also Chapter 3). The meaning of the score used, such as rank, standard score or percentile depends on this relationship. For example, 'Jane was top of the class this year' is a norm-referenced statement of Jane's ability. It tells us nothing about what Jane actually did, only that whatever she did, it was better than anyone else. Here the standard shifts according to the performance of the class as a whole.

The simplest method of norm-referencing is thus ranking. Many commercial tests that compare students to some general population are also norm-referenced. IQ tests, for example, usually are designed to give an average of 100: the average score of the population is in fact set at 100, and other scores are expressed as a deviation from that average. In this case, the scores are made to fit a normal curve, so that most cluster around the mean or average, with progressively fewer and fewer people at either extreme (see Figure 10.1). In the case of intelligence, that is not a bad assumption to make.

The normal curve is not, however, the only distribution in frequent use. HSC scores are spread along a rectangular distribution and expressed in deciles. That is, the bottom 9.9 per cent of scores are collectively given the score '1'; the next 10 per cent (10 per cent to 19.9 per cent) are given a score '2', and so on, with the top 10 per cent (i.e. the best in the State) getting a score '10'.

All these scores, of course, like ranks themselves, are 'content-free': they say *nothing* about absolute standards. They are simply a way of discriminating between students in a performance domain. Of course, in very large populations, one assumes that standards remain constant, so that one can say that a decile of 9 in maths is worth 9 in science; or that a score of 5 in English this year will reflect the same standard as 5 in English last year. That is, however, still an assumption, and when norm-referenced scores are derived from small groups of students, such as a class, cross-class comparisons *cannot* be made. All teachers know how drastically one class of the same grade and year level can differ from another.

Norm-referenced measures are useful when we wish to compare students with each other or against some reference group. In vocational guidance, for example, it is helpful to know that the profile of abilities matches that of the normal population or matches that of a particular occupational group.

Figure 10.1   The normal curve, IQ and percentage of population
               (where IQ = 100 and SD = 15)

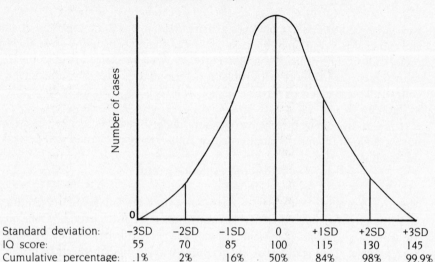

Standard deviation:	−3SD	−2SD	−1SD	0	+1SD	+2SD	+3SD
IQ score:	55	70	85	100	115	130	145
Cumulative percentage:	.1%	2%	16%	50%	84%	98%	99.9%

The main reason why we want to rank order students, however, is in 'rationed' situations. This becomes starkly clear in most moderation procedures (see Section B). In essence, a school is told that there is to be, for example, one '10' and three '9s' in the HSC this year. That situation absolutely guarantees that at least four students in that school will be engaged in some pretty cut-throat competition during the year: and given the place for teachers' ratings in the final result, that means that teachers may be placed in quite an invidious situation.

There have to be better ways.

Criterion-referencing. Criterion-referenced measures are used to make a different sort of decision about individuals, concerning particular task requirements only (i.e. whether or not an objective has been met). Can this person (irrespective of how others perform) carry out long division, swim 50 metres or sing in tune?

Glaser and Nitko (1971) defined criterion-referenced tests as those which 'yield measurements that are directly interpretable in terms of specified performance standards'. This means, as Popham and Husek (1969) pointed out, that the individual is evaluated in terms of some prescribed standard *irrespective* of the performance of other individuals. Airasian and Madaus (1972) argued that criterion-referenced measurement focuses attention where it belongs: on whether or not the learner has learned what was intended to be learned. If teachers decide that a certain objective is important, then presumably their major concern is with whether or not a particular student has achieved it, rather than how much of it was achieved relative to others in the class.

A common example of a criterion-referenced test is a driving test. In order to pass the test, one has typically to demonstrate (a) verbal knowledge of the traffic rules (usually around 80 per cent accuracy); and (b) pass-fail prowess in driving around a set route. If everyone, or nobody, passed the test on the first go, then no doubt questions might be asked about the suitability of the standards; but that is a separate issue.

We should consider the relationship between norm and criterion referencing, and formative and summative evaluation. Formative evaluation only makes sense when it is criterion-referenced: the student gets 17 words correct out of 20; regularly makes errors in a particular mathematical operation; keeps confusing response learning with respondent conditioning, etc. The formative function is not furthered by pointing out that he or she is better or worse than others in the class at doing these things.

Summative evaluation, on the other hand, may quite logically be either norm- *or* criterion-referenced. There are two stages to summative evaluation. First, we must derive the standard for awarding a mark or grade; second, we may then determine how each student is to be awarded that grade. In norm-referenced evaluation, both stages are amalgamated: the group characteristics (e.g. how far above or below the mean) determine simultaneously what the standard is and where the student stands in relation to that standard. In criterion-referenced evaluation, however, the standard is determined first. This may quite reasonably be done by using a norm-determined standard (e.g. the quality of work of the previous year's top 20 per cent of students). Or it may be done *a priori*: by deciding that, given the nature of the task, such-and-such a standard is 'reasonable'. Then, once the standard has been fixed, the final grade or statement as to the student's performance is determined (this is, of course, independent of the grade or statement made about any other student in the group). Determining the standard first is important because many students confuse a norm-determined *standard* with norm-referenced *evaluation*. It is only in the second step, deciding each student's grade, that the norm- versus criterion-referenced issue arises.

It is worth noting that as far back as 1918, Thorndike distinguished what we today would call norm-referenced and criterion-referenced measurement, and predicted that 'the latter seems to represent the type which will prevail if education follows the course of development of the physical Sciences' (quoted in Airasian and Madaus, 1972). However, as these two authors commented, the course of development was *not* the logical one followed by the sciences. Instead, educators in general, and test constructors in particular, used a model of evaluation that *maximised differences between individuals*, not one that assessed the differences between an individual's performance and some absolute standard.

Latent trait theory: the Rasch model. One of the troubles with norm-referencing is that the unit of measurement is completely bland: a statistical deviation unit that has little relation to what has been taught, and that means nothing to a teacher. Another trouble is that even that unit is dependent on the underlying distribution: unless the samples are large and random, the unit changes. In the last 25 years or so a new model of measurement has arisen that meets these difficulties (see Thorndike, 1971, and Izard and White, in Spearritt, 1982). In this model it is assumed that the chances of a student getting an item correct depend on the difficulty of the item, *and* on the ability of the student in that content area. The 'ability' referred to is a 'latent trait' or personal characteristic that accounts for performance. By this is not meant an innate ability, but any trainable competency in the sense meant in Chapter 9 — bridge-playing, adding involving carrying — *any* domain of competency that can be accessed by performance items of some kind, and where items vary in difficulty, but not too widely. Knowing the difficulty of the items, it is possible to estimate the ability of the student with respect to the trait underlying the items. There are several ways of doing this; the Rasch model is the simplest, and the one most widely used. The mathematics need not concern us here, but the principle is an important one.

There are several *advantages* of the Rasch model:

- Student performance on different tests can be calibrated on what may be assumed to be the same scale, which combines the advantages of both norm referencing and criterion referencing.
- Maximum information is squeezed out of a small number of items, so tests can be quite short and still yield reliable and valid information.
- Items can be calibrated and placed in an *item bank*, so that completely parallel or equivalent tests can be constructed very quickly. For example, teachers could give a short test before instruction and again afterwards, using completely different items, but remaining sure that they are measuring the same underlying competency (e.g. adding with carrying).
- Item banking could be used to overcome the clumsiness of present moderation procedures, and the pain and unfairness induced by 'rationing' the top decile scores.
- Instruction may be completely individualised.
- Microcomputers can be used at all stages: calibrating items, testing individuals and providing sealed scores on the competencies in question; and (a separate issue) for maintaining complete and highly accessible records of student progress.

The main disadvantage of the Rasch model is the obvious one. It seems complicated and mystifying, even though micros can do all the dirty work, and professional organisations such as ACER all the development and banking of items. As Spearritt (1982) remarked on this point: 'one must view with some trepidation the public's likely degree of understanding of a student's score on ∴ a scale that does not range from 0 to 100. A great deal of effort will have to be expended in communicating the meaning of new scale scores to teachers and the public' (p. 251).

It is to be hoped that such effort will be expended, because appropriate use of such scaled tests can in certain areas greatly simplify instruction in such areas as science and mathematics, where performance skills can be tested accurately. Izard and White (1982) for example describe *review* and *progress* tests (RAPT) in mathematics: the review test (which is quite short, only 10 or so items) covers the competency needed for completing a set of objectives, while the progress tests address each objective (and are even shorter). The review tests can be used as a pre-test to determine the level of each student before teaching a particular topic: students can then be taken individually (or in small groups according to competency) in a mastery format (see Section B) until the particular objectives identified in the progress tests have been mastered. A review test can also be given after a period of teaching to determine where the students stand with respect to the topic. The point is that all review and progress scores are expressed in units that may be directly compared with each other.

Two properties of a test

Reliability. An important property of a test is its stability or *reliability*. The test, like any measuring instrument, should perform identically from day to day, irrespective of who is administering it. A clock that is unpredictably running fast and then slow is obviously unreliable; so is an elastic tape-measure. Thus we have to assume any test we administer is a reliable estimate of the student's level of achievement. Variations in the test score must be assumed to be due to variations in the characteristic being measured, rather than to unrelated factors which therefore become errors of measurement. There is always some error of measurement present, but this should be as small as possible.

There are three main sources of error.

1. In the testing environment. If the test is administered in a noisy room, with many distractions, students' performance is likely to be erratic. There may be a tendency to misinterpret or skip items or make mistakes. Another factor in the testing environment is the way the test is presented. Are instructions given clearly? Is the manner of presentation likely to arouse or reduce anxiety? If the test is timed, is it timed accurately? Standardised administration is particularly important in norm-referenced tests (e.g. IQ tests), because the basis of norm-referencing is comparison (of individual with group norms). In both latent trait (Rasch) and criterion-referenced tests, however, the test conditions should be *optimal* for each student, so that the *best* performance is extracted. Thus, criterion-referenced tests may quite reasonably be administered under differing conditions: some students might need a longer time than others; some will do well under pressure, others under relaxed conditions. Teachers need to be very careful about whether they standardise or optimise the test environment.

2. In the learner. The reliability of the test will also be affected by changing factors in the learner. These might include tiredness or illness on the day of the test, poor reading skills so that test items are capriciously misread or misunderstood, feelings of anxiety, and so on.

3. In the test itself. A most important source of unreliability is in the test itself. If items are poorly or ambiguously worded, they may be interpreted differently by different people; or one person may interpret the same item differently on different occasions. Likewise, the scoring of the test must be consistent and free of bias, so that the same scores are obtained by different competent markers.

Unreliability thus has several sources: in the testing situation, in the learner and in the test itself. How do we know whether a test gives a reliable score or not?

Test–retest reliability. If one person, under identical conditions on the same test, achieves the same score on two separate occasions, the score is said to be reliable or stable. Test–retest reliability makes good theoretical sense, but there are two practical reasons that may make it unsatisfactory. First, practice may have an effect: having done the test once, the student will find it easier to do next time, and hence will get a higher score. Second, he or she might actually have changed in the interim, having learned or forgotten something that affects the score. The test may reflect these changes accurately — but it would appear to be unstable.

Split-half reliability. One way of beating these problems is to divide the test into two halves: the odd items and the even items are scored separately, and the two scores are correlated. If the correlation is high (e.g. + .85 or above), the two half-tests are yielding compatible scores.

Internal consistency. A test is internally consistent if all items intercorrelate: whatever they are measuring, at least they are consistent. Internal consistency is maximised by the process of *item analysis* (this procedure is discussed in more detail in Section B): items that are found *not* to correlate with the total score on the test are simply not scored. The resulting test score is thus reliable, because each item is contributing to it.

Inter-judge agreement. A test must be 'marker-proof'. Two teachers marking an exam must be able to agree, within limits, about the marks awarded to a student's responses; equally, the same person must be able to make the same judgment about a response on two different occasions.

Validity. The validity of a test is its ability to measure what it is supposed to measure. This is the most important property of a test. There are several kinds of validity.

Face validity. Competent judges would agree that the test *appears* to be measuring what it is intended to measure. Particularly with attainment and ability tests, this agreement is fairly easily obtained; it is considerably more difficult in the case of some personality tests, which may be deliberately disguised. This form of validity is a good start, but it is not in itself sufficient to establish validity.

Content validity. Test scores should relate to other measures, the validity of which is known or assumed. IQ items were originally validated, for example, by comparing responses to teachers' ratings of students' intelligence. In a science test, scores could be correlated with laboratory performance, or some problem-solving task.

Predictive validity. The test should be able to predict future performance (e.g. a maths test should correlate with the final examination). Predictive validity is particularly important when the test is used for selection purposes; it must be demonstrable that those selected actually do perform better than those rejected.

Factorial validity. Factor analysis is a means of reducing the number of tests to a fewer number of factors, without significant loss of information. It may be used, for example, where there are five tests which *appear* to measure science achievement but of which the testers are not sure. In this case, they may end up with one or two factors, whose nature can be interpreted from the correlations between all the tests and each factor. There are, however, many ways of using factor analysis: the issue is too complex to deal with any further in the present context.

Construct validity. How well do test scores relate to the construct being measured? This can usually only be established by research and, like factor analysis, is not an issue with which teachers need be concerned.

The proper determination of validity requires experimental work, statistical know-how and facilities that the classroom teacher will not usually have. The only kind of validity check readily available is that of face validity, where a teacher uses his or her own judgment and possibly that of a colleague.

Test publishers (e.g. ACER, State Curriculum Branches, Educational Testing

Service, Psychological Corporation, Science Research Associates), on the other hand, can do all the basic groundwork. The teacher has only to provide a course and then use one of the offered attainment tests. This solution appears a logical one, but there may be problems involved. In particular, teachers tend to teach to the test; the test then sets the curriculum rather than the other way round (Hoffman, 1962). It is important to note, however, that this is *not* true with item banking on the Rasch model: the test items are constantly changed and cannot directly be 'taught'.

Test distortion: A special case of validity. Test distortion is a consistent tendency for scores to be influenced (positively or negatively) by characteristics of the learner that are independent of the content measured (Andrews, 1968).

Test distortion relates to all forms of testing. The objective test, for example, requires that the learner focus on the one correct answer. As we saw in Chapter 9, this is a characteristic of the high converger. Thus, Biggs (1973b) found that students who did better on objective tests than on essays used the convergent strategy of focusing on and rote-learning essential detail in the course. Essays, on the other hand, do not necessarily show distortion in favour of divergers; it depends upon how the essays are marked, and what characteristics the marker (consciously or unconsciously) favours.

It is important to recognise the presence of test distortion. In some cases, it works in favour of good decision-making. For example, it is obviously reasonable to include oral assessments of teachers or barristers in training because their careers require them to be competent in oral skills. Similarly, if one wished to sort out students who could write fluently and stylishly about current affairs, it would be inappropriate to examine their knowledge of current affairs by objective test. On the other hand, evaluation is often undertaken for the purpose of finding out a student's general achievement. In this case, the tests used should be *distortion-free*. Such tests are hard to find, so the obvious strategy is to use a *variety* of evaluational instruments.

SUMMARY

Learning and evaluation: Two sides, same coin. Evaluation, properly conceived, involves a qualitative conception of learning. Terms like 'assessment', 'grading' or 'measurement' imply a quantitative conception. We are concerned here to see that evaluation is involved as an integral part of learning and instruction, not as a one-off exercise for grading and labelling students at the end of a learning episode.

Evaluation logically relates to all stages of learning: *presage* (curriculum objectives), *process* (how the students approach the learning task) and *product* (whether or not the objectives have been achieved satisfactorily). The setting of curriculum objectives and their evaluation requires that the outcomes of learning are appropriately realised, in terms of structural organisation and level of abstraction of the data. Testing theory and practice has traditionally emphasised *quantitative* outcomes of learning; modern practice must also come to terms with the need to take *qualitative* outcomes of learning into consideration.

Some basic concepts in evaluation. A *test* is designed as an instrument for measuring educational outcomes; tests may take several forms, such as essay, multiple choice, interview, observation, etc.

There are two basic functions of evaluation:

- to provide feedback information *during* learning (formative), and
- to state some kind of standard that has been achieved *after* learning has been completed (summative).

Student strategies are very different if they perceive the function as formative as opposed to summative. The latter, for example, rewards students for concealing error, the former for revealing error.

Test scores may be determined in three different ways. Each way has its advantages:

Norm-referencing determines the scores in relation to other students' performance. This method has been traditionally used, ranking being the stereotypical example; other examples would include moderation procedures. Norm-referencing maximises the differences between students as the basis for expressing scores. When competition is the issue — as when scholarships or prizes are to be awarded — norm-referencing is quite appropriate. Often, however, it is used when the competitive implications are inappropriate.

Criterion-referencing ties the test score to a predetermined standard, as in a driving licence: the candidate's performance does/does not meet the pre-set criterion, independently of how other individuals perform. The criterion for deciding whether performance is adequate or not is determined in advance: on educational or 'reasonable' grounds. Such grounds should be stated in the curriculum objectives, based on sound curriculum development.

Latent trait theory is a sophisticated method of combining the advantages of criterion and norm referencing. The statistics may be complicated but the theory is simple. A coherent set of test items is presumed to address a competency: a student's score on a test can be used to determine that individual's ability or competence, in units that are transferable across tests. Latent trait theory (and the Rasch version in particular) do validly what 'per cents' have done invalidly for many years.

Necessary properties of a test are *reliability* and *validity*. Reliability refers to the stability of a score: the chances that a retest would produce the same answer. Whether or not that is so depends on the test itself, the way it is administered, and the test-taker (illness, nervousness at the time of testing).

Validity refers to whether or not the test measures what it is supposed to measure. The determination of validity is quite technical, requiring that scores be associated with an independent criterion. One area where tests may be reliable but invalid is distortion, where an irrelevant characteristic of the learner may distort the score, positively or negatively.

SECTION B

LEARNING THROUGH EVALUATION: MASTERY LEARNING STRATEGY

Mastery learning is a teaching strategy that presupposes the closest links between learning and evaluation (Block, 1971; Bloom, Hastings and Madaus, 1971). It is used in areas such as core skills which all or most students may reasonably be expected to master (see Box 10.2). Testing is criterion-referenced: what is considerd 'mastery' is defined in advance, usually to a criterion — 90 per cent of the items in the test are answered correctly. The technology has thus emphasised a quantitative view of learning success, but this is not inherent in the strategy itself: mastery could just as easily be defined qualitatively (e.g. reaching a relational level of response in the topic).

The point is that where core skills can be defined fairly exactly — for example, spelling or calculation is correct or incorrect; facts are known or they are not known —mastery learning becomes a very logical way of approaching the task. If the student fails the first test, one does not award an 'F' and then move on to the next topic; the teacher uses the formative feedback provided by the test — what items were failed? what appears to be the difficulty? — reteach, and then test again. This procedure is repeated until the test is passed at the criterion level of mastery. Then the next topic in the sequence is taken.

The theory behind mastery learning is that performance is a function of two main factors: time on task and ability. Simply, bright students need to take less time to learn

---

BOX 10.2   THE PLACE FOR MASTERY LEARNING

A level of performance is specified for mastery of the tasks set. If a student reaches this level, the instructional sequence is considered to have been successful for that student. If a student does not reach the mastery level, then additional teaching or alternative approaches will need to be used until he has mastered the objectives of the program. There is no place in this process for comparisons between one student and another. It is not helpful to demonstrate that Bill Smith is not as good as Mary Jones at long division, but just that he is not yet good enough to perform this operation confidently and needs further tuition. This approach to assessment would seem to be essential in the core area of the basic skills if all students are to reach a predefined standard of competence.

Source: Keeves, Matthews and Bourke, 1978, p. 59.

something to the same level of competence as do dull students. Thus — conversely — dull students can be brought up to the level of competence displayed by brighter students *if they spend more time on task*. There are obvious limits to this: the performance in question must be 'reasonable' for that person. In practice the time needed for some people may be too long; the longer the time, and the more the repeats, the more bored and alienated the student may become.

All these qualifications are true and need to be taken into account. That is why mastery learning is reserved for basic skills, such as literacy and numeracy, on which it *is* reasonable to expect mastery from most students. Second, while one would not prescribe too much time on task, for both logistic and motivational reasons, when we look at what happens in school we see a very odd thing: *time is held constant* for all students, regardless of ability — and yet we expect most to achieve mastery! Of course, most do not, and we wonder why. It is for that reason that we find that IQ correlates with school performance: teach every student a topic for 40 minutes and then test them, and the distribution of scores will follow the normal curve (a few do well, most so-so, a few badly). If we decide to teach each person for as long as it took to reach mastery, we would find that *time spent teaching* would follow a normal curve — but the performance scores would all be at or above 90 per cent. One might be forgiven for thinking that what is important is to arrange the school day so that teachers can conveniently move around in 40 minute time slots — not that students should learn what they are supposed to learn.

Bloom emphasises the affective consequences of mastery learning: that students in a mastery model have a better self-concept. He argues that it is better for the slower students to know a few things competently than fail at most things; and he is probably right, particularly in those areas where society expects competence, such as literacy and numeracy.

Mastery learning, then, is not a method of teaching so much as a logistic; a decision not to teach an individual more until mastery in the preceding material is displayed. It is therefore best suited for content that is sequential and that permits clear-cut decisions as to learning progress. The test material and format is therefore crucial, and is one area where latent trait tests, such as the RAPT battery in mathematics mentioned in Section A, may be particularly useful, as one is expressing learning in constant units throughout.

METHODS OF TESTING

Teachers are continually evaluating and testing students in an informal way — observing, questioning, getting them to question each other, asking students to give talks or displays, correcting work, and so on. The methods of formal testing are more limited, and it is with the more important of these that we are concerned in this section.

The essay

The essay may be defined as a continuous piece of prose written in response to a question or problem. It appears to be a simple and direct way of finding out what students know, and how well they think about a topic. A question is asked, and students are then given what should be sufficient time to organise their thoughts and express them succinctly. There are many variations of the essay technique:

- the *timed* examination, students having no prior knowledge of the question;
- the *open-book* examination, where students usually have some prior knowledge and are allowed to bring reference material into the exam room;
- the *untimed* exam, where students can take as long as they like, within reason;
- the *take-home*, where students are given notice of the questions and several days to prepare their answers in their own time;
- the *assignment*, which is an extended version of the take-home and which comprises the most common of all methods of evaluating by essay;
- the *dissertation*, which is an extended report of independent research.

We have of course looked at the essay in some detail in Chapter 7, and many of the points made there about appropriate discourse structure, answering the question, the dangers of knowledge-telling, and the like, still apply here. We are concerned in this section with the reliability of essays, rather than in content, the quality of which must of course be the marker's first priority.

Reliability in marking essays. Years ago the essay was almost the exclusive method of formal evaluation. Its prestige received a serious blow as far back as 1912, when Starch and Elliott (1912; 1913a, 1913b) originated a devastating series of investigations into the reliability of essay-marking. They sent copies of two student papers in each of English, geometry and history to 180 teachers and asked that they grade the papers on a 100-point scale, with 75 as a pass mark. The range in marks in one English paper was 47 points (50 per cent to 97 per cent); and was even greater in geometry — some teachers marking for neatness, showing calculations, etc., while others did not.

A more recent investigation by Diederich (1974) confirmed these findings. This study involved the marking of 300 English essays by 53 judges (including academics from different disciplines, professional writers and business executives) all of whom were deeply concerned about the quality of students' writing. They were told they were free to grade as they liked, on a nine-point scale (1–9). The median correlation out of all those generated (nearly 3,000) was only +.31, which is quite low (see Section A): for example, 101 of the 300 papers received *every grade* from 1 to 9!

Such results strongly suggest that different markers are looking for different things. Diederich factor–analysed the variables, and found that there were five quite distinct characteristics emphasised by different markers:

- *ideas:* logical coherence, relevance to topic, originality and wit;
- *skills:* correct usage of words, sentence structure, punctuation and spelling;

- *organisation:* correct format, presentation, structure;
- *vocabulary:* use of precise but uncommon words and phrases;
- *personal style:* individual expression and style.

It is clear that a person keen on organisation would mark a well-organised but dull essay higher than a disorganised but highly original one. It is also very important that markers become *aware* of the criteria they are in fact using during marking.

Further, personal characteristics of the marker can influence judgment. For example, markers who are untidy writers mark neat and untidy essays equally; neat writers, however, tend to downgrade untidy essays heavily (Huck and Bounds, 1970). These findings suggest that, unless all essays are typewritten, only teachers with untidy writing should be permitted to mark them!

Diederich's study confirms the common belief that markers are swayed by their own prejudices in awarding marks for quality. If so, then students will get higher grades than they deserve if they correctly divine what the marker wants to read. There is some evidence for this: students who adopted a 'give-teachers-what-they-want' strategy did achieve higher grades than their general attainment in class would have indicated (Biggs, 1973b).

Not only may different markers vary greatly, but the same marker can also vary from script to script. Apart from momentary lapses, fatigue, and so on, one systematic source of unreliability is the *order* effect. When a marker sits down to a batch of thirty or so essays (the more there are, the worse the effect), the first half-dozen tend to set the standard for the next half-dozen, which in turn reset the standard for the next. Also, a moderately good essay following a run of poor ones tends to be marked higher than it deserves; similarly, if it follows a run of very good ones, it would be marked down (Hales and Tokar, 1975). The marker's standards thus tend to slide up or down according to the quality of the essays he or she happens to be marking at the time.

Reactions to findings such as these have been in two directions. One is that the essay medium is so unreliable that it should be replaced by objective tests. This implies, however, that students would be given less and less opportunity to carry out writing in continuous prose, when they are already given too little. The other is that, despite its obvious limitations, the essay is a useful technique and it would be worthwhile improving the faults of essay-marking.

Improving the reliability of marking essays. The following are some precautions which may help mitigate the above effects:

All marking should be done 'blind' (i.e. the marker is unaware of the identity of the student, and is thus less likely to be influenced by irrelevant factors). For example, Hore (1972) demonstrated that attractive female students tend to receiver higher grades than unattractive ones. Blind marking makes it less possible for teacher expectations to become a self-fulfilling prophecy.

'Blind' rechecking (i.e. with the original mark concealed, to ensure that standards are remaining fairly constant).

Decide what criteria are to be used in marking, for example, one, two or all of Diederich's list of characteristics, or others that suit one's own judgment.

Grade generally at first, say into 'Excellent', 'Pass' and 'Fail', and later try to discriminate more finely within these categories. All borderline cases should be reviewed, or re-viewed.

Spot-checks, with particular care for borderline cases, should be carried out by an independent marker. Gross disagreements should be resolved between the markers or by recourse to a third marker.

The wording of the original questions should be checked for ambiguities by an independent marker.

Guard against bias due to handwriting, by first quickly scanning all papers and deciding whether there are any particular ones that need to be rewritten.

Each question should be marked across all students, if several questions per student are involved (e.g. where an exam booklet is used). This procedure sets a standard for each question, and prevents 'halo effects' from question to question. Between questions, the papers should be shuffled to prevent systematic order effects.

Use a 'model answer', with points awarded for each congruence between the model and the student's essay. This is particularly important where essays are sectioned off to different markers. On the other hand, this procedure does away with one of the major advantages of the essay — the fact that students can structure their own responses. Clearly, the unthinking application of the model-answer technique would penalise the highly original student, and may decrease the range of cognitive processes that the essay is capable of tapping.

In summary, there are certain difficulties in obtaining reliable essay ratings but it is possible to do so if one can afford to devote a rather large amount of time to marking and checking. Because of the peculiar benefits of the essay — not least that it allows the student to indulge in continuous writing — this time is usually worth investing.

The objective test

The objective test is 'objective' only in the sense that the scoring and collation of marks is, in principle, independent of the prejudices and judgment of the scorer: indeed, scoring is now often done by machine. However, the prejudices of the test-constructor can very easily show themselves in the alternatives chosen and in the ones designated as correct.

Two main forms of the objective test are in common use: where two alternatives are provided (the true-false test), and where several — usually four or five — alternatives are provided (the multiple-choice test). Other versions involve matching procedures (e.g. States with capital cities, pictures with descriptive phrases, etc.), filling in blank diagrams, completing sentences, and so on. Of all these techniques, the multiple-choice format is the most widely used and the most acceptable. True-false is open to the obvious objection that a score of 50 per cent could be obtained by guessing, although it is possible to offset this by penalising wrong replies. We shall mainly be concerned with the multiple-choice format here.

Constructing norm-referenced tests. Say we are to construct a 50-item test, with four choices per stem, for a course in English literature. There are three stages involved:

1. Deciding what kind of items would relate to the intentions of the teacher (e.g. if appreciation of English literature would be tested adequately by items requiring the ability to recognise an author's style from selected unseen excerpts from his or her works).
2. Constructing a pool of potential items (three times the number required is a common rule-of-thumb), and testing these out by the process of item analysis (described below).
3. Deriving the final version of the test.

First one defines the item types, and then collects examples of possible items. These should be checked for wording, etc., preferably with a colleague's help, and then roughly 150 items would be administered to a few classes. The test papers are then scored and placed in rank order, with the highest scorer on top, the next second, and so on, with the poorest last.

Table 10.1   A typical item-analysis chart (simplified)

	Students	Items 1	2	3	4	5	6	7	8	9
Top third	1	X	0	X	X	X	X			
	2	X	0	X	X	X	0			
	3	X	0	X	X	X	0			
	4	0	0	X	X	0	0	etc.		
	5	X	0	X	X	0	0			
	6	X	0	X	X	0	0			
	7	X	X	X	X	X	0			
Number correct		6	1	7	7	4	1			
Bottom third	15	X	X	X	0	X	0			
	16	0	X	0	0	0	0			
	17	X	X	0	0	0	0			
	18	X	X	0	0	0	0	etc.		
	19	X	X	0	0	0	0			
	20	X	X	0	0	0	0			
	21	X	0	0	0	0	0			
Number correct		6	6	1	0	1	0			

X = item correctly answered
0 = item incorrectly answered

To illustrate the principle of item analysis, let us simplify by reducing the number of students taking the test to 21. We mark the test, and divide into top-scoring and lowest-scoring students. We then take the top third of seven students and the bottom third of seven students and draw up a checklist, classifying each student's responses by each item. This is illustrated in Table 10.1, with the responses of the top seven students, and those of the bottom seven, listed in full. The assumption behind the item analysis is that the total score of all items is a better index of the student's knowledge than one single item. If we look down the column for Item 1, we see that six of the top students got this right, but that six of the bottom students did too. Obviously this item is too easy, and it is not discriminating between good and poor students. Item 2 is worse than useless: only one top student got it, but six of the bottom students did. If this score was counted in, the worst students would get a better mark than the best students. Items 3 and 4 are both very good — especially 4 which all the good students got correct, and none of the poor students did. Item 5 is difficult, answered correctly by only five out of the 14 students. It was moderately discriminating: four of these five were in the top group. Item 6 is very difficult and could be answered by only the best student.

There are proper procedures for analysing such a chart, but inspection gives a rough idea of what are good items and what are not. Generally speaking, a 'good' item is one that is answered correctly by all the good students and incorrectly by the poor students, and is of middling difficulty. If an item is either to easy or too difficult, it clearly cannot discriminate. Item analysis usually results in the discovery that an awful lot of items are inadequate — hence the threefold increase in the numbers required for pre-testing. To obtain the final score, then, the students' responses on the surviving 50 items are added up, *not* their responses on the original 150. For future administrations of the test, only the remaining 50 items would be used.

Items selected in this way need to address the same domain: if one wanted to address different levels of the Bloom taxonomy, say, it would be necessary to do such an item analysis within each level: knowledge, comprehension, etc.

Constructing tests of this nature clearly requires a lot of work. We have described the manual way of doing this to show the principle: all that work would now of course be done inside a microcomputer. Item analysis programs are readily available and they do all the sorting and correlating, and also produce a reliability coefficient for the test. These refinements are, however, beyond our present scope: teachers wanting to move into this area need to consult the particular program manuals concerned.

Constructing tests on the Rasch model. Although latent trait theory is undoubtedly where the future of formalised testing lies, we shall not elaborate on the techniques of test construction on these lines because the mathematics involved — as opposed to the basic principles — is rather complex and beyond an introductory chapter such as this. For the foreseeable future, the construction and development will take place in institutions such as the Australian Council for Educational Research, and State Testing Branches rather than in classrooms.

Constructing criterion-referenced tests. So far, we have been talking about constructing norm-referenced tests: items are selected as good or bad depending upon whether or not they *discriminate the good from the poor students*. Test items that discriminate most effectively are those that are answered correctly by about 50 per cent of the students: the *best* 50 per cent. Selecting items and constructing a test in this way, however, has the undesirable effect of automatically limiting the number of students who can achieve mastery on the test.

Popham and Husek (1969) pointed out that the statistics used in constructing and evaluating tests rely upon the fact that the item and test scores vary widely and are normally distributed. These techniques of test construction therefore cannot be applied to criterion-referenced tests.

Airasian and Madaus (1972) suggest three steps in the development of criterion-referenced tests:

1.   *Specify instructional objectives prior to instruction.* As has been previously stressed, effective instruction in content means that the objectives of each learning episode need to be determined and stated clearly beforehand. Each objective should contain an operational verb: one that describes what the student must do to demonstrate that learning has taken place. The essence of criterion-referenced evaluation is in demonstrating that the student can, or cannot, meet the objectives that have been prescribed.

2.   *Decide on criteria that define adequate knowledge or performance.* Deciding whether or not a student has met the objectives is essentially a yes/no matter. The logical criterion is perfection — but humans always make errors, and so a more realistic question would ask *how much* error is permitted. It has become recognised that mastery in basic skills falls short of perfection by 10–20 per cent (i.e. it is usually acceptable if the student is correct 80–90 per cent of the time). This figure is arbitrary, however, and to a large extent depends on the teacher's judgment. For example, if the objective is the multiplication of three-digit by two-digit numbers, and the target consists of random computations of this kind, how much slip should the teacher allow for *simple* computational error? For *serious* computational error?

There is no really objective answer to such questions: basically the teacher must decide if 15 out of 20 is unacceptable, but 16 out of 20 is acceptable. In fact, the target falls into place when testing is in a formative context. If a person just misses the target 80 per cent and commits five errors, the fact of missing the target is far less important than *why* it was missed. What kinds of errors were made? Perhaps they all are concerned with multiplying when zero is involved, or with a particular multiplication combination: missing the target simply indicates that something needs to be diagnosed and remedied.

The seemingly arbitrary question of percentage error that should be tolerated now becomes much more meaningful. It is not a simple 'If 80 per cent correct or more — *Pass*, if 79 per cent correct or less — *Fail*', but rather 'If 79 per cent or less — *Why*?'. The answer then becomes an instructional objective in itself; we would drill the student in the erring combination or help him or her to understand handling zero. When that has been successfully accomplished, the student will be well into the 90 per cent mastery zone (if that was the only difficulty).

Sensible criterion-referenced testing therefore does not only give a final pass-fail statement, or a formula leading to that. It provides a list of diagnostic check-points that will give information as to *why* the goal was not reached satisfactorily. Sensible instruction demands that students should know what kinds of errors they are making, be instructed in their rectification, and permitted another go. The teacher using criterion-referenced evaluation has therefore to be very analytical about what is involved in teaching a certain topic, in selecting items that will test that topic, and structuring those items in a test.

In criterion-referenced testing, then, items are selected on the basis of their relationship to the *curriculum objectives*. A good item would therefore reflect instruction: for example, before instruction, only 10 per cent of students could pass the item, but after instruction the figure is 90 per cent. A poor item would be one that might be passed by 50 per cent before instruction and 60 per cent after.

    3. Devising testing situations. The final step is committing the objectives to some form of test format. A test format may involve pencil-and-paper items (as in the usual objective test) or, because instructional objectives should be behavioural where possible, use of a *practical* context, in which student behaviours are evaluated (see the list of illustrative verbs supplied by Gronlund, 1970).

A criterion-referenced test might have subsections, with several items in each, dealing with 'enabling' objectives which lead progressively towards the terminal objective. Instead of a final total score, the ideal test would break this down into a series of subscores so that one could tell at a glance a student's progress in relation to the final goal. Gagné (1967) described how such a test may be constructed. If the successful completion of an enabling objective is dependent upon the successful completion of the one preceding it, then the student's sub-test scores in the instructional episode would look like a staircase: to do Section 2, one must master Section 1, to do 3, one must master 2 (and 1), and so on. Gagné used this progressive dependence as a means of ensuring the validity of the tests: if the items do not form a staircase in this way, then they should be rearranged; and if they cannot, they are probably unreliable or invalid. The staircase approach to reliability and validity is appropriate only when the content to be learned is also, in fact, structured in this way.

Other approaches to reliability are summarised in Hambleton (1972). If the score on a criterion-referenced test is the same when it is given to two strictly comparable groups (e.g. two halves of the same class, divided randomly), then the test is clearly reliable. Correspondingly, if parallel forms of the same test could be given to the same group, again results should be the same.

Super-items. Objective tests, whether norm- or criterion-referenced, are often criticised for being both trivial and limited to assessing only the quantitative aspects of learning. Neither criticism need be true, at least of criterion-referenced tests, which are as trivial or as significant as the curriculum objectives they should be addressing.

An example of a criterion-referenced test that stretches a student 'vertically' was devised by Collis and Davey (1984) on a series of science concepts in the middle secondary curriculum (referred to in Chapter 5). They use the notion of 'super-items' (Cureton, 1965): each concept has several responses, requiring the student to produce a correct answer, and those responses are structured hierarchically. The student is scored, for that concept, at the *highest* level of understanding that is obtained: if the test is designed properly, it is found that there is a clear cut-off level, below which the student gets all items right, and above which no items are correct.

Collis and White used the SOLO taxonomy to structure the responses, giving unistructural, multistructural, relational and extended abstract alternatives: a student failing the unistructural item would of course be scored as prestructural with respect to that concept. An example of a science super-item is given in Box 10.3, and a mathematics super-item in Box 10.4.

This notion is potentially an extremely useful one, as it provides a way of criterion-referencing students' *levels of understanding* of particular curriculum topics after instruction. Obviously much care and pretesting is needed in the construction of super-items, but once they are developed, it becomes possible to check very quickly where an individual or a class is with respect to their grasp of a concept.

The short-answer test

A test format that falls between the objective and the essay is the short-answer technique, where essay-type questions are set, and the student is asked to answer in note form, using abbreviations and avoiding elaboration. This format is useful for getting at fairly factual and straightforward material, particularly for addressing or interpreting diagrams, charts and tables.

BOX 10.3   A SCIENCE SUPER-ITEM

An unmanned spacecraft landed on Mars and sent back only the following information about two samples, x and y, found on the surface. Nothing else is known about them.

Property	Sample x	Sample y
Colour	White	White
Texture	Rough	Smooth
Volume	8cc	9cc
Lustre	Dull	Dull

Target mode is concrete-symbolic.

Unistructural — What is the texture of sample x?

Multistructural — The samples x and y differ in two of their directly observable properties. Name the properties.

Relational — Can you be certain that x and y are different substances? Why do you think that?

Extended abstract — Subsequent chemical analysis of the samples showed that both x and y contained only the elements iron and oxygen. On what basis (principle) does quantitative analysis allow us to establish that the samples are different?

Source: Collis and Davey, 1984.

BOX 10.4   A MATHEMATICS SUPER-ITEM

This is a machine that changes numbers. It adds the number you put in three times and then adds 2 more. So, if you put in 4, it puts out 14.

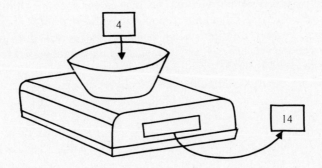

Unistructural — If 14 is put out, what number is put in?
Multistructural — If we put in a 5, what number will the machine put out?
Relational — If we got out a 41, what number was put in?
Extended abstract — If *x* is the number that comes out of the machine, when the number *y* is put in, write down a formula which will give us the value of *y* whatever the value of *x*.

The stem provides all the necessary information and each question requires reasoning at a different level with the target mode being concrete-symbolic.

Unistructural answer: 4. One piece of information used, one answer required, the information is obtainable from either the last sentence in the stem, or from the diagram.

Multistructural answer: 17. All the information is used in a sequence of discrete answers. The stem is seen as a set of instructions to be followed in order.

Relational answer: 13. All the information is used but, in addition, the student has to extract the principle involved in the problem to solve it — in this case to use it in reverse.

Extended abstract answer: $y = \frac{x-2}{3}$. The student has to extract the abstract general principle from the information and write it in its abstract form. This involves dismissing distracting cues, perhaps forming hypotheses and testing them, and zeroing in on the relationships involved.

Source: Collis and Biggs, 1986.

The usual presupposition behind the short-answer test is that the examiner is after something quite specific (i.e. it too is a one-correct-answer format). The use of the model-answer technique is more justifiable here than in the essay proper. The short answer is thus well suited to criterion-referenced testing where the answer is too complex (or otherwise inappropriate) to put into a standard multiple-choice format. Another advantage of the short answer is that it is less susceptible to test-taking strategies than the ordinary multiple choice. In the latter, it is possible to give a correct response by a process of elimination (i.e. the student does not know enough to decide that a response is correct, but knows enough to realise that three of the four alternatives are *incorrect*). Further, multiple choice depends on a process of *recognition*, whereas the short answer depends on *recall*; and it is much easier to recognise something as familiar than it is to recall it. If the examiner felt that it was more appropriate to test recall rather than recognition, then the choice is the short-answer format.

The practicum

Here the student is put in a practical situation that is identical to the behaviour that will be required when instruction has ceased. This is particularly useful in courses with practical objectives, where indeed it is the only logical way of evaluating.

In teacher-education courses, student teachers are required to demonstrate at some point that they have acquired teaching skills, as opposed to passing a written examination in teaching method. Examples are manifold: students in woodworking should have to demonstrate that they can actually operate power tools, make a rubbed-glue joint, etc.; chemistry students, that they can set up the apparatus and carry out a quantitative analysis in the laboratory. Of course it may be necessary to supplement such evaluation with pencil-and-paper tests on relevant content, but the *critical* evaluations are in practical contexts.

Criterion-referenced evaluation is most appropriate for evaluating the practicum. The objectives should be quite clear-cut: the student has to perform certain behaviours to a specified standard. It should therefore be a simple matter in most cases to specify what these behaviours are, whether the learner passes muster, and if not, why not. Let us take, for example, a particular segment of teaching behaviour: the student teacher is adopting a lecturing style which requires telling the class a certain principle and then questioning the pupils. The desired behaviours are placed on a checklist (see Table 10.2): many behaviours might appear on such a list, depending on circumstances. Students should be well aware in advance of what such a list might contain, and be given fairly immediate feedback, perhaps in conjunction with a video-taping (in which case, students would find it valuable to rate their own performance before discussing the supervisor's rating).

The diagnostic value of such a checklist is considerable, far more so than a typical norm-referenced evaluation of a practical teaching session, which might read:

A: Definitely superior, among the best in the year;
B: Above average;

Table 10.2   Checklist of student teaching behaviours

The dimensions in this profile carry differential importance in the assessment of teaching performance. It is not considered appropriate that a student's overall performance be determined by a simple summation of the ratings assigned to the various dimensions.

Professional qualities   *Year one*

1.	Relation with school personnel	U	W	S	G	V	E
2.	Relation with children	U	W	S	G	V	E
3.	Approach to teaching	U	W	S	G	V	E
4.	Attempts to improve teaching competence	U	W	S	G	V	E

General teaching skills

5.	Oral communication	U	W	S	G	V	E
6.	Written communication	U	W	S	G	V	E
7.	Lesson planning	U	W	S	G	V	E
8.	Organisation of classroom	U	W	S	G	V	E
9.	Lesson implementation	U	W	S	G	V	E
10.	Lesson evaluation	U	W	S	G	V	E

Classroom management and control

11.	Classroom interpersonal skills	U	W	S	G	V	E
12.	Classroom control	U	W	S	G	V	E
13.	Anticipation of pupil disruptions	U	W	S	G	V	E
14.	Coping with pupil disruptions	U	W	S	G	V	E

Specific teaching skills

15.	Preparation of lesson notes	U	W	S	G	V	E
16.	Lesson introduction	U	W	S	G	V	E
17.	Explanation skills	U	W	S	G	V	E
18.	Demonstration skills	U	W	S	G	V	E
19.	Basic questioning skills	U	W	S	G	V	E
20.	Use of media and materials	U	W	S	G	V	E
21.	Closure of lesson	U	W	S	G	V	E
22.	Reinforcement of pupil behaviour	U	W	S	G	V	E
23.	Ability to create pupil involvement	U	W	S	G	V	E
24.	Ability to monitor the quality of pupil involvement	U	W	S	G	V	E

Diagnostic skills

25.	Planning skills	U	W	S	G	V	E
26.	Evaluation skills	U	W	S	G	V	E

(U) *Unsatisfactory*	(S) *Satisfactory*	(V) *Very Good*
(W) *Weak*	(G) *Good*	(E) *Excellent*

General observations. (Optional Comments)

Source: Newcastle College of Advanced Education, 1986.

C: Average;
D: Below average, but meets minimal standards;
E: Not up to standard.

Clearly, such a rating is singularly uninformative. Is the 'A' student *really* a good teacher, or merely the best of a bad bunch? Students of 'B' gradings and below have no idea, in the absence of other information, what was really wrong with their performance. A criterion checklist, moreover, is likely to lead to more reliable measurement than an overall grading: two raters are more likely to agree on more specific, detailed behaviours (e.g. a student's audibility or skill in question-handling) than on whether he or she is 'average' or 'above average' overall. The critical point with the checklist approach is whether the items of listed behaviours include the most important aspects of teaching. Again, we come back to the matter of professional judgment.

One general advantage of the practicum as a medium of evaluation is its apparent face validity: the student is being assessed in a situation that models reality. The closer the practicum is to the real thing, the greater its validity. It is, however, often difficult to get psychologically close to actuality. Even in the practice teaching session, the presence of the evaluator (either in person or by one-way screens or recording devices) distorts the situation so that nervous students in particular are likely to behave quite differently from the way they *would* behave if they were not being observed, and if the children in the class were all personally known to them. Nevertheless, the amount of distortion introduced by such factors is probably less than would occur if practice teaching were assessed exclusively by written examinations; which are themselves likely to be affected by anxiety and other factors.

Oral tests: Presentations and interviews

A common oral test is the class presentation, which is evaluated in terms of the content conveyed and the effectiveness of presenting that content. It is similar to the teaching practicum, but class presentation is not necessarily meant to reproduce a situation in which students will later find themselves.

Another oral form of evaluation is the interview, where the teacher questions the student on a one-to-one basis. The great advantage is that this is a two-way process. Skilful examiners can plumb the depths of the student's knowledge and abilities in ways that they may not be able to prescribe in advance. They can also provide feedback to the student, and thus serve a valuable formative function. On the other hand, the success of the technique depends to a large extent on the mental chemistry of the participants: some such interviews go off with a bang, with enjoyment and stimulation to both parties; others can be painfully embarrassing. This instability is reflected in the extraordinarily low reliability of the interview, which is in fact lower than any other evaluation medium. It should be noted that this unreliability applies only to the open-ended interview: a structured interview that is conducted with a criterion-referenced checklist (e.g. a practicum on conversational skills) is not open-ended and may be quite reliable.

A COMPARISON OF EVALUATION METHODS

Now for an overall view of the media we have been discussing, with a quick look at the advantages and disadvantages of each. Comparisons are made in terms of both general properties of all tests, and some educational or practical points.

Properties of tests

There are four general properties to be considered:

1.   *Validity.* The validity of the essay depends on whether examiners set unambiguous questions, and whether they mark in terms of the qualities they think they are marking. The objective format is valid if the appropriate pre-testings are carried out, and if some kind of logical taxonomy (e.g. Bloom) is used to clarify the levels to be tested. Without some kind of theory of relevant cognitive process, markers can go quite astray, for example over-emphasising computation in a maths concept test. The short answer is probably a valid medium as far as it goes, but it is more restricted in scope than either the essay or the objective. The practicum has excellent face validity: it makes clear sense to both student and evaluator, although there may be difficulties in reproducing the terminal situation exactly. The validity of the interview depends much on the participants.

2.   *Reliability.* The oral is the least reliable of all media, followed by the essay, then the short answer, with the objective being most reliable. The practicum can be very reliable if the behaviours are scheduled in advance on a checklist: if, however, general ratings of performance constitute the method of scoring, then the practicum would be on a par with the essay.

3.   *Distortion.* The question of distortion is complicated by the fact that so little research has been done on it, despite the fact that it is of great practical concern to both teachers and students. Distortion is not always bad: if evaluators are aware of the kinds of distortion most likely to be influential in a particular format, they can capitalise on this. This applies particularly to essay-marking: if markers know the kinds of things they reward in students which are independent of strict content-related material (e.g. ability to write fluently and wittily), they should make this clear to students. It is also important that markers become aware of undesirable things they mark up (e.g. reproduction of teacher's words), and desirable things they mark down (e.g. originality). Objective tests favour convergent abilities, as may the short answer.

4.   *Suitability of norm or criterion referencing.* All media *can* be either norm- or criterion-referenced. In the case of media which involve the judgment of the marker, there is a strong tendency to make comparisons between individuals if the criteria are not absolutely clear. The marker may start with every intention of rating the candidate in terms of particular criteria, but when pinned down to make a decision, prevaricates: 'Well, if I pass her, then I've got to pass Tom whom I already have decided should fail ...'

Everyone who has ever attempted evaluation knows how often it comes to this in the end, which is one reason why good criterion-referenced checklists are so useful.

Each specific piece of behaviour can be rated unequivocally and the outcome should be clear — and can be made clear to the candidate. In a global rating, the internal means of arriving at a decision so often involves purely personal like–dislike factors. Students are, of course, fully aware of this, and when they fail under a global-rating type of evaluation, they tend to feel that they have also been failed as a person. Wherever personal judgment is involved, then, the evaluator should be extra careful about making the criteria clear to the students.

Practical aspects

There are several practical aspects of testing media, four of which are dealt with here.

1. *Trouble in preparation.* Essays and short answers are the easiest of all tests to prepare, objective tests and practicums the most difficult. Oral interviews may be extremely easy, or require a lot of preparatory work, depending on the context.

2. *Coverage.* One of the major advantages of objective tests is their enormous potential for coverage: items may be selected so that every important aspect of the course is sampled. At the other extreme is essay-writing, which takes a considerable amount of time relative to selecting a multiple-choice item. While this means that a particular issue can be addressed in depth, it is difficult, in the time available for examinations, to test coverage. Unless there is considerable choice offered in an essay exam, it becomes something of a lottery. The shorter time required on short-answer formats means that coverage here can be better than in the essay proper, but not as good as the objective test. Coverage in the practicum should be close to total: if it is not, one of its major advantages (resemblance to a real situation) is lost. The interview can ask questions in depth or range widely (or both if time permits) — a degree of flexibility which is of great advantage.

3. *Freedom for student to demonstrate relevant knowledge and skills.* The objective format is clearly very limited in this respect: the student can either check the correct alternative or not. It is possible to allow students to explain their choice, offer alternatives different from those presented, but to do so weakens one of the main advantages of the objective test, ease of scoring.

The essay leaves a lot more scope for students to justify their interpretation of the question, and to allow them freedom to angle the question so that it best reflects their thinking on the issue. Rigid marking of essays can of course make the medium just as restricted as an objective test. The short answer is more restricted than the essay, but less so than the objective test. In a well-conducted practicum, the student ought to be required to show all relevant abilities (this is, of course, the purpose of a practicum). On the other hand, there may be little freedom for the student if a criterion checklist is being used. If a student teacher has a particularly individual style of teaching which does not match the categories in the list then, however effective that style could be, it will not be evaluated as effective. However, it would make little sense if the evaluator stuck rigidly to the checklist if all *other* indications were that the student was doing extremely well. The interview is as free as the interviewer will allow it to be: either to leave the student no choice but to answer the questions and follow the leads given, or to give the student complete responsibility for self-revelation.

4. *Ease of scoring.* This factor probably accounts for the popularity of the objective test. Once the test has been set, the scoring is extremely quick and easy. This is in direct contrast to the essay, which is easy to set but difficult to score reliably. The short answer is a great improvement on the essay in this respect, although ease of scoring is offset by restricted freedom for the student. The practicum is easy to score once the checklist has been well established, but it does mean that the evaluator has to concentrate long and hard while he or she is observing the student. Scoring an interview may be difficult, for if preparation is inadequate the interview often results in a general gut-level rating: the interviewer builds up a general feeling that the interviewee is excellent, good, passable or not up to standard (we each have our own peculiar calculus to arrive at this decision).

These are some of the more important characteristics of the main forms of testing. The next important step in the evaluation procedure is to move from the test itself to the final distribution of grades.

GRADING

Implementing the results of evaluation involves that aspect of summative evaluation that causes most worries: grading. By grading, most people mean the award of labels (e.g. Distinction, Credit, Pass, Fail, or a numerical equivalent). Two particular aspects of the usual grading systems cause concern among teachers, students, parents, employers and the general public:

1. Grading is a system of *discriminating* between people.
2. These discriminations are made *public*. Kirschenbaum, Napier and Simon (1971) referred to grading as public evaluation: it consists of data that are to be made available to employers or educational institutions, and on the basis of such data, decisions will be made that seriously affect the student's life.

Some forms of grading include:

Written evaluations. These are qualitative statements made about each student for each subject: a criterion checklist, simple statements about each student's strengths and weaknesses, and so on. Such statements, if they are to be meaningful, need to be criterion-referenced, which also helps to avoid the subjectivity and unreliability of overall ratings. Such evaluations, however, take a long time to prepare and a lot of space to report. Further, they hardly meet the requirements of public evaluation: their main value is for the student, future teachers, parents, etc. Really, of course, they should be provided *whatever* other forms of grading are used.

Self-evaluation. Self-evaluation is not the same as self-grading. In the latter, students actually set their own grade, which may or may not then be averaged with the teacher's grade. In self-evaluation, students evaluate their own work qualitatively (either in writing or in conference) in line with their own and their teachers' criteria. The teacher then incorporates the students' evaluations into the final evaluation. Kirschenbaum et al. comment that self-evaluation is in itself an important learning experience. The disadvantages are that pressure for high grades strains the student's honesty, and that in some subjects the student may not have the content expertise to make appropriate judgments. Once self-evaluation is put into context, however, it seems that it might be a *component* of most evaluational schemes. We have much more to say about this below.

The contract system. Contracts between student and teacher are becoming increasingly popular. They can be devised either on an individual basis, whereby each student negotiates his or her own contract, or on a class basis, where the terms of the contract apply to everyone in the class. In either case, it is agreed between students and teacher that so much work is worth an 'A' (or whatever labels are used), so much a 'B', and so on. Where a student fails to meet the terms of the contract, a new one can be negotiated, or the outcome left to the teacher's judgment. A class contract could consist of something like the following (in this case the teacher likes good attendance ...):

F: Failing to hand in any assignments, and failing to attend more than two-thirds of the classes;
D: Attendance satisfactory but assigned work unsatisfactory;
C: Attendance satisfactory: at least one satisfactory assignment;
B: Attendance satisfactory: at least two satisfactory assignments;
A: Attendance satisfactory: assignments unusually good *or* extra work undertaken.

Very similar to the class contract is the point-accumulation system, according to which points are awarded for amount *and* quality of work. An A may be worth 10–12 points; B, 7–9; C, 4–6; D, 2–4; and F, zero or 1 point. There is no need for students actually to sign a contract; they know the rules (and may well have a hand in deciding them), and each works until sufficient credit is gained towards a grade that satisfies. (Under this kind of system, a student should be permitted to re-submit a poor paper.) Points can be awarded for quantity or for quality, but preferably for both (e.g. 0 for unsatisfactory, 1 for pass, and 2 for excellent). This tends to avoid one disadvantage of contracting — that it can reinforce sheer quantity of output. It does mean, however, that the teacher's workload is much increased: a determined student can easily wear a teacher down with requests for re-submissions or detailed evaluations.

Taylor (1971) surveyed students' attitudes towards contract and conventional systems and found that students did see the contract system as fairer, but they did not actually perform at a higher level.

Mastery learning. Mastery learning is not so much a grading procedure as a total instructional approach (which we have already discussed at some length). Mastery learning can be used in connection with a letter-grade system by either defining mastery in terms of 'per cent error = A, per cent error = B,' and so on; or by using one criterion for a variety of tasks (giving A if all tasks are complete, B if most are, etc.).

Meskauskas (1976) gave a highly technical analysis of the problems presented by mastery models.

Pass/fail. Pass/fail is usually part-and-parcel of a criterion-referenced approach (student does or does not meet the specified standards), but it can stand as a grading method in its own right. Pass/fail is where the only statement on a student's report or transcript is whether the course is passed or failed. Many schools and universities now work on this basis in at least some courses; its application in non-mastery courses is simply that the higher grades are all compressed into one overall P. Variations of the method retain an 'excellent' category in addition to pass and fail.

Pass/fail removes much of the pressure to compete for higher grades, and this often results in a more pleasant classroom atmosphere, which may be important in certain courses involving a high degree of participation and discussion. In other courses, however, some of the more ambitious students may not feel it worth their while to work hard for 'only a P'.

Credit/no credit. A version of pass/fail is the credit/no credit system, which is preferable in many ways and strongly endorsed by Glasser (1969) in his book *Schools Without Failure*. The student receives credit for *passing* a course, but there is no permanent record of *failing*. It is important under this system that the student has plenty of reasonable opportunities for gaining credit (e.g. students can re-sit an examination), although Glasser realistically stated that in the student's own interests (not to mention the teacher's) there should be some kind of limit to the number of attempts permitted. The point is that these attempts are nowhere recorded officially, which removes some of the pressure on the borderline student.

From test marks to final grade

Whatever grading system is used, the educator has to move from the student's performance — which is usually expressed in marks, percentages, number correct, etc. — to the grading category (i.e. B, Credit, Pass, or some qualitative comment). The problem is easier where a dual (Pass/Fail, Credit/No credit) system is used; harder where three (Honours/Pass/Fail), or more (A, B, etc.) categories are used. There are two main problems involved: moving from a mark to a grading category, and combining several marks or grades to form a final grade.

Determining grade from a continuous distribution. The first problem arises where marking is along a continuous scale, as where points are awarded for various aspects of a paper (e.g. 5 marks for organisation, 1 mark for title, 15 marks for evidence of wide background reading, 10 marks for originality of approach, etc.), or where the marks of several raters are to be added in.

A typical score distribution (where 50 students have been given a 20-item objective test, with each correct response gaining one mark), and some suggested grading schemes, are outlined in Table 10.3. (The figures are taken from an actual class list.) Scores on the test ranged from 0 to 20: one student got all 20 correct; two got 19 correct; three 18, one 17, and so on. As can be seen, the test is of moderate difficulty: most scores are around the halfway mark (this is clearly not a mastery test). If, for example, it is decided to give the conventional letter grade, there are two real alternatives. The first is norm-referenced, and the agreed 'ration' is that approximately 10 per cent of the class should get As, 20 per cent Bs, 40 per cent Cs, 20 per cent Ds and 10 per cent Fs, which gives a nice symmetrical near-enough-to-normal curve.

Table 10.3   Some alternative grading schemes

Final score dsitribution	Number of students	Norm-referenced compromises 1	2	3
20 (max.)	1			
19	2	6 As	7 As	Excellent
18	3	(nearest 10%)		
17	1			
16	0		2 Bs	
15	2	8 Bs		
14	0	(nearest 20%)		
13	2			
12	3			Satisfactory
11	6		29 Cs	
10	8	19 Cs		
9	5	(nearest 40%)		
8	5			
7	0			
6	0	10 Ds		
5	2	(nearest 20%)		
4	3		9 Ds	Doubtful (borderline)
3	4			
2	0	7 Fs		
1	2	(nearest 10%)	3 Fs	Unsatisfactory
0	1			
TOTAL	50			

We count down the list and mark off the appropriate percentages: this is done in Column 1. We cannot get exactly 10 per cent As: if we allow 20 and 19 items correct, we have three students (6 per cent); and if 18 items correct is also allowed, six students (12 per cent). Twelve per cent is nearer, so we will give As to students scoring 18 and above. Similarly, we cannot get exactly 20 per cent for Bs — eight students (16 per cent) is the nearest, if we make the cutting point for Bs at 12 correct. For C, 11, 10 and 9 correct gives 19 students (near enough to 40 per cent) so the cut-off here is at 9. We can get exactly 20 per cent for Ds, so that cut-off is at 4 items correct. This leaves seven students as Fs, with 3 or fewer items correct.

This system is very logical, but hardly good sense — look for example, at the 'gaps' in the distribution. A more reasonable compromise is to let the shape of the distribution, together with the teacher's sense of what is or is not a good score, decide the cut-off points. This is done in Column 2. We can see that the top seven students form a group: let us call them all As. The two who scored 15 correct would be Bs. There is now a run of students, from 13 to 8 items correct, that cluster around the halfway mark: evidently these should all be Cs. A cluster of nine students with 3, 4 and 5 correct then become Ds — which leaves three clear Fs. This is not a symmetrical distribution, but it makes intuitive sense. It avoids the arbitrary (and to the students, perceptibly unjust) decision in the simple norm-referenced solution — where four students scoring 3 correct items were failed, whereas their colleagues with only one more correct item were passed.

The main advantage of this method is that it is non-competitive: the grades are not rationed, they just follow the natural 'fall-out' of marks. If 40 students scored 18 and above, then all 40 would receive As. The main disadvantage with the method is that it relies on uneven fall-out. If it so happened that every possible score from 0 to 20 was represented by two to three students, it would be impossible to locate natural cut-offs. Further, the teacher has to rely on the coincidence that the number of breaks in the distribution corresponds to the number of categories used in grading. The present example worked out rather well (if it is agreed that 3 correct out of 20 justifies a D), but another example may not.

Obviously, the method is more likely to work where there are fewer categories, the case given in Column 3. A logical way of interpreting the distribution — and one which is more likely to be compatible with what the percentage correct on a test of 20 items indicates about the students' learning — is in terms of *four* categories. There are seven students whose group shows 'excellent' learning; 31 students showing 'satisfactory' or 'pass-level' learning; nine 'doubtfuls'; and three clear 'fails' or 'unsatisfactories'. This solution is partly norm-referenced (in that the group to a certain extent sets its own standards), but it may be adjusted to the quality of the learning. If the teacher decided in advance, for instance, that anyone scoring less than 50 per cent correct ought to be considered as a 'doubtful', we would add another 10 students to the nine already in this category. What should be done with these 'doubtfuls' is for the teacher to decide. One desirable approach would be to find out what was wrong, teach the students again, and give them another test — in the hope they would all move into the 'satisfactory' category. In this case, the 'unsatisfactories' might also be included, although one or zero items correct out of 20 looks rather like a total breakdown in learning which would require little short of complete reteaching. If it was not practically possible to give remedial work, or to administer another test, the 'doubtful' group would have to be evaluated on the basis of other information: performance in class, knowledge of illness or stress on the day of the test, opinions of other teachers, and so on.

Combining grades. The second problem to be considered is that of combining marks to form a final grade. To illustrate this, assume that the teacher is taking the following into account:

- a term paper;
- a research project;
- an objective examination;
- an essay examination.

Logically, there are two alternative models of using these marks.

1.   *Combining them all.* The first and most common model is one in which each set of marks counts, the assumption being that they all assess something different and are all thus important. A good student has to do a good term paper, a good project *and* good finals: the final grade is then composed of the sum (*union*) of the several sets of marks.

The next problem is to decide how to combine the marks. If it is simply by adding them up, there are two further problems:

(a) each mark has to be converted into units that are equivalent; and
(b) one has to decide what weight to give each mark (e.g. is the project to count equally with the final objective?).

Traditional statistics would suggest *normalising* the scores: we have already met the problems associated with that. A common practice is to convert them all into percentages, misleading though that might be (see Section A). Second, it is necessary to decide on a reasonable weighting system. Factor loadings are technically a good solution but this is impractical in schools. A simple solution is to say that each is worth 33 per cent — all receive equal weight — or the students could decide in a class discussion.

2.   *Grading on the best result.* The second alternative allows for both individual differences and the fact that test distortion might penalise students in areas that are actually irrelevant educationally. Here, the teacher's objectives are different: to pass this course, a student must show progress by writing a good term paper or doing a good research project *or* by passing a final exam — either in essay or in objective format. This allows for the fact that individuals do differ: students can arrive at different goals by different routes and still be competent.

It is obviously a matter of educational philosophy as to which of the two models is considered more appropriate in a particular course. Biggs and Braun (1972) looked at the characteristics distinguishing those students who did best on the first model with those who did best on the second. Students who did best by using all tests and papers were surface-achievers: teacher-dependent, organised in their approach and rote learned a great deal. Students who did best when their best paper was selected had a deep approach to learning: not surprisingly they put all their efforts into what they were most interested in.

It does matter, therefore, how tests and assignment results are combined: it looks like the familiar dichotomy between quantity and quality of work. Clearly, teachers will have to do what they see as best for their own particular educational objectives.

School reports

A final matter, which should be considered briefly, is the question of reporting grades on a transcript, report card or other document. Although this might be considered largely an administrative issue, different evaluational philosophies will obviously have a great effect on what student data are recorded officially, and in what form. There are three main classes of reportable information:

1. information for other educators and institutions, such as progress reports which start in Year 1 and follow students through their school careers;
2. information meant for students and parents (e.g. the usual term report card);
3. semi-public information, on transcript, which is intended for employers or other interested parties.

Information for other educators. One of the most important implications of Rosenthal's work on the self-fulfilling prophecy (Rosenthal, 1971; Rosenthal and Jacobson, 1968) is that information about a child tends to create expectations about the child which so guide the teacher's own behaviour that those expectancies are fulfilled. If a teacher writes on the Year 1 progress report card that the child is 'a behaviour problem', when the Year 2 teacher sees that information the chances are increased that that child will remain (or become) a behaviour problem. If the child is designated 'a slow learner' he or she has an additional burden placed on his or her unknowing shoulders in following years. Sarason (1971) pointed out that a major constraint on a teacher is to produce results that are compatible with those produced for that child by preceding teachers. Letter grades, particularly those with a vague 'below average' translation, tend to act as pointers to colleagues.

One solution is to make progress reports criterion-referenced, by listing all curriculum-based skills that the child has mastered. If this is efficiently done, it tells the next teacher precisely where to start; and it does so without making invidious comparisons or floating estimates about what the child is *not* capable of doing.

Information for parents. The problem of term reports to parents is rather more difficult. Most parents think they understand a norm-referenced grade: they were themselves brought up with quantities, rankings and the rest. As we have seen in this chapter, however, such information can be highly misleading. On the other hand, a criterion-referenced statement or checklist is not necessarily the answer, especially where parents are not familiar with educational terminology. And even if there is a checklist, many parents still want some easy-to-grasp label so that they can, for example, work out where their child stands in relation to the one next door.

There is no easy answer. One could compromise by giving both norm- and criterion-referenced evaluations; or by taking quite a tough line and saying that on educational grounds the school had decided to forego grading for term reports. This is obviously an issue that would depend on both school policy and the relationship between staff and their students' parents. It would be a pity, however, if teachers were unable to implement a system of grading that they firmly believed to be educationally desirable because of the non-educational issue of public relations. It is likely that, with ingenuity, a mutually acceptable system of public reporting could be devised that would combine the educational benefits of criterion-referenced reports with communicability.

Semi-public information. Norm-referenced grades are not as informative as most people believe. A general criterion-referenced grade (such as Credit or Pass/Fail) can very easily be filled out with explanatory comments that would be fairer to the student, and more meaningful to a future employer or teacher, than a letter-grade or grade-point average. Such comments could point out that although the student got a string of Cs in his or her school career he or she does, for instance, have a flair for straight dealing with people. In any case, those Cs might be equivalent to As on someone else's transcript. But there is another more basic issue: while it is perhaps reasonable that a school is the appropriate institution to detail semi-publicly what a child has learned, is it reasonable that the school should do the main task of job selection for an employer? Or that the teacher's own educational philosophy should be overridden by those whose concern is *not* primarily with the education of the child?

EVALUATING AT THE PROCESS LEVEL

There are two main aspects of evaluation at the level of process: evaluation *as* a process that students should experience, and evaluation *of* process. The first aspect was introduced in the introduction to this chapter: that the notion of educating people to become autonomous operators — in whatever field — means that they should be able to evaluate their own work at presage, process and product levels. That in turn means that they must be given the opportunity to assess their own work.

Self-assessment

We should repeat first that self-*assessment* does not necessarily mean self-*grading*: that is, the evaluation that the students produce about their own work may, or may not, be incorporated into the final grade for a course. The main point is that assessing one's own work is a learning experience that is rarely encountered prior to entry into the real world where it is an immediate and natural expectation of the professional person. It seems reasonable that students be given the chance of that experience before entering that world. For example, Boud (1985b) reports a survey of nearly 2,000 graduates of the University of New South Wales, who ranked 'Evaluating one's own work' as second (to 'Solving problems') in a list of nine skills in importance to them in their work; only 20 per cent felt that the university had contributed 'considerably' towards acquiring that skill. Boud argues that self-assessment (not necessarily involving self-grading) 'is an important skill which all graduates should possess and which universities do insufficient towards acquiring' (p. 1).

That is all very well when talking about graduates. The question is: does self-assessment have a legitimate place in the school curriculum? Another question is: why not? As noted, there are good reasons why it should.

Assessment of any kind involves two stages: *setting the criteria* for assessing the work; and *making a judgment* about the extent to which these criteria have been met. Students may be involved in setting the criteria, then in judging in accordance with them; or they may be involved only in judging, using the teacher's criteria. The last case is the most conservative. Let us take that first.

Self-assessment on teacher's criteria. Boud reports a conventional case of a mid-session examination, where students (in an electrical engineering course and after the examination) were provided with a paper of an unnamed fellow student and a detailed model answer. They were asked to mark their colleague's paper in line with the model answer, indicating exactly where the student had deviated from the model. They returned the papers, and then received their own paper. They then applied the same procedure to their own paper, without knowing what marks someone else might have given it. The self- and other- marks were then compared: if the mark was within 10 per cent of what the other student had awarded, the self-mark was given. If the discrepancy was greater than 10 per cent, the lecturer in charge of the course remarked the script. Boud reports that the saving in staff time was considerable, especially in large classes.

Apart from the staff saving of time, however, there were considerable improvements in content: the students not only learned the curriculum content to the extent usual for sitting exams, they then studied a model exam, another student's paper, and then their own paper. In other words, they studied the specific exam content several times, and had thought about it in a very generative kind of way because they had to assess another student's paper, as well as their own. On the other hand, this technique would work only in a highly convergent or closed topic, where it was possible to write a model answer and use that with such precision. The method could not work in a more open or divergent area, where a great deal of judgment is necessary.

To deal with this latter kind of situation, student involvement is also necessary at the stage of setting the criteria. Boud refers to a 'nominal group technique' for arriving at these criteria.

Self-assessment on student-generated criteria. The class is brainstormed for points that should be included in the assignment, which may be an essay, a project, a lab report, whatever. A large number of criteria are obtained: these are written up on a board and regrouped into smaller categories. It is important that the teacher keep out of the business of suggesting criteria, so that the students feel a genuine 'ownership' about them. *They* are the ones who decide what constitutes a good essay/project/etc. In fact, Boud reports that no group he has ever attended has ever omitted a significant feature: for example, clarity of expression, coverage of literature, proper structure giving aims, method, conclusions, etc. All these features are then regrouped — from sometimes over 100 to about five or six headings. The class then decides which to use and with what emphasis. A marking sheet is then drawn and distributed to the class.

The class then go and do the assignment, mark their own work in terms of the criteria, and place that marking and its justification in a sealed envelope, which is returned to the teacher, with the assignment itself. It is up to the teacher what happens next. Whether or not the teacher uses the mark summatively or formatively is an open question: in either case the students have gone through an important learning experience. They have decided the important features of the assignment; they have evaluated their own work in terms of those features. The end-product is greatly enhanced in quality as a result.

There are many variations on the self-assessment theme. One is to mix group and individual aims, whereby some of the course content and agreed activities can be decided by the majority and other aspects negotiated with each individual. In the latter case, a *learning portfolio* can be maintained by the student: a record of everything to do with the course is kept, including a diary on feelings about the course, interactions with individuals in and out of the class, and evidence of learning from these activities. A variation would include a partnership between two members of the class with similar aims towards the course. In such a course, students would state their aims in undertaking the course, and then decide whether or not their aims had been met, and the evidence they had in their portfolios for coming to that conclusion.

These kinds of activities might sound very advanced and tertiary level, but this is not necessarily so. Portfolios could easily be maintained in such courses as creative writing in secondary school, in which students could state their aims and include a published short story or article as a necessary criterion for a higher level pass.

Evaluation of process in specific tasks

The second aspect to process evaluation is evaluating the processes used in a specific task, or towards learning in general. We have come across the notion of evaluating in specific content areas, or with respect to particular tasks, earlier. In Chapter 6, for example, we referred to deep process in essay writing: students could easily be marked on their 'deepness' — both in terms of outcome, and in relation to an interview in which they might be asked how they went about their essays: did they review in terms of main ideas or themes or only in terms of words and sentences? Did they revise with a view to the overall sequence and main idea or only in terms of correct wording and orthographics? In the case of reading, Paris in his ISL program assessed children's metacognitive knowledge of reading strategies. Similar approaches could be made in other tasks.

In Chapter 9 it was suggested that process be assessed in terms of divergence, but within specific content areas. Thus, in social studies, teachers could address the ability to test hypotheses (e.g. that family structure is related to social stability). Divergence could be addressed with test items like 'What would happen if ...' (e.g. Western Australia seceded from the Commonwealth); 'Think of as many different ways as you can of slowing the drift from rural areas to the cities'. This kind of process-testing is, in effect, using the psychological process variables as a *structure* for constructing the test items.

Another way of getting at both cognitive and affective process evaluation would be in terms of the student's overt behaviour in problem-solving. It should be comparatively simple to make up a list of behaviours that defines whether or not the student is able to deal effectively and autonomously with particular situations (Biggs, 1973a). Such a list might include (suitably worded for the occasion):

1. possessing or locating relevant information;
2. being able to apply relevant skills and operations;
3. using general strategies that avoid either being snowed under with too much information, or of being starved with too little;
4. being able to set one's own objectives;

5. evaluating the products of one's own thinking internally, and checking the truth and falsity of hypotheses as a matter of course;
6. being able to persist in the absence of extrinsic reinforcers.

Such a checklist would vary both for different tasks and for different levels of learning; each item would become a process objective.

Evaluation of process with regard to general approach to learning

Reference has been made to several studies where students' approaches to learning have been assessed for research purposes. Two ways of going about this are using general purpose self-rating questionnaires, and using one-to-one observation and/or interview. Self-rating questionnaires can be administered in groups and are quick and easy to administer and score. Students rate themselves on items referring to their usual or typical reactions in general learning situations (see Table 10.4 for examples). Scores thus give an indication of students' tendencies or predilections for surface or deep processing; they do not guarantee that that approach is applying at any particular time.

Table 10.4   Typical items from the learning process questionnaire

Surface motive	I chose my present subjects mainly because of career prospects when I leave school, not because I'm particularly interested in them.
Surface strategy	I tend to study only what's set; I usually don't do anything extra.
Deep motive	I find that many subjects become very interesting once you get into them.
Deep strategy	I try to relate what I have learned in one subject to what I already know in other subjects.
Achieving motive	I see doing well in school as a sort of game, and I play to win.
Achieving strategy	I usually try to read all the references and things my teacher says we should.

Researchers interested in relationships between processes and outcomes with respect to particular tasks prefer to observe students while they perform, or to interview them during or immediately after they have completed a particular task. Such information is of course more difficult to obtain, but it does enable one to infer more accurately what the student actually did when the task was undertaken.

Each kind of information has its uses and the generalisations made in Chapter 4 about the different approaches to learning were based on research using both kinds of data. What exactly constitutes a deep or a surface approach with respect to a particular task is something that needs working out for each task: in Chapter 6, for instance, this is done in the case of writing a typical essay assignment. Here we look at assessing how students may approach their learning in general.

The Entwistle and Ramsden (1983) *Approaches to Study Inventory* was developed for British tertiary students, while the *Learning Process Questionnaire* (LPQ) (Biggs, 1986b) and *Study Process Questionnaire* (SPQ) (Biggs, 1986c) are designed for Australian middle to upper secondary schools, and colleges and universities, respectively. The 36 item LPQ and the 42 item SPQ are scored by adding the student's self-ratings on the items comprising each subscale. There are six subscale scores, three motives and three strategies. The sum of the three motive and strategy subscales gives the approach score (see Figure 10.2).

The instruments were normed on national samples, and the scores are expressed in deciles, separately for males and females and, in the case of the LPQ, for middle and senior secondary school, and of the SPQ, for university or CAE, and for different faculties. By looking at a student's decile on any scale, or more importantly, by looking at the profile of scores over all scales, one can tell at a glance how *typical* that student's approach to learning is compared to otherwise similar Australian students: this is an example where norm-referencing may be useful for making decisions about individual students.

There are many ways in which teachers, counsellors and researchers can make use of LPQ and SPQ scores. It is possible for instance to design various forms of instruction that take best advantage of the learning profiles of one's students, to screen students for profiles that may indicate future difficulties, or to use the scores to monitor attempts to change students' approaches to learning. These and other uses of the scale are, however, specialised, and the reader is advised to turn to the appropriate manuals for further discussion. The present point is a more general one: by drawing attention to students' motives for learning and strategies of going about learning, we acknowledge that the focus and the impact of teaching is not limited to the formal performance outcomes, and that these are even enhanced when we start asking about the effects on students' learning processes.

Figure 10.2 Structure of LPQ and SPQ scales

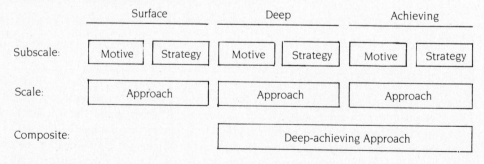

THE AWARD AT THE END OF SCHOOLING

The Radford Scheme was implemented in 1973 in Queensland in response to a problem resulting from the changing population of Years 11 and 12 in high schools. Traditionally, senior high school was intended for tertiary preparation, and the curriculum was narrowly academic. Societal values, however, were changing; high schools also were seen to have a function in developing individual potential. Consequently, many more 'non-academic' students attended senior high school than hitherto. This situation is now much more the case than it was in 1967; and in all States.

The moment of truth came in Queensland when 3,150 out of 4,400 candidates failed in the senior physics external examination in 1967: the chief examiner blamed poor teaching and the lack of intellectual ability of many candidates (Campbell and Campbell, 1978). Such a situation could not continue, and in 1970 the Radford Committee was appointed to propose a solution.

That solution centred on school-based assessment. In Years 10 and 12, it was proposed that all examining be carried out in the schools. That model has been adopted by several other States, at least in Year 10 if not in Year 12. There are, however, grave difficulties in this. Schools differ in both student and teacher quality, so standards are likely to vary considerably from school to school. How can employers and universities be assured that the standards of excellence are the same for students from different schools? At least, they argued, the old external examination, with all its faults, was a broad yardstick (with some semblance of criterion-referencing) that applied equally to all schools.

The solution is ingenious and complicated. Essentially, schools are given 'reference tests' around mid-year, the average of which establishes the relative academic standard of each *school*. On the basis of these results, so many grades are allocated to the school: some schools are allowed a relatively large number of the top grades if they perform well in the reference tests; others very few or none, if they perform poorly. The teacher's job is then simply to rank order the students in the class, on the basis of tests (some external in some States) and ratings (including attitude) and the certificate gradings are determined on that basis. In case of gross discrepancies between teacher assessments and externally examined data, and also to collate and standardise results, an elaborate system of scaling is used (termed 'a mathematical fairyland' by a former member of the New South Wales Higher School Examination Committee in the *Sydney Morning Herald* of 13 March 1979).

Much can be said about such a system. It presupposes that teachers will not 'load' the allocation of grades by encouraging absenteeism among the poorer students during the reference tests, thereby obtaining a larger ration of higher grades. It means that very bright students who transfer from poorer schools *after* the evaluation tests have less hope of obtaining the top grades which they would otherwise have obtained. The detailed workings of the scheme are virtually incomprehensible to many students, and more parents.

However, the most cogent criticisms with respect to student motivation are expressed by Campbell and Campbell. The system inevitably (although it could be otherwise) leads to norm-referenced evaluation of the most obvious kind:

*Will external marking become
a thing of the past with new
modes of assessment?*

A careful examination of relevant educational literature reveals that normative (norm-referenced) assessments almost inevitably heighten anxiety in secondary-school students, and foster a sense of 'pawnship' in both students and teachers. Thus the expectation must be that Queensland students will experience high anxiety, disillusionment, and resentment towards 'the system', and that teachers will strike out at the futility of trying to motivate their students. This is precisely what one finds (1978, p. 51).

External examinations of the traditional kind also have their problems with respect to teacher and student motivation. Wherever it is adopted, however, moderation leads to other problems: most notably by forcing the teachers and students into a competition to win the greatest proportion of high grades for their school; and the individual students within the school, into competition with each other for those grades that are eventually allocated. The results may be very convenient for employers and universities, but they play motivational havoc with the learning process.

Different States are now developing new ways of handling this problem (Box 10.5, for example, gives details of the Queensland model in 1985). The future is

---

BOX 10.5   CALCULATING THE TERTIARY ENTRANCE SCORE

The Board of Secondary School Studies is keen for all interested members of the public to understand the various aspects of the TE Score. The following statements may be helpful:

- The TE Score represents a place in the rank order (reported in bands) of all eligible Year 12 students in the State in a particular year.
- Eligible students are those who have fulfilled the requirements for eligibility set down by the Board of Secondary School Studies. Not all Year 12 students are eligible. Some students choose subjects at school with no intention of undertaking tertiary studies.
- TE Scores are calculated by using the individual student's subject results and group results in ASAT (Australian Scholastic Aptitude Test).
- The highest TE Score in any year is 990: the lowest TE Score changes from year to year, depending on the number of eligible students. As the number increases, more and more bands are required.

The number of students in each band is a fixed percentage of the 17-year-old population in Queensland in each year. In 1985, when the population is approximately 41,000 about 410 students (1 per cent) will receive 990. All the other bands will contain about 205 students (½ per cent). If the whole 17-year-old population in Queensland were at school and were eligible, then the bands would extend from 990 to 5.

The middle TE Score in 1985 is 760 and the lowest TE Score is 530.

As the name implies, the primary purpose of the TE Score is for use by the tertiary institutions in making decisions about offering places. For other purposes, the student's Senior Certificate, listing all subjects and levels of achievement attained, provides comprehensive information.

John A. Pitman
Executive Officer

Source: The Australian, 21–22 December 1985, p. 6.

unpredictable: it may be that the Rasch model will be used more widely (despite Spearritt's concerns about communicability); it may also be that universities, employers and other users of public statements of academic progress will devise their own means of selection.

SUMMARY

Learning through evaluation: Mastery learning strategy. *Mastery learning* is based on the decision not to teach students more until they demonstrate mastery over materials already presented. It is common in core skill areas such as literacy and numeracy, which all students have to master. Student performance is a function of time on task and ability: but there are practical limits on the amount of time available.

Methods of testing. *The essay technique* has a number of variations:

- the timed examination;
- the open-book examination;
- the untimed examination;
- the take-home examination;
- the assignment;
- the dissertation.

The essay can be made more reliable by:

- concealing the writer's identity;
- rechecking with the earlier mark concealed;
- deciding on marking criteria;
- first allocating general grades on a coarser scale;
- spot checks;
- checking the wording of the original questions for looseness;
- guarding against bias due to handwriting;
- marking each question across all answers;
- using a model answer.

Objective tests consist either of those with only two alternatives provided (as in the true/false question) or those where several alternatives are provided (as in multiple choice; matching; filling in blanks or completion tests). There are three stages in constructing a *norm-referenced* test:

1. deciding the type of items;
2. constructing a pool of items;
3. deriving the final version.

Criterion-referenced tests are developed by:

1. specifying instructional objectives before teaching commences;
2. deciding criteria which define adequate knowledge or performance;
3. devising testing situations.

A qualitative dimension can be introduced to objective tests by using super-items which have a hierarchy of correct answers.

Short answer tests combine an open-end format with the specificity of the multiple choice test; they test recall of particular information rather than the rather lower level process of recognition.

The *practicum* is an evaluation based on performance in a practical situation, and is particularly appropriate where practical skills need to be displayed at or beyond a given level of competence, as in practice teaching. Criterion-referenced checklists are particularly useful in this kind of evaluation.

Oral tests, such as interviews, are expensive and unreliable, but they do have their advantages for in-depth probing.

A comparison of evaluation methods. In deciding what evaluation methods to use, four general properties might be borne in mind: validity, reliability, distortion, and suitability for norm- or criterion-referencing. These need to be balanced against the practical considerations: trouble in preparation, coverage, freedom for students to demonstrate relevant knowledge, and skills and ease of scoring. Each of the testing media considered have their advantages and disadvantages in terms of these properties and practical considerations.

Grading. The award of summative grades is the aspect of evaluation that causes most worries to students, teachers, employers, parents and administrators. There are several forms of grading, the most basic distinction being between norm-referenced and criterion-referenced grading systems. A practical problem for teachers is how to derive a final grade from several sets of test results. Decisions must be made about the weighting of individual tests, and then moving from the combined distribution to graded categories of results. Such decisions force teachers to think very carefully about the purpose of the components in a course. An aspect of grading refers to school reports, and how information is best presented here, particularly in balancing the needs-to-know of different interest groups: students, other educators, parents or employers.

Evaluating at the process level. At the level of process, evaluation can become a learning experience for students as well as an actual evaluation of the learning process. Teachers can establish criteria for students to use in self-assessment, or the students can generate their own. Process can be evaluated in terms of a specific task or with regard to a general approach to learning (usually by means of self-rating questionnaires, one-to-one observation or interviews).

The award at the end of schooling. In order to maintain parity of standards when school-based assessment is used for senior students, moderation is carried out to establish the relative academic standing of each school. Teachers then rank their students to fill the grades allocated to the school on the basis of the results of the moderating tests. Scaling is used to minimise discrepancies and to standardise the results. Although convenient for employers and tertiary institutions, the system has defects: the worst being its effect on student motivation and the competition for high grades for the school. The future is unpredictable, but alternatives to moderation, such as the Rasch model, are promising.

FURTHER READING

On evaluation in general
R. L. Thorndike (ed.), *Educational Measurement*, American Council on Education, Washington, DC, 1971.
W. A. Mehrens and I. J. Lehmann, *Measurement and Evaluation in Education and Psychology*, Holt, Rinehart and Winston, New York, 1978.

Thorndike has edited a collection of papers written by experts in different aspects of evaluation: should be read by anyone seriously interested in the subject, especially the paper by Glaser and Nitko. Test construction is well covered in the early part of the book, also the most recent work on essays, and the theory of measurement. Mehrens and Lehmann provide a comprehensive coverage of most topics dealt with in this chapter, and in much greater depth.

On criterion-referenced evaluation
J. H. Block (ed.), *Mastery Learning*, Holt, Rinehart and Winston, New York, 1971.
W. J. Popham, *Educational Evaluation*, Prentice-Hall, Englewood Cliffs, NJ, 1975.

See especially Block's discussion of the normal curve, and the papers by Carroll and Airasian on problems of criterion-referenced measurement and evaluation. Popham is an easy-to-read account of most of the points raised in this chapter, with particular emphasis on criterion-referenced testing.

On grading
H. Kirschenbaum, R. Napier and S. B. Simon, *Wad-ja-get? The Grading Game in American Education*, Hart, New York, 1971.

Just about all that needs to be said on grading practices in the American context. Very easy to read, very well researched (with a useful annotated bibliography on some of the more important research reports on grading) and presented in fictional form: the dilemma facing the staff and students of 'Mapleton High School'. Can be read with profit by Australian teachers at all levels. Nevertheless, an up-to-date Australian version would be most valuable.

On school-based assessment and curriculum development
Parliament of New South Wales, *Report from the Select Committee of the Legislative Assembly upon the School Certificate* (The McGowan Report), Government Printer, Sydney, 1981.

The McGowan Report examines the development of a school-based curriculum and the need for increased flexibility and autonomy in educational programs in schools. It aroused considerable reaction from teacher and parent groups to its recommendations concerning pupil failure, provision of alternative courses for pupils who are not progressing, and a diversity of curriculum packages from school to school with dezoning to enable students to attend schools of their choice.

On the Rasch model
D. Spearritt (ed.), *The Improvement of Measurement in Education and Psychology*, The Australian
   Council for Educational Research, Hawthorn, Victoria, 1982.

This is a report on a conference at ACER in 1980 on the use of latent trait models in education. The chapters by Thorndike, Choppin, Izard and White, and Spearritt are useful; others are rather technical for general purposes. A simple approach to Rasch is badly needed.

On self-assessment
D. Boud, *Studies in Self-Assessment*, Tertiary Education Research Centre, The University of New
   South Wales, Occasional Publication No. 26, 1985.

This is a simplified account of five cases where self-assessment of various kinds had been applied successfully to university professional courses, mainly law, engineering and education. The principles are, however, easily transferred to the secondary school.

QUESTIONS

Questions for self-testing

1. At what three stages should monitoring of learning occur?
2. How can 'horizontal' and 'vertical' outcomes of learning be distinguished?
3. What is the focus of quantitative evaluation?
4. Name the six levels of response, in order of increasing quality, in the Bloom taxonomy.
5. Distinguish between formative and summative evaluation.
6. Name three ways of calibrating tests.
7. What is a common example of a criterion-referenced test?
8. Explain what is meant by a latent trait.
9. What are the advantages of the Rasch model of evaluation?
10. What is its major disadvantage?
11. What sort of test is the RAPT?
12. How do we know if a test gives a reliable score?
13. Distinguish between five types of validity.
14. What is meant by test distortion?
15. Give six variations of the essay technique used as a test.
16. What are eight ways of improving the reliability of essay marking?

17. Provide four types of objective tests.
18. List the three steps in constructing a criterion-referenced test.
19. What is a super-item?
20. Name four general properties of a test.
21. What are six ways of grading students?

Questions for discussion

1. 'Assessing one's own work is a learning experience that is rarely experienced until the real world is encountered. There it is an immediate and natural expectation of the professional person. It seems reasonable that students be given the chance of that experience before entering that world.'
   (a) What do you think of this proposition?
   (b) Why?
   (c) Design a self-assessment component for one syllabus topic.
2. What sort of award should be given at the successful end of secondary education? Briefly describe the basis upon which awards would be made, how they would discriminate between the relative success of students and how the award could be used to determine entrance to tertiary education or employment. Or do we really need such awards at all?
3. Which methods of assessment will you use with your pupils? List the methods and state why you intend to use them.
4. In a staff meeting one of your colleagues is insisting that students should be able to opt for an ungraded pass (that is, either pass or fail), another is arguing that results should be graded to reward achievement. Who will you support? Why?
5. You have been asked to present your philosophy of evaluating learning to a meeting of parents. What will you say?

Part 5

Product: From espoused theory to practice

Chapter 11 is the final link between espoused theory and your theory-in-use. It is not, however, a simple task to go from this point to immediate competence as a teacher. As you go 'out there' to teach, we hope that as problems arise you may come back to this book, and read and think about each problem constructively.

For the moment, there are two main jobs to be done:

- to review and synthesise some of the more important matters that have emerged in previous chapters;
- to suggest how that synthesis might be used.

The last might sound a little presumptuous. Schools will continue to change, easily as much as they have in the five or six years separating the first and second editions of this book: but we will not indulge in unnecessary futurology. Pointers already exist in schools as to how things may change; the exciting part of all this is that these changes in approach and values are just those ones that fit the new direction emerging from psychology. As we pointed out in Part 1, there is a confluence that augurs well.

The aim issued by the New South Wales State Department — 'toward perceptive understanding, mature judgment, responsible self-direction, and moral autonomy' — seemed almost a joke to some people when it was first promulgated in 1973. While many genuinely believed that this was an attainable goal, the Director General of the time found it necessary to distance himself, and the boards, from 'any derivable courses of action' that might be thought to be involved. Certainly the fate of 'community involvement' did not inspire confidence, nor the overkill on the three Rs (second set) backed up, then, by what was all to often the first, not the last, resort. And in any case, if one did take it seriously, what *would* have been done, and on what theoretical basis? The psychology of the time did not really address any of the stated aims, except in 'Kohlberg programs'.

Since then public attitudes have changed, laws have changed, teachers and schools have changed; and psychology and high technology are beginning to say something that does directly address 'responsible self-direction'. We are getting there.

11

The second set of 3Ps: From learning to teaching

OVERVIEW

How do you move from knowledge about learners to effectiveness in teaching? That is the basic question addressed in this, the final, chapter. To structure discussion we reconsider the presage-process-product model of learning and present a 'second set of 3Ps':

- What are the aims of education? What is an appropriate context for teaching, and what experiences should be provided for students? What aspects of the curriculum can be presented as attainable instructional objectives?
- What conditions are associated with good student learning? Can these conditions be used to categorise effective teaching practices?
- How does the teacher use this knowledge to teach more effectively? What levels of decision-making are necessary to teach effectively?

These and other questions are answered in this chapter, and when you have read this chapter you should be able to do the following:

1. teach;
2. and, with more teaching experience as a teacher to guide a rereading of this book, teach even better.

The 3P model has been used to organise our discussion of the process of learning in Parts 2, 3 and 4.

- The first P referred to *presage* factors, which affect learning prior to actual engagement in the task. Such factors include those belonging to the individual learner, such as abilities, experience, prior knowledge; and those inhering in the situation, such as course structures, curriculum content, methods of instructing and evaluating.
- The second P referred to the learning *process*; in particular, that derived by the learner to meet personal intentions with respect to the task as presented.
- The third P referred to the *product*, the outcome of learning. All this was discussed in the Section As; the implications for teaching in the Section Bs.

Our present task is to bring these multistructural components into some sort of relational order that may be used as a framework to guide teaching practice. For that we need a model of teaching, a second set of three Ps.

- Presage now involves prior planning in terms of *goals* and contexts for learning.
- Process refers to *teaching procedures* most likely consistently to produce the conditions for optimal learning leading to the desired outcomes.
- The product becomes the professional person who can integrate theory and practice: that person is you, the reader.

THE FIRST P: EDUCATIONAL GOALS

In Chapter 1 we discussed the aims of schooling in broad terms: process and content aims, and cognitive and affective targets. That was useful in order to contrast various tasks the school had to do, but we have moved a little since then. We have come to see that it is not a matter of process *versus* content, but process *through* content: process aims are achieved by learning content in a particular way. Likewise affect — motives, values and feelings about learning — is intertwined with cognitive processes. The creation of a particular kind of affective climate is related to achieving otherwise cognitive aims; and the affective goals of multiculturalism are taught using cognitive content.

So let us now talk about educational goals. Goals are usually expressed, first in general terms (such as aims, rationale, etc.) then as more specific objectives that reflect more exactly what the teacher has to do.

- The general directions have to be decided. These are stated as educational *aims*. Aims signal broad intentions with respect to schooling in general.
- Some aspects of the aims are open-ended: We can say certain *contexts* and *experiences* are desirable, and teachers should provide them, and avoid others.
- Some particular aspects of the aims are specifiable and can be stated as instructional *objectives* with respect to particular content topics.

Aims

Educational aims are frequently broad and rhetorical, referring to the production of a highly desirable kind of student: for example, an autonomous learner who can cope with the complexities of a rapidly changing future. They usually comprise a heady mixture of affective and cognitive qualities of a 'motherhood' kind with which few could disagree (Sarason, 1971): these are the stuff of governmental reports and departmental papers. Disagreement is not so much about the aims or broad intentions of schooling, as about the means of realising those intentions. Good intentions may pave roads leading anywhere.

Nevertheless, some statement of general direction is obviously needed; all State departments provide them, and each resembles the other. When, however, we look closely at what those statements *mean*, we see that some directions are implied very much more strongly than are others: most imply metacognitive activity (autonomy, self-management, reflective self-awareness), and often post-conventional values such as moral autonomy. When we look further at what all that might mean in terms of action, a clear and consistent picture emerges, having implications right along the line, from the provision of a certain kind of school and classroom climate, to teaching particular curriculum topics in ways in which both specifiable levels of attainment and methods of handling the task are addressed.

Our discussion of general educational aims (in Chapters 1 and 5 particularly) leads us to the following general conclusions with which few, we think, could disagree.

- Schools should produce individuals who will be able to cope both with existing vocational and societal tasks, and with future tasks that are at the moment largely undefined. If this means anything, it means that school-leavers will need to feel sufficiently self-confident to cope autonomously with new circumstances.
- Students should be able to enter responsibly and co-operatively into arrangements and agreements with others.
- Students should, for any task they may reasonably be expected to undertake, possess the metacognitive skills to plan ahead, to devise strategies, to monitor their progress and to judge when the task is completed.
- Such planning and judgmental skill requires both a background of content knowledge, and the basic skills of literacy and numeracy.

If that sounds like producing a society consisting of all chiefs and no Indians, it is not. Metacognitive skills apply to all levels of a task; obviously different people will display different levels of competence, both cognitively and metacognitively. Everyone has some metacognitive potential: it is simply that that potential is not encouraged or deliberately fostered in today's schools to any significant extent (Wagner and Sternberg, 1984). Whatever the task, where few algorithms or directions exist, to cope at all implies metacognition; and that in turn requires an approach to learning and teaching that is signalled in the *aims* of education, and frequently ignored in *practice*.

So much for good intentions. What *courses of action* are implied if they are to be brought about?

Prescribing contexts and experiences

Educating, like any complex human enterprise, is not always predictable. What educational benefits do we expect from a trip overseas? Some we can specify, some we cannot. Often the most valuable turn out to be the least expected. We thus make a distinction between *open* outcomes and *closed* outcomes. The latter we can specify in terms of quite clear curriculum objectives; the former we can only specify by prescribing *contexts* and *experiences*. The important thing is not to prescribe what the teacher does, but what the students will experience.

Eisner (1971) drew a distinction between expressive objectives and instructional objectives: what he meant by expressive objectives is roughly what we mean by these prescriptions. Expressive objectives require that *an experience be provided* and it is in the course of that experience that the objectives are recognised and formulated (if at all): usually it is the learner who recognises that *this* is what the experience was about. A writer has this experience continually: it is not the 'preplanned' sentence, but the one that tumbles out in the heat of the moment that feels 'right'. Theory, past experience, deep-seated feelings and emotions all say 'Do it'; but what will be the end result simply cannot be foreordained. What one prescribes, in other words, is the experience, not the outcome.

Such contexts can be very broad or quite specific. For example, one might prescribe that:

*Expressive objectives require
that an experience be provided.*

- The school atmosphere should be such as to encourage an 'origin' self-concept rather than a 'pawn' self-concept. Rules and regulations are to be minimal, consistent with efficient administration and smooth running; student opportunity for exercising choice is to be maximal.
- The whole of Year 11 is to spend a week camping out in the Flinders Ranges (given parental agreement).
- Some aspects of self-assessment are to be introduced into all classes from Years 7 to 12; whether that is to involve self-grading and if so, to what extent, are matters to be decided by each class in consultation with the teacher concerned.

So many 'process' outcomes are of this experiential nature. What figures in the teaching objectives is not therefore any particular cognitive or affective outcomes, but the prescription of what theory and sense and intuition tell us are likely to be contexts providing rich experiences.

The adult mode of learning. By 'rich' we mean experiences likely to lead to both learning and metalearning. What might they be? All the evidence reviewed here points to the *adult mode* of learning, which in Chapter 5 was contrasted to the traditional 'fill-the-tanks' mode of traditional schooling. In his discussion of adult learning, Knowles (1978) thought that the way adults go about learning was sufficiently different from the way children go about learning to justify the title 'androgogy' to distinguish adult education from traditional education or 'pedagogy'.

One can highlight the differences between the psychology of mature and immature learners: one can also seek the similarities. Allowing for the situational context, Davies (1982) saw striking similarities between children's and adult culture. The mechanisms children use to derive and validate explanations of natural phenomena are just like those used by scientists in certain crucial respects; what was once thought to be different 'logical programming' between children and adults, might better be seen as different levels of abstraction with which one may deal with otherwise similar tasks and levels of explanation (see Chapter 5). Many child-adult differences in cognitive functioning are due to expert knowledge acquired from appropriately rich experience (Chi, 1978; Chipman, Segal and Glaser, 1984). We could of course emphasise more differences; our point for the moment is that both similarities and differences exist.

Now, it would be possible to design a school system that is to prepare children to operate as adults in an emerging adult world in either of two ways:

1. by concentrating on the *differences* between child and adult thinking and operating, and building a school system that emphasises the differences between children and adults and the way each operates;
2. by concentrating on the *similarities* between child and adult thinking and operating, and designing a school system that is maximally attuned to those similarities.

The first model is, of course, that upon which traditional schooling has been based. It leads to:

- a sharp distinction between declarative knowledge (knowing that) and procedural knowledge (knowing how). Procedural knowledge is driven by a need-to-know: adults acquire their learnings in such a context and so do children. Declarative, or as Connell (1985) more simply calls it, *school*, knowledge is self-referring and abstract, which 'strongly separates what is learned from the personal and social experiences of the learner' (p. 87). Children's need-to-know instead produces procedural knowledge out of alternative frameworks — that the school then spends years in trying to counter;
- highly structured and directive teaching that in turn causes many students to surface learn in order to satisfy institutional demands, rather than to deep learning that satisfies ecologically valid needs;

- an institutional atmosphere that maximises differences between children and adults; in dress, mode of address, behavioural expectations, assumptions as to self-direction and capability, ability to accept responsibility, and the like. Children learn to become dependent or to prolong their dependence in such a climate. Box 3.3 illustrates how even sophisticated adults are transformed by situation into pawns; Box 11.1 makes the link with the school;
- assumptions about the nature of learning (filling the tanks with declarative knowledge), the production of new knowledge, and societal needs, that are just plain wrong.

One reaction to that traditional model has been *home learning*. This is a concept by which parents retain their children at home and educate them there. One of the major advocates of this alternative is John Holt (as in Holt, 1970) who visited Australia in 1981: since then hundreds of Australian families are exercising their right to withhold their children from school (if they can convince their State department that they can

Preparing for an adult world
using adult modes of learning.

BOX 11.1   STUDENT IS TO CHILD AS TEACHER IS TO ADULT?

Well basically, this is the thing that I've got against this authoritarianism. That teachers are made to feel that — and I guess it's true in a school like this — that if they are not going to be strict with the kids, the kids are going to riot, and go all over them. And so they have to be strict with the kids and sort of authoritarian. And because they are authoritarian, they act — not as a normal adult would act, towards a child that age. And therefore the children don't regard them as a normal adult they would see outside the school grounds.
> — 'Joe Guaraldi', a teacher interviewed in Connell (1985, p. 104)

And the consequence? Connell comments:
Joe Guaraldi is right; this is not as a normal adult would act. And the result is, exactly as he says, that the kids do not treat the teachers as normal adults. Arlette herself spells out a striking example of the consequences ... The school set up special classes about sex and contraception. They don't work. Arlette heard one girl tell her girlfriends that her older sister had told her, 'Don't go on the pill, it screws up your insides and later on you can't have any babies.' The girls, Arlette says, will believe a mother, or a virgin aunt, or a sister. They will not believe the scientific information they are given in the special classes, as she pointed out to the teacher in charge, 'because you are a teacher'. The curriculum breaks down because there is no trust.

Source: Connell, 1985, p. 105.

---

provide adequate education at home). An article in *The National Times* (28 June–4 July 1985) explained why and how this is done, and what the results are ('When home learning does work, it can be spectacular', p. 13). A typical reason was given by one mother (who wished to remain anonymous as her husband taught at a State school):

> We were worried because the children have the control of their own lives taken away from them. We were worried because schools don't try to develop self-discipline, they organise them from without. We were worried because at that time academic training was lockstep, they were moved along in batches rather than being allowed to progress at their own rate.
>
> Schools squashed initiative. They make people think they can only learn things if they have someone else to teach them. And the 'hidden curriculum' was the most dangerous thing of all: being taught that you obey authorities unquestioningly just because they are authorities (*The National Times*, 28 June–4 July 1985, p. 9).

Although the above quotation is comparatively recent, all the signs are that we are already moving away from the context that made those sorts of reasons valid. Given parental commitment — which has to be enormous, in every sense — there is much to be said for home learning. There are, however, aspects, particularly those relating to social learning and plain feasibility for most parents, where home learning cannot compete with formal schooling. As we said in Chapter 5, we do not believe that the deschooling proposed by Holt and Illich will work. Rather, schooling will change so that many of the reasons for deschooling will become less pressing.

What sort of change that might be is indicated by the second model, which is what the home learners were after: concentrating on adult–child *similarities*. This model leads to:

- a climate emphasising self-choice, delegating as much responsibility as may safely be done, and the minimisation of child-adult differences;
- a classroom atmosphere built along management lines rather than discipline-obedience lines;
- teaching from a perceived need-to-know wherever possible — often it is not possible but it is more often than is currently recognised;
- minimising differences between school, community and society.

In short the school is run along the same general lines as the adult world: not *identically*, because it is not the adult world, but *generally*. It is recognised in the workplace, for instance, that offices should be comfortable and pleasant to look at: open spaces, indoor plants, art work, carpet and decor which often has little functional use. Such things do have an *existential* use: they recognise that people have the right to work in pleasant surroundings. That recognition in schools was unheard of even as late as 1970; it is not fully realised today. Further examples include the use of community resources, and vice versa, the community use of school resources and community say in the staffing and running of schools. Following from this, it would allow that sharp cutoffs between school-age — and the school-leaving rituals, which emphasise separateness — would go. As is happening in many matriculation colleges, teenagers and adults sit side by side, learning the same material, subject to the same rules and procedures. What better way of learning to become an adult than being treated like one?

This is all very well, but what about the differences between adults and children? A problem-based education can be used in the professions (Boud, 1985a) precisely because students are old enough to know what they want, and sophisticated enough to handle real-life problems and case studies responsibly. To base education on what students perceive at a particular time to be relevant is thought by some to be 'trivial relevance' that leads to 'mediocrity' (see Box 11.2).

The point should be taken. What worries Kramer and others is the use of (a) specific vocational goals, such as teaching only what a truckdriver or typist might need to know, to define educational objectives; and (b) passing fads and trends — or worse, controversial issues — to structure the curriculum. Triviality may be found in both left and right wings of the political spectrum.

It is not, however, trivial to use active experience as a basis for building knowledge of the physical and biological worlds; to co-operate with other students to find out both how they learn, and how you operate as learner, thinker and decision-maker; to learn by direct experience (how else?) to plan, monitor, act and to evaluate the outcome with minimal external support.

The expressed aims of present school systems — except some independent and private systems — imply the provision of a learning context that derives from the adult

BOX 11.2 'TRIVIAL RELEVANCE' IMPOSING MEDIOCRITY ON STUDENTS

The drive for relevance in Australian education threatened to create a restrictive school system which imposed mediocrity on pupils and narrowed their minds, Dame Leonie Kramer said yesterday.

The Professor of Australian Literature at Sydney University and the former chairman of the ABC, Dame Leonie said 'trivial relevance' had become the central principle governing education policy.

'The relevance now being so zealously promoted is despotic in the restrictions it seeks to impose on the undeveloped capacities of young people,' Dame Leonie said in Sydney.

Award

'Education is about enlarging the mind, not narrowing its range to immediately visible targets.'

Dame Leonie said that an education system oriented to 'teaching what was topical, controversial, expedient, entertaining and utilitarian' would train workers rather than educate children.

She was speaking after becoming the first Australian to receive the annual Britannica Award from the Encyclopaedia Britannica for her contribution to the dissemination of knowledge.

'The common notion is that what a student needs is what is relevant to specific employment. This view can appear remarkably authoritarian ... for needs then become what the marketplace dictates and even what society appears to require,' she said.

If school subjects were broken down into skills and studies as an aid to contemporary living, she said, literature would have no place in schools, and art and music would become non-essential options.

'Such a curriculum is narrowly prescriptive by catering for the existing rather than potential interests of students on the one hand and on the other for the supposed needs and requirements of society.

'It proposes restricting the educational experience of students by endorsing a facile notion of relevance which does not recognise the distinction between education and training.'

Dame Leonie said the 'dreary functionalism' of the drive towards relevance in education was supported by a growing number of educators and politicians.

While there was a need to impart useful, up-to-date skills to young people, the 'lasting relevance of a general education' should not be ignored.

Source: Melissa Roberts, *The Weekend Australian,* 22–23 March 1986, p. 3.

world, not that of childhood. Obviously there need to be differences in structure between infant, primary and secondary schools in the extent to which the adult mode may successfully be implemented. The extraordinary thing is that when we look at these levels of schooling, it is possible in many current instances to see, if anything, an *inverse* correlation. Co-operative group activity and decision-making, interpersonal warmth and mutual respect, responsibility by older for younger students, the use of direct personal experience as a medium for guiding learning, and similar manifestations of Theory Y, are more likely to be found in the lower levels of schooling. Rigid adherence to procedure, imposed decisions about what, when and how to learn, intolerance of deviant behaviours, harsh and punitive modes of interpersonal interaction, and like expression of Theory X, are more frequent in secondary levels, at least up to Year 10. Yet Theory X underpins an adult-child model of schooling; Theory Y, adult-adult modes of interaction. If theory Y can work in the kindergarten, it is surely more appropriate still nearer adulthood.

As soon, then, as you promulgate an aim addressing independence and other adult characteristics, you are committed to the provision of a context likely to develop or to encourage the expression of those characteristics. Such a context derives from adult-adult interaction.

Instructional objectives

Finally, we come to specific content objectives: these are the topics that are outlined in the curriculum documents in the various subject areas, and that can be specified in advance. Unlike expressive objectives, curriculum and instructional objectives are most meaningfully linked to outcomes. It makes most sense when talking about the level of competence required of students in a given subject at a particular year level, to determine the extent to which those curriculum objectives are in fact met.

In the traditional model, objectives and outcomes have usually not been inter-linked. As noted in Chapter 8, teachers frequently plan their lessons not with respect to what the students are to learn, but what they are themselves to do in the course of the lesson (provide this, explain that, set so many problems, so much question time). Student learning is then assessed in a norm-referenced context, rank ordering a student's performance with respect to the performance of the group as a whole and independently of the original objectives. Some teachers object to linking instructional objectives with outcomes, and evaluating the latter in relation to the pre-set criteria in the curriculum, because they see instructional objectives as behavioural, and that to reduce many forms of learning to behavioural terms is to trivialise them (McDonald Ross, 1973). If, however, objectives were stated in a qualitative way that recognises their complexity, and outcomes assessed to see whether or not they measure up to the desired standard of complexity, then whatever force that argument had is considerably lessened.

We saw in Chapter 5 that it is possible to express objectives in terms that reflect their complexity (see Table 5.1, for some illustrations from the science curriculum). It is also possible to index learning outcomes — either in open-end responses or in closed 'super-items' (see Boxes 10.3 and 10.4) — so that one can judge whether or not the required level of complexity in learning that topic has yet been achieved by the student.

With school-based curriculum development and assessment becoming more and more common, it is important that some non-trivial way of expressing curriculum objectives, and of assessing them, be used. Chapter 5 outlined some suggestions that helped, first, to determine the level of abstraction or mode in which the task ought generally to be expressed; and then the point in the learning cycle at which learning is sufficiently well structured for present purposes. The distinction is made beween the accretion of knowledge (knowing something about), and the structuring of knowledge (understanding how aspects of a topic meaningfully inter-relate). The first is in SOLO terms a multistructural level of response, and might be accepted for some aspects of schooling. The 'natural' end-point of a learning episode is, however, relational, which is the level required for explanation or for meaningful action. Writing an essay that addresses the question usually requires a discourse structure of relational level; solving a maths problem requires more than knowing how to carry out various number operations; knowing the climatological facts is in itself insufficient for explaining coastal rain.

Whether or not the student arrives at an adequate level of learning in relation to an objective can be determined by appropriate evaluation; this may include formal testing, observing performance in some appropriate context, predicting-and-explaining as used in alternative frameworks research, or whatever is appropriate to the situation. Whatever the particular methods of evaluation, the present point is that many important topics can be expressed as instructional objectives in ways that are not trivial, and that guide the teacher through the other processes of teaching and evaluation.

Summary

In sorting out presage factors at the teaching level, then, we find it convenient to refer to educational goals at three levels:

- *Aims* with respect to the desired qualities and competencies of the school leaver. Mostly such aims refer to content knowledge and adult characteristics such as autonomy and independence. Most people agree with the rhetoric in which aims are expressed; where they disagree is when one begins to specify how they might be actualised.
- Prescribed *contexts* and *experiences*. It is not always possible accurately to foreshadow outcomes, beyond saying that some outcomes need to be left open. In that case we try to achieve a climate and atmosphere that is compatible with those aims, and certain experiences that are likely to be fruitful ones, in terms both of particular outcomes and of longer term effects on the learner. As current aims emphasise the adult features of self-management and responsibility a learning context derived by dwelling on the similarities between children and adults seems more appropriate to those aims than one constructed by dwelling on the differences.
- Where particular curriculum statements about *instructional objectives*, and the exit level appropriate for different students at different year levels can be made, they should be made.

There is some difference of opinion among educators as to the relative emphasis one should place on expressive and instructional objectives or, in other words, on how open or closed the educational process is. Humanities tend to be treated more openly than science subjects; some topics can be treated in both open and closed ways (for example see 'activity-centred excursions' below). The material reviewed in this book has something to say about clarifying all three levels of goals, and about suggesting how they may be achieved.

THE SECOND P: FROM LEARNING TO TEACHING PROCESSES

What kinds of teaching processes have we found to have been associated with best learning? It is possible to make some strong and mutually consistent generalisations.

Motivational context

- The best learning, leading to richer outcomes, is when learning is intrinsically motivated.
- This is most likely to be when the learner is actively involved, feels competent and in charge, and has some proprietorial interest or 'ownership' in the task.
- Learning arises out of a perceived need-to-know, a need that may variously have co-operative, competitive, intrinsic and even instrumental roots.

Learner activity

- Learning is always associated with learner activity.
- Activity may be physical, social or metacognitive, but the more ways in which the learner is involved, and the more senses invoked, the stronger will be the learning.
- Activity not only enriches the connections between learnings, it is motivationally important as it is likely to lead to perceived needs-to-know.

Interactive context

- Learning is interactive as well as active; it requires immediate and finely tuned feedback, from other people and even from machines.
- Different people serve different interactive functions.
- Adults (or other experts) serve a supportive or embedded function that leads to modelling and reliance on structure.
- Peers serve a more metacognitive function: learning about yourself, what and how you think, in comparison to others like yourself.
- Some learners have a much stronger need for contextual support than do others.

Content

- Deep learning builds on past experience.
- Prior knowledge and experience is vital for deriving good learning and problem-solving strategies.
- Content that is taught piecemeal, isolated from other related content, leads to surface learning.

As can be seen, there are points in common between these headings: activity relates to motivation, social or machine interaction implies activity by the learner, and interaction is motivating. All take place with respect to content — the task is central — and with more or less structure. When all come together, the result is deep learning, implying good cognitive and metacognitive involvement. Figure 11.1 attempts to illustrate this relationship with a Venn diagram.

Figure 11.1 presents a useful way of categorising some of the more important teaching strategies and techniques that have been mentioned in the Section Bs. Content enters into some techniques peripherally, in others it is quite central; and most techniques involve medium to high structure or direction. Let us start with 'learner activity' and move clockwise.

1.   Learner activity. In this category, we consider techniques where the focus is on activity by the individual learner, not as part of a group.

Learning mathematics by multiple embodiment (Bruner, 1964; Dienes, 1963). Multiple embodiment is strongly content based: the concepts to be learned are embodied in a variety of concrete actions that the learner has to carry out. Doing different things achieves the same conceptual result. In true concrete-symbolic mode, mathematics is recording how operations on various manifestations in the physical world may be carried out and match symbolic operations, not just manipulating the symbols themselves.

Activity-centred excursions (Mackenzie and White, 1982). Again physical activity is emphasised: wading through mangrove swamps, jumping around cliff platforms, chewing leaves for salinity. These actions are not disjointed or bizarre: they are keyed into preset instructional objectives, linking a particular highlighted action with a feature of the natural phenomenon to be learned.

Self-assessment (Boud, 1985b). Here the learner activity is centred on two strongly content-based foci: deriving criteria for assessing a project or assignment, then judging one's own, and frequently another student's, work on that basis.

Metacognitive activity. We refer here to metacognitive activity that mainly involves the learner, rather than the learner in interaction with others: guided self-questioning (Baird, in press; Baird and White, 1984) for teaching senior high school biology; Informed Strategies for Learning (Paris, in press) for reading comprehension; SQ3R, (Robinson, 1946), SHEIK (Jackson, Reid and Croft, 1980), heuristics (Polya, 1945; Bransford and Stein, 1984), for study skills and problem solving. All these techniques require the learner to stop and self-question at various stages of the activity in progress.

Reflective writing (Chapter 6). A deep approach to writing requires a strong content orientation, at a high level of abstraction, but a division of focus according to

Figure 11.1   Interaction of learner activity, motivational context, interactive context and content to produce deep learning

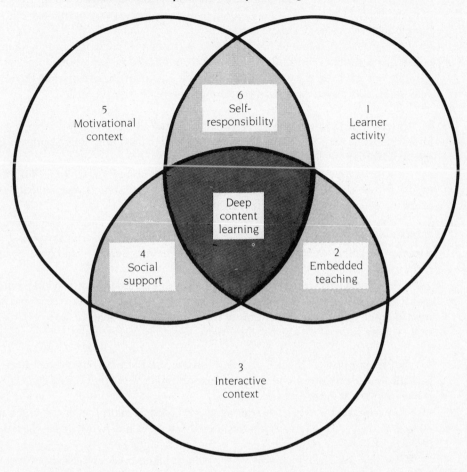

concentration on content or mechanics: planning, monitoring and reviewing all follow much the same pattern as in more open or heuristic approaches to a task. Again, the emphasis is on *planful activity*, which is greatly enhanced by word processer, which highlights the crucial activities (revising).

2.   Embedded teaching. We have used the term 'embedded' to emphasise the strong interactivity between the learner and some other who *leads* in some sense that closely lines up with the learner's immediate behaviour. The prototypical example is parent–child interaction in early childhood (Fischer and Bullock, 1984).

CAI, especially interactive video (IV). Webster's (1986) model used both visual and software (symbolic) input (thus exemplifying multiple embodiment as well), and found IV to be superior in most respects to small group interactive teaching, and greatly superior to non-interactive video, although the latter used the *same* visual input material. Requiring the learner to do something, which is immediately responded to and challenged, is clearly a powerful means of learning.

Conferencing in writing (Graves, 1983; Turbill, 1982). An adult (although peers can do this) reflects students' thinking to help them in redrafting and focusing. There is a lot of motivational support in this, including ownership, but the essence seems to lie in the interaction embedded in the story content.

Expert-novice (Case, 1985; Glaser, 1984). A strong content orientation with implied embedded activity is recommended by Case, and is also present in the expert-novice paradigm of teaching: the expert leads the novice by directing attention to the relevant next steps, and structuring progress through them.

3.   Interactive context. Most of these techniques directly involve peers for the interaction, one important result being the self-insight that interaction with others like oneself affords.

Judgment groups, syndicate groups (Abercrombie Johnson, 1969; Collier, 1983). Mostly used at tertiary level, these kinds of groups require deep interaction around a cognitive issue: the teacher's role is as facilitator only.

Values clarification, role play, the bull-ring (Brady, 1979; Grainger, 1970; Rest, 1974; SEMP). All these techniques use peer group interaction in various ways in the affective domain — values, interpersonal feelings, moral development — and have been used from upper primary levels upwards.

Peer teaching (Allen, 1976; Palincsar and Brown, 1984). Peer teaching is heavily focused on content: teaching others helps one to develop an 'audience sense' and a more rounded and viable comprehension of the content to be taught. Most peer teaching studies show little or no loss for the taught, and considerable gains for the teacher.

4.   Social support. The intersection between interactive context and motivation basically refers to the social or peer support given by others (as opposed to the leader-support of embedded teaching).

The sociocentric 'collaborative network' constructed by skilful teachers which incorporates a co-operative let's-work-together theme. The non-worker, the slacker, then becomes the deviate (Chapter 7).

Peer support and family grouping, where older students take responsibility for younger ones, in both academic and social roles (Chapters 5 and 8).

Think-aloud modelling (Chapter 4). The teacher becomes a public model of how to do it (the example we used in Chapter 4 was writing). Here the teacher relies on expertise and some kind of identification and modelling. Clearly this is only a first step to provide sufficient structure to let students know where they are to go, but it is one that is often ignored.

5.   Motivational context. Strictly motivational techniques would rely on the 'centre of interest'; that is, building a lesson or task around an existing interest of the student. This is often hard to do as such; frequently, motivational techniques rely on interaction, or learner activity to generate the interest. Nevertheless, we would include here:

Organic reading (Ashton Warner, 1980). The teacher takes the child's own words, often referring to important personal happenings, and uses them to build 'organic readers' for each child. Freire's (1970) technique with adult illiterates is similar.

Variability and surprise (Berlyne, 1966; Suchman, 1961). Content is used to create contradictory, surprising or conflicting results that prompt learner curiosity, and a perceived need-to-explain: it also permeates the whole alternative frameworks approach (Chapter 5). Most obvious applications are in science and mathematics teaching.

6.   **Self-responsiblity.** The intersection between motivation and learner activity is extremely important, bringing in the questions of attribution and self-efficacy on the one hand; and, a short step from variability and surprise above, problem-based learning, on the other.

Climate: the whole atmosphere of school and of classroom that allows the learner freedom of choice and the opportunity to develop an 'origin' self-concept. This has two further aspects:

- *'Ownership'* or proprietorial interest in the task. The learner feels a special relationship to the task.
- A *self-concept of self-efficacy* based on beliefs of competence with respect to that particular task.

Problem-based learning (Boud, 1985a). In a sense this is a highly structured version of the centre-of-interest, where a real experimental situation is arranged which requires the learner to do something: usually, to first find out some pertinent knowledge on which to base a decision. This usually provides a powerful link between content, motivation and a perceived-need-to-know, and learner activity.

Summary: Teaching processes. The learning process is unified, but it does consist of various facets and — depending on resources, the topic, the teacher's own knowledge and expertise, the relationship with the students, and a host of other factors — the teacher can devise teaching processes and techniques that call upon one or several of these aspects. Figure 11.1, and the preceding section based on it, simply illustrates the point made in Chapter 8: teaching is a complex process requiring a great deal of professional knowledge and personal skill. By the same token, that also means that teachers are not born; they are made in a process that requires much to be learned and practised. Indeed, the first few years of teaching will be 'problem-based learning' in a very real sense.

We cannot therefore hope to be all-inclusive in our coverage of teaching processes. We can, however, on the basis of our survey of human learning, draw attention to some of the key aspects that seem to be associated with deep learning.

These include: learner *activity* (probably that first), *interactivity* with peers, experts and machines, and *motivation*, which is as much a consequence of the first two as a stimulus to learning; and their various interactions, which deeply involve immersion in *content*, and a facilitative *structure*.

We are not saying that learning takes place at the learner's beck and call. Learning in close collaboration with others — particularly with seniors who are more expert and who often take the initiative, set the pace and call the shots — seems very much to be biologically prepared (see Chapter 1): which is very fortunate, for otherwise we should not have acquired much as infants or children before schools were invented. But schools need to join with that embedded framework for learning, not to fight it as they have done, with the emphasis on packaged knowledge, heavy evaluation (academic, behavioural and personal), and 'neutral', disembedded teaching contexts.

Paradoxically, that embedded one-to-one interaction, in which both parties have their own stake and responsiblities, is characteristic *both* of the adult world as well as that of early childhood. The adult mode is obviously *different* from that of early childhood, but the sense of interaction within an experienced context is the same. The school could provide continuity by making use of the contexts and interactions that characterise both ends of the lifespan.

In very brief, then, what does our school look like, if it followed the aims contexts and experiences, and the teaching processes arising therefrom, that have been suggested here?

- The atmosphere will resemble that of a well-run adult enterprise, with shared responsibilities, rather than a total institution whose nature elicits the alternately rebellious and overly dependent behaviours it purports to be eliminating.
- Activities will become more group and co-operatively centred, less competitive.
- Educational goals will be directed towards instilling a pleasant working atmosphere and rich experiences eliciting high student activity and co-operation, on the one hand; and developing specific currriculum objectives where appropriate, specifying expected standards of competence, and evaluating with respect to those standards, on the other.
- The school will be integrated much more with the local community, and encourage tolerance of diverse community values; de-emphasising differences due to age, race and sex.

It is a bit of a mixture: at the same time 'progressive' but concerned with results and standards. It is less concerned with competition and heavy rules, but nevertheless emphasises structure, competence and expertise. How realistic, psychologically and socially, even politically, is such a picture of the school?

Visions of the future

As parents were busy choosing their school for the 1986 academic year or reconciling themselves to what fate had decreed to be their 'zoned' local school, Box 11.3 appeared in a Sydney newspaper.

The general picture is a familiar one: emphasis on relaxed atmosphere and management skills, open relations, community input, but also an emphasis on results, in the sense of learning outcomes.

It is interesting to compare these observations with an article that appeared in the *Sydney Morning Herald*, Tuesday 8 May 1979: 'The shape of schools to come' in which two Sydney principals predicted what would happen in the eighties. Some excerpts are given in Box 11.4.

BOX 11.3   WHAT MAKES A GOOD SCHOOL?

Top HSC results ... A reputation for success in sport? ... The jobs of ex-students? ... Smart presentation? ...

What does a parent look for in trying to identify a really worthwhile school?

Over recent years educational researchers in many countries have been trying to find out what it is that makes a particular school a place that is good both for children and for the general community.

Various types of school have been identified as those most likely to promote academic achievement as well as develop some of the many personal qualities that contribute to the living of full, effective and happy lives.

It seems that our best schools have these qualities:

- They are run by principals who are skilled instructional leaders. This is a key finding: successful principals are much more than efficient managers and smooth public relations officers; they have a clear understanding of children and learning and they are able to share their knowledge and skills with their more junior colleagues.
- They have very clear and agreed-upon goals. The teachers and parents share a sense of common purpose. The staff know where they want to go and they regularly evaluate how successful they are in achieving their objectives.
- They have high expectations of their pupils. And the pupils, in turn, tend to respond to these expectations.
- They provide a climate which is orderly yet stimulating. The pupils feel safe while enjoying appropriate challenges.
- They have a strong sense of community. Members are caring and supportive of each other. Parents are welcomed and valued. There is a general sense of belonging.

The message from a host of research studies is insistent: it is in this kind of place that our children are most likely to learn things that are worth knowing.

Well, what does this mean for parents who are trying to make an informed assessment of any particular school?

Perhaps, in talking with the principal, teachers and other parents, and making their own careful observations, they might consider the following basic questions:

1. In this school there an observable balance between freedom and order, and a general atmosphere of kindness-calmness and absorption in worthwhile activities?

2. Is there an emphasis on caring for individuals and catering for their needs rather than on institutional image-making and on whole-class movement through inflexible routines?

3. Do the individual children, at all levels of ability, seem to be enjoying a real sense of achievement?

4. Does the curriculum appear to be balanced, with plenty of opportunity for drama, art, craft and music as well as the traditional academic subjects?

5. Do the members of the school community speak to each other courteously? Do they appear sensitive to each other's needs?

6. Is there a clearly understood and enforced discipline policy that is characterised by fairness as well as firmness, and that always places children's welfare above organisational convenience?

7. Does the school environment suggest by its appearance that the people here care about the place they work in?

8. Are there ample opportunities for parents to communicate with the school and to be involved in its day-to-day life?

9. Most importantly, are the values demonstrated and taught at the school the same as your own? If they are significantly different, this school, no matter how effective in some ways, is not for your child.

Source: Barry Dwyer, *The Sun Herald*, 26 January 1986, p. 19.

Increased community involvement, adult learners and adult modes of learning, recognition of diversity, training for a complex professional task, management skills ... these things were foreshadowed by experienced practising educators in 1979, and in 1986 recognised as the criteria for a good school; and they are attainable through recent research into people learning. As has been suggested, both in this and in Chapter 8, both society and schools are moving together on the question of the sort of schooling we are needing.

So we are agreed on the theory, the goals, the contexts and the methods. How do we put all that into practice?

THE THIRD P: THE PROFESSIONAL TEACHER

Moving from theory to practice occurs on two levels. The first is more deliberate, referring to the kinds of management issues talked about in Chapter 8. Planning, setting up operational procedures in the classroom, 'negotiating' with the class, and so on. These are long-term decisions and evolve gradually, both formally and informally.

The second level is more spontaneous. Usually we are talking of quick decisions that need to be made in the heat of the moment, often with respect to just one student or another staff member: these are the routine decisions that have to be made every day, and for which there is usually insufficient time to plan a proper strategy.

BOX 11.4   THE SHAPE OF SCHOOLS TO COME: TWO VIEWS
OF THE EIGHTIES

Mrs Jo Dunbar, then principal, Enfield Primary School
... it's not an Anglo-Saxon Australia, it's a multicultural Australia. I'll be looking
very closely at what things are accepted as Australian culture ... the Australian
child should not be disadvantaged by not having a second language.
Computers will come with a big bang ... suddenly we are actually going into the
computer age. Schools will be invovled in retraining ... we will have to do
continuous retraining for the rest of our lives ... Systems in a government
department are very rigid ... to add flexibility you have to hasten slowly. From
the director downward, we are trying to do something about the flexibility of
our system ... One of the major changes ahead ... schools being the centre of
the community where people will attend for their needs for the rest of their
lives. Even the senior citizens have a section in the schools I have seen in
Canada. It is a fantastic idea; they use all the facilities available.

And Mr Geoff Vardrop, then principal, Newtown Boys' High School
Curriculum in the eighties will have to have relevance for a changing society,
with its expanding technology and increasing leisure ... these changes in
curriculum must have corresponding flexibility in the staffing of high schools
... Teacher training ... needs to have closer and longer association with schools
and practising teachers. School-based teacher training programs seem to me
to be the model of the eighties ... Secondary education will have to be much
more flexible ... flexible school leaving age, vocational and social skill
experience, a closer consideration of the senior college concept in schools,
acceptance of mature students, part-time daytime experiences ... parents
getting involved in school programs. The decision-making and sharing
process in education is one that has enduring effects on pupils, staff and
community ...

Source: Education Herald, *The Sydney Morning Herald*, 8 May 1979.

Management issues: Long-term planning

Some of the more important aspects that needed to be brought into a management
strategy were discussed in Chapter 8. It is hopefully clearer by now how these fit into
context: in particular, what we mean by 'managing' as opposed to 'disciplining' a class.
The connotations of 'discipline' suggest a hierarchical adult–child mode of interaction,
which as we have seen (Box 11.1 provides a powerful example) locks both teacher and
student in roles neither wants and which are counter-productive. This is not to say that

the management model of negotiations between responsible parties will always work. There will always be students, as happens with adults too, who will not behave responsibly no matter what the opportunities to do so.

The evidence is, however, that when it has been tried it has worked. What is equally true is that the traditional model *is not* working. It might have done in the past; it is anachronistic today. What most certainly does not work is the *mixture* of traditional and management models. As Connell comments on precisely this point: 'This clash of strategies was plainly one of the most divisive and intractable issues among the staff of these schools' (Connell, 1985, p. 108). All too frequently, as Connell comments, when this clash becomes such a major issue, the solution has been to bring in the 'iron man deputy' who imposes a rugged disciplinary mode from the top down, which is precisely counter to the general evolution of schooling, and which brings in all the attendant counter-productive problems we have listed before: all due to sociocentrism defining 'us' and 'the enemy' (teachers). The sad thing is that the alternative would be so much easier and more effective: sociocentrism then can be brought into play to define 'There is no doubt that the 'iron man' concept is on the way out, but particularly in 'tough' areas and in more conservative schools it is still perceived as the quick solution to a very real problem.

But we are writing for the near-future, not for a receding past (even if it is receding in some areas and States more gradually than in others). Given that, we return to implementing the management model. Managers are professionals. Professionalism relies on expertise, impartially administered. The question of expertise bears on planning; the question of impartiality on everyday decisions is discussed in the following section.

The first step, then, is to clarify goals to oneself. General aims exist already: they are implicit guidelines. We refer to:

- arranging the context: school and classroom climate;
- inventing or arranging for rich experiences;
- clarifying instructional objectives, and their evaluation.

Planning those experiences, arranging objectives into lesson topics, and choosing suitable instructional and evaluational procedures, then follow for each lesson.

Operational procedures, rewards and (possibly) punishment, and general modes of teacher–student interaction then need to be decided, with low- and high-structure alternatives — which depends on what you can personally tolerate and work within, what the school climate is, and what is most compatible with the kind of climate or atmosphere you want eventually to create.

In this way, the *teacher's agenda* can be prepared. The next major step is to take the *students' agenda* into account: that is why we used the 'eventually' above. A 'contract' has yet to be struck; a collaborative network to be established — and the dominance of the teacher's agenda is affected by 'gravity' whereas the students' appears not to be (see Chapter 8).

Two things need to be emphasised about establishing the management model. First, while the procedure should be as open as possible it can rarely be a completely open negotiation. Matters are too complicated for that. Nevertheless, the main features relating to *operational procedures* in the classrooms (what the rules are, what the penalties are for breaking them) and to *academic goals* (where we are heading, what the purpose of this activity is) should wherever possible be made *completely clear* to the students. They will only be clear if the teacher is also completely clear about them. As Davies' (1982) work shows, the sudden discovery of a tacit rule, which overrides an explicit rule, provokes outrage in sociocentric thinkers (the Mr Bell and the blankets instance).

Second, the 'negotiating' process is continual. The teacher needs to be constantly engaged in metateaching by seeking feedback about each decision; did it have the effect intended or was there a hidden agenda as far as the students were concerned? Depending on such feedback, the teacher then needs to be open to change: to blunder on regardless shows little metacognitive awareness, in teaching or in any other activity.

Teachers often seem to think that to change direction — a policy on evaluation, a topic being taught, a method of teaching, following through with any proposal — is a sign of weakness that they can ill afford. Again, that seems to reflect an outmoded and insecure bargaining position. Inflexibility in and of itself is unreasonable: the management model, being founded on reasonableness, cannot work on unreason.

In short, a management policy is long term and will be continually modified with experience, and with increasing knowledge of new techniques and teaching processes. Essentially, it involves coming to terms with a policy that:

- the teacher can live with;
- the students can live with;
- the school can live with;
- the community can live with.

Complicated, but all that does imply freedom to move; teaching does not imply the unilateral take-it-or-leave-it stance that has been common in the past.

Everyday decisions: Short-term acting

It is one thing to plan and negotiate policy on the grand scale. It is another to make the right decisions in the heat of the moment. Ideally, teachers educated in the declarative knowledge of espoused theory (educational psychology for instance) would act on that knowledge, so that it became procedural knowledge, the theory-in-use. To what extent do teachers do this?

One of the authors ran an in-service class in educational psychology and asked the group to think up incidents in which they or another teacher said or did something to a student in the expectation that the student would learn something, or change behaviour appropriately, as a result. Two such incidents are reported below.

Example 1   A matter of damages
Ms X arrives at her GA classroom one morning to find two Year 7 boys brawling quite viciously. She breaks them up, and discovers one was a 'foreigner' from another class, and was being forcibly removed by a boy from the home class. There was only minor damage

to the boys concerned, but a bicycle parked in the racks outside the classroom had been knocked in the scuffle and a lamp broken. The owner of the bike was not involved at all.

Having got the general picture, Ms X then asked them both what was to be done about the damage to the bike. Both boys agreed spontaneously to pay for the damage.

'Very good,' she said, 'that was an excellent decision. I think the principal would be pleased to hear that you have settled the matter this way. Why don't you see him just after lunch, and explain the matter, and then we'll forget about it.'

Over lunch, Ms X described to the principal what had happened.

'Hmmmmm,' was the ominous, and only, response.

'Oh dear,' thought Ms X. 'Have I blown it?'

She *had* blown it, in fact. As soon as the two lads entered his office, the principal got stuck into them:

'What's all this I hear? Were you fighting? And did you break the bicycle lamp?'

'Well, yes sir, but sir, we'll pay ...'

'QUIET! Now listen to me, you two young louts, I will not, do you understand, I will NOT, tolerate fighting in my school ...' And so on. He did not comment on the fact that they had offered to pay restitution; in his eagerness to prove the intractability of GAs, or to play his traditional role, he had completely overlooked why they had been sent to him.

Ms X was convinced that her decision to allow the boys time to decide what they thought they should do, and then let them relate their ideas to the principal, was a *professionally correct* one. (Her natural, commonsense reaction to the incident would have been — she thought — one of anger and moral outrage.) What she had overlooked, in the detachment of espoused theory, was that the principal might act less professionally than she (he, of course, had not had her advantage of a year's in-service course of educational psychology). Paradoxically, had she operated from her theory-in-use, the confrontation between the boys and the principal would not have taken place. On the other hand, her own personal relationship with the boys might well have suffered more than it did in the event.

Example 2   Room to save face

Tom was a sullen 15-year-old, given to bouts of depression. During such a bout, he was requested by the teacher to answer a question.

Silence.

'Tom! I asked you a question!' Loudly, this time.

Silence.

Furious, the teacher strode to Tom's desk and, lowering his face to the level of the other's, repeated slowly, '*I — asked — you — a — question!*'

Mumble — which sounded rather like 'F..k off'.

'What?? *What* did you say?'

'F..k off.' No mistake this time.

'*Apologise this instant*, or you'll go to the principal.'

'F..k off.'

'*Right*! Off we go!'

And so the feuding ended up in the principal's office. The principal was relatively young, and a female. She remembered something from conventional wisdom which said, 'Always allow the other person room to save face'; and something else about self-concept theory (Chapter 3), arousal and its effect on working memory and quality of decision-making (Chapter 2). With this unformulated but happily compatible mixture, she knew she had to keep them in her office until they had cooled down to the point where each could give just a little. Otherwise, it was a complete impasse and she would have a recurrent problem on her hands — not to mention a couple of unhappy people, and an unpleasant backwash throughout the school.

She talked her way through the '*Apologise*'/'*Make me*' volleys until they subsided. Both parties by now were beginning to sense the impossibility of the situation they had constructed. In a few minutes the boy apologised to the teacher, both returned to the classroom; the principal slumped on her desk with relief.

There is a striking contrast here — the reverse of the first example — between the professionalism of teacher and principal. The teacher was operating affectively (on an emotional level): all he could see was the affront to his authority, and his concern to protect that authority had pushed him into a corner from which there was no exit — unless the pushing ceased.

Fortunately, thanks to the principal's professionalism, it did. Had the principal relied on the traditional theory-in-use ('The authority of a teacher must always be upheld'), she would have sided with the teacher. Together they would have tried to dragoon the boy into an apology, at the expense of either the boy's self-respect or their own future comfort.

The professionalisation of education involves increasing reliance on espoused theory, as far as possible, in everyday decision-making. We have seen in the above examples that espoused theory has the following characteristics:

- Decisions can be *justified* in terms of a public theory, the validity of which may be tested scientifically. Commonsense decisions are often hard to justify beyond, 'Well it's obvious ... you can't let 'em get away with that!' or, 'I've always found that it works in the past, so you'd do well to take my advice ...' Unless one understands *why* 'it' worked, the chances are that the time will come when it does not; and, equally, that one will not know why.
- Decisions are *non-personal* (this does not mean *impersonal* or uncaring). One does not decide to do this or that because *Smith* is involved ('and we all know what a little rat *he* is').
- Closely related to this, decisions are *value free* as far as possible. In the two examples we looked at above, the commonsense theory-in-use involved *value judgments* (i.e. deciding what is 'good', 'the thing to do', etc.) instead of simply deciding — without emotion — what the most productive outcome would be. As we saw in Chapter 2, becoming emotional about a complex issue is very likely to diminish the chance of ever arriving at a good decision.

Well, where does all this leave the preservice student, about to embark on a career in teaching? Clearly, the development of professionalism takes time: it will not happen in a preservice course. As we said before, the first few years will be problem-based learning with a vengeance. That experience will bring a new perception of the application of this book to teaching.

Meantime there are a few points to remember. Teachers *are* made; but it takes time and expertise to make one. The expertise operates at two levels: long-term policy planning, and everyday decision-making. Given that, it is certain that you will be able to negotiate a position you can live with. Basically, if:

- the total school climate is appropriate;
- a variety of experiences is established, involving high student input and activity;
- curriculum goals are clear, and management rules and the 'contract' are made explicit;
- the students are treated with respect and with a reasonable simulation of adult–adult interaction;
- the teacher is an efficient organiser, and sufficiently expert in both teaching content and educational processes, to make everyday decisions unemotionally; then
- learning and teaching will be effective and enjoyable.

It is going to take time, and probably much in-service workshopping and course-taking as experience defines problems, but Connell is right when he says (quoted already in Box 8.4):

> Teaching can also be an exhilarating and joyful experience, expanding the teacher's life through skills, or human relations, or both. Teaching well is a thrill (Connell, 1985, p. 127).

SUMMARY AND CONCLUSIONS

In this final chapter, the 3P model of learning was adapted to a model of teaching, to provide the integration and application of the preceding chapters:

- presage: educational goals;
- process: teaching procedures and techniques;
- product: the professional teacher.

The first P: Educational goals. Aims set the general direction. Usually educational aims are stated broadly and rhetorically, with reference to the desirable personal characteristics of future citizens. It is usually hard to disagree with most official statements of aims. They do, however, point in a certain direction, and when we follow that direction through, we see it leads to specifiable aspects of schooling.

Most State departments refer to independence, autonomy, creativity, as well as to mastery of particular content, including basic literacy and numeracy skills. Following that through, we arrive at an *adult* mode of learning, rather than the adult–child mode that characterises traditional and most current schooling.

To actualise that direction, we need to refer to two distinct situations:

- where goals are open, and outcomes cannot accurately be specified in advance;
- where goals are closed, and outcomes can be specified.

In the first case we specify *contexts*, leading to rich experiences that theory, experience and intuition tell us students should undergo in realising the main aims; and in the second, where outcomes are both predictable and attainable, we specify instructional objectives on particular topics and means of monitoring their attainment.

The second P: From learning to teaching processes. A survey of all the research on student learning (the Section As) shows that good learning involves some or all of the following:

- learner activity;
- an interactive context, involving others or interactive software;
- a motivational context;
- all focused on a particular task content;
- and all within a facilitative structure, involving direction and forethought.

People vary in their need for high and low structure: in simulating the adult mode, structure should decrease throughout the school years. The first four factors interact to form a means of classifying the teaching techniques and procedures referred to in the Section Bs.

There were well over 20 distinct teaching processes that could be classified in this way, variously using co-operative peer group structures, carefully planned physical activities keyed to defined instructional objectives, heuristic and other metacognitive procedures, and all within a climate and atmosphere that encouraged the attributions leading to appropriate feeling about the self and the task.

The use of such procedures, and the creation of the appropriate climate, builds up quite a distinct picture of the school, and one which contrasts sharply with the traditional picture. We checked this picture with that foreshadowed some years ago by two school principals, and with that currently published as the image of a 'good' school. All three pictures tallied: we are not being fanciful and futuristic.

The third P: The professional teacher. When aims, contexts and procedures are clarified, they need to be put into action: that is the third P, a teacher professionally expert enough to do that. Professionalism addresses two levels of decision-making: the big ones involved in an overall management strategy, and the little ones involved in everyday interaction with students, other staff and parents.

Our picture of a school emphasises strongly that teaching is complex but manageable. Our management model uses the analogy of parties coming together for their mutual advantage: the initiative is strongly with the teacher to clarify and define the terms, but those terms are still negotiable and need to be seen to be negotiable. There is difficulty in a school when one teacher's policy is out of line with general school policy, but indications are that schools are moving towards the kind of model we are advocating, so that planning, expertise and flexibility are paramount rather than 'strength of personality'.

The second level of decision-making emphasises the use of espoused theory as a basis for everyday decisions: such decisions are 'cool', non-personal and justifiable on public grounds. That sounds like a counsel for perfection, particularly for beginning teachers about to enter the teaching force.

The fill-the-tanks model of education is, however, as invalid for teacher education as it is for schooling in general. Teachers will quickly find that their teacher education is life-long and problem-based. We feel that our part in that process will have been successful if this book is treated as a continuing source of espoused theory, enabling you to make those professional decisions that the future is going to require you to make.

FURTHER READING

R. W. Connell, *Teachers' Work*, George Allen & Unwin, Sydney, 1985.

As final 'further reading' we suggest only one title: the most up-to-date, realistic, and yet (if you read closely) optimistic we could find. This book was recommended too at the end of Chapter 1: we recommend a reread in light of what has been said in this chapter. Compare notes: our guess is that your second reading will be more encouraging than the first.

QUESTIONS

Questions for discussion

If you have completed all the self-testing questions from Chapters 1 to 10, you will have no need for any this chapter. There remains, however, plenty to discuss. We suggest the following:

1. A topic for a debate: 'Primary/secondary school children (take your pick according to professional interest, or have a separate debate on each) differ from adults in the ways that matter for the purposes of schooling to such an extent that the proposition that schools should use adult-to-adult modes of interaction as a basis for educating children is simply unrealistic.'

Prepare two debating teams, one for the above proposition, one against. Each side is to use points gleaned from *The Process of Learning* itself, or from other sources as convenient.

2. Take a curriculum statement for one subject for one year level (e.g. Year 7 English or Year 9 Social Science) and divide into 'open' and 'closed' outcomes. What aspects or topics of the curriculum would you allocate to 'open' treatment by prescribing certain *contexts and experiences*, and what to 'closed' treatment by deriving a list of *instructional objectives*? What may be treated by either approach?
3. Take Figure 11.1 and describe a teaching process or technique to treat a particular topic for each of the three intersections:

   - embedded teaching;
   - social supports;
   - self-responsibility.

4. From practice teaching, observation or some other source, give an account of the process of *negotiation* between teacher and class. Describe what you saw of the initial teacher's agenda, and the students' agenda. What kind of collaborative network evolved? How could things have been improved if the final result was not really a viable one?
5. Give an example of recent teacher–student interaction in which the teacher did (or conspicuously did not) rely on espoused theory. Comment freely on the result, and on how else it might have been.

GLOSSARY

ability   A stable tendency to perform well on a *range* of tasks. Abilities are part-learned, part-inherited traits that underlie and 'explain' test performance. Abilities may be classified in terms of content (e.g. number ability) or process (e.g. divergent ability).

accommodation   The term used by Piaget to describe the process whereby COGNITIVE STRUCTURES (CODES) are made richer and more complex through modification by new experiences. Exactly equivalent to RECODING.

accountability   The view that teachers and SCHOOLING can be held responsible for the amount of learning that students evidence. A nineteenth-century version of accountability held that teachers should be paid according to the examination results of their students ('payment by results').

acculturation   Refers (a) to the socialising or 'taming' of the individual to the norms of society; and (b) to the mutual interaction between minority and majority groups in a MULTICULTURAL society.

achievement motivation   Motivation for academic learning that is based on the ego-enhancement achieved by winning in a competitive situation; desire to achieve success, as opposed to desire to avoid failure.

achieving   Applies to MOTIVES, STRATEGIES and APPROACHES TO LEARNING: associated with institutionally desirable LEARNING OUTCOMES (high grades). Achieving strategy comprises typical study skills.

activation   See AROUSAL.

advance organiser   A PRE-INSTRUCTIONAL STRATEGY suggested by Ausubel that involves prefacing information to be learned with a brief statement that organises the concepts involved at a high level of abstraction.

affective domain   The domain that emphasises feelings, motivation and reactions to other people and oneself; to be distinguished from the COGNITIVE DOMAIN, which is concerned with thought.

aggression   Thought or action that wilfully inflicts psychological or physical hurt on another; to be contrasted with ASSERTION and ALTRUISM.

allocentric   Thought (and sometimes feeling) that is centred around the way other people think and feel; as opposed to SOCIOCENTRIC and EGOCENTRIC.

alternative frameworks   'Children's science': the explanations children create to explain phenomena for themselves. These explanations fall short of the PARADIGMATIC or accepted frameworks of science in that they are expressed in a lower MODE, or in a sub-RELATIONAL level in the learning cycle, or both.

altruism   Helping others without regard for the MATERIAL CONSEQUENCES to oneself which will result from the action.

anxiety   A feeling of threat, accompanied by high AROUSAL. Trait anxiety is a predisposition for some individuals to react to a variety of situations with anxiety. State anxiety refers to the anxiety felt in a particular situation, such as TEST ANXIETY.

approach to learning   A consistent way of going about a particular task, or learning/study, in general, that derives from the student's METACOGNITION, linking MOTIVE and STRATEGY, with perceived task demands and desired type of LEARNING OUTCOME. Approaches, as may MOTIVES and STRATEGIES, can be referred to as DEEP, SURFACE and ACHIEVING, with deep-achieving and surface-achieving as other possible combinations.

arousal   Arousal or activation is a generalised motivation to behave, irrespective of the direction of behaviour. Low arousal is associated with low drive; high arousal with 'hyper' behaviour. The physiological source of arousal is the reticular arousal system (RAS), which is located in the brain stem.

assertion   Treating others firmly, but with no deliberate intention of harming them, in order to obtain one's own ends. High-STRUCTURE teaching requires that teachers be assertive.

assessment   In general, the quantitative EVAL-UATION of student performance, after a teaching episode. In progressive assessment, the student's final grade is determined by performance throughout the course; in terminal assessment, the grade is determined by performance in a final examination at the end of the course. See also SELF-ASSESSMENT.

assimilation   (a) The merging of minority groups so that they become indistinguishable from the majority group. (b) The term used by Piaget to describe the understanding and interpretation of experiences in terms of the individual's existing COGNITIVE STRUCTURES. Exactly equivalent to ENCODING (or coding).

associative interference   A theory of forgetting based on the similarity between items learned. Interference is retroactive when recall of previously learned material is inhibited by later material, proactive when recently learned material is inhibited by material that has been previously learned. This theory is mostly relevant for ROTE rather than MEANINGFUL learning.

attainment   Performance on a *particular* test, as opposed to ABILITY, which refers to a range of tests.

attending   Selecting relevant from irrelevant material in the SENSORY REGISTER through a process of PRECODING; being aware of material in WORKING MEMORY.

attribution theory   A theory which bases motivation for performance of a particular task on previous performance of that task. Specifically, attribution theory emphasises the factors (such as ability, luck, effort or task difficulty) to which the subject attributes his or her performance.

autonomy (as in moral).   Acting out of principle, rather than out of CONFORMITY or self-interest. The highest level of moral development, ahead of SOCIOCENTRISM and EGO-CENTRISM.

baseline   The level of performance, in a BEHAVIOUR MODIFICATION program, that is obtained in the absence of any deliberate rewards or CONTINGENCIES.

behaviour modification   A technique of changing the behaviour of individuals by deliberately altering the consequences of a particular behaviour in order to change the frequency of future occurrence of that behaviour, based on Skinner's principles of OPERANT CONDITIONING.

behavioural objective   An educational goal that specifies the learned behaviours a student is to exhibit after a laerning episode (lesson or series of lessons). The objective usually details the conditions under which the learning is to occur, and the level of performance expected (see INSTRUCTIONAL OBJECTIVE).

behaviourism   A school of psychology which is concerned only with the conditions associated with changes in behaviour. Internal ('mentalistic' or 'cognitive') events are regarded as irrelevant. Behaviourist psychologists rely on (CLASSICAL and OPERANT CONDITIONING as explanatory models of human behaviour.

burn-out   Various physical and psychological reactions to prolonged job stress, particularly noted in helping professions, including teaching, resulting in poor morale, irritability and depression.

chunks   The units of information, grouped in WORKING MEMORY, that determine the amount of information a person can handle at any given time. A phrase-length unit of meaning.

classical conditioning   See CONDITIONING.

codes (elaborated and restricted)   Elaborated codes of communication are learned, according to Bernstein, by middle-class children, and emphasises public and formal rules of grammar. Restricted codes — where language is limited to personal reference, following instructions, and particularly to context — are said to be learned by working-class children.

codes (in general)   Codes ar the part of COGNITIVE STRUCTURE which allow input to be incorporated with previous learnings. Generic codes have a high degree of access to cognitive structure; surface codes access to only a few, limited aspects of cognitive structure.

coding   See ENCODING.

cognitive domain   That aspect of human functioning that refers to thought; as opposed to the AFFECTIVE DOMAIN, which refers to feeling, emotion and motivation.

cognitive psychology   A school of thought in psychology that refers to a MODEL OF HUMAN NATURE in which humans are represented as thinkers. As opposed to HUMANIST PSYCHOLOGY and BEHAVIOURISM.

cognitive structure   The internal organisation of CODES or SCHEMATA that determine how information will be ENCODED. Cognitive structure generally grows more complex with development.

cognitive style   A qualitatively distinct and consistent way of encoding, storing and performing that is mostly independent of INTELLIGENCE.

comprehension (in reading)   The final phase, after PREREADING and DECODING, where the reader synthesises meaning from the text, using 'top-down' and 'bottom-up' processes for clues. Comprehension can be enhanced by METACOGNITION, using HEURISTICS to self-check on understanding.

computer assisted instruction (CAI)   The use of computers in actually instructing students. This may range from reactive, as in PROGRAMMED INSTRUCTION, to highly interactive, as in EMBEDDED TEACHING. CAI includes simulations, word processing and teaching writing, problem solving, etc.

computer managed instruction (CMI)   The use of computers in administering instruction, for example establishing data bases, testing students and scoring their results, report writing, etc. CMI does not use computers in an instructional role.

conception of learning   The view a person holds about what constitutes learning. Conceptions are basically quantitative ('a good learner knows a lot') or qualitative ('a good learner understands and can reapply what is learned'); conceptions affect APPROACH TO LEARNING and LEARNING OUTCOME.

concrete-symbolic   The mode of development, typical of middle to late childhood, wherein children learn to use symbol systems to refer to their experienced world.

conditioning   A form of learning (and of motivation) that suggests that the performance

of responses is conditional on the intervention of the external environment. In classical conditioning, responses are emitted as a function of the association between an unconditioned and a conditioned stimulus; operant (or instrumental) conditioning occurs when the responses are associated with rewarding or punishing consequences. Both forms of conditioning are examples of BEHAVIOURISM.

conferencing (in writing)   A technique of one-to-one interaction between the writer and (usually) the teacher, to assist primarily in PARAWRITING and REVISING activities.

conformity   Changing behaviour because of perceived pressure from others; in particular, from the peer group, and from authority. Conformity to peers is the hallmark of SOCIOCENTRIC behaviour and thought.

conservation   A concept, emphasised by Piaget, according to which properties of an object (e.g. length, weight, quantity) remain the same regardless of any changes that may be made to the object (e.g. pouring into a different container) which do not alter the fundamental constancy of the object.

content learning   Learning in which the main interest of both teacher and student is the subject matter to be learned, rather than any effects the learning experience may have on the learner (see PROCESS LEARNING).

contingency   A result (rewarding or punishing) signalled prior to the elicitation of a response, in order to affect the frequency of that response.

conventional   In Kohlberg's theory of moral development, the middle level (SOCIOCENTRIC), where right and wrong are determined according to conformity with peer (Stage 3) or societal (Stage 4) norms. Preconventional judgments are EGOCENTRIC, and are based on avoidance of punishment (Stage 1) or maximisation of reward (Stage 2). Post-conventional judgments rely on FORMAL principles; societal (Stage 5) or universal (Stage 6).

convergence   A type of thinking that emphasises arriving at the 'one correct answer' to a problem. Convergent thought can be measured, particularly, by IQ tests.

core (curriculum) Generally, the subjects that should be taught to all students, comprising basic skills, knowledge and concepts in all subject areas that are thought to be the minimum necessary for effective citizenship.

correlation A statistical technique that expresses the degree of relationship between two variables: +1.00 indicates a perfect positive relationship (rarely obtained); –1.00, a perfect negative relationship (also rare); and 0.00, no relationship at all.

creative writing Writing, in either prose or poetry, in which the writer's intention is to entertain or express emotion and/or ideas, rather than to pass on information.

creativity A type of thinking that emphasises flexible, original and productive ways of responding. Related to DIVERGENCE.

credentialling Providing a SUMMATIVE formal statement of standards of attainment either with respect to an individual, or to the level of courses offered in an institution.

criterion-referenced evaluation Evaluation of student performance in terms of how well the student meets pre-set standards, as opposed to NORM-REFERENCED EVALUATION.

curriculum In general, the total process of instruction from setting OBJECTIVES, through teaching method, to EVALUATION. In Australia, the term 'curriculum' has tended to become equated with 'syllabus', that is, the selection and arrangement of content to be taught in particular subjects to particular year groups. Curriculum development is becoming increasingly SCHOOL-BASED.

declarative knowledge Knowing about a topic so that one may declare that knowledge; an aspect of espoused THEORY. Often contrasted with PROCEDURAL KNOWLEDGE.

decoding (a) retrieving material from long-term memory (see also DISMEMBERING), (b) the second phase, after PRE-READING, in which the particular association between visual symbols and sounds are handled, and words are recognised. This should merge with COMPREHENSION.

deductive process Learning by moving from general concepts to more specific ones, according to logical principles.

deep INTRINSIC when applied to MOTIVE: meaning-oriented, to STRATEGY. Deep APPROACH leads to highly structured LEARNING OUTCOMES.

development (cognitive) The description of shifts in level of abstraction in MODES within which LEARNING takes place.

direct teaching A high-STRUCTURE method teaching, where OBJECTIVES are clear and student performance is systematically evaluated. Direct teaching is expository, competency-based and prescriptive.

discipline (a) painful consequences that are natural or endemic, as opposed to PUNISHMENT, (b) a mode of classroom control based on the implied authority of the teacher, as opposed to (a) above, and to MANAGEMENT, (c) a body of knowledge organised at the RELATIONAL level of the FORMAL–1 mode.

disembeddedness See EMBEDDEDNESS.

dismembering Based on the theory of memory, according to which individuals CODE the different aspects of an experience in semantic, temporal, logical or spatial codes, and reassemble these components on recall.

divergence A type of thinking that generates many novel alternatives to a given situation; often equated with creativity (see CONVERGENCE).

drive See AROUSAL.

editing Changing and correcting text at the mechanical and orthographic levels (grammar, spelling, etc.).

egocentricism In Piaget's theory, a viewpoint of the world and other people that takes into account only the perspective of the individual; a period of development covering early to middle childhood. This meaning must be distinguished from the non-technical one.

embeddedness Donaldson's term to account for stage-like progressions in cognitive development. To the young child, a problem is embedded in its context and its crucial aspects hidden. Complete disembedding occurs only in the FORMAL mode. Embedded teaching involves close one-to-one interaction.

encoding (or coding) Reading in, interpreting and understanding input in terms of existing coded knowledge.

English-as-a-Second-Language (ESL), English-as-a-Foreign-Language (EFL) The teaching of English to non-English speakers, for example, migrants in Australia, whose mother tongue (L1) is not English.

entering behaviour(s) Glaser's term for those behaviours (such as previous knowledge, skills, attitudes) that a student has developed before he or she enters a learning situation in which they are relevant to its successful completion.

essay tests Tests or examinations in which students structure their own responses in continuous prose.

evaluation Sampling student performance and making a judgment as to its adequacy. Evaluation may be NORM REFERENCED, CRITERION-REFERENCED, FORMATIVE or SUMMATIVE.

exit levels Curriculum statements specifying the TARGET MODE and level in LEARNING CYCLE when a particular topic may be judged to have been learned adequately, and at which point the student's performance may be accredited with some SUMMATIVE EVALUATION statement.

exophoric reference The use of a pronoun, which is separated from its referent and accordingly may lead to ambiguity; for example, 'Jim and his brother arrived. He said ...'

extended abstract A sophisticated response that 'overshoots' the TARGET MODE. See also SOLO TAXONOMY.

external examination A system of assessment in which exams are set and marked outside the institution which teaches in the subject (as opposed to SCHOOL-BASED assessment).

extinction The weakening and disappearance of a learned response through lack of reinforcement (e.g. in operant conditioning by withholding reward, and in classical conditioning by not periodically presenting the unconditioned stimulus with the conditioned stimulus).

extrapunitive An individual who blames others for the fact that he or she is punished for wrongdoing (as opposed to INTROPUNITIVE).

extrinsic motivation Where learning or performance takes place as a means of gaining some material reward or avoiding a punishment, it is extrinsically motivated; learning undergone for MATERIAL CONSEQUENCES.

formal The most abstract MODES of thought: formal–1 develops in early adolescence, but does not mature at all in some people; formal–2 develops in early adulthood and is comparatively rare.

formative evaluation Evaluation conducted during the performance of a task to provide feedback information on how well the task is being performed and how performance may be improved.

free schools Schools, in which STRUCTURE is at a minimum, founded on the theory that the child's learning and development is best left to evolve 'naturally', with minimal constraints imposed from outside. These schools also emphasise interpersonal feeling as more important than cognitive abilities or expertise.

generativity Wittrock's term to emphasise the view in cognitive psychology that learning and recall are constructive processes, involving active participation by the learner.

heuristics Guided self-questioning whereby, in the course of some task, the learner asks an open-ended question that prompts META-COGNITION and hopefully improved performance.

humanist psychology A philosophical position, as much as a scientific one, that emphasises human values, authentic relationships and feelings about oneself and others as being the proper concern of psychology.

ikonic A mode of cognitive development in which information is processed in terms of unidimensional codes, often of a perceptual or emotional nature.

implicit (hidden) curriculum Teaching particular values by requiring the student to do things that imply those values; such values are not examined consciously by the student.

individualised instruction Instruction designed to meet the needs of the individual student in terms both of content and method of teaching. In particular, individualised, or personalised, systems of instruction (PSI) often mean just that the student proceeds at his or her own pace until the instructional objectives are met, as in MASTERY LEARNING.

inductive process Learning general principles from specific concrete examples, as in discovery learning.

information integration A theory of intellectual functioning proposed by Das and Kirby that involves the process ABILITIES of SIMULTANEOUS and SUCCESSIVE SYNTHESIS, and PLANNING.

information processing theories A form of the COGNITIVE theory of learning in which human behavoiur is described in terms of the individual selectively interpreting, storing and recalling the information in the environment. This concept is analogous to that of a self-programming computer.

instrumental motivation see EXTRINSIC MOTIVATION.

intelligence A hypothetical factor of wide generality that is presumed to underlie an individual's competence in performing cognitive tasks. A great deal of controversy surrounds the nature, generality and modifiability of intelligence.

intrinsic motivation Where learning or performance takes place in the absence of any INTRINSIC, SOCIAL or ACHIEVEMENT motivation, it is positively intrinsically motivated; where learning is abruptly terminated for no evident reasons it is negatively intrinsically motivated. Positive intrinsic motivation usually signals high quality learning.

intropunitive An individual who blames him or herself for the fact that he or she is punished for wrongdoing (as opposed to EXTRAPUNITIVE).

IQ Intelligence quotient (IQ) is the score yielded by an intelligence test, which measures a person's general ability in relation to the population (see also INTELLIGENCE).

latent trait theory See RASCH MODEL.

learned helplessness A state of depression and inability to cope brought about by the realisation that one has no control over one's environment.

learning The acquisition of skills or information through interaction with the environment. See also LEARNING CYCLE.

learning cycle The levels of complexity achieved with respect to a TARGET MODE. Three major transitions are involved: from uni- to multistructural (the accretion of knowledge); from multistructural to relational (the structuring of knowledge); and from relational to extended abstract (the generalisation of knowledge).

learning outcome The product of a learning experience; may be construed or evaluated quantitatively or qualitatively, expressed in terms of structure-to-data (S–D) ratio. Qualitative aspects can be assessed by the SOLO TAXONOMY.

literacy Displayed competence in reading and writing.

locus of control A concept introduced by Rotter describing how individuals perceive themselves in relation to the external world. Individuals with an external locus of control perceive themselves as being controlled by chance, other people or 'fate'; those with an internal locus of control perceive themselves as having control over their decisions and what happens to them.

long-term memory (LTM) Storage of previous learning to be reconstructed when appropriate in WORKING MEMORY.

look-and-sayu A method of teaching reading (also called 'whole word approach') which relies on recognising each word in its entirety, as opposed to breaking the word into letter-sound components.

management A view of classroom control that is 'adult mode': a mutually acceptable 'contract' is negotiated to the mutual advantage of teacher and class. Teaching is characterised by planning, expertise and mutual regard. Contrasted to classroom control based on DISCIPLINE.

mastery learning An INDIVIDUALISED method of teaching and CRITERION-REFERENCED evaluation, based on the assumption that virtually all students can learn basic CORE content, if given sufficient time and adequate instruction.

match-mismatch The state in which input is to be interpreted by cognitive structure. Match implies complete interpretation (ENCODING); mismatch the need for RE-CODING. According to the degree of mismatch, INTRINSIC MOTIVATION will be positive or negative.

material consequences The pleasant and/or unpleasant results of a particular behaviour; these consequences are manipulated in behaviour modification programs in order to change a person's behaviour.

mean   The average of a distribution of scores, that is, the sum of the scores divided by the number of scores.

meaningful learning   Learning verbal material by the method of coding (ENCODING) with the intention of understanding the message well enough to be able to express the sense of the message in different words.

median   In a distribution of scores from lowest to highest, the median score is the one at the midpoint of the distribution. In a NORMAL CURVE the median is the same as the mean.

memory   The storage and retrieval of information. Three levels, based on period of retention, are postulated: ultra-short (SENSORY REGISTER), short (WORKING MEMORY), and long (LONG-TERM MEMORY).

mental set   A condition where the PLAN is consciously adjusted to attend to a particular task or train of information.

metacognition   Awareness of one's own cognitive processes rather than of the content of those processes. Use of that self-awareness in controlling and improving cognitive processes such as study skills, reading comprehension, writing.

metalearning   METACOGNITION applied to student learning, whereby students derive APPROACHES TO LEARNING.

mnemonic   An artificial device to aid memory by linking new information to well-known material, for example, 'ROY G. BIV' for the colours of the spectrum.

nodality   A sensory channel of information, for example, verbal, visual, kinaesthetic (touch), etc. Cross-modal coding occurs when material is deliberately linked to more than one mode (e.g. writing down a new word, as well as listening to it).

model of human nature   A personal set of assumptions about the nature of humans, which may be fairly primitive or highly sophisticated. Three models underlie the main schools of psychology: reaction (BEHAVIOURISM), thought (COGNITIVE PSYCHOLOGY) and feeling (HUMAN PSYCHOLOGY).

modelling   Learning that takes place as a result of seeing someone else carry out the

performance.

moderation   A technique for equating schools by a pre-test, and then 'rationing' final grades on the basis of the result.

monitoring   A metacognitive activity in which one checks that one's processing and outcomes are in line with PLANS.

morality   The rules that govern interpersonal behaviour. In Piaget's theory, moral absolutism results where the rules are perceived as unalterable and imposed by authority; moral relativism where they arise from group consensus (SOCIOCENTRISM) or from a principled consideration of others (ALLOCENTRISM). (See also CONVENTIONAL.)

motive   The reason(s) why a student approaches a task. In general, motives may be INSTRUMENTAL, INTRINSIC, ACHIEVING and SOCIAL. In connection with APPROACHES TO LEARNING, motives corresponding to the first three categories are referred to as SURFACE, DEEP and ACHIEVING.

multiculturalism   A view of society that advocates maintaining and respecting the cultural diversity found in society. *Bicul*turalism, in Australia, refers to Aboriginal education.

multiple-choice   A form of OBJECTIVE test in which the 'stem' of the item is presented, and the student has to select the correct response to the stem from, usually, four or five alternatives.

multistructural   The middle point in the LEARNING CYCLE; data-rich but inadequately structured. See also SOLO TAXONOMY.

myelin sheath   A coating around neurones that grows progressively at different stages of development, improving the efficiency of neuronal transmission. Progressive myelinisation could help account for our ability to think more abstractly as we grow older.

narrative   A way of knowing used to understand the world in terms of meaningful myth, parable and 'understanding'. Contrasted to PARADIGMATIC way, narrative develops earlier but is also present in highly creative adult thought and feeling.

need-achievers   Individuals who are highly ACHIEVEMENT motivated.

non-standard English   A form of dialect of

English that is used by people to communicate in informal contexts, and which differs in vocabulary, phonology and grammatical structure from STANDARD ENGLISH; for example, 'This joker come up to me' for 'The man approached me'.

norm-referenced evaluation   Evaluation of student performance in terms of how well the student compares to some reference group such as class, age peers, etc; as opposed to CRITERION-REFERENCED EVALUATION.

normal curve   A bell-shaped curve that is assumed to correspond to the distribution of many ability test scores.

numeracy   Displayed competence in calculating correctly and in understanding and applying the four rules of number to real-life situations.

objective (instructional)   A precise statement of the teacher's intentions when designing a learning episode; of the various types of instructional objective, the BEHAVIOURAL OBJECTIVE is the most rigorous.

objective test   A test format in which the student chooses from a limited number of alternatives to indicate his response. This obviates subjective judgment in scoring, though it does not necessarily eliminate bias in choosing the 'correct' alternatives.

open education   A process of educating that relies on discovery learning, student activity and carefully monitored experiences, usually in the physical context of open-plan architecture.

operant   See CONDITIONING.

oracy   Displayed competence in speaking and listening.

origin   Individuals with an internal LOCUS OF CONTROL who see their behaviour as being caused by their own decisions. De Charms links this belief with INTRINSIC MOTIVATION.

paradigmatic   The way of knowing used by scientists and encouraged by schooling. Contrasted to the NARRATIVE way of knowing.

parawriting   Processes involved in writing that are distinguishable from actually creating text. Planning and composing are parawriting activities; transcribing and editing are writing activities.

pawn   Individuals with an external LOCUS OF CONTROL who see their behaviour as being directed from outside themselves.

percentiles   Rank ordering converted to a percentage basis; 99th percentile indicates a score at the top one per cent of the population. The 50th percentile is the same as the median. A decile occurs every 10 percentiles, and a quartile every 25 percentiles.

phoneme   A linguistic term referring to the smallest complete sounded unit in a word and written /th/.

phonics   A method of teaching reading which relies on breaking a word into PHONEMES, and relating each phoneme to a letter(s) (as opposed to LOOK-AND-SAY).

plan   The 'executive' system that controls and integrates cognitive processes from selective attention, coding and/or rehearsal, and storage and retrieval. More generally, planning is an essential metacognitive activity that distinguishes a STRATEGY from a TACTIC.

post-test   In an experiment, a test conducted after the experimental treatment (as opposed to PRE-TEST).

practicum   An instructional situation that involves practising a role or learning a skill through active participation, for example, practice teaching in teacher education.

precoding   The process, which takes place in the SENSORY REGISTER, of selecting a particular train of information for conscious attention on the basis of its current importance.

preinstructional strategies   Teaching strategies that attempt to focus and 'sensitise' the learner's attention on particularly relevant items of content before it is actually taught, for example, a list of questions, an overview, an ADVANCE ORGANISER.

Premack principle   A principle suggested by Premack to help the selection of suitable reinforcers in behaviour modification. It states that if behaviour A is more frequent than behaviour B, the frequency of behaviour B can be increased by making behaviour A contingent on behaviour B (see CONTINGENCY).

preparedness   A biologically based theory explaining why skills that were basic to survival early in the evolutionary history of humans (e.g. ORACY) are acquired more easily than historically recent ones that are not basic to survival (e.g. LITERACY).

pre-reading   An orientation phase, before DECODING and COMPREHENSION, in which the child 'relates' to the text.

presage   The first of the '3Ps'. Presage factors are those that exist prior to the actual ongoing learning situation; and derive from the *learner* (e.g. abilities, prior knowledge) and the *teaching situation* (e.g. curriculum, course demands, pressures, etc.).

prestructural   A response that falls short of the required TARGET MODE. See also SOLO TAXONOMY.

pre-test   In experiment, a test conducted prior to any experimental treatment (as opposed to POST-TEST).

problem-based learning   Learning DECLARATIVE knowledge in a context that has defined a need for that knowledge.

procedural knowledge   Knowing *how* to do something; THEORY-in-use. Often contrasted with DECLARATIVE KNOWLEDGE.

process learning   Learning in which the main emphasis is on the effects the learning experience has on the learner (particularly the way one goes about learning), rather than on the CONTENT learned.

programmed instruction   Instructional materials, self-administered, in which a topic is broken down into small sequential steps (frames), which require a response from the learner. Immediate feedback to the learner is provided.

punishment   An unpleasant event that follows a particular behaviour as a result of a deliberate decision by an authority figure. Reactions to punishment may be INTROPUNITIVE or EXTRAPUNITIVE.

rank order   Placing scores in order from lowest to highest.

Rasch model   A technique for determining, in units that are comparable across tests and samples of students, the 'latent trait' or ABILITY of students in a category of performance.

readiness   The notion that a student is cognitively, socially and physically developed to an extent that a particular topic may be taught; for example, reading readiness. Piaget's stages have been interpreted as signifying a general readiness for undertaking certain kinds of conceptual tasks.

reciprocity   Piaget's term for the idea of moral obligation: an ALTRUISTIC act puts the person helped in a situation of obligation to the helper.

recoding   Change in CODES or COGNITIVE STRUCTURE brought about as a result of mismatch (see also MATCH). With the optimal degree of mismatch, cognitive structures grow more complex and INTRINSIC MOTIVATION is experienced.

reconstruction   A theory of memory which postulates that recall of previously learned material is not so much a matter of retrieving stored information as reconstructing the original event from stored 'clues' (see also GENERATIVITY).

reflective   A METACOGNITIVE process: thinking about one's own thoughts and actions, as REFLECTIVE WRITING.

reflective writing   Writing that clarifies the thinking of the writer on the topic in question; contrasted to 'knowledge-telling', or writing that simply conveys information.

rehearsal   Storing material by repeated practice rather than by linking to previously learned material (ENCODING). In the case of verbal material, rehearsal produces ROTE LEARNING.

reinforcement   The process whereby a (rewarding) consequence of a response results in the increased likelihood of that response occurring in future. A positive reinforcer refers to a pleasant consequence; a negative reinforcer to the avoidance of an unpleasant consequence. Reinforcements may be allocated according to various schedules, such as partial, interval, self-administered, and so on.

relational   The highest point in the LEARNING CYCLE within the TARGET MODE. See also SOLO TAXONOMY.

reliability (test)   A test is reliable if it is internally consistent (the items measure the same construct) and the scores are stable over time.

remediation   Reviewing prior learning where it has been incorrect or otherwise inadequate, and taking steps to rectify the faults.

reticular arousal system   See AROUSAL.

retrieval   The usual, if somewhat misleading, term for recalling previously learned information and material. See also RECONSTRUCTION.

reversibility A logical concept which implies that a logical operation may be cancelled by its inverse. Reversibility first appears in conceptual operations in CONCRETE OPERATIONS.

revising (in writing) Rewriting text, with a focus on the meaning of the theme and main ideas. Contrasted to EDITING.

rote learning Learning verbal material by the method of REHEARSAL with the intention of exactly reproducing the original, with or without understanding it.

schema A schema (pl. schemata) is the term used by Piaget for CODE; the units used by individuals to organise their experience.

school-based In general, the location of a function in the individual school rather than externally (e.g. the State Department of Education). Curriculum development and assessment are two common functions that are becoming increasingly school-based in Australia.

selective attention The process of attending to particular stimuli and not to others (see also PRECODING).

self-assessment Requiring the student to contribute towards his or her own assessment, by (a) determining the criteria for assessment, (b) judging in accordance with those criteria, or both (a) and (b). Self-assessment may or may not be used in grading or SUMMATIVE EVALUATION.

self-efficacy A person's expectation that he or she will perform a task at a particular level of effectiveness. Beliefs in self-efficacy have a strong effect on INTRINSIC MOTIVATION.

self-concept The image or concept people have of themselves, particularly of their abilities (physical, mental and social), and the value (positive or negative) they place on these self-evaluations.

self-fulfilling prophecy Occurs when believing or saying something is true actually causes it to happen; for example, not giving a student enough work in the belief that he or she is stupid, and 'proving' the belief by the lack of output.

semantic Refers to word meanings: semantic input or semantic coding thus refer to verbal messages, and to storing information according to word meaning. Semantic processing is believed to occur mainly in the left hemisphere of the brain.

sensori-motor In general, learning that involves linking perceptions with motor responses. In particular, the term describes the stage of development taking place during INFANCY.

sensory input Information supplied by the senses: vision, touch, hearing, taste, smell, etc.

sensory register The first stage in information processing; a brief (about ¼–1 sec.) period during which information is held and scanned (PRECODING).

sexism Making discriminatory and prejudicial decisions or statements about individuals or groups because of one's beliefs about their gender.

simultaneous synthesis An ABILITY to hold two or more items in mind at once while attempting to find a relationship between them. See also INFORMATION INTEGRATION theory.

social motivation Where learning or performance takes place because of the influence of one or more other people, as in MODELLING, or conforming to a group.

social learning The theory that much (particularly MORAL) behaviour is learned in particular situations, rather than being innate, or developmental, in nature.

sociocentrism Piaget's middle stage of moral development, during which judgments of 'right' and 'wrong' are dictated by social norms.

socioeconomic status A term referring to the relative power or prestige of different groups of people in society.

SOLO taxonomy A classification system that may be used both for setting curriculum objectives, and for evaluating the quality of learning outcomes. There are three levels of complexity within the TARGET MODE (UNISTRUCTURAL, MULTISTRUCTURAL and RELATIONAL); PRESTRUCTURAL outcomes are inadequate, falling within a mode of a lower level of abstraction than the target; EXTENDED ABSTRACT outcomes fall within the next higher mode.

spatial Refers to information pertaining to the arrangement of objects in space, for example, a map. Spatial coding would refer to the storage of information in visual terms, for example, an image. Spatial processing is believed to occur mainly in the right hemisphere of the brain.

standard English The formal version of English used in official and public communications; standard English is minimally EMBEDDED, and makes no assumptions about non-verbal support (gestures, etc.).

standardised tests Tests that have been previously trialled and revised, and which yield reliable (usually NORM-REFERENCED) information. The conditions of testing and scoring must be carefully adhered to.

strategy A way of tackling a type of problem, or learning material, that may be applied to a whole class of learnings, not just to the particular problem in question. Strategies, unlike TACTICS, involve forethought and METACOGNITION.

streaming Placing students of similar ability in one class for learning purposes (also called 'grading', 'ability grouping'). Streaming can be a basis for one, several, or all subjects in the curriculum.

stress Heavy psychological or physical pressure that results in strong increases in AROUSAL. Mild stress may improve performance, but heavy stress usually impairs performance (see YERKES–DODSON LAW).

structure (of individuals) See COGNITIVE STRUCTURE.

structure (of instructional settings) There are three aspects of structure: *instructional*, which minimises the learner's decisions about his or her learning; *motivational*, which involves EXTRINSIC (positive and negative) REINFORCERS, SOCIAL MOTIVATION, and ACHIEVEMENT MOTIVATION; and *situational*, the provision of space and facilities for instruction.

structure (of subject matter) The fundamental ideas and relationships that make up a discipline.

structure-data (S–D) ratio See LEARNING OUTCOMES.

successive synthesis An ABILITY to hold information in WORKING MEMORY when there is no relationship between items apart from their sequence. See also INFORMATION INTEGRATION theory.

summative evaluation Evaluation conducted after a task or learning episode has been completed in order to see how well it has been done; grading a task. Summative evaluation may be NORM-REFERENCED or CRITERION-REFERENCED.

super-items A form of CRITERION-REFERENCED OBJECTIVE test that extends the student's ability to answer until a cutoff is reached for each item. Super-items show that objective tests can test for quality as well as quantity.

surface Instrumental when applied to motive; reproductive to STRATEGY. Surface APPROACH leads to low structure OUTCOMES.

tactic An algorithm or set procedure for producing an answer. Requires little planning or monitoring; contrasts with STRATEGY.

target behaviour The particular behaviour(s) in a behaviour modification program that are to be the subject of modification. They must be specified exactly, and measures of their emission rate taken.

target mode The level of abstraction chosen for presenting a task or a curriculum objective. The quality of learning within the selected mode may be evaluated by the SOLO TAXONOMY. Target modes are selected from SENSORI-MOTOR, IKONIC, CONCRETE-SYMBOLIC, FORMAL–1 and FORMAL–2 levels of abstraction.

tautology A statement that rephrases what is known and thus conveys no further information; for example, 'I couldn't sleep because I had insomnia'.

teacher anxiety A form of state ANXIETY experienced by classroom teachers. In beginner teachers, a common focus of teacher anxiety is discipline.

temporal Refers to the relationships between events in time. Temporal coding is using chronological order as a basis for storing and remembering information: for example, historical events.

test A task presented to the learner to assess performance; an important component in ASSESSMENT and EVALUATION.

test anxiety   A form of state ANXIETY that is focused on the TEST situation, and specifically on the individual's fear that he or she will fail. Test anxiety usually impairs performance.

test distortion   Occurs when a particular test format, for example, ESSAY or OBJECTIVE, consistently inflates or depresses a person's performance because of some PERSONALITY characteristic, for example, MULTIPLE-CHOICE tests favour CONVERGENT thinkers over DIVERGENT thinkers when their content knowledge is identical.

theory   An integrated statement of what is known about a particular area of study or practice. Argyris distinguishes between espoused theory, as the 'official' statement to which lip-service is paid, and theory in-use, as the often unrecognised statement that is implicit in a person's actions. Professionalised theory consists in integrating the two, so that the theory actually used is the espoused one.

Theory X   A set of assumptions about humanity which asserts that individuals cannot be trusted to work or to learn unless it is made worth their while — usually by coercion. Contrasts to THEORY Y.

Theory Y   A set of assumptions about humanity which asserts that individuals work and learn at their best when they are trusted, are not under surveillance, and can feel 'ownership' in their product.

time-out   A procedure used in some behaviour modification programs whereby a student is removed from the room as a consequence of inappropriate behaviour. Time-out is meant to relate more to EXTINCTION than to PUNISHMENT.

token economy   A behaviour modification program in which the reinforcers (see also REINFORCEMENT) are tokens (tallies or buttons) that may later be exchanged for material goods, privileges, etc.

traditional schools   Schools which appear to have a strong COGNITIVE emphasis, but the practices of which carry a strong IMPLICIT CURRICULUM. For example, motivation is usually controlled by devices that emphasise reward, competition and punishment, and which tend to preclude intrinsic motivation. The basics of traditional schooling have changed little in the last 100 years.

transductive process   A primitive form of reasoning which precedes DEDUCTIVE and INDUCTIVE processes, in which a conclusion is drawn (usually incorrectly) on the basis of preference or coincidence, rather than of logic or fact.

unistructural   The lowest point in the LEARNING CYCLE; one relevant datum is learned. See also SOLO TAXONOMY.

validity   The extent to which a test measures what it is designed to measure.

value   A belief in the worth of a class of activities, people or objects, and deriving from the AFFECTIVE rather than the COGNITIVE DOMAIN. A value judgment is a judgment about a particular person's behaviour, an object or an event that reflects one's own value system rather than the properties of the item judged.

values clarification   Classroom experiences which encourage students to discover their own values, reflect on them and compare them to others, while avoiding teaching specific values to students.

variability (of teaching)   Switching from one pattern of interaction teaching medium, style and content to another in order to maintain student interest.

variability (of test scores)   The extent to which a set of test scores vary from the MEAN of the group; usually expressed as standard deviations (SD) or variance (SD^2).

working memory   The short-term memory system in which conscious thought takes place; roughly equivalent to 'span of attention'.

Yerkes–Dodson Law   A law of motivation formulated early this century stating that under increasing motivation (AROUSAL), performance in complex tasks will be impaired before that in simple tasks. In the latter, performance may show improvement before impairment.

REFERENCES

Airasian P. and Madaus G. (1972), 'Criterion-referenced Testing in the Classroom', *Measurement in Education*, special reports of the National Council on Measurement in Education 3, No. 4, East Lansing, Mich.

Allen V. L. (1976), 'The Helping Relationship and Socialisation of Children: Some Perspectives on Tutoring', in V. Allen (ed.), *Children as Teachers*, Academic Press, New York.

Anderson C. C. and Cropley A. J. (1966), 'Some Correlates of Originality', *Australian Journal of Psychology*, **18**, pp. 218–27.

Anderson R. C. (1972), 'How to Construct Achievement Tests to Assess Comprehension', *Review of Educational Research*, **42**(2), pp. 145–70.

_____ and Anderson R. M. (1963), 'Transfer of Originality Training', *Journal of Educational Psychology*, **54**, pp. 300–4.

Andrews A. S. (1968), 'Multiple Choice and Essay Tests', *Improving College and University Teaching*, **16**, pp. 61–6.

Angus M. J. (1979), *The Australian Open Area Schools Project*, Western Australian Education Department, Perth.

_____ (1981), 'Children's Conceptions of the Living World', *Australian Science Teachers Journal*, **29**(3), pp. 65–8.

Applebee A. N. (1984), 'Writing and Reasoning', *Review of Educational Research*, **54**, pp. 577–96.

Ardrey R. (1976), *The Hunting Hypothesis*, Atheneum Press, New York.

Argyris C. (1976), 'Theories of Action that Inhibit Individual Learning', *American Psychologist*, **31**, pp. 638–54.

Aronson E. (1980), *The Social Animal*, W.H. Freeman, San Francisco, Calif.

_____ (1984), *The Social Animal* (4th ed.), W.H. Freeman, San Francisco, Calif.

Asch S. (1956), 'Studies of Independence and Conformity: A Minority of One Against a Unanimous Majority', *Psychological Monographs*, **70** (9 and whole 416).

Ashman A. F. (September 1985), *Group and Individual Differences following Process Training*, paper presented at the meeting of the Australian Group for the Scientific Study of Mental Deficiency, Brisbane.

_____ and Das J. (1980), 'Relations between Planning and Simultaneous and Successive Processing', *Perceptual and Motor Skills*, **51**, pp. 371–82.

Ashton–Warner S. (1980), *Teacher*, Virago Press, London.

Atkinson J. W. (1964), *An Introduction to Motivation*, Van Nostrand, New York.

_____ (1966), 'Mainsprings of Achievement-oriented Activity', in J. D. Krumboltz (ed.), *Learning and the Educational Process*, Rand McNally, Chicago, Ill.

Atkinson R. C. and Shiffrin R. M. (1968), 'Human Memory: A Proposed System and Its Control Processes', in J. Spence and K. Spence (eds), *The Psychology of Learning and Motivation*, **2**, Academic Press, New York.

Australian Broadcasting Corporation (first broadcast May 1981), *Taim Bilong Masta*, Episode: 'Masta Me Laik Work'.

Australian Department of Education (1975), *Inquiry into Schools of High Migrant Density*, a study done in 1974 based on selected schools in New South Wales and Victoria, Canberra.

Ausubel D. P. (1968), *Educational Psychology: A Cognitive View*, Holt, Rinehart & Winston, New York.

_____ (1978), 'Defence of Advance Organisers', *Review of Educational Research*, **48**, pp. 251–7.

Axelrod S. (1977), *Behaviour Modification for the Classroom Teacher*, McGraw–Hill, New York.

_____ (September 1979), 'Comparison of Two Common Classroom Seating Arrangements', *Academic Therapy*.

Baddeley A. D. (1976), *The Psychology of Memory*, Basic Books, New York.

Baer D. M. (October 1971), 'Let's Take Another Look at Punishment', *Psychology Today*, **5**, p. 32.

Bailey C. (1979), 'Morality, Reason and Feeling', *Journal of Moral Education*, **9**, pp. 114–21.

Baird J. R. (in press), 'Improving Learning through Enhanced Metacognition: A Classroom Study', *European Journal of Science Education*, **8**.

_____ and White R. T. (1984), 'Improving Learning through Enhanced Metacognition:

A Classroom Study', paper read to American Educational Research Association Annual Conference, New Orleans.

Bandura A. (1969), *Principles of Behaviour Modification*, Holt, Rinehart & Winston, New York.

——(1977), 'Self-efficacy: Toward a Unifying Theory of Behavioural Change', *Psychological Review*, **84**, pp. 191–215.

Barcan A. R. (1977), 'The Decline in Teaching', in A. D. Spaull (ed.), *Australian Teachers*, Macmillan, Melbourne.

Barclay J. R. (1978), 'Temperament Cluster and Individual Differences in the Elementary Classroom: A Summary', paper read to American Educational Research Association Annual Conference, Toronto.

Barker R., Dembo T. and Lewin K. (1941), 'Frustration and Regression: An Experiment with Young Children', *University of Iowa Studies in Child Welfare*, **18**, pp. 1–314.

Barker–Lunn J. B. (1970), *Streaming in the Primary School*, National Foundation for Educational Research, London.

Barrish H. H., Saunders M. and Wolf M. M. (1969), 'Good Behaviour Games: Effects of Individual Contingencies for Group Consequences on Disruptive Behaviour in a Classroom', *Journal of Applied Behaviour Analysis*, **2**, pp. 119–24.

Bar–Tal D. (1978), 'Attributional Analysis of Achievement-related Behaviour', *Review of Educational Research*, **48**, pp. 259–71.

Bartlett F. C. (1982), *Remembering*, Cambridge University Press, London.

——(1958), *Thinking*, Allen & Unwin, Reading, Mass.

Bassett G. W., Cullen P. and Logan L. (1984), *Australian Primary Schools and their Principals*, Harcourt Brace Jovanovich, Sydney.

Bates J. A. (1979), 'Extrinsic Reward and Intrinsic Motivation: A Review with Implications for the Classroom', *Review of Educational Research*, **49**, pp. 557–76.

Bates R. and Kynaston E. (1983), 'Thinking Aloud: Interviews with Australian Educators', Deakin University Press, Geelong, Vic.

Becker W. C., Madsen C. H., Arnold C. and Thomas D. R. (1971), 'The Contingent Use of Teacher Attention and Praise in Reducing Classroom Behaviour Problems', in W. C. Morse and G. M. Wingo (eds), *Classroom Psychology*, Scott, Foresman, Glenview, Ill.

Beez W. V. (1970), 'Influence of Biased Psychological Reports on Teacher Behaviour and Pupil Performance', in M. Miles and W. W. Charters (eds), *Learning in Social Settings*, Allyn & Bacon, Boston, Mass.

Bennett N. (1976), *Teaching Styles and Pupil Progress*, Open Books, London.

Benware C. A. and Deci F. C. (1984), 'Quality of Learning with an Active Versus Passive Motivational Set', *American Educational Research Journal*, **21**, p. 755–65.

Bereiter C. (1980), 'Development in Writing', in L. Gregg and E. Steinberg (eds), *Cognitive Processes in Writing*, Lawrence Erlbaum, Hillsdale, NJ.

—— and Engelmann S. (1966), *Teaching Disadvantaged Children in the Pre-school*, Prentice-Hall, Englewood Cliffs, NJ.

Berliner D. (Autumn 1980), 'Using Research on Teaching for the Improvement of Classroom Practice', *Theory into Practice*, **19** (4).

—— (1984), *Research and Teacher Effectiveness*, ERIC Microfishe, ED249584.

Berlyne D. E. (1966), 'Curiosity and Education', in J. Krumboltz (ed.), *Learning and the Educational Process*, Rand McNally, Chicago, Ill.

Bernard J. and Delbridge A. (1980), *Introduction to Linguistics: An Australian Perspective*, Prentice-Hall of Australia, Sydney.

Berne E. (1964), *Games People Play*, Grove, New York.

Bernstein B. (1961), 'Social Structure, Language and Learning', *Educational Research*, **3**, pp. 163–76.

—— (1965), 'A Sociolinguistic Approach to Social Learning', in J. Gould (ed.), *Penguin Survey of Social Sciences*, Penguin, Harmondsworth, Middlesex.

—— (1970), 'A Sociolinguistic Approach to Socialisation with Some Reference to Educability', in F. Williams (ed.), *Language and Poverty: Perspectives on a Theme*, Markham, Chicago, Ill.

Bessant B. and Spaull A. (1976), *Politics of Schooling*, Pitman Pacific, Carlton, Vic.

Beswick D., Hayden M. and Schofield H. (1983), 'Evaluation of the Tertiary Assistance Scheme', Australian Government Publishing Service (AGPS), Canberra.

Beveridge M. (1985), 'The Development of Young Children — Understanding of the

Process of Evaporation', *British Journal of Educational Psychology*, **55**, pp. 84–90.

Biggs J. B. (1959), 'The Teaching of Mathematics Part I. The Development of Number Concepts in Children', *National Foundation for Educational Research*, **1**, pp. 17–34.

―――― (1962), *Anxiety, Motivation and Primary School Mathematics*, National Foundation for Educational Research, Occasional Publication, No. 7, London.

―――― (1966), *Mathematics and the Conditions of Learning*, National Foundation for Educational Research, London.

―――― (1968), *Information and Human Learning*, Cassell Australia, Melbourne.

―――― (1970), 'Personality Correlates of Some Dimensions of Study Behaviour', *Australian Journal of Psychology*, **22**, pp. 287–97.

―――― (1973a), 'Content to Process', *Australian Journal of Education*, **17**, pp. 225–38.

―――― (1973b), 'Study Behaviour and Performance in Objective and Essay Formats', *Australian Journal of Education*, **17**, pp. 157–67.

―――― (1976), 'Schooling and Moral Development', in P. Williams and V. Varma (eds), *Piaget, Psychology and Education*, Hodder & Stoughton, London.

―――― (August 1979a), 'Making Community Involvement Work', *Parent and Citizen*, **30**(7), pp. 4–5.

―――― (1979b), 'Individual Differences in Study Processes and the Quality of Learning Outcomes', *Higher Education*, **8**, pp. 381–94.

―――― (1985), 'The Role of Metalearning in Study Processes', *British Journal of Educational Psychology*, **55**, pp. 185–212.

―――― (1986a), *Student Approaches to Learning and Studying*, J. B. Acer, Hawthorn, Vic.

―――― (1986b), *The Study Process Questionnaire (SPQ) Users' Manual*, J. B. Acer, Hawthorn, Vic.

―――― (1986c), *The Learning Process Questionnaire (LPQ): Users' Manual*, J. B. Acer, Hawthorn, Vic.

―――― (in press), 'Approaches to Learning and to Essay Writing', in R. R. Schmeck (ed.), *Learning Styles and Learning Strategies*, Plenum Press, New York.

―――― and Braun P. H. (1972), 'Models of Evaluation and Student Characteristics', *Journal of Educational Measurement*, **9**, pp. 303–9.

―――― and Collis K. F. (1982a), *Evaluating the Quality of Learning: The SOLO Taxonomy*, Academic Press, New York.

―――― and Collis K. F. (1982b), 'The Psychological Structure of Creative Writing', *Australian Journal of Education*, **26**(1), pp. 59–70.

―――― Fitzgerald D. and Atkinson S. M. (1971), 'Convergent and Divergent Abilities in Children and Teachers' Ratings of Competence and Certain Classroom Behaviours', *British Journal of Educational Psychology*, **41**, pp. 277–86.

―――― and Rihn B. (1984), 'The Effects of Intervention on Deep and Surface Approaches to Learning', in J. Kirby (ed.), *Cognitive Strategies and Educational Performance*, Academic Press, New York.

Binet A. and Simon T. (1908), 'Le Développement de l'Intelligence Chez les Enfants', *Année Psychologique*, **14**, pp. 1–94.

Blasi A. (1980), 'Bridging Word Cognition and Moral Action: A Critical Review of the Literature', *Psychological Bulletin*, **88**, pp. 1–45.

Block J. H. (1971), *Mastery Learning*, Holt, Rinehart & Winston, New York.

Bloom B. S. (ed.), Engelhart M. D., Furst E. J., Hill W. H. and Krathwohl D. R. (1956), *Taxonomy of Educational Objectives I: Cognitive Domain*, McKay, New York.

―――― Hastings J. T. and Madaus G. F. (1971), *Handbook of Formative and Summative Education of Student Learning*, McGraw–Hill, New York.

―――― Krathwohl D. and Masia P. (1960), *Taxonomy of Educational Objectives II: Affective Domain*, McKay, New York.

Bond G. L. and Dykstra R. (1967), 'The Co-operative Research Program in First Grade Reading Instruction', *Reading Research Quarterly*, **2**(4), pp. 5–142.

Borg W. R. (1964), *An Evaluation of Ability Grouping*, Co-operative Research Project No. 577, Utah State University.

Borke H. (1978), 'Piaget's View of Social Interaction and the Theoretical Construct of Empathy', in L. S. Siegel and C. J. Brainerd (eds), *Alternatives to Piaget*, Academic Press, New York.

Boud D. (1985a), *Problem-based Learning in Education for the Professions*, Higher Education Research and Development Society of Australasia, Sydney.

_____ (1985b), *Studies in Self-assessment*, Tertiary Education Research Centre, UNSW, Occasional Publication, No. 26, Kensington.

Bourke S. F. and Keeves J. P. (1977), *Australian Studies in School Performance, Vol. III — The Mastery of Literacy and Numeracy: Final Report*, Educational Research and Development Committee, Report No. 3, AGPS, Canberra.

_____ and Lewis R. (1976), *Australian Studies in School Performance, Vol. II — Literacy and Numeracy in Australian Schools: Interim Report*, AGPS, Canberra.

Bower G. H. (1970), 'Analysis of a Mnemonic Device', *American Scientist*, **58**, pp. 496–510.

Brady L. (1979), *Feel, Value, Act: Learning About Values, Theory and Practice*, Prentice-Hall of Australia, Sydney.

Braggett E. J. (1983), IQ 130+: A Study of Individual and Family Backgrounds, *Education Research and Perspectives*, **10**, pp. 172–84.

_____ (1984), 'A Differentiated Curriculum Model for the Education of Gifted and Talented Children', *Curriculum Perspectives*, **4**(2), pp. 31–40.

_____ (1985), *Education of Gifted and Talented Children: Australian Provision*, Commonwealth Schools Commission, Canberra.

Brainerd C. J. (1975), 'Structures-of-the-whole and Elementary Education', *American Educational Research Journal*, **12**, pp. 369–78.

Bransford J. D. and Stein B. S. (1984), *The Ideal Problem Solver*, W. H. Freeman, New York.

Bringuier J. C. (1980), *Conversations with Jean Piaget*, quoted in *Psychology Today*, July 1980, p. 41, University of Chicago Press, Chicago, Ill.

Britton J., Burgess T., Martin N., McLeod A. and Rosen H. (1975), *The Development of Writing Abilities*, pp. 11–18, Macmillan Educational, London.

Brophy J. E. (March 1983), 'Classroom Organisation and Management', *The Elementary School Journal*, **83**(4), pp. 265–85.

Brown A., Bransford S., Ferrara R. and Campione J. (1983), 'Learning, Remembering and Understanding', in P. H. Musson (ed.), *Handbook of Child Psychology (4th ed.), Vol. III, Cognitive Development*, Wiley, New York.

Brown P. (1971), *An Exploratory Study of Teacher–Pupil Verbal Interaction in Primary Reading Groups*, unpublished Ph.D. thesis, University of Alberta, Alberta.

Bruner J. S. (1960), *The Process of Education*, Harvard University Press, Cambridge, Mass.

_____ (1964), 'Some Theorems on Instruction Illustrated with Reference to Mathematics', in E. R. Hilgard (ed.), *Theories of Learning and Instruction*, 63rd Yearbook of the National Society for the Study of Education, University of Chicago Press, Chicago, Ill.

_____ (1966), *Towards a Psychology of Instruction*, University Press, Cambridge, Mass.

_____ (1985), 'Narrative and Paradigmatic Modes of Thought', in E. Eisner (ed.), *Learning and Teaching the Ways of Knowing*, 86th Yearbook of the National Society for the Study of Education, Part II, University of Chicago Press, Chicago, Ill.

Budby J. (December 1982), 'A Blueprint for the Future — Integrating Aboriginal Studies into the Curricula', *Education News*, **18**(2), pp. 42–3.

Bugelski B. R. (1958), *The Psychology of Learning*, Henry Holt, New York.

Buggie J. (18 November 1975), reported in *The Australian*.

Burt C. (1966), 'The Genetic Determination of Differences in Intelligence: A Study of Monozygotic Twins Reared Together and Apart', *British Journal of Psychology*, **57**, pp. 137–53.

Burtis P. J., Bereiter C., Scardamalia M. and Tetroe J. (1984), 'The Development of Planning in Writing', in B. Kroll and C. G. Wells (eds), *Exploration of Children's Development in Writing*, Wiley, Chichester.

Butts R. F. (1955), *Assumptions Underlying Australian Education*, Australian Council for Educational Research, Melbourne.

Calder, B. J. and Staw B. M. (1975), 'Self-perception and Intrinsic and Extrinsic Motivation', *Journal of Personality and Social Psychology*, **31**, pp. 599–605.

Callan V. J. (1986), *Australian Minority Groups*, Harcourt Brace Jovanovich, Sydney.

Campbell W. J. (1975), *Being a Teacher in Australian State Government Schools*, Australian Advisory Committee on Research and Developmental Education, Report No. 5, AGPS, Canberra.

_____ (21 April 1980), 'What Australian Society Expects of its Schools, Teachers and Teaching', *Education*, pp. 156–7.

_____ and Campbell E. M. (1978), *School-based Assessments: Aspirations and Achievements of the Radford Scheme in Queensland*, Educational

Research and Development Committee, Report No. 7A, AGPS, Canberra.

_____ and Robinson N. M. (1979), *What Australian Society Expects of its Schools, Teachers and Teaching*, Department of Education, University of Queensland.

Canter L. and Canter M. (1979), *Assertive Discipline*, Canter and Associates, Los Angeles.

Carmi G. (1981), 'The Role of Context in Cognitive Development', *The Quarterly Newsletter of the Laboratory of Comparative Human Cognition*, **3**(3), pp. 46–54.

Carpenter P. (March 1985), 'Does the School Make a Difference?', *Education News*, **19**(2), pp. 12–15.

_____ and Western J. S. (1984), 'Origins, Aspirations and Early Career Attainments', report to the Department of Education and Youth Affairs, Canberra.

Case R. (1985), *Cognitive Development*, Academic Press, New York.

Cattell R. B. (1971), *Abilities: Their Structure, Growth and Action*, Houghton Mifflin, Boston, Mass.

Chapman J. D. (1984), 'The Selection and Appointment of Australian School Principals', Commonwealth Schools Commission, Canberra.

Charles C. M. (1985), *Building Classroom Discipline: From Models to Practice*, Longman, New York.

Chi M. (1978), 'Knowledge Structures and Memory Development', in R. Siegler (ed.), *Children's Thinking: What Develops?*, Lawrence Erlbaum, Hillsdale, NJ.

Chipman L. (October 1980), 'The Menace of Multicuralism', *Quadrant*, pp. 3–6.

Chipman S., Segal J. and Glaser R. (eds) (1984), *Thinking and Learning Skills*, Current Research and Open Questions, Lawrence Erlbaum, Hillsdale, NJ.

Chomsky N. (1957), *Syntactic Structures*, Mouton, The Hague, Netherlands.

Clarke R. M. and Newble D. (in press), 'Students' Approaches to Learning in an Innovative Medical School: A Cross-sectional Study', *British Journal of Educational Psychology*.

Clements D. H. and Gullo D. F. (1984), 'Effects of Computer Programming on Young Children's Cognition', *Journal of Educational Psychology*, **76**, pp. 1051–88.

Clendening C. P. and Davies R. A. (1980),

Creating Programs for the Gifted: A Guide for Teachers, Librarians and Students, Bowker, New York.

Clough E. and Driver R. (1984), 'A Study of Consistency of Students' Conceptual Frameworks across Different Task Contexts', unpublished paper, Centre for Studies in Science and Mathematics Education, University of Leeds.

_____ and Driver R. (1985a), 'Secondary Students' Conceptions of the Conduction of Heat: Bringing Together Scientific and Personal Views', *Physics Education*, **20**, pp. 176–82.

_____ and Driver R. (1985b), 'What do Children Understand About Pressure in Fluids?', *Research in Science and Technology Education*, **3**(3), pp. 210–20.

Cloward R. D. (1976), 'Teenagers as Tutors of Academically Low-achieving Children', in V. L. Allen (ed.), *Children as Teachers*, Academic Press, New York.

Coates T. J. and Thoreson C. E. (1976), 'Teacher Anxiety: A Review with Recommendations', *Review of Educational Research*, **46**, pp. 159–84.

Coleman J. (1966), *Equality of Educational Opportunity*, United States Government Printing Office, Wash., DC.

Collier K. G. (1983), *The Management of Peer-group learning: Syndicate Methods in Higher Education*, Society for Research in Higher Education, Guildford.

_____ (1985), 'Teaching Methods in Higher Education: The Changing Scene, with Special Reference to Small-group Work', *Higher Education Research and Development*, **4**(1), pp. 3–26.

Collis K. F. (1975), *A Study of Concrete and Formal Operations in School Mathematics: A Piagetian Viewpoint*, Australian Council for Educational Research, Melbourne.

_____ and Biggs J. (1983), 'Matriculation, Degree Requirements, and Cognitive Demands in University and CAEs', *Australian Journal of Education*, **27**, pp. 41–51.

_____ and Biggs J. (1986), 'Using the SOLO Taxonomy', SET, **1**(1), Item 3A.

_____ and Davey H. (1984), 'The Development of a Set of SOLO Items for High School Science', State Education Department, Hobart.

Connell R. W. (1985), *Teachers' Work*, George Allen & Unwin, Sydney.

Connors L. (1978), 'School-based Decision Making', *Education News*, **16**(7), p. 4.

Condry J. (1977), 'Enemies of Exploration: Self-initiated Versus Other-initiated Learning', *Journal of Personality and Social Psychology*, **35**, pp. 459–77.

Conway R. (1975), 'On Mutual Liberation: The Need for a Liberated Female and a Liberated Male', *Education News*, **15**(4), pp. 22–9.

Cooper C. R. and Odell L. (eds) (1978), *Research on Composing: Points of Departure*, National Council of Teachers of English, Urbana, Ill.

Cox D., Chiu E., Dileo P., MacKenzie A. and Taylor J. (eds) (1978), *An Uneasy Transition — Migrant Children in Australia*, 9th International Congress of International Association of Child Psychiatry and Allied Professions, Melbourne.

Craik F. I. M. and Lockhart R. S. (1972), 'Levels of Processing: A Framework for Memory Research', *Journal of Verbal Learning and Verbal Behaviour*, **11**, pp. 671–84.

—— and Tulving E. (1975), 'Depth of Processing and the Retention of Words in Episodic Memory', *Journal of Experimental Psychology*, **104**, pp. 268–94.

Cramer J. C. (1936), *Australian Schools Through American Eyes*, Melbourne University Press, Melbourne.

Creed K. (ed.) (1984), *Free to Be*, Talented and Gifted Children Curriculum Committee, Camberwell.

Cronbach L. J. and Snow R. E. (1977), *Aptitudes and Instructional Methods*, Irvington (Wiley), New York.

Cropley A. J. (1966), 'Creativity and Intelligence', *British Journal of Educational Psychology*, **36**, pp. 259–66.

—— (1967), *Creativity*, Longmans Green, London.

—— (1976), 'Some Psychological Reflections on Lifelong Education', in R. Davel (ed.), *Foundations of Lifelong Education*, Pergamon Press, Oxford.

—— and Field T. W. (1968), 'Intellectual Style and High School Science', *Nature*, **217**, pp. 1211–12.

Cruickshank D. R. (September 1985a), 'Teacher Clarity', *International Journal for Teacher Education*.

—— (1985b), *Reflective Teaching: The Preparation of Students of Teaching*, the Ohio State University, Columbus.

—— (February 1986), 'A Synopsis of School Effectiveness Research', *Illinois School Research and Development*.

—— Holton J., Fay D., Williams J., Kennedy J., Myers B. and Hough J. B. (1981), *Reflective Teaching*, Phi Delta Kappan, Bloomington, Ind.

—— Kennedy J., Williams J., Holton J. and Fay D. (1981), 'Evaluation of Reflective Teaching Outcomes', *Journal of Educational Research*, **75**(1), pp. 26–32.

Cummins J. (1979), 'Linguistic Interdependence and the Educational Development of Bilingual Children', *Review of Educational Research*, **49**, pp. 222–51.

Cureton E. E. (1965), 'Reliability and Validity: Basic Assumptions and Experimental Designs', *Educational and Psychological Measurement*, **25**, pp. 327–46.

Das J. P., Kirby J. and Jarman R. F. (1979), *Simultaneous and Successive Cognitive Processes*, Academic Press, New York.

Davey C. P. (1973), 'Exertion Arousal, Personality and Mental Performance', unpublished Ph.D. dissertation, University of Alberta, Alberta.

Davies B. (1982), *Life in the Classroom and Playground: The Accounts of Primary School Children*, Routledge & Kegan Paul, Henley.

—— (1983), 'The Role Pupils Play in the Social Construction of Classroom Order', *British Journal of Sociology of Education*, **4**, pp. 55–69.

—— (1984a), 'Children Through their Own Eyes', *Oxford Review of Education*, **10**, pp. 225–92.

—— (1984b), 'Friends and Pupils', in M. Hammersley and P. Woods (eds), *Life in Schools*, Open University Press, Milton Keynes, p. 256.

Davis S. (1980), *Aboriginal Science: Language, Learning and World View*, paper presented to the Teacher–Linguist Conference, Northern Territory Department of Education.

de Charms R. (1968), *Personal Causation: The Internal Affective Determinants of Behaviour*, Academic Press, New York.

—— (1972), 'Personal Causation Training in the Schools', *Journal of Applied Psychology*, **2**, pp. 95–113.

Deci E. L. (1971), 'Effects of Externally Mediated Rewards on Intrinsic Motivation', *Journal of Personality and Social Psychology*, **18**, pp. 105–15.

—— (August 1972), 'Work — Who Does Not Like It and Why?', *Psychology Today*, p. 57ff.

—— (1975), *Intrinsic Motivation*, Plenum, New York.

de Lacey P. (1974), *So Many Lessons to Learn — Failure in Australian Education*, Penguin, Ringwood, Vic.

—— and Poole M. E. (eds) (1979), *Mosaic or Melting Pot: Cultural Evolution in Australia*, Harcourt Brace Jovanovich, Sydney.

de Lemos M. (1975), *Study of the Educational Achievement of Migrant Children*, final report, Australian Council for Educational Research, Melbourne.

Dempster F. N. (1981), 'Memory Span: Sources of Individual and Developmental Differences', *Psychological Bulletin*, **89**, pp. 63–100.

Dettman H. W. (1972), *Discipline in Secondary Schools in Western Australia: Report of the Committee*, Education Department, Perth.

Deutsch J. A. and Deutsch D. (1963), 'Attention: Some Theoretical Considerations', *Psychological Review*, **70**, pp. 80–90.

de Villiers P. A. and de Villiers J. G. (1979), *Early Language*, Harvard University Press, Cambridge, Mass.

Diederich P. B. (1974), *Measuring Growth in English*, National Council of Teachers of English, Urbana, Ill.

Dienes Z. P. (1963), *An Experimental Study of Mathematics Learning*, Hutchinson Educational, London.

Directorate of Special Programs (1985a), *Towards Non-sexist Education — Curriculum Ideas — English*, NSW Department of Education.

—— (1985b), *Towards Non-sexist Education — Curriculum Ideas — Industrial Arts*, NSW Department of Education.

—— (1985c), *Towards Non-sexist Education — Curriculum Ideas — Music*, NSW Department of Education.

—— (1985d), *Towards Non-sexist Education — Curriculum Ideas — Visual Arts*, NSW Department of Education.

Disibio M. (1982), 'Memory for Connected Discourse: A Constructivist View', *Review of Educational Research*, **52**, pp. 149–74.

di Vesta F. J. and Palermo D. (1974), 'Language Development', in J. Carroll (ed.), *Review of Educational Research*, **2**, Peacock, Itasca, Ill.

Doenau S. (undated), 'Have School Standards Declined?', Edvance Publications, Pennant Hills, NSW.

Donaldson M. (1978), *Children's Minds*, Fontana, Glasgow.

Doyle W. and Rutherford B. (Winter 1984), 'Classroom Research on Matching Learning and Teaching Styles', *Theory into Practice*, **23**(1), pp. 20–5.

Dreeben R. (1968), *On What is Learned in School*, Addison–Wesley, Reading, Mass.

Dreikurs R. and Cassel P. (1972), *Discipline Without Tears*, Hawthorn, New York.

—— Grunwald B and Pepper F. C. (1971), *Maintaining Sanity in the Classroom — Illustrated Teaching Technique* (2nd ed.), Harper & Row, New York.

Driver R. (1981), 'Pupils' Alternative Frameworks in Science', *European Journal of Science Education*, **3**, pp. 93–101.

—— (1983), 'The Pupil as Scientist', The Open University Press, Milton Keynes.

—— (1985), 'Cognitive Psychology and Pupils' Frameworks in Mechanics', in P. Lijnse (ed.), *The many Faces of Teaching and Learning Mechanics*, WCC Publications, Utrecht.

—— and Bell B. (December 1985), 'Students' Thinking and the Learning of Science', *School Science Review*.

—— and Easley J. (1978), 'Pupils and Paradigms: A Review of Literature Related to Concept Development and Adolescent Science Studies', *Studies in Science Education*, **5**, pp. 61–84.

—— and Warrington L. (1985), 'Students Use of the Principle of Energy Conservation in Problem Situations', *Physics Education*, **20**, pp. 171–5.

Duhs C. A. (1979), 'MACOS/SEMP Debate in Queensland, 1978: Some Central Issues', *The Australian Journal of Education*, **23**, pp. 270–83.

Duke D. L. and Meckel M. A. (1984), *Teachers' Guide to Classroom Management*, Random House, New York.

Dulay H. C. and Burt M. K. (1974), 'Errors and Strategies in Child Second Language Acquisition', *TESOL Quarterly*, **8**, pp. 129–36.

Dunkin M. J. and Biddle B. J. (1974), *The Study of*

Teaching, Holt, Rinehart & Winston, New York.

Dweck C. S. (1975), 'The Role of Expectations and Attributions in the Alleviation of Learned Helplessness', *Journal of Personality and Social Psychology*, **31**, pp. 674–85.

Easley J. (August 1984), 'A Teacher Educator's Perspective on Students' and Teachers' Schemes', paper presented to Conference on Thinking, Harvard Graduate School of Education, Boston.

Ebbinghaus H. (1913), *Memory*, Teacher College Press, New York.

Education Commission of NSW (1986), *Multicultural Education*, Information Sheet No. 6.

Edwards A. D. (1976), *Language in Culture and Class*, Heinemann, London.

Edwards J. (1986), *The Effects of Metacognitive Training in Study Skills on Students' Approaches to Learning and Examination Performance*, unpublished Masters of Psychology (Educational) thesis, University of Newcastle.

Egan K. (1984), *Educational Development*, Oxford University Press, New York.

Eisner E. W. (1971), 'Instructional and Expressive Educational Objectives', in M. D. Merrill (ed.), *Instructional Design: Readings*, Prentice-Hall, Englewood Cliffs, NJ.

Elashoff J. and Snow R. E. (eds) (1971), *Pygmalion Revisited*, C. A. Jones, Worthington, Ohio.

Elkind D. (1967), 'Egocentrism in Adolescence', *Child Development*, **38**, pp. 1025–34.

—— (1968), 'Adolescent Cognitive Development', in J. F. Adams (ed.), *Understanding Adolescence*, Allyn & Bacon, Boston.

Elliott I. and Margitta I. (1975), *Child Migrant Education Survey: Research Report 5/74*, Curriculum and Research Branch, Education Department, Victoria.

Elliott W. J. (1936), *Secondary Education in NSW*, Melbourne University Press, Melbourne.

Entwistle N. (1984), 'Contrasting Perspectives on Learning', in E. Marton, D. Hounsell and N. Entwistle (eds), *The Experience of Learning*, Scottish Academic press, Edinburgh.

—— and Ramsden P. (1983), *Understanding Student Learning*, Croom Helm, London.

Epstein H. T. (1978), 'Growth Spurts During Brain Development: Implications for Educational Theory and Practice', in J. S. Chall and A. F. Mirsky (eds), *Education and the Brain*, 77th Yearbook of the National Society for the Study of Education, Part II, University of Chicago Press, Chicago, Ill.

Erikson E. (1959), *Identity and the Life Cycle*, International Universities Press, New York.

Evans G., Georgeff M. and Poole M. E. (1980), 'Training in Information Selection for Communication', *The Australian Journal of Education*, **24**(2), pp. 137–54.

Evertson C. M. and Emmer E. T. (1982), 'Preventive Classroom Management', in D. L. Duke, *Helping Teachers Manage Classrooms*, Association for Supervision and Curriculum Development, Alexandria, Va.

Ewanyk D. (1973), 'Disequilibrium as a Source of Inducing Higher Moral Reasoning in Delinquent Boys', unpublished M.Ed. thesis, University of Alberta, Alberta.

Farber J. (1970), *The Student as Nigger*, Pocket Books, New York.

Faw H. W. and Waller T. G. (1976), 'Mathemagenic Behaviours and Efficiency in Learning from Prose Materials: Review, Critique and Recommendations', *Review of Educational Research,* **46**, pp. 691–720.

Feigelson N. (1970), *The Underground Revolution*, Funk & Wagnalls, New York.

Fensham P. (1980), 'A Research Base for New Objectives of Science Teaching, *Research in Science Education*, **10**, pp. 23–33.

Fesl E. (July 1983), 'The Irrelevance of Literacy', *Education News*, **18**(5), pp. 14–15.

Festinger L. (1968), 'The Psychological Effects of Insufficient Rewards', in W. H. Bartz (ed.), *Readings in General Psychology*, Allyn & Bacon, Boston, Mass.

Field T. W. and Poole M. (1970), 'Intellectual Style and Achievement of Arts and Science Undergraduates', *British Journal of Educational Psychology*, **40**, pp. 338–41.

Finn J. D. (1972), 'Expectations and the Educational Environment', *Review of Educational Research*, **42**, pp. 387–410.

Fischer K. and Bullock D. (1984), 'Cognitive Development in School-age Children: Conclusions and new Directions', in W. Collins (ed.), *Development during Middle Childhood: The Years from Six to Twelve*, National Academy of Sciences Press, Wash., DC.

—— and Pipp S. (1984), 'Process of Cognitive Development: Optional Level and Skill

Acquisition', in R. Sternberg (ed.), *Mechanics of Cognitive Development*, W. H. Freeman, New York.

_____ and Silvern L. (1985), 'Stages and Individual Differences in Cognitive Development', *Annual Review of Psychology*, **36**, pp. 613–48.

Fixx J. (1977), *The Complete Book of Running*, Random House, New York.

Flanders N. S. (1967), 'Teachers' Influence in the Classroom', in E. J. Amidon and J. B. Hough (eds), *Interaction Analysis: Theory, Research and Application*, Addison–Wesley, Reading, Mass.

Flavell J. H. (1976), 'Metacognition Aspects of Problem Solving', in L. B. Resnick (ed.), *The Nature of Intelligence*, Lawrence Erlbaum, Hillsdale, NJ.

_____ Botkin P., Fry G., Wright J. and Jarvis P. (1968), *The Development of Role-taking and Communication Skills*, John Wiley, New York.

_____ and Wellman H. (1977), 'Metamemory', in R. V. Kail and J. W. Hagen (eds), *Perspectives on the Development of Memory and Cognition*, Lawrence Erlbaum.

Flower L. (1981), *Problem Solving Strategies for Writing*, Harcourt Brace Jovanovich, New York.

Flynn C. and Savage W. (1980), *Who's Talking in Class*, Curriculum Development Centre, ACT.

Foster V. (ed.) (1981), *The Consultants' Role in Non-sexist Education — A Resource Book*, Central Metropolitan Region, Department of Education, Sydney.

Fransson A. (1977), 'On Qualitative Differences in Learning IV — Effects of Intrinsic Motivation and Extrinsic Test Anxiety on Process and Outcome', *British Journal of Educational Psychology*, **47**, pp. 244–55.

Fraser B. J. (1981), *Learning Environment in Curriculum Evaluation: A Review*, Evaluation in Education Series, Pergamon, London.

Freire P. (1970), *Pedagogy of the Oppressed*, Herder & Herder, New York.

French J. R. P. and Raven B. (1959), 'The Bases of Social Power', in D. Cartwright (ed.), *Studies in Social Power*, Institute for Social Research, Ann Arbor, Mich.

Freud S. (1905), *The Basic Writings of Sigmund Freud*, Random House, New York.

Furth H.G. (1970), *Piaget for Teachers*, Prentice–Hall, Englewood Cliffs, NJ.

Gagné E. D. (1978), 'Long-term Retention of Information Following Learning from Prose', *Review of Educational Research*, **48**, pp. 629–65.

Gagné R. M. (1967), 'Curriculum Research and the Promotion of Learning', in R. Tyler, R. Gagné and M. Criven (eds), *Perspectives of Curriculum Evaluation*, Rand McNally, Chicago, Ill.

_____ and Briggs L. J. (1974), *Principles of Instructional Design*, Holt, Rinehart & Winston, New York.

_____ and White R. (1978), 'Memory Structures and Learning Outcomes', *Review of Educational Research*, **48**, pp. 187–222.

Gantt W. (1981), 'Classroom Observations of Task Attending Behaviours of Good and Poor Readers', *Journal of Educational Research*, **74**, pp. 400–5.

Garbarino J. (1975), 'The Impact of Anticipated Rewards on Cross-age Tutoring', *Journal of Personality and Social Psychology*, **32**, pp. 421–8.

Gardner J. M. (1976), 'Cross-cultural Diffusion of Behaviour Modification', in P. W. Sheehan and K. D. White (eds), *Behaviour Modification in Australia*, Monograph Supplement No. 3, *Australian Psychologist*, p. 11.

Gaudry E. and Bradshaw G. (1970), 'The Differential Effect of Anxiety on Performance in Progressive and Terminal School Examinations', *Australian Journal of Psychology*, **22**, pp. 1–4.

_____ and Spielberger C. (1971), *Anxiety and Educational Achievement*, Wiley, Sydney.

Gerencser S. (1979), 'The Calasanctius Experience', in A. H. Passow (ed.), *The Gifted and The Talented: Their Education and Development*, 78th Yearbook of the National Society for the Study of Education, pp. 127–37, University of Chicago Press, Chicago, Ill.

Getzels J. W. and Jackson P. (1962), *Creativity and Intelligence*, Wiley, New York.

Gibbs G. (1977), 'Can Students be Taught to Study?', *Higher Education Bulletin*, **5**, pp. 107–18.

_____ (1981), 'Teaching Students to Learn: A Student-centred Approach', Milton Keynes, The Open University Press.

Gibbs J. and Schnell S. (1985), 'Moral Development Versus Socialisation', *American Psychologist*, **40**, pp. 1071–80.

Gilbert J., Osborne R. and Fensham P. (1982), 'Children's Science and its Consequences for

Teaching', *Science Education*, **68**, pp. 623–33.

———— and Watts M. (1983), 'Concepts, Misconceptions and Alternative Conceptions: Changing Perspectives in Science Education', *Studies in Science Education*, **10**, pp. 61–98.

———— Watts M. and Osborne R. (1982), 'Students' Conceptions of Ideas in Mechanics', *Physics Education*, **17**, pp. 62–6.

Gilchrist M. (1972), *The Psychology of Creativity*, Melbourne University Press, Melbourne.

Gilligan C. (1982), *In a Different Voice: Psychological Theory and Women's Development*, Harvard University Press, Cambridge, Mass.

Ginott H. (1971), *Teacher and Child*, Macmillan, New York.

Ginsburg H. and Opper S. (1979), *Piaget's Theory of Intellectual Development*, Prentice–Hall, Englewood Cliffs, NJ.

Glaser R. (1984), 'Education and Thinking: The Role of Knowledge', *American Psychologist*, **39**, pp. 93–104.

———— and Nitko A. J. (1971), 'Measurement in Learning and Instruction', in R. L. Thorndike (ed.), *Educational Measurement*, American Council on Education, Wash., DC.

Glasser W. (1969), *Schools Without Failure*, Harper & Row, New York.

———— (November–December 1977), '10 Steps to Good Discipline', *Today's Education*.

Gmelch W. H. (Winter 1983), 'Stress for Success — How to Optimise Your Performance', *Theory into Practice*, **22**(1), pp. 7–14.

Gnagey W. (1975), *The Psychology of Discipline in the Classroom*, Macmillan, New York.

Goleman D. (February 1980), '1,528 Little Geniuses and How They Grew', *Psychology Today*, **13**(9).

Good T. (April 1985), 'Goodbye, Little Red Schoolhouse', *Creative Computing*, pp. 64–76.

Gordon D. (1980), 'The Immorality of the Hidden Curriculum', *Journal of Moral Education*, **10**, pp. 3–8.

———— and Brophy J. (1973), *Looking in Classrooms*, Harper & Row, New York.

———— and Grouws D. (1977), 'Teaching Effects: A Process — Product Study in Fourth-grade Mathematics Classrooms', *Journal of Teacher Education*, **28**, pp. 49–54.

Gordon T. (1974a), *TET — Teacher Effectiveness Training*, Wyden, New York.

———— (1974b), *PET — Parent Effectiveness Training*, Wyden, New York.

Goyen J. D. (1974), 'Incidence of Adult Illiteracy in Sydney Metropolitan Area', *Literacy Discussion*, **7**(3), pp. 63–71.

Graham D. (1972), *Moral Learning and Development*, Angus & Robertson, Sydney.

Grainger A. J. (1970), *The Bullring: A Classroom Experiment in Moral Education*, Pergamon Press, Oxford.

Grassby A. J. (1978), 'It's Time for Migrant Education to Go', in P. R. de Lacey and M. E. Poole (eds), *Mosaic or Melting Pot? Cultural Evolution in Australia*, Harcourt Brace Jovanovich, Sydney.

Graves D. (1983), *Writing: Teachers and Children at Work*, Heinemann Educational, Exeter, New Hampshire.

Green K. and Stager S. (22–24 August 1985), 'Improving Performance Assessment: A Study of Teachers' Coursework in Testing, Attitude, Toward Testing and Use of Classroom Tests', paper presented to Higher Education Research and Development Society of Australasia, Annual Conference, Auckland, New Zealand.

Griffin J. H. (1961), *Black Like Me*, Houghton–Mifflin, Boston, Mass.

Gronert R. R. (1970), 'Combining a Behavioural Approach with Reality Therapy', *Elementary School Evidence and Counselling*, **5**, pp. 104–12.

Gronlund N. E. (1970), *Stating Behavioural Objectives for Classroom Instruction*, Macmillan, New York.

Guilford J. P. (1956), 'The Structure of Intellect', *Psychological Bulletin*, **53**, pp. 267–93.

———— (1967), *The Nature of Human Intelligence*, McGraw–Hill, New York.

Gunstone R., Champagne A. and Klopfer L. (1981), 'Instruction for Understanding: A Case Study', *Australian Science Teachers Journal*, **27**(3), pp. 27–32.

———— and White R. (1981), 'Understanding of Gravity', *Science Education*, **65**, pp. 291–9.

Guthrie E. R. (1977), *Sexism in Education — The Report of the Minister's Committee*, AGPS, Sydney.

Guthrie E. S. (1952), *The Psychology of Learning*, Harper & Row, New York.

Haddon F. A. and Lytton H. (1968), 'Teaching Approach and the Development of Divergent Thinking Abilities in Primary Schools', *British*

Journal of Educational Psychology, **38**, pp. 171–80.

———and Lytton H. (1971), 'Primary Education and Divergent Thinking Abilities — Four Years On', *British Journal of Educational Psychology*, **41**, pp. 136–47.

Hales L. W. and Tokar E. (1975), 'The Effect of Quality of Preceding Responses on the Grades Assigned to Subsequent Responses to an Essay Question', *Journal of Educational Measurement*, **12**, pp. 115–17.

Halford G. S. (1982), *The Development of Thought*, Lawrence Erlbaum, Hillsdale, NJ.

Hall R. V., Panyan M., Rabon D. and Broden M. (1968), 'Instructing Beginning Teachers in Reinforcement Procedures which Improve Classroom Control', *Journal of Applied Behaviour Analysis*, **1**, pp. 315–22.

Halpin A. W. (1966), *Theory and Research in Administration*, Macmillan, New York.

Hambleton R. K. (1972), 'Towards a Theory of Criterion-referenced Tests', paper presented to the National Council on Measurement in Education, Chicago, Ill.

Hamilton R. (1985), 'A Framework for the Evolution of the Effectiveness of Adjunct Questions and Objectives', *Review of Educational Research*, **55**, pp. 47–86.

Hanley E. N. (1970), 'Review of Research Involving Applied Behaviour Analysis in the Classroom', *Review of Educational Research*, **40**, pp. 597–625.

Haring N. G. and Whelan R. F. (1966), 'Modification and Maintenance of Behaviour through Systematic Appliation of Consequences', *Exceptional Children*, **32**, pp. 281–9.

Harlow H. F. (1953), 'Mice, Monkeys, Man and Motives', *Psychological Review*, **60**, pp. 23–32.

Hart N. W. M. (1976), *The Mt. Gravatt Developmental Reading Programme*, Addison–Wesley, Sydney.

Hartley J. and Davies I. K. (1976), 'Preinstructional Strategies: The Role of Pretests, Behavioural Objectives, Overviews and Advance Organisers', *Review of Educational Research*, **46**, pp. 239–65.

Hartshorne H. and May M. (1928), *Studies in the Nature of Character: Vol. 1 Studies in Deceit*, Macmillan, New York.

Harvey O., Hunt D. and Schroder H. (1961), *Conceptual Systems and Personality Organisation*, Wiley, New York.

Hasan P. and Butcher H. (1966), 'Creativity and Intelligence: A Partial Replication with Scottish Children of Getzel's and Jackson's Study', *British Journal of Psychology*, **57**, pp. 129–35.

Hausen E. (1968), 'Linguistics and Language Planning', in W. Bright (ed.), *Sociolinguistics*, Mouton, The Hague.

Hearnshaw L. S. (1979), *Cyril Burt, Psychologist*, Hodder & Stoughton, London.

Hebb D. O. (1946), 'On the Nature of Fear', *Psychological Review*, **53**, pp. 259–76.

———(1949), *The Organisation of Behaviour*, Wiley, New York.

———(1955), 'Drives and the CNS (Conceptual Nervous System)', *Psychological Review*, **67**, pp. 243–54.

Heckhausen H. (1975), 'Fear of Failing as a Self-reinforcing Motive System', in I. G. Sarason and C. Spielberger (eds), *Stress and Anxiety*, Hemisphere, Washington, DC.

Hemming J. (1980), 'Another Prospect in Moral Education', **9**, pp. 75–80.

Henry J. (1963), *Culture Against Man*, Penguin Books, Harmondsworth, Middlesex (first published, Random House, New York, 1963).

Hepworth A. J. (1979), 'Vales Education —Some New South Wales Experiences', *Journal of Moral Education*, **8**, pp. 193–202.

Hess R. D. (1970), 'Social Class and Ethnic Influences upon Socialisation', in P. Mussen (ed.), *Carmichael's Manual of Child Psychology*, Wiley, New York.

Hocking H. (1984), 'Interpreting Disruptive Behaviour by High School Students and its Implications for Curriculum and School Management', paper presented to the Australian Association for Research in Education National Conference, Perth.

Hoffman B. (1962), *The Tyranny of Testing*, Collier, New York.

Hoggart R. (1959), *The Uses of Literacy*, Chatto & Windus.

Holland J. L. (1959), 'Some Limitations of Teacher Ratings as Predictors of Creativity', *Journal of Educational Psychology*, **50**, pp. 219–23.

Holt J. (1970), *How Children Fail*, Dell, New York.

Horn J. L. (1968), 'Organisation of Abilities and the Development of Intelligence', *Psychological Review*, **75**, pp. 242–59.

Horne M. S. (1968), 'Sex Differences in Achievement, Motivation and Performance in Competitive and Non-competitive Situations', unpublished Ph.D. thesis, University of Michigan, Mich.

Horner R. (1984), *The Health Revolution*, Happy Landings Press, Sydney.

Hounsell D. (1984), 'Learning and Essay-writing', in F. Marton, D. Hounsell and N. Entwistle (eds), *The Experience of Learning*, Scottish Universities Press, Edinburgh.

Howe M. J. A. (1970a), 'Repeated Presentation and Recall of Meaningful Prose', *Journal of Educational Psychology*, **61**, pp. 214–9.

—— (1970b), 'Positive Reinforcement: A Humanising Approach to Teacher Control in the Classroom', *The National Elementary Principal*, **49**, pp. 31–4.

—— (1972), *Understanding School Learning: A New Look at Educational Psychology*, Harper & Row, New York.

Huck S. W. and Bound W. G. (1972), 'Essay Grades: An Interaction Between Graders, Handwriting Clarity and the Neatness of Examination Papers', *American Journal of Educational Research*, **9**, pp. 279–83.

Hudson L. (1966), *Contrary Imaginations*, Methuen, London.

—— (1968), *Frames of Mind*, Methuen, London.

Huey E. B. (1968), *The Psychology and Pedagogy of Reading*, MIT Press, Cambridge, Mass.

Hull C. L. (1943), *Principles of Behaviour*, Appleton-Century, New York.

Humphreys M. and Revelle W. (1984), 'Personality, Motivation and Performance: A Theory of the Relationship between Individual Differences and Information Processing', *Psychological Review*, **91**, pp. 153–84.

Hunt D. E. (1971), *Matching Models in Education*, Ontario Institute for Studies in Education, monograph series No. 10, Toronto.

Illich I. (1971), *Deschooling Society*, Harper & Row, New York.

Isaacs E. (1979), 'Social Control and Ethnicity: The Socialisation and Repression of a Greek Child at School', in P. de Lacey and M. Poole (eds), *Mosaic or Melting Pot? Cultural Evolution in Australia*, Harcourt Brace Jovanovich, Sydney.

Izard J. and White J. D. (1982), 'The Use of Latent Trait Models in the Development and Analysis of Classroom Tests', in D. Spearritt (ed.), *The Improvement of Measurement in Education and Psychology*, Australian Council for Educational Research, Hawthorn, Vic.

Jackson B. (1964), *Streaming: An Education System in Miniature*, Routledge & Kegan Paul, London.

Jackson P., Reid N. and Croft A. (1980), 'Study Habits Evaluation and Instruction Kit (SHEIK)', Australian Council for Educational Research, Hawthorn, Vic.

Jackson R. W. B. (1961), *Emergent Needs in Australian Education*, University of Toronto, Toronto.

James W. (1890), *The Principles of Psychology*, Vol. I, Henry Holt, New York.

—— (1962), *Talks to Teachers on Psychology*, Dover, New York (original edition, Henry Holt, New York, 1899).

Jensen A. R. (1969), 'How Much Can We Boost IQ and Scholastic Achievement?', *Harvard Educational Review*, **39**, pp. 1–123.

—— (1970), 'A Theory of Primary and Secondary Familial Mental Retardation', in N. R. Ellis (ed.), *International Review of Research in Mental Retardation*, **4**, Academic Press, New York.

—— (1972), *Genetics and Education*, Methuen, London.

—— (1973), *Educational Differences*, Methuen, London.

Johnson D. W. and Johnson F. P. (1975), *Joining Together — Group Theory and Group Skills*, Prentice–Hall, Englewood Cliffs, NJ.

—— and Johnson R. T. (1975), *Learning Together and Alone: Co-operation, Competition and Individualisation*, Prentice–Hall, Englewood Cliffs, NJ.

—— and Johnson R. (April 1982), 'Co-operation — The Key to Success', *Education News*, **17**(10), pp. 17–19.

Johnson Abercrombie M. (1969), *The Anatomy of Judgment*, Penguin Books, Harmondsworth, Middlesex.

Johnston J. M. (1972), 'Punishment of Human Behaviour', *American Psychologist*, **27**, pp. 1033–54.

Jones R. M. (1968), *Fantasy and Feeling in Education*, New York University Press, New York.

Jung C. G. (1956), *The Integration of the Personality*, Routledge & Kegan Paul, London.

Kagan J. (1965), 'Reflection-impulsivity and Reading Ability in Primary Grade Children',

Child Development, **36**, pp. 609–28.

———— (1966), 'Reflection and Impulsivity: The Generality and Dynamics of Conceptual Tempo', *Journal of Abnormal and Social Psychology*, **71**, pp. 17–24.

Kamin L. J. (1974), *The Science and Politics of IQ*, Lawrence Erlbaum, Potomac, Ill.

Kamler B. and Klarr G. (1984), Chapter in B. Kroll and C. G. Wells (eds), *Exploration of Children's Development in Writing*, Wiley, Chichester.

Kandel I. L. (1960), *Types of Administration: With Particular Reference to the Educational Systems of New Zealand and Australia*, Melbourne University Press, Melbourne.

Karmel P. H. (1973), *Schools in Australia: Report of the Interim Committee for the Australian Schools Commission*, AGPS, Canberra.

Katz M. B. (1968), *The Irony of Early School Reform*, Harvard University Press, Cambridge, Mass.

Kaufman H. (1970), *Aggression and Altruism*, Holt, Rinehart & Winston, New York.

Keavney G. and Sinclair K. E. (1978), 'Teacher Concerns and Teacher Anxiety: A Neglected Topic of Classroom Research', *Review of Educational Reserach*, **48**, pp. 273–90.

Keeves J. P. and Bourke G. F. (1976), *Australian Studies in School Performance, Vol. 1, Literacy and Numeracy in Australian Schools: A First Report*, Educational Research and Development Committee (ERDC), report No. 8, Woden, ACT.

———— Matthews J. K. and Bourke S. F. (1978), *Educating for Literacy and Numeracy in Australian Schools*, Australian Council for Educational Research (Australian Education Review No. 11), Hawthorn, Vic.

Keller F. (1968), 'Goodbye Teacher ...', *Journal of Applied Behaviour Analysis*, **1**, pp. 79–89.

Kelly G. A. (1955), *The Psychology of Personal Constructs*, Norton, New York.

———— (1974), *The Psychology of Personal Constructs*, Norton, New York.

Killen L. (1983), *Applications of the SOLO Taxonomy in Technical and Further Education*, extended essay (unpublished), Master of Educational Studies, Faculty of Education, University of Newcastle.

Kirby J. R. (1980), 'Individual Differences and Cognitive Processes', in J. R. Kirby and J. B. Biggs (eds), *Cognition, Development and Instruc-* *tion*, Adademic Press, New York.

———— (ed.) (1984a), *Cognitive Strategies and Educational Performance*, Academic Press, New York.

———— (1984b), 'Educational Roles of Cognitive Plans and Strategies', in J. R. Kirby (ed.), *Cognitive Strategies and Educational Performance*, Academic Press, New York.

———— (1984c), 'Strategies and Processes', in J. R. Kirby (ed.), *Cognitive Strategies and Educational Performance*, Academic Press, New York.

———— (in press), 'Style, Strategy and Skill in Reading', in R. R. Schmeck (ed.), *Learning Style and Learning Strategies*, Plenum, New York.

———— and Biggs J. (1981), 'Learning Styles, Information Processing Abilities and Academic Achievement', final report, Australian Research Grants Committee, Belconnen, ACT.

———— and Moore P. (in press), 'Metacognitive Knowledge and Reading Ability', *Journal of Psychoeducational Assessment*.

Kirschenbaum H., Napier R. and Simon S. B. (1971), *Wad-ja-get? The Grading Game in American Education*, Hart, New York.

Klich L. and Davidson G. (1984), 'Toward a Recognition of Australian Aboriginal Competence in Cognitive Functions', in J. Kirby (ed.), *Cognitive Strategies and Educational Performance*, Academic Press, New York.

Knowles M. (1978), *The Adult Learner: A Neglected Species*, Gulf, Houston.

Knox A. B. (1977), *Adult Development and Learning*, Jersey Bass, San Francisco.

Koestler A. (1969), 'Abstract and Picture Strip', in G. Talland and N. Waugh (eds), *The Pathology of Memory*, pp. 261–70, Academic Press, New York.

Kogan N. (1971), 'Educational Implications of Cognitive Styles', in G. Lesser (ed.), *Psychology and Educational Practice*, Scott, Foresman, Glenview, Ill.

Kohlberg L. (1969), 'Stage and Sequence: The Cognitive-developmental Approach to Socialisation', in D. Goslin (ed.), *Handbook of Socialisation Theory and Research*, Rand McNally, Chicago.

———— (1970), 'Stages of Moral Development as a Basis for Moral Education', in C. Beck and E. Sullivan (eds), *Moral Education*, University of Toronto, Toronto.

———and Turiel E. (1971), 'Moral Development and Moral Education', in G. S. Lesser (ed.), *Psychology and Educational Practice*, Scott, Foresman, Glenview, Ill.

Kounin J. (1967), *Discipline and Group Management in Classrooms*, Holt, Rinehart & Winston, New York.

——— and Gump P. (1961), 'The Comparative Influence of Punitive and Non-punitive Teachers for Children's Concepts of School Misconduct', *Journal of Educational Psychology*, **52**, pp. 44–9.

Kruglanski A., Riter A., Amitai A., Bath–Shevah M., Shabtai L. and Zaksh D. (1975), 'Can Money Enhance Intrinsic Motivation: A Test of the Content-consequence Hypothesis', *Journal of Personality and Social Psychology*, **31**, pp. 744–50.

Krywaniuk L. (1974), *Patterns of Cognitive Abilities of High and Low Achieving School Children*, unpublished Ph.D. thesis, University of Alberta, Alberta.

Kunzelmann H. P. (ed.) (1970), *Precision Teaching: An Initial Training Sequence*, Special Child Publications, Seattle, Wash., DC.

Kurtines W. and Greif E. (1974), 'The Development of Moral Thought: Review and Evaluation of Kohlberg's Approach', *Psychological Bulletin*, **81**, pp. 453–70.

Kurzeja D. (1986), *An Intervention using Cognitive Modelling and Verbal Mediation for the Induction of a Problem — Solving Heuristic in Primary School Children*, unpublished Master of Education dissertation, School of Education, Murdoch University.

Labov W. (1970), 'The Logic of Non-standard English', in F. Williams (ed.), *Language and Poverty*, Markham, Chicago, Ill.

Lashley K. S. (1960), 'In Search of the Engram' (1950), in F. A. Beach, D. O. Hebb, C. T. Morgan and N. W. Nissen (eds), *The Neuropsychology of Lashley*, McGraw–Hill, New York.

Lawrence J., Dodds A. E. and Volet S. (1983), *An Afternoon Off: A Comparative Study of Adults and Adolescents' Planning Activities*, paper presented to Australian Educational Research Association Annual Conference, Canberra.

Lawson M. (1984), 'On Being Executive about Metacognition', in J. R. Kirby (ed.), *Cognitive Strategies and Educational Performance*, Academic Press, New York.

Le Fevre J. (September 1985), 'Education Fails to Graduate', *Computing Australia*, p. 22.

Lenneberg E. H. (1969), 'On Explaining Language', *Science*, **64**, pp. 635–43.

Lepper M. and Greene D. (1975), 'Turning Play into Work: Effects of Adult Surveillance and Extrinsic Rewards on Children's Intrinsic Motivation', *Journal of Personality and Social Psychology*, **31**, pp 479–86.

——— Greene D. and Nisbett R. I. (1973), 'Undermining Children's Intrinsic Interest with Extrinsic Reward: A Test of the "Overjustification" Hypothesis', *Journal of Personality and Social Psychology*, **28**, pp. 129–37.

Lesser G. S. (1971), 'Matching Instruction to Student Characteristics', in G. S. Lesser (ed.), *Psychology and Educational Practice*, Scott, Foresman, Glenview, Ill.

Lett W. R. (1971), 'Teacher Games and the Problems of Control', in S. d'Urso (ed.), *Counterpoints — Critical Writings on Australian Education*, Wiley, Sydney.

Levinson D., Darrow C., Klein E., Levinson H. and McKee B. (1978), *The Seasons of a Man's Life*, Knopf, New York.

Liebert R. M. and Caron R. A. (1972), 'Some Immediate Effects of Televised Violence on Children's Behaviour', *Developmental Psychology*, **6**, pp. 469–75.

Lippman L. (1977), *The Aim is Understanding — Educational Techniques for a Multicultural Society*, Australian and New Zealand Book Company, Sydney.

Lloyd P. (1970), *Our Wide Wonderful World: Compass Series*, **1A**, p. 49, Thomas Nelson, Australia.

Locke J. (1969), *Some Thoughts Concerning Education*, A. and J. Churchill, London.

Lovell K. (1961), *The Growth of Understanding in Mathematics: Kindergarten Through Grade III*, Holt, Rinehart & Winston, New York.

Lovibond S. H., Mithiran T. and Adams W. G. (1979), 'The Effects of Three Experimental Prison Environments on the Behaviour of Non-convict Volunteer Subjects', *Australian Psychologist*, **14**, pp. 273–87.

Luria A. R. (1966), *Human Brain and Psychological Processes*, Harper & Row, New York.

McClelland D. C., Atkinson J. W., Clark R. W. and Lowell E. L. (1953), *The Achievement Motive*, Appleton–Century–Crofts, New York.

McCutchen D. (1985), *Sources of Developmental Differences in Children's Writing: Knowledge of Topic and Knowledge of Discourse and Linguistic Form*, unpublished Ph.D. dissertation, University of Pittsburgh.

McDiarmid G. and Pratt D. (1971), *Teaching Prejudice*, Ontario Institute for Studies in Education, curriculum series No. 12, Toronto.

McDonald-Ross R. M. (1973), 'Behavioural Objectives: A Critical Review', *Instructional Science*, **2**, pp. 1–52.

McGeoch J. A. and Irion A. L. (1952), *The Psychology of Human Learning*, Longmans Green, New York.

McGregor D. (1960), *The Human Side of Enterprise*, McGraw–Hill, New York.

McKeachie W., Pintrich P. and Lin Y. G. (September 1984), *Learning to Learn*, paper given to 23rd International Congress of Psychology, Acapulco, Mexico.

MacKenzie A. and White R. (1982), 'Fieldwork in Geography and Long-term Memory Structures', *American Educational Research Journal*, **19**(4), pp. 623–32.

McKenzie B. (1980), 'Review of Vernon's Intelligence: Heredity and Environment', *Australian Journal of Psychology*, **32**, pp. 155–61.

McLuhan M. (1970), 'Education in the Electronic Age', *Interchange*, **1**(4), pp. 1–12.

McNally D. W. (1975), *Piaget, Education and Training*, Hodder & Stoughton, Sydney.

McQuinn T. (1979), 'An ESL Perspective on a Child's Language', TEFL/TESL *Newsletter*, **4**(3), pp. 14–22.

Mackay C. K. and Cameron M. (1968), 'Cognitive Bias in Scottish First Year Science and Arts Undergraduates', *British Journal of Psychology*, **38**, pp. 315–18.

Mackay D. (1971), *Schools Council Program in Linguistics and English Teaching*, Longman, London.

Madsen C. H. and Madsen L. K. (1970), *Teaching/Discipline*, Allyn & Bacon, Boston.

Madsen M. (1971), 'Developmental and Cross-cultural Differences in the Co-operative and Competitive Behaviour of Young Children', *Journal of Cross-cultural Psychology*, **2**, pp. 365–71.

Maehr M. and Sjogren D. (1971), 'Atkinson's Theory of Achievement Motivation: First Step Toward a Theory of Academic Motivation?', *Review of Educational Research*, **41**, pp. 143–61.

Mager R. (1961), *Preparing Instructional Objectives*, Fearon, San Francisco.

Mandaglio S. (April 1984), 'The Helping Professional and Teacher Burnout', *The South Pacific Journal of Teacher Education*, **12**(1).

Marsh R. (1985), 'Phrenoblysis: Real or Chimera?', *Child Developmental*, **56**, pp. 1059–61.

Martin E. and Ramsden P. (18–21 July 1985), 'Learning Skills or Skills in Learning?' paper presented to a Joint International Conference of the Society for Research in Higher Education and the Cognitive Psychology section of the British Psychological Society, University of Lancaster.

Marton F. (1975), 'On Non-verbatim Learning — I: Level of Processing and Level of Outcome', *Scandinavian Journal of Psychology*, **16**, pp. 273–9.

—— (1981), 'Phenomenography — Describing Conceptions of the World Around Us', *Instructional Science*, **10**, pp. 177–200.

—— Hounsell D. and Entwistle N. (eds) (1984), *The Experience of Learning*, Scottish Academic Press, Edinburgh.

—— and Saljo R. (1976a), 'On Qualitative Differences in Learning — I: Outcome and Process', *British Journal of Educational Psychology*, **46**, pp. 4–11.

—— and Slajo R. (1976b), 'On Qualitative Differences in Learning — II: Outcome as a Function of the Learner's Conception of the Task', *British Journal of Educational Psychology*, **46**, pp. 115–27.

—— and Saljo R. (1984), 'Approaches to Learning', in F. Marton, D. Hounsell and N. Entwistle (eds), *The Experience of Learning*, Scottish Academic Press, Edinburgh.

Maslow A. H. (1954), *Motivation and Personality*, Harper & Row, New York.

Meacham M. L. and Wiesen A. E. (1974), *Changing Classroom Behaviour* (2nd ed.), International Textbook Co., New York.

Mehrabian A. (1970), *Tactics of Social Influence*, Prentice–Hall, Englewood Cliffs, NJ.

Mehrens W. A. and Lehmann I. J. (1978), *Measurement and Evaluation in Education and Psychology*, Holt, Rinehart & Winston, New York.

Mercurio J. A. (1975), *Caning: Educational Ritual*, Holt, Rinehart & Winston, Sydney.

Merrill M. D. (ed.) (1971), *Instructional Design: Readings*, Prentice–Hall, Englewood Cliffs, NJ.

Meskauskas J. (1976), 'Evaluation Models for Criterion-referenced Testing: Views Regarding Mastery and Standard Setting', *Review of Educational Research*, **46**, pp. 133–8.

Metcalfe L. (1971), *Values Education: Rationale, Strategies and Procedures*, National Council for the Social Studies, 41st Yearbook, Wash., DC.

Meyer P. (February 1970), 'If Hitler Asked You to Electrocute a Stranger, Would You? Probably', *Esquire*.

Milgram S. (1964), 'Group Pressure and Action Against a Person', *Journal of Abnormal and Social Psychology*, **69**, pp. 137–43.

Miller G. A. (1956), 'The Magical Number Seven, Plus or Minus Two', *Psychological Review*, **63**, pp. 81–97.

Miller I. W. and Norman W. H. (1979), 'Learned Helplessness in Humans: A Review and Attribution-theory Model', *Psychological Bulletin*, **86**, pp. 93–118.

Miller J. S. (1979), 'What Science Teaching Needs', *The Primary Journal*, **1**, p. 51.

Miller L. R. (August 1985), 'Teacher Absenteeism — What are the Realities?', *Australian Educational Research*, pp. 29–41.

Molloy G. N. and Pierce C. (1980), 'Do Token Rewards Lead to Token Learning — A Note on the Use of Extrinsic Incentives', *Australian Behaviour Therapist*, **7**, pp. 33–42.

Moore P. G. and Kirby J. (1981), 'Metacognition and Reading: A Replication and Extension of Myers and Paris in an Australian Context', *Educational Inquiry*, **4**(1), pp. 18–29.

Morgan M. (1984), 'Reward-induced Decrements and Increments in Intrinsic Motivation', *Devices of Educational Research*, **54**, pp. 5–30.

Morine–Dershimer G. (1978–79), 'Planning in Classroom Reality — An In-depth Look', *Educational Research Quarterly*, **3**, pp. 83–99.

Morris D. (1969), *The Human Zoo*, Jonathan Cape, London.

Morrison T. (August 1979), 'Classroom Structure, Work Involvement and Social Climate in Elementary School Classrooms', *Journal of Educational Psychology*.

Moston M. (1972), *Teaching: From Command to Discovery*, Wadsworth, Belmont, Calif.

Moulton R. W. (1969), 'Effects of Success and Failure on Level of Aspiration as Related to Achievement Motives', *Journal of Personality and Social Psychology*, **1**, pp. 399–406.

Myers M. and Paris S. (1978), 'Children's Metacognitive Knowledge about Reading', *Journal of Educational Psychology*, **70**, pp. 680–90.

Neill A. S. (1960), *Summerhill*, Hart, New York.

Neisser U. (1967), *Cognitive Psychology*, Appleton–Century–Crofts, New York.

Newell P. (ed.) (1972), *A Last Resort: Corporal Punishment in the Schools*, Pelican, United Kingdom.

Newman D. (February 1985), 'So You Want to Leave Teaching', *The Australian Teacher*, **11**, pp. 11–12.

Newman F. and Oliver D. W. (1970), *Classifying Public Controversy: An Approach to Teaching Social Studies*, Little, Brown & Co., Boston.

Newman H. H., Freeman F. N. and Holzinger K. J. (1937), *Twins: A Study of Heredity and Environment*, University of Chicago Press, Chicago, Ill.

New South Wales Department of Education (1971), *Migrant Education in NSW*, Research Bulletin No. 34, Division of Research and Planning, Department of Education, NSW.

———— (1980), *Towards Non-sexist Education — Policies and Guidelines for Schools*, Pre-school–Year 12.

New South Wales Teachers' Federation (1979), *Non-sexist Teaching — Some Practical Hints*, Sydney.

———— (11 February 1985), 'The Case For and Against Corporal Punishment', *Education*, p. 5.

Norman D. A. (1976), *Memory and Attention*, Wiley, New York.

Novak J. D. and Gowin D. B. (1984), *Learning How to Learn*, Cambridge University Press, Cambridge, United Kingdom.

Nuthall G. and Lee A. A. (1982), *Measuring and Understanding the Way Children Learn in Class*, Technical Report: Teaching Research Project, Education Department, University of Canterbury, Christchurch, New Zealand.

Olson D. R. (1977), 'The Language of Instruction: On the Literate Bias of Schooling', in R. C. Anderson, R. J. Spiro and W. Montague (eds), *Schooling and the Acquisition of Knowledge*, Lawrence Erlbaum, Hillsdale, NJ.

O'Neill A., Speilberger C. and Hansen D. (1969), 'Effects of State-anxiety and Task Difficulty on Computer-assisted Learning', *Journal of Educational Psychology*, **60**, p. 343–50.

O'Neill M. and Reid J. A. (1985), *Educational and Psychological Characteristics of Students Gifted in English*, Commonwealth Schools Commission, Canberra.

Packard R. G. (1970), 'The Control of "Classroom Attention": A Group Contingency for Complex Behaviour', *Journal of Applied Behaviour*, Analysis 3, pp. 13–28.

Palincsar A. S. and Brown A. L. (1984), 'Reciprocal Teaching of Comprehension — Monitoring Activities', *Cognition and Instruction*, **1**(2), pp. 117–75.

Pallett R. (1985), *SOLO Taxonomy in Teaching Science*, Education Department Bulletin, Hobart.

Paris S. (24 April 1984), 'Improving Children's Metacognition and Reading Comprehension with Classroom Instruction', paper read to American Educational Research Association — Annual Conference, New Orleans.

_____ (1985), 'Teaching Children to Guide their Reading and Learning', in T. E. Raphael and L. Reynolds (eds), *Contexts of Literacy*, Longman, New York.

_____ (in press), 'Using Classroom Dialogues and Guided Practice to Teach Comprehension Strategies', in E. Cooke and T. Harris (eds), *Reading, Thinking and Concept Development: Tuteractive Strategies for the Classroom*, The College Brand, New York.

_____ Cross D. R. and Lipson M. (1984), 'Informed Strategies for Learning: A Program to Improve Children's Reading Awareness and Comprehension', *Journal of Educational Psychology*, **76**, pp. 1239–52.

_____ and Lindauer B. (1982), 'The Development of Cognitive Skills during Childhood', in B. Wolman (ed.), *Handbook of Developmental Psychology*, Prentice–Hall, Englewood Cliffs, NJ.

_____ and Oka E. R. (in press), Children's Reading Strategies, Metacognition and Motivation, *Developmental Review*.

Parliament of New South Wales (1981), *Report from the Select Committee of the Legislative Assembly Upon the School Certificate* (The McGowan Report), Government Printer, Sydney.

Pask G. and Scott B. C. E. (1972), 'Learning Strategies and Individual Competence', *International Journal of Man–Machine Studies*, **4**, pp. 217–53.

Pauk W. (1974), *How to Study in College*, Houghton, Boston.

Pearson P. D. and Tierney R. J. (1984), 'On Becoming a Thoughtful Reader: Learning to Read like a Writer', in A. Purves and O. Niles (eds), *Becoming Readers in a Complex Society*, 83rd Yearbook of the National Society for the Study of Education, Part I, University of Chicago Press, Chicago.

Peddiwell J. A. (1959), *The Saber-tooth Curriculum*, McGraw–Hill, New York.

Penny H. H. (March 1980), *The Training of Aborigines for Teaching in Aboriginal Schools of the Northern Territory*, report to the Education Department of the Northern Territory, the National Aboriginal Education Committee, and the Education Research and Development Committee.

Perfetti C. A. and Lesgold A. M. (1977), 'Discourse Comprehension and Sources of Individual Differences', in M. Just and P. Carpenter (eds), *Cognitive Process in Comprehension*, Lawrence Erlbaum, Hillsdale, NJ.

Perry W. G. (1970), *Forms of Intellectual and Ethical Development in the College Years: A Scheme*, Holt, Rinehart & Winston, New York.

Peters R. S. (1963), 'Reason and Habit: The Paradox of Moral Education', in W. R. Niblett (ed.), *Moral Education in a Changing Society*, Faber, London.

Peters W. (1971), *A Class Divided*, Doubleday, New York.

Peterson C. (1984), *Looking Forward Through the Life Span*, Prentice–Hall of Australia, Sydney.

Pezzullo T. R., Thorsen E. and Madaus G. (1972), 'The Heritability of Jensen's Level 1 and Level 2 and Divergent Thinking', *American Educational Research Journal*, **9**, pp. 539–46.

Pflaum S. W., Walberg H., Karegianes M. and Rasher R. (1980), 'Reading Instruction: A Quantitative Analysis', *Educational Research*, **9**(7), pp. 12–18.

Phillips D. C. and Nicolayev J. (1978), 'Kohlbergian Moral Development: A Progressing or Degenerating Research Program?', *Educational Theory*, **28**, pp. 286–301.

Phillips S. (1979), *Young Australians: The Attitudes of Our Children*, Harper & Row, Sydney.

Piaget J. (1926), *The Language and Thought of the Child*, Routledge & Kegan Paul, London.

—— (1932), *The Moral Judgment of the Child*, Routledge & Kegan Paul, London.

—— (1950), *The Psychology of Intelligence*, Routledge & Kegan Paul, London.

—— (1958), *The Growth of Logical Thinking from Childhood to Adolescence*, Basic Books, New York.

—— and Inhelder B. (1973), *Memory and Intelligence*, Basic Books, New York.

—— and Weil A. M. (1951), 'The Development in Children of the Idea of the Homeland and of Relations with Other Countries', *International Social Science Bulletin*, **3**, p. 561.

Pickens K. A. (1980), 'Recent Research on Open Education', *SET: Research Information for Teachers*, special issue No. 1, Australian Council for Educational Research.

Pimsleur P., Mosberg L. and Morrison A. L. (1962), 'Student Factors in Foreign Language Learning', *Modern Language Journal*, **46**.

Pines M. (June 1979), 'Good Samaritans at Age Two', *Psychology Today*, **13**(1), pp. 66–77.

—— Ronsen E. A and Kafry D. (1981), *Burnout — from Tedium to Personal Growth*, Free Press, New York.

Polya G. (1945), *How to Solve It*, Princeton University Press, Princeton, NJ.

Poole M. E. (1971), 'Social Class Differences in Code Elaboration: A Study of Oral Communication at the Tertiary Level', *Australian Journal of Education*, **15**, pp. 152–60.

—— de Lacey P. R. and Randhawa B. S. (1985), *Australia in Transition*, Harcourt Brace Jovanovich, Sydney.

Popham W. J. (1970), *Systematic Instruction*, Prentice–Hall, Englewood Cliffs, NJ.

—— (1975), *Educational Evaluation*, Prentice–Hall, Englewood Cliffs, NJ.

—— and Husek T. R. (1969), 'Implications of Criterion-referenced Measurement', *Journal of Educational Measurement*, **6**, pp. 1–9.

Premack D. (1959), 'Toward Empirical Behaviour Laws: I. Positive Reinforcement', *Psychological Review*, **66**, pp. 219–33.

Pribram K. H. (1969), 'The Amnestic Syndromes: Disturbances in Coding?', in G. Talland and N. Waugh (eds), *The Pathology of Memory*, Academic Press, New York.

Probert P. J. (1985), *Computer-assisted Instruction*, Bachelor of Educational Studies Extended Essay, Faculty of Education, University of Newcastle.

Purkey W. W. (1970), *Self-concept and School Achievement*, Prentice–Hall, Englewood Cliffs, NJ.

Ramsden P. (1984), 'The Context of Learning', in F. Marton, D. Homsell and N. Entwistle (eds), *The Experience of Learning*, Scottish Universities Press, Edinburgh.

—— (1985), 'Student Learning Research: Retrospect and Prospect', *Higher Education Research and Development*, **5**(1), pp. 51–70.

Raths L. E., Harmin M. and Simon S. B. (1970), *Values and Teaching*, Merrill, Columbus, Ohio.

Raucher H. (1970), *Watermelon Man*, Ace, New York.

Read D. A. and Simon S. B. (eds) (1975), *Humanistic Education Sourcebook*, Prentice–Hall, Englewood Cliffs, NJ.

Reavis G. H. (1968), 'The Animal School', in E. C. Short and G. D. Marconnit (eds), *Contemporary Thought on Public School Curriculum*, Brown, Dubuque, Iowa.

Rees J. A. (1977), 'The Development of an Instrument for Assessing the Learning Environment of Australian Secondary Schools — The School Climate Profile', unpublished Ph.D. thesis, University of Newcastle.

Renzulli J. S. (November 1978), 'What Makes Giftedness? Re-examining a Definition', *Phi Delta Kappan*, **60**, pp. 180–4.

Rest J. (1974), 'Developmental Psychology as a Guide to Value Education: A Review of "Kohlbergian" Programs', *Review of Educational Research*, **44**, pp. 214–59.

—— Turiel E. and Kohlberg L. (1969), 'Relations between Level of Moral Judgment and Preference, and Comprehension of the Moral Judgment of Others', *Journal of Personality*, **37**, pp. 225–52.

Robinson E. (1983), 'Metacognitive development', in S. Meadows (ed.), *Developing Thinking*

Approaches to Children's Cognitive Development, Methuen, London.

Robinson F. P. (1946), *Effective Study*, Harper & Row, New York.

Rogers C. R. (1951), *Client-centred Therapy*, Houghton Mifflin, Boston, Mass.

_____ (1969), Freedom to Learn, Merrill, Columbia, Ohio.

_____ (1983), *Freedom to Learn in the 80s*, Charles E. Merrill, Columbia.

Rose M. (1984), *Writer's Block: The Cognitive Dimension*, Universities Press, Carbondale, Ill.

Rosenshine B. (1978), 'Review of N. Bennett's Teaching Style and Pupil Progress', *American Educational Research Journal*, **15**, pp. 163–9.

_____ (1983), 'Teaching Functions in Instructional Programs', *The Elementary School Journal*, **83**(4), pp. 335–52.

Rosenthal R. (1971), 'Teacher Expectations and Their Effects upon Children', in G. Lesser (ed.), *Psychology and Educational Practice*, Scott, Foresman, Glenview, Ill.

_____ and Jacobson L. (1968), *Pygmalion in the Classroom*, Holt, Rinehart & Winston, New York.

Rotter J. B. (1966), 'Generalised Expectancies for Internal Versus External Control of Reinforcement', *Psychological Monograph*, **80**.

_____ (June 1971), 'Who Rules You? External Control and Internal Control', *Psychology Today*, **5**,(1).

Ruitenbeek H. M. (1970), *The New Group Therapies*, Discus, New York.

Rushton J. and Littlefield C. (1979), 'The Effects of Age, Amount of Modelling and a Success Experience on Seven-to-eleven-year-old Children's Generosity', *Journal of Moral Education*, **9**, pp. 55–6.

Ryba A. K. and Chapman J. W. (August 1983), 'Toward Improving Learning Strategies and Personal Adjustment with Computers', *The Computing Teacher*, pp. 48–53.

Salgado G. (1980), 'The Novelist at Work', in M. Seymour–Smith (ed.), *Novels and Novelists*, St Martin's Press, New York.

Sarason S. B. (1971), *The Culture of the School and the Problem of Change*, Allyn & Bacon, Boston.

_____ et al. (1960), *Anxiety in Elementary School Children*, Wiley, New York.

Scardamalia M. (1980), 'How Children Cope with the Cognitive Demands of Writing', in C. H. Frederiksen, M. R. Whiteman and J. F. Dominic (eds), *Writing: The Nature, Development and Teaching of Written Communication*, Lawrence Erlbaum, Hillsdale, NJ.

_____ and Bereiter C. (1982), 'Assimilative Processes in Composition Planning', *Educational Psychologist*, **17**, pp. 165–71.

Schaie K. W. (1979), 'The Primary Mental Abilities in Adulthood: An Exploration in the Development of Psychometric Intelligence', in B. Baltes and O. Brim (eds), *Life Span Development and Behaviour*, Academic Press, New York.

Schatzman L. and Strauss A. (1955), 'Social Class and Modes of Communication', *American Journal of Sociology*, **60**, pp. 329–38.

Schlaefli A., Rest J. and Thoma S. (1985), 'Does Moral Education Improve Moral Judgment?', A Meta-analysis of Intervention Studies Using the Defining Issues Test, *Review of Educational Research*, **55**, pp. 319–52.

Schmuck R. A. (1971), 'Influence of the Peer Group', in G. Lesser (ed.), *Psychology and Educational Practice*, Scott, Foresman, Glenview, Ill.

_____ (1977), 'Peer Groups as Settings for Learnings', *Theory Into Practice*, **16**(4), pp. 272–9.

Schofield M. and Krafer N. (1985), 'Children's Understanding of Friendship Issues: Developmental by Stage or Sequence?', *Journal of Social and Personal Relationships*, **2**, pp. 151–65.

Schwartz M. (November 1982), 'Computers and the Teaching of Writing', *Educational Technology*, pp. 27–9.

Scriven M. (1967), 'The Methodology of Evaluation', in R. Tyler, R. Gagnă and M. Scriven (eds), *Perspectives of Curriculum Evaluation*, Rand McNally, Chicago, Ill.

Seligman M. E. P. (1970), 'On the Generality of the Laws of Learning', *Psychological Review*, **77**, pp. 406–18.

_____ (1975), *Helplessness: On Depression, Development and Death*, W. H. Freeman, San Francisco.

Selman R. L. (1980), *The Growth of Interpersonal Understanding*, Academic Press, New York.

Selye H. (1974), *Stress Without Distress*, Lippincott, Philadelphia.

Shavelson R. and Stern P. (1981), 'Research on

Teachers Pedagogical Thoughts, Judgments, Divisions and Behaviour', *Review of Educational Research*, **51**(4), pp. 455–98.

Shayer M. and Adey P. (1981), *Towards a Science of Sincere Teaching*, Heinemark Educational, London.

Sheehy G. (1976), *Passages*, Dutton, New York.

Shuy R. (1973), 'The Language that the Child Brings with Him to School', in *The Teaching of English*, proceedings of the National Seminar on the Teaching of English, AGPS, Sydney.

Sieber J. (1969), 'A Paradigm for Experimental Modification of the Effects of Test Anxiety on Cognitive Processes', *American Educational Research Journal*, **6**, pp. 46–61.

Silberman C. E. (1970), *Crisis in the Classroom*, Random House, New York.

Silberman M. L. (ed.) (1971), *The Experience of Schooling*, Holt, Rinehart & Winston, New York.

Skinner B.F. (1949), *Walden Two*, Macmillan, New York.

—— (1957), *Verbal Behaviour*, Appleton, New York.

—— (1965), *Science and Human Behaviour*, Free Press, New York.

—— (1968), *The Technology of Teaching*, Appleton–Century–Crofts, New York.

Smith F. (1971), *Understanding Reading*, Holt, Rinehart & Winston, New York.

Smith R. A. and Knight J. (1978), 'MACOS in Queensland: The Politics of Educational Knowledge', *The Australian Journal of Education*, **22**, pp. 225–48.

Snow R. E. (1976), 'Research on Aptitude for Learning: A Progress Report', in L. S. Shulman (ed.), *Review of Educational Research*, **4**, Peacock, Itasca, Ill.

—— (1977), 'What Do We Know About ATI? What Should We Learn?', in L. Cronbach and R. E. Snow (eds), *Aptitude-treatment Interaction*, Wiley, New York.

Snowman J. (in press), 'Learning Tactics and Strategies', in G. D. Phye and T. Andre (eds), *Cognitive Instructional Psychology: Components of Classroom Learning*, Academic Press, New York.

Solomon J. (August 1984), 'The Social Construction of Children's Knowledge and the Epistemology of Jean Piaget', paper presented to British Educational Research Association, University of Lancaster.

—— (May 1985), 'Children's Explanations!', paper read to American Educational Research Association Annual Conference, Chicago, Ill.

Spalding I. (February 1974), 'Race Bias in Social Studies', *The Aboriginal Child at School*, **2**(1), pp. 20–30.

Sparkes R et al. (1970), *Australia's Heritage* (2nd ed.), p. 52, Jacaranda Press, Brisbane.

Spearman C. (1927), *The Abilities of Man*, Macmillan, New York.

Spearrit D. (ed.) (1982), *The Improvement of Measurement in Education and Psychology*, The Australian Council for Educational Research, Hawthorn, Vic.

Sperling G. (1960), 'The Information Available in Brief Visual Presentations', *Psychological Monographs*, **74** (whole No. 498).

Spuck D. W. and Atkinson G. (Fall/Winter 1984), 'Administrative uses of the Micro-computer', *AEDS Journal*, **17**(1 and 2), pp. 83–90.

Staines J. W. (1968), 'Levelling-sharpening and Academic Learning in Secondary School Children', *Australian Journal of Psychology*, **20**, pp. 123–8.

Starch D. and Elliott E. C. (1912), 'Reliability of the Grading of High School Work in English', *School Review*, **20**, pp. 442–57.

—— (1913a), 'Reliability of Grading Work in Mathematics', *School Review*, **21**, pp. 254–9.

—— (1913b), 'Reliability of Grading Work in History', *School Review*, **21**, pp. 676–81.

Steinberg E. R. (1984), *Teaching Computers to Teach*, Lawrence Erlbaum, Hillsdale, NJ.

Stelzer E. (1975), 'Writing about Writing', *Language in Education*, **1**, Tasmanian Department of Education, pp. 37–42.

Sternberg R. J. (1980), 'Towards a Unified Componential Theory of Human Intelligence', by M. Friedman, J. P. Bas and N. O'Connor (eds), *Intelligence and Learning*, Plenum, New York.

Storr A. (1970), *Human Aggression*, Bantam, New York.

Suchman J. R. (1961), 'Inquiry Training: Buildings Skills for Autonomous Discovery', *Merrill–Palmer Quarterly Behaviour Development*, **7**, pp. 148–69.

Suppes P. (June 1974), 'The Place of Theory in Educational Research', *Educational Researcher* **3**(6), pp. 3–10.

Sylvester R. (Winter 1983), 'The School as a Stress Reduction Agency', *Theory into Practice*, **22**(1), pp. 3–6.

Taba H. (1962), 'Curriculum Development: Theory and Practice', Harcourt Brace Jovanovich, New York.

Tabberer R. (1984), 'Introducing Study Skills at 16–19', *Educational Research*, **26**, pp. 1–6.

Taylor E. (1984), 'Orientation to Study: A Longitudinal Investigation', unpublished Ph.D. dissertation, University of Surrey.

Taylor H. (1971), 'Student Reaction to the Grade Contract', *Journal of Educational Research*, **64**, pp. 311–4.

Taylor J. (1986), *The Organisation and Structure of Knowledge Underlying Cognition Skill Performance*, unpublished Ph.D. dissertation, University of Queensland.

Telfer R. (1979a), 'A Teaching Problem Questionnaire', *The Forum of Education*, **38**(1), pp. 27–32.

_____ (13 February 1979b), 'The Use of Behavioural Objectives in Flight Instruction', paper presented to the Flight Instructor Examiners' Conference, Department of Transport, Melbourne.

_____ (January 1981), 'Analysing Parochial Teaching Problems : A Nomothetic Approach', *Journal of Teacher Education*, **32**(1), pp. 39–45.

_____ (1982), 'Teaching Problems of Beginning Teachers', *The Forum of Education*, **40**(1), pp. 23–6.

_____ (1985), *Program Equity and Participation — A Report of an Evaluation Study of Garokan High School*, Research Report, Department of Education, University of Newcastle.

_____ and Rees J. (1975), *Teacher Tactics*, Symes, Sydney.

Terman L. M. (1954), 'The Discovery and Encouragement of Exceptional Talent', *American Psychologist*, **9**, pp. 221–30.

Thomas A. (1979), 'Learned Helplessness and Expectancy Factors: Implications for Research in Learning Disabilities', *Review of Educational Research*, **49**, pp. 208–21.

Thomas D. B. and McLain D. H (Fall/Winter 1983), 'Selecting Microcomputers for the Classroom: A Rethinking after Four Years', *AEDS Journal*, **17**(1 and 2), pp. 9–22.

Thomas, D. R., Becker W. C. and Armstrong M.

(1968), 'Production and Elimination of Disruptive Classroom Behaviour by Systematically Varying Teacher's Behaviour', *Journal of Applied Behaviour Analysis*, **1**, pp. 35–45.

Thomas P. R. and Bain J. D. (1984), 'Contextual Dependence of Learning Approaches: The Effects of Assessments', *Human Learning*, **3**, pp. 227–40.

Thorndike E. L. (1898), 'Animal Intelligence: An Experimental Study of the Associative Processes in Animals', *Psychological Review*, Monograph Supplement.

Thorndike R. L. (1968), 'Review of Pygmalion in the Classroom', *Educational Research Journal*, **5**, pp. 709–11.

_____ (ed.) (1971), *Educational Measurement*, American Council on Education, Wash., DC.

Thurstone L. L. (1938), 'Primary Mental Abilities', *Psychometric Monographs*, No. 1, University of Chicago Press, Chicago, Ill.

Tibbetts S. L. (November 1978), 'Wanted: Data to Prove that Sexist Reading Material has an Impact on the Reader', *The Reading Teacher*, **32**(2), pp. 165–9.

Tiger L. and Fox R. (1974), *The Imperial Animal*, Granada, St. Albans.

Toffler A. (1971), *Future Shock*, Random House, New York.

Tomlinson P. (1980), 'Moral Judgment and Moral Psychology: Piaget, Kohlberg and Beyond', in S. and C. Modgil (eds), *Toward a Theory of Psychological Development*, National Foundation for Educational Research, Windsor, Berks.

Torrance E. P. (1960), *Educational Achievement of the Highly Intelligent and the Highly Creative: Eight Partial Replications of the Getzels–Jackson Study*, Bureau of Educational Research, University of Minnesota, Minneapolis.

_____ (1961), 'Priming Creative Thinking in the Primary Grades', *Elementary School Journal*, **62**, pp. 34–41.

_____ (1963), *Education and the Creative Potential*, University of Minnesota Press, Minneapolis.

_____ (1965a), *Gifted Children in the Classroom*, Macmillan.

_____ (1965b), *Guiding Creative Talent*, Prentice-Hall, Englewood Cliffs, NJ.

_____ and Myers R. E. (1970), *Creative Learning and Teaching*, Harper & Row, New York.

Tough A. (1971), *The Adult's Learning Projects*, Ontario Institute for Studies in Education, Toronto.

Tulving E. (1972), 'Episodic and Semantic Memory', in E. Tulving and W. Donaldson (eds), *Organisation and Memory*, Academic Press, New York.

Tunmer W., Pratt C. and Herriman M. (eds) (1984), *Metalinguistic Awareness in Children*, Springer–Verlag, Berlin.

Turbill J. (ed.) (1982), *No Better Way to Teach Writing*, Primary English Teaching Association, Rozelle, NSW.

Turiel E. (1966), 'An Experimental Test of the Sequentiality of Developmental Stages in the Child's Moral Judgments', *Journal of Personality and Social Psychology*, **3**, pp. 611–18.

Turney C. and Cairns L. G. (1976), *Sydney Micro Skills: Series 3 Classroom Management and Discipline*, Sydney University Press, Sydney.

―――― Eltis K. J., Hatton N., Owens L. C., Towler J. and Wright R. (1983), *Sydney Microskills Redeveloped, Series 1 Handbook, Reinforcement Basic Questionning, Variability*, Sydney University Press, Sydney.

―――― and Ryan C. (1978), *Inner-city Teaching: Awareness and Simulation Materials*, Sydney University Press, Sydney.

Tyler L. E. (1978), *Individuality*, Jossey–Bass, San Francisco, Calif.

Tyler R. W. (1980), *Basic Principles of Curriculum Instruction*, University of Chicago Press, Chicago, Ill.

Van Rossum E. J. and Schenk S. M. (1984), 'The Relationship between Learning Conception, Study Strategy and Learning Outcome', *British Journal of Educational Psychology*, **54**, pp. 73–83.

Vaughan W. J. A. (1973), *Aims and Objectives of Secondary Education in NSW*, Directorate of Studies, NSW Department of Education, Sydney.

Veenman S. (1984), 'Perceived Problems of Beginning Teachers', *Review of Educational Research*, **54**(2), pp. 143–78.

Vernon P. E. (1950), *The Structure of Human Abilities*, Methuen, London.

―――― (1969), *Intelligence and Cultural Environment*, Methuen, London.

―――― (1979), *Intelligence: Heredity and Environment*, W. H. Freeman, San Francisco, Calif.

Veroff J. (1969), 'Social-comparison and the Development of Achievement Motivation', in C. P. Smith (ed.), *Achievement Related Motives in Children*, Russell Sage, New York.

Victorian Education Gazette, 13 February 1980.

Viney L. (1980), *Transitions*, Cassell, Melbourne.

Vivian W. (1984), 'The Twang Factor', *Education News*, pp. 36–9.

Vorrath H. A. and Brendiro L. K. (1979), *Positive Peer Culture*, Aldine, Hawthorne.

Vygotsky L. S. (1962), *Thought and Language*, Wiley, New York.

―――― (1978), *Mind and Society*, Harvard University Press, Cambridge, Mass.

Wagner R. K. and Sternberg R. J. (1984), 'Alternative Conceptions of Intelligence and their Implications for Education', *Review of Educational Research*, **54**, pp. 179–223.

Wall M., *The Effects of Exertion on the Mental Performance of Fit, Medium Fit and Unfit Primary School Children*, unpublished dissertation, Master of Psychology (Educational), University of Newcastle, in progress.

Wallace I., Wallechinsky D. and Wallace A. (1984), *The Book of Lists — 3*, pp. 67–9, Corgi Books, London.

Wallach M. and Wallach L. (1983), *Psychology's Sanction for Selfishness*, W. H. Freeman, San Francisco.

―――― and Wing C. (1969), *The Talented Student*, Holt, Rinehart & Winston, New York.

Watkins D. (1983), 'Depth of Processing and the Quality of Learning Outcomes', *Instructional Science*, **12**, pp. 49–58.

―――― and Hattie J. (1981), 'The Learning Processes of Australian University Students: Investigations of Contextual and Physiological Factors', *British Journal of Educational Psychology*, **51**, pp. 384–93.

―――― and Hattie J. (1985), 'A Longitudinal Study of the Approach to Learning of Australian Tertiary Students', *Human Learning*, **4**(2), pp. 127–42.

Watson H. J., Vallee J. M. and Mulford W. R. (1981), *Structured Experiences and Group Development*, Curriculum Development Centre, Canberra.

Watson J. B. (1924), *Behaviourism*, People's Institute, New York.

Watson P. G. (1971), 'From the Educational Technologist's Point of View', *Educational Horizons*, **49**, pp. 81–7.

Watt D. (1984), 'Tools for Writing', *Popular Computing*, **78**, pp. 75–6.

Watts D. and Zylbersztajn A. (1981), 'A Survey

of Some Children's Ideas about Force', *Physics Education*, **16**, pp. 360–5.

Watts M. D. (1983), 'A Study of School Children's Alternative Frameworks of the Concept of Force', *European Journal of Science Education*, **5**, pp. 217–30.

_____ and Bentley D. (1984), 'The Personal Parawriting of Cognition: Two Personal Aims in Science Education', *Oxford Review of Education*, **10**(3), pp. 309–17.

_____ and Gilbert J. (1983), 'Enigmas in School Science Students' Conceptions for Scientifically Associated Words', *Research in Science and Technological Education*, **1**, pp. 161–71.

Waymouth P. (1983), *A Study of Classroom Climate Comparisons between Streamed Schools and Non-streamed Schools*, Master of Psychology (Educational) thesis, Department of Psychology, University of Newcastle.

Wax R. (1971), *Doing Fieldwork*, pp. 253–4, University of Chicago Press, Chicago, Ill.

Webster L. (1986), 'The Development and Evaluation of a Computer-assisted Video Instruction System', unpublished BA (Honours) thesis, University of Newcastle.

Wechsler D. (1949), *Wechsler Intelligence Scale for Children: Manual*, Psychological Corporation, New York.

_____ (1955), *Wechsler Adult Intelligence Scale Manual*, Psychological Corporation, New York.

Weiner B. (1967), 'Implications of the Current Theory of Achievement Motivation for Research and Performance in the Classroom', *Psychology in the Schools*, **4**, pp. 164–71.

_____ (1972), 'Attribution Theory, Achievement Motivation and the Educational Process', *Review of Educational Research*, **42**, pp. 203–15.

_____ (1977), 'An Attributional Approach for Educational Psychology', in L. Shulman (ed.), *Review of Educational Research*, **4**, Peacock, Itasca, Ill.

White K. A. (1978), *Volunteerism and Bureaucracy: Trends in the Utilisation of Volunteers in Adult Literacy Programs*, unpublished M.Ed. Admin. dissertation, University of New England, Armidale, NSW.

White R. T. (1984), 'Understanding and its Measurement', paper read to Australian Educational Research Association Annual Conference, Perth.

_____ and Tisher R. (1983), 'Research on Natural Science', in M. Wittrock (ed.), 3rd Handbook of Research on Teaching, Rand McNally, Chicago.

White R. W. (1959), 'Motivation Reconsidered: The Concept of Competence', *Psychological Review*, **66**, pp. 297–333.

Whyte J., Deem R., Kant L. and Cruickshank M. (eds) (1985), *Girl Friendly Schooling*, Methuen, London.

Williams J. K. (February/March 1977), 'Imparting Basic Skills', *ACES Review*, **4**(1), pp. 8–10.

Williams N. (1969), 'Children's Moral Thought', *Moral Education*, **1**, pp. 3–12.

Wilson G. (1979), 'The Sociobiology of Sex Differences', *Bulletin of the British Society*, **32**, pp. 350–3.

Wilson J. (1979), 'Moral Education: Retrospect and Prospect', *Journal of Moral Education*, **9**, pp. 3–9.

_____ (1981), *Student Learning in Higher Education*, Croom Helm, London.

Winkler R. L. (1976), 'New Directions for Behaviour Modification in Homosexuality, Open Education and Behavioural Economics', in P. W. Sheehan and K. D. White (eds), *Behaviour Modification in Australia*, Monograph Supplement No. 5, *Australian Psychologist*, **11**.

Witkin H., Lewis H., Hutzman M., Machover K., Meissner P. and Wagner S. (1954), *Personality through Perception*, Harper, New York.

_____ Moore C. A., Goodenough D. R. and Cox P. W. (1977), 'Field-dependent and Field-independent Cognitive Styles and Their Educational Implications', *Review of Educational Research*, **47**, pp. 1–64.

Wittrock M. C. (1977), 'The Generative Processes of Memory', in M. C. Wittrock (ed.), *The Human Brain*, Prentice–Hall, Englewood Cliffs, NJ.

Wong B. (1985), 'Self-questioning Instructional Research', *Review of Educational Research*, **55**, pp. 227–68.

Wrightsman L. S. (1962), 'The Effects of Anxiety, Achievement Motivation and Task Importance upon Performance on an Intelligence Test', *Journal of Educational Psychology*, **53**, pp. 150–6.

Yamamoto K. (1963), 'Relationships between Creative-thinking Abilities of Teachers, and

Achievement and Adjustment of Pupils',
Journal of Experimental Education, **32**, pp. 3–25.
―――― (1965), 'Effects of Restriction of Range
and Test Unreliability on Correlation between
Measures of Intelligence and Creative Think-
ing', *British Journal of Educational Psychology*, **35**,
pp. 300–5.

Yinger R. (June 1979), 'Routines in Teacher
Planning', *Theory into Practice*, **18**(3), pp. 163–9.
Zimbardo P. G., Haney C., Banks W. C. and
Jaffe D. (8 April 1973), 'A Pirandellian Prison:
The Mind is a Formidable Jailer', *New York
Times Magazine*, pp. 38–60.

AUTHOR INDEX

SUBJECT INDEX

Note: **A bold** entry refers to Glossary where the term is defined.